P9-CJP-838

Beginning
Lua Programming

Beginning
Lua Programming

Kurt Jung and Aaron Brown

Wiley Publishing, Inc.

Beginning Lua Programming

Published by
Wiley Publishing, Inc.
10475 Crosspoint Boulevard
Indianapolis, IN 46256
www.wiley.com

Copyright © 2007 by Wiley Publishing, Inc., Indianapolis, Indiana

Published simultaneously in Canada

ISBN: 978-0-470-06917-2

10 9 8 7 6 5 4 3 2

1MA/SS/QR/QX/IN

Library of Congress Cataloging-in-Publication Data

Jung, Kurt, 1956-
 Beginning Lua programming / Kurt Jung and Aaron Brown.
    p. cm.
 ISBN-13: 978-0-470-06917-2 (pbk.)

 1. Lua (Computer program language) I. Brown, Aaron, 1973- II. Title.
 QA76.73.L82J96 2007
 005.13′3--dc22

2006036460

No part of this publication may be reproduced, stored in a retrieval system or transmitted in any form or by any means, electronic, mechanical, photocopying, recording, scanning or otherwise, except as permitted under Sections 107 or 108 of the 1976 United States Copyright Act, without either the prior written permission of the Publisher, or authorization through payment of the appropriate per-copy fee to the Copyright Clearance Center, 222 Rosewood Drive, Danvers, MA 01923, (978) 750-8400, fax (978) 646-8600. Requests to the Publisher for permission should be addressed to the Legal Department, Wiley Publishing, Inc., 10475 Crosspoint Blvd., Indianapolis, IN 46256, (317) 572-3447, fax (317) 572-4355, or online at http://www.wiley.com/go/permissions.

LIMIT OF LIABILITY/DISCLAIMER OF WARRANTY: THE PUBLISHER AND THE AUTHOR MAKE NO REPRESENTATIONS OR WARRANTIES WITH RESPECT TO THE ACCURACY OR COMPLETENESS OF THE CONTENTS OF THIS WORK AND SPECIFICALLY DISCLAIM ALL WARRANTIES, INCLUDING WITHOUT LIMITATION WARRANTIES OF FITNESS FOR A PARTICULAR PURPOSE. NO WARRANTY MAY BE CREATED OR EXTENDED BY SALES OR PROMOTIONAL MATERIALS. THE ADVICE AND STRATEGIES CONTAINED HEREIN MAY NOT BE SUITABLE FOR EVERY SITUATION. THIS WORK IS SOLD WITH THE UNDERSTANDING THAT THE PUBLISHER IS NOT ENGAGED IN RENDERING LEGAL, ACCOUNTING, OR OTHER PROFESSIONAL SERVICES. IF PROFESSIONAL ASSISTANCE IS REQUIRED, THE SERVICES OF A COMPETENT PROFESSIONAL PERSON SHOULD BE SOUGHT. NEITHER THE PUBLISHER NOR THE AUTHOR SHALL BE LIABLE FOR DAMAGES ARISING HEREFROM. THE FACT THAT AN ORGANIZATION OR WEBSITE IS REFERRED TO IN THIS WORK AS A CITATION AND/OR A POTENTIAL SOURCE OF FURTHER INFORMATION DOES NOT MEAN THAT THE AUTHOR OR THE PUBLISHER ENDORSES THE INFORMATION THE ORGANIZATION OR WEBSITE MAY PROVIDE OR RECOMMENDATIONS IT MAY MAKE. FURTHER, READERS SHOULD BE AWARE THAT INTERNET WEBSITES LISTED IN THIS WORK MAY HAVE CHANGED OR DISAPPEARED BETWEEN WHEN THIS WORK WAS WRITTEN AND WHEN IT IS READ.

For general information on our other products and services please contact our Customer Care Department within the United States at (800) 762-2974, outside the United States at (317) 572-3993 or fax (317) 572-4002.

Trademarks: Wiley, the Wiley logo, Wrox, the Wrox logo, Programmer to Programmer, and related trade dress are trademarks or registered trademarks of John Wiley & Sons, Inc. and/or its affiliates, in the United States and other countries, and may not be used without written permission. All other trademarks are the property of their respective owners. Wiley Publishing, Inc., is not associated with any product or vendor mentioned in this book.

Lua 5.0 Copyright © 1994-2006, Lua.org, PUC-Rio

Lua 5.1 Copyright © 2006, Lua.org

The Lua logo was designed by Alexandre Nakonechnyj.

Wiley also publishes its books in a variety of electronic formats. Some content that appears in print may not be available in electronic books.

About the Authors

Between his first programs submitted to a Burroughs 5500 on Hollerith punch cards and his latest programs tapped into a Palm Pilot, **Kurt Jung** has been the principal programmer on various projects ranging from airline yield management to state machine–driven workflow.

Aaron Brown began programming in elementary school on a Commodore 64. He plays various musical instruments and speaks Esperanto.

Credits

Acquisitions Editor
Kit Kemper

Development Editor
Maryann Steinhart

Technical Editor
Adam Dumas

Production Editor
Rachel Meyers

Copy Editor
Kathryn Duggan

Editorial Manager
Mary Beth Wakefield

Production Manager
Tim Tate

Vice President and Executive Group Publisher
Richard Swadley

Vice President and Executive Publisher
Joseph B. Wikert

Graphics and Production Specialists
Denny Hager
Shane Johnson
Barry Offringa
Heather Ryan

Quality Control Technician
John Greenough
Jessica Kramer

Project Coordinator
Erin Smith

Proofreading and Indexing
Techbooks

Anniversary Logo Design
Richard Pacifico

Acknowledgments

This project has had strong and capable guidance from Kit Kemper and Maryann Steinhart at Wiley Publishing. Maryann was remarkably responsive in making sure our questions were answered promptly. May Kit and Maryann land leading roles when Hollywood makes *Beginning Lua Programming* into a major motion picture.

Laurels and commendations go to Adam Dumas, the best technical editor a book could possibly have. Adam's thoroughness and attention to detail uncovered a humbling number of issues with the manuscript, all of which were brought to our attention in the most courteous and constructive way and often with insightful corrections.

The Lua community provided much help and many answers. Thanks go to Roberto Ierusalimschy, Waldemar Celes, and Luiz Henrique de Figueiredo for creating a remarkable language about which it is easy to remain enthusiastic. Roberto and Luiz Henrique also answered some specific questions related to this book. The following people were very helpful in answering questions about their respective projects: André Carregal (LuaForge and the Kepler Project), Mark Hamburg (Adobe Lightroom), Asko Kauppi (LuaSDL and LuaX), and Kein-Hong Man (ChunkSpy and the No-Frills Introduction to Lua 5.1 VM Instructions).

From Kurt Jung: Collaborating with an individual as gifted and inventive as Aaron has been an entirely rewarding experience. It's with great pleasure that I look forward to future projects together. *Multajn dankojn, mia bonamiko.*

The encouragement of my mother and other family members has been greatly appreciated. Although writing this book may have given me a great excuse to delay various chores (most notably the one involving a lawn mower) and household repairs, it never interfered with the frequent, pleasurable, and bonding walks I take with my wife Maura, daughter Laura, and our bundle of canine energy, Brilla. I owe the greatest thanks to Maura for her support during this endeavor.

From Aaron Brown: Apart from being my programming mentor, inviting me to collaborate on this book with him, and being an all-around nice guy, Kurt Jung is one of the few true kindred spirits I have encountered. *Mia teraplano estas plena je angiloj!*

Cathy Lewis gave advice on the writing process at a pivotal moment. She (in her capacity as my girlfriend), my bandmates, and family also deserve thanks for their understanding of my reduced availability while slaving in the book mines.

Special thanks to Mom (a.k.a. Marty Brown), who bought me that first computer so long ago.

Contents

Acknowledgments   ix
Introduction   xxiii

Chapter 1: Getting Situated   1

Choosing How to Install Lua   1
  Building Lua Yourself   2
  Selecting Prebuilt Lua   3
Finding Your System's Shell   3
  Windows Shells   3
  Shells on Unix and Unix-Like systems   3
  Shell Features   4
  The Environment   4
    Environment Variables on Unix-Like Systems   4
    Environment Variables on Windows   5
Dealing with Tarballs and Zip Files   6
Compiling Lua   7
  The Lua Source Tarball   7
  Compiling Lua on Linux and Other Unix-Like Systems   8
  Compiling Lua on Windows   12
    Building Lua with Microsoft Visual C++   13
    Building Lua with the Tiny C Compiler   14
    Building Lua with MinGW   16
Binary Packages   18
  Selecting a Prebuilt Binary Package   18
  Installing a Prebuilt Binary Package on a Unix-Type System   19
  Installing a Prebuilt Binary Package on Windows   20
Additional Tools   21
  Programmer's Editor   21
  Revision Control System   22
Summary   22

Chapter 2: First Steps   23

Numbers and Arithmetic Operations: Basic Interpreter Usage   23
  Addition, Subtraction, Multiplication, Division, and Exponentiation 24
  Interacting with the Interpreter   24
  Other Notations for Numbers   25

Contents

Interpreter Know-How   **26**
Quitting the Interpreter   26
Interpreter Shortcuts   26
Numerical Gotchas   **27**
Division by Zero and Overflow   27
Floating-Point Rounding   28
Variables and Assignment   **28**
Assignment Basics   29
Multiple Assignment   31
Variables on the Right Side of Assignments   32
Strings   **32**
Quoting Strings   32
Quoting Strings with Double Quotes   32
Quoting Strings with Single Quotes   33
Quoting Strings with Square Brackets   33
Backslash Escaping   35
Relational Operators and Boolean Values   **37**
Comparing Numbers   37
Comparing Strings   38
The nil Value   **40**
Boolean Operators   **41**
The and Operator   42
The or Operator   43
The not Unary Operator   44
The Concatenation, Length, and Modulo Operators   **45**
The String Concatenation Operator   45
The Length Operator   46
The Modulo Operator   47
Automatic Conversion of Operands   **48**
Precedence and Associativity   **49**
Variables and Values   **51**
Comments   **52**
Expressions and Statements   **53**
Compound Statements   **54**
The if Statement   55
The while Loop   58
The for Loop   60
The repeat Loop   62
The break and do Statements   63
Summary   **66**
Exercises   **66**

Contents

Chapter 3: Extending Lua with Functions   **69**

Return Values   **72**
   Using a Function that Returns a Value   72
   Defining a Function that Returns a Value   73
   Using return to Alter Control Flow   74
   Returning Nothing   76
   Returning Multiple Values   77
   Adjusting Value Lists   78
      Using Multiple-Valued Functions in Value Lists   78
      Using Valueless Functions in Value Lists   79
Chunks as Functions   **81**
Variable Scope   **84**
   Actual and Formal Arguments   84
   Local Variables   85
Understanding Side Effects   **91**
   Ordering Side Effects   91
   Short-Circuit Evaluation   93
Functions Calling Functions   **95**
   The Call Stack   95
   Recursion   97
   Stack Overflow   98
   Tail Calls   99
Functions as Values   **102**
   Replacing Built-In Functions   102
   Comparing and Printing Functions   103
   Function Definitions as Assignments   103
   Local Functions   105
Whitespace, Semicolons, and Function Calls   **106**
Upvalues and Closures   **108**
   Defining Functions that Create Functions   108
   Defining Functions with Private State   110
   Figuring Out Tricky Scope Situations   111
Summary   **113**
Exercises   **114**

Chapter 4: Working with Tables   **117**

Tables Introduced   **117**
A Shorter Way to Write Some Keys   **119**
Altering a Table's Contents   **120**
Tables as Arrays   **121**
Array Length   **123**

Contents

Looping through Tables   **124**

Tables of Functions   **128**

     The Table Library   128

         table.sort   128

         table.concat   131

         table.remove   132

         table.maxn   132

     Object-Oriented Programming with Tables   133

Functions with Variable Numbers of Arguments   **136**

     Defining Vararg Functions   136

     Scripts as Vararg Functions   140

Keyword Arguments   **143**

Different but the Same   **144**

     Table Equality   144

     Avoiding Bugs by Understanding Mutability   145

     Variables and Mutable Values   145

     Tables and Functions   147

     Copying Tables   148

Building Other Data Structures from Tables   **152**

Custom-Made Loops   **158**

Global Variable Environments   **163**

Summary   **168**

Exercises   **169**

Chapter 5: Using Strings   **171**

Basic String Conversion Functions   **171**

String Length   **173**

Converting Between Characters and Character Codes   **173**

Formatting Strings and Numbers with string.format   **174**

Input/Output   **180**

     Writing to and Reading from a File   181

Pattern-Matching   **185**

     Searching for a Specific String   186

     Matching Any of Several Characters   186

     Matches of Varying Lengths   193

     Captures   198

     Matching Balanced Delimiters   202

     More on string.find, string.match, and string.gsub   202

     Iterating Through All Matches   204

     Tricks for the Tricky   207

     Magic Characters Chart   209

Summary   **210**

Exercises   **210**

Chapter 6: Handling and Avoiding Errors   213

Kinds of Errors   213
Syntax Errors   213
Runtime Errors   217
Handling Errors   218
Default Error Behavior   218
Checking Assumptions   219
    Code Errors   220
    Data Errors   220
    The assert and error Functions   220
    Defining Your Own Error Condition   221
Anticipating Error Conditions   222
Working with Return Values   222
Structuring Code   224
Error-Containment Functions   227
    The pcall Function   227
    The xpcall Function   229
    User-Written Scripts   230
Locating Errors   230
Summary   230
Exercises   231

Chapter 7: Using Modules   233

Interfaces and Implementations   233
The require Function   234
Where to Put Modules   235
Creating a Module Directory   235
Setting Lua's Environment Variable   236
Preserving a Module's Interface   236
Module Bookkeeping   240
Bytecode   241
Namespaces   242
Creating and Reusing Namespaces   242
Avoiding Global Variables   244
    Using the strict Module   244
    Reporting All Global Assignments   244
The module Function   245
C Modules   247
Summary   247
Exercises   247

Contents

Chapter 8: Extending Lua's Behavior with Metamethods   **249**

Using Concatenation and Arithmetical Operators on Tables   **249**
Relational Metamethods   **257**
Indexing and Call Metamethods   **258**
Non-Tables with Metamethods   **265**
Non-Syntactical Metamethods   **267**
Metamethod Applicability   **268**
Summary   **268**
Exercises   **269**

Chapter 9: Handling Events Naturally with Coroutines   **271**

Coroutines and Program Control   **271**
Coroutines Are Not Functions   272
How Coroutines Are Like Programs   272
Coroutines Transfer Control   273
Wrapping a Coroutine   273
Coroutines Are Cooperative   273
Outside Looking In   275
Coroutines Have Status   278
Rules of Conduct   279
Work Shoulder-to-Shoulder   279
Trust the Dispatcher   280
Expect the Best, Prepare for the Worst   280
Play on Your Side of the Fence   280
Avoid the Deep End   281
Managing Concurrent Tasks   **281**
Retaining State   **282**
Exercising a Coroutine's Memory   282
Iterating with Coroutines   286
Handling Events Simply   **287**
The Event Loop   288
Yielding to Another Coroutine   296
Summary   **297**
Exercises   **297**

Chapter 10: Looking Under the Hood   **299**

Bytecode and luac   **299**
Garbage Collection   **303**
The Implementation of Tables and Strings   **307**

Contents

The Debug Library	**308**
Inspecting and Manipulating Running Code	308
Hooks	315
Other Functions in the Debug Library	321
Summary	**321**
Exercises	**322**
Chapter 11: Exploring Lua's Libraries	**325**
Core Library	**325**
Environment Functions	326
Metatable Functions	326
Chunk-Loading Functions	328
Error-Containment Functions	330
Module Functions	331
The Garbage-Collection Function	332
Type and Conversion Functions	333
Basic Output	333
Error-Condition Functions	333
Table Traversal Functions	334
Vararg-Related Functions	335
Coroutine Library	**336**
Package Library	**338**
String Library	**340**
Pattern-Based String Functions	340
String-Conversion Functions	342
Table Library	**344**
Math Library	**345**
Trigonometric Functions	345
Inverse Trigonometric Functions	348
Hyperbolic Functions	351
Exponent Functions	354
Logarithm Functions	356
Adjustment Functions	358
Floating Point Representation	360
Angle Conversion Functions	361
Pseudo-Random Number Functions	362
Modulus Functions	362
Minimum and Maximum Functions	363
Constants	363
Input/Output Library	**364**

Contents

Operating System Library   **368**
CPU Timing   368
Time and Date Functions   368
Filesystem Functions   369
Other Operating System Functions   370
Debugging Library   **370**
Summary   **373**

Chapter 12: Using Community Libraries   **375**

Library Overview   **375**
Dynamically Linked Libraries   376
Resolving External References   376
Configuration Options   376
Libraries Built from Source Code   377
Building Libraries on Unix-Like Systems   378
Building Libraries on Windows   378
Limits to Portability   379
How Lua Interacts with Libraries   **379**
The Variable Registration Process   379
Calling a C Function from Lua   380
The pack Binary Structuring Library   **383**
Building the pack Library on Unix-type Systems   383
Building and Installing the pack Library on Windows   384
Testing the pack Library   384
Installing the pack Library   385
Using the pack Library   385
The cURL File Transfer Library   **389**
Building libcurl   389
Building libcurl on Unix-Like Systems   390
Building libcurl on Windows   391
Building luacurl   392
Building luacurl on Unix-Like Systems   392
Building luacurl on Windows   393
Using luacurl   393
The gd Graphics Library   **395**
Building gd   395
Building gd on Unix-Like Systems   396
Installing gd on Windows   396
Building lua-gd   397
Building lua-gd on Unix-Like Systems   397
Building lua-gd on Windows   398
Using lua-gd   399

Contents

The SQLite Database Library   **405**

Building SQLite3   405

    Building SQLite3 on Unix-Like Systems   405

    Building SQLite3 on Windows   406

Building lua-sqlite3   407

    Building lua-sqlite3 on Unix-Like Systems   407

    Building lua-sqlite3 on Windows   408

Using lua-sqlite3   409

Summary   **411**

Exercises   **412**

Chapter 13: Interfacing Lua with Other Languages   **413**

How C Programs Use Lua   **413**

Embedding Lua   414

Extending Lua   414

Embedding or Extending: Which Is Best?   414

Communicating Between Lua and C   **415**

Calling Lua from C   **421**

Obtaining a Lua Function   421

Calling a Lua Function   421

Protected Calls   422

Working with Userdata   **423**

Indexing Values in C   **436**

Retrieving Indexed Values   436

Setting Indexed Values   437

Retaining Values in C   **438**

The Registry   438

C Function Environments   439

Upvalues in C   439

Referencing Values   440

The Thread Environment   441

Layering Your Extension Library   **441**

Summary   **447**

Exercises   **448**

Chapter 14: Managing Information with Databases   **449**

Some Basic Relational Database Concepts   **449**

SQL, LuaSQL, and MySQL   **458**

Summary   **466**

Exercises   **466**

Contents

Chapter 15: Programming for the Web   **467**

A Web Server Primer   **467**
Dynamic Web Content   **468**
    Embedded Web Server   468
    Extended Web Server   469
    Creating Content at Run Time with Lua   469
Executing CGI Scripts   **469**
    CGI Scripts on Unix-Type Systems   470
    CGI Scripts on Windows   470
Installing a Web Server   **471**
    Apache   471
    TinyWeb   472
Testing Your Web Server with Static Content   **474**
Serving Dynamic Web Content   **474**
    Problems with CGI Scripts   475
    Asynchronous Calls to the Server   476
    Producing a Calendar Dynamically   478
    Producing Charts Dynamically   481
Interactive CGI Applications   **489**
    CGI Helper Routines   489
    Developing CGI Scripts   498
    Security Issues   498
The Kepler Project   **498**
    CGI the Kepler Way   499
    Lua Pages   500
Summary   **501**
Exercises   **501**

Chapter 16: Connecting to a Larger World   **503**

Installing LuaSocket   **503**
    Compiling LuaSocket   504
        Compiling on Linux and Other Unix-Like Systems   504
        Compiling on Windows   504
    Installing Windows Binaries   505
Network Overview   **506**
    Routed Packets   506
    Addresses   507
    Domain Names   507
    Identifying Internet Resources   508
    Transport Protocols   509
    Sockets: Streams and Datagrams   510
    TCP Socket Sociology   511

Contents

Using LuaSocket for Network Communication **512**

Handling Multiple Persistent Connections **518**

Using Lua Coroutines with the select Function 518

Multiple Connections on the Server Side 522

Setting Timeout Values for the Server Socket 523

The Application Protocols **524**

Filtering the Flow of Data 524

Accessing Web Pages 527

Sending and Receiving E-mail Messages 529

Networking with Lua and Streams **536**

On the Server Side: inetd and Friends 536

On the Client Side: ssh and Friends 538

Summary **541**

Exercises **542**

Chapter 17: Programming Games with Lua **543**

Understanding Why and When to Use Lua **543**

Simple 2-D Action Game Using SDL **544**

Installing SDL and LuaCheia 544

Using SDL 546

Summary **562**

Exercise **562**

Chapter 18: Carrying Lua with You **565**

Getting Started with Plua **565**

Obtaining Plua 566

Examining the Distribution Contents 566

Exploring Plua's Features **567**

Running the Plua Application 567

Saving Plua Programs 569

Reading the Online Documentation 570

Using Palm OS Streams 571

Compiling Applications 572

Compiling Libraries 573

Plua on the Mothership **576**

The Command-Line Compiler 576

The Palm OS Emulator 577

Obtaining the Emulator 577

Installing on Windows 578

Configuring POSE 578

Running Plua in the Emulator 578

Contents

Compiling a Program in the Emulator   580

Exiting the Emulator   580

The Palm OS Simulator   581

Obtaining the Simulator   581

Using the Simulator   581

Programming with Plua   **581**

Generating Graphics   582

Programming the User Interface   583

Accessing Databases   590

Summary   **592**

Exercises   **593**

Chapter 19: Fitting into the Lua Community   **595**

The Lua Web Site   **596**

The Lua Reference Manual   **596**

Framing Questions   **597**

The Lua Mailing List   **597**

Viewing and Searching the Archives   597

Downloading the Archives   598

Using a Web Browser to Access the List   599

Using a Newsreader to Access the List   599

Subscribing to the List Server   599

Posting Messages   600

The Lua Chat Room   **601**

Forums   **601**

The Lua Wiki   **601**

LuaForge   **602**

Annual Workshops   **603**

Summary   **603**

Appendix A: Answers   **605**

Index   **629**

Introduction

Perhaps you need one or more of these things:

- ❏ A way to present dynamic information, both textual and graphical, on your website
- ❏ A means to transfer legacy data to a modern database
- ❏ Nonprogrammers or end users to augment your application with additional functionality
- ❏ A custom program for your handheld device that you can use in the field
- ❏ Scripts to drive the user interface and business logic of an enterprise-level application
- ❏ An engine to run gaming scripts
- ❏ An interface language for scientific instrumentation
- ❏ A scripted way to monitor the health of a computer network
- ❏ A robust mechanism to allow end users to set application options in an easy-to-understand configuration file

If so, you'll find this versatile and fast programming language called Lua to be the perfect tool. Lua has a gentle learning curve that will enable you to write effective programs after only a short introduction. With it, simple programs *look* simple—there is no extraneous baggage you need to add to your programs or peculiar syntax to which you need to conform to make them run. From the examples in the preceding list, you can see that Lua is quite appropriate for use by technically adept individuals who aren't necessarily programmers.

At the other end of the continuum, Lua has features that support advanced program requirements. It imposes very few conventions on the way you write your programs, instead providing mechanisms with which you can construct clear and maintainable solutions to your programming tasks. Even experienced software developers find novel and powerful ways of using Lua to extend and simplify their applications.

Lua is robust, yet its mild entry curve makes it quite suitable as a first programming language. In combination, these make Lua an attractive language for students and professionals alike.

The Facets of Lua

Lua is, first and foremost, a tool for creating software. You can use the standalone interpreter that is packaged with the Lua distribution to great advantage, and fit it seamlessly into your applications.

Lua Is a Programming Language

Lua as a language has its own grammar and idioms. Like all languages, it is a means to communicate, and like all programming languages, it can be used to convey instructions to a computer. But this connection to hardware isn't essential. In fact, Edsger Dijkstra, one of the towering figures of computer science, emphasized the importance of programming without a computer to really understand and verify programs. Lua's syntax—the rules that dictate how its language pieces may fit together correctly—is small, clean, and straightforward. This syntax includes ways to convey instructions as well as to describe data.

Lua Is an Implementation

Lua is also a functioning software system. A part of what we call Lua is an actual computer application that can interpret programs written in the Lua programming language. The Lua interpreter is written in ANSI C, which because of its wide support, allows Lua to run on a vast spectrum of devices from high-end network servers to small devices.

Both Lua's language and its interpreter are mature, small, and fast. Both have been synthesized from some of the best ideas and practices in computer science. The smallness of Lua is by design, and has advantages well beyond Lua's capability to run on tiny hardware. A few visits to Lua's mailing list will assure you that there are enthusiasts who understand every nook and cranny of this language and its implementation. Its source code has been scrutinized. It can be argued that these insights, and the suggestions for refinements that these insights foster, would be much less likely with a larger language and implementation.

Lua Is Fast

Traditionally, programming language ease-of-use has come at the cost of performance. The C programming language is known for its speed and extensive library support, but it is rarely categorized as easy to use. Lua alters the playing field somewhat by being both easy to use and fast, and it has the ability to interface smoothly with C libraries. How fast is Lua? In a word: *very*. A visit to the programming language shootout site (`shootout.alioth.debian.org`) should convince you that with Lua, speed and expressivity are not mutually exclusive.

Lua Is Free and Open

Lua is open-source software. You can use it in personal, academic, and commercial applications at no cost. Your essential requirements when using Lua are to properly ascribe its copyright (Lua.org, PUC-Rio) and to not hold its authors or copyright holders liable if anything goes wrong. You can read its license at `www.lua.org`. Be aware that some of the libraries you will use with Lua are licensed under different terms. Please understand and adhere to these licenses. A lot of hard work and ingenuity goes into the creation of software, and your respect for its authors' intentions helps keep the open software community vibrant and active.

Who This Book Is For

This book is for students and professionals who are intrigued by the prospect of learning and using a powerful language that provides a rich infrastructure for creating programs. No programming knowledge is necessary to benefit from this book except for the section on Lua bindings, which requires some familiarity with the C programming language. A certain comfort level with command-line operations, text editing, and directory structures is assumed.

Software developers who have experience with functions, strings, and associative arrays can skim Chapters 2 through 5 with the caveat that certain Lua colloquialisms are introduced there along with programming concepts.

Throughout the text, sections pertaining to a particular operating system are clearly marked and can be skipped by readers working on a different platform.

How This Book Is Structured

This book is organized to guide you through the basics of using Lua. Its structure is as follows:

- ❑ Installing Lua on your system (Chapter 1)
- ❑ Learning the fundamentals of programming in Lua (Chapters 2 through 10)
- ❑ Reviewing standard Lua functions (Chapter 11)
- ❑ Exploring application development with Lua using packages contributed by the community (Chapters 12 through 18)
- ❑ Using Lua's many community resources (Chapter 19)

Chapters 2 through 10 each build on concepts that are presented in its predecessors, so a sequential reading of this part of the book is advised. The summary of Lua's built-in libraries contains examples that assume you have a good grasp of the materials presented in the first 10 chapters.

Some of the libraries and techniques presented in Chapters 12 and 13 are needed in the remaining chapters of the book. Chapters 14 through 19 are relatively independent of one another and can be read out of sequence.

What You Need to Use This Book

You need surprisingly little in the way of computer resources to learn and use Lua. This book focuses on Windows and Unix-like (including Linux) systems, but any operating system that supports a command shell should be suitable. You'll need a text editor to prepare and save Lua scripts.

If you choose to extend Lua with libraries written in a programming language like C, you'll need a suitable software development kit. Many of these kits are freely available on the Internet but, unlike Lua, they can consume prodigious amounts of disk space and memory.

Chapter 18 discusses using Lua on a Palm Pilot. Even if you don't own or have access to one of these devices, this chapter shows how you can simulate one on the major desktop systems.

Conventions

To help you get the most from the text and keep track of what's happening, a number of conventions are used throughout the book.

Try It Out

This is an exercise you should work through, following the text in the book.

1. A Try It Out usually consists of a set of steps.
2. Each step has a number.
3. Complete all the steps, sequentially, to produce the intended results.

How It Works

After each Try It Out, the code you've typed is explained in detail.

Boxes like this one hold important, not-to-be forgotten information that is directly relevant to the surrounding text.

Tips, hints, tricks, and asides to the current discussion are offset and placed in italics like this.

As for styles in the text:

❑ New terms and important words are *highlighted* when they're introduced.

❑ Keyboard strokes look like this: Ctrl+A.

❑ Filenames, URLs, and code within the text look like so: `persistence.properties`.

❑ Code is presented in two different ways:

```
In code examples, new and important code is highlighted with a gray background.
```

```
The gray highlighting is not used for code that's less important in the present
context, or has been shown before.
```

Some of the code examples are mixtures of your input and Lua's output:

```
> In such examples, your input is bold
and Lua's output is not.
```

Source Code

As you work through the examples in this book, you may choose either to type in all the code manually or to use the source code files that accompany the book. All of the source code used in this book is available for download at www.wrox.com. On this site, you can simply locate the book's title (either by using the Search box or by using one of the title lists) and click the Download Code link on the book's detail page to obtain all the source code for the book.

> *Because many books have similar titles, you may find it easiest to search by ISBN. This book's ISBN is 978-0-470-06917-2.*

Alternatively, you can go to the main Wrox code download page at http://wrox.com/dynamic/books/download.aspx to see the code available for this book and all other Wrox books.

After you download the code, just decompress it with your favorite compression tool.

Errata

We make every effort to ensure that there are no errors in the text or in the code. However, no one is perfect, and mistakes do occur. If you find an error in one of our books, like a spelling mistake or faulty piece of code, we would be very grateful for your feedback. By sending in errata you may save another reader hours of frustration, and at the same time, you will be helping us provide even higher quality information.

To find the errata page for this book, go to www.wrox.com and locate the title using the Search box or one of the title lists. Then, on the book details page, click the Book Errata link. On this page, you can view all errata that has been submitted for this book and posted by Wrox editors. A complete book list including links to each book's errata is also available at www.wrox.com/misc-pages/booklist.shtml.

If you don't spot "your" error on the Book Errata page, go to www.wrox.com/contact/techsupport.shtml and complete the form there to send us the error you found. We'll check the information and, if appropriate, post a message to the book's errata page and fix the problem in subsequent editions of the book.

p2p.wrox.com

For author and peer discussion, join the P2P forums at p2p.wrox.com. The forums are a Web-based system for you to post messages relating to Wrox books and related technologies and interact with other readers and technology users. The forums offer a subscription feature to e-mail you topics of interest of your choosing when new posts are made to the forums. Wrox authors, editors, other industry experts, and your fellow readers are present on these forums.

At http://p2p.wrox.com you will find a number of different forums that will help you not only as you read this book, but also as you develop your own applications. To join the forums, just follow these steps:

1. Go to p2p.wrox.com and click the Register link.
2. Read the terms of use and click Agree.
3. Complete the required information to join as well as any optional information you wish to provide and click Submit.
4. You will receive an e-mail with information describing how to verify your account and complete the joining process.

You can read messages in the forums without joining P2P but to post your own messages, you must join.

After you join, you can post new messages and respond to messages other users post. You can read messages at any time on the Web. If you would like to have new messages from a particular forum e-mailed to you, click the Subscribe To This Forum icon by the forum name in the forum listing.

For more information about how to use the Wrox P2P, be sure to read the P2P FAQs for answers to questions about how the forum software works as well as many common questions specific to P2P and Wrox books. To read the FAQs, click the FAQ link on any P2P page.

Getting Situated

The first order of business in learning to program in Lua is to acquire and install the necessary tools. For your initial steps, all you need is the Lua *interpreter*, a small program that enables you to type Lua commands and have them executed immediately. As you advance through this book, you will need additional tools such as a text editor and the Lua compiler.

If you want to write web applications, you'll need access to a web server such as Kepler (a versatile Lua-based web server) or Apache (an industry-wide standard). These and other web servers are freely available on the Internet.

If you want to extend Lua with low-level libraries or to embed Lua into your application, you'll need a *software development kit* (often referred to as SDK) with a compiler that is compatible with Lua's *application program interface* (referred to as API).

Lua is written in the C programming language, and a C compiler turns a program written in this language into something that can run on your computer. Most C compilers work fine, as do Delphi and the cross-platform Free Pascal Compiler.

This chapter is unlike the others in this book, because it has little to do with Lua and much to do with setting up programs on your system. Although Lua doesn't have a setup program that handles installation details, you'll find the steps are straightforward. In addition to guiding you through the process, this chapter briefly explores programming editors and revision control systems — tools that can enhance your productivity as you become proficient in Lua.

Choosing How to Install Lua

Lua can be installed on a wide variety of platforms and, after it is installed, it will function similarly on all of them. Unlike most of the material that follows in this book, this chapter necessarily delves into some platform-specific details. Basically, there are two categories that are covered here: Windows desktop systems (including Windows 95 and up) and Unix-type systems, including GNU/Linux, Mac OS X, AIX, BSD, and Solaris. (The many other operating systems and hardware platforms capable of running Lua are outside the scope of this book.)

Lua Versions

In the instructions that follow, you'll see references to version 5.1.1. A later version of Lua may be available as you read this. As Lua evolves, some improvements are made that require changes to existing scripts. Your decision is either to install a version of Lua later than 5.1.1 and encounter possible instances where you have to modify the scripts and libraries in this book, or to install version 5.1.1 and forgo any improvements that may have been made to Lua. The Lua manual includes a section at the end named "Incompatibilities with Previous Versions" that can help you decide. If you install a later version, you'll need to make corresponding changes to the commands and directory names used in this chapter.

There are two excellent open-source packages for Windows that blur the Windows-Unix distinction somewhat. One of them, the Cygwin system, provides many GNU and Linux tools (including various shells and development tools) for Windows platforms. It is available at www.cygwin.com. Applications that you build with this environment will run only on systems that have Cygwin installed. If you want to install Lua in this environment, follow the directions for building Lua on Unix-type systems.

The other package is the MinGW system, which enables you to use standard Unix-like tools to build applications that run on all 32-bit desktop versions of Windows without any extra support libraries. This first-rate system is available at www.mingw.org.

As you read this chapter, section headers will indicate whether a Unix-like system or Windows is being discussed. You can skip the sections that don't apply to your platform.

The Lua interpreter, typically named `lua.exe` in Windows and `lua` in Unix and friends, is a small command-line program that executes your scripts either interactively or noninteractively. You'll become familiar with the Lua interpreter and both of these modes in the first chapters of this book.

A note about these names: In this book, Lua refers to the Lua programming language or implementation, and `lua` refers to the Lua interpreter.

To install Lua, you can download a package that has been compiled for your particular operating system platform, or download the source code and compile it yourself. There are the advantages and disadvantages to each approach, as the following sections discuss.

Building Lua Yourself

Compiling Lua is straightforward. Lua, including the language processor and its core libraries, is written in plain vanilla C so that it can be built on a wide variety of platforms with any ANSI-compliant C compiler. The advantage is that the resulting libraries and interpreter program are compatible with the system on which it's built. This is one of the principal advantages of open-source software in general. As long as the target platform supports the tools and libraries needed to compile the source code — in Lua's case, this is a standard C compiler — the resulting binary program is compatible with the platform.

The disadvantage of compiling Lua is that the system you intend to build it on must have a complete C development environment. That is generally not a problem on Unix and Unix-like operating systems where such development tools are part of a long-standing tradition. However, on platforms such as Windows, a C compiler and its related tools and files are not installed by default. Such a development package can require a surprisingly large amount of disk space and present a bewildering number of options. One refreshingly small exception to this rule is the Tiny C Compiler (TCC), which runs on Linux and Windows on the 80×86 platform. Building Lua with TCC is described later in this chapter.

Selecting Prebuilt Lua

Besides being able to skip the compilation step, an advantage of selecting a prebuilt version of Lua is that it will be compatible with a number of libraries that conform to its dependency conventions. These conventions involve issues such as which runtime libraries are used and whether those libraries are safe to use with multiple threads of execution.

If you are a Windows user and don't have a C development environment set up on your system, installing the appropriate binary Lua package may be your best option. You'll see how to do that in the section on installing binary packages later in this chapter.

Finding Your System's Shell

Most computer systems have a *shell*, also known as a *command-line interface*. This is a program you can use to type commands to the computer. These commands can tell the computer to copy, move, delete, and otherwise manipulate files, and to start programs, including (of course) Lua programs and Lua itself. In several places in this book, you'll need to access your system's shell; in particular, everything in this chapter that you need to type, you need to type into the shell. You can perform some of the operations, such as creating directories and moving files, using visual tools (such as Explorer on the Windows platform). Only the shell commands are presented here, but feel free to use whatever tools you are most comfortable with to accomplish the task at hand.

Windows Shells

To access your shell on Windows XP or Windows 2000, select Start⇨Run, type cmd, and press Enter. On Windows Me, Windows 98, or Windows 95, select Start⇨Run, type command, and press Enter (Return on some keyboards — just substitute "Return" for "Enter" whenever it's mentioned in this book).

Shells on Unix and Unix-Like systems

On Mac OS X, open your Applications folder (on your startup disk). Inside it, open the Utilities folder; inside that, open Terminal. On other systems with a graphical user interface (GUI), look in the menu that you start programs from for a program with a name like xterm, Konsole, or Terminal. On systems without a graphical user interface, you are already at the shell, as you are if you use a program such as ssh, telnet, or PuTTY to connect to a remote Unix(-like) server.

Shell Features

Shells vary greatly in appearance and functionality, but each of them presents some form of a prompt to let you know that it's waiting for you to issue a command. In general, you type a command following the prompt and press the Enter key to submit the command to the shell. When you are working in a shell, there is always one directory that is considered your current working directory. Most shell prompts contain that directory to make it easier for you to keep your bearings as you move from directory to directory. For example, a typical prompt in Windows shells may look something like the following:

```
C:\Program Files>
```

and in Unix-type shells, something like the following:

```
mozart maryann /usr/local/bin>
```

To exit the shell, type `exit` and press Enter.

The Environment

Each shell also has a pool of variables, known as the *environment*, available to programs. The environment typically holds information about where the system should look for programs and libraries, what the shell prompt should look like, and so forth. You can view this information by issuing the following command at the shell prompt:

```
set
```

Regardless of the platform you use, you will want to modify the shell environment to let Lua know where to find extension modules. Additionally, if you intend to compile Lua or libraries, you'll need to set up environment variables that your SDK will look for.

Environment Variables on Unix-Like Systems

On Unix-like systems, you generally modify the shell environment in one of the shell startup scripts. For example, if you use the `bash` shell, it will process `/etc/bashrc` and, in your home directory, `.bashrc` when it starts. The first file is used for system-wide settings, and the second is used for your own private settings. You'll need root privileges to modify the first. Within these files, you set an environment variable by including a line that looks like the following:

```
export LUA_DIR=/usr/local/lib/lua/5.1
```

When you reference environment variables in shell scripts, you precede the name with $, as in `echo $LUA_DIR`.

In this book, the following environment variables are recommended for Unix-like systems:

```
LUA_DIR=/usr/local/lib/lua/5.1
LUA_CPATH=?.so;$LUA_DIR/?.so
LUA_PATH=?.lua;$LUA_DIR/?.lua
```

Restart the shell for changes to take effect.

Now create the actual directory that LUA_DIR identifies. Do this, as root, with the following command:

```
mkdir -p /usr/local/lib/lua/5.1
```

Environment Variables on Windows

Depending on which version of Windows you use, you modify the shell environment either through the autoexec.bat file (Window 95, 98 and ME) or, for later versions, through a dedicated dialog box that you get to through the System Properties dialog box. If you use autoexec.bat, you set environment variables with lines that look like the following:

```
SET LUA_DIR="c:\program files\lua\5.1"
```

If you use the dedicated dialog box, you'll need to choose between system variables and user variables. In this window, you can add a new variable, edit an existing variable, or delete an existing variable. When you add or edit a variable, there are separate input fields for the variable name and its value.

Within a shell script, surround an environment variable name with the % character, as in — echo %LUA_DIR%.

The Windows Search Path

On a Windows system, whether you compile Lua or acquire a precompiled package, you'll want to put the Lua interpreter, compiler, and dynamic link library in a location that makes them easy to use. From a shell prompt, the system should launch the interpreter when you execute the lua command. There are two practical approaches you can take: using aliases or using the search path.

When you're at the shell prompt, Windows enables you to use a simple alias — lua, for example — as a replacement for a more complicated command, such as c:\program files\utility\lua.exe. It implements aliases like these, in addition to command-line editing and history, using doskey. This method may locate the aliased program slightly faster, but you cannot use the alias in a batch script. Consult the output of the following to read more about this utility:

```
doskey /?
```

You can also use the Windows search path mechanism. When a command is invoked that is not internal (such as dir or del) and is not qualified with path information, Windows examines the search path, looking for a matching executable. To see the current search path from the shell, execute this command:

```
path
```

In the following steps, you work with files and directories so you can use Windows Explorer if you like. Complete these steps to move the Lua executables to a directory that is included in the Windows search path:

1. If your current search path does not include a directory where you store utilities, create one now (the directory c:\program files\utility is assumed for this example, but the choice is yours). Note that quotes are necessary when specifying names with spaces:

```
mkdir "c:\program files\utility"
```

2. Add this directory to the Windows search path. On older versions of Windows, use the `autoexec.bat` file in the root directory of the boot drive. (More recent versions of Windows still support this, but they also provide a graphical environment editor that you by opening the System applet from the Control Panel.)

   If the text field containing the path variable is too small to see the entire value, cut and paste the value to your text editor, make the appropriate change, and then cut and paste the modified value back to the path edit field.

3. The new search path applies only to shells that are opened after the change, so exit and restart your shell.

Recommended Settings for Windows

For this book, the following environment variables are recommended on Windows systems:

```
UTIL_DIR=c:\program files\utility
LUA_DIR=c:\program files\lua\5.1
LUA_CPATH=?.dll;%LUA_DIR%\?.dll
LUA_PATH=?.lua;%LUA_DIR%\?.lua
```

The UTIL_DIR variable identifies the utility directory you created in the preceding section. Additionally, if you have a software development kit and intend to compile Lua and possibly libraries for Lua, set the following environment variables:

```
SDK_DIR=c:\program files\msc
INCLUDE=%SDK_DIR%\include;%SDK_DIR%\include\usr
LIB=%SDK_DIR%\lib;%SDK_DIR%\lib\usr
```

The SDK_DIR depends on where you installed your SDK.

Restart your shell for environment changes to take effect. Then use Windows Explorer or the command shell to create the various directories that these environment variables identify.

Dealing with Tarballs and Zip Files

Whether you install Lua using precompiled packages or compile it from a source code package, you will be dealing with a packaging form colloquially known as a *tarball*. Files of this type have the extension `.tar.gz` or `.tgz`. A tarball bundles a group of files that can be distributed over one or more directories. The contents, owners, permissions, and timestamps of the bundled files are preserved using the `tar` utility, whose name derives from its original purpose of transferring files to and from a tape archive. The amalgamated file is then compressed using the `gzip` utility or, for tarballs with the `.tar.bz2` extension, using the slower and more aggressive `bzip2` compression utility. Although tarballs are part of the Unix tradition, tools for managing them on Windows are freely available. In particular, one versatile open-source utility for Windows that handles any type of package you are likely to encounter is `7z`. Both graphical and shell-oriented versions are available from `www.7-zip.org`. Whichever version you use, make sure the directory in which you install 7-zip is included in your system search path. Extracting the contents of a tarball in Windows is a two-step process. Here's how to do it from the shell. First, unzip the embedded tarball using a command like the following:

```
7z x somefile.tar.gz
```

In a standard package, this creates the file `somefile.tar`. Extract the contents of this tarball with a command like the following:

```
7z x somefile.tar
```

Another packaging format, more common for Windows-based projects, is the zip file, which has a `.zip` extension. The `zip` and `unzip` utilities on Unix-style systems manage files of this type. On Windows, you can extract the contents of a zip file using `7z` with a command like the following:

```
7z x somefile.zip
```

Compiling Lua

In the general sense, compiling an application refers to the process of building an executable program from source components. The executable program comprises processor instructions that a computer can follow. It may also contain certain resources such as embedded icons and copyright notices. Source code is the text that is created in a programming language by a programmer. Strictly speaking, compilation is the intricate step that translates a source-code text file to a machine-code object file. Object files usually contain references to other object files that may or may not be part of the same package. A *linker* generates an executable program by combining all required object files and resolving their references to one another. Sometimes the compilation and linking steps are combined by a wrapper program.

The Lua Source Tarball

The contents of the Lua tarball are organized as follows:

```
lua-5.1.1
  doc
  etc
  src
  test
```

In the first level of this directory, you can read various text documents prepared by the Lua authors. The README file explains what Lua is, the terms by which it is available, how to install it, and its origin. The HISTORY file tracks the changes to the Lua language, its application programming interface (API), and its implementation. Read the relevant portion of that file when upgrading to a new version of Lua to understand the changes that have been made. The INSTALL file has information about building Lua.

You can read these files using a text viewer or editor. If you are using a Unix-type system, the `less` command is convenient for scanning text files. The `lynx` character-mode web browser is great for exploring the distribution: use the arrow keys to drill into and out of directories and the contents of text and HTML files. Press **Q** to exit `less` or `lynx` when you are ready to return to the shell itself. If you are a Windows user, note that the files have Unix-style line endings that will not be properly handled by Windows Notepad, so you should use a programmer's editor or a web browser to read them.

With your web browser, you can explore the hyperlinked Lua manual in the `doc` subdirectory. The `src` subdirectory contains all of the source code for the Lua interpreter, compiler, and core libraries. The `etc` subdirectory contains miscellaneous files such as the Lua icon and the source code for an especially small interpreter with reduced functionality. The `test` subdirectory contains a number of Lua scripts that provide an excellent survey of Lua's capabilities. Some of these scripts push at the far reaches of Lua's domain, so don't be dismayed if some appear rather dense at first.

Compiling Lua on Linux and Other Unix-Like Systems

One of the first things you should do at your shell is to check whether you have a functioning C compiler. To do so, execute the following command:

```
cc -v
```

If version and configuration information is displayed, then it's likely that you've got everything you need to successfully build Lua. If you receive a message indicating that the command `cc` could not be found, try executing `gcc -v` instead. If neither of these commands work, you need to find out if either the C development tools have not been installed or some configuration setting is simply keeping them from being available to you.

Where you build Lua depends on your purposes. If you intend for Lua to be used by other users on your system, and you have the appropriate privileges, you'll want to select a standard location for source code such as `/usr/local/src`. Otherwise, your home directory is a logical choice. In the shell, change your default working directory with the following command:

```
cd /usr/local/src
```

Alternatively, simply use `cd` to go to your home directory.

Assuming you are connected to the Internet, acquire the source package as follows:

```
wget http://www.lua.org/ftp/lua-5.1.1.tar.gz
```

The program `wget` is a standard tool for retrieving Internet resources such as web pages and other files. If your system doesn't have it, you can try `curl` or an interactive web browser. The file you download will be in the form of a tarball that has the extension `.tar.gz`. Extract the contents as follows:

```
tar xzvf lua-5.1.1.tar.gz
```

The `tar` utility will recreate the same directory structure that the Lua authors used to package the source materials. Drop into the newly created directory by executing the following command:

```
cd lua-5.1.1
```

You'll use the `make` utility to control the build process. This utility reads a script, typically named `makefile`, that describes the dependency relationships between the various source files and intermediate and final targets. For example, one of the lines in Lua's `makefile` is as follows:

```
lua.o: lua.c lua.h luaconf.h lauxlib.h lualib.h
```

Here, `lua.o` is the object file that corresponds to `lua.c`, the main source file of the Lua interpreter. The other files that have the extension .h are header files that contain definitions and prototypes. This line is interpreted as: If `lua.o` is missing or if its timestamp is older than any of the timestamps of `lua.c`, `lua.h`, `luaconf.h`, `lauxlib.h`, or `lualib.h`, then invoke the appropriate rule to generate `lua.o`. The `make` utility is indispensable for keeping track of this kind of dependency and for automating the build process.

If you type `make` by itself, as shown in the following line, you get a list of the various platforms on which you can build Lua:

```
make
```

The output looks like this:

```
Please do
    make PLATFORM
where PLATFORM is one of these:
    aix ansi bsd generic linux macosx mingw posix solaris
```

Select the platform that you're on. For example, if you are compiling on Linux, execute the following command:

```
make linux
```

You'll see the commands displayed on the console as they are executed.

If you are familiar with building other open-source packages, you'll notice that Lua's approach is a little different. There is no configuration stage to identify the characteristics of the system and create a tailor-made makefile. Instead, the platform argument you provide is all the information make needs to select the correct commands and parameters.

Because Lua has such standard requirements, it is unlikely that you will encounter any problems building it. If errors do occur at this stage, they are likely to be related to an incomplete installation of the C development tools or incorrectly configured search paths for header files or libraries. If that happens, read the documentation for your operating system distribution to install and configure the development tools properly.

With the default settings used here, `make` will generate the Lua interpreter (`lua`) and the Lua byte-code compiler (`luac`). These will be created in the `src` subdirectory. No shared libraries will be created — all of the Lua internals required by each of these executables will be statically linked. For example, components such as the parser will be embedded into both `lua` and `luac`, but the byte-code interpreter will be embedded only into `lua`.

After make completes, your shell prompt is displayed. If no error messages were encountered during the building process, you can test the Lua interpreter by executing the following command:

```
make test
```

That should result in output that looks like

```
Hello world, from Lua 5.1!
```

In the unlikely event that you don't get this response, the probable culprit is the unavailability of one or more runtime libraries. Although the Lua internals are statically linked into lua, other libraries are expected to be available for dynamic linking when lua is actually run. These runtime dependencies include the math library, the general purpose C library, and, depending on your platform, libraries that support screen formatting and text input editing and recall. List the shared library dependencies with the following ldd command:

```
ldd src/lua
```

The result is a series of lines such as this:

```
libm.so.6 => /lib/libm.so.6 (0x40024000
libdl.so.2 => /lib/libdl.so.2 (0x40047000)
```

If, in the output, you see one or more "not found" lines such as the following, you'll know that the referenced library is not present on your system or that the dynamic loader is unable to find it:

```
libncurses.so.5 => not found
```

In this case, consult your operating system documentation to guide you through the process of installing the missing library. Alternatively, you can rebuild lua with fewer dependencies with the command make clean generic.

If you have root privileges on your system and would like lua and luac to be available for other users, you should become root at this point. Do this with the following command:

```
su -
```

Alternatively, you can use the sudo command to elevate your privilege level for particular commands. In this case, prefix the command requiring root authority with sudo. In general, using sudo requires some configuration using the visudo command.

The hyphen tells the command that you want the root's environment, including its search paths, to be loaded. Doing so will likely change your default working directory, so you may need to return to the lua directory by using the cd command. For example:

```
cd /usr/local/src/lua-5.1.1
```

You're now ready to install the Lua executables, static library, header files, and manual pages. To do so, execute the following command:

```
make install
```

Then execute the following command to return to your nonroot session:

```
exit
```

The following command should present the lua manual page:

```
man lua
```

You can scroll up and down through the document by using the standard navigation keys. Press **Q** to return to the shell itself.

Now enter following command:

```
lua -v
```

This should present you with a version statement like the following:

```
Lua 5.1.1 Copyright (C) 1994-2006 Lua.org, PUC-Rio
```

Any problem at this point indicates an issue that you can clarify with the following which command:

```
which lua
```

The response should be a line like this:

```
/usr/local/bin/lua
```

A response like the following means that lua was installed into a directory that is not in your *search path*, which is an ordered list of directories that the operating system examines to resolve external commands:

```
which: no lua in (/usr/local/bin:/usr/bin)
```

You can remedy this by editing the PATH variable in your shell startup script to include the directory in which lua and luac were installed. You need to exit and restart the shell for these changes to take effect.

If you don't have root privileges or simply want to test the installation locally, you can execute the following command:

```
make local
```

This creates several additional directories such as bin and man beneath the current directory.

Alternatively, you can specify some other location for the installation. For example, if you want to install in /tmp/lua-5.1.1, execute the following command:

```
make INSTALL_TOP=/tmp/lua-5.1.1 install
```

In these last cases, you'll need to specify a full or relative path to lua, luac, and the man pages because the default search path won't include them. For example, to read the man page installed with the last example, execute the following:

```
man /tmp/lua-5.1.1/man/man1/lua.1
```

Then, to test lua, execute the following command:

```
/tmp/lua-5.1.1/bin/lua -v
```

This section led you through a basic build of Lua on Unix-like systems. Many options exist for configuring Lua in different ways. For example, you can configure Lua to use a primitive data type other than double for numbers. The curious can examine src/luaconf.h to see the configurable options. Your best approach at this point is to leave them at their default settings. This book assumes that you are using Lua with its default options.

Compiling Lua on Windows

Although Lua compiles cleanly on Windows, the makefile that comes with the Lua source package is oriented toward Unix-style systems. Unless you are using a Unix emulation layer such as Cygwin, you'll need to craft your own approach to the task of creating the Lua interpreter and byte-code compiler.

A lot of C/C++ compilers exist for Windows, and many of them are available for free. The tools in these SDKs generally have their own particular set of command line switches, configuration conventions, and system dependencies, making it impractical to cover more than one Windows SDK in this book. The instructions in this book assume you are using the Microsoft Visual C++ 6.0 SDK. Later versions of this kit have been released, but Visual C++ 6.0 is still widely used in the industry because of its support for a broad range of Windows versions. You can configure it to generate programs that use MSVCRT.DLL, a system library that is available on all 32-bit desktop versions of Windows. An effort has been made in this book to provide instructions that will generate applications and libraries that are compatible with the Lua binaries for Windows available on LuaForge. These binaries are easy to deploy, because they depend only on libraries that come with Windows.

If you have a later version of Visual C++ or are using another SDK (such as a product from Pelles C or Borland) you will need to consult the appropriate documentation to find how to build and deploy applications and libraries. Recent versions of the Microsoft C++ SDK require manifest files to be deployed along with applications and libraries.

The directions that follow create the Lua interpreter and compiler. Three approaches are shown. The first works well with Visual C++ 6.0. If you are some other large-scale C development system, follow these directions with the understanding that you may need to make toolkit-specific changes. The second approach is suitable for users of TCC, and the third applies to the MinGW SDK.

Building Lua with Microsoft Visual C++

First, make sure that the SDK's bin directory has been included in your system's search path. Under the SDK's include directory, make a subdirectory named usr. Similarly, under the SDK's lib directory, make a subdirectory named usr. Additionally, as covered in the environment section, you should set the LIB environment variable to the SDK's lib and lib\usr directories, and the INCLUDE environment variable to the SDK's include and include\usr directories. Your SDK may include a batch file named vcvars32.bat that can help with this. If you modify these environment variables, exit and restart the shell to have your changes take effect.

Create a directory in which to build Lua. The following lines assume that this will be c:\dev:

```
c:
cd \
mkdir dev
cd dev
```

Download lua-5.1.1.tar.gz and place it in this directory. Extract the contents. Here are the commands you would use with 7-zip:

```
7z x lua-5.1.1.tar.gz
7z x lua-5.1.1.tar
```

This creates a subdirectory named lua-5.1.1. Delete lua-5.1.1.tar at this point, like this:

```
del lua-5.1.1.tar
```

Drop into the src subdirectory like this:

```
cd lua-5.1.1\src
```

Create a new text file and add the following lines:

```
cl /MD /O2 /W3 /c /DLUA_BUILD_AS_DLL *.c
del *.o
ren lua.obj lua.o
ren luac.obj luac.o
ren print.obj print.o
link /DLL /IMPLIB:lua5.1.lib /OUT:lua5.1.dll *.obj
link /OUT:lua.exe lua.o lua5.1.lib
lib /out:lua5.1-static.lib *.obj
link /OUT:luac.exe luac.o print.o lua5.1-static.lib
```

Save the file as build.bat in the current directory (c:\dev\lua-5.1.1\src).

While you're still in the src subdirectory, run the newly created batch script from the shell:

```
build
```

This compiles each of the source files into a corresponding object file. Prior to linking these object files into a dynamic link library, three object files are renamed to keep them from being included in the library. These are the interpreter, the compiler, and a support file for the compiler. Finally, the interpreter and compiler executables are created. The Lua interpreter is quite small, because its main functionality comes from the dynamic link library. To test the Lua interpreter, execute the following command:

```
.\lua ..\test\hello.lua
```

This should result in the following output:

```
Hello world, from Lua 5.1!
```

Copy the import library and header files associated with the dynamic-link library to standard development directories where your compiler and linker can find them. The approach taken here is to place them in the usr subdirectory beneath the SDK's lib and include directories. These subdirectories can then hold third-party files where they won't be confused with toolkit files.

To install Lua, create a file with the following contents:

```
xcopy lua5.1.lib "%SDK_DIR%\lib\usr\*.*" /y
xcopy lua5.1-static.lib "%SDK_DIR%\lib\usr\*.*" /y
xcopy lua.exe "%UTIL_DIR%\*.*" /y
xcopy luac.exe "%UTIL_DIR%\*.*" /y
xcopy lua5.1.dll "%UTIL_DIR%\*.*" /y
xcopy lua.h "%SDK_DIR%\include\usr\*.*" /y
xcopy luaconf.h "%SDK_DIR%\include\usr\*.*" /y
xcopy lualib.h "%SDK_DIR%\include\usr\*.*" /y
xcopy lauxlib.h "%SDK_DIR%\include\usr\*.*" /y
```

Save this file as install.bat in the src directory. Copy the files by executing this batch script:

```
install
```

Building Lua with the Tiny C Compiler

The Tiny C Compiler (TCC) is a freely available C development system that you can use to build Lua on both Linux and Windows. It is discussed here because it is an excellent way for Windows users who don't have a C toolkit to familiarize themselves with developing programs in C. The TCC web site (http://fabrice.bellard.free.fr/tcc) contains a link to the Window binary distribution in the form of a zip file that includes everything you need to compile Lua.

TCC is perfectly suitable for building Lua itself, but you may want to consider a more full-featured SDK if you intend to build extension libraries for Lua.

Download the zip file and place it in the directory above the point where you want to install TCC. Assuming you are using the 7-zip utility and the version of the file is 0.9.23, extract the contents of the file as follows:

```
7z x tcc-0.9.23.zip
```

This creates the following subdirectory structure:

```
tcc-0.9.23
  doc
  examples
  include
    sys
    winapi
  lib
  tcc
```

With this particular version of TCC, you need to make two small adjustments before proceeding. In the include/winapi directory, open the winnt.h file with your text editor. On lines 1814 and 2288, change the occurrences of Value to _Value.

Change your working directory to Lua's source directory. For example, if you extracted the Lua tarball in c:\dev, use the following shell commands:

```
c:
cd \dev\lua-5.1.1\src
```

TCC requires a change to the file ldo.c. Open this file with your text editor and find line 487, which reads as follows:

```
static void f_parser (lua_State *L, void *ud) {
```

Just beneath it, add the following line:

```
typedef Proto* (* load_func) (lua_State*, ZIO*, Mbuffer*, const char*);
```

Several lines lower, find the line that includes

```
((c == LUA_SIGNATURE[0]) ? luaU_undump : luaY_parser)
```

and replace

```
luaU_undump
```

with

```
(load_func) luaU_undump
```

and

```
luaY_parser
```

with

```
(load_func) luaY_parser.
```

Use your text editor to prepare the following batch file. Adjust the first line if necessary to specify the directory in which you installed TCC. The second line begins with SET TCCCMD and ends with -lkernel32 — make sure it is all on one line. (The ⊃ symbol indicates that the code line is too long to print on one line in the book; the code that follows is a continuation of the first line. In other words, ⊃ tells you to keep typing on the same line.)

```
SET TCCDIR=c:\program files\tcc-0.9.23
SET TCCCMD="%TCCDIR%\tcc\tcc" -D_WIN32 -I"%TCCDIR%\include" ⊃
  -I"%TCCDIR%\include\winapi" -L"%TCCDIR%\lib" -lkernel32
ren luac.c luac.c0
ren print.c print.c0
%TCCCMD% -o lua.exe *.c
ren lua.c lua.c0
ren luac.c0 luac.c
ren print.c0 print.c
%TCCCMD% -o luac.exe *.c
ren lua.c0 lua.c
SET TCCDIR=
SET TCCCMD=
SET TCCIMP=
```

Save this file as build.bat in the current directory. Build Lua by running this batch script:

```
.\build
```

Although TCC can generate dynamic link libraries, the code that is shown here builds statically linked versions of lua.exe and luac.exe. Copy these to your utility directory as follows:

```
xcopy lua.exe "%UTIL_DIR%\*.*" /y
xcopy luac.exe "%UTIL_DIR%\*.*" /y
```

Building Lua with MinGW

The MinGW package provides you with all the command-line tools you need to develop Windows applications. An optional related package, MSYS, includes a Unix-like shell and, among other tools, awk, bzip2, find, grep, sed, tar, vi, and which. The instructions that follow cover only the use of MinGW, but MSYS is definitely worth investigating if you want the power and flexibility of working in a Unix-like development environment. The MinGW website has an excellent FAQ (Frequently Asked Questions) page as well as a comprehensive wiki to help you use the MinGW and MSYS systems to their fullest.

The following instructions show you how to install the MinGW system. You need about 50MB of space available on your disk. Obtain the following files (or more recent versions if they are available) from the current section of download page of the MinGW site, www.mingw.org:

```
binutils-2.15.91-20040904-1.tar.gz
w32api-3.6.tar.gz
mingw-utils-0.3.tar.gz
gcc-core-3.4.2-20040916-1.tar.gz
mingw-runtime-3.9.tar.gz
```

Create a directory for the MinGW files as follows:

These instructions assume you will install MinGW in `c:\mingw`, *but you can choose another location if you like. If you do, make the appropriate changes in the following lines.*

```
c:
mkdir \mingw
cd \mingw
```

Extract the contents of the tarballs as follows, changing all occurrences of `\path\to` to the directory where you placed the downloaded files:

The 7-zip tool is used in this example; remember that its directory must be in the Windows search path. If you have downloaded more recent versions of any of these files, be sure to make the appropriate file-name changes. .

```
7z x \path\to\binutils-2.15.91-20040904-1.tar.gz
7z x \path\to\w32api-3.6.tar.gz
7z x \path\to\mingw-utils-0.3.tar.gz
7z x \path\to\gcc-core-3.4.2-20040916-1.tar.gz
7z x \path\to\mingw-runtime-3.9.tar.gz
7z x -y *.tar
del *.tar
```

Place `c:\mingw\bin` in your Windows search path. (See "The Windows Search Path" earlier in this chapter for more details on setting this.)

Create a directory in which to build Lua. The following lines assume that this will be `c:\dev`:

```
c:
mkdir \dev
cd \dev
```

Extract the contents. Here's how to do this if you are using the 7-zip tool:

```
7z x \path\to\lua-5.1.1.tar.gz
7z x lua-5.1.1.tar
del lua-5.1.1.tar
```

Drop into the `src` subdirectory as follows:

```
cd lua-5.1.1\src
```

With your Windows text editor, create a new file with the following contents:

```
gcc -O2 -Wall -c *.c
ren lua.o lua.obj
ren luac.o luac.obj
ren print.o print.obj
gcc -shared -Wl,--export-all-symbols -o lua5.1.dll *.o
strip --strip-unneeded lua5.1.dll
gcc -o lua.exe -s lua.obj lua5.1.dll -lm
gcc -o luac.exe -s -static luac.obj print.obj *.o -lm
```

Save the file as `build.bat` in the `c:\dev\lua-5.1.1\src` directory. While you're still in Lua's src directory, invoke this batch file to build Lua:

```
.\build
```

The batch script generates three files: `lua.exe`, `luac.exe`, and `lua5.1.dll`. You can verify that they use only standard Windows libraries as follows:

If you have installed the MSYS tools, replace `find` *with* `grep`.

```
objdump -x lua.exe | find "DLL Name"
```

This will print the following import references:

```
DLL Name: KERNEL32.dll
DLL Name: msvcrt.dll
DLL Name: lua5.1.dll
```

You can repeat this for `luac.exe` and `lua5.1.dll`. Notice that `luac.exe` does not depend on `lua5.1.dll`.

Install the three files in your utility directory as follows:

```
xcopy lua.exe "%UTIL_DIR%\*.*" /y
xcopy luac.exe "%UTIL_DIR%\*.*" /y
xcopy lua5.1.dll "%UTIL_DIR%\*.*" /y
```

Binary Packages

Unlike source code that can conform to a wide spectrum of environments, binary applications (that is, those that have already been compiled) function only in a particular niche. Binary packages need to distinguish a number of factors, including the following:

❑ Operating system (such as AIX, Solaris, Linux, or Windows)

❑ Hardware architecture (such as 32-bit versus 64-bit or Intel versus PowerPC)

❑ Required C runtime library (such as the various versions of the Microsoft Visual C runtime library)

These are mostly issues that you don't have to be concerned with when compiling Lua from source code, but you do need to pay attention to when the packages are precompiled. Despite the plethora of different platforms, there is a good chance that you can find a binary package for your particular environment.

Selecting a Prebuilt Binary Package

To acquire a Lua package precompiled for your platform, visit LuaForge (`http://luaforge.net/`), a web site devoted to open-source projects created and maintained by members of the growing Lua community.

One of the most popular packages maintained at LuaForge is LuaBinaries, a set of ready-made Lua packages (http://luaforge.net/projects/luabinaries/). In the file download section of the LuaBinaries site is a list of files that includes entries like these:

```
lua5_1_Win32_bin.tar.gz      82060  1,376  Intel x86 .gz
lua5_1_Linux26_bin.tar.gz   127132     80  Intel x86 .gz
```

The names of these files include abbreviated information about their contents. For more detailed information about each of the packages, read the packaging file (apackaging_lua5.1.html) located in the same directory. It will help you select the appropriate package for your platform.

Installing a Prebuilt Binary Package on a Unix-Type System

After you have selected the appropriate tarball from the LuaBinaries site, download it and place it in the /tmp directory. The following commands assume you have selected lua5_1_Linux24g3_bin.tar.gz — make the appropriate changes if necessary. Unpack it as follows:

```
cd /tmp
tar xzvf lua5_1_Linux24g3_bin.tar.gz
```

This creates the following directory structure:

```
lua5.1
  bin
    Linux24g3
```

In the Linux24g3 subdirectory are three files: the interpreter (lua5.1), the byte-code compiler (luac5.1), and a utility that helps with embedding Lua scripts into C programs (bin2c5.1). Make sure the interpreter works with your system, as follows:

```
lua5.1/bin/Linux24g3/lua5.1 -v
```

This should result in the following output:

```
Lua 5.1 Copyright (C) 1994-2006 Lua.org, PUC-Rio
```

You should get the same response when invoking the compiler with the -v switch. If you don't get this, you've likely selected a binary package that is incompatible with your operating system.

If the interpreter and compiler work with your system, move them to a location in your search path. If you have root privileges and want to make Lua available to all users of your system, the location /usr/local/bin is traditional. If you lack sufficient privileges or are interested only in using Lua yourself, the bin directory beneath your home directory is a good location. In this last case, you may need to create the bin subdirectory and set it as part of your PATH environment variable.

Assuming you have root privileges and want to make Lua available to all users of your system, execute these commands:

```
su -
cd /tmp/lua5.1/bin/Linux24g3
mv lua5.1 /usr/local/bin/lua
mv luac5.1 /usr/local/bin/luac
chown root.root /usr/local/bin/{lua,luac}
chmod u=rwx,go=rx /usr/local/bin/{lua,luac}
cd /tmp
rm -fr lua5.1
exit
```

Now you should be able to execute lua without any path qualification, like this:

```
lua -v
```

Installing a Prebuilt Binary Package on Windows

If you are installing onto a 32-bit version of Windows, a safe bet is to select the package named lua5_1_Win32_bin.tar.gz. This package uses the C runtime library MSVCRT.DLL, which is available on all recent versions of Windows.

After you download one of the tarballs, you need to extract the package contents to a suitable location using a utility such as Winzip or 7-zip. The following instructions assume you have downloaded the package lua5_1_Win32_bin.tar.gz and are using the 7-zip command-line utility — make the appropriate changes if you have selected a different package or are using a different extraction utility. Place the package in the directory of your choice, and then execute the following commands at a shell prompt:

```
7z x lua5_1_Win32_bin.tar.gz
7z x lua5_1_Win32_bin.tar
del lua5_1_Win32_bin.tar
```

The following directory structure will be created:

```
lua5.1
  bin
    Win32
```

Four files are included in the Win32 subdirectory: the interpreter (lua5.1.exe), the byte-code compiler (luac5.1.exe), the Lua core in dynamic link library form (lua5.1.dll), and an embedding tool (bin2c5.1.exe). Change your default working directory to Win32 with the following command:

```
cd lua5.1\bin\Win32
```

Install the dynamic link library and executables as follows:

```
copy /b lua5.1.exe "%UTIL_DIR%\lua.exe"
copy /b luac5.1.exe "%UTIL_DIR%\luac.exe"
copy /b lua5.1.dll "%UTIL_DIR%\"
copy /b bin2c5.1.exe "%UTIL_DIR%\bin2c.exe"
```

You do not rename the library, `lua5.1.dll`, because references to it are embedded in the interpreter and compiler.

Type **lua -v** and **luac -v** from any working directory to make sure the two programs are accessible on the search path.

An additional nicety is to add the Lua icon to this directory. You can copy the icon named `lua.ico` in the `etc` directory of the Lua source package to the utility directory.

Additional Tools

While on the topic of getting situated with Lua, a few notes about programming editors and script management are appropriate. Although these tools and methods are not required to create programs, their use definitely makes you more productive.

Programmer's Editor

One tool you want to choose carefully is your text editor. You'll use it not only to create Lua scripts, but also to read and search through them. A vast number of free and commercial text editors are available for all mainstream platforms. Wikipedia has a comprehensive summary of their availability and features at `http://en.wikipedia.org/wiki/Comparison_of_text_editors`. Programmer's editors provide features well beyond the basic editing of text including features such as the following:

❑ Advanced search and replace using regular expressions, a powerful form of recognizing patterns in text

❑ Syntax highlighting that gives you visual confirmation that your script is properly structured

❑ Multiple undoing and redoing

❑ Bracket matching

❑ The capability to automatically hide portions of text and code

❑ Macros to automatically repeat time-consuming or error-prone operations

❑ The capability to filter selected portions of text through an external program (that is, one written in Lua) to process text in ways that might be awkward or complicated using the editor's own commands

Most programmer's editors enable you to configure syntax highlighting for various programming languages, and syntax highlighting for Lua is provided as part of many editor packages. An editor's highlighting mechanism might have trouble with Lua's novel way of handling multiline comments and strings, but you can usually configure it to handle those constructions at least gracefully if not perfectly.

Revision Control System

Organizing your Lua scripts in a directory or directory tree makes it easier to reuse code that you have written. It also simplifies your managing those scripts with a revision control system such as CVS or Subversion. A revision control system enables you to do the following:

- ❑ Recover an earlier revision of a script
- ❑ Review the history of a script's progress in the form of commit log entries
- ❑ Safely develop scripts from more than one machine
- ❑ Back up your work easily because only the repository needs to be backed up
- ❑ Create and merge multiple sets of files — known as *branches* — to distinguish between the installed and developmental versions of your scripts

One advanced system, Monotone, uses distributed repositories with Lua as a scripting language. Revision control is usually associated with collaborative team efforts, but it has many benefits for the independent programmer as well. The usual cycle is to edit and test your script until you reach some sort of milestone, and then commit the script with a note to the revision control system's repository.

Many well-written books and how-to guides exist for setting up and using open-source revision control systems.

Summary

You now have a working Lua interpreter and compiler on your system.

In this chapter, you learned about the following:

- ❑ Lua's package structure
- ❑ How to build Lua from scratch
- ❑ How to install a precompiled Lua package
- ❑ The advantages of a programmer's editor
- ❑ The advantages of a revision control system for your source code

You'll use the various shell operations you learned about in the chapters ahead. When you extend Lua's functionality with libraries, you'll use the same techniques to obtain and install the libraries as you did in this chapter for Lua itself.

First Steps

This chapter and the next two lay the foundation you need to understand the rest of the book. As such, they cover a great deal of material, although they're still very basic. If you've never programmed before, you'll learn a lot of new concepts; if you're an experienced programmer, you'll see a lot of things that you already know. In the latter case, you are encouraged to skim, but be warned: Some of the Lua building blocks covered in these three chapters may have no counterpart in the languages you are familiar with.

This chapter explains the:

- ❏   Arithmetic operations
- ❏   Variables and assignment
- ❏   Strings
- ❏   *true*, *false*, and *nil* values
- ❏   *if* statements and *while*, *for*, and *repeat* loops

Numbers and Arithmetic Operations: Basic Interpreter Usage

The Lua interpreter — lua — is a program that can execute Lua code that you type right after you type it.

> *This is how the term* interpreter *is used in this chapter, but it can also refer to a particular internal component of the Lua implementation — more on this in the next chapter and Chapter 10.*

In this section, you explore the basics of using lua.

Addition, Subtraction, Multiplication, Division, and Exponentiation

Start with something simple — adding two and two. Access your system's shell, as described in Chapter 1. When you're there, type **lua** and press Enter (Return on some keyboards). You should see something like the following:

```
Lua 5.1.1  Copyright (C) 1994-2006 Lua.org, PUC-Rio
>
```

Typing `lua` starts the Lua interpreter. When it starts, it prints its version number and copyright information, and then it prints the following:

```
>
```

This Lua prompt tells you it's waiting for you to give it something to do.

Now type the following (the part you type is **bold**):

```
> print(2 + 2)
```

Then press Enter. You should see the following:

```
4
>
```

Lua looked between the parentheses, saw 2 + 2, added two and two, and followed the `print` command and output the result to the screen. It then displayed another prompt to tell you it was ready for more.

Lua can handle subtraction, negative numbers, numbers with decimal points, multiplication (using *), division (using /), exponentiation (using ^), and combinations of these. Here are some examples:

```
> print(2 - 2)
0
> print(-2 + -2)
-4
> print(2.5 + 2.75)
5.25
> print(3 * 3)
9
> print(100 / 4)
25
> print(3 ^ 2)
9
> print(5 * -5 + 1 + 1 + 0.5)
-22.5
```

Interacting with the Interpreter

The interpreter knows how to respond when you type Lua code that either contains a mistake or is incomplete. Sooner or later, you'll type something that makes no sense to Lua. In case you haven't already done this accidentally, now is the time to do it on purpose to see what happens. Type **print (2 + + 2)** and press Enter. Here's what you get:

```
> print(2 + + 2)
stdin:1: unexpected symbol near '+'
>
```

Lua sees something that doesn't make sense (two plus signs next to each other), so it prints a short explanation of why it doesn't make sense. The explanation is also known as an *error message*.

Because Lua is only a computer program, its explanations aren't always easy to understand at first, but this one (unexpected symbol near '+') is fairly straightforward. Next to a plus sign, Lua found something it wasn't expecting—in this case another plus sign.

After printing the error message, Lua displayed another prompt to let you know it was ready for more.

You'll get similar error messages if you leave out print or its parentheses, like this:

```
> 2 + 2
stdin:1: unexpected symbol near '2'
> print 2 + 2
stdin:1: '=' expected near '2'
```

If you type something that makes sense except that it's incomplete, Lua lets you finish it on another line. For example, press Enter before the close parenthesis, type the close parenthesis, and press Enter again, like this:

```
> print(2 + 2
>> )
4
```

Lua sees that the first line you typed was incomplete, so it printed >>. This is a *continuation prompt*, Lua's way of letting you know that it's waiting for you to finish what you started. When Lua got the close parenthesis on the next line, it was able to print the result.

Other Notations for Numbers

You can also write numbers using *scientific notation*, where the part before the upper- or lowercase e is multiplied by 10 to the power after the e. For example, 5e2 means 5 times 10 to the 2nd power, or 500. Scientific notation is normally used to write extremely large or extremely small numbers, or for Lua to print them. Here are some examples:

```
> print(5e2)
500
> print(5e-2)
0.05
> print(1.2193263111264E17 / 987654321)
123456789
> print(123456789 * 987654321)
1.2193263111264e+17
> print(2.3283064365387e-10 * 4294967296)
1
```

The numbers you use in daily life (and have used so far in this chapter) are decimal, or base 10. This means that there are 10 digits, 0-9. Lua also understands hexadecimal (base 16) numbers, using the letters a-f (or A-F) to represent 10 through 15. Hexadecimal numbers should start with 0x or 0X. (That's a zero before the x, not a letter O.) They have to be *integers* (whole numbers). Take a look at these examples:

```
> print(0x1)
1
> print(0x10)
16
> print(0xff)
255
> print(0XA)
10
> print(0x03e8)
1000
> print(-0xf000)
-61440
> print(0xff.ff)
stdin:1: ')' expected near '.'
```

Lua 5.0 did not understand hexadecimal numbers.

Interpreter Know-How

Before learning any more about the Lua language, you should know a couple things about the interpreter.

Quitting the Interpreter

Sooner or later, you'll want to take a break. There are three ways to get out of the interpreter:

❑ Press Ctrl+C. This sends the interpreter what is called an *interrupt signal*. If the interpreter is waiting for you to type something, this will exit the interpreter. If the interpreter is stuck, doing something (or nothing) over and over without stopping, then this same key combination will get you back to the state where the interpreter is waiting for you to type something.

❑ Press Ctrl+Z (or on Unix-like platforms, including Mac OS X, press Ctrl+D) at the beginning of an empty line and press Enter. This sends an *end-of-file* (*EOF*). It's a signal to Lua that it should give up trying to get input from you.

❑ The most typing-intensive way to stop the interpreter is to type the following line:

```
os.exit()
```

Interpreter Shortcuts

Depending on your system, you may be able to scroll through an editable history of previous lines you've typed by using the up- and down-arrow keys on your keyboard.

On Windows XP and Windows 2000, this history feature is handled by the cmd *shell. On Windows 95,
98, and Me, it is handled by the* doskey *utility (if it's running). On Unix-like systems, it's handled by
the GNU Readline and History libraries, if they were linked to when your copy of Lua was compiled.*

Here's another typing saver. When the interpreter sees a line that starts with =, such as the following, it
treats the rest of the line as though it came between the parentheses of a print:

```
> =2 + 2
4
```

This is not part of the Lua language proper — it only works when you're typing something into the interpreter interactively. This means it's not to be confused with the use of the equal sign that *is* part of Lua
proper, which you'll learn about in the next section. You can substitute this typing-saver use of = for
print() in some of the examples in this chapter, but not all of them. Roughly speaking, you can only use
it if what you're typing is a line unto itself, and not part of one of the multiline structures you'll learn
about later. For consistency, this book generally uses print(), but you should substitute = when possible.

*If you can access the history of what you've typed with the arrow keys, you may (depending on your
system) see that lines that start with = have been transformed into lines that start with* return*. You'll
learn about* return *in the next chapter.*

Numerical Gotchas

At the intersection of the elegant world of mathematics and the sometimes rough-and-ready world of
computers, nonintuitive things may happen. This section explains the major ones.

Division by Zero and Overflow

In arithmetic, dividing a number by zero is undefined. It's also undefined in Lua, which in practice
means that what happens when you divide by zero depends on the C compiler used to compile your
copy of Lua. To find out what happens on your own system, simply divide something by zero and
observe the result. Here is an incomplete list of the possibilities:

❑   Lua may abruptly exit (with no error message).

❑   Lua may freeze and your operating system may display an error message. (If necessary, use
    Ctrl+C to get out of Lua.)

❑   The calculation may succeed and give a result. This result may not be a regular number but may
    instead look like -1.#IND, 1.#INF, Inf, or NaN.

If you do get a pseudo-number like NaN, beware: These generally have unusual behavior, sometimes to
the extent of not being equal to themselves.

Unless you're prepared for the results, never divide by zero.

On most systems, the highest and lowest possible numbers have more than 300 digits (when written in regular base-10 notation). If you happen to go beyond these limits, the same division-by-zero warnings discussed in this section apply.

Floating-Point Rounding

Decimal-point notation cannot accurately express fractions unless they can be expressed in tenths, hundredths, and so on. For instance, ½ is ⁵⁄₁₀, or 0.5; ¼ is ²⁵⁄₁₀₀ or 0.25; but ⅓ is somewhere between 0.33333333 and 0.33333334. Most computer hardware stores numbers in base-2 format, which has a similar problem — numbers not expressible as halves, quarters, eighths, and so on must be rounded to the nearest such fraction before they can be stored. This means that even a seemingly simple number like 0.1 cannot be accurately represented.

Another type of rounding takes place when a number is printed — if it would have an absurdly long number of decimal places, it is rounded to a nearby number. The following example demonstrates both types of rounding:

> *This example uses some things you won't learn until later in this chapter. It's shown here for reference purposes only.*

```
> AlmostOne = 0.1 + 0.1 + 0.1 + 0.1 + 0.1 +
>>    0.1 + 0.1 + 0.1 + 0.1 + 0.1
> print(AlmostOne < 1)
true
> print(AlmostOne)
1
```

Don't let this scare you off — in most situations problems like this don't arise. However, if you do run into two numbers that look alike but are not equal to each other, you now know a possible cause.

If you want to know more about these issues, go to the library or the web. One standard reference is David Goldberg's paper "What Every Computer Scientist Should Know About Floating-Point Arithmetic," which is available at http://docs.sun.com/source/806-3568/ncg_goldberg.html.

> *By default, Lua uses what are known as* double-precision floating-point numbers. *It's possible to recompile Lua to use another representation for numbers. Unless you're using special hardware, doing this will not avoid the problems just discussed (or it will trade them for another set of problems).*

Variables and Assignment

Like almost all programming languages, Lua has *variables*. For now, you can think of these as named cubbyholes or storage containers for values. (Numbers are the only values you've encountered so far, but you'll learn about other types later in the chapter.) After you put a value into a variable, you can refer to it using the variable's name.

Assignment Basics

Putting a value into a variable is called *assignment*. Here are two examples of assignment (along with some `print`s that show what's going on):

```
> NumberA = 2
> print(NumberA)
2
> NumberB = 2 + 2
> print(NumberB)
4
> print(NumberA + NumberB)
6
```

An equal sign assigns a value to a variable. In these examples, the value 2 is assigned to the variable `NumberA`, and the value 4 (the result of 2 + 2) is assigned to the variable `NumberB`.

After a value has been assigned to a variable, you can access the value again using the variable's name, such as `print(NumberA)` or `print(NumberA + NumberB)`.

Notice that Lua's equal sign means a different thing than the one in algebra. The algebraic equal sign is a statement of fact indicating that two things are equal. Lua's equal sign is a command to Lua to make two things equal, so that the one on the left can be used in place of the one on the right. Because of this, a particular variable may contain different values at different points in a program. Here's an example:

```
> Sum = 2 + 2
> print(Sum)
4
> Sum = 2 + 5000
> print(Sum)
5002
```

There are rules for variable names, or *identifiers*: An identifier has to start with a letter or an underscore. It can't contain anything other than letters, underscores, or digits. Nor can it be one of Lua's *reserved words* or *keywords*, which are and, break, do, else, elseif, end, false, for, function, if, in, local, nil, not, or, repeat, return, then, true, until, and while. The following are all valid identifiers:

- ❏   a
- ❏   A
- ❏   ABC
- ❏   _xyz
- ❏   something_55
- ❏   AnotherThing
- ❏   _____

None of the following are valid identifiers:

- ❑ `function` (a keyword)
- ❑ `this-var` (contains something other than a letter, number, or underscore)
- ❑ `1stThing` (starts with something other than a letter or underscore)

Lua is case-sensitive, which means that `NUM`, `Num`, and `num` are all different identifiers:

```
> NUM = 1
> Num = 2
> num = 3
> print(NUM)
1
> print(Num)
2
> print(num)
3
```

This also means that `FUNCTION`, `Function`, and `fUnCtIoN` are all valid identifiers, because none of them is the keyword `function`.

There are various styles for identifiers:

- ❑ `totalsales`
- ❑ `total_sales`
- ❑ `totalSales`
- ❑ `TotalSales`

Some programmers even use different styles for different types of variables. If you're working on someone else's code, use the style used by that code. In your own code, pick a style and stick to it. This book uses the style `TotalSales`. Lua itself generally uses the `totalsales` style, so in this book, you can tell by looking whether a variable is defined in an example or built into Lua.

Lua has a few special variables that start with an underscore followed by capital letters (and possibly a number), such as `_G` or `_PROMPT2`. Avoid using names like that so that your variables don't clash with them.

A single underscore (`_`) is often used as a variable for *junk values* — values that need to be assigned, but won't be used. (You see this in Chapter 4 and elsewhere in the book.)

Multiple Assignment

You can assign multiple values to multiple variables at the same time. You can also print multiple values at the same time. The comma is used for both. Here's how you use the comma for multiple assignment, and for printing multiple values at the same time:

```
> Sum, Product, Exponent = 10 + 10, 10 * 10, 10 ^ 10
> print(Sum, Product, Exponent)
20        100        10000000000
```

In this example, three values were generated by adding 10 to itself, multiplying it by itself, and raising it to the 10th power. These three values were assigned respectively to the three variables Sum, Product, and Exponent. These three variables (more specifically, the values in these variables) were then printed.

You can also use multiple assignment to swap, rotate, or otherwise interchange the contents of variables. Here's an example:

```
> A, B = 1, 2
> print(A, B)
1        2
> A, B = B, A
> print(A, B)
2        1
> John, Jane, Jolene = "chips", "lemonade", "egg salad"
> print(John, Jane, Jolene)
chips    lemonade        egg salad
> John, Jane, Jolene = Jane, Jolene, John
> print(John, Jane, Jolene)
lemonade         egg salad        chips
```

Notice that without multiple assignment, swapping the contents of two variables would require a third variable for temporary storage:

```
> A = 1
> B = 2
> print(A, B)
1        2
> Tmp = A
> A = B
> B = Tmp
> print(A, B)
2        1
```

Variables on the Right Side of Assignments

As you may have noticed in some the previous examples, and as shown in the following example, the thing to the right of the equal sign can also be a variable:

```
> A = 10
> B = A
> print(B)
10
```

Even if a variable got its value from another variable, the two variables are independent. For example:

```
> A = 10
> B = A
> print(A, B)
10      10
> A = 555
> print(A, B)
555     10
```

This is because once the assignment gets the value of a variable that's on its right side, it forgets what variable the value came from (or even that it came from a variable at all).

Strings

Numbers are nice, but most programs need to deal with *strings*, which are sequences of *characters* (a letter, digit, space, or punctuation mark) or *control characters* (such a newline or formfeed).

Quoting Strings

A string can contain any text — even something that itself looks like Lua code — so it needs to be separated from the actual Lua code that comes before and after it. This is called *quoting* the string.

There are three ways to quote strings: with double quotes, with single quotes, and with square brackets.

Quoting Strings with Double Quotes

The double quote characters (") mark the beginning and end of the string. Marking the beginning and end is all they do; they are not actually part of the string, which is why print doesn't print them, as in this example:

```
> print("This is a string!")
This is a string!
```

Like numbers, strings are values, which means they can be assigned to variables. Here's an example:

```
> Name, Phone = "Jane X. Doe", "248-555-5898"
> print(Name, Phone)
Jane X. Doe      248-555-5898
```

The same variable can contain both a string and a number at different times, as shown here:

```
> Var = 42
> print(Var)
42
> Var = "forty-two"
> print(Var)
forty-two
```

You can also have an *empty string*, which contains no characters between the quote marks. For example:

```
> print("")

>
```

Quoting Strings with Single Quotes

You can also quote strings by using the single quote (or apostrophe) character ('), like this:

```
> print('This is also a string.')
This is also a string.
```

Single quotes work exactly like double quotes except that a single-quoted string can contain a double quote (without that double quote marking the end of the string). Similarly, a double-quoted string can contain a single quote (without that single quote marking the end of the string). Here are some examples:

```
> print('Cry "Havoc," and let slip the dogs of war')
Cry "Havoc," and let slip the dogs of war
> print("Cry 'Havoc,' and let slip the dogs of war")
Cry 'Havoc,' and let slip the dogs of war
```

Other than how they treat embedded double and single quotes, single and double quotes work exactly the same, and you can use either one. The best practice is to pick one and stick with it in all cases except those in which the other is more convenient.

Quoting Strings with Square Brackets

You can also quote strings with pairs of square brackets. Square brackets are used mainly for strings that would be too unwieldy to quote with double or single quotes, like this one:

```
> print([[There are some
>> funky "\' characters
>> in this string.]])
There are some
funky "\' characters
in this string.
```

If you mark the beginning of a string with two open square brackets ([[), then you mark the end with two close square brackets (]]). Inside such a string, no characters have any special meaning — a double quote represents a double quote, a *newline* (the invisible character that marks the end of a line, as when you press Enter) represents a newline, a backslash represents a backslash, a backslash followed by a letter n represents a backslash followed by a letter n, and so on. Strings quoted this way are sometimes called *long strings*, because they can be spread out over several lines, but they work fine on one line too.

If the first character of a square-bracket string is a newline, it is ignored. This allows you to write multi-line square-bracket strings in an easier-to-read way. The following two `print`s print exactly the same thing, but the second looks more like its result:

```
> print([[+-----+
>> | Lua |
>> +-----+
>> ]])
+-----+
| Lua |
+-----+

> print([[
>> +-----+
>> | Lua |
>> +-----+
>> ]])
+-----+
| Lua |
+-----+
```

What if you wanted to print two close square brackets inside a long string? For example:

```
> print([[Here ]] are some square brackets.]])
stdin:1: ')' expected near 'are'
```

The square brackets are interpreted by Lua as the end of the string. A backslash (the Lua escape character, discussed in the following section) won't prevent this from happening, because backslashes have no special meaning inside square-bracket strings. Instead, put an equal sign between the string's opening square brackets, and another between the closing square brackets:

```
> print([=[Here ]] are some square brackets.]=])
Here ]] are some square brackets.
```

If you need to, you can use multiple equal signs — the same number at the beginning and the end — like this:

```
> print([=[babble ]=] burble]=])
stdin:1: ')' expected near 'burble'
> print([==[babble ]=] burble]==])
babble ]=] burble
> print([====[babble ]=]==]===] burble]====])
babble ]=]==]===] burble
```

In other words, a square-bracket string starts with an open square bracket, zero or more equal signs, and another open square bracket, and it ends with a close square bracket, the same number of equal signs, and another close square bracket.

Lua 5.0 had a slightly different quoting method for long strings: The beginning was always `[[` *(never* `[=[` *or* `[==[`*), and the end was always* `]]` *(never* `]=]` *or* `]==]`*). Also, matching sets of bracket pairs could nest —* `[[[ ]]]` *was legal and equivalent to* `"[ ]"`*. The equivalent Lua 5.1 long string would be* `[=[[ ]]=]`*.*

Backslash Escaping

You can use the backslash character (\)inside double- and single-quoted strings to do things that would otherwise be inconvenient or impossible.

When the double quote character occurs within a double-quoted string, it has a special meaning: end of string. As you saw earlier, one way to avoid this special meaning (so that a double quote can be part of a string) is to quote the string with single quotes. Here's another way, using the backslash:

```
> print("Cry \"Havoc\"")
Cry "Havoc"
```

When a double quote is preceded by a backslash, the double quote's end-of-string meaning is taken away (escaped), and it becomes a part of the string. The backslash itself is not part of the string (in the same way that the quotes at the beginning and end of the string aren't part of it).

In other words, a backslash followed by a double quote represents a double quote. In the same way, a backslash followed by a single quote represents a single quote. For example:

```
> print('Ain\'t nobody\'s business if you do!')
Ain't nobody's business if you do!
```

A backslash followed by a backslash represents a backslash (just one):

```
> print("1 backslash: \\ 2: \\\\ 3: \\\\\\")
1 backslash: \ 2: \\ 3: \\\
```

And a backslash followed by a newline represents a newline:

```
> print("one\
>> two")
one
two
```

Different systems have different conventions for what character or character sequence is used to mark the end of a line. Lua accounts for this automatically — if any of the common end-of-line characters or character sequences occur in Lua code, inside or outside of string quotes, they are silently translated to newlines.

Normally, breaking a string into two lines would result in an error such as this:

```
> print("one
>> two")
stdin:1: unfinished string near '"one'
```

In addition to letting double quotes, single quotes, backslashes, and newlines represent themselves, the backslash also gives special meanings to some characters. For example, a backslash followed by a lower-case letter n represents a newline:

```
> print("one\ntwo")
one
two
```

These sequences of characters that start with a backslash are called *escape sequences*, because they temporarily escape from the normal interpretation of characters. Here are all of them:

Escape Sequence	Meaning
\a	\Bell (in certain circumstances, printing this character causes the computer to beep—a stands for "alert")
\b	Backspace
\f	Formfeed
\n	Newline
\r	Carriage return (some operating systems use this by itself or in combination with newline to represent the end of a line)
\t	Tab (used to format text in columns)
\v	Vertical tab
\\	Backslash
\"	Double quote
\'	Single quote (apostrophe)
\99	The character whose numeric representation is 99 (described next)
\	Newline (a backslash followed by a literal newline represents a newline)

A backslash followed by one, two, or three decimal digits represents the character whose numeric representation (inside the computer's memory or on a disk) is that number. This varies from system to system, but on most systems "\99" is the same as "c"—of course, in most circumstances it would make more sense to use the latter form rather than the former.

Lua's escape sequences are similar to those of the C language. The most important difference is that numeric escapes like \123 are interpreted as decimal (base 10), not octal (base 8).

Lua strings can include any character, including the *null byte*: the (invisible) character whose numeric representation is 0. However, parts of Lua that depend on the C language to handle strings will consider that character to mark the end of the string. For example:

```
> EmbeddedNull = "BEFORE\0after"
> print(EmbeddedNull)
BEFORE
```

Relational Operators and Boolean Values

+, -, *, /, and ^ are called operators, or more specifically, *arithmetic operators*. Arithmetic operators ask "how much" questions. In this section you learn about *relational operators*, which ask yes-or-no questions.

Comparing Numbers

The operators in this section are relational because they ask about the relation between two values: whether one value is less than the other, greater than it, equal to it, and so on.

Here's how to ask Lua whether one number is less than another:

```
> print(4 < 5)
true
> print(5 < 4)
false
```

You've learned about two *types* of values so far: numbers and strings. The less-than operator always gives true or false as a result. true and false look like strings at first glance, but actually they are a new type, called *Boolean* values (named after the 19th-century mathematician George Boole). There are lots of numbers (1, -300, 3.14159) and lots of strings ("Hello there!", "apple", "asdfjkl;"), but true and false are the only Booleans. Because they are values, they can be assigned to variables. To hard-code a Boolean value into a program, just type true or false (with no quotes), like this:

```
> Boolean1, Boolean2, Boolean3 = true, false, 1 < 2
> print(Boolean1, Boolean2, Boolean3)
true    false   true
```

There are six relational operators:

❑   A < B Is A less than B?

❑   A > B Is A greater than B?

❑   A <= B Is A less than or equal to B?

❑   A >= B Is A greater than or equal to B?

❑   A == B Is A equal to B?

❑   A ~= B Is A not equal to B?

Of these six, <, >, <=, and >= determine what order two values are in. == and ~= just determine whether two values are equal. For example:

```
> print(1 > 1)
false
> print(1 > 2)
false
> print(1 >= 1)
true
> print(1 >= 2)
false
> print(1 == 1)
true
> print(1 == 2)
false
> print(1 ~= 1)
false
> print(1 ~= 2)
true
```

> **Two values of different types are never considered equal, even if they look similar. So the number 1 is not equal to the string "1", and the string "true" is not equal to the Boolean true. Also, unlike some other languages, the number 0 is not equal to either the empty string "" or the Boolean false, and the number 1 is not equal to the Boolean true.**

Here are a couple common errors:

```
> Num == 42
stdin:1: '=' expected near '=='
> print(Num = 42)
stdin:1: ')' expected near '='
```

A single equal sign is used for assignment and a double equal sign is used for equality comparison. It's very common to mix these up, but Lua always spots the error.

Comparing Strings

If two strings have the same characters in them (in the same order), then they are considered the same string, which means they are equal to each other (because a value is always equal to itself). For example:

```
> Str1 = "Jane X. Doe"
> Str2 = "Jane X. Doe"
> print(Str1 == Str2)
true
```

<, >, <=, and >= can be used on strings as well. Single-character strings compare based on their collation (sorting) order in the current *locale*. In the simplest case, this is their order in your system's character set. (Locale is a system setting that determines, among other things, the appropriate alphabetization order for the language being used.) Here are some examples:

```
> print("a" < "b")
true
> print("a" < "a")
false
> print("a" <= "a")
true
> print("A" < "a")
true
> print(" " > "\n")
true
```

Multiple-character strings compare based on the first character that is different, like this:

```
> print("abcd" < "abce")
true
```

The absence of a character is considered less than any character, as these examples illustrate:

```
> print("" < "A")
true
> print("" < "\0")
true
> print("abc" < "abcd")
true
```

Although == and ~= can be used with values of any type, even values of two different types, the <, >, <=, and >= operators can only be used with two numbers or two strings. Anything else causes an error, as these examples show:

```
> print(false < true)
stdin:1: attempt to compare two boolean values
stack traceback:
        stdin:1: in main chunk
        [C]: ?
> print(42 >= "41")
stdin:1: attempt to compare string with number
stack traceback:
        stdin:1: in main chunk
        [C]: ?
```

The rule that <, >, <=, and >= can only be used to compare two strings or two numbers is not strictly true. You'll learn how to bypass this rule — and several other rules given in this chapter — with metatables in Chapter 8.

The nil Value

Assigning an initial value to a variable is called *initializing* it. A variable that has had no value assigned to it is said to be *uninitialized*. You've learned about three types of value (also known as *datatypes*) so far: numbers, strings, and Booleans. There's one more type to learn about in this chapter, and you'll see it if you print the value of an uninitialized variable such as the following:

```
> print(Asdf)
nil
```

This is the value `nil`. Its type is also named `nil`; in fact it is the only value whose type is `nil`. It is used mainly to represent the absence of any other value. Any uninitialized variable has `nil` as its value.

You can also explicitly assign `nil` to a variable, which you might do if you want Lua to forget about the variable's previous value. For example:

```
> Password = "$xa(yb`y"
> print(Password)
$xa(yb`y
> Password = nil
> print(Password)
nil
```

`nil` also comes into play when an assignment is made that has more variables on its left side than values on its right side. Here's an example:

```
> C, D = 3, 4
> A, B, C, D = 1, 2
> print(A, B, C, D)
1       2       nil     nil
```

If there are more variables on the left side of an assignment than there are values on the right side, the list of values is *adjusted* to the correct length by adding `nil`s to the end. So the line where A and B are assigned as follows:

```
> A, B, C, D = 1, 2
```

acts just as though it had been written like this:

```
> A, B, C, D = 1, 2, nil, nil
```

This means that extra variables (C and D in this example) are set to `nil`, even if they already have been set to another value.

If there are more values on the right than variables on the left, the list of values is adjusted by throwing away the extra values, like this:

```
> A, B = 1, 2, 3, 4
> print(A, B)
1       2
```

`nil` is different from `false`, `0`, and the string `"nil"`. But, like all values, it's equal to itself:

```
> print(nil ~= false)
true
> print(nil ~= 0)
true
> print(nil ~= "nil")
true
> print(nil == nil)
true
```

If a `nil` turns up where you don't expect it, a typo is usually the cause. In the following example, the variable `LoginCount` is initialized, but then its name is miscapitalized as `LogInCount`, which is a different variable:

```
> MaxLoginCount = 100
> LoginCount = 50
> print(LogInCount > MaxLoginCount)
stdin:1: attempt to compare number with nil
stack traceback:
        stdin:1: in main chunk
        [C]: ?
```

Because `LogInCount` is uninitialized, its value is `nil`, which can't be compared to a number.

In the next example, `Joe` and `Mike` were intended as strings, but because they are not quoted, they're treated as (uninitialized) variables:

```
> FirstNameA, FirstNameB = Joe, Mike
> print(FirstNameA < FirstNameB)
stdin:1: attempt to compare two nil values
stack traceback:
        stdin:1: in main chunk
        [C]: ?
```

Boolean Operators

The three *Boolean operators* — and, or, and not — are handy for working with Boolean values. However, as you will see, they can also be given non-Boolean values, and two of them (and and or) don't always even give Boolean results.

The and Operator

Like the other operators you've seen so far, the and operator takes two values, one to its left and one to its right. The values given to an operator are called *operands*. The simple explanation of and is that it gives a true result only if both of its operands are true, as follows:

```
> print(false and false)
false
> print(false and true)
false
> print(true and false)
false
> print(true and true)
true
```

One way that you can use this is to check if a number is within a range. In the following example Num > 10 is true *and* Num < 20 is true, so the result is true:

```
> Num = 15
> print(Num > 10 and Num < 20)
true
```

If you use operands that aren't Booleans, the behavior of and is a bit more subtle. Here are some examples — see if you can figure out what rules and is following in them:

```
> print(false and nil)
false
> print(nil and false)
nil
> print(false and 1)
false
> print(1 and false)
false
> print(nil and 1)
nil
> print(1 and nil)
nil
> print(nil and true)
nil
> print(true and nil)
nil
> print(true and 1)
1
> print(1 and true)
true
> print("a" and 1)
1
> print(1 and "a")
a
```

The more complicated explanation of the and operator is that if its first operand is `false` or `nil`, then the first operand is used as the result; otherwise the second operand is used as the result. Mentally apply that rule to the preceding examples to see if you come up with the same answer as Lua.

Notice that the complicated explanation is the same as the simple explanation if you consider both `false` and `nil` to be false values and everything else to be true values. There's a distinction here between `true` and `false`, which are proper names for specific values in Lua, and "true" and "false," which are adjectives. In this book, the adjectives will always be in the same typeface as the surrounding text, and the names will be in `this typeface`, like so:

`false` and `nil` are false. `true` and `"Jane Doe"` are true.

> Remember, `false` and `nil` are the two false values, and every other value is a true value. This means that, unlike some other languages, the number `0` and the empty string are both true.

The or Operator

The `or` operator gives a false result only if both its operands are false, as follows:

```
> print(false or false)
false
> print(false or true)
true
> print(true or false)
true
> print(true or true)
true
```

Like and, the result of `or` is always one of its operands. If its first operand is something other than `false` or `nil`, then the first operand is used as the result; otherwise the second operand is used as the result. For example:

```
> print(42 or nil)
42
> print(nil or 42)
42
> print(false or nil)
nil
> print(nil or false)
false
> print("first" or "second")
first
> print(false or "second")
second
```

This behavior comes in handy in the following example.

```
> print(FavoriteFruit or "apple")
apple
> FavoriteFruit = "kiwi"
> print(FavoriteFruit or "apple")
kiwi
```

The `print` line (which occurs twice in the example) is the interesting one here. If there's a favorite fruit, that line prints it. If, however, `FavoriteFruit` is uninitialized (and therefore is `nil`), there's no favorite fruit, and the default (`"apple"`) is printed.

There can be chains of these, in which case, the result is the first value that is true. Here's an example:

```
> Choice1, Choice2, Choice3 = nil, "pencil", "pen"
> print(Choice1 or Choice2 or Choice3)
pencil
```

Mathematicians consider the or *operator to be the Boolean equivalent of addition, and the* and *operator to be the Boolean equivalent of multiplication.*

The not Unary Operator

Most of the operators you've learned about so far are *binary*; that is, they take two operands, one to the left of the operator and one to the right. (This meaning of binary is not to be confused with the *base-two number system*.) You've seen one *unary* (a one-operand) operator as well, although you may not have realized it. It's the so-called unary minus, and you've already used it to make negative numbers, like this:

```
> print(-50)
-50
> print(-2 + -2)
-4
```

You can also use it to make any positive value negative, or make a negative value positive. :

```
> Two = 2
> print(-Two)
-2
> MinusTwo = -Two
> print(-MinusTwo)
2
```

– is both a binary and a unary operator, but Lua never gets these two uses confused, because it's always visible from the context which one you intended:

```
> print(-13 - -2)
-11
```

and and or are both binary, but the remaining Boolean operator, not, is unary. As with -, the not operand goes to its right. If that operand is false or nil, then the result of not is true; otherwise, it's false:

```
> print(not false)
true
> print(not nil)
true
> print(not true)
false
> print(not 50)
false
> print(not "Hello")
false
```

If a true value is preceded by two nots, the result is true; if a false value (that is, false or nil) is preceded by two nots, the result is false:

```
> print(not not true)
true
> print(not not 50)
true
> print(not not "Hello")
true
> print(not not false)
false
> print(not not nil)
false
```

The Concatenation, Length, and Modulo Operators

There are three other operators you need to know about: concatenation, length, and modulo. You'll examine all three in the following sections.

The String Concatenation Operator

The string concatenation operator is written like this: .. (two periods, with no spaces between them). It takes two strings as operands and *concatenates* them, or splices them together. Here are some examples:

```
> print("App" .. "le")
Apple
> print("a" .. "b" .. "c" .. "d")
abcd
> Name = "dear reader"
> print("Hello, " .. Name .. ", how are you?")
Hello, dear reader, how are you?
```

The .. operator creates a new string by putting its two operands together with no space between them. If you want a space (or some other separator), explicitly include it in the concatenation, like this:

```
> print("Jane" .. "Doe")
JaneDoe
> print("Jane" .. " " .. "Doe")
Jane Doe
```

As mentioned previously, two strings with the same characters in the same order are the same string. This means that two different concatenations can have equal results. For example:

```
> OneAndTwoThree, OneTwoAndThree = "1" .. "23", "12" .. "3"
> print(OneAndTwoThree, OneTwoAndThree)
123     123
> print(OneAndTwoThree == OneTwoAndThree)
true
```

Concatenating a string to the empty string gives the same string:

```
> print("abcd" .. "" == "abcd")
true
```

The Length Operator

The length operator #, like not and one version of -, is a unary operator. It measures the length of a string. (It also measures the length of a table, which you'll learn about in Chapter 4.) Take a look at these examples:

```
> print(#"")
0
> print(#"!")
1
> print(#"\n")
1
> print(#"abcd")
4
> VerbForms = "see saw seen"
> print(#VerbForms)
12
```

The length of a string is simply the number of characters in it. (Notice that "\n" is a single character, even though it is typed as two.)

Lua considers a character to be exactly one *byte*—a small chunk of memory just big enough to be able to take on one of 256 different values. (To be pedantic, Lua considers a character a C char, but that will be one byte on any system you're likely to use.) This makes a difference if you're using a character encoding (UTF-8, for example) in which some characters take up more than one byte; the following word looks like it's four characters long, but Lua sees it as five:

```
> print(#"fi_o")
5
```

Lua counts the null byte just like any other character:

```
> NullByte = "\0"
> NullBytes = NullByte .. NullByte .. NullByte
> print(#NullByte)
1
> print(#NullBytes)
3
> print(#"before\0between\0behind")
21
```

Lua 5.0 didn't have the length operator #. To get the length of a string, use the function `string.len`; *to get the length of a table, use the function* `table.getn`.

The Modulo Operator

Imagine the hour hand of a clock. If it's pointed at 3 and you turn it two hours forward, it's now pointed at 5. This can be modeled by addition: 3 plus 2 equals 5. But what if, when it's pointed at 5, you turn it 144 hours forward? The answer is that it will still be pointed at 5 because 144 is divisible by 12. After the hour hand passes 12, the addition model breaks down (in this case giving the answer 149). The modulo operator, %, is good for modeling cyclical things like hours in a day, days in a week, or musical pitches in an octave.

Try It Out   **Using % to Model a Clock Face**

The following example models setting an hour hand to 3, moving it two hours forward, moving it 144 hours forward, and moving it 149 hours backward. For this example, pretend that the top of the clock says 0 instead of 12 (the fact that real clocks go from 1 to 12 rather than 0 to 11 could be adjusted for by adding and subtracting 1 at the appropriate points, but that would needlessly complicate this example).

```
> Hour = 3
> Hour = Hour + 2
> Hour = Hour % 12
> print(Hour)
5
> Hour = Hour + 144
> Hour = Hour % 12
> print(Hour)
5
> Hour = Hour - 149
> Hour = Hour % 12
> print(Hour)
0
```

How It Works

The lines where addition or subtraction is done represent turning the hour hand, but they can leave Hour either too high (greater than or equal to 12) or too low (negative). The lines where % is used adjust for this. Hour % 12 is pronounced "hour modulo twelve" or "hour mod twelve," and it means "What would Hour be if I added or subtracted enough 12s so that it was less than 12 and greater than or equal to zero?"

For positive numbers (even fractional ones), this is the same as the remainder of a division. For example, 35 % 12 is 11 because 12 goes into 35 two times with a remainder of 11. This can be used to check whether a number is divisible by another number. For instance, if X is even, then X % 2 will be 0.

In other languages, the modulo operators and functions treat negative numbers differently than the Lua % operator does. The Lua operator follows the definition of modulo most commonly used by mathematicians. One way of stating this definition is as follows:

> To find X % Y, add Y to (or subtract it from) X as many times as necessary until a number between 0 and Y is reached. (This number can be exactly equal to 0, but it cannot be exactly equal to Y.)

This definition allows the clock-face example to work even when Hour briefly becomes negative.

As with division by zero, using zero as the second operand of % is undefined.

> *Lua 5.0 didn't have the % operator. Use the function* math.mod *instead, but be warned that it has different behavior with negative numbers.*

Automatic Conversion of Operands

Some operators (such as ==) can take operands of any type. Other operators (such as <) expect operands of a certain type and produce an error message if given the wrong type. The arithmetical operators (+, -, *, /, ^, and %) fall into this second category, except that they will attempt to convert string operands into numbers, like this:

```
> print("2" + "2")
4
```

The result is still a number, not a string. If the conversion attempt fails, an error message like the following results:

```
> print("x" + "y")
stdin:1: attempt to perform arithmetic on a string value
stack traceback:
        stdin:1: in main chunk
        [C]: ?
```

> *If the string is a hexadecimal number, it must be positive. (Negative hexadecimal numbers may be converted correctly, but this is not guaranteed — it depends on the C library used to compile Lua.)*

The string concatenation operator also does an automatic conversion, from number to string. For example:

```
> print(111 .. 999)
111999
```

Precedence and Associativity

You may remember from math class that both 5 * 5 + 1 and 1 + 5 * 5 give the same result — multiplication is done before addition even if it comes later. Multiplication is therefore said to have a higher *precedence* than addition. However, if you want to do a lower-precedence operation before a higher-precedence one, you can surround the lower-precedence one in parentheses.

The following shows that, no matter what the left-to-right order, multiplication will always be done before addition, unless the addition is wrapped in parentheses, in which case it will be done first:

```
> print(5 * 5 + 1)
26
> print(1 + 5 * 5)
26
> print(5 * (5 + 1))
30
> print((1 + 5) * 5)
30
```

Notice that parentheses are being put to two different uses here — to override precedence and to wrap the thing being printed. These two uses are completely unrelated, but in both cases each open parenthesis must have a corresponding close parenthesis. If the open and close parentheses don't match up, you'll get either an error message or a continuation prompt telling you to finish what you started:

```
> print((1 + 5) * 5))
stdin:1: unexpected symbol near ')'
> print(5 * (5 + 1)
>>
```

What about two operators that have the same precedence? In some cases, it doesn't matter what order they're done in: (2 + 3) + 4 and 2 + (3 + 4) are both 9. But how about 2 - 3 + 4? This will give a different answer depending on whether the subtraction or the addition is done first, and precedence can't be used to decide this because addition and subtraction have the same precedence. In this case, the subtraction is done first because it's on the left, and + and - are both *left-associative* operators. Anytime two operators are the same precedence, they are done from left to right if they're left associative, and right to left if they're right associative. Lua only has two right-associative operators: .. (string concatenation) and ^ (exponentiation). (That's not counting unary operators, which are done from right to left because that's the only way that makes sense.)

The following chart lists all of Lua's operators, from highest precedence to lowest. (All operators are binary unless marked as unary, and all binary operators are left associative unless marked as right associative.)

^ (exponentiation; right-associative)

not (Boolean negation; unary), - (unary minus), # (length; unary)

* (multiplication), / (division), % (modulo)

+ (addition), - (subtraction)

.. (string concatenation; right-associative)

< (less than), > (greater than), ~= (not equal to), <= (less than or equal to), == (equal to), >= (greater than or equal to)

and (Boolean "multiplication")

or (Boolean "addition")

Most experienced programmers do not memorize this whole chart, nor do they check it every time they can't remember a precedence. Rather, they memorize a handful of the most commonly used precedences and use parentheses for anything they're not sure of. It doesn't hurt to add parentheses even if they're not strictly necessary according to the precedence chart, and it often makes your code easier for you and others to understand.

On the other hand, Lua's precedence chart is well thought out, and many common idioms do not require parentheses. For example, relational operators have comparatively low precedence, which means that arithmetic results don't need to be wrapped in parentheses before being compared:

```
> CreditA, DebitA, CreditB, DebitB = 1000, 150, 500, 25
> print(CreditA - DebitA == CreditB - DebitB)
false
> print(CreditA - DebitA > CreditB - DebitB)
true
```

and and or both have very low precedence, so you don't need to wrap comparisons in parentheses before using and or or:

```
> CreditA, DebitA, CreditB, DebitB = 1000, 150, 500, 505
> print(CreditA >= DebitA and CreditB >= DebitB)
false
> print(CreditA >= DebitA or CreditB >= DebitB)
true
```

and has higher precedence than or, so you can use A and B or C to mean "if A, then B, otherwise C."

Here's the A and B or C trick in action:

```
> B, C = "B was chosen", "C was chosen"
> A = true
> print(A and B or C)
B was chosen
> A = false
> print(A and B or C)
C was chosen
```

A is anded with B and the result (A if A is false, otherwise B) is ored with C. The upshot is that whether A is true or false determines whether the result is B or C. This would have worked the same if A had been set to any true value instead of true, or nil instead of false. It would not have worked, though, if B had been nil or false:

```
> B, C = false, "C was chosen"
> A = true
> print(A and B or C)
C was chosen
```

This is a limitation of this idiom — the middle value must be true.

Variables and Values

Earlier you read that variables are like named cubbyholes or containers for values. This means that the following assignment finds the three cubbyholes Number, Greeting1, and Greeting2 (creating them if they don't already exist) and puts 123 in Number, "Hello" in Greeting1, and "Hello" in Greeting2:

```
Number, Greeting1, Greeting2 = 123, "Hello", "Hello"
```

This is illustrated in Figure 2-1.

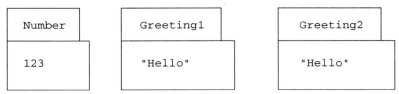

Figure 2-1

For everything you've done and will do in this chapter, that's a perfectly accurate mental model, but later you'll run into situations where it would lead you astray. Before you get it too ingrained in your head, a somewhat more accurate model is that the following finds the three names Number, Greeting1, and `Greeting2` (creating them if they don't already exist) and points `Number`'s arrow at `123` and `Greeting1`'s and `Greeting2`'s arrows at `"Hello"`:

```
Number, Greeting1, Greeting2 = 123, "Hello", "Hello"
```

This is illustrated in Figure 2-2.

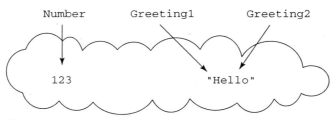

Figure 2-2

The difference is that instead of `Greeting1` and `Greeting2` each containing `"Hello"`, they only point to it. Chapter 4 explains why this is important.

Comments

If Lua sees two consecutive hyphens outside of a string, it considers everything until the end of that line a *comment* and ignores it. For example:

```
> print("Hello") -- This is a comment.
Hello
> print("Goodbye") -- So is this.
Goodbye
```

Comments are useful to explain your code's purpose to other programmers (or to remind yourself when you return to the code after a few months). Whenever you change your code, make certain you update your comments appropriately.

Comments can also be used to temporarily comment out code that you want Lua to ignore but don't want to delete entirely, like this:

```
> -- print("Hello")
>
```

If the two hyphens are immediately followed by an open square bracket, zero or more equal signs, and another open square bracket, then Lua uses the rules described previously for long strings (square bracket strings) to ignore the following text (including the rule about nested sets of square brackets needing different numbers of equal signs). This is most often used for multiline comments such as the following:

```
> --[[ This is
>>    a multi-line
>>    comment.]]
>
```

It can also be used to temporarily comment out code in the middle of a line, like this:

```
> print(2 + --[[2 +]] 2)
4
```

Or to temporarily comment out multiple lines of code, like this:

```
> --[[
>> print("Multiple")
>> print("lines.")
>> --]]
>
```

Notice that the closing brackets have -- in front of them. This lets you add a single - in front of the opening brackets (turning that line into a single-line comment rather than the start of a multiline comment) without the closing brackets causing an error:

```
> ---[[
> print("Multiple")
Multiple
> print("lines.")
lines.
> --]]
>
```

That looks pretty silly typed into the interpreter, but you'll find it useful for debugging when you start saving code to (and executing it from) files.

Even though code typed directly into the interpreter is normally short-lived and not commented, much of the following example code is commented for your benefit.

Expressions and Statements

For most of this chapter, you've been using expressions and statements. For the rest of the chapter to make sense, these terms need to be defined.

An *expression* is something that has a value. As you've used `print`, you've been putting expressions (separated by commas when there is more than one) between its parentheses. An expression can be a *literal* value, such as a quoted string, `true`, `false`, or `nil`. *Literal* means that you can tell just by looking at it what it is. For example, a variable named `Count` may contain a number (and probably does, given its name), but it's not a literal number, like `42` is.

An expression can also be a variable name, like `Count`. It can also be an expression preceded by a unary operator, an expression wrapped in parentheses, or two expressions separated by a binary operator. For example, `-Count` is an expression because `Count` is an expression, and an expression preceded by a unary operator is also an expression. `2 + 3` is an expression because `2` and `3` are expressions, and separating two expressions with a binary operator makes another expression. Take a look at the following example:

```
Count > 5 and #(FirstNameStr .. LastNameStr) <= 20
```

Even a complicated expression like this can be explained as the literals `5` and `20` and the variable names `Count`, `FirstNameStr`, and `LastNameStr` combined according to the preceding rules.

There are other rules for making expressions, but these are the only ones relevant to this chapter.

A *statement* is the smallest complete unit of Lua code. A Lua program is simply one or more statements (actually zero or more, because if you enter an empty line into the interpreter, you're executing a valid program that does nothing). Lua doesn't know what to do with an expression unless it's wrapped in a statement such as the following:

```
> 2 + 2
stdin:1: unexpected symbol near '2'
> print(2 + 2)
4
```

As this example implies, `print (...)` is a statement. Assignment is also a statement, and these are the only two types of statement you've learned about so far in this chapter. You'll learn more in the next section.

For the most part, expressions and statements are two different things. There is one type of expression that can be used as a statement, and you'll learn about it next chapter.

Compound Statements

Compound statements are statements that can contain other statements. The following sections describe five of Lua's compound statements: the *if* statement; the *while*, *for*, and *repeat* loops; and the *do* statement.

At any time during the execution of a program, a certain part of the program is in control. By default, control flows from each statement to the one after it, but most compound statements are *control structures*, so-named because they are structures (with multiple parts), and they alter the flow of control. The *if* statement is one of these control structures.

The if Statement

Say you have two strings, Str1 and Str2, and you want to concatenate them in (the < operator's version of) alphabetical order. To do so, you need to test whether Str1 comes before Str2 and, if it does, concatenate them with Str1 first, but otherwise concatenate them with Str2 first. You already know enough to do this, if you use the A and B or C trick described earlier. Give it a try.

You should come up with the following:

```
> Str1, Str2 = "aardvark", "zebra"
> print(Str1 < Str2 and Str1 .. Str2 or Str2 .. Str1)
aardvarkzebra
>
> Str1, Str2 = "zebra", "aardvark"
> print(Str1 < Str2 and Str1 .. Str2 or Str2 .. Str1)
aardvarkzebra
```

There's another way to do this, using the if control structure.

Try It Out   **Using if to Make a Choice**

The if version is a bit wordier but, at least in this case, it's easier to read, and it scales up more easily to more complicated things. Here's the code:

```
> Str1, Str2 = "aardvark", "zebra"
> if Str1 < Str2 then
>>    print(Str1 .. Str2)
>> else
>>    print(Str2 .. Str1)
>> end
aardvarkzebra
> -- Do it again with the strings swapped:
> Str1, Str2 = "zebra", "aardvark"
> if Str1 < Str2 then
>>    print(Str1 .. Str2)
>> else
>>    print(Str2 .. Str1)
>> end
aardvarkzebra
```

How It Works

In English: If the two strings are in the right order, then print them; otherwise, print them in reverse order.

The `if` control structure has the following form:

```
if an expression then
   zero or more statements
else
   zero or more statements
end
```

The expression is *evaluated*, that is, its value is checked. If the value is true (that is, something other than `false` or `nil`), then only the statements between the `then` and the `else` are executed; if the expression is false (that is, `false` or `nil`) then only the statements between the `else` and the `end` are executed.

An `if` statement doesn't have to be spread out across several lines. If it's not too long, you can fit it on one line. If you do spread it across several lines, indent the statements before and after the `else`, as the preceding example shows. Lua doesn't care about indentation, but humans find it much easier to read properly indented code.

If you have no statements to put in the `else` clause (the part between the `else` and the `end`), just leave the `else` out. For example:

```
if not Asdf then print("Asdf is false") end

if "X" .. "Y" .. "Z" == "XYZ" then
   Name = "Virginia"
   print("Yes, " .. Name .. ", it's \"XYZ\"")
end
```

It's possible to rewrite the alphabetical concatenation example with no `else` clause. Give it a try before you look at the following example. (Hint: the `print` statement needs to come after the `end`.)

```
> Str1, Str2 = "aardvark", "zebra"
> if Str1 > Str2 then
>>    Str1, Str2 = Str2, Str1
>> end
> print(Str1 .. Str2)
aardvarkzebra
> -- Do it again with the strings swapped:
> Str1, Str2 = "zebra", "aardvark"
> if Str1 > Str2 then
>>    Str1, Str2 = Str2, Str1
>> end
> print(Str1 .. Str2)
aardvarkzebra
```

In English: If the two strings are in the wrong order, swap them. Then print them (whether they were swapped or not).

This code does one thing if `Str1` is greater than `Str2` and does something else if `Str1` is less than or equal to `Str2`. Similarly, the first version does one thing if `Str1` is less than `Str2` and something else if `Str1` is greater than or equal to `Str2`. Because an `if` structure is a statement, it can be put inside a `then` clause or an `else` clause. This fact can be used to do one thing if `Str1` is less than `Str2`, another thing if `Str1` is greater than `Str2`, and yet another if they are equal. Write a version that concatenates `Str1` and `Str2` in order as before if they are inequal, but only prints one of them if they are equal. This means that the following:

```
Str1, Str2 = "aardvark", "aardvark"
```

should result in this:

```
aardvark
```

After you've written your code, test it and make sure it works. Testing it in this case means trying it out with all three cases: two strings in the right order, two strings in the wrong order, and two identical strings.

There are several correct ways to write this code. Here's one:

```
if Str1 == Str2 then
  -- Str2 is a duplicate of Str1; replace it with the
  -- empty string:
  Str2 = ""
else
  if Str1 > Str2 then
    -- They're in the wrong order; swap 'em:
    Str1, Str2 = Str2, Str1
  end
end
print(Str1 .. Str2)
```

Because the inner `if` doesn't have an `else`, the strings are only executed if one of the two tests turns out true; if not, none of the statements except the final `print` is executed.

Notice that the contents of the outer `if` statement's `then` and `else` clauses are indented one level (which is two spaces in this book), and the inner `if` statement's `then` clause is indented one more level.

If an `if` statement is nested inside the `else` clause of another `if` statement, Lua allows them to be combined into one `if` statement using the keyword `elseif`.

Here's the nested-`if` version of alphabetical concatenation rewritten using `elseif`:

```
if Str1 == Str2 then
  -- Str2 is a duplicate of Str1; replace it with the
  -- empty string:
  Str2 = ""
elseif Str1 > Str2 then
  -- They're in the wrong order; swap 'em:
  Str1, Str2 = Str2, Str1
end
print(Str1 .. Str2)
```

The `elseif` test (to see if the strings are in the wrong order) is only done if the `if` test (to see if the strings are equal) turned out false.

An `if` statement can have zero or more `elseif`s, and zero or one `else`. If there is an `else`, it has to be the last part of the `if`:

```
if N == 1 then
   print("N is one")
elseif N == 2 then
   print("N is two")
elseif N == 3 then
   print("N is three")
else
   print("N is neither one nor two nor three")
end
```

In an `if` like this, the test expressions (right before `then`) are evaluated from the first one downward, until the first true one is found, at which point the next statement block (the part between the `then` and the next `elseif`, `else`, or `end`) is executed, and the `if` is exited. The statement block after the `else` is only executed if none of the test expressions are true. In this example, you can tell at a glance that only one of the `print`s will be executed.

The while Loop

The `if` control structure gives a program the power to decide *whether* something gets executed. Lua's other control structures — `while`, `repeat`, and `for` — give a program the power to decide *how many times* something gets executed. They are called *loops*, and the simplest is `while`, whose form is as follows:

```
while an expression do
   zero or more statements
end
```

The expression is evaluated. If it's true, the statements between `do` and `end` are executed, and then the expression is evaluated again. If it is still true, the statements are executed again, and the cycle continues. If the expression evaluates as false at any time (including the first time it's evaluated), the `while` statement is exited, which means that the statements are not executed and the expression is not evaluated again. For example, the following code does nothing:

```
while false do
   print("This will")
   print("never print.")
end
```

On the other hand, here's an example that will run forever — (or until you stop it by pressing Ctrl+C):

```
while true do
   print("It keeps")
   print("going and going.")
end
```

More interesting cases are those where the expression starts out true, and then becomes false, like in the following example, which uses `while` to count to 10:

```
> Counter = 1
> while Counter <= 10 do
>>    print(Counter)
>>    Counter = Counter + 1
>> end
1
2
3
4
5
6
7
8
9
10
>
```

Here, `Counter` is set to 1, and as long as it's less than or equal to 10, it is printed and then *incremented* (increased by one). At the end of the tenth time through the loop, `Counter` is set to 11. The test — whether `Counter` is less than or equal to 10 — is done an eleventh time, this time with a false result, which means the loop is done.

A *factorial* is a number formed by multiplying a sequence of consecutive integers starting with 1. For example, the factorial of 5 (notated by mathematicians as "5!") is 1×2×3×4×5, or 120. (Apart from their use in the mathematical field of combinatorics, factorials are quite handy for writing examples in programming books.)

The following code prints all the factorials less than 100:

```
> N, F = 1, 1
> while F < 100 do
>>    print(N .. "! is " .. F)
>>    N = N + 1
>>    -- Compute the factorial of the new N based on
>>    -- the factorial of the old N:
>>    F = F * N
>> end
1! is 1
2! is 2
3! is 6
4! is 24
```

The first line *initializes* (gives initial values to) N and F, setting N to 1 and F to the factorial of 1, which also happens to be 1. The expression after `while` makes sure that F is less than 100. Inside the loop's body, N and F are printed, N is incremented, and the factorial of the new value of N is computed, using the fact that n! equals (n – 1) !×n.

The for Loop

One difference between the factorial loop and the 1-to-10 loop is that you knew the 1-to-10 loop's body would be executed 10 times, but you didn't know how many times the factorial loop's body would be executed (unless you figured the factorials out in your head). To know when to exit the loop, Lua had to compute 4!, see that it was less than 100, and then compute 5! and see that it was not less than 100. The `while` loop is for situations where you don't know how many times you want the loop to repeat. When you do know how many times you want the loop to repeat, use Lua's `for` loop. (It's called `for` because it does things *for* a certain number of times.)

Here's the 1-to-10 loop rewritten with `for`:

```
> for Counter = 1, 10 do
>>    print(Counter)
>> end
1
2
3
4
5
6
7
8
9
10
```

Notice how much simpler it is than the first version. The `for` loop has the following form:

```
for variable = start number, end number, step do
   zero or more statements
end
```

The value `start number` is assigned to `variable`, the `zero or more statements` are executed, `step` is added to `variable` (`step` is optional and usually left out, in which case 1 is used), and if `variable` is still less than or equal to `end number`, then the loop body is executed again.

If Lua sees that the variable will never either reach or go beyond `end number`, then the body is never executed:

```
> for N = 1, 0 do
>>    print(N)
>> end
>
```

The right thing is done for negative and fractional values and cases where the difference between the start number and the end number is not divisible by the step value:

```
> for N = 3, 1, -1 do
>>    print(N)
>> end
3
2
1
> for N = -50, -45.25, 2.5 do
>>    print(N)
>> end
-50
-47.5
> for N = 2, 5, 2 do
>>    print(N)
>> end
2
4
```

The start number, end number, and step value don't need to be, and often aren't, literal numbers — they can be any expressions that evaluate to numbers. This evaluation takes place once, at the beginning of the loop (unlike a `while` loop's test expression, which is evaluated over and over as the loop loops). That's why the following example loops five times, even though End gets lower and lower:

```
> End = 5
> for I = 1, End do
>>    End = End - 1 -- The loop doesn't care that End is being
>>       -- changed.
>>    print("I is " .. I .. " and End is " .. End)
>> end
I is 1 and End is 4
I is 2 and End is 3
I is 3 and End is 2
I is 4 and End is 1
I is 5 and End is 0
```

`for` loops can be nested inside each other. For example:

```
> for Outer = 1, 3 do
>>    for Inner = 1, 3 do
>>       print("Outer: " .. Outer .. "; Inner: " .. Inner)
>>    end
>> end
Outer: 1; Inner: 1
Outer: 1; Inner: 2
Outer: 1; Inner: 3
Outer: 2; Inner: 1
Outer: 2; Inner: 2
Outer: 2; Inner: 3
Outer: 3; Inner: 1
Outer: 3; Inner: 2
Outer: 3; Inner: 3
```

> A common mistake is to forget the do after a for or while, or the then after an if or elseif. If you do this, you'll get an error message:
>
> ```
> > for N = 1, 10
> >>    print(N)
>
> stdin:2: 'do' expected near 'print'
> ```

Another way to say something loops is to say that it *iterates*. Looping in general is called iteration, but each time the body of a loop is executed is called *an* iteration.

On each iteration of a for loop, there's an implicit assignment to the *loop variable* (the variable named right after for). This variable has a behavior that you might not expect. In the following example, N is used both outside the loop and as a loop variable:

```
> N = "outside"
> for N = 1, 3 do
>>    print(N)
>> end
1
2
3
> print(N)
outside
```

The outside value of N was unaffected by the numbers that were assigned to N inside the loop. A for loop's variable is only visible inside the loop — if you look at it outside the loop, you'll get any value it was given outside the loop (nil if it hasn't been given a value outside the loop). This is because the N inside the loop and the N outside the loop are actually two different variables — they're in two different *scopes*. (You learn more about this in the next chapter.)

The repeat Loop

The repeat loop is different in three ways from the while loop:

❑ Its expression is tested *after* its body (the statements between do and end), which means that the body is always executed at least once.

❑ The sense of the test is reversed — the while loop keeps going *while* the expression is true; the repeat loop, whose expression comes after the keyword until, keeps going *until* the expression is true.

❑ A repeat loop, unlike a while (or any other compound statement for that matter), does not end with the keyword end.

Here's the factorial example rewritten to use a `repeat` loop:

```
> N, F = 1, 1
> repeat
>>    print(N .. "! is " .. F)
>>    -- Compute the next N and its factorial:
>>    N = N + 1
>>    F = F * N
>> until F >= 100
1! is 1
2! is 2
3! is 6
4! is 24
```

There's sort of an incipient bug in this version. It is that if you had wanted to see all factorials less than 1, then the `while` version would have given you the correct answer (none), but the `repeat` version would have incorrectly printed like this:

```
1! is 1
```

That's why you only use `repeat` when you know that you want the loop's body to be executed at least one time.

The `repeat` loop is the least commonly used control structure. There are a few examples of it in Chapter 18.

The break and do Statements

The `break` statement exits a `while`, `for`, or `repeat` loop prematurely. For example:

```
> for N = 1, 10 do
>>    if N > 5 then
>>       break
>>    end
>>    print(N)
>> end
1
2
3
4
5
>
```

If a `break` is inside more than one loop, it only breaks out of the innermost one as follows:

```
> for Outer = 1, 3 do
>>    for Inner = 101, 103 do
>>       print("Outer: " .. Outer .. "; Inner: " .. Inner)
>>       if Inner == 102 then
>>          print("Breaking out of inner loop; 103 won't be reached.")
>>          break
>>       end
>>    end
>> end
Outer: 1; Inner: 101
Outer: 1; Inner: 102
Breaking out of inner loop; 103 won't be reached.
Outer: 2; Inner: 101
Outer: 2; Inner: 102
Breaking out of inner loop; 103 won't be reached.
Outer: 3; Inner: 101
Outer: 3; Inner: 102
Breaking out of inner loop; 103 won't be reached.
```

Use `break` with caution; sometimes it's the simplest way to do what you want, but more often it makes code hard to understand. If the following loop has no `break`s in it, you can tell at a glance that it will execute 10 times:

```
for Times = 1, 10 do
  A bunch
  of code
  goes here.
end
```

But if the line `if Times == 5 then break end` is in the middle, the loop will execute 4½ times, which is a bit harder to hold in your head while you're looking for a bug.

A `break` must be the last statement in a *block*. A block is a group of statements between the following:

- ❏ `do` and `end`
- ❏ `repeat` and `until`
- ❏ `then` and `elseif`, `else`, or `end`
- ❏ `elseif` and `end`
- ❏ `else` and `end`

In other words, a block is a do block (more about these in a moment), a loop, or a branch of an `if` statement. There are other blocks too, but these are the ones relevant to `break`. The following example demonstrates the error caused by trying to use `break` as something other than the last statement in a block:

```
> while true do
>>    break
>>    print("Never reached")
stdin:3: 'end' expected (to close 'while' at line 1) near 'print'
```

This limitation is not a hardship, because even if you could put statements after a break, they would never get executed. During debugging, however, it can be convenient to break out of the middle of a block, and you can do this by wrapping the break in its own block. Lua's final compound statement, the do block, is useful for this, as you can see in the following example:

```
> for N = 1, 10 do
>>    print("Before")
>>    do break end
>>    print("After")
>> end
Before
>
```

The do block has the following form:

```
do
    zero or more statements
end
```

It can also be used to force code typed directly into the interpreter to be executed as one unit, as in the second of the following examples, which, unlike the first, has all of its output in the same place, instead of it being interleaved with the code:

```
> print("\nHere are some numbers:")

Here are some numbers:
> for N = 1, 5 do
>>    print(N)
>> end
1
2
3
4
5
> print("There were some numbers.")
There were some numbers.

> do
>>    print("\nHere are some numbers:")
>>    for N = 1, 5 do
>>        print(N)
>>    end
>>    print("There were some numbers.")
>> end

Here are some numbers:
1
2
3
4
5
There were some numbers.
```

Summary

This chapter introduced you to the most fundamental elements of the Lua programming language. Most of the examples were given as typed into `lua`, the Lua interpreter. In this chapter, you learned the following:

❑ Numbers, strings, Booleans, and `nil` are different types of values.

❑ To print a value, use `print` and parentheses.

❑ You can use operators to do math, compare values, concatenate strings, and do various other things with values.

❑ Operators are applied in order of their precedence, but you can use parentheses to control this.

❑ You use a single equal sign to assign a value to a variable.

❑ Variable names (identifiers) must include only letters, digits, and underscores, and begin with a letter or an underscore. You cannot use keywords such as `and`, `true`, and `if` as variable names.

❑ Comments start with two dashes.

❑ Literal values and variables are expressions. You can build more complex expressions from less complex ones with operators and parentheses.

❑ Statements are the smallest complete unit of Lua code.

❑ To determine whether to do something, or how many times to do something, you use the control structures `if`, `for`, `while`, and `repeat`.

Often in this chapter, you have given names to values using assignment. It's possible to give names to pieces of code too. For example, you can write a big `if` structure and give it a name, and then when you want to use it, you don't have to type the whole thing in again, you just need to type the name. Pieces of code that are nameable like this are called functions, and they're the subject of the next chapter. Before leaving this chapter, though, take some time to do the exercises and test your understanding of what you've learned so far. You'll find answers in the appendix.

Exercises

1. Why does the following code give an error message rather than printing "Hello"?

```
> Print("Hello")
stdin:1: attempt to call global 'Print' (a nil value)
stack traceback:
        stdin:1: in main chunk
        [C]: ?
```

2. Assuming X is `true` and Y is `nil`, what is the value of the following expression?

```
(X and "ABC") .. (Y and "DEF" or 123)
```

3.   The expression from the previous exercise does not have a value if X is `false`. Why is that?

4.   Consider the following `if` statement:

```
if N < 10 then
   print("x")
elseif N > 0 then
   print("x")
end
```

If N is 5, how many x's will be printed?

5.   Write a `for` loop that prints out the even numbers between 2 and 10, inclusive, in reverse order.

Extending Lua with Functions

One of the key concepts in programming is *abstraction*, which means ignoring unimportant details. Consider the following set of instructions:

1. Get two slices of bread, a jar of peanut butter, a jar of jelly, and a butter knife.
2. Using the butter knife, spread a thin layer of peanut butter on one side of one piece of bread.
3. Using the butter knife, spread a thin layer of jelly on one side of the other piece of bread.
4. Attach the two pieces of bread together by pressing the peanut-buttered side of the one to the jellied side of the other.

Now compare those instructions with the following:

1. Make a peanut-butter-and-jelly sandwich.

The first set of instructions is less abstract than the second, because it contains details that would only be helpful to someone naïve in the ways of sandwich preparation. The second set of instructions *abstracts away* these details. Consider the following code:

```
print(1)
print(2)
print(3)
print(4)
print(5)
print(6)
print(7)
print(8)
print(9)
print(10)
```

This is less abstract than the following code:

```
for I = 1, 10 do
  print(I)
end
```

Both examples do the same thing, but the second one takes advantage of the fact that Lua knows how to count. This demonstrates one of the benefits of abstraction — there's less to type! A related benefit is that it makes code easier to understand: When you know how `for` loops work, you can tell at a glance that the second example prints the numbers from 1 to 10, whereas you'd only know that for sure about the first one if you were to proofread it and make sure that (for instance) it doesn't print two sixes in a row.

Functions are the most important means of abstraction in Lua. You've already used one function in the previous chapter: `print`. In the following example, the `print` function is being told to do its thing with two pieces of data — the string `"The answer is"` and the number 42:

```
print("The answer is", 42)
```

Another way of saying this is that `print` is being *called* with two *arguments*. `print` is only one of many built-in functions that Lua has, but almost any program you write will involve you defining your own functions.

Take a look at the following example:

```
> function Greet(Name)
>>    print("Hello, " .. Name .. ".")
>> end
> Greet("John")
Hello, John.
> Greet("Jane")
Hello, Jane.
> Greet("Aloysius")
Hello, Aloysius.
```

The first line ("`function Greet(Name)`") tells Lua that you're defining a function, that the function's name will be `Greet`, and that it will take one argument, whose value will be placed into the variable `Name`. When the function is called, the second line concatenates the string `"Hello, "` with (the contents of) `Name` and a period, and prints the result. The last line of the function tells Lua that you're done defining the function. A function definition like this is a *statement*.

The function is then called three times, each time with a different name as an argument, and prints a greeting customized for a person with that name. Because the details of how to greet someone are only in one place, you only need to make any change you want once, rather than every time you greet someone.

The inside of a function definition is executed only when or if the function is called. In the preceding example, because the call to `print` is inside `Greet`, nothing is printed when `Greet` is defined, but something is printed each time `Greet` is called. This point may seem obvious, but if you're a beginning programmer, you might find yourself forgetting it when confronted with more complex pieces of code.

Functions can have more than one line of code inside them. In fact, they can include all the things covered in the preceding chapter. Here's one that includes assignment and an `if` control structure:

```
function Greet(Name)
   if Name == "Joe" then
     MsgStr = "Whaddya know, Joe?"
   else
     MsgStr = "Hello, " .. Name .. "."
   end
   print(MsgStr)
end
```

For that matter, functions can even contain no lines of code, in which case they do nothing. Functions can also take any number of arguments, or none, as in the following example:

```
> function NoNameGreet()
>>    print("Hello.")
>> end
> NoNameGreet()
Hello.
> function TwoNameGreet(Name1, Name2)
>>    print("Hello, " .. Name1 .. " and " .. Name2 .. ".")
>> end
> TwoNameGreet("Mutt", "Jeff")
Hello, Mutt and Jeff.
```

If a function is called with more arguments than it was written for, the extra arguments are thrown away, like this:

```
> NoNameGreet("Cathy")
Hello.
> TwoNameGreet("Larry", "Moe", "Curly", "Shemp")
Hello, Larry and Moe.
```

If a function is called with fewer arguments than it was written for, the remaining arguments are (inside the function) set to `nil` as follows:

```
> function Print2Args(Arg1, Arg2)
>>    print(Arg1, Arg2)
>> end
> Print2Args("1st argument", "2nd argument")
1st argument    2nd argument
> Print2Args("1st argument")
1st argument    nil
> Print2Args()
nil     nil
```

Notice that this behavior (discarding extra arguments and setting missing ones to `nil`) exactly parallels the behavior of multiple assignment (described in Chapter 2):

```
> Var1, Var2 = "1st value", "2nd value", "3rd value"
> print(Var1, Var2)
1st value       2nd value
> Var1, Var2 = "1st value"
> print(Var1, Var2)
1st value       nil
```

This chapter is all about functions. It explains how to do the following:

❏   Give names to pieces of code and refer to them by those names (this is one of the most important methods used to structure a program)

❏   Execute a file that contains Lua code

❏   Use variables that are only valid in limited parts of a program

❏   Use the same variable name to refer to different variables in different parts of a program

Return Values

Functions — both ones built into Lua and ones that you define — can *return* values. This means that a function call can result in a value that you can then pass to another function, use in a variable assignment, or otherwise operate on. In other words, function calls are actually expressions that, like `print` and `Greet`, you can use as statements.

Using a Function that Returns a Value

You can return values from functions that you've defined. But first, you should see how to get a return value from a function that's already built into Lua.

Lua's built-in `type` function is a good example of a function that returns a value. Here are some examples of this function:

```
> print(type(42))
number
> print(type("Hello, Aloysius."))
string
> print(type(true))
boolean
> print(type(type(true)))
string
> print(type(nil) .. type(false))
nilboolean
> SomeType = type(42)
> print(SomeType)
number
```

The `type` function takes one argument, which can be any value. It always returns a string that names the datatype of its argument, which will be — one of the following eight strings: `"boolean"`, `"function"`, `"nil"`, `"number"`, `"string"`, `"table"`, `"thread"`, or `"userdata"`. So, when `type` is called with a number as an argument, it returns the string `"number"`; when `type` is called with `nil` as an argument, it returns the string `"nil"`; and so on.

> *These eight strings represent all eight Lua types. Booleans, nils, numbers, and strings were covered last chapter. Right now you're learning about functions. Tables, threads, and userdata will be explained in Chapter 4, Chapter 9, and Chapter 13, respectively.*

As the preceding examples show, a call to `type` is an expression and can be used wherever an expression is legal. You can use it as the argument to another function:

```
print(type(type(true)))
```

Or as an operator's operand:

```
print(type(nil) .. type(false))
```

Or in an assignment:

```
SomeType = type(42)
```

If you call `type` in the interpreter without doing anything with its value, nothing happens (the value is thrown away):

```
> type(42)
>
```

This is why the `type` result has been passed to `print` in the preceding examples.

Defining a Function that Returns a Value

Unsurprisingly, Lua makes it easy to define your own functions that have return values. You use the `return` statement.

The following function, `Average`, uses `return` to return the average of its two arguments:

```
> function Average(Num1, Num2)
>>    return (Num1 + Num2) / 2
>> end
> Average(0, 10)
> print(Average(0, 10))
5
> print(Average(Average(10, 20), Average(30, 40)))
25
```

The first time `Average` is called, nothing is done with the result, so the result is thrown away, and you never see it. The second time it is called, the result (5) is passed to `print`, so you do see it. On the next line, `Average` is called twice, and the results are passed to a third call of `Average`. This is equivalent to the following:

```
Avg1, Avg2 = Average(10, 20), Average(30, 40)
print(Average(Avg1, Avg2))
```

Using the return values of function calls as arguments to other function calls is very common. If carried to an extreme, it can get a bit hard to read, in which case assigning intermediate results to variables (like `Avg1`) can make things more legible.

> *This `Average` function can only average two numbers. In the next chapter, you'll learn how to write a function that can average however many numbers you give it.*

Using return to Alter Control Flow

Functions, just like the `break` statement and the `if`, `for`, and `while` control structures, alter the flow of control through a program. The `return` statement also alters the flow of control.

In the following example, `return` is used to jump past the bottom of the function:

```
> -- Returns true if Str has an even number of characters;
> -- otherwise returns false:
> function EvenLen(Str)
>>    if #Str % 2 == 0 then
>>       return true
>>    else
>>       return false
>>    end
>>    print("This will never get printed!")
>> end
> print(EvenLen("Jane"))
true
> print(EvenLen("Joe"))
false
>
```

The `if` tests whether the length of `Str` is evenly divisible by 2. If it is, the function immediately returns `true`, which means that the rest of the function (in this case, the final `print` call) never gets executed. If the length is not evenly divisible by 2, the function immediately returns `false`, and the `print` is again not reached.

If this sounds familiar, it's because `return` is very similar to `break`, which you learned about in the last chapter. In fact, there are two differences:

❑ `break` exits the innermost loop; `return` exits the innermost function (functions, like loops, can be nested).

❑ Because loops don't return values, `break` cannot be followed by an expression like `return` can.

Like `break`, `return` must be the last statement in a block. In the last chapter, an incomplete list of blocks was given (do blocks; `for`, `while`, and `repeat` loops; branches of `if` statements). The only other blocks are functions and *chunks*. A chunk is a piece of code executed as a unit, such as the following:

❑ A complete file

❑ A single line typed into the Lua interpreter without causing the continuation prompt to appear

❑ Multiple lines typed into the Lua interpreter, of which all but the last cause the continuation prompt to appear

Again as with `break`, if you want (for debugging purposes) to return from the middle of a block, just use a dummy do block like this:

```
> function ReturnFromMiddle()
>>    print("Does get printed")
>>    do return true end
>>    print("Doesn't get printed")
>> end
> ReturnFromMiddle()
Does get printed
>
```

In the last chapter, you saw how `break` can sometimes make loops, especially long ones, harder to understand. For similar reasons, returning from the middle of functions, particularly long ones, can make them harder to understand. To verify that the last line of EvenLen will never be executed, you need to examine the whole function, a small hardship which would be greater with a larger function.

This book often has you write functions like this:

```
function EvenLen(Str)
   if #Str % 2 == 0 then
     Ret = true
   else
     Ret = false
   end
   return Ret
end
```

The return value is assigned to Ret in the middle of the function, but Ret is only returned at the very end, so the function has only one exit point, while the earlier version of EvenLen had two. (There's actually something wrong with this example — Ret is visible outside the function, when it really should be the function's own private variable. You'll learn how to avoid this later in this chapter.)

> *The practice of having only one exit point from each block is part of what is known as structured programming, a school of thought most identified with programming pioneer Edsger Dijkstra (1930-2002). Structured programming is much less controversial now than when it was first introduced in the 1960s, but it is by no means universally regarded as correct. We, the authors of this book, think of it as a rule of thumb to which exceptions can be made.*

Returning Nothing

Before you learned about return, you saw how to write functions that don't include return. What do such functions return? It's easy enough to find out. When print is called with no arguments, it just prints an empty line, like this:

```
> print()

>
```

If you create a function that does nothing and has no return statement, and print its result, you get an empty line as shown here:

```
> function DoNothing()
>> end
> print(DoNothing())

>
```

If functions like this returned nil, you would see it here. This is a strong hint that functions that don't use return really do not return a value. You can verify this by trying to print the following DoNothing return value, which results in type complaining that it wasn't given a value:

```
> print(type(DoNothing()))
stdin:1: bad argument #1 to 'type' (value expected)
stack traceback:
        [C]: in function 'type'
        stdin:1: in main chunk
        [C]: ?
```

To explicitly return no value, use return with no value. The following version of DoNothing behaves exactly the same as the previous version:

```
function DoNothing()
   return
end
```

And the following function also does nothing and returns nothing:

```
function DoNothing()
   do return end
   print("This will never print.")
end
```

Not having a `return` **statement at the end of a function has exactly the same effect as having a** `return` **that returns no values.**

Returning Multiple Values

So far, you've seen functions that return one value and functions that return no values. Functions can also return more than one value, and this turns out to be a particularly handy feature of Lua.

Here's a function that takes three arguments and returns all of them.

```
> function ReturnArgs(Arg1, Arg2, Arg3)
>>    return Arg1, Arg2, Arg3
>> end
> print(ReturnArgs(1, 2, 3))
1        2        3
> print(ReturnArgs(ReturnArgs(1, 2, 3)))
1        2        3
> A, B, C = ReturnArgs("alpha", "bravo", "charlie")
> print(A, B, C)
alpha    bravo    charlie
```

To return multiple values, simply separate the values with commas. Just from reading the following line, you might think that `print` is being given only one argument:

```
print(ReturnArgs(1, 2, 3))
```

But it actually gets three arguments — the three values returned by `ReturnArgs`. The next line is just a generalization of this. `ReturnArgs` is given three arguments; it returns three values; those three values are given to another call of `ReturnArgs`, which itself returns three values; and those values are given to `print` (which prints them):

```
print(ReturnArgs(ReturnArgs(1, 2, 3)))
```

You can also use a call to a function that returns multiple values as the right side of an assignment, like this:

```
A, B, C = ReturnArgs("alpha", "bravo", "charlie")
```

Adjusting Value Lists

You just saw that you can use a function that returns multiple values as the first and only argument to another function (in which case it's as though the function was called with multiple arguments) or as the entire right-hand side of an assignment (in which case it's as though multiple values were assigned). What if you use a function that returns multiple values as one of several arguments to another function, or as only part of the right side of an assignment? As you know, if you call a function with more than one argument, then the arguments are separated with commas. The same applies to assignment statements that assign more than one value and return statements that return more than one value. These lists of zero or more (in the case of functions and return) or one or more (in the case of assignment) values are called *value lists*.

When you call functions in value lists, their return values are adjusted. This is similar to the process of adjustment (described in Chapter 2) that happens in assignment statements.

Using Multiple-Valued Functions in Value Lists

Here's how multiple-valued functions work in various positions in value lists of various lengths, using the ReturnArgs function defined in the previous section:

```
> print(1, ReturnArgs("a", "b", "c"))
1       a       b       c
> print(ReturnArgs(1, 2, 3), "a")
1       a
> print(ReturnArgs(1, 2, 3), ReturnArgs("a", "b", "c"))
1       a       b       c
```

The rule that Lua follows it this:

> **If a function call returning multiple values is the last (or only) expression in a value list, then all the function's return values are used. If a function call returning multiple values is in a value list but is not the last expression, then only its first return value is used; its remaining return values are discarded.**

This explains why the following:

```
print(ReturnArgs(1, 2, 3), ReturnArgs("a", "b", "c"))
```

printed this:

```
1       a       b       c
```

ReturnArgs(1, 2, 3) was not the last expression in the print list of arguments, so only its first return value (1) was used, and its second and third values were thrown away. The ReturnArgs("a", "b", "c") was the last expression in print's argument list, so all three of its return values ("a", "b", and "c") were passed as (the second, third, and fourth) arguments to print.

The rule also applies to value lists with more than two expressions in them, such as these:

```
> print(
>>    ReturnArgs(1, 2, 3),
>>    ReturnArgs(4, 5, 6),
>>    ReturnArgs(7, 8, 9),
>>    ReturnArgs(10, 11, 12))
1        4        7        10       11       12
```

Although these examples were given using the print function, the value lists in return and assignment statements work the same way:

```
> function Test()
>>    return ReturnArgs(1, 2, 3), ReturnArgs(4, 5, 6)
>> end
> print(Test())
1        4        5        6
> A, B, C, D = ReturnArgs(1, 2, 3), ReturnArgs(4, 5, 6)
> print(A, B, C, D)
1        4        5        6
```

Using Valueless Functions in Value Lists

What about functions that return no values, such as the following:

```
> function DoNothing()
>> end
> print(1, DoNothing())
1
> print(DoNothing(), 2)
nil      2
> print(DoNothing(), DoNothing())
nil
```

This is just an application of the same rule: When the call to DoNothing is the last expression in the value list, no adjustment is made and no corresponding value is passed to print, and when the call to DoNothing is not the last expression in the value list, it is adjusted from no values to one value, namely nil. Here's the rule rephrased to cover functions that return no values:

> **If a function call is the last (or only) expression in a value list, then all (if any) values returned by the function are used. If a function call is in a value list but is not the last expression, then its first return value (or nil, if it returns nothing) is used and any remaining return values are discarded.**

This rule (adjust every expression except the last to one value) may seem more complicated than necessary, but there is good reasoning behind it. If every expression in a value list were adjusted to one value, there would need to be a special way to override this, which would make the ability of Lua functions to return multiple values harder to use. If no expressions in a value list were adjusted to one value, then any function returning less or more than one value would throw off the positioning of everything that came after it in the value list.

As you saw with type, *a function call used as a statement is adjusted to no return values, because there's nowhere for those values to go.*

As covered in the previous chapter and earlier in this one, the whole value list involved in an assignment or a function call is adjusted to the right size by discarding values or adding nils. That adjustment happens after the adjustment of individual expressions in the value list that this section has been describing:

```
> A, B = DoNothing(), 1, 2
> print(A, B)
nil     1
> A, B, C = ReturnArgs(1, 2, 3), 4
> print(A, B, C)
1       4       nil
```

To force a function call at the end of a value list to be adjusted to one value, surround the whole function call (including its parentheses) with parentheses:

```
> print("a", (ReturnArgs("b", "c", "d")))
a       b
> print("a", (DoNothing()))
a       nil
```

You've seen three uses for parentheses: function calls, controlling precedence in expressions, and function definitions. It may seem as though adjusting to one value is yet another use of parentheses, but in Lua, these are the same type of parentheses used to control precedence. You can use a function to return less or more than one value only when a call to it is the last expression in a value list. Wrapping such a call in parentheses has no effect on precedence, because there are no operators and therefore no precedence to control, but it does cause the last expression in the value list to no longer be a function call (even though it contains one), and to therefore no longer be eligible for multiple- or zero-value treatment.

return is not a function. This means that you should not surround whatever comes after it in parentheses, unless you want to force adjustment to one value as shown in the following example:

```
> -- This example requires the ReturnArgs function used
> -- earlier.
> function Test()
>>    return (ReturnArgs(1, 2, 3))
>> end
> print(Test())
1
```

Chunks as Functions

Earlier in this chapter, a *chunk* was defined as a piece of code executed as a unit. The simplest example is code typed into the interpreter. When you enter a line into the interpreter, it checks whether you typed any complete statements. If so, it executes those statements as a chunk. If not, it prints a continuation prompt so you can finish. After it has amassed a whole number of statements, it *compiles* (converts) them into *bytecode*—an internal representation much more efficient than the text that you type in (which is also known as *source code*). This bytecode is meant for the internal component of Lua also known as the interpreter, which is the second meaning of the term *interpreter* mentioned in the previous chapter. When there is a possibility for confusion, the first interpreter can be called `lua` or the *command-line interpreter*, and the second can be called the *bytecode interpreter*.

> *The command-line interpreter and the bytecode interpreter are not two independent things. Rather, the command-line interpreter uses (and depends on) the bytecode interpreter.*

After a chunk has been compiled into bytecode, it is a function (albeit one without a name). This means that chunks, including those typed into the interpreter, can be returned from the following:

```
> return
>
```

The return can even come from deep within a chunk, like this:

```
> for I = 1, 10 do
>>    print(I)
>>    if I == 5 then return end
>> end
1
2
3
4
5
>
```

If values are returned, `lua` passes them to `print` so you can see them, as shown here:

```
> return nil, "Hello", nil
nil     Hello   nil
```

This is how the equal-sign typing saver described in the last chapter works. When the interpreter sees a chunk that starts with an equal sign, it replaces the equal sign with `"return "` before compiling the chunk like this:

```
> =nil, "Hello", nil
nil     Hello   nil
```

When a chunk typed into the interpreter is executed as a function, no arguments are passed to it.

Another important type of chunk is a file containing Lua code. Such a file is often called a *script*.

Try It Out   Writing Your First Lua Script

Unlike code typed directly into the interpreter, scripts are self-contained programs, which you can run repeatedly without having to type them in again. The following very simple script gives a greeting that is traditional in programming examples.

1.   Create a file with the following contents and name it **hello.lua**:

```
-- This is the first file-based example in the book.
print("Hello, world!")
```

2.   Access your system's shell, and make sure you're in the same directory as the file you just created (as described in Chapter 1). Then type the following and press Enter:

```
lua hello.lua
```

You should see the following:

```
Hello, world!
```

How It Works

When lua is started with a filename, it loads that file as a chunk and executes it. As with any chunk, a file can be returned from it, and values can be returned from it, but if the file is executed as shown in this example, these values will simply be thrown away. Arguments can be given to a file, as you'll learn in the next chapter.

From here on, many of the examples will be presented as scripts to be executed by giving the filename to lua.

*If you don't want to have to type **lua** every time you run a file like this, you can make it directly executable. On Unix-like platforms this is done by making its first line something like #!/usr/local/bin/lua or #!/usr/bin/env lua, and marking the file as executable with chmod a+x followed by the file's name. (If Lua saw #! in the middle of a script, it would complain, but if it sees # as the very first character, it just skips to the second line.)*

There are several ways to do it on Windows. Ussing hello.lua as an example, one method is to make a file called hello.cmd that consists of a line like this:

```
@lua "C:\Your\Dirs\Here\hello.lua" %*
```

Or if that doesn't work because you are running an earlier version of Windows, you can use the following method, which limits the number of command-line arguments to nine (replace "C:\Your\Dirs\Here\" with the full path to the Lua file):

```
@lua "C:\Your\Dirs\Here\hello.lua" %1 %2 %3 %4 %5 %6 %7 %8 %9
```

The `.cmd` *file must be in a directory in your system's search path. After you do this, typing* `hello` *will run the file.*

You can also execute a string as a chunk. First use the built-in function `loadstring` to convert it to a function, and then call the function like this:

```
> Fnc = loadstring("print('Hello!')")
> Fnc()
Hello!
```

`loadstring` is an excellent example of the usefulness of multiple return values. If it succeeds in converting the string to a function, it returns that function; otherwise, it returns `nil` and an error message. That's demonstrated by the following example, which also shows that `loadstring` takes an optional second argument—a a string used as a name for the chunk in any error messages:

```
> Fnc, ErrStr = loadstring("print(2 + + 2)", "A STRING CHUNK")
> if Fnc then
>>    Fnc()
>> else
>>    print(ErrStr)
>> end
[string "A STRING CHUNK"]:1: unexpected symbol near '+'
```

You can use the `vararg` mechanism described in the next chapter to access any arguments given to the function returned by `loadstring` (although not in Lua 5.0).

Like all chunks, a chunk compiled by `loadstring` has no access to local variables from other chunks. For example:

```
> Test = "global"
> do
>>    local Test = "local"
>>    Fnc = loadstring("print(Test)")
>>    Fnc() -- This prints Test's global value.
>> end
global
```

> `loadstring` **may seem like a very powerful function, but it's seldom necessary. If you feel a need to use it, chances are that what you want to do should be done another way instead (with the closures described later in this chapter, for example, or with the** `getfenv` **and** `setfenv` **functions described in the next chapter). An exception to this is a program that (like the Lua interpreter) accepts code while it's running, and runs that code. That type of thing is the ideal use of** `loadstring`**.**

Variable Scope

In the last chapter, you saw that the variable created by a `for` loop is only visible inside the loop, and that a variable outside the loop can have the same name without them affecting each other. (*Visible* here means that it can be assigned to and its value can be read.) This is possible because Lua, like most modern programming languages, has *variable scopes*, which are regions within which certain variables are visible.

> *In early computer languages, all variables were in the same scope, which made it hard to write large programs, because you needed to make sure that the same name wasn't used for two different things.*

The first step in understanding scopes is learning the distinction between a function's *actual arguments* and its *formal arguments*. This is explained by the next section.

Actual and Formal Arguments

In the following example, what is `PrintArg`'s argument?

```
> -- Prints its one argument:
> function PrintArg(Arg)
>>    print(Arg)
>> end
> PrintArg(true)
true
```

There are two answers to that question. The argument `PrintArg` is defined with is `Arg`, but the argument it's called with is `true`. The arguments that a function is defined to take are called *formal arguments*; the arguments that it is called with are called *actual arguments*.

> *This terminology is not totally standardized. For instance, some people call formal arguments* parameters *and reserve the word* argument *for actual arguments.*

Formal arguments are just the names by which actual arguments are referred to inside a function when it is called. This is why using something other than a name as a formal argument is an error, such as the following:

```
> function Oops(true)
stdin:1: <name> or '...' expected near 'true'
```

Local Variables

A function's formal arguments are only visible inside the function, and any variable from outside the function is only visible if it does not share a name with a formal argument. For example:

```
> Arg, NotShadowed = "Outside 1", "Outside 2"
>
> -- Prints its one argument and the value of NotShadowed:
> function ScopeTest(Arg)
>>    print(Arg, NotShadowed)
>> end
>
> ScopeTest(true)
true    Outside 2
> print(Arg)
Outside 1
```

When `ScopeTest` is called, a new variable is created, named `Arg`, and the actual argument for `ScopeTest` is assigned to it. Because this variable is only visible inside the function, it is called a *local* variable. When the value of `Arg` is printed, it's the local `Arg` (whose value is `true`) that gets printed, and not the outer `Arg` (whose value is `"Outside 1"`). For this reason, the local `Arg` is said to *shadow* the outer `Arg`. On the other hand, `NotShadowed`, which does not share a name with any variable local to the function, is not shadowed, and is therefore accessible in the normal way.

After `ScopeTest` returns, the outer `Arg` is unaffected.

Scopes can be nested inside each other, as shown in this rather contrived example:

```
> function ScopeTest2(LclA)
>>    print("LclA is " .. LclA)
>>    for LclB = 1, 5 do
>>       print("LclB is " .. LclB)
>>       LclA = LclA + 1
>>    end
>>    print("LclA is now " .. LclA)
>> end
>
> ScopeTest2(100)
LclA is 100
LclB is 1
LclB is 2
LclB is 3
LclB is 4
LclB is 5
LclA is now 105
```

The scope of `LclA` is the whole function. The scope of `LclB` is just the loop. The example also shows that you can assign to local variables from containing scopes.

Functions and `for` loops create their own local variables, but you can create local variables too.

This example introduces the keyword `local`:

```
> function ScopeTest3(Lcl)
>>    for I = 1, 5 do
>>        Lcl = Lcl .. "a"
>>        print(Lcl)
>>        local Lcl = ""
>>        Lcl = Lcl .. "z"
>>        print(Lcl)
>>    end
>>    print("The loop is done.")
>>    print(Lcl)
>> end
>
> ScopeTest3("")
a
z
aa
z
aaa
z
aaaa
z
aaaaa
z
The loop is done.
aaaaa
```

`local Lcl = ""` is a statement that creates a new local variable named `Lcl` and initializes it to the empty string. This new local variable's scope starts on the statement after the `local` statement. Because it's inside the scope of another variable also named `Lcl` (the function's formal argument), it shadows that outer variable.

Every time the `local` statement is executed, a new local variable is created and initialized. That's why the outer `Lcl` becomes a longer and longer string of a's, whereas the inner `Lcl` is never longer than one z, because it keeps getting recreated and hence doesn't remember its previous value.

The scope of a local variable created with the `local` statement has to end somewhere. In this example, it ends at the end of the loop (the same place that the scope of the loop variable `I` ends). You can see that this is true, because when the value of `Lcl` is printed after the loop is done, it's the outer `Lcl` whose value get printed.

> **A local variable's scope extends to the end of the innermost block that encloses it. A block is a do block, the body of a `while` or `for` loop, the body of a `repeat` loop plus its `until` expression, a branch of an `if` statement, a function, or a chunk.**

Figure 3-1 shows all the scopes in `ScopeTest3`, and clearly illustrates why the two `Lcl`s are called outer and inner. The scope of the outer `Lcl` starts at the top of the function's body and ends at the bottom of the function's body; the scope of the `I` loop variable starts at the top of the loop body and ends at the bottom of the loop body; the scope of the inner starts right after the `local` statement and ends at the bottom of the loop body.

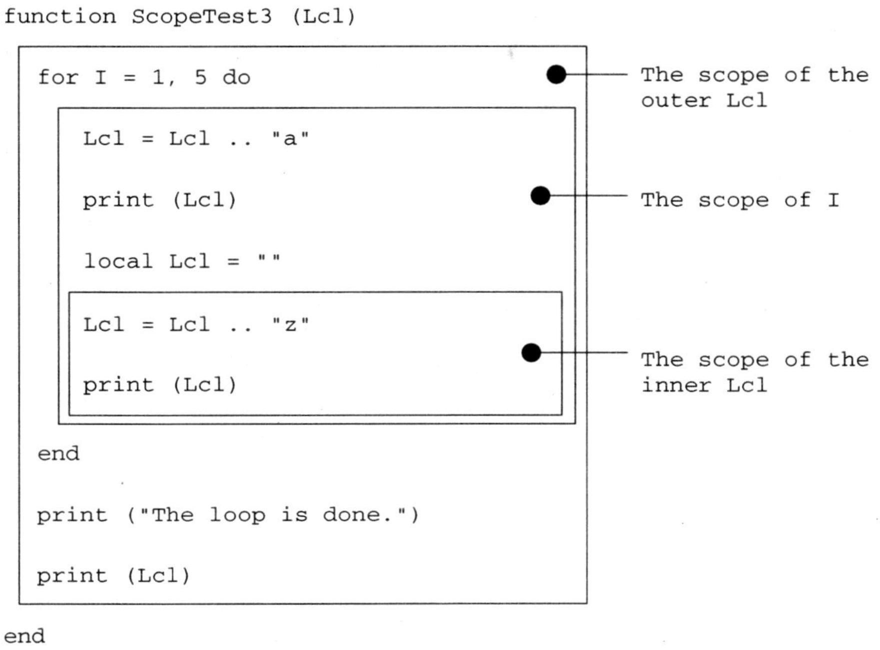

```
function ScopeTest3 (Lcl)
```

The scope of the outer Lcl

The scope of I

The scope of the inner Lcl

```
    end
```

Figure 3-1

Variables from outer scopes are always visible in inner scopes, unless they are shadowed. This is easier to show using the following `do` blocks to delimit scopes without altering control flow:

```
> do
>>   local A = "A1"
>>   do
>>     local B = "B1"
>>     do
>>       local A = "A2"
>>       do
>>         local B = "B2"
>>         B = "still B2"
>>       end
>>       do
>>         local C = "C1"
>>         print(A, B, C)
>>       end
>>     end
>>   end
>> end
A2       B1        C1
```

The inner A is printed because it shadows the outer one, but the first B is printed because the second B is not in a containing scope. By the time C's scope starts, the second B scope has already ended. Figure 3-2 illustrates this:

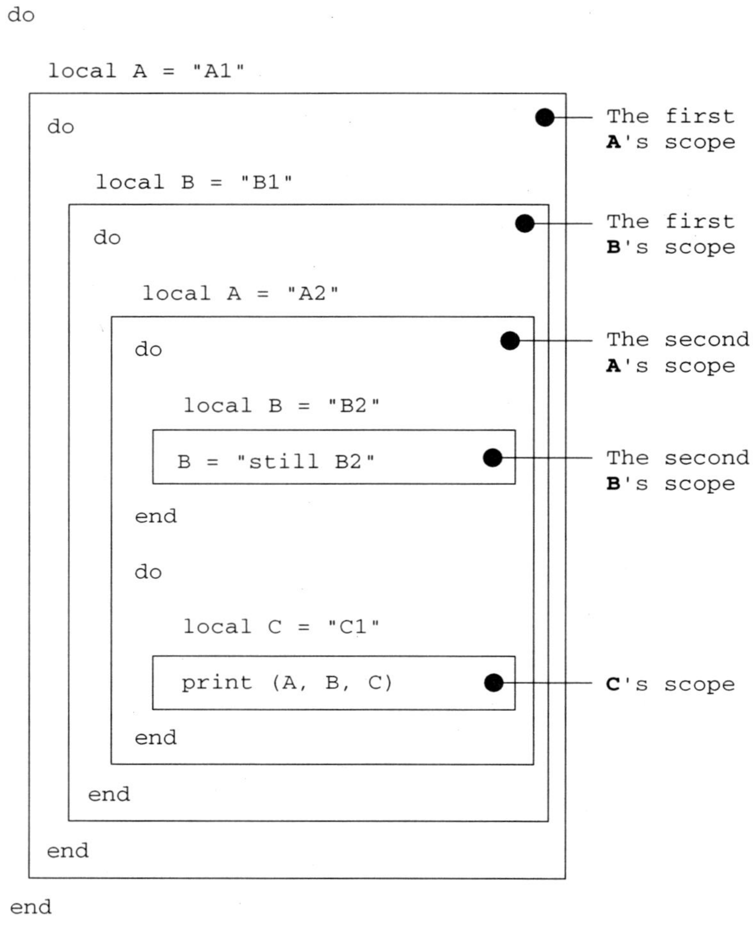

```
do

    local A = "A1"

    do                                          ●──── The first
                                                       A's scope
        local B = "B1"

        do                                      ●──── The first
                                                       B's scope
            local A = "A2"

            do                                  ●──── The second
                                                       A's scope
                local B = "B2"

                B = "still B2"                  ●──── The second
                                                       B's scope
            end

            do

                local C = "C1"

                print (A, B, C)                 ●──── C's scope

            end

        end

    end

end
```

Figure 3-2

One of the benefits of indenting by block is that it makes scopes easier to see. To find out where the inner Lcl's scope ends in ScopeTest3, all you need to do is find the first line below the local line that's farther to the left — Lcl's scope includes everything up to that line:

```
function ScopeTest3(Lcl)
    for I = 1, 5 do
        Lcl = Lcl .. "a"
        print(Lcl)
        local Lcl = ""
        Lcl = Lcl .. "z"
```

```
        print(Lcl)
    end
    print("The loop is done.")
    print(Lcl)
end
```

As mentioned earlier (and illustrated by the positioning of the boxes in Figures 3-1 and 3-2), the scope of a variable created by a `local` statement doesn't begin until the following statement. This means that if a variable name appears on both sides of a `local` statement's equal sign, the one on the left names the variable whose scope is about to begin, and the one on the right names a variable in a containing scope:

```
> do
>>    local Lcl = "aardvark"
>>    -- The first Lcl's scope starts here.
>>    local Lcl = Lcl .. "zebra"
>>    -- The second Lcl's scope starts here.
>>    print(Lcl)
>>    -- Both scopes end here.
>> end
aardvarkzebra
```

A chunk is a block, which means that if a local variable is not contained within any other blocks, its scope ends when the chunk ends. This means that a local variable is never visible in two different files. It also means that a local variable is never visible in two different chunks of interpreter input. Here's an example:

```
> City = "New York"
> local City = "London"
> print(City)
New York
```

In this example, the first line gives a value to the variable `City`, which is not a local variable. The second line creates and initializes a local variable, also named `City`, which is forgotten about as soon as the line is done executing. The third line prints the value of a variable named `City`. Because there is no containing block with a local variable of that name, the `City` from the first line is used.

Variables that aren't local are called *global* variables. They are called this because they are visible globally, everywhere in the program, even across different chunks. Their scopes begin and end at the beginning and end of the program. Not counting `for` loop variables, all the variables you used in the previous chapter were global.

You can shadow global variables by local variables as follows:

```
> Var = "global"
> do
>>    local Var = "local"
>>    print(Var)
>>    Var = "still local"
>>    print(Var)
>> end
local
still local
> print(Var)
global
```

You can create and initialize multiple local variables at the same time. Other than creating new local variables, you follow the same rules as for multiple assignment (for example, `nil`s are used if the list of values is too short):

```
> do
>>    local A, B = 1, 2
>>    print(A, B)
>>    local A, B = 1
>>    print(A, B)
>>    local A, B = 1, 2, 3
>>    print(A, B)
>> end
1       2
1       nil
1       2
```

You can create local variables without initializing them. This is exactly like initializing them to `nil`:

```
> do
>>    local A
>>    print(A)
>>    local B, C
>>    print(B, C)
>> end
nil
nil     nil
```

Whether you make the `nil` implicit (`local A`) or explicit (`local A = nil`) is a stylistic choice. Generally, you shouldn't use the explicit version if the `nil` will never be seen because it will be replaced with another value. An example of this is the following rewritten version of the `EvenLen` function:

> Remember that the second version of `EvenLen` given earlier (the one with only one exit point) had a problem. The problem was that, before returning its return value, it stored it in the global variable `Ret`, which means that if `Ret` was used as a global anywhere else, calling `EvenLen` would rudely overwrite its value. (You can verify this by calling `EvenLen` and then printing `Ret`.) This is exactly the problem that local variables are meant to solve. Here, `EvenLen` is rewritten so that the `Ret` it uses is only visible inside it.

```
function EvenLen(Str)
  local Ret
  if #Str % 2 == 0 then
    Ret = true
  else
    Ret = false
  end
  return Ret
end
```

> Don't make the mistake of thinking that regular assignment (an equal sign but no `local` keyword) is for assigning to global variables and the `local` keyword is for assigning to local variables. Rather, regular assignment assigns to either globals or locals (whichever is visible, scopewise), and the `local` keyword creates new locals and optionally assigns initial values to those very locals.

Understanding Side Effects

If a statement or expression causes something to change, this is called a *side effect*, such as when the `print` function changes what's on the screen. For example, the following function changes the value of the global variable `G1`:

The `Val` variable created in this example is not part of the side effect, because creating a new local variable doesn't change the value of a variable that already exists.

```
function SetG1(Val)
   G1 = Val
end
```

On the other hand, the `type` function has no side effects — all it does is return a value. However, this value may then be used by another function or statement that does have a side effect.

Ordering Side Effects

If two functions are free of side effects, it doesn't matter which order they're called in. In the following example, it is impossible to tell whether the `type` on the left was called before or after the one on the right, but that's okay, because all that matters is that the left one's return value was used as the first `print` argument (and the right return value as the second):

```
> print(type(1), type("a"))
number   string
```

If two functions do have side effects, though, you can see which order they're called in. This will be easiest to demonstrate with a function that has both a return value and a side effect:

```
-- Prints a message with Val, then returns Val:
function PrintReturn(Val)
  print("Returning: " .. tostring(Val))
  return Val
end
```

`PrintReturn` takes a single argument. It prints a message that it is about to return this argument, and then it does so. It uses the built-in Lua function `tostring` to convert the argument to a string (otherwise the concatenation operator would choke on `nil` and Booleans):

```
> print(PrintReturn(1), PrintReturn(2), PrintReturn(3))
Returning: 1
Returning: 2
Returning: 3
1        2        3
```

This example showed that the three calls to `PrintReturn` are made from left to right, but don't rely on this — the order is actually undefined and only happens to be left to right in the current implementation. If you want to make sure that function calls are made in a particular order, make them part of different statements like this:

```
> do
>>    local Val1 = PrintReturn(1)
>>    local Val2 = PrintReturn(2)
>>    local Val3 = PrintReturn(3)
>>    print(Val1, Val2, Val3)
>> end
Returning: 1
Returning: 2
Returning: 3
1        2        3
```

This holds for function calls used in expressions, too — they're done left to right, but don't rely on it:

```
> print(PrintReturn(1) + PrintReturn(2))
Returning: 1
Returning: 2
3
```

Similarly, the current implementation of Lua assigns from right to left, but this behavior shouldn't be relied on:

```
> A, A = 1, 2
> print(A)
1
```

What is guaranteed is that all function calls to the right of an assignment will be made before any of the variables to the left are assigned to. This is just a special case of the rule that all expressions to the right of an assignment are evaluated before any assigning is done. (If it weren't for that rule, you couldn't use multiple assignment to swap values, which was demonstrated in the previous chapter.) In the following example, when 1 is added to B, the initial value of B is used, and when 1 is added to A, the initial value of A is used. Only after both calls to `PrintReturn` are made (with these incremented values) do A and B get new values:

```
> A, B = 1, 10
> A, B = PrintReturn(B + 1), PrintReturn(A + 1)
Returning: 11
Returning: 2
```

```
> print(A, B)
11      2
```

It's also guaranteed that any function call used as an argument (or part of an argument) to another function will be made before the other function is called. So, the innermost `PrintReturn` is called before the one whose parentheses it is inside (which would be true even if the outer `PrintReturn` never did anything with its argument):

```
> print(PrintReturn(PrintReturn(1) + 1))
Returning: 1
Returning: 2
2
```

Functions that don't have side effects are easier to decipher than those that do because you don't have to think about how many times or in what order they're executed. Side effects that are only visible within a small part of the program (that is, assigning to a local variable) are easier to decipher than those visible throughout the whole program, because you don't have to consider them while thinking about the rest of the program. This doesn't mean that you should completely avoid side effects. It does mean that, when faced with the choice of writing a function with side effects or without, you should write it without side effects unless there's a good reason to write it with them. It also means that, unless a variable needs to be visible throughout the entire program, it should be made local with as narrow a scope as possible.

The and and or operators have a special behavior regarding side effects. This behavior is called *short-circuit* (or *shortcut*) *evaluation*, and it is demonstrated next.

Short-Circuit Evaluation

Remember that the length operator # gets the length of a string. If it's given something that doesn't have a length (a Boolean in the following example), it will error out, but notice that there is no error when `Len` is given a Boolean, even though `Len` returns an expression that includes an attempt to get its argument's length:

```
> print(#true)
stdin:1: attempt to get length of a boolean value
stack traceback:
        stdin:1: in main chunk
        [C]: ?
>
> -- Returns Val's length, or false if Val isn't a string:
> function Len(Val)
>>    return type(Val) == "string" and #Val
>> end
>
> print(Len(""))
0
> print(Len("abc"))
3
> print(Len(true))
false
```

In the previous chapter, you learned that and uses its second operand as its result only if its first operand is true. However, if its first operand is false, then not only does it not use its second operand as its result, but it doesn't even evaluate the second operand, so any side effects the second operand might have had will not happen. This also applies to errors; giving a Boolean to the # operator causes an error, but in the previous example, Val is only given to # if it's a string. The following examples, which use the PrintReturn function, will make this clearer:

```
> print(PrintReturn(1) and PrintReturn(2))
Returning: 1
Returning: 2
2
> print(PrintReturn(1) and PrintReturn(false))
Returning: 1
Returning: false
false
> print(PrintReturn(nil) and PrintReturn(2))
Returning: nil
nil
> print(PrintReturn(nil) and PrintReturn(false))
Returning: nil
nil
```

The first operand of an and is always evaluated (which means any side effects it has will happen). The second operand is only evaluated if it needs to be — if the first operand is false (false or nil), then that's the result of the and, which means that there's no need to evaluate the second operand.

This also applies to or — if the first operand of or is true (anything other than false or nil), then that's the result, and the second operand is not evaluated. For example:

```
> print(PrintReturn(1) or PrintReturn(2))
Returning: 1
1
> print(PrintReturn(1) or PrintReturn(false))
Returning: 1
1
> print(PrintReturn(nil) or PrintReturn(2))
Returning: nil
Returning: 2
2
> print(PrintReturn(nil) or PrintReturn(false))
Returning: nil
Returning: false
false
```

Every function, even a supposedly side effect-free function like type, has the side effect of taking awhile to execute. Normally, this can be ignored, but not if a function takes a particularly long time to execute, or if it's in a time-critical section of a program. To see what this has to do with short-circuit evaluation, imagine that you have a function called Search that always returns some true value and takes a long time to run. It may or may not have been run earlier in the program. If it was run, its result will be in the variable SearchResult. In this situation, the following statement is a concise way of printing the search result while making sure that Search is not called unnecessarily:

```
print(SearchResult or Search(SearchStr))
```

Short-circuit evaluation doesn't do anything that couldn't be done with `if` statements—and vice versa, for that matter. Use whichever one is easier to understand in a given case.

Functions Calling Functions

From within many of the preceding functions, you called `print`. You can also call your own functions from within functions.

The Call Stack

When a function calls another function, the calling function gets put on hold while the called one is doing its thing. Lua keeps track of which function is active and which ones are on hold with something called the *call stack*. Explaining how the call stack works will require an example (given in the following Try It Out) in which function calls are nested within other function calls.

Try It Out　　　　　　**Use Creating Nested Function Calls**

1. Save the following code under the filename **nestedcalls.lua:**

```
-- A demonstration of functions calling functions.

function A()
  print("  About to enter B")
  B()
  print("  Just exited B")
end

function B()
  print("    About to enter C")
  C()
  print("    Just exited C")
end

function C()
  print("      Inside C")
end

print("About to enter A")
A()
print("Just exited A")
```

2. As you did with `hello.lua` earlier, run it by typing this into your shell:

   lua nestedcalls.lua

   You should see this:

```
About to enter A
  About to enter B
    About to enter C
      Inside C
    Just exited C
```

```
        Just exited B
    Just exited A
```

How It Works

Lua keeps a *stack* of information about all currently running functions. It's called a stack because things are only put onto or taken off of the top. When a function is called, information about it is put on the top of the stack (making the stack taller), and when a function returns, that function's information is removed from the top of the stack (making the stack shorter). Because this stack grows every time a function is called, it's called the *call stack*. The information about one function call is said to occupy one *stack frame*.

A stack is also used to keep track of C function calls. This type of stack is called the C stack, *and it's separate from Lua's call stack. Functions written in C also use a stack to interact with Lua, called the* Lua API stack, *and it is actually a little window on part of the call stack. This glosses over some details, but if you really want to know how it works, look at Lua's source code.*

In this example, the prints are formatted so as to be more and more indented as the stack gets taller. At the stack's tallest point — the line where Inside C is printed — the stack frame at the top of the stack (not counting print's stack frame) contains (among other things) the current location inside C. (*Location* here means the location of control: which statement is being executed and which expression is being evaluated.) The stack frame underneath that contains the current location inside the function that called C, namely B. This is the point to which control will return when C returns. The next stack frame contains the current location inside A, and the bottom one contains the current location inside the function that called A, which is the whole file. (Remember that files are chunks, which are executed as functions.) All of these locations are highlighted here:

```
-- A demonstration of functions calling functions.

function A()
    print("  About to enter B")
    B()
    print("  Just exited B")
end

function B()
    print("    About to enter C")
    C()
    print("    Just exited C")
end

function C()
    print("      Inside C")
end

print("About to enter A")
A()
print("Just exited A")
```

These locations will be listed (in stack order) if an error happens inside C. For instance, if two `nil`s are added together like this:

```
function C()
   print(nil + nil)
   print("     Inside C")
end
```

then the result will be three `About to enter` messages, followed by the error message, followed by a *stack traceback*, which is a multiline message showing the current location of control in each function on the stack, from the top down:

```
About to enter A
  About to enter B
    About to enter C
lua: nestedcalls.lua:16: attempt to perform arithmetic on a nil value
stack traceback:
        nestedcalls.lua:16: in function `C'
        nestedcalls.lua:11: in function `B'
        nestedcalls.lua:5: in function `A'
        nestedcalls.lua:21: in main chunk
        [C]: ?
```

The bottom of the stack is `[C]: ?`. This just means that the main chunk was called by a C program (the Lua interpreter).

You'll learn more about stack tracebacks in Chapter 6. The reason for introducing the concept of the call stack now is that it makes it much easier to explain the concepts of *recursion*, *stack overflow*, and *tail calls*.

Recursion

If a function calls itself, it is said to be *recursive*. Lua uses the call stack to store local variables, which means that multiple calls to the same function can be active at the same time without one call's local variables stomping on those of another call.

Recursion is most often used when the problem to be solved is defined in terms of itself. The factorials in the previous chapter are an example of this: a number's factorial is defined as that number times the factorial of that number minus one (for example, the factorial of 5 is 5 times the factorial of 4). By itself, this is a circular definition and hence useless. Circularity is avoided by defining the factorial of 0 to be 1. This is easily translated into a Lua function. One branch of an `if` statement handles the *base case* — the part of the definition that isn't self-referential. The `if`'s other branch handles the self-referential, or recursive, case:

```
> -- Returns the factorial of N:
> function Fact(N)
>>    local Ret
>>    if N == 0 then
>>       -- Base case:
>>       Ret = 1
>>    else
```

```
>>      -- Recursive case:
>>        Ret = N * Fact(N - 1)
>>     end
>>     return Ret
>> end
>
> for N = 0, 5 do
>>    print(N .. "! is " .. Fact(N))
>> end
0! is 1
1! is 1
2! is 2
3! is 6
4! is 24
5! is 120
```

A step-by-step breakdown of the call Fact(2) would look like this:

1. N is 2. Because it is not equal to 0, Fact is called recursively with 1 as an argument.

2. This recursive call to Fact creates a new variable N (local to this call) and sets it to 1. This N is completely independent of the N from the previous call. Because it's not 0, Fact is called yet again, with 0 as an argument.

3. At this point, the call stack is at its tallest — three stack frames taller than before the first call to Fact was made. This third call does take the base case, returning 1.

4. Control returns to the second call, which receives the 1 returned by the third call. It multiplies this 1 by N, which is also 1, and returns the result (also 1).

5. The first call receives this 1, multiplies it by 2, and returns the result (also 2). After the return, the stack will be back to the height it started at.

If you've worked with recursion before, this will all be old news to you. If you haven't worked with recursion before and you're having trouble wrapping your head around it, try going step-by-step through another call or two to Fact with slightly higher numbers. You'll find that, to keep track of each call's location of control and value of N, you need to simulate a stack (mentally or on paper).

Stack Overflow

If the call stack gets too tall, it can run out of space. This is called *stack overflow*, and it is an error.

Fact only works on non-negative integers. If it's given a negative or fractional number, a stack overflow occurs, as shown in the following example:

```
> print(Fact(-1))
stdin:8: stack overflow
stack traceback:
        stdin:8: in function 'Fact'
        stdin:8: in function 'Fact'
        stdin:8: in function 'Fact'
        stdin:8: in function 'Fact'
        stdin:8: in function 'Fact'
```

```
stdin:8: in function 'Fact'
stdin:8: in function 'Fact'
stdin:8: in function 'Fact'
stdin:8: in function 'Fact'
stdin:8: in function 'Fact'
...
stdin:8: in function 'Fact'
stdin:8: in function 'Fact'
stdin:8: in function 'Fact'
stdin:8: in function 'Fact'
stdin:8: in function 'Fact'
stdin:8: in function 'Fact'
stdin:8: in function 'Fact'
stdin:8: in function 'Fact'
stdin:1: in main chunk
[C]: ?
```

A negative or fractional number is handled with the recursive case, but the base case is never reached, which means that the stack gets taller and taller (which takes awhile) until it *overflows*, or tries to go beyond its maximum size. The stack traceback in the error message only shows the top and bottom of the stack (the dots represent the middle).

For most purposes, you are not likely to run out of stack space if your program isn't buggy. Stack overflow is usually a sign of an infinite recursion, as the previous example shows. If you do want to keep the stack from growing unnecessarily, there are two ways to do it. One is to use iteration (a loop) instead of recursion, like this:

```
-- Returns the factorial of N (iteratively):
function Fact(N)
  local Ret = 1
  for I = 1, N do
    Ret = Ret * I
  end
  return Ret
end
```

The other way is to make sure that a recursive call is a *tail call*, which means it has a certain form explained in the next section.

If for some reason you need to change how big the stack gets before it overflows, edit the value of LUAI_MAXCALLS *in* src/luaconf.h *before compiling Lua. Due to the way the stack is grown, this value should be twice the maximum number of stack frames you need to use.*

Tail Calls

In the recursive version of Fact, there's still more work to be done after the recursive call returns. You need to multiply the recursive call's result by N, and assign that value to Ret, which you must then return. Here's how:

```
-- Returns the factorial of N:
function Fact(N)
```

```
   local Ret
   if N == 0 then
      -- Base case:
      Ret = 1
   else
      -- Recursive case:
      Ret = N * Fact(N - 1)
   end
   return Ret
end
```

If there were nothing left to do but return the recursive call's result after it returned, you wouldn't need to make a new stack frame for it. Instead, you could overwrite the current function's stack frame (the information in it no longer being necessary).

This type of function call whose result is immediately returned by the calling function is called a *tail call*. When Lua sees a tail call, it does the preceding optimization, reusing the calling function's stack frame rather than making a new one. Therefore, the following function will run forever (or until interrupted), continually calling itself but never consuming more than one stack frame:

```
function ForeverTail()
   return ForeverTail()
end
```

When you do interrupt it, it looks like the stack is big, but it isn't really. Lua keeps track of how many tail calls have happened and shows them in the traceback, but they don't take up any space in the actual call stack:

```
> ForeverTail()
stdin:2: interrupted!
stack traceback:
        stdin:2: in function 'ForeverTail'
        stdin:2: in function <stdin:1>
        (tail call): ?
        (tail call): ?
        (tail call): ?
        (tail call): ?
        (tail call): ?
        (tail call): ?
        (tail call): ?
        (tail call): ?
        ...
        (tail call): ?
        (tail call): ?
        (tail call): ?
        (tail call): ?
        (tail call): ?
        (tail call): ?
        (tail call): ?
        stdin:1: in main chunk
        [C]: ?
```

In the following function, it may seem that there is nothing left to do after the call, and that the call is therefore a tail call:

```lua
function ForeverNotTail()
  ForeverNotTail() -- Is this a tail call?
end
```

This is not a tail call, though, because there is something left to do before returning: the list of `ForeverNotTail` return values must be adjusted to zero. Therefore, `ForeverNotTail`, unlike `ForeverTail`, will overflow the stack.

A tail call is always a `return` statement whose expression is a single function call.

None of the following are tail calls — the first because there's no `return`, the rest because the `return`'s expression is something other than a single function call:

```lua
Fun()
```

```lua
return Fun() + 1
```

```lua
return X and Fun()
```

```lua
return (Fun()) -- This expression is a single function call
  -- surrounded in parentheses, which is different than the
  -- required single function call (the parentheses adjust
  -- Fun to one return value).
```

```lua
return Fun(), Fun()
```

A recursive function that uses a tail call to call itself is said to be *tail recursive*. The recursive version of `Fact` is not tail recursive, but you can rewrite it to be tail recursive by introducing an *accumulator* — a variable that keeps track of all the multiplications done so far:

```lua
-- Returns the factorial of N (tail-recursively).  Calls
-- itself with two arguments, but when you call it, you need
-- supply only one argument (like the other Fact functions).
function Fact(N, Acc)
  -- Initialize the accumulator to 1:
  Acc = Acc or 1
  if N == 0 then
    -- Base case:
    return Acc
  else
    -- Recursive case:
    return Fact(N - 1, N * Acc)
  end
end
```

This version of `Fact` will recurse forever (instead of overflowing the stack) if you give it a negative or fractional number.

Although none of the preceding examples show it, a tail call is still a tail call even if it's not a recursive call.

Functions as Values

Functions are values (as are numbers, strings, Booleans, and `nil`). For example, take a look at the following:

```
print(type("Hello"))
```

This operates by looking in the global variable `type`, finding a function there, calling that function with the value `"Hello"`, looking in the global variable `print`, finding a function there, and calling that function with the value returned by the function in `type`.

If you call `type` with a function as an argument, it returns the string `"function"`:

```
> print(type(print))
function
```

Replacing Built-In Functions

You can demonstrate that functions are values by replacing the `print` function with your own function:

```
> -- Give the print function another name, so it'll still be
> -- accessible:
> RealPrint = print
>
> -- Prints a message and its one argument:
> function FakePrint(Val)
>>    RealPrint("Inside FakePrint:", Val)
>> end
>
> -- Replace print with FakePrint:
> print = FakePrint
> -- Use print:
> print("Hello")
Inside FakePrint:        Hello
> print(true)
Inside FakePrint:        true
> -- Undo the damage:
> print = RealPrint
> -- Back to normal:
> print("Hello")
Hello
> print(true)
true
```

There are two reasons that you need to assign the real `print` function to `RealPrint` before assigning the `FakePrint` function to `print`. One is to give `FakePrint` some way to print things; the other is to allow the real `print` function to be put back in its rightful place afterwards.

If you play around a bit, you'll find that the Lua interpreter actually uses whatever function it finds in the global variable `print` to print any values returned from interpreted chunks, like this:

```
> print = FakePrint
> return "abc"
Inside FakePrint:        abc
```

Comparing and Printing Functions

You can compare functions for equality (or inequality), like this:

```
> print = RealPrint
> print(print == RealPrint)
true
> print(print == type)
false
```

If you print a function (or convert it to a string with `tostring`), it will appear as the word *function*, followed by a colon, a space, and a number (a hexadecimal number on most systems):

```
> print(print)
function: 0x481720
```

The only thing you need to know about this number is that two different functions that exist at the same time will have different numbers.

Under the hood, this number represents the function's location in memory.

Function Definitions as Assignments

Because functions are values and function names are variable names, it could be deduced that the `function` statement is a type of assignment. This is indeed true. Take a look at the `function` statement:

```
function name(formal arguments)
   statements
end
```

This does exactly the same thing as the following assignment statement of the form:

```
name = function(formal arguments)
   statements
end
```

To the right of the equal sign (and spilling out onto the next two lines) is a *function expression*—an expression whose value is a newly created function.

You can use a function expression wherever you can use any other expression. You can print it, pass it to another function, assign it, compare it, and so on. In the following example, function() end is a function expression representing a function that takes no arguments, does nothing, and returns nothing:

```
> print(function() end)
function: 0x493888
> print(type(function() end))
function
```

As this example shows, you do not need to give a function a name. A function without a name is called an *anonymous function*. You can call an anonymous function by wrapping the function expression that created it in parentheses (and following that with the usual parentheses used in function calls), like this:

```
> (function(A, B)
>>    print(A + B)
>> end)(2, 3)
5
```

Calling an anonymous function (or anything that doesn't look like the part of a function call before the arguments) is yet another use for parentheses, but as far as Lua is concerned, these are the same parentheses used to control precedence and to adjust to a single value.

Every time a function expression is evaluated, a new function is created. That's why DoNothing1 and DoNothing2 are not equal in the following example, even though the expressions that created them look alike:

```
> DoNothing1, DoNothing2 = function() end, function() end
> print(DoNothing1, DoNothing2)
function: 0x493f20        function: 0x493f38
> print(DoNothing1 == DoNothing2)
false
```

For the same reason, both times MakeDoNothing is called in the following example, it returns a different function, even though each of those functions is created by literally the same function expression:

```
> -- Returns a do-nothing function:
> function MakeDoNothing()
>>    return function() end
>> end
>
> print(MakeDoNothing() == MakeDoNothing())
false
```

> Two different function **expressions or** function **statements will always create two different functions, even if the text of the expressions or statements is the same. A single** function **expression or statement will create two different functions if it is executed twice.**

As shown by the `MakeDoNothing` *example, you can return functions just like other values. In Lua, unlike in some other languages, there are no arbitrary limits on what can be done with functions (as compared with other values). For this reason, Lua functions are said to be first-class values.*

Local Functions

You can also assign functions to local variables. This can be done either with a `function` expression, like this:

```
> do
>>    local LclAverage = function(Num1, Num2)
>>      return (Num1 + Num2) / 2
>>    end
>>    print(LclAverage(10, 20))
>> end
15
> -- This will print the global variable LclAverage, which
> -- will be nil:
> print(LclAverage)
nil
```

Or with a local form of the `function` statement, like this:

```
> do
>>    local function LclAverage(Num1, Num2)
>>      return (Num1 + Num2) / 2
>>    end
>>    print(LclAverage(10, 20))
>> end
15
> -- This will print the global variable LclAverage, which
> -- will be nil:
> print(LclAverage)
nil
```

Because they can be hidden from the rest of a program, local functions have the same benefits as local variables of other types. More specifically, a function is a good candidate for localization if it only makes sense in one small part of a program—especially if it's a closure that will be recreated several times as a program runs.

Another use of local functions is to speed up time-critical loops. This works because access to local variables is faster than access to global variables. For example, if you use the (global) `type` function inside a loop that needed to run as quickly as possible, you could precede the loop with the following:

```
local type = type
```

However, optimizations like this should be done only if they're necessary, as discussed in Chapter 4.

Because the scope of a variable created by a `local` statement starts on the next statement, creating a recursive local function like the following will not work because the F referred to inside the function is a global variable (or possibly a local in a containing scope):

```
local F = function()
  code that does something or other
  F() -- A failed attempt at a recursive call -- the local F
    -- is not visible here.
  more code that does something or other
end
```

Instead, you need to create the `local` first, and then assign the function:

```
local F
F = function()
  something or other
  F() -- This really is a recursive call.
  more something or other
end
```

Conveniently, the `local function` statement does exactly that for you behind the scenes:

```
local function F()
  something or other
  F() -- This, too, really is a recursive call, because the
    -- "local function" statement arranges for the body of
    -- the function to be within the scope of the function's
    -- name.
  more something or other
end
```

In the same way that an assignment such as A = 5 assigns to either a local variable or a global one (depending on whether a local variable named A is visible), a function statement such as `function F()` creates either a local function or a global one, depending on whether a local named F is visible.

Whitespace, Semicolons, and Function Calls

This is a convenient time to cover some topics that aren't all directly related to functions.

Characters that have no visual appearance other than moving other characters farther apart (such as the space and newline characters) are called *whitespace*. Outside of strings, Lua is very tolerant of different uses of whitespace. It treats the following pieces of code the same:

```
for I=1,10 do local X=I*7 print(I,X)end--Cramped!
```

```
    for

    I
    = 1
    , 10 do
  local   X
```

```
   = I * 7
  print   (
  I  ,   X  )
 end  --  Spacy!!
```

The first example is cramped and hard to read, and the second is just silly, but in between these two extremes, you'll see variation from programmer to programmer. In your own code, you should pick a whitespace style that is not too far from the mainstream, but you should also cultivate an eye for variations, so that if you work with other people on a project that has a consistent whitespace style, you can pick it up easily. For instance, did you notice that the comment markers in this book have spaces separating them from any code before or comments after them? Did you notice that commas in this book have spaces after (but not before) them?

Another point of variation among Lua programmers is the use of the semicolon. You can follow any statement by a semicolon if you want. For example:

```
> print("Test");
Test
```

Semicolons can ease the transition for programmers used to languages where semicolons are required. Most Lua programmers do not use semicolons, or if they do, they use them only to separate multiple statements on the same line, like this:

```
function Avg(A, B) local Sum = A + B; return Sum / 2; end
```

There is a situation where a semicolon is required, and it's related to a situation where a newline is prohibited. For example, Lua reads the following in a single chunk:

```
Fun1()
(function() return Fun2 end)()
```

But Lua doesn't know whether this is supposed to be one statement (call Fun1 with no arguments, call its return value with the anonymous function as an argument, and call that function's return value with no arguments) or two statements (call Fun1, and then call the anonymous function). For this reason, Lua doesn't allow a newline before the open parenthesis of a function call, as in the following example:

```
> print
>> ("Lua")
stdin:2: ambiguous syntax (function call x new statement) near '('
```

If you follow this rule, and you still get the ambiguous syntax message, you'll need to put a semicolon at the end of the statement before the line where the error occurs, like this:

```
> do
>>    print("2 plus 3 is:")
>>    (function(A, B)
stdin:3: ambiguous syntax (function call x new statement) near '('
> do
>>    print("2 plus 3 is:");
>>    (function(A, B)
```

```
>>        print(A + B)
>>    end)(2, 3)
>> end
2 plus 3 is:
5
```

A function call variant that you'll run into is this: When a function is called with one argument, and that argument is a literal string, the parentheses can be left out. For example:

```
> print "with a space"
with a space
> print"or without"
or without
```

Upvalues and Closures

You saw earlier that if the same `function` statement or expression is executed twice, it creates two different functions. The reason for this is that two functions created by the same source code can act differently from each other if they have *upvalues* and are therefore *closures*. Definitions of these terms will have to wait until after the following example.

Defining Functions that Create Functions

You've already seen one function that created (and returned) other functions: `MakeDoNothing`. That was a bit boring, though, because even though it created a unique function each time it was called, all those functions did the same thing (which was nothing). The following function, `MakeLessThan`, creates less-than functions, each of which tests whether its argument is less than a particular number:

```
> -- Returns a function that tests whether a number is
> -- less than N:
> function MakeLessThan(N)
>>    return function(X)
>>       return X < N
>>    end
>> end
>
> LessThanFive = MakeLessThan(5)
> LessThanTen = MakeLessThan(10)
> print(LessThanFive(4))
true
> print(LessThanTen(4))
true
> print(LessThanFive(5))
false
> print(LessThanTen(5))
true
> print(LessThanFive(9))
false
> print(LessThanTen(9))
```

```
true
> print(LessThanFive(10))
false
> print(LessThanTen(10))
false
```

Remember that when you call a function, a new local variable is created for each of its arguments. So when MakeLessThan is called with 5 as an argument, a local variable N is created and initialized to 5. Normally, this N would no longer be visible after MakeLessThan returns, but because there's a function (the anonymous one after return) in N's scope that uses N, N will last as long as the function does. MakeLessThan returns the function and assigns it to LessThanFive.

Next, MakeLessThan is called with 10 as an argument. At this point, a local variable N is created and initialized to 10. This is a newly created variable — it's different from the other N created for the previous call. MakeLessThan returns a function that uses this new N, and this function is assigned to LessThan Ten. Calling LessThanFive and LessThanTen with various values shows that they live up to the names given to them. LessThanFive tests whether its argument is less than 5, and LessThanTen does the same with 10.

When a function uses a variable that is local to a containing scope (such as N in this example), that variable is called an *external local variable* or an *upvalue*. The term "upvalue" is somewhat misleading, because an upvalue is *not a value*, but a variable used in a certain context. (The term dates back to Lua 3.1, when it was more accurate.) Despite this, it is used in this book because it's in common use among Lua programmers, and it's much shorter than the more accurate "external local variable." A function that has one or more upvalues is called a *closure*. (All functions, even those with no upvalues, are represented in the same way internally. For this reason, "closure" is sometimes used as a synonym for "function.")

Earlier it was said that local variables reside on the stack, but the stack is not a good place for long-term storage; when a function returns, its stack frame is abandoned, and when a function does a tail call, its stack frame is overwritten. Lua handles this by making sure that an upvalue is migrated from the stack to a safe place elsewhere in memory whenever the block it was created in is exited. Knowing that Lua initially stores local variables on the stack and migrates them elsewhere only if needed is good background information, but it is not strictly necessary for an understanding of either local variables or upvalues. An implementation of Lua could be written that always kept local variables somewhere other than the stack. It would act the same as the real implementation of Lua, except that it would be slower. (Actually, it would be different in one other way — it would not impose a limit on the number of local variables visible at one time. In practice, though, this limit in the real implementation is high enough that it is seldom if ever reached.)

You can call a function returned by another function directly, without giving it a name first. In the following example, MakeLessThan is called with 10 as an argument. The function it returns is then called with 5 as an argument. Because 5 is less than 10, true is printed:

```
> print(MakeLessThan(10)(5))
true
```

Two closures can share an upvalue, and upvalues can be assigned to. Both of these facts are demonstrated by the following example.

Defining Functions with Private State

The following MakeGetAndInc example makes and returns two functions: one that gets a value, and another that increments that value. These functions have *private state* — "state" because there's changeable data that's remembered in between calls, and "private" because this data is stored in a local variable visible to only these functions.

```
> -- Returns two functions: a function that gets N's value,
> -- and a function that increments N by its argument.
> function MakeGetAndInc(N)
>>     -- Returns N:
>>     local function Get()
>>        return N
>>     end
>>
>>     -- Increments N by M:
>>     local function Inc(M)
>>        N = N + M
>>     end
>>
>>     return Get, Inc
>> end
>
> -- Make two pairs of get and increment functions, one
> -- pair initialized to 0 and the other initialized to 100:
> GetA, IncA = MakeGetAndInc(0)
> GetB, IncB = MakeGetAndInc(100)
> -- Try them out:
> print(GetA())
0
> print(GetB())
100
> IncA(5)
> print(GetA())
5
> IncA(5)
> print(GetA())
10
> IncB(1)
> print(GetB())
101
> IncA(1)
> print(GetA())
11
```

As you can see, GetA and IncA both refer to the same N, but GetB and IncB both refer to another N. GetA and IncA refer to the N created by the first call to MakeGetAndInc. The initial value of this N is 0, but it gets a new value every time IncA is called, and that new value is visible to GetA. GetB and IncB act the same way, except their value is stored in the N created by the second call to MakeGetAndInc.

This is also a good example of local functions. The names Get and Inc are only visible inside MakeGetAndInc. Because there's no need to make them globally visible, it would have been a programming no-no to do so, because then MakeGetAndInc would not be usable in a program that already used one or both of those names for global variables.

> There are two ways to accidentally use a global when a local was intended. One is to misspell the name of a local variable. The other is to forget the `local` keyword. Both of these are common sources of bugs.

Figuring Out Tricky Scope Situations

Every iteration of a `for` loop creates a new local loop variable. This is demonstrated by the following example:

```
> for I = 1, 2 do
>>    if I == 1 then
>>       function One()
>>          return I
>>       end
>>    else
>>       function Two()
>>          return I
>>       end
>>    end
>> end
> print(One())
1
> print(Two())
2
```

Both `One` and `Two` return variables named `I`, but they are different variables — if they were the same `I`, then `One` and `Two` would return the same value.

> *`for` loops in Lua 5.0 actually did use the same loop variable for each iteration. If this example is tried in Lua 5.0, both `One` and `Two` return 2 because they refer to the same `I`, whose value when the loop ends is 2. Additionally, assigning to the loop variable (which is fine in Lua 5.1) has undefined behavior in Lua 5.0.*

If you are ever in doubt about the scope of a variable, start from the statement where the variable's name is used and search upwards for the following:

❑   A `local` statement that creates a variable of this name, or a `local function` statement that creates a function of this name

❑   A function definition (a `function` statement, `local function` statement, or `function` expression) that uses this name as a formal argument

❑   A `for` loop that uses this name as a loop variable

The first one of these that you run into whose scope extends to the statement where you started searching is the place where your (local) variable was created. (Remember that the scope of a variable created with `local` extends to the end of the innermost block that encloses it; this also applies to the scope of a function created with a `local function` statement.) If your search hits the top of the file without finding anything, the variable is global.

If your program is properly indented, this is a simple up-and-out search. You never need to look at a line that is indented further (to the right) than any line you have already looked at.

In the following example, `PrintStr` prints `"Inside first do block"` even though the call to it is in the scope of a local `Str` whose value is `"Inside second do block"`:

```
> do
>>    local Str = "Inside first do block"
>>
>>    function PrintStr()
>>       print(Str)
>>    end
>> end
> do
>>    local Str = "Inside second do block"
>>    PrintStr()
>> end
Inside first do block
```

It doesn't matter where the call is. What matters is where `Str` is actually named, and that's inside the *definition* of `PrintStr` (which is inside the first do block). A function cannot see local variables from the scope that called it (unless that happens to be the same scope in which it's defined). This means that you can tell everything you need to know about a variable's scope by looking at the program's source code, without having to figure out which functions call which. In the same way, Lua itself can tell everything it needs to know about a variable's scope when it compiles source code into bytecode, rather than having to wait till *runtime* (when the program is running).

> Because variable scope is determined by the structure of a program's source code, Lua is said to have lexical scope *(The term "lexical" here means "based on source code.")*
>
> *Actually, although whether a variable is global or local is determined lexically, Lua global variables are not lexically scoped. In most cases they can be treated as if they are; the exception happens when the function* setfenv *is used. You'll learn about* setfenv *in the next chapter.*

Lua's scoping rules allow arbitrarily complex combinations of global variables, local variables, closures with upvalues from multiple scopes, closures that share some upvalues but not others, upvalues that themselves contain closures, and so on. But the rules themselves are relatively simple, considering their power. Here they are:

❑ Each time a `local` or `local function` statement is executed, a new local variable (or possibly several, in the case of `local`) is created. Its scope extends downward to the end of the inner-most enclosing block.

❑ Each time a `for` loop iterates, a new local variable (or possibly several, in the case of the *generic* `for` loop you'll learn about next chapter) is created. Its scope extends to the end of the loop.

❑ Each time a function is called, a new local variable is created for each formal argument. The scope of these variables extends to the end of the function.

❑ If a variable was not created in any of the three aforementioned ways, it's global.

❑ Each time a `function` or `local function` statement is executed, or a `function` expression is evaluated, a new function is created.

❑ There is no limitation on reading from or assigning to a visible local variable from within a function. (In other words, closures are possible.)

So if you find yourself not understanding why a program is doing what it's doing, and you think it may be a scoping issue, ask yourself these questions:

❑ Is this a global or local variable?

❑ Where and when was this local variable created?

❑ Where and when was this function created?

Summary

In this chapter, you learned almost everything you need to know about functions. Namely:

❑ Functions allow complexity to be compartmentalized, and let you use the same code in different places in a program.

❑ A chunk is treated by Lua as a function.

❑ To run a Lua script, give `lua` a filename when you start it.

❑ Functions can take zero or more arguments and return zero or more values.

❑ When a function is called, a local variable is created for each of its formal arguments. These local variables are only visible inside the function.

❑ The `local` keyword and the `for` loop also create local variables.

❑ A function can call itself, which is called recursion. During recursion, or in any case where two calls are made to the same function, each call has its own local variables.

❑ A stack is used to keep track of function calls. You can us tail calls to avoid exhausting the large but finite space available for this stack.

❑ A function is a type of value (as are numbers, strings, Booleans, and `nil`). You can create functions at runtime, pass them as arguments, return them, assign them, compare them, used them without naming them, and so on.

❑ A function has full access to all local variables that are visible where the function is defined. A function that takes advantage of this is called a closure, and the variables from outer scopes that it accesses are called upvalues. You can use upvalues to create (from the same definition, at runtime) functions with different behavior, as well as to create functions that retain state between calls.

There are a couple remaining facts about functions that weren't covered in this chapter. For example, how do you create a function that (like `print`) can take an indefinite number of arguments? You'll learn this and more in the next chapter, which is about *tables*, Lua's tool for combining multiple pieces of data into one. When you complete the next chapter, you'll understand all of the basic elements of Lua, and you'll be ready to start applying that knowledge in the chapter after that. This chapter ends with some exercises to test your understanding of functions. The answers are in the appendix.

Exercises

1. Write a `TypedToString` function that converts a value to a string and prefixes that string with the value's type. (You don't have to deal specially with the fact that a function converted to a string already has its type prefixed to it.)

```
> print(TypedToString("abc"))
string: abc
> print(TypedToString(42))
number: 42
> print(TypedToString(true))
boolean: true
> print(TypedToString(function() end))
function: function: 0x485a10
```

2. Write a function `SumProd` that returns both the sum and the product of two numbers:

```
> print(SumProd(1, 1))
2       1
> print(SumProd(2, 2))
4       4
> print(SumProd(3, 5))
8       15
```

3. Using `SumProd` from the previous exercise, what will the following print?

```
print(SumProd(3, 3), SumProd(5, 5))
```

4. What does the following print?

```
Continent = "North America"

function F(Continent)
  Continent = "Australia"
end

F(Continent)
print(Continent)
```

5. The following `MakeDotter` function is intended to return a function that appends N dots to its argument (and returns the result). It almost works, but every time it's used to make a new dotter function, the old ones stop working right. Why does this happen, and what one-line change can be made to make it work right?

```
> function MakeDotter(N)
>>    Dots = ""
>>    for I = 1, N do
>>       Dots = Dots .. "."
>>    end
>>    return function(Str)
>>       return Str .. Dots
>>    end
>> end
>
> -- Make a function that appends one dot to its argument:
```

```
> OneDotter = MakeDotter(1)
> print(OneDotter("A"))
A.
> print(OneDotter("B"))
B.
> -- Make a function that appends three dots to its argument:
> ThreeDotter = MakeDotter(3)
> print(ThreeDotter("C"))
C...
> print(ThreeDotter("D"))
D...
> -- OneDotter now appends three dots instead of one:
> print(OneDotter("E"))
E...
```

Working with Tables

This chapter explores a new data type called a *table*. It's a *data structure*, which means that it lets you combine other values. Because of its flexibility, it is Lua's only data structure. (It is possible to create other, special-purpose data structures in C.)

In this chapter, you learn how to do the following:

❑   Create and modify tables

❑   Loop through the elements of tables

❑   Use Lua's built-in table library

❑   Write programs in an object-oriented style

❑   Write functions that take variable numbers of arguments

Tables Introduced

The following example creates a table and assigns it to the variable `NameToInstr`, and then looks around inside the table:

```
> NameToInstr = {["John"] = "rhythm guitar",
>>    ["Paul"] = "bass guitar",
>>    ["George"] = "lead guitar",
>>    ["Ringo"] = "drumkit"}
> print(NameToInstr["Paul"])
bass guitar
> A = "Ringo"
> print(NameToInstr[A])
drumkit
> print(NameToInstr["Mick"])
nil
```

A table is a collection of *key-value pairs*. In this example, the expression that starts and ends with { and } (curly braces) is a *table constructor* that creates a table that associates the key "John" with the value "rhythm guitar", the key "Paul" with the value "bass guitar", and so on. Each key is surrounded in [and] (square brackets) and is separated from its value by an equal sign. The key-value pairs are separated from each other by commas.

After the table is created and assigned to NameToInstr, square brackets are used to retrieve the values for particular keys. When NameToInstr["Paul"] is evaluated, the result is "bass guitar", which is the value associated with the key "Paul" in the NameToInstr table.

> *The term "value" is used here to mean "the second half of a key-value pair." Both this sense and the broader sense used in Chapters 2 and 3 are used in this chapter; which sense is intended should be clear from the context. A "key" is a value in the broader (but not the narrower) sense.*

As the line with NameToInstr[A] shows, the expression in between the square brackets doesn't have to be a literal string. Here it is a variable, but it can be any expression. (This also applies to the square brackets inside table constructors — if an expression inside square brackets is a function call, it is adjusted to one value.)

If you ask a table for the value of a key it doesn't contain, it gives you nil:

```
> print(NameToInstr["Mick"])
nil
```

This means that nil cannot be a value in a table. Another way of saying this is that there is no difference between a key not existing in a table, and that key existing but having nil as its value. Keys cannot be nil, although if the value of a nil key is asked for, the result will be nil:

```
> Tbl = {}
> print(Tbl[nil])
nil
```

Both keys and values can be any type other than nil. For example:

```
> T = {[print] = "The print function",
>>    ["print"] = print,
>>    [0.1] = 0.2}
> print(T[print]) -- Function key, string value.
The print function
> print(T["print"]) -- String key, function value.
function: 0x481720
> print(T[0.1]) -- Number key, number value.
0.2
```

The association between a key and a value is one-way. NameToInstr["Ringo"] is "drumkit", but NameToInstr["drumkit"] is nil. A given value can be associated with multiple keys, but a given key can only have one value at a time. For example:

```
> T = {["a"] = "duplicate value",
>>    ["b"] = "duplicate value",
>>    ["duplicate key"] = "y",
```

```
>>    ["duplicate key"] = "z"}
> print(T["a"])
duplicate value
> print(T["b"])
duplicate value
> print(T["duplicate key"])
z
```

Keys follow the same equality rules as other values, so (in the following example, 1 and "1" are two distinct keys:

```
> T = {[1] = "number", ["1"] = "string"}
> print(T[1], T["1"])
number  string
```

A Shorter Way to Write Some Keys

A key is often called an *index* to a table, and accessing a key's value (like T[X]) is called *indexing* the table.

> *The word "index" has other uses too. For example, getting the nth character of a string is "indexing" that string, and a loop variable, particularly one with an integer value, can be called an index (which is why some of the loop variables in this book are named I).*

The value of a particular index of a particular table is often called a *field*, and the index itself is called a *field name*. This terminology is used especially when the field name is a valid identifier. If a field name is a valid identifier, you can use it in a table constructor without the square brackets or quotes. The following is another way to write the constructor for NameToInstr:

```
NameToInstr = {John = "rhythm guitar",
   Paul = "bass guitar",
   George = "lead guitar",
   Ringo = "drumkit"}
```

That doesn't work with any of the following tables, because none of the keys are valid identifiers (notice that the error messages are different, because the keys are invalid identifiers for different reasons):

```
> T = {1st = "test"}
stdin:1: malformed number near '1st'
> T = {two words = "test"}
stdin:1: '}' expected near 'words'
> T = {and = "test"}
stdin:1: unexpected symbol near 'and'
```

You can also access fields in an existing table (if the field names are valid identifiers) by using . (a dot) instead of square brackets and quotes, like this:

```
> print(NameToInstr.George)
lead guitar
```

You can index a table within a table in one step, as follows:

```
> Tbl1 = {Tbl2 = {Bool = true}}
> print(Tbl1.Tbl2.Bool)
true
> print(Tbl1["Tbl2"].Bool)
true
> print(Tbl1.Tbl2["Bool"])
true
> print(Tbl1["Tbl2"]["Bool"])
true
```

This works for tables within tables within tables, as deep as you want to go. If there are enough nested tables, then `Tbl.Think.Thank.Thunk.Thenk.Thonk` is perfectly valid.

Don't let the flexibility of tables and the variety of methods for accessing them confuse you. In particular, remember that `NameToInstr["John"]` and `NameToInstr.John` both mean "get the value for the `"John"` key," and `NameToInstr[John]` means "get the value for whatever key is in the variable `John`." If you find yourself getting a `nil` when you don't expect to, make sure you're not mixing these up.

Altering a Table's Contents

After you create a table, you can modify or remove the values already in it, and you can add new values to it. You do these things with the assignment statement.

Try It Out   **Assigning to Table Indexes**

Type the following into the Lua interpreter:

```
> Potluck = {John = "chips", Jane = "lemonade",
>>    Jolene = "egg salad"}
> Potluck.Jolene = "fruit salad" -- A change.
> Potluck.Jayesh = "lettuce wraps" -- An addition.
> Potluck.John = nil -- A removal.
> print(Potluck.John, Potluck.Jane, Potluck.Jolene,
>>    Potluck.Jayesh)
```

Here's the result:

```
nil      lemonade      fruit salad      lettuce wraps
```

How It Works

In this exercise, you create a table with three people and their foods. You then use assignment to change one person's food, to add a new person-food pair to the table, and to remove an existing person-food pair.

`Potluck.Jolene = "fruit salad"` overwrites the previous value of `Potluck.Jolene` (`"egg salad"`).

`Potluck.Jayesh = "lettuce wraps"` adds a new key (and its value) to the table. The value of `Potluck.Jayesh` before this line would have been `nil`.

`Potluck.John = nil` overwrites the previous value of `Potluck.John` with `nil`. This is another way of saying that it removes the key `"John"` from the table (because there's no difference between a `nil`-valued key and a nonexistent key).

Notice that, except in the line with the table constructor, the variable `Potluck` is never assigned to. Rather, individual fields of the table in `Potluck` are being assigned to. This is called *indexing assignment*.

> *The Lua reference manual actually calls table fields a third type of variable (after globals and locals). This usage makes some things clearer, but it isn't widespread, so it isn't followed in this book.*

Often the most convenient way to populate a table is to start with an empty table and add things to it one at a time. Here's an example of creating a table of the first five perfect squares and then printing it:

```
> Squares = {} -- A table constructor can be empty.
> for I = 1, 5 do
>>    Squares[I] = I ^ 2
>> end
> for I = 1, 5 do
>>    print(I .. " squared is " .. Squares[I])
>> end
1 squared is 1
2 squared is 4
3 squared is 9
4 squared is 16
5 squared is 25
```

You can assign to nested tables in one step, as in `Tbl.Think[Thank].Thunk = true`.

Here are a couple of other table constructor tidbits. You can optionally follow the final value in a table constructor by a comma: `{A = 1, B = 2, C = 3, }`. This is convenient for automatically generated table constructors, and for frequently edited ones (so you don't have to always make sure to delete a comma if a value becomes the last one). And instead of commas, you can use semicolons (or a mixture of commas and semicolons): `{A = 1; B = 2; C = 3}`.

Tables as Arrays

It's common for the keys of a table to be consecutive integers, starting at 1. For example:

```
> Months = {[1] = "January", [2] = "February", [3] = "March",
>>    [4] = "April", [5] = "May", [6] = "June", [7] = "July",
>>    [8] = "August", [9] = "September", [10] = "October",
>>    [11] = "November", [12] = "December"}
> print(Months[11])
November
```

A table used in this way is sometimes called an *array* (or a *list*). To emphasize that a table is *not* being used as an array, it can be called an *associative table*.

You can write table constructors that build arrays in a more concise, less error-prone way that doesn't require writing out each integer key. For example:

```
> Months = {"January", "February", "March", "April", "May",
>>   "June", "July", "August", "September", "October",
>>   "November", "December"}
> print(Months[11])
November
```

Inside a table constructor, the first value that doesn't have a key (and an equal sign) in front of it is associated with the key 1. Any subsequent such values are given a key one higher than that given to the previous such value. This rule applies even if key-value pairs with equal signs are intermixed, like this:

```
> T = {A = "x", "one", B = "y", "two", C = "z", "three"}
> print(T[1], T[2], T[3])
one     two     three
```

Usually this sort of mixed table constructor is easier to read if the consecutive-integer values are all together and the other key-value pairs are all together.

If a function call is used as the value of an explicit key ({K = F()}, for example), it's adjusted to one return value. If it's used as the value of an implicit integer key, it's only adjusted to one return value if it's not the last thing in the table constructor; if it is the last thing, no adjustment is made:

```
> function ReturnNothing()
>> end
>
> function ReturnThreeVals()
>>   return "x", "y", "z"
>> end
>
> TblA = {ReturnThreeVals(), ReturnThreeVals()}
> print(TblA[1], TblA[2], TblA[3], TblA[4])
x       x       y       z
> TblB = {ReturnNothing(), ReturnThreeVals()}
> -- The following nil is the result of adjustment:
> print(TblB[1], TblB[2], TblB[3], TblB[4])
nil     x       y       z
> TblC = {ReturnThreeVals(), ReturnNothing()}
> -- The following three nils are not the result of adjustment;
> -- they're there because TblC[2] through TblC[4] were not
> -- given values in the constructor:
> print(TblC[1], TblC[2], TblC[3], TblC[4])
x       nil     nil     nil
> TblD = {ReturnNothing(), ReturnNothing()}
> -- The first nil that follows is the result of adjustment; the
> -- second is there because TblD[2] was not given a value
> -- in the constructor:
> print(TblD[1], TblD[2])
nil     nil
```

Array Length

The # (length) operator can be used to measure the length of an array. Normally, this number is also the index of the last element in the array, as in the following example:

```
> Empty = {}
> One = {"a"}
> Three = {"a", "b", "c"}
> print(#Empty, #One, #Three)
0        1        3
```

Apart from arrays with gaps (discussed shortly), the length operator gives the same result whether a table got the way it is purely because of its constructor (as previously shown) or because of assignments made to it after it was created like this:

```
> Empty = {"Delete me!"}
> Empty[1] = nil
> Three = {"a"}
> Three[2], Three[3] = "b", "c"
> print(#Empty, #Three)
0        3
```

It also doesn't matter whether the constructor uses implicit or explicit integer indexing, as shown here:

```
> print(#{[1] = "a", [2] = "b"})
2
```

Noninteger indexes (or nonpositive integer indexes, for that matter) do not count — the length operator measures the length of a table as an array as follows:

```
> Two = {"a", "b", Ignored = true, [0.5] = true}
> print(#Two)
2
```

An array is said to have a *gap* if there are is a nil somewhere between element 1 and the highest positive integer element with a value that is not nil. Here is an example of a gap in an array:

```
T1 = {nil, "b", "c"} -- Gap between beginning and
    -- element 2.
T2 = {"a", "b", nil, nil, "e"} -- Gap between element 2 and
    -- element 5.
T3 = {"a", "b", "c", nil} -- No gap!  (Element 3 is the last
    -- element in the array.)
```

Arrays with gaps cause the length operator to behave unpredictably. The only thing you can be sure of is that it will always return the index of a non-nil value that is followed by a nil, or possibly 0 if element 1 of the array is nil. For example:

```
> T = {"a", "b", "c", nil, "e"}
> print(#T)
5
```

```
> -- Equivalent table; different result:
> T = {}
> T[1], T[2], T[3], T[4], T[5] = "a", "b", "c", nil, "e"
> print(#T)
3
```

For this reason, it's generally a good idea to avoid having gaps in your arrays. However, an array is just a table used in a certain way, not a separate datatype, so this warning about avoiding gaps only applies if you're planning to use a table as an array. This means there's nothing wrong with the following table:

```
-- Considered as an array, this would have gaps, but it's
-- obviously intended as an associative table:
AustenEvents = {[1775] = "born",
    [1811] = "Sense and Sensibility published",
    [1813] = "Pride and Prejudice published",
    [1814] = "Mansfield Park published",
    [1816] = "Emma published",
    [1817] = "died",
    [1818] = "Northanger Abbey and Persuasion published"}
```

You can define # operator to always give either the first element followed by nil *or the last, but both of these approaches require searches through the table much more time-consuming than the way that # actually works.*

Lua 5.0 dealt with array length differently. In addition to the nonexistence of the # operator, the main differences were that the functions table.getn *and* table.setn *were used to get and set the length of an array, and a table's* "n" *field could be used to store its array length.*

Looping through Tables

Printing a table gives similar results to printing a function:

```
> print({})
table: 0x493bc0
```

This means that to see what's inside a table, you need to look at each key-value pair in turn. In the previous Squares example, this was done with a for loop hardcoded to run to 5 (the length of Squares). You could improve this by using the # operator, so that if the array's length is changed, you only need to it in one place:

```
> Squares = {}
> for I = 1, 5 do
>>    Squares[I] = I ^ 2
>> end
> for I = 1, #Squares do
>>    print(I .. " squared is " .. Squares[I])
>> end
1 squared is 1
2 squared is 4
3 squared is 9
4 squared is 16
5 squared is 25
```

This is better, but there's an even better way to loop through an array, as you'll see in the following Try It Out.

Using ipairs to Loop through an Array

Type the following into the interpreter. The first of the two loops is the `for` loop you already know from Chapter 2. The second is still a `for` loop, but it looks and works a bit differently.

```
> Squares = {}
> for I = 1, 5 do
>>    Squares[I] = I ^ 2
>> end
> for I, Square in ipairs(Squares) do
>>    print(I .. " squared is " .. Square)
>> end
1 squared is 1
2 squared is 4
3 squared is 9
4 squared is 16
5 squared is 25
```

How It Works

The first `for` loop in this example loops through a series of numbers. The second one is a new type of `for` loop that loops (in this case) through an array. It's called the *generic* `for` loop because, as you will see soon, it is able to iterate through anything at all (including tables that aren't arrays and even things other than tables). The `for` loop you learned about in Chapter 2 is called the *numeric* `for` loop. You can tell the difference between them because the generic `for` will always include the keyword `in`.

The thing that makes this example's generic `for` treat `Squares` as an array is the use of the function `ipairs` in the line:

```
for I, Square in ipairs(Squares) do
```

This line means "loop (in order) through each key-value pair in the array `Squares`, assigning the key and value to (respectively) the loop variables `I` and `Square`." To write your own similar loop, replace `Squares` with the array you want to loop through, and replace `I` and `Square` with the names you want to give to its keys and values. (As you'll soon see, `ipairs` can be replaced when you don't want to treat the thing being looped through as an array.)

`Squares` itself never needs to be indexed in the body of the loop, because `Square` is available.

———————————

If you use a generic `for` loop with `ipairs` to loop through an array that has gaps, it will stop when it reaches the first gap, as follows:

```
> for Number, Word in ipairs({"one", "two", nil, "four"}) do
>>    print(Number, Word)
>> end
1       one
2       two
```

That means that, if an array has gaps, looping through it with a generic for and ipairs will not necessarily give the same results as looping through it with a numeric for whose end value is the length of the array.

A generic for loop that uses ipairs after the in keyword is often called an *ipairs loop* for short. If pairs is used instead of ipairs, then all key-value pairs, not just the array ones, are looped through.

A pairs loop has the same form as an ipairs loop:

```
for Key, Val in ipairs(Tbl) do
```

```
for Key, Val in pairs(Tbl) do
```

Try this pairs loop:

```
> NameToInstr = {John = "rhythm guitar",
>>    Paul = "bass guitar",
>>    George = "lead guitar",
>>    Ringo = "drumkit"}
> for Name, Instr in pairs(NameToInstr) do
>>    print(Name .. " played " .. Instr)
>> end
Ringo played drumkit
George played lead guitar
John played rhythm guitar
Paul played bass guitar
```

This is similar to an ipairs loop in that on each iteration, the first loop variable (Name) is set to a key in the table given to pairs, and the second loop variable (Instr) is set to that key's value. One difference is that the first value no longer has to be a positive integer (although it could be, if there happened to be any positive integer keys in NameToInstr).

The second difference is that the key-value pairs are looped through *in an arbitrary order*. The order in which pairs occur in the table constructor does not matter. Nor is there any significance to the order in which keys are added or removed after a table is constructed. The only guarantee is that each pair will be visited once and only once. Tables in general have no intrinsic order (other than the arbitrary order shown by a pairs loop). Even the order shown by an ipairs loop is only a result of adding 1 to each index to get the next one. pairs often visits integer keys all together and in the correct order, but it's not guaranteed to do so. For example:

```
> T = {A = "a", B = "b", C = "c"}
> T[1], T[2], T[3] = "one", "two", "three"
> for K, V in pairs(T) do
>>    print(K, V)
>> end
A         a
1         one
C         c
B         b
3         three
2         two
```

Both ipairs *loops and* pairs *loops have the property that neither loop variable is ever* nil. *(This can be deduced from what has been said about* nil *keys and* nil *values.)*

Like the loop variable in a numeric `for`, the loop variables in a generic `for` are local to each iteration. They can be assigned to, although because of their limited scope, there's seldom a reason to do this:

```
> T = {Gleep = true, Glarg = false}
> for Fuzzy, Wuzzy in pairs(T) do
>>    Fuzzy, Wuzzy = Fuzzy .. "ing", #tostring(Wuzzy)
>>    print(Fuzzy, Wuzzy)
>> end
Gleeping        4
Glarging        5
> -- The table itself is unchanged:
> print(T.Gleep, T.Glarg)
true    false
> print(T.Gleeping, T.Glarging)
nil     nil
```

Because the assignments are made to the loop variables, and not to fields in the table itself, they do not alter the table's contents. If you do want to alter the table's contents, do an indexing assignment on the table itself, like this:

```
> T = {"apple", "banana", "kiwi"}
> for I, Fruit in ipairs(T) do
>>    T[I] = Fruit .. "s"
>> end
> print(T[2])
bananas
```

Adding a previously nonexistent key to a table while looping over it with `pairs` has undefined results. If you need to do this, save a list of the changes you need to make in another table and apply them after the loop is over. You can remove a key (by setting its value to `nil`) and change a key's value during a `pairs` loop.

You can use loop variables as upvalues to closures. As shown in the previous chapter (with a numeric `for`), each iteration means a new upvalue:

```
> -- A table that maps numbers to their English names:
> Numbers = {"one", "two", "three"}
> -- A table that will contain functions:
> PrependNumber = {}
> for Num, NumName in ipairs(Numbers) do
>>    -- Add a function to PrependNumber that prepends NumName
>>    -- to its argument:
>>    PrependNumber[Num] = function(Str)
>>      return NumName .. ": " .. Str
>>    end
>> end
> -- Call the second and third functions in PrependNumber:
> print(PrependNumber[2]("is company"))
two: is company
> print(PrependNumber[3]("is a crowd"))
three: is a crowd
```

In this example, each time the loop iterates, a new function is created that *prepends* (appends to the front) a spelled-out number name to its argument and returns the result. These functions are placed, by number, into the PrependNumber table, so that when, for example, PrependNumber[2] is called, it prepends "two: " to its argument.

> *The notes about Lua 5.0's numeric* for *in the previous chapter also apply to the generic* for. *Assigning to the first (that is, leftmost) loop variable has undefined results, and the scope of the loop variables extends over the entire loop (not each individual iteration). This means that if you tried the* PrependNumber *example on Lua 5.0, you would get "*attempt to concatenate a nil value*" errors because both loop variables are set to* nil *when the end of the table is reached.*

To loop through a table in a way not supported by either ipairs or pairs, use either while or the numeric for (along with some extra bookkeeping), or structure your data differently. An example of the latter is the following loop, which is a rewrite of the earlier pairs loop through NameToInstr that goes in the order specified by the table (it also serves as an example of tables within tables):

```
> NamesAndInstrs = {
>>    {Name = "John", Instr = "rhythm guitar"},
>>    {Name = "Paul", Instr = "bass guitar"},
>>    {Name = "George", Instr = "lead guitar"},
>>    {Name = "Ringo", Instr = "drumkit"}}
> for _, NameInstr in ipairs(NamesAndInstrs) do
>>    print(NameInstr.Name .. " played " .. NameInstr.Instr)
>> end
John played rhythm guitar
Paul played bass guitar
George played lead guitar
Ringo played drumkit
```

Yet another option is to write your own function to use instead of ipairs or pairs. This is covered later in this chapter.

Tables of Functions

Using tables that contain functions is a handy way to organize functions, and Lua keeps many of its built-in functions in tables, indexed by strings. For example, the table found in the global variable table contains functions useful for working with tables. If you assign another value to table, or to one of the other global variables used to store built-in functions, the functions won't be available anymore unless you put them somewhere else beforehand. If you do this accidentally, just restart the interpreter.

The Table Library

The functions contained in table are known collectively as the *table library*.

table.sort

One function in the table library is table.sort. Here is an example of how you use this function:

```
> Names = {"Scarlatti", "Telemann", "Corelli", "Purcell",
>>    "Vivaldi", "Handel", "Bach"}
```

```
> table.sort(Names)
> for I, Name in ipairs(Names) do
>>    print(I, Name)
>> end
1       Bach
2       Corelli
3       Handel
4       Purcell
5       Scarlatti
6       Telemann
7       Vivaldi
```

The `table.sort` function takes an array and sorts it *in place*. This means that, rather than returning a new array that's a sorted version of the one given to it, `table.sort` uses indexing assignment (a side effect) on the given array itself to move its values to different keys. (See Chapter 3 for an explanation of side effects.)

`table.sort` uses the < operator to decide whether an element of the array should come before another element. To override this behavior, give a *comparison function* as a second argument to `table.sort`. A comparison function takes two arguments and returns a true result if and only if its first argument should come before its second argument.

`table.sort` only looks at a table as an array. It ignores any noninteger keys and any integer keys less than 1 or greater than the table's array length. To sort a table that isn't an array, you need to put its contents into an array and sort that array. The following Try It Out demonstrates this, as well as the use of a comparison function.

Try It Out   **Sorting the Contents of an Associative Table**

1.   Save the following as **sortednametoinstr.lua**:

```lua
-- A demonstration of sorting an associative table.

NameToInstr = {John = "rhythm guitar",
   Paul = "bass guitar",
   George = "lead guitar",
   Ringo = "drumkit"}
-- Transfer the associative table NameToInstr to the
-- array Sorted:
Sorted = {}
for Name, Instr in pairs(NameToInstr) do
   table.insert(Sorted, {Name = Name, Instr = Instr})
end
-- The comparison function sorts by Name:
table.sort(Sorted, function(A, B) return A.Name < B.Name end)
-- Output:
for _, NameInstr in ipairs(Sorted) do
   print(NameInstr.Name .. " played " .. NameInstr.Instr)
end
```

2.   Run `sortednametoinstr.lua` by typing `lua sortednametoinstr.lua` into your shell.

The output is as follows (in alphabetical order by the player's name):

```
George played lead guitar
John played rhythm guitar
Paul played bass guitar
Ringo played drumkit
```

How It Works

The contents of `NameToInstr` are transferred, one-by-one, into `Sorted` using the `table.insert` function. This function, like `table.sort`, works by side-effecting the table given to it rather than by returning a value. Specifically, it puts its second argument at the end of the array given as the first argument. For example, if the first argument is a fifteen-element array, it will be given a sixteenth element (the second argument). Take a look at the following argument:

```
table.insert(Arr, Val)
```

This has the same effect as the following:

```
Arr[#Arr + 1] = Val
```

Both `table.sort` and `table.insert` could be rewritten to have no side effect on the tables they are given, but they would then need to spend time making independent copies of those tables to return.

After `Sorted` has been populated, it can be passed to `table.sort`, but because each of its elements is itself a table, a comparison function needs to be given as well (otherwise `table.sort` would use < to compare the subtables, which would cause an error). The comparison function is quite simple. It just asks whether the `Name` element of its first argument is less than that of its second argument. It would be very easy to change it to sort by `Instr` instead, or (by using >) to have it sort in reverse order.

The comparison function accepted by `table.sort` is an example of a *callback*. A callback is a function that you write to be called by a library function. It gets its name from the fact that it allows a library to call back into code you have written (reversing the normal situation, in which you call a function in the library).

For efficiency, `table.sort` performs an *unstable* sort, which means that two elements that are considered equal by the comparison function may end up in a different order than they started in.

If you need a stable sort, one solution is to record all the elements' original positions and have the comparison function use that as a tiebreaker.

If you're using `table.sort` with a comparison function, and you're getting errors that you can't make sense of within your comparison function or within `table.sort` itself, your comparison function may be at fault. `table.sort` relies on a comparison function having consistent results — it should always return false for things that it considers equal, it should never say that A is less than B if it's already said that B is less than A, it should say that A is less than C if it's already said that A is less than B and B is less than C, and so on.

In the following example, the comparison function returns inconsistent results. It says that, for sorting purposes, 5 is less than 5. This confuses `table.sort`, hence the following error:

```
> T = {5, 5, 10, 15}
> table.sort(T,
```

```
>>    function(A, B)
>>       return not (A < B) -- BAD COMPARISON FUNCTION!
>>    end)
stdin:3: attempt to compare nil with number
stack traceback:
          stdin:3: in function <stdin:2>
          [C]: in function 'sort'
          stdin:1: in main chunk
          [C]: ?
```

The desired effect of not (A < B) was presumably to sort in reverse order. Either A > B or B < A would have had that effect.

table.concat

The function table.concat takes an array of strings (or numbers) and concatenates them all into one string, as follows:

```
> print(table.concat({"a", "bc", "d"}))
abcd
```

If given a second argument, it puts it in between the elements of the array like this:

```
> -- Returns a string showing an array's elements separated by
> -- commas (and spaces):
> function CommaSeparate(Arr)
>>    return table.concat(Arr, ", ")
>> end
>
> print(CommaSeparate({"a", "bc", "d"}))
a, bc, d
```

Normally, all elements from the first to the last will be concatenated. To start concatenating at a different element, give its index as the third argument of table.concat; to stop concatenating at a different element, give its index as the fourth argument of table.concat:

```
> Tbl = {"a", "b", "c", "d"}
> -- Concatenate the second through last elements:
> print(table.concat(Tbl, "", 2))
bcd
> -- Concatenate the second through third elements:
> print(table.concat(Tbl, "", 2, 3))
bc
```

If any of the second through fourth arguments are nil, the defaults of (respectively) the empty string, 1, and the length of the array are used, as follows:

```
> print(table.concat(Tbl, nil, nil, 3))
abc
```

If the third argument is greater than the fourth argument, the empty string is returned, like this:

```
> print(table.concat(Tbl, "-", 4, 1) == "")
true
```

131

table.remove

The `table.insert` function (seen in the most recent Try It Out) has a counterpart that removes elements from an array, `table.remove`. By default, both work on the last element of the array (or the top element when viewing the array as a stack). `table.remove` works by side effect like `table.insert` does, but it also returns a useful value — the element it just removed — as follows:

The following examples use the `CommaSeparate` *function defined in the previous example.*

```
> T = {}
> table.insert(T, "a")
> table.insert(T, "b")
> table.insert(T, "c")
> print(CommaSeparate(T))
a, b, c
> print(table.remove(T))
c
> print(CommaSeparate(T))
a, b
> print(table.remove(T))
b
> print(CommaSeparate(T))
a
> print(table.remove(T))
a
> -- T is now empty again:
> print(#T)
0
```

Both of these functions take an optional second argument that specifies the position at which to insert or remove an element. (In the case of `table.insert`, this means that the thing to be inserted is either the second or the third argument, depending on whether a position argument is given.) Any elements above that inserted or removed are shifted up or down to compensate, like this:

```
> T = {"a", "b", "c"}
> table.insert(T, 2, "X")
> -- C is now the fourth element:
> print(CommaSeparate(T))
a, X, b, c
> print(table.remove(T, 2))
X
> -- C is the third element again:
> print(CommaSeparate(T))
a, b, c
```

table.maxn

The function `table.maxn` looks at every single key-value pair in a table and returns the highest positive number used as a key, or 0 if there are no positive numbers used as keys. For example:

```
> print(table.maxn({"a", nil, nil, "c"}))
4
> print(table.maxn({[1.5] = true}))
1.5
```

```
> print(table.maxn({["1.5"] = true}))
0
```

One possible use for `table.maxn` is to find the length of arrays with gaps, but keep in mind both that it is time-consuming in proportion to the size of the table (including nonnumeric keys) and that it considers fractional keys as well as integers.

That covers all the functions in Lua's built-in table library. Among Lua's other built-in libraries are the string library (whose functions are found in the `string` table), the mathematical library (in the `math` table), the input/output library (in the `io` table), and the basic or base library (functions like `print`, `tostring`, and `pairs`). You'll learn about these and other built-in libraries throughout the book. In particular, the next chapter will discuss the string library in detail.

Object-Oriented Programming with Tables

Another use for tables is in what is known as *object-oriented programming*. In this style of programming, functions that deal with a particular type of value are themselves part of that value. Such a value is called an *object*, and its functions are called *methods*.

The term "object" is also sometimes used in a more general sense, to mean a value (such as a table or function) that is not equal to any other value created at a different time.

It's quite easy to rewrite the `MakeGetAndInc` example from Chapter 3 to return a two-method object rather than two functions. Here's how:

```
-- Returns a table of two functions: a function that gets
-- N's value, and a function that increments N by its
-- argument.
function MakeGetAndInc(N)
  -- Returns N:
  local function Get()
    return N
  end

  -- Increments N by M:
  local function Inc(M)
    N = N + M
  end

  return {Get = Get, Inc = Inc}
end
```

An object is created and used like so:

```
> -- Create an object:
> A = MakeGetAndInc(50)
> -- Try out its methods:
> print(A.Get())
50
> A.Inc(2)
> print(A.Get())
52
```

This is an improvement on the previous technique in that only the newly created object needs to be given a name (rather than both functions), and in that the functions are bundled up into an object (so that the whole object can be passed around the program as a unit).

Both of these advantages are greater the more methods there are, and this is an acceptable way of implementing objects. But it has two disadvantages: each time an object is created (or *instantiated*), a closure needs to be created for each method, and an object's state is stored in multiple places (as an upvalue in each method) rather than in one place.

The creation of a closure for each method is really only a disadvantage for efficiency reasons. In a program that instantiates several new multiple-method objects a second, creating all those closures could have a noticeable speed impact.

The second point, about state being stored as an upvalue within each method, means that you can use a method apart from its object, as shown here:

```
> A = MakeGetAndInc(50)
> Inc, Get = A.Inc, A.Get
> A = nil
> -- The methods are still usable even though A is no longer
> -- accessible:
> Inc(2)
> print(Get())
52
```

This might occasionally be convenient, but it's usually just confusing.

A technique that avoids these problems is to store the object's state in the object (table) itself, and have the methods be, rather than closures, just regular functions that take the object as an argument:

```
-- Returns Obj.N:
function Get(Obj)
   return Obj.N
end

-- Increments Obj.N by M:
function Inc(Obj, M)
   Obj.N = Obj.N + M
end

-- Creates an object:
function MakeGetAndInc(N)
   return {N = N}
end
```

The Inc method of an object A would then be called like Inc(A, 5), which means you'd need to keep track of which methods go with which objects. You wouldn't need to keep track of this if the methods were (as in an earlier example) fields of their objects, but you'd still need to type the object's name twice: **A.Inc(A, 5)**.

To get around this problem, Lua offers a bit of *syntactic sugar*. *Syntax* just means grammar — the rules of how operators, variable names, parentheses, curly braces, and so on can fit together to make a valid Lua program. And syntactic sugar just means an extension to Lua's syntax that doesn't give Lua any new powers, but does make programs easier to type or read. For example, the equivalence between a `function` statement and an assignment statement with a `function` expression as a value (which you learned about in the previous chapter) is due to the former being syntactic sugar for the latter.

Similarly, when Lua sees something that looks like `A:Inc(5)` (note the colon), it treats it as though it were `A.Inc(A, 5)`. A is used both as the source for the `Inc` function and as the first argument to that function. Because the methods in the previous example are written to expect their first argument to be the object, the only change you need to make in order to use colon syntax is to include `Get` and `Inc` in the object that `MakeGetAndInc` returns. (`Get` and `Inc` are also made local below this, because they no longer need to be used anywhere but inside `MakeGetAndInc`.) Now the methods are called right from the object, just as in the example at the beginning of this section, but with a colon substituted for the dot:

```
> do -- Local scope for Get and Inc.
>>    -- Returns Obj.N:
>>    local function Get(Obj)
>>       return Obj.N
>>    end
>>
>>    -- Increments Obj.N by M:
>>    local function Inc(Obj, M)
>>       Obj.N = Obj.N + M
>>    end
>>
>>    -- Creates an object:
>>    function MakeGetAndInc(N)
>>       return {N = N, Get = Get, Inc = Inc}
>>    end
>> end
>
> -- Create an object:
> A = MakeGetAndInc(50)
> -- Try out its methods:
> print(A:Get())
50
> A:Inc(2)
> print(A:Get())
52
```

There's also syntactic sugar for defining methods: `function T:F(X)` is equivalent to `function T.F(self, X)`, which itself is equivalent to `T.F = function(self, X)`. You can rewrite the preceding example to use this if you make a table in which you can put `Get` and `Inc`, and if you have them use `self` instead of `Obj` as a name for their (now implicit) first argument. Here's how:

```
do -- Local scope for T.
   -- A table in which to define Get and Inc:
   local T = {}

   -- Returns self.N:
   function T:Get()
     return self.N
   end

   -- Increments self.N by M:
```

```
    function T:Inc(M)
      self.N = self.N + M
    end

    -- Creates an object:
    function MakeGetAndInc(N)
      return {N = N, Get = T.Get, Inc = T.Inc}
    end
  end
```

Note the following about this example:

❏   If the colon syntax is used to define a function, Lua itself will take care of inserting the formal
     self argument. If you forget this and try do to it yourself by typing **function T:Get(self)**, then Lua
     will treat that as though it were function T.Get(self, self), which is not what you want.

❏   Get and Inc are neither local nor global — they are fields of a (local) table. local function
     T:Get() would be wrong for the same reason that local T.Get = function(self) would be
     wrong — the local keyword is for creating new local variables, but T.Get is not a variable
     name (it's the name of a table field).

❏   Because the colon syntaxes for function calls and function definitions are just syntactic sugar,
     you can mix and match them. You can use the dot syntax to call a function defined with the
     colon syntax, and you can use the colon syntax to call a function defined with the dot syntax
     (assuming, of course, that the actual arguments correspond with the formal arguments after
     translating from colon syntax to dot syntax).

❏   T is only used as a container for Get and Inc up to the point they're put into a real object. If
     there were something else that all objects needed to have in common (for instance, a default
     value for N), T would be a good place to put it.

Later in this chapter, you'll see an extended example that uses the colon syntax for something more
interesting than incrementing numbers.

Functions with Variable
Numbers of Arguments

Functions that accept variable numbers of arguments are called *vararg* functions and, as promised in the
previous chapter, you'll now learn how to write them.

Defining Vararg Functions

The Average function returns the average of all its arguments. It also introduces the built-in function
assert, which does nothing if its first argument is true and triggers an error if it's false. (The second
argument is used as the error message.) Here's an example of how you use the Average function:

```
> -- Returns the average of all its arguments:
> function Average(...)
>>    local Ret, Count = 0, 0
>>    for _, Num in ipairs({...}) do
```

```
>>        Ret = Ret + Num
>>        Count = Count + 1
>>     end
>>     assert(Count > 0, "Attempted to average zero numbers")
>>     return Ret / Count
>> end
>
> print(Average(1))
1
> print(Average(41, 43))
42
> print(Average(31, -41, 59, -26, 53))
15.2
> print(Average())
stdin:7: Attempted to average zero numbers
stack traceback:
        [C]: in function 'assert'
        stdin:7: in function 'Average'
        stdin:1: in main chunk
        [C]: ?
```

The Average function's formal argument list consists only of . . . (three dots), which tells Lua that Average is a vararg function. Within a vararg function, three dots can be used as an expression, which is called a *vararg expression*. A vararg expression, like a function call, can evaluate to zero or more values. The vararg expression in Average is inside a table constructor. When Average is called with 1 as an argument, it is as though the table constructor looked like {1}. When it's called with 41 and 43 as arguments, it's as though the table constructor looked like {41, 43}. When it's called with 31, -41, 59, -26, and 53 as arguments, it's as though the table constructor looked like {31, -41, 59, -26, 53}. And when it's called with no arguments, it's as though the table constructor looked like {}.

You can use a vararg expression anywhere any other expression can be used. It follows exactly the same adjustment rules as a function call. For example, the vararg expression in the following assignment would be adjusted to two values:

```
Var1, Var2 = ...
```

Both vararg expressions in the following return statement would be adjusted to one value:

```
return ..., (...)
```

And the one in the following function call would not be adjusted at all — all of its zero or more values would be passed along to print:

```
print("args here:", ...)
```

A vararg expression includes any nil passed to the function, as follows:

```
> function F(...)
>>    print(...)
>> end
>
> F(nil, "b", nil, nil)
nil     b       nil     nil
```

A vararg function can also have regular (named) formal arguments, in which case the three dots come last and catch any actual arguments that are left over after the leftmost ones are assigned to the named formal arguments. Here's an example that makes that clearer:

```
> function F(Arg1, Arg2, ...)
>>    print("Arg1 and Arg2:", Arg1, Arg2)
>>    print("The rest:", ...)
>> end
>
> F()
Arg1 and Arg2:  nil     nil
The rest:
> F("a")
Arg1 and Arg2:  a       nil
The rest:
> F("a", "b")
Arg1 and Arg2:  a       b
The rest:
> -- Now there will be arguments left over after Arg1 and
> -- Arg2 have been taken care of:
> F("a", "b", "c")
Arg1 and Arg2:  a       b
The rest:       c
> F("a", "b", "c", "d")
Arg1 and Arg2:  a       b
The rest:       c       d
```

A vararg expression cannot be used as an upvalue. Again, this will make more sense with an example. Let's say you want to write a `MakePrinter` function. `MakePrinter` will return a function that takes no arguments and prints all the arguments given to `MakePrinter`. The obvious way to write this is like this:

```
function MakePrinter(...)
  return function()
    print(...) -- THIS DOESN'T WORK!
  end
end
```

But if you type that in, Lua will complain partway through:

```
> function MakePrinter(...)
>>    return function()
>>      print(...) -- THIS DOESN'T WORK!
stdin:3: cannot use '...' outside a vararg function near '...'
```

The anonymous function is not a vararg function. The vararg expression used in it is local to `MakePrinter`, which makes it an upvalue in the anonymous function, and because vararg expressions can't be used as upvalues, another way needs to be found to make the `MakePrinter` arguments available inside the anonymous function. That part is actually quite easy — just put the vararg expression inside a table constructor, and use the variable holding that table as the upvalue. The hard part is calling `print` with each of the table's values as arguments. That's easy to do with the `unpack` function, which takes an array as its first argument and returns, in order, all of the elements of that array (up to the array's length). For example:

```
> function MakePrinter(...)
>>     local Args = {...}
>>     return function()
>>         print(unpack(Args))
>>     end
>> end
>
> Printer = MakePrinter("a", "b", "c")
> Printer()
a       b       c
```

Because unpack uses its argument's length, it may not act right with an array that has gaps, which Args will if MakePrinter is given any nil arguments. The fix for this involves extra arguments to unpack, as well as a new built-in function, select.

The first select argument is a positive integer. If it's 1, select will return all its additional arguments; if it's 2, select will return all its additional arguments except for the first; and so on:

```
> print(select(1, "a", "b", "c"))
a       b       c
> print(select(2, "a", "b", "c"))
b       c
> print(select(3, "a", "b", "c"))
c
> -- This returns nothing:
> print(select(4, "a", "b", "c"))

>
```

As a special case, if the first select argument is the string "#", then it returns how many additional arguments it received, as follows:

```
> print(select("#"))
0
> print(select("#", "a"))
1
> print(select("#", "a", "b"))
2
> print(select("#", "a", "b", "c"))
3
```

It's this "#" usage that lets you find out how many values (including nils) are in a vararg expression (or in any expression that can have multiple values, for that matter):

```
> function F(...)
>>     print(select("#", ...))
>> end
>
> F(nil, "b", nil, nil)
4
```

You might think that #... would get the length of a vararg expression, but all it really does is get the length of the first element of the vararg expression (which, being used as an operand, is not eligible for multiple-value treatment and so is adjusted to one value).

unpack takes a second and third argument specifying where it starts and stops, getting values out of the table given to it:

If these arguments are not given, they default to 1 and the length of the table.

```
> -- Get elements 2 through 4 (inclusive):
> print(unpack({"a", "b", "c", "d", "e"}, 2, 4))
b        c        d
```

Here's the rewritten version of MakePrinter that handles nils properly. It uses select("#", ...) to count MakePrinter's arguments, and when it calls unpack, it unpacks all elements from the first up to however many arguments it counted:

```
> function MakePrinter(...)
>>    local Args = {...}
>>    local ArgCount = select("#", ...)
>>    return function()
>>       print(unpack(Args, 1, ArgCount))
>>    end
>> end
>
> Printer = MakePrinter(nil, "b", nil, nil)
> Printer()
nil      b        nil      nil
```

If a vararg function doesn't contain any vararg expressions, then a local arg variable is created and initialized to a table of all the extra arguments. arg.n is the number of extra arguments. It is as though the first lines of the function were as follows:

```
local arg = {...}
arg.n = select("#", ...)
```

This is done so that vararg functions written for Lua 5.0 will run on Lua 5.1. Lua 5.0 had no vararg expression, so vararg arguments were always put in such an arg table.

In addition to the lack of the vararg expression and use of arg, Lua 5.0 did not have the select function, and its unpack function took only one argument.

Scripts as Vararg Functions

You already know that chunks are functions. In this section, you'll see that they are vararg functions. In particular, Lua scripts are vararg functions and they can be given arguments on the command line.

Try It Out   Creating Command-Line Arguments

1.   Save the following as **cmdlineargs.lua**:

```
-- This script lists (by number) all arguments given to it
-- on the command line.

local Count = select("#", ...)
if Count > 0 then
```

```
    print("Command-line arguments:")
    for I = 1, Count do
      print(I, (select(I, ...))) -- The parentheses adjust
        -- select to one value.
    end
  else
    print("No command-line arguments given.")
  end
```

2.   Run it by typing the following into your shell:

```
lua cmdlineargs.lua this is a test
```

The output should be as follows:

```
Command-line arguments:
1       this
2       is
3       a
4       test
```

How It Works

When you type the name of a program (lua) into the shell, the words that come after it are called *command-line arguments*. The shell passes these arguments along to the program. In this case, lua treats the first command-line argument, cmdlineargs.lua, as the name of a program. It compiles that program into a function, and calls the function with the remaining command-line arguments (the strings "this", "is", "a", and "test").

This example also shows how you can use select to access arguments without putting them into a table first.

The shell gives special meaning to some characters. For example, it treats spaces as argument separators. If you want to include a special character in an argument, you need to escape it or quote it. The exact rules for escaping or quoting characters vary from shell to shell, but something like the following:

```
lua cmdlineargs.lua "this is a test" "" "<*>"
```

generally results in this:

```
Command-line arguments:
1       this is a test
2
3       <*>
```

The second argument is the empty string.

Command-line arguments are always strings, which means you don't have to worry about a gap caused by a nil.

lua treats some of its command-line arguments specially. These are called *options*, and they all start with a hyphen. The following table lists the lua options:

Option	Action
-e	Executes the following command-line argument as Lua code.
-l	Uses the `require` function on the library named by the following command-line argument. (You'll learn about `require` in Chapter 7.)
-i	Enters interactive mode after running the script named after all the options (or executing any `-e` arguments).
-v	Prints version information.
--	Stops handling options (this is useful if you want to run a script whose name starts with "-").
-	Stops handling options and executes `lua`'s input as a single chunk.

Here are a couple examples. Starting `lua` like this

```
lua -e "print('Hello')"
```

prints "Hello", but does not enter interactive mode (the Lua interpreter). Starting it like this:

```
lua -i sortednametoinstr.lua
```

runs `sortednametoinstr.lua` and then enters interactive mode, where you have access to any global variables it created (which in this case are `NameToInstr` and `Sorted`):

```
Lua 5.1.1  Copyright (C) 1994-2006 Lua.org, PUC-Rio
George played lead guitar
John played rhythm guitar
Paul played bass guitar
Ringo played drumkit
> print(NameToInstr.John)
rhythm guitar
> print(Sorted[4].Name)
Ringo
```

The options `-e` and `-l` can be combined with the command-line arguments immediately following them. The following example of `-e` does exactly the same thing as the one given earlier:

```
lua "-eprint('Hello')"
```

A script's command-line arguments are also available in the global table `arg`, even if a vararg expression is used in the script. This is done to give access to the script's name (found at `arg[0]`) and the interpreter's name and any options (found at negative indexes). If `lua` is started with the following:

```
lua -i cmdlineargs.lua this is a test
```

then this is the `arg`:

```
{[-2] = "lua",
 [-1] = "-i",
```

```
[0] = "cmdlineargs.lua",
[1] = "this",
[2] = "is",
[3] = "a",
[4] = "test"}
```

Notice that, unlike the `arg` described in the previous section, this one doesn't have its length in `arg.n`. The length is easy enough to find out, though (for instance, with `#arg`, or with a loop if you want to count the nonpositive indexes).

Keyword Arguments

In the previous chapter, you saw that a function call whose sole argument is a literal string doesn't require parentheses. The same applies to table constructors. For example:

```
> print {}
table: 0x493760
> print{}
table: 0x493978
```

This can be used to simulate *keyword arguments* — arguments that are identified not by their position, but by being associated with an identifier. In all three of the following examples, a function called `Sort` is being called with its `Arr` keyword argument set to `T` and its `CompFnc` keyword argument set to `F` (the last example reveals that all that's really going on is that an associative table is being passed to `Sort`):

```
Sort{Arr = T, CompFnc = F}
```

```
Sort{CompFnc = F, Arr = T}
```

```
Sort({Arr = T, CompFnc = F})
```

There is no special syntax for defining functions with keyword arguments — they're just defined to take a single table as an argument. For example, you could define `Sort` as follows:

```
-- A wrapper for table.sort that takes keyword arguments:
function Sort(KeyArgs)
  local Arr = KeyArgs.Arr -- The array to be sorted.
  local CompFnc = KeyArgs.CompFnc -- Comparison function.
    or function(A, B) return A < B end -- Default.
  if KeyArgs.Reverse then
    -- Reverse the sense of the comparison function:
    local OrigCompFnc = CompFnc
    CompFnc = function(A, B)
      return OrigCompFnc(B, A)
    end
  end
  table.sort(Arr, CompFnc)
  return Arr
end
```

The `Reverse` argument reverses the sense of the comparison function. When no `CompFnc` is given, but `Reverse` is set to `true`, the sense of the default comparison function is reversed, which sorts the table in reverse order:

```
> Letters = {"a", "b", "c"}
> Sort{Reverse = true, Arr = Letters}
> print(table.concat(Letters))
cba
```

The usual reasons for writing a function to take keyword arguments are that it has a lot of optional arguments, or that it has so many arguments that it's hard to remember what order they go in.

Different but the Same

A common problem in understanding how Lua works comes from the fact that tables are *mutable*, which means they can be changed. Side-effecting a table — changing it using indexing assignment — is called *mutating* the table. There's no way to mutate a string (or a number, Boolean, or `nil`) — it can only be replaced with a different value. (Strings, numbers, Booleans, and `nil` are therefore said to be *immutable*.) But a table can be mutated, and afterward it will have different content, but it will still be the same table.

Table Equality

Because tables are mutable, there needs to be a way to tell whether two tables are really the same table or not (so that you can tell if a mutation of one will be visible in the other). You do this with the `==` (equality) operator. When two tables are tested for equality, their contents are not looked at. Rather, they are considered equal if and only if they were created by the same table constructor at the same time (and are therefore the same table). In the following example, A and B are equal because they were created by the same table constructor at the same time:

```
> A = {}
> B = A
> print(A == B)
true
```

In the next example, C and D are unequal because they were created by two different table constructors, and E and F are unequal because they were created by the same table constructor at different times:

```
> C, D = {}, {}
> print(C == D)
false
>
> function CreateTbl()
>>    return {}
>> end
>
> E, F = CreateTbl(), CreateTbl()
> print(E == F)
false
```

Functions follow the same equality rule as tables: Two functions are equal if and only if they were created by the same `function` expression (or `function` statement) at the same time. This is because both table constructors and `function` expressions *create new objects* (using the term "object" in the broad sense).

Avoiding Bugs by Understanding Mutability

Among other things, you can use mutability to model things in the real world, most of which are mutable. For example, this book would still be the same book if you "mutated" it by writing your name in it. But mutability can also be a source of bugs, if you don't keep track of what's what. In the real world, you would never confuse having both hands on the same book with having each hand on a different book. But in Programming Land, it's not too tough to forget that two variables (or two table fields, or a variable and a table field) both contain the same table.

For example, imagine the following variant of `table.sort`, which still sorts its first argument in place but also returns it:

```
function TableSort(Arr, CompFnc)
    table.sort(Arr, CompFnc)
    return Arr
end
```

This would be convenient in some cases, letting you sort an array and pass it to another function in one statement like this:

```
SomeFnc(TableSort(SomeArr))
```

instead of in two statements like this:

```
table.sort(SomeArr)
SomeFnc(SomeArr)
```

But it might also imply `Sorted` is sorted and `SomeArr` is unsorted after the following line:

```
local Sorted = TableSort(SomeArr)
```

If you write a function that side-effects a table given to it, make sure that's clear in any documentation you write for the function. If you're using a function that someone else wrote, make sure you know if the function causes side effects in any tables given to it.

Variables and Mutable Values

In Chapter 2, you saw an illustration of the cubbyhole model (shown in Figure 4-1) and the arrow model (shown in Figure 4-2) of the association between variables and their values.

Number	Greeting1	Greeting2
123	"Hello"	"Hello"

Figure 4-1

145

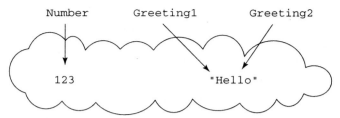

Figure 4-2

Both of these models are accurate for immutable values (ignoring memory usage). But the cubbyhole model doesn't work for mutable values. Consider the following code:

```
> A, B = {}, {}
> C = B
> -- Before
> B.Test = "test"
> -- After
> print(C.Test)
test
```

An arrow diagram of the variables as of the `Before` comment (shown in Figure 4-3) reflects the fact that B and C are the same table.

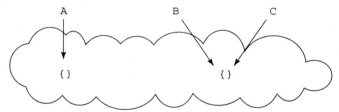

Figure 4-3

It's an easy step from there to an accurate arrow diagram of the variables as of the `After` comment, as shown in Figure 4-4.

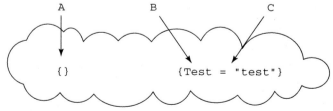

Figure 4-4

A cubbyhole diagram as of the `Before` comment (see Figure 4-5) does not show that B and C are the same table.

146

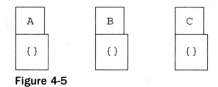

Figure 4-5

It thus could lead to an *incorrect* diagram as of the `After` comment, as shown in Figure 4-6):

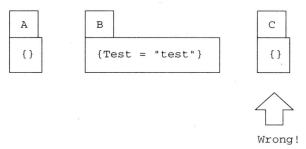

Wrong!

Figure 4-6

Tables and Functions

You saw earlier that functions follow the same equality rule as tables. Another thing that functions have in common with tables is mutability. Closure functions can be mutated by calling them, as is done with `Counter` in the following example:

```
> do
>>    local Count = 0
>>
>>    function Counter()
>>       Count = Count + 1
>>       return Count
>>    end
>> end
> print(Counter())
1
> print(Counter())
2
> print(Counter())
3
```

A difference between tables and functions is that tables do not have upvalues. A local variable inside a function is evaluated every time the function is called, but a local variable inside a table constructor is evaluated only once, while the table is being constructed. That's why, in the following code, `Tbl.Str` is still `"before"` even after `Str` has been set to `"after"`:

```
> do
>>    local Str = "before"
>>    Fnc = function() return Str end
```

```
>>     Tbl = {Str = Str}
>>     Str = "after"
>> end
> print(Fnc())
after
> print(Tbl.Str)
before
```

It's easy to get an upvalue-like effect by assigning to a table field instead of a local, like this:

```
> do
>>     local Str = "before"
>>     Tbl = {Str = Str}
>>     Tbl.Str = "after"
>> end
> print(Tbl.Str)
after
```

If you want multiple tables to share state, have them share a subtable, as Tbl1 and Tbl2 share SubTbl here:

```
> do
>>     local SubTbl = {Str = "before"}
>>     Tbl1 = {SubTbl = SubTbl}
>>     Tbl2 = {SubTbl = SubTbl}
>> end
> Tbl1.SubTbl.Str = "after"
> print(Tbl2.SubTbl.Str)
after
```

If you're familiar with the distinction between pass by value and pass by reference, you may think that Lua passes immutable values by value and mutable values by reference, but that isn't true — arguments are always passed by value. A function's caller can tell whether the function did an indexing assignment to a table the caller gave it, but not whether the function did a regular assignment to one of its arguments.

If you absolutely needed to use the language of values versus references to describe Lua's treatment of mutable values, you could say that mutable values themselves are references.

Copying Tables

Sometimes you need to make a copy of a table. For example, if you want to sort a table without altering the unsorted table, you need to make a copy and sort that. The simplest way (which is all you need in many circumstances) is to make a *shallow copy*:

```
-- Makes a shallow copy of a table:
function ShallowCopy(Src)
  local Dest = {}
  for Key, Val in pairs(Src) do
    Dest[Key] = Val
  end
  return Dest
end
```

In this example, `ShallowCopy` creates a fresh table (`Dest`) and then loops through all key-value pairs in `Src`, putting each value into `Dest` at the appropriate key. (`Src` and `Dest` stand for "source" and "destination.") This is called a shallow copy because it doesn't burrow deep into `Src`—if any of `Src`'s values or keys are tables, those very tables will be put into `Dest`, not copies of them. Copying subtables as well as the top level of a table is called making a *deep copy*. You can change a `ShallowCopy` to make a deep copy by adding the following two lines (and the name, of course):

```
-- Makes a deep copy of a table.  Doesn't properly handle
-- duplicate subtables.
function DeepCopy(Src)
  local Dest = {}
  for Key, Val in pairs(Src) do
    Key = type(Key) == "table" and DeepCopy(Key) or Key
    Val = type(Val) == "table" and DeepCopy(Val) or Val
    Dest[Key] = Val
  end
  return Dest
end
```

The new lines test whether a key or value is a table. If it is, they call `DeepCopy` recursively to make a deep copy of it. Unlike `ShallowCopy`, a copy made by `DeepCopy` will never have any subtables in common with the original, which means that the copy can have side effects without affecting the original. For example:

```
> Body1 = {Head = {"Eyes", "Nose", "Mouth", "Ears"},
>>    Arms = {Hands = {"Fingers"}},
>>    Legs = {Feet = {"Toes"}}}
> Body2 = DeepCopy(Body1)
> print(Body1.Legs.Feet[1], Body2.Legs.Feet[1])
Toes    Toes
> Body2.Legs.Feet[1] = "Piggies"
> -- If ShallowCopy had been used, this would print
> -- Piggies Piggies:
> print(Body1.Legs.Feet[1], Body2.Legs.Feet[1])
Toes    Piggies
>
```

There are two problems with this version of `DeepCopy`. One is that it treats functions the same as it treats anything else that isn't a table—it doesn't make copies of them. There are ways to copy functions, but none of them is completely general, unless you use an add-on library such as Pluto. (A general solution needs to treat upvalues correctly, including upvalues shared between functions.) Copying functions is seldom necessary, though, so you can ignore this problem here.

> *Pluto is a persistence library, which means that it allows arbitrary Lua values to be saved to disk and reloaded later, even after Lua has been restarted. It's available at* `luaforge.net`.

The other problem is more serious. If a table appears more than once within the table being copied, it shows up as different tables in the copy. For example:

```
> SubTbl = {}
> Orig = {SubTbl, SubTbl, SubTbl}
> Copy = DeepCopy(Orig)
> -- Orig contains the same table three times:
```

```
> for I, SubTbl in ipairs(Orig) do
>>    print(I, SubTbl)
>> end
1         table: 0x4a0538
2         table: 0x4a0538
3         table: 0x4a0538
> -- Copy contains three different tables:
> for I, SubTbl in ipairs(Copy) do
>>    print(I, SubTbl)
>> end
1         table: 0x4a0a08
2         table: 0x4a0a48
3         table: 0x4a0a98
```

Something even more interesting happens when you pass DeepCopy a table that has a *cycle*. A table is said to have a cycle if it contains any table (including itself) that directly or indirectly contains itself. In the following example, T is such a table; to copy it, DeepCopy first needs to copy T.T, but to copy that, it needs to copy T.T.T, and so on. Because these are all the same table, DeepCopy keeps recursing until it runs out of stack space or you interrupt it:

```
> T = {}
> T.T = T
> -- The same table, within itself:
> print(T, T.T.T.T.T.T.T)
table: 0x495478 table: 0x495478
> T2 = DeepCopy(T)
stdin:3: stack overflow
stack traceback:
        stdin:3: in function 'DeepCopy'
        stdin:5: in function 'DeepCopy'
        stdin:5: in function 'DeepCopy'
        stdin:5: in function 'DeepCopy'
        stdin:5: in function 'DeepCopy'
        stdin:5: in function 'DeepCopy'
        stdin:5: in function 'DeepCopy'
        stdin:5: in function 'DeepCopy'
        stdin:5: in function 'DeepCopy'
        ...
        stdin:5: in function 'DeepCopy'
        stdin:5: in function 'DeepCopy'
        stdin:5: in function 'DeepCopy'
        stdin:5: in function 'DeepCopy'
        stdin:5: in function 'DeepCopy'
        stdin:5: in function 'DeepCopy'
        stdin:5: in function 'DeepCopy'
        stdin:5: in function 'DeepCopy'
        stdin:1: in main chunk
        [C]: ?
```

There is a general solution to this problem, and it involves keeping track of what tables have already been copied. You use it in the following Try It Out.

Try It Out   **Copying Subtables Correctly**

1.   Enter this version of DeepCopy into an interpreter session:

```
-- Makes a deep copy of a table.  This version of DeepCopy
-- properly handles duplicate subtables, including cycles.
-- (The Seen argument is only for recursive calls.)
function DeepCopy(Src, Seen)
  local Dest
  if Seen then
    -- This will only set Dest if Src has been seen before:
    Dest = Seen[Src]
  else
    -- Top-level call; create the Seen table:
    Seen = {}
  end
  -- If Src is new, copy it into Dest:
  if not Dest then
    -- Make a fresh table and record it as seen:
    Dest = {}
    Seen[Src] = Dest
    for Key, Val in pairs(Src) do
      Key = type(Key) == "table" and DeepCopy(Key, Seen) or Key
      Val = type(Val) == "table" and DeepCopy(Val, Seen) or Val
      Dest[Key] = Val
    end
  end
  return Dest
end
```

2.   Now test it with a particularly hairy case — a table that contains itself as both a key and a value:

```
> T = {}
> T[T] = T
> T2 = DeepCopy(T)
> -- T2 really is cyclical:
> print(T2[T2][T2][T2][T2][T2])
table: 0x703198
> -- And a side effect to it isn't visible in the source
> -- table:
> T2.Test = "test"
> print(T2[T2][T2][T2].Test)
test
> print(T[T][T][T].Test)
nil
```

How It Works

This version of DeepCopy works by storing every copy it makes as a value in an associative table, the key being that copy's source table. That lets it avoid making more than one copy of a given table. This mapping between already seen source and destination tables is in the second argument of DeepCopy, which is Seen.

When you called DeepCopy, you gave it only one argument. It saw that Seen was nil and initialized it to an empty table. It then saw that Dest was nil (because it hadn't been found in Seen), so it created a fresh destination table, assigned it to `Dest`, and established an association between the source table and the destination table in `Seen`. Then it looped through `Src`. This part of `DeepCopy` is almost the same as the previous version. The only difference is that recursive calls pass the `Seen` argument. When the first recursive call (for `Key`) was made, that call saw that `Seen` was set, so it assigned `Seen[Src]` to `Dest`. If `Src` had not been seen yet, that assignment would have done nothing, and the loop inside the next `if` statement would have been entered. But in this case, a table got assigned to `Dest`, so the loop was skipped. The same happened with the second recursive call (for `Val`).

Building Other Data Structures from Tables

In Lua, tables serve the same purposes as what other languages call tables, dictionaries, associative arrays, or hash tables, such as the following:

```
Potluck = {John = "chips", Jane = "lemonade",
  Jolene = "egg salad"}
```

and what other languages call arrays or vectors, such as these:

```
Days = {"Monday", "Tuesday", "Wednesday", "Thursday",
  "Friday", "Saturday", "Sunday"}
```

You can build other data structures out of tables as well. For example, you can use `table.insert` and `table.remove` to treat a table as a stack, and use tables within tables to represent *tree-structured* data — data that branches out like a tree, as shown in Figure 4-7.

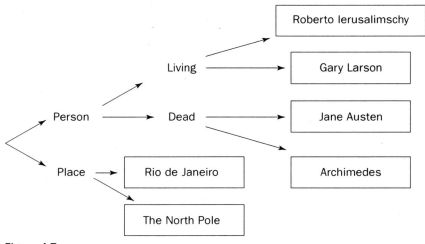

Figure 4-7

The diagram in the figure could be represented as follows:

```
{Person = {
    Living = {"Roberto Ierusalimschy", "Gary Larson"},
```

```
            Dead = {"Jane Austen", "Archimedes"}},
        Place = {"Rio de Janeiro", "The North Pole"}}
```

Special-purpose data structures like these can be accessed and manipulated like ordinary tables, but if they behave differently enough from tables, you can write special-purpose functions that work with them. It may be convenient to use the colon syntax to attach such functions to the data structures themselves. The following Try It Out is an example of this. It's an implementation of a *ring*, a data structure that is something like a stack, except the top (referred to in the exercise as the current element) can be moved, and the top and bottom act like they're hooked onto each other.

Try It Out   Using a Table as a Ring

1. Save the following file as `ring.lua`:

```
-- A ring data structure:

-- Returns X mod Y, but one-based: the return value will
-- never be less than 1 or greater than Y.  (Y is assumed to
-- be positive.)
local function OneMod(X, Y)
  return (X - 1) % Y + 1
end

-- A table in which to create the methods:
local Methods = {}

-- Inserts a new element into self:
function Methods:Push(Elem)
  table.insert(self, self.Pos, Elem)
end

-- Removes the current element from self; returns nil if
-- self is empty:
function Methods:Pop()
  local Ret
  if #self > 0 then
    Ret = table.remove(self, self.Pos)
    -- Keep self.Pos from pointing outside the array by
    -- wrapping it around:
    if self.Pos > #self then
      self.Pos = 1
    end
  end
  return Ret
end

-- Rotates self to the left:
function Methods:RotateL()
  if #self > 0 then
    self.Pos = OneMod(self.Pos + 1, #self)
  end
end

-- Rotates self to the right:
```

153

```
function Methods:RotateR()
  if #self > 0 then
    self.Pos = OneMod(self.Pos - 1, #self)
  end
end

-- Returns the ring's size:
function Methods:Size()
  return #self
end

-- Returns a string representation of self:
function Methods:ToString()
  -- Convert the parts of self to the left and to the right
  -- of self.Pos to strings:
  local LeftPart = table.concat(self, ", ", 1, self.Pos - 1)
  local RightPart = table.concat(self, ", ", self.Pos, #self)
  -- Only put a separator between them if neither is the
  -- empty string:
  local Sep
  if LeftPart == "" or RightPart == "" then
    Sep = ""
  else
    Sep = ", "
  end
  -- RightPart's first element is self.Pos, so put it first:
  return RightPart .. Sep .. LeftPart
end

-- Instantiates a ring:
function MakeRing(Ring)
  -- Make an empty ring if an array of initial ring values
  -- wasn't passed in:
  Ring = Ring or {}
  -- Ring.Pos is the position of the current element of the
  -- ring; initialize it to 1 (all methods that expect
  -- there to be a current element first make sure the ring
  -- isn't empty):
  Ring.Pos = 1
  -- Give the ring methods and return it:
  for Name, Fnc in pairs(Methods) do
    Ring[Name] = Fnc
  end
  return Ring
end
```

2. Start lua as follows (this will run ring.lua and then enter interactive mode):

```
lua -i ring.lua
```

3. Within interactive mode, use the function MakeRing to create a ring, and use that ring's methods to manipulate it:

```
> R = MakeRing{"the", "time", "has", "come"} -- Another use
>    -- for the syntax from the "Keyword Arguments" section.
> print(R:ToString())
the, time, has, come
> print(R:Pop())
the
> R:Push("today")
> print(R:ToString())
today, time, has, come
> R:RotateL()
> print(R:ToString())
time, has, come, today
> print(R:Pop(), R:Pop(), R:Pop())
time        has        come
> R:Push("here")
> print(R:ToString(), R:Size())
here, today        2
> R:Push("tomorrow")
> R:Push("gone")
> print(R:ToString())
gone, tomorrow, here, today
> R:RotateR()
> print(R:ToString())
today, gone, tomorrow, here
> R:RotateR()
> print(R:ToString())
here, today, gone, tomorrow
```

How It Works

MakeRing instantiates a new ring. If you call it with no argument, it makes an empty ring, but if you call it with an array, it uses that array's elements as the elements of the ring (the first element is the initial current element). A ring has the following six methods:

- ❑ Push — Adds a new element to the ring.

- ❑ Pop — Removes the current element from the ring and returns it.

- ❑ RotateL — Rotates the ring left by one element.

- ❑ RotateR — Rotates the ring right by one element.

- ❑ Size — Returns the size of the ring.

- ❑ ToString — Returns a string listing all elements of the ring, with the current one first.

    When used in the context of stacks and related structures, Push and Pop mean insert and remove.

A ring is represented as an array with a Pos field that points to its current element. For example, take a look at the ring in Figure 4-8.

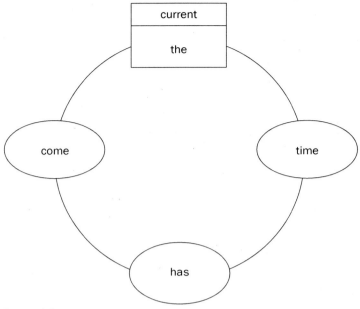

Figure 4-8

This ring could be represented as any of the following (the methods are left out for clarity):

```
{"the", "time", "has", "come", Pos = 1}
```

```
{"come", "the", "time", "has", Pos = 2}
```

```
{"has", "come", "the", "time", Pos = 3}
```

```
{"time", "has", "come", "the", Pos = 4}
```

Rotating a ring takes the same amount of time no matter how big the ring is. But pushing or popping an element can take an amount of time proportional to the size of the ring. More specifically, it takes an amount of time proportional to the number of elements from Pos to the end of the array. That's because when `table.insert` and `table.remove` insert or remove an item into or from the middle of an array, they need to go through every element between there and the end of the array and shift them up or down to compensate. This implementation of rings was written that way because it's simple and easy to understand, and the time that it takes to push or pop is not even noticeable in most circumstances.

If pushing and popping does consume a problematic amount of time, either because of the sheer size of a ring, or because a bunch of pushes or pops were being done in a time-critical section of code, then you could *optimize* the rings — reimplementing them in a more efficient way using a different representation. One simple optimization would be to arrange for Pos to go up on pushes and down on pops. This way, when Pos hits the sweet spot at the end of the array, it would stay at the end unless the ring was rotated.

Another optimization would be to represent each element as a table with a `Val` field (that element's value), and `Left` and `Right` fields (the tables of the elements counterclockwise and clockwise from that element). Doing it that way has the advantage of making pushes and pops take the same amount of time no matter how big the ring is. It's more complicated, though, because pushes and pops have to do the correct relinking of the `Left` and `Right` fields of the element in question, and those of its two neighbors. Additionally, each push creates a new table, which takes more time than simply inserting a value sufficiently close to the end of an array, so for rings with less than 50 or 60 elements, this approach is actually slower than the worst case of the version given in `ring.lua`.

A good rule of thumb is to first write something in as simple and clear a way as possible, test it to make sure it's correct, and then *don't* optimize it — unless it's slowing the whole program down enough to detract from the program's usability.

Here are a few more comments:

❑ Other than `ToString`, which expects everything in the ring to be a string or a number, `ring.lua`'s rings can hold any value — except for `nil`. There are (at least) a couple ways to fix this. One is to replace `table.insert` and `table.remove` with code that can handle a `nil`, and use a field in `self` to keep track of the size instead of `#`. The other is to create a value that won't be equal to any other value that might be pushed into the ring, and use that value to represent `nil`. So `Push`, when given a `nil`, would push that value instead, and `Pop`, when popping that value, would return `nil`. You can use a do-nothing function or an empty table for the value.

❑ The size of the ring is measurable with the `#` operator, but that might no longer be true if the implementation were changed. That's why there's a `Size` method: it hides the details of how the size is kept track of.

❑ The only global variable set by `ring.lua` is `MakeRing` because it's the only thing needed to create a ring.

❑ The local function `OneMod` is there to make the rotation methods easier to read by abstracting away a bit of arithmetic.

❑ You can use `lua -i filename` to write, test, and debug code. If you make a change in the file, and you don't want to exit the interpreter just to reload it, call `dofile` with the filename, such as `dofile("ring.lua")`. If you want to test a local function (such as `OneMod`), you can make it global for long enough to test it and then relocalize it.

❑ The guts of this implementation are not hidden, which means that goofy fiddling like `R.Pos = -1` can be done. This is fine in a prototype, but you want to prevent it in code intended for serious use. One way would be to put nothing but methods in the tables returned by `MakeRing`. There would be an upvalue containing a table whose keys would be the tables returned by `MakeRing`, and whose values would be tables with `Pos` and the contents of the corresponding ring. Only `MakeRing` and the methods would have access to that upvalue. When a method wanted to get at the contents or position of its ring, it would index the upvalue with `self`. Another way of protecting an object's guts from fiddling is described in Chapter 11.

Because of tables' flexibility, you often don't need a customized data structure. Just ask yourself how you most often want to access your data — usually an associative table or an array will do the job. For instance, the task of finding a user's information based on his or her username is obviously suited to an associative table whose keys are usernames and whose values are tables of information about each user. The task of displaying all users in alphabetical order by username is suited to a sorted array. It's common to create ad hoc tables to do something that the main table you're using can't do. If you were working with an associative table like the one described previously, keyed by usernames, but you wanted to do something that grouped users by last name, you could create a table like the following, with last names as keys and arrays of users as values:

```lua
local LastUsers = {} -- Keys: last names; vals: arrays of
  -- UserInfos.
for Username, UserInfo in pairs(Users) do
  -- If this last name hasn't been seen yet, make an empty array:
  LastUsers[UserInfo.LastName] = LastUsers[UserInfo.LastName] or {}
  table.insert(LastUsers[UserInfo.LastName], UserInfo)
end
```

Custom-Made Loops

Most times when you want to loop through a table, `pairs` or `ipairs` is appropriate, but if neither is, you can instead write and use your own function. Here, for example, is a function similar to `ipairs`, but it goes through the array given to it in reverse order:

```lua
-- An iterator factory -- like ipairs, but goes through the
-- array in reverse order:
function ReverseIpairs(Arr)
  local I = #Arr

  local function Iter()
    local Ret1, Ret2
    if I > 0 then
      Ret1, Ret2 = I, Arr[I]
      I = I - 1
    end
    return Ret1, Ret2
  end

  return Iter
end

for I, Str in ReverseIpairs({"one", "two", "three"}) do
  print(I, Str)
end
```

The output is as follows:

```
3       three
2       two
1       one
```

The `Iter` function is what is known in the Lua world as an *iterator*. In the simplest terms, an iterator is a function that, each time you call it, returns the next element or elements from the thing you're looping through. The generic `for` expects to find an iterator to the right of the keyword `in`. `ReverseIpairs` is not an iterator — it, like `ipairs` and `pairs`, is an *iterator factory* — a function that returns an iterator.

(This book follows that terminological distinction, but elsewhere, you may see iterator factories referred to as iterators, when the context makes it clear what's being talked about.) In this example, the `for` does not find `ReverseIpairs` to the right of the `in`, but `Iter`, because that's what the call to `ReverseIpairs` returns. The `for` then calls `Iter`, puts its results into the newly created local `I` and `Str` variables, and executes the body of the loop. It keeps on doing this until `Iter`'s first return value is `nil`, at which point the loop is exited.

That last sentence is a rule about all iterators. That is, when an iterator returns `nil` as its first value (or when it returns nothing, which `for` adjusts to `nil`), the loop is ended. For this reason, the leftmost loop variable (which receives the iterator's first return value) is called the loop's *control variable*.

This implementation of `ReverseIpairs` returns what is called a *stateful* iterator because it includes (as the upvalues `Arr` and `I`) the current state of the iteration. You can also write *stateless* iterators, which depend on `for` to keep track of the current state of the iteration for them.

Try this stateless version of `ReverseIpairs`:

```
do -- Local scope for Iter.
  -- ReverseIpairs's iterator; Arr is the "invariant state",
  -- and I is the control variable's previous value:
  local function Iter(Arr, I)
    if I > 1 then
      I = I - 1
      return I, Arr[I] -- Violates structured programming
        -- (not a severe misdeed in such a small function).
    end
  end

  -- An iterator factory -- like ipairs, but goes through
  -- the array in reverse order:
  function ReverseIpairs(Arr)
    return Iter, Arr, #Arr + 1
  end
end

for I, Str in ReverseIpairs({"one", "two", "three"}) do
  print(I, Str)
end
```

It prints the same thing as the stateful version:

```
3       three
2       two
1       one
```

The generic `for` actually expects up to three values to the right of the `in`:

❑   The iterator itself

❑   An *invariant state* (`nil` in a stateful iterator, and usually the table being looped through in a stateless iterator)

❑   A seed value for the loop's control variable (`nil` in a stateful iterator and in some stateless iterators)

159

Every time `for` calls the iterator, it passes it two arguments: the invariant state and the value of the control variable from the previous iteration. That's why it needs the seed value — to have something to pass the iterator before the first iteration.

In the example, `ReverseIpairs` returns `Iter`, the array it was given (the invariant state), and the length of the array plus one (the seed value for the control variable). `for` then calls `Iter` with the array and the seed value. `Iter` doesn't know that it's being called on the first iteration. It just sees that its second argument is 4 and, in effect, thinks to itself: "If the last value of the control variable was 4, then it's time for me to return 3 and the 3rd element of my first argument." `for` assigns these values to `I` and `Str`, and executes the body of the loop. Then it calls `Iter` again, with the array and 3 as arguments. This process continues until the last time `Iter` is called. Because its second argument is 1, it returns nothing. `for` looks at `Iter`'s first return value and, seeing it to be (after adjustment) `nil`, ends the loop.

The built-in function `next` is a stateless iterator. It takes a table and a key in that table and returns the "next" key-value pair in the table, like this:

```
> NameToInstr = {John = "rhythm guitar",
>>    Paul = "bass guitar",
>>    George = "lead guitar",
>>    Ringo = "drumkit"}
> print(next(NameToInstr, "Ringo"))
George   lead guitar
> print(next(NameToInstr, "George"))
John     rhythm guitar
> print(next(NameToInstr, "John"))
Paul     bass guitar
```

If given the seed value `nil`, it returns the "first" key-value pair in the table, and if given the "last" key in the table, it returns `nil`, like this:

```
> print(next(NameToInstr))
Ringo    drumkit
> print(next(NameToInstr, "Paul"))
nil
```

"Next," "first," and "last" are in quotes here because the order of the table is arbitrary. But it's the same arbitrary order in which `pairs` loops through a table. In fact, all `pairs` does is return `next`, the table given to it, and `nil`, so that if you write one of the following:

```
for Key, Val in next, Tbl, nil do
```

```
for Key, Val in next, Tbl do
```

it's the same as writing this:

```
for Key, Val in pairs(Tbl) do
```

`pairs` has parentheses after it and `next` doesn't because `pairs` is an iterator factory and needs to be called, but `next` is an iterator and needs to be given straight to `for`.

If you check it out, you'll see that next *and the iterator returned by* pairs *are actually different functions, but that's just a quirk of the Lua implementation. Both are just wrappers around the same function written in C.*

ipairs is similar. It returns a stateless iterator, the table given to it, and a seed value of 0. The iterator (called IpairsIter in the following example) works by adding one to its second argument and returning that key-value pair of its first argument:

```
> IpairsIter, Arr, Seed = ipairs({"one", "two", "three"})
> print(IpairsIter, Arr, Seed)
function: 0x480c68     table: 0x496230 0
> print(IpairsIter(Arr, 0))
1       one
> print(IpairsIter(Arr, 1))
2       two
> print(IpairsIter(Arr, 2))
3       three
> print(IpairsIter(Arr, 3)) -- This will return nothing.

>
```

IpairsIter is not a built-in function, but it's easy to write. Here's how:

```
function IpairsIter(Arr, PrevI)
  local CurI = PrevI + 1
  Val = Arr[CurI]
  if Val ~= nil then
    return CurI, Val
  end
end
```

The behavior of the generic for is complex, but it allows for to be both flexible and efficient — flexible because an iterator can be written for anything you want to loop through, and efficient because a stateless iterator factory can return the same iterator every time, rather than creating a new closure each time it's called. If you're writing an iterator, and you can easily tell just by looking at the control variable's previous value what the next value should be, then write a stateless iterator; otherwise write a stateful one.

All of the iterator factories you've seen so far have only taken one argument, and all their iterators have returned two values after each iteration, but that's only because they're all for iterating through key-value pairs of tables. The following Subseqs iterator factory takes an array and a Len number, , and then returns an iterator that loops through the array's subsequences, each subsequence being Len elements long:

```
> -- Returns an iterator that goes through all Len-long
> -- subsequences of Arr:
> function Subseqs(Arr, Len)
>>    local Pos = 0
>>
>>    return function()
>>       Pos = Pos + 1
>>       if Pos + Len - 1 <= #Arr then
```

```
>>          return unpack(Arr, Pos, Pos + Len - 1)
>>       end
>>    end
>> end
>
> Nums = {"one", "two", "three", "four", "five", "six"}
> for Val1, Val2, Val3, Val4 in Subseqs(Nums, 4) do
>>    print(Val1, Val2, Val3, Val4)
>> end
one      two      three    four
two      three    four     five
three    four     five     six
```

Here's an iterator (meant to be part of `ring.lua`) that only returns one value after each iteration — it loops through all values in the ring, starting with the current one:

```
-- Returns an iterator that iterates through all self's
-- elements.
function Methods:Elems()
  local IterPos -- The position of the element the iterator
    -- needs to return

  return function()
    local Ret
    if IterPos then
      if IterPos ~= self.Pos then
        Ret = self[IterPos]
      else
        -- Back at the beginning; do nothing (which ends the
        -- loop by returning nil).
      end
    else
      -- At the beginning: initialize IterPos:
      IterPos = self.Pos
      Ret = self[IterPos] -- If the ring is empty, this'll
        -- end the loop by returning nil.
    end
    IterPos = OneMod(IterPos + 1, #self)
    return Ret
  end
end
```

Here it is in use:

```
> dofile("ring.lua")
> Days = MakeRing{"Monday", "Tuesday", "Wednesday",
>>    "Thursday", "Friday", "Saturday", "Sunday"}
> Days:RotateR()
> for Day in Days:Elems() do
>>    print(Day)
>> end
Sunday
Monday
```

```
Tuesday
Wednesday
Thursday
Friday
Saturday
```

The normal rules for adjustment apply to iterators and loop variables:

```
> Letters = {"a", "b", "c"}
> for I in ipairs(Letters) do
>>    print(I)
>> end
1
2
3
> for I, Letter, Junk1, Junk2 in ipairs(Letters) do
>>    print(I, Letter, Junk1, Junk2)
>> end
1       a       nil     nil
2       b       nil     nil
3       c       nil     nil
```

You can write stateless iterators that ignore their second argument (and keep track of where they are by side-effecting the table given as the first argument), but this technique is seldom used.

You'll learn one more method for writing iterators in Chapter 12.

Global Variable Environments

You may have noticed similarities between global variables and table keys, such as their lack of distinction between nil and nonexistence. These similarities are not coincidental. Global variables are actually stored in a table. This table can be found in the global variable _G, as you can see in the following example:

You can tell by looking at the numbers that print *and* _G.print *are the same value, as are* _G *itself and* _G._G._G._G, *because* _G, *being both a global variable and a table containing all the global variables, contains itself.*

```
> print(print, _G.print)
function: 0x481720    function: 0x481720
> MyGlobal = "Hello!"
> print(MyGlobal, _G.MyGlobal)
Hello!  Hello!
> print(_G, _G._G._G._G)
table: 0x4806e8 table: 0x4806e8
```

This means that you can access global variables whose names are strings built at run time (without resorting to loadstring), like this:

```
> Abcd = "test 1"
> print(_G["Ab" .. "cd"])
```

```
test 1
> _G["Wx" .. "yz"] = "test 2"
> print(Wxyz)
test 2
```

For more on `loadstring`, see Chapter 3.

You can also loop through all global variables. Give the following code a try:

print *already puts a tab character between the things it prints. The extra* print *in the following example just makes it easier to read.*

```
for Name, Val in pairs(_G) do
   print(Name, "\t", Val)
end
```

A table used to store global variables is called an *environment*, and every function has one. Usually they're all the same environment, but you can give a function its own environment with the function `setfenv` (short for set function environment). In the following example, you create a `Greet` function and give it an empty environment. This function tries to call `print`, but the `"print"` key in its environment is not set, so there's an error:

```
> function Greet(Name)
>>    print("Hello, " .. Name .. ".")
>> end
> setfenv(Greet, {})
> Greet("Syd")
stdin:2: attempt to call global 'print' (a nil value)
stack traceback:
        stdin:2: in function 'Greet'
        stdin:1: in main chunk
        [C]: ?
```

When you give it an environment whose `"print"` key is set to the `print` function, it works as desired:

```
> setfenv(Greet, {print = print})
> Greet("Syd")
Hello, Syd.
```

Of course, the function could be called `print` but could do something different than the real `print`, as in the following example:

```
> Env = {print = function(Str)
>>    print("<<<" .. Str .. ">>>")
>> end}
> setfenv(Greet, Env)
> Greet("Syd")
<<<Hello, Syd.>>>
```

Earlier it was said that some closures can be side-effected by calling them. Now you see that you can give side effects to all functions by calling `setfenv` on them.

A function's environment can be retrieved with the `getfenv` ("get function environment") function. For example:

```
> PrintEnv, GreetEnv = getfenv(print), getfenv(Greet)
> -- print's environment is different than Greet's environment:
> print(PrintEnv, GreetEnv)
table: 0x4806e8 table: 0x493958
> -- print's environment is the one in _G, Greet's isn't:
> print(PrintEnv == _G, GreetEnv == _G)
true    false
```

Environment tables are just ordinary tables, and behave accordingly. In the previous example, because `PrintEnv` is the same as `_G`, any changes you make to `PrintEnv` will show up in `_G`:

```
> PrintEnv.Test = "test"
> print(_G.Test)
test
> print(Test)
test
```

Function environments can be used to modularize code by making global variables not so global. An example of this (the `module` function) is given in Chapter 7.

Another common use is *sandboxing*, which means running code with a limited or otherwise specialized set of global variables. The environment you gave to `Greet` that only had `print` in it was a sandbox — `Greet` had no way of accessing any of Lua's other built-in functions. This sort of thing is useful if your program needs to run code supplied by a user, but you want to limit the power of the user to mess things up (either by assigning to global variables, or by calling functions that he or she shouldn't be calling). One way to make a sandbox is to make a table with all the globals that the sandboxed function is supposed to have access to — this is the technique you used in the `Greet` example. (It may be easier to use a function like `DeepCopy` to copy `_G`, and then remove anything you don't want it to contain.) Another, more flexible technique is explained in Chapter 11.

The first argument to `setfenv` or `getfenv` can be a number instead of a function. The number is treated as a stack level, and the function at that level of the stack has its environment set or gotten. Lower numbers are closer to the top of the stack: 1 is the current function (the one calling `setfenv` or `getfenv`); 2 is the function that called the current function (and hence is right below it on the stack); 3 is the function that called the function that called the current function; and so on. (Calling `getfenv` with no argument is the same as calling it with an argument of 1 — it returns the current function's environment.) For example:

```
> -- Gives its caller an empty environment:
> function PwnMe()
>>    setfenv(2, {})
>> end
>
> do
>>    PwnMe()
>>    -- Global variables are missing now:
>>    print("test")
>> end
```

```
stdin:4: attempt to call global 'print' (a nil value)
stack traceback:
        stdin:4: in main chunk
        [C]: ?
> -- Since this is a new chunk now, things are back to
> -- normal.  That wouldn't be the case if this were a
> -- script, and therefore all one chunk.
> print("test")
test
```

For more on chunks, see Chapter 3.

This means that if you're sandboxing a function to prevent it from messing with its caller's global variables, you should not include either setfenv or getfenv in the sandbox.

When you create a function, it inherits the environment of its source function. That's why DoNothing1 and DoNothing2 have different environments in the following code, and they'll keep these environments until and unless you use setfenv on them:

```
> -- Returns a do-nothing function:
> function MakeDoNothing()
>>    return function() end
>> end
>
> EmptyTbl1, EmptyTbl2 = {}, {}
> setfenv(MakeDoNothing, EmptyTbl1)
> DoNothing1 = MakeDoNothing()
> setfenv(MakeDoNothing, EmptyTbl2)
> DoNothing2 = MakeDoNothing()
> -- DoNothings 1 and 2 have the environments that
> -- MakeDoNothing had when it created them:
> print(getfenv(DoNothing1) == EmptyTbl1)
true
> print(getfenv(DoNothing2) == EmptyTbl2)
true
```

You cannot alter an environment of a function not written in Lua, as shown here:

```
> -- This causes an error because print is written in C:
> setfenv(print, {})
stdin:1: 'setfenv' cannot change environment of given object
stack traceback:
        [C]: in function 'setfenv'
        stdin:1: in main chunk
        [C]: ?
```

This restriction is to protect functions written in low-level languages like C (which have much more power to mess things up) from unauthorized meddling by Lua functions.

Like many restrictions in Lua, this one can be bypassed with the debug library, described in Chapter 10.

There is a way, though, for you to set the environment used by the bottom frame of the stack. You'll learn how to do this in a moment, but first, here's a bit of background. The bottom frame of the stack is always in C (which is why stack tracebacks always end with "[C]: ?"). Its environment is called the *global environment*. (This term is a bit confusing because all references to global variables are resolved by looking in an environment, but even if various functions/stack frames have different environments, only one of them is the *global* environment.)

If you try to change the global environment by figuring out what stack level it's at, you'll get the same error given previously when you tried to give setfenv the print function:

```
> setfenv(2, {})
stdin:1: 'setfenv' cannot change environment of given object
stack traceback:
        [C]: in function 'setfenv'
        stdin:1: in main chunk
        [C]: ?
```

The way to work around this is to use the magic number 0 as the first argument to setfenv. Chunks typed into the interpreter inherit the global environment. Then you set the global environment to a table with nothing in it but _G (the original global environment). After you do this, every chunk inherits that environment and thus can't access the standard global variables under their usual names. For example:

```
> setfenv(0, {_G = _G})
> -- Error message won't have tracebacks, as explained below.
> print("This won't work.")
stdin:1: attempt to call global 'print' (a nil value)
> _G.print("This won't either, since print calls tostring.")
attempt to call a nil value
> tostring = _G.tostring
> _G.print("Now that tostring is in place, this will work.")
Now that tostring is in place, this will work.
> -- Undo the damage by putting the original global
> -- environment back in place:
> _G.setfenv(0, _G)
> print("This works again!")
This works again!
```

Note the following in this example:

❑   Although you can't access it with setfenv or getfenv, print has its own environment. That environment is unaffected by changing the global environment, because it is the original global environment, inherited by print when it was created. If print looked for tostring, it would find it, but it looks instead in the current global environment, where tostring is nil. (There's no hidden meaning to print looking in the global environment rather than its own; that's just how it was written.)

❑   The error message has no stack traceback. That's because the stack traceback is created by calling the function debug.traceback. When the interpreter sees that this function is missing, it doesn't even try to call it.

setfenv returns the function whose environment it just set, or nothing if it's used to set the global environment, as shown here:

```
> DoNothing = function() end
> print(setfenv(DoNothing, _G) == DoNothing)
true
> print(select("#", setfenv(0, _G)))
0
```

In Lua 5.0, setfenv *never returns a value.*

If getfenv is passed a non-Lua function, it returns the global environment (not that function's real environment).

A function returned by loadstring (or by one of its cousins load and loadfile) inherits the current global environment.

_G is just a regular global variable, with no magic behavior. When Lua starts up, it puts the global environment into _G, but if the global environment is changed to a different table, _G is not updated, and if you put a different table into _G, no environments are changed. _G is purely a convenience, and in the previous examples, it saved you from having to type a lot of getfenv(0).

Summary

In this chapter, you examined tables and some other things that are easier to understand in relation to tables. What you learned included the following:

❑ Tables are collections of key-value pairs, and they are Lua's only data structure.

❑ Curly braces are used to create tables; square brackets and dots are used to read and assign to table fields.

❑ There is no difference between a key not existing in a table, and that key existing but being associated with the value nil.

❑ You can use tables as arrays by using consecutive integer keys (starting at one).

❑ You can use pairs and ipairs with the generic for to loop through tables.

❑ The table global variable contains a table, which in turn contains functions useful for dealing with tables (as in table.sort).

❑ The colon syntax makes writing in an object-oriented style more convenient.

❑ You can access the extra arguments of a vararg function with . . . (the vararg expression). You can use the select and unpack functions when dealing with vararg functions.

❑ All chunks are compiled into functions. For example, scripts are vararg functions, which allows access to their command-line arguments.

❑ Tables are mutable, so that when you alter a table's contents, it is still the same table.

❑ pairs and ipairs are iterator factories. You can write iterator factories of your own.

❑   Global variables are stored in tables called environments. You use the `getfenv` and `setfenv` functions to manipulate these environments.

Numeric, string, Boolean, and `nil` values; operators; expressions; statements; control structures; functions; tables — these are the building blocks of Lua and, as now that you know them, you know Lua.

You may have noticed that through this and the previous two chapters, there were an increasing proportion of examples that look like they could be useful in real programs. This trend continues in the next chapter, which has lots of code relevant to the real world — code for searching, matching, substituting, and otherwise manipulating strings and their characters and substrings. First, though, try the exercises for this chapter (answers are in the appendix).

Exercises

1.   In your head, figure out what the following prints:

```
A = {}
B = "C"
C = "B"
D = {
   [A] = {B = C},
   [B] = {[C] = B},
   [C] = {[A] = A}}
print(D.C["B"])
```

2.   By default, `table.sort` uses < to compare array elements, so it can only sort arrays of numbers or arrays of strings. Write a comparison function that allows `table.sort` to sort arrays of mixed types. In the sorted array, all values of a given type should be grouped together. Within each such group, numbers and strings should be sorted as usual, and other types should be sorted in some arbitrary but consistent way.

Test the function out on an array like this:

```
{{}, {}, {}, "", "a", "b", "c", 1, 2, 3, -100, 1.1,
   function() end, function() end, false, false, true}
```

3.   The `print` function converts all its arguments to strings, separates them with tab characters, and outputs them, along with a trailing newline. Write a function that, instead of giving that as output, returns it as a string, so that the following:

```
Sprint("Hi", {}, nil)
```

returns this:

```
"Hi\ttable: 0x484048\tnil\n"
```

which, if printed, would look like this:

```
Hi      table: 0x484048 nil
```

4. In `ring.lua`, the `RotateL` method only rotates its object one element to the left, as shown here:

```
-- Rotates self to the left:
function Methods:RotateL()
  if #self > 0 then
    self.Pos = OneMod(self.Pos + 1, #self)
  end
end
```

Rewrite it to take an optional numeric argument (defaulting to 1) and rotate the object by that many elements. (This requires neither a loop nor recursion.)

5. Write a stateful iterator generator, `SortedPairs`, that behaves just like `pairs`, except that it goes through key-value pairs in order by key. Use the `CompAll` function from exercise 2 to sort the keys.

Using Strings

The last chapter covered tables and the table library. You already know strings, but you don't know the string library, and that's the main topic of this chapter. Among many other things, you'll learn about the following:

❏   Converting between uppercase and lowercase

❏   Getting individual characters and substrings out of strings

❏   Getting user input

❏   Reading from and writing to files

❏   Doing pattern matching and replacement on strings (which is very powerful, and accounts for more than half of the chapter)

Basic String Conversion Functions

Many of the functions in the string library take a single string argument (and, in a few cases, one or two numeric arguments) and return a single string. In the following example, string.lower takes a string and returns a string that's the same except that any uppercase letters have been converted to lowercase:

```
> print(string.lower("HELLO there!"))
hello there!
```

Of course, string.lower doesn't care if the string given to it contains no uppercase letters, or no letters at all — it just returns the same string as shown here:

```
> print(string.lower("hello there!"))
hello there!
> print(string.lower("1 2 3 4"))
1 2 3 4
```

You may occasionally find yourself doing something like the following, and wondering why `Str` hasn't been changed to `"abc"`:

```
> Str = "ABC"
> string.lower(Str)
> print(Str)
ABC
```

If you think about it, you'll see that this is because strings are immutable, so it's impossible for a function like `string.lower` to work by side effect the way functions like `table.sort` do. Instead, `string.lower` (and all string functions) works by return value:

```
> Str = "ABC"
> Str = string.lower(Str)
> print(Str)
abc
```

It's convenient to say things like "`string.lower` converts any uppercase characters in a string to lowercase" (instead of the previous wordier "takes a string and returns a string" phrasing). Saying it this way doesn't mean that `string.lower` changes the characters right in the string itself, which is impossible. Rather, the conversion process creates a new string, which is the function's return value.

`string.upper` is the obvious counterpart to `string.lower`:

```
> print(string.upper("HELLO there!"))
HELLO THERE!
```

Both `string.lower` and `string.upper` use the current locale to decide what characters are uppercase or lowercase letters. There's a short example of this later in this chapter.

`string.reverse` reverses a string, character by character, like this:

```
> print(string.reverse("desserts"))
stressed
```

> *Lua 5.0 didn't have `string.reverse`. It can be written by looping through a string backwards, putting its characters in an array, and passing that array to `table.concat`.*

`string.rep` takes a string and a number, and repeats the string that many times, like this:

```
> print(string.rep("a", 5))
aaaaa
> print(string.rep("Hubba", 2))
HubbaHubba
```

`string.sub` returns a substring of the string given to it. The second and third arguments of `string.sub` are the (one-based) numeric positions of the desired first and last characters. For example:

```
> Str = "alphaBRAVOcharlie"
> print(string.sub(Str, 1, 5))
alpha
> print(string.sub(Str, 6, 10))
BRAVO
```

```
> print(string.sub(Str, 11, 17))
charlie
```

Negative numbers can be used as positions: -1 means the last character in the string, -2 means the second-to-last, and so on:

```
> print(string.sub(Str, -7, -1))
charlie
> print(string.sub(Str, 6, -8))
BRAVO
> print(string.sub(Str, -17, 5))
alpha
```

All of the built-in functions that take character positions understand negative ones.

If string.sub's last argument is omitted, it defaults to -1 (or, equivalently, the length of the string), as follows:

```
> print(string.sub(Str, 1))
alphaBRAVOcharlie
> print(string.sub(Str, -7))
charlie
```

String Length

string.len (like the # operator) returns the length of the string given to it. For example:

```
> print(string.len(""))
0
> print(string.len("ABCDE"))
5
```

Converting Between Characters and Character Codes

string.byte returns the numerical byte values used by your system to represent the characters of the substring specified (string.sub-style) by its second and third arguments. For example:

```
> print(string.byte("ABCDE", 1, 5))
65       66       67       68       69
> print(string.byte("ABCDE", 2, -2))
66       67       68
```

The third argument defaults to the value of the second argument (so only one character's byte value is returned):

```
> print(string.byte("ABCDE", 2))
66
```

```
> print(string.byte("ABCDE", -1))
69
```

`string.byte` is often called with only one argument, in which case the second argument defaults to 1:

```
> print(string.byte("ABCDE"))
65
> print(string.byte("A"))
65
```

The Lua 5.0 `string.byte` *only took two arguments and therefore never returned more than one value.*

`string.char` takes integers like those returned by `string.byte` and returns a string composed of those characters, as follows:

```
> print(string.char(65))
A
> print(string.char(65, 65, 66, 66))
AABB
```

If called with no arguments, it returns the empty string.

The byte values used by `string.byte` and `string.char` are not necessarily the same from system to system. Most of the examples in this book assume that ASCII characters have their ASCII values. (If this is not true on your system, you probably know it.)

Formatting Strings and Numbers with string.format

The code you've seen and written so far has formatted its output using string concatenation: `tostring`, and the automatic insertion of tabs with `print`. A more powerful tool for formatting output is `string.format`, which can do the following:

❑   Pad strings with spaces and pad numbers with spaces or zeros

❑   Output numbers in hexadecimal or in octal (base 8)

❑   Trim extra characters from a string

❑   Left- or right-justify output within columns

Try It Out   Outputting Data in Columns

Imagine you have a bulletin board system, and you want a report of how many new posts and replies to existing posts each user has made. If you wanted to read this report in a web browser, you could format it as HTML, but if you want to read it on the command line or in a text editor, then it'll be easier to read if you format it in columns. (This works only with fixed-width fonts like Courier or Fixedsys, which you should be using to read and write code anyway.)

1. Define the following function:

```
-- Prints a report of posts per user:
function Report(Users)
  print("USERNAME       NEW POSTS  REPLIES")
  for Username, User in pairs(Users) do
    print(string.format("%-15s  %6d    %6d",
      Username, User.NewPosts, User.Replies))
  end
end
```

2. Run it as follows:

```
Report({
  arundelo = {NewPosts = 39, Replies = 19},
  kwj = {NewPosts = 22, Replies = 81},
  leethax0r = {NewPosts = 5325, Replies = 0}})
```

The output should be this:

```
USERNAME       NEW POSTS  REPLIES
arundelo              39       19
leethax0r           5325        0
kwj                   22       81
```

How It Works

The `string.format` function takes as its first argument a *format string* that includes *format placeholders* like `"%-15s"` and `"%6d"`. It returns a string constructed by replacing the placeholders by the rest of the `string.format` arguments.

All format placeholders start with the `%` character. A placeholder that ends in the character `s` inserts the corresponding arguments as a string:

```
> print(string.format("-->%s<--", "arundelo"))
-->arundelo<--
```

A number that's between the `%` and the `s` uses spaces to pad the string out to that many characters:

```
> print(string.format("-->%15s<--", "arundelo"))
-->       arundelo<--
```

A - (minus sign) in front of the number left-justifies the string:

```
> print(string.format("-->%-15s<--", "arundelo"))
-->arundelo       <--
```

A placeholder that ends in the character `d` inserts the corresponding argument as a decimal integer:

```
> print(string.format("-->%d<--", 39))
-->39<--
```

A number in between the % and the d uses spaces to pad the number out to that many characters (numbers can also be left-justified just like strings, but that's not done in this example):

```
> print(string.format("-->%6d<--", 39))
-->    39<--
```

There should be a one-to-one correspondence between placeholders and extra arguments ("extra arguments" here refer to arguments after the format string). The first placeholder corresponds to the first extra argument, the second placeholder to the second extra argument, and so on:

```
> print(string.format("%-15s  %6d   %6d", "arundelo", 39, 19))
arundelo           39     19
```

Apart from its ability to format strings and numbers to certain lengths, string.format is also a useful alternative to string concatenation. Both of the following two lines insert the variables Link and LinkText into an HTML <a> (anchor) element. The second has the disadvantage of greater length, but it's arguably more readable, especially after your eye gets used to picking out the two format placeholders:

```
Anchor = '<a href="' .. Link .. '">' .. LinkText .. '</a>'
```

```
Anchor = string.format('<a href="%s">%s</a>', Link, LinkText)
```

This readability advantage ramps up the more alternating literal strings and variables you're dealing with. If you find yourself using string.format a lot in a particular piece of code, you can give it a shorter name, like this:

```
local Fmt = string.format
```

A single percent sign in string.format's output is represented by two consecutive ones in the format string, as in the following example. This %% pseudo-placeholder is the only exception to the one-to-one correspondence between format placeholders and the rest of the string.format arguments:

```
> print(string.format("We gave %d%%!", 110))
We gave 110%!
```

When necessary, string.format converts strings to numbers and numbers to strings, but any other conversions need to be done by hand. For example:

```
> print(string.format("%d-%s", "50", 50))
50-50
> print(string.format("%s", {}))
stdin:1: bad argument #2 to 'format' (string expected, got table)
stack traceback:
        [C]: in function 'format'
        stdin:1: in main chunk
        [C]: ?
> print(string.format("%s", tostring({})))
table: 0x4927e8
```

The %d placeholder only works for integers. For fractional numbers, use `%f` as follows:

```
> print(string.format("We gave %f percent!", 99.44))
We gave 99.440000 percent!
```

By default, six digits are printed after the decimal point. To control this, supply a *precision*, which should be an integer preceded by a dot. For example:

```
> print(string.format("%.0f | %.1f | %.2f | %.3f",
>>    99.44, 99.44, 99.44, 99.44))
99 | 99.4 | 99.44 | 99.440
```

If there's a *width* (the number used to control column widths in the previous Try-It-Out example), put it before the precision. The width includes any digits after the decimal point, and the decimal point itself, if there is one. Here's an example:

For readability, this example uses a square-bracket string, as covered in Chapter 2.

```
> print(string.format([[
>> -->%5.0f<-- width: 5; precision: 0
>> -->%5.1f<-- width: 5; precision: 1
>> -->%5.2f<-- width: 5; precision: 2]], 99.44, 99.44, 99.44))
-->   99<-- width: 5; precision: 0
--> 99.4<-- width: 5; precision: 1
-->99.44<-- width: 5; precision: 2
```

If either a string or a number is longer than the width allotted for it, it will spill over — no characters or digits will be removed:

```
> -- Print some usernames in a 15-character column:
> print(string.format([[
>> -->%-15s<--
>> -->%-15s<--
>> -->%-15s<--
>> -->%-15s<--]],
>>    "arundelo", "kwj", "leethax0r", "reallylongusername"))
-->arundelo       <--
-->kwj            <--
-->leethax0r      <--
-->reallylongusername<--
> -- Print various numbers in a 4-character column:
> print(string.format([[
>> -->%6.1f<--
>> -->%6.1f<--
>> -->%6.1f<--]], 1, 99.44, 123456789))
-->   1.0<--
-->  99.4<--
-->123456789.0<--
```

If you give a `%s` placeholder a precision, it's treated as a maximum width—characters will be trimmed from the end of the string to make it fit. The following strings are printed with a width (the minimum width) of 2 and a precision (the maximum width) of 2:

```
> print(string.format([[
>> -->%2.2s<--
>> -->%2.2s<--
>> -->%2.2s<--]], "a", "ab", "abc"))
--> a<--
-->ab<--
-->ab<--
```

Along with the – (left-justification) character, you can place the following characters right after the percent sign (that is, before the width and precision, if any):

```
> -- "+" -- all numbers are printed with a sign:
> print(string.format("%+d", 1))
+1
> -- " " -- use a space if a sign is omitted on a positive
> -- number:
> print(string.format("% d", 1))
 1
> -- "0" -- pad numbers with zeros instead of spaces:
> print(string.format("%05d", 1))
00001
> -- "#" -- various uses -- with %f, output always has a
> -- decimal point; with %x, output always has "0x":
> print(string.format("%#.0f", 1))
1.
> print(string.format("%#x", 31))
0x1f
```

These characters don't have to be in any particular order when combined. For example:

```
> print(string.format("-->%-+5d<--", 11))
-->+11  <--
> print(string.format("-->%+-5d<--", 11))
-->+11  <--
```

The `%q` placeholder ("q" stands for quote) surrounds a string with double quotes, backslash-escapes any double quotes, backslashes, or newlines in it, and converts any zero bytes to `"\\000"`:

```
> print(string.format("%q", [[backslash: \; double quote: "]]))
"backslash: \\; double quote: \""
> print(string.format("%q", "\0\n"))
"\000\
"
```

In other words, it converts a string into a representation of that string usable in Lua source code:

```
> WeirdStr = "\"\\\n\0"
> Fnc = loadstring(string.format("return %q", WeirdStr))
```

```
> print(Fnc() == WeirdStr)
true
```

This lets you save data for subsequent use by formatting it as a valid Lua script and putting it into a file. When you want to retrieve the data, you load the file into a string, pass it to loadstring, and call the resulting function. (You'll see how to save and load files in the next section.)

This kind of data file can consist of a single return statement (like the string passed to loadstring in the previous example). It can also be a series of function calls whose arguments are the data in question, like this:

```
Record{Username = "arundelo", NewPosts = 39, Replies = 19}
Record{Username = "kwj", NewPosts = 22, Replies = 81}
Record{Username = "leethax0r", NewPosts = 5325, Replies = 0}
```

The function called (Record in this example) is one that you define to do what's necessary to make the data available to the main program. If this function is given to the loadstring function by setfenv, then there's no need for the data file to have access to any other functions.

If you want to save a table, you need to build up a string by splicing together the table's keys and values with the appropriate curly braces, square brackets, commas, and so on. Chapter 7 has an example of this.

Other common placeholders include %x and %X for hexadecimal output, %o for octal output, %e and %E for scientific notation, %g and %G for automatic selection between scientific notation and standard notation, and %i, which is just a synonym for %d. Here are some examples:

```
> print(string.format("%%x: %x\t%%o: %o", 31, 31))
%x: 1f   %o: 37
> print(string.format("%%e: %e\t%%g: %g", 3.1, 3.1))
%e: 3.100000e+00        %g: 3.1
> print(string.format("%%e: %e\t%%g: %g", 11 ^ 13, 11 ^ 13))
%e: 3.452271e+13        %g: 3.45227e+13
```

Placeholders that come in both uppercase and lowercase differ only in the case of any letters they might print. For example:

```
> print(string.format("%x, %X", 255, 255))
ff, FF
```

More detail on format strings is available in books on the C programming language, because the string.format format placeholders are almost exactly the same as those used by the C language's printf family of functions.

The differences are as follows: C doesn't understand the %q placeholder, and Lua doesn't understand the h, L, or l modifiers, the %n or %p placeholders, or the * character used as a width or precision. To compensate for the second difference, you can build a format string in Lua at run time.

A lot of string.format's work is actually done by the C function sprintf. This means that you should not include any "\0" characters in strings you give to string.format (unless they'll be formatted by %q placeholders).

179

Input/Output

It's time to take a brief break from the string library, and detour through the topic of *input/output* (I/O). You've already used `print` for output, but `print` does things in addition to output data — it converts everything to strings, separates multiple arguments with tabs, and appends a newline. This is convenient for debugging because you can see what values a function returns, but a more fundamental output function is `io.write`. This function expects all of its arguments to be strings or numbers, and it outputs each of the arguments without adding anything. The > character that appears to be at the end of the following output is really just the Lua prompt — it didn't get put on its own line because no newline was outputted:

```
> Str1, Str2 = "Alpha", "Bravo"
> io.write(Str1, Str2)
AlphaBravo>
```

Here's the same thing, with a space and a newline:

```
> io.write(Str1, " ", Str2, "\n")
Alpha Bravo
>
```

And in the following, `io.write` is used like a `print` that uses neither the concatenation operator nor `table.concat`; (trace its execution for a few sample arguments so that you can see how it works, especially how it builds one line of output with several iterations of `io.write`):

```
function Print(...)
  local ArgCount = select("#", ...)
  for I = 1, ArgCount do
    -- Only print a separator if one argument has already
    -- been printed:
    if I > 1 then
      io.write("\t")
    end
    io.write(tostring(select(I, ...)))
  end
  io.write("\n")
end
```

The function `io.read` reads (by default) one line of input. Call it like so:

```
Line = io.read()
```

Your cursor will move to the next line, but there'll be no Lua prompt. Type some random text and press Enter. The Lua prompt will reappear. Print `Line` and you'll see that it contains whatever you typed.

To write to or read from a file, you need a *handle* to that file. A file handle is an object with methods like `write` and `read`. Getting a handle to a file is called *opening* the file.

Writing to and Reading from a File

The following example will write to a file named `test.txt` in your current directory. (If you already have a file of this name that you don't want overwritten, move it or use a different name.) Do the following in the interpreter:

```
> FileHnd, ErrStr = io.open("test.txt", "w")
> print(FileHnd, ErrStr)
file (0x485ad4) nil
> FileHnd:write("Line 1\nLine 2\nLine 3\n")
> FileHnd:close()
> FileHnd, ErrStr = io.open("test.txt")
> print(FileHnd, ErrStr)
file (0x485ad4) nil
> print(FileHnd:read())
Line 1
> print(FileHnd:read())
Line 2
> print(FileHnd:read())
Line 3
> print(FileHnd:read())
nil
> FileHnd:close()
> print(os.remove("test.txt"))
true
```

The first `io.open` argument is the name of the file to be opened. Its second argument, `"w"`, means that the file will be opened in *write mode*, making it possible to write to it but not read from it. If the file is successfully opened, a handle to it will be returned, but if for some reason it can't be opened, then it returns a `nil` value and an error message. (You can print the file handle and the error message in the context of an actual program with something like `"if FileHnd then"`. There's an example of this in the next chapter.)

The file handle has a `write` method, which works just like `io.write`, but writes to the file instead of your screen. The following line writes three lines (each one terminated with a newline character) to the file:

```
FileHnd:write("Line 1\nLine 2\nLine 3\n")
```

After this, calling the file handle's `close` method *closes* the file. This ensures that all output actually makes it to the hard drive, and that any system resources associated with the open file aren't tied up any longer than they need to be. After the file is closed, an attempt to use any of the handle's methods will cause an error.

Next, the file is reopened, but this time in read mode instead of write mode. (The second `io.open` argument defaults to `"r"`.)

The first three times `FileHnd:read` is called, it returns the file's three lines, one after the other. Notice that the newline characters marking the ends of these lines are *not* returned. (You can tell this because, if they were returned, then `print` would appear to print an extra blank line after each line.)

The fourth time `FileHnd:read` is called, it returns `nil`, which means that the end of the file has been reached. The file is then closed with `FileHnd:close` and removed with `os.remove`, whose return value of `true` just means that the removal was successful. If you skip the removal step, you can look at `test.txt` in your text editor.

The first character of the second `io.open` argument must be an `r` (for read mode), a `w` (for write mode, which discards any contents the file may have already had), or an `a` (for append mode, which writes to the end of the file, preserving any previous contents). This letter can optionally be followed by (in any order) a "+" character and/or a "b" character. Including `"+"` opens the file in one of three different versions of read/write mode, depending on the first letter. Including `"b"` opens the file in *binary mode* (specifically binary read, binary write, or binary append mode).

There's more discussion of the distinction between binary mode and text mode (the default) in Chapter 13, but here's the essence. Some systems use something other than `"\n"` to mark the end of a line. Lua (actually, the C I/O library that Lua uses) does a translation that lets you ignore this and always use `"\n"`. That's a good thing, but if you're working with a file that isn't text, and you don't want the library messing with any bytes that happen to look like end-of-line markers, or if you have to deal with text files that were created on a system with a different end-of-line convention, a mode string with `"b"` turns off this translation.

If given no arguments, `read` (either `io.read` or the `read` method of a file handle) reads and returns one line (with no trailing `"\n"`) or returns `nil` on end-of-file. If it's given an argument, the argument should be one of the following:

Argument	Description
`"*l"`	Reads and returns one line (with no trailing `"\n"`) or returns `nil` on end-of-file.
`"*a"`	Reads and returns the whole file, minus anything that's already been read. This will be the empty string if the whole file has already been read.
`"*n"`	Reads and returns a number, or returns nil if a number can't be read (possibly because there's something other than whitespace that needs to be read first before a number can be reached).
a number	Reads and returns a string with this many characters (or less, if end-of-file is reached). If end-of-file is reached without needing to read any characters, nil is returned.

`read` can be given multiple arguments, in which case it reads and returns multiple values.

The I/O library supplies the following three pre-opened file handles to virtual files (things that act like files, but don't actually reside on the hard disk):

❑ `io.stdin` is the *standard input* file handle (read-only). By default, it reads from the keyboard. `io.stdin:read` acts the same as `io.read`.

❑ `io.stdout` is the *standard output* file handle (write-only). By default, it writes to the screen. `io.stdout:write` acts the same as `io.write`.

❑ `io.stderr` is the *standard error* file handle (write-only). By default, it too writes to the screen.

Now that you know the basics of I/O, you can write a script that works with files.

Try It Out   Sorting and Eliminating Duplicate Lines in a File

1. Create a file with the following contents, and save it as **sortuniq.lua**:

```lua
-- This script outputs all unique lines of a file, sorted.
-- It does no error checking!
--
-- Usage:
--
--    lua sortuniq.lua INFILE OUTFILE
--
-- If OUTFILE is not given, standard output will be used.  If
-- no arguments are given, standard input and standard output
-- will be used.

-- Like pairs, but loops in order by key.  (Unlike the
-- version in Chapter 4, this only handles all-string or
-- all-numeric keys.)
function SortedPairs(Tbl)
  local Sorted = {} -- A (soon to be) sorted array of Tbl's keys.
  for Key in pairs(Tbl) do
    Sorted[#Sorted + 1] = Key
  end
  table.sort(Sorted)
  local I = 0

  -- The iterator itself:
  return function()
    I = I + 1
    local Key = Sorted[I]
    return Key, Tbl[Key]
  end
end

function Main(InFilename, OutFilename)
  -- Make the lines of the input file (standard input if no
  -- name was given) keys of a table:
  local Lines = {}
  local Iter = InFilename and io.lines(InFilename) or io.lines()
  for Line in Iter do
    Lines[Line] = true
  end
  -- Get a handle to the output file (standard output if no
  -- name was given):
  local OutHnd = OutFilename
    and io.open(OutFilename, "w")
    or io.stdout
  -- Write each line in Lines to the output file, in order:
  for Line in SortedPairs(Lines) do
    OutHnd:write(Line, "\n")
  end
  OutHnd:close()
end

Main(...)
```

2. Create a file with the following contents, and save it as **testin.txt**:

```
bravo
alpha
charlie
alpha
charlie
charlie
alpha
```

3. At your shell, type this:

```
lua sortuniq.lua testin.txt testout.txt
```

4. Open the `testout.txt` file in your text editor. Here's what it should contain:

```
alpha
bravo
charlie
```

How It Works

`io.lines` is an iterator factory. If given a filename, it opens that file and returns an iterator that loops through all lines in the file. If called with no argument, it returns an iterator that loops through all lines found on standard input (by default, the lines you type).

`sortuniq.lua` is written to use either of these. If no input file is given as a command-line argument, `io.lines` would be called with no argument and loop through standard input. In the previous example, though, `InFilename` is `testin.txt`, each line of which is made a key in the table `Lines` inside the loop. This has the effect of ignoring duplicate lines:

```lua
local Lines = {}
local Iter = InFilename and io.lines(InFilename) or io.lines()
for Line in Iter do
  Lines[Line] = true
end
```

When the iterator hits the end of `testin.txt`, it closes the file right before the loop is exited. Next, `testout.txt` (the file named by `OutFilename`) is opened. Again, the following is done so that standard output will be used if no output file was specified on the command line:

```lua
local OutHnd = OutFilename
  and io.open(OutFilename, "w")
  or io.stdout
```

Next, the `SortedPairs` function loops through `Lines` in order by key, and each key is written to `testout.txt`, along with a newline — the `io.lines` iterator, like `io.read`, doesn't include newlines on the lines it returns:

```lua
for Line in SortedPairs(Lines) do
  OutHnd:write(Line, "\n")
end
```

Finally, `testout.txt` is closed and the program is exited.

If you don't supply an output file at the command line, then standard output is used, which means the output will get written right to your screen (as though io.write had been used instead of OutHnd:write). If you also omit the input file, then standard input is used, which means you can type the input instead of saving it in a file. (Use Ctrl+D or Ctrl+Z to send an EOF when you're done typing.)

Omitting the filenames also lets you use your shell's *redirection operators* (<, >, and |) to make standard input come from a file or another program instead of your keyboard, and standard output go to a file or another program instead of your screen. For example, the following code:

```
lua sortuniq.lua < testin.txt > testout.txt
```

does the same thing as this:

```
lua sortuniq.lua testin.txt testout.txt
```

except that in the version with < and >, the shell opens testin.txt and testout.txt and sortuniq.lua just uses standard input and standard output.

This script does no error checking. If, for instance, the output file can't be created or is read-only, then the io.open will fail, and output will default to standard output with no explanation of why that happened. You'll learn how to check for and handle errors in the next chapter, but for now just remember that most I/O library functions will return nil and an error string if something unexpected happens.

For example, a file's write function simply triggers an error when you give it bad arguments or use it with a closed file, but when it doesn't trigger an error, it returns true or nil depending on whether it successfully wrote what you wanted it to write. If it returns a nil then the second return value will be an error message. Accidentally writing to a file opened in read mode gives the cryptic "No error", and writing to a disk drive that has no more space might give an error message like "No space left on device". The former is just a programmer error, but the latter is something that the program can't prevent. If a program doesn't check the write return values, it won't know if something like this happens. That's fine for scripts where the likelihood or harmfulness of a disk drive filling up is small, for example, but something mission-critical may merit more care.

Some functions (such as io.open), are more likely to fail in this way, so their return values should always be checked, except in interactive use or quick-and-dirty scripts where you can spot problems and fix them on the fly.

> *When an I/O function returns nil and an error message, it also returns, as an undocumented third value, the numeric error code from C. Later in this chapter, you'll find out about the implications of using undocumented features.*

Pattern-Matching

Other than the string.dump function (to be covered in Chapter 10), the rest of the functions in the string library are all for finding or replacing substrings. (In some cases, the substring being searched for is the entire string being searched.) A string being searched is called a *subject*. A substring to be searched for is specified with a string called a *pattern*, and the substring, if found, is called a *match*.

Searching for a Specific String

A single pattern can have different matches. For example, a pattern that searched for "sequences of 1 or more whitespace characters" would match both the `" "` and `"\t\n\t\n"` substrings, among others. However, you can also use a pattern to search for one specific match. In the simplest case, such a pattern is identical to the substring it matches, like this one:

```
> Str = "The rain in Spain stays mainly in the plain."
> print(string.gsub(Str, "ai", "oy"))
The royn in Spoyn stays moynly in the ployn.         4
```

`string.gsub` searches its first argument (the subject) for substrings that match the pattern given as its second argument, and replaces any that it finds with its third argument. Thus every occurence of `"ai"` in `Str` is replaced with `"oy"`. As a second result, `string.gsub` returns the number of substitutions done (4 in this case).

> `gsub` *stands for global substitute. It's global because all matches are replaced, not just the first one.*

If there are no matches, then no substitutions are done, meaning that `string.gsub` returns the subject and `0`. Here's an example:

```
> print(string.gsub("A shrew in Kew glues newbies to a pew.",
>>    "ai", "oy"))
A shrew in Kew glues newbies to a pew.  0
```

If a fourth argument is given, then at most that many substitutions are done (starting from the beginning of the string), like this:

```
> Str = "The rain in Spain stays mainly in the plain."
> print(string.gsub(Str, "ai", "oy", 2))
The royn in Spoyn stays mainly in the plain.         2
> print(string.gsub(Str, "ai", "oy", 999))
The royn in Spoyn stays moynly in the ployn.         4
```

The replacement string can be a different length than the pattern, as shown here:

```
> print(string.gsub(Str, "ai", "izzai"))
The rizzain in Spizzain stays mizzainly in the plizzain.    4
```

In particular, replacing matches with the empty string deletes them. For example:

```
> print(string.gsub(Str, "ai", ""))
The rn in Spn stays mnly in the pln.         4
```

Matching Any of Several Characters

How often have you been buying something online and seen a message like "when entering credit card number, please enter only numbers without spaces or dashes"? This is *bad programming* — a user should be able to enter their credit card number with separators, so they can more easily double-check it. It takes only a few lines of code to allow this and still make sure the user didn't type in something that obviously isn't a credit card number.

Try It Out   **Validating Credit Card Numbers**

1.   Define the following function:

```
-- Returns Str without any whitespace or separators, or nil
-- if Str doesn't satisfy a simple validity test:
function ValidateCreditCard(Str)
  Str = string.gsub(Str, "[ /,.-]", "")
  return string.find(Str, "^%d%d%d%d%d%d%d%d%d%d%d%d%d%d%d%d$")
    and Str
end
```

2.   Test it out like this:

```
> print(ValidateCreditCard("1234123412341234"))
1234123412341234
> print(ValidateCreditCard("1234 1234 1234 1234"))
1234123412341234
> print(ValidateCreditCard("1234-1234-1234-1234"))
1234123412341234
> print(ValidateCreditCard("1234-1234-1234-123"))
nil
> print(ValidateCreditCard("221B Baker Street"))
nil
```

How It Works

This example introduces several new concepts. The first one is that a pattern can include *bracket classes*, which are lists of characters enclosed by square brackets. The bracket class [/,.-] matches a character if it's a space, a slash, a comma, a dot, or a dash:

```
> print(string.gsub("The rain? -- the plain!", "[ /,.-]", ""))
Therain?theplain!       6
```

The user can use any of those characters as separators, anywhere in the credit card number, and `string.gsub` will remove them, but leave intact any digits, letters, or other characters:

```
Str = string.gsub(Str, "[ /,.-]", "")
```

After separators have been removed, the string will be considered valid only if it's nothing more and nothing less than 16 digits. %d is shorthand for the bracket class [0123456789] — it matches any decimal digit:

```
> print(string.gsub("52 pickup", "%d", "Digit"))
DigitDigit pickup       2
> print(string.gsub("52 pickup", "%d%d", "TwoDigits"))
TwoDigits pickup        1
```

Patterns can include %d and other combinations of the percent sign with other characters. Although they look the same, these are unrelated to string.format *placeholders.*

If a pattern's first character is ^ (a caret), it means that the rest of the pattern will only match at the beginning of the subject. In this example, not only is "ab" contained in "abc", but "ab" is right at the beginning of "abc", so a substitution is made:

```
> print(string.gsub("abc", "^ab", "XX"))
XXc     1
```

In the next example, "bc" is contained in "abc", but it's not right at the beginning, so no substitution is made:

```
> print(string.gsub("abc", "^bc", "XX"))
abc     0
```

The caret is said to *anchor* the pattern at the beginning. A pattern is anchored at the end if it ends with $ (a dollar sign):

```
> print(string.gsub("abc", "ab$", "XX"))
abc     0
> print(string.gsub("abc", "bc$", "XX"))
aXX     1
```

So the pattern "^%d%d%d%d%d%d%d%d%d%d%d%d%d%d%d%d$", anchored both at the beginning and the end, matches a subject only if it contains 16 digits and nothing else.

The function string.find returns the positions of the first and last character of the *first* match, or nil if there is no match:

```
> print(string.find("duck duck goose", "duck"))
1       4
> print(string.find("duck duck goose", "goose"))
11      15
> print(string.find("duck duck goose", "swan"))
nil
```

ValidateCreditCard, however, depends only on the fact that string.find's first result will be true if there's a match and nil if there's no match. When this result is anded with Str itself, the effect is that the function returns nil if Str is something other than 16 digits, and Str if it is 16 digits:

```
return string.find(Str, "^%d%d%d%d%d%d%d%d%d%d%d%d%d%d%d%d$")
   and Str
```

Characters like [, %, and ^ are called *magic* characters, because they have special meanings rather than representing themselves the way a standard character does (for example, "a"). To match a magic character, escape it with a percent sign. For example, "%[" matches "[", "%^" matches "^", "%%" matches "%", and so on, as follows:

```
> -- If not for the extra %, this would give an error message:
> print(string.gsub("90%, 100%, 110%", "110%%", "a lot!"))
90%, 100%, a lot!       1
```

```
> -- If not for the %, this would replace the zero-length
> -- string before the 3:
> print(string.gsub("3^10", "%^", " to the power of "))
3 to the power of 10    1
```

All magic characters are punctuation characters. This means that nonpunctuation characters—including letters, digits, whitespace, and control characters—always represent themselves and don't need to be percent-escaped.

Backslash-escaping is decoded when a chunk is compiled, so the pattern-matching functions don't even know about it. The pattern "\\" contains only one character (the backslash), which it matches. If you have trouble separating percent-escaping and backslash-escaping in your mind, you can quote the troublesome pattern with square brackets: [[\]].

Not all punctuation characters are magic, but a punctuation character (or any nonalphanumeric character) escaped by a percent sign always represents itself, whether it's normally magic or not. In the following example, both "@" and "%@" match the at-sign, which is not magic:

```
> print(string.gsub("somebody@example.com", "@", " AT "))
somebody AT example.com 1
> print(string.gsub("somebody@example.com", "%@", " AT "))
somebody AT example.com 1
```

The reasoning behind this is that anytime you want to match a punctuation character, you don't have to remember whether it's magic or not, you can just go ahead and escape it. This also applies to characters that are only magic in certain contexts. For example, the dollar sign has its magic anchoring meaning only at the very end of a pattern, and anywhere else it represents itself, but rather than thinking about that, you can feel free to escape it wherever it occurs if you don't want it to be magic. Here's how:

```
> print(string.gsub("I have $5.", "$%d", "some money"))
I have some money.      1
> print(string.gsub("I have $5.", "%$%d", "some money"))
I have some money.      1
```

The individual units of a pattern are called *pattern items*. Pattern items that produce matches that are one character in length are called *character classes*. Some character classes are themselves one character long ("a"), and some are longer ("%d", "[/, .-]").

In addition to character classes, you've seen pattern items with zero-character matches ("^" and "$"). In the next section, you'll see how to make pattern items whose matches are longer than one character. All this complexity can make it hard to decode patterns, but a useful technique is to write them down on scratch paper and break them into their elements. For example, you could diagram the "p[aeiou]t" pattern as shown in Figure 5-1.

If it wasn't obvious from the pattern itself, it's easy to see from this diagram that "p[aeiou]t" will match any of the character sequences "pat," "pet," "pit," "pot," and "put" (wherever they may occur in the subject, because there's no anchoring).

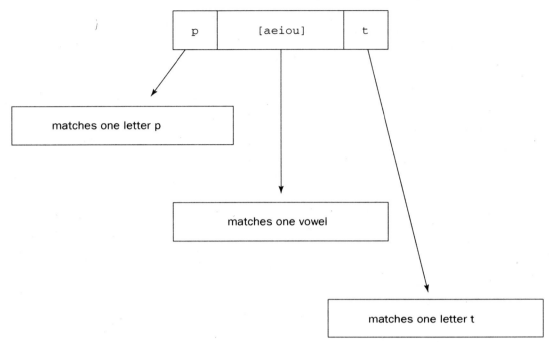

Figure 5-1

Bracket classes have a few other features. One is that you can specify a *range* of characters, with the lowest character in the range followed by a - (hyphen) character and the highest character in the range (with "lowest" and "highest" being defined in terms of `string.byte`). In the following example, `"[0-4]"` is equivalent to `"[01234]"`, and `"[a-e]"` is equivalent to `"[abcde]"`:

```
> print(string.gsub("0123456789", "[0-4]", "n"))
nnnnn56789      5
> Str = "the quick brown fox jumps over the lazy dog"
> print(string.gsub(Str, "[a-e]", "!"))
th! qui!k !rown fox jumps ov!r th! l!zy !og     7
```

Actually, although `"[0-9]"` is guaranteed to match all and only the decimal digits, the meaning of other ranges is dependent on your system's character set. Chances are, however, that your system uses the ASCII character set or some superset of it, so that `"[a-z]"` matches all and only the 26 lowercase letters of the English alphabet, and `"[A-Z]"` matches the 26 uppercase letters. This will be assumed in the examples.

Because the hyphen has a magic meaning inside bracket classes, it generally needs to be escaped to be included in a bracket class: `"[a%-z]"` matches the letter a, the hyphen, and the letter z. The only reason that you didn't need to escape the hyphen in `"[ /,.-]"` (from the `ValidateCreditCard` example) because it did not have a character to its right, so it was in a nonmagical position. Alternatively, you could have written that bracket class as `"[ /,.%-]"`.

You can combine ranges with other ranges, and with other things in a bracket class. "[a-emnv-z]" matches the letters a through e, the letters m and n, and the letters v through z.

If a bracket class starts with ^ (a caret), it matches all characters that would *not* be matched without the caret. "[aeiou]" matches all vowels, so "[^aeiou]" matches any character that *isn't* a vowel in the following example:

```
> Str = "the quick brown fox jumps over the lazy dog"
> print(string.gsub(Str, "[^aeiou]", ""))
euioouoeeao     32
```

There are other character classes that, like "%d", use a percent sign followed by a letter and match some predefined category of characters. A complete list is provided later in the chapter, but here is an example that uses "%a" (letters), "%u" (uppercase letters), and "%l" (lowercase letters):

```
> Str = "abc Abc aBc abC ABc AbC aBC ABC"
> print(string.gsub(Str, "%u%l%l", "Xxx"))
abc Xxx aBc abC ABc AbC aBC ABC 1
> print(string.gsub(Str, "%a%a%a", "!!!"))
!!! !!! !!! !!! !!! !!! !!! !!! 8
```

Just as "%d" is another way of writing "[0-9]", "%l" is another way of writing "[a-z]" and "%a" is another way of writing "[A-Za-z]". Unlike bracket classes, which are based on your system's character set, character classes like "%a" are based on your system's locale settings, so they may give different results with non-English characters.

Unfortunately, a full explanation of locales and other character-encoding issues is outside the scope of this book, but the following example (which may not work as-is on your system) shows that the %a character class and the string.upper function use the current locale. The example uses the os.setlocale function to manipulate the ctype locale setting, which governs the categorization of characters:

```
> -- Change the ctype (character type) locale, saving the
> -- current one:
> OrigCtype = os.setlocale(nil, ctype)
> print(OrigCtype)
C
> -- Set the ctype locale to Brazilian Portuguese:
> print(os.setlocale("pt_BR", "ctype"))
pt_BR
> -- Test [A-Za-z] versus %a:
> Str = "Pontif\237cia Universidade Cat\243lica do Rio de Janeiro"
> print(Str)
Pontifícia Universidade Católica do Rio de Janeiro
> print(string.gsub(Str, "[A-Za-z]", "."))
......í... ............ ...ó.... .. ... .. ....... 42
> print(string.gsub(Str, "%a", "."))
.......... ............ ......... .. ... .. ....... 44
> -- Also test string.upper:
> print(string.upper(Str))
PONTIFÍCIA UNIVERSIDADE CATÓLICA DO RIO DE JANEIRO
```

```
> -- Go back to the original ctype locale:
> print(os.setlocale(OrigCtype, "ctype"))
C
> -- Test string.upper again, with the original ctype locale
> -- which, being "C", will not recognize the non-English
> -- characters:
> print(string.upper(Str))
PONTIFÍCIA UNIVERSIDADE CATóLICA DO RIO DE JANEIRO
```

Locales use 8-bit character encodings, where each character is one byte. A more flexible encoding system is Unicode. In Unicode's UTF-8 format, ASCII characters ("regular" characters) are one byte long and other characters are two or more bytes. Lua has no built-in support for Unicode (for example, it measures string length in bytes), but it does nothing to prevent you from using Unicode. In UTF-8, the character ı happens to be represented as "\195\173", so if the string "Pontif\195\173cia" is written to a file, and that file is opened with a text editor that reads it as UTF-8, then the editor will show "Pontifícia."

To do more complicated things with Unicode and other character encodings, try the Selene Unicode library (slnunicode), available at luaforge.net. For more information on Unicode and other character encoding issues, check out the Joel Spolsky article at joelonsoftware.com/articles/Unicode.html.

"%D" matches any character that isn't a digit, "%L" matches any character that isn't a lowercase letter, and "%A" matches any character that isn't alphabetical. In fact, any pattern item that is a percent sign followed by a lowercase letter has a counterpart with an uppercase letter that matches all the characters not matched by the lowercase version.

Any character class that isn't itself a bracket class can be included in a bracket class. This includes character classes like "%d" and "%a"; both "[%d.]" and "[0-9.]" match digits and decimal points. However, the two endpoints of a hyphen-separated range must be single characters (representing themselves), not longer character classes like "%d", "%a", "%%", or "%]".

The only characters that are magic inside a bracket class are "-", "^", "]", and "%", and of these, only "%" is magic in all positions. But unless it's the endpoint of a range, a punctuation character can be escaped even when that's not strictly necessary, like this:

```
> print(string.gsub("!@#$%^&*", "[%!%@%#%$]", "."))
....%^&*        4
```

As with patterns as a whole, you can understand complex bracket classes better if you diagram them. Often, all you need to do is show how the parts are divided up. For example, Figure 5-2 is a diagram of "[aq-z%]%d]" — it makes clear that the characters matched are the letter a, the letters q through z, the] character, and all digits.

| a | q-z | %] | %d |

Figure 5-2

To match any character at all, including whitespace and control characters, use the `.` (dot) character class. Here are some examples:

```
> print(string.find("abc", "a.c"))
1       3
> print(string.find("a c", "a.c"))
1       3
> print(string.find("a!c", "a.c"))
1       3
> print(string.find("a\0c", "a.c"))
1       3
> -- It matches one and only one character:
> print(string.find("abbc", "a.c"))
nil
> print(string.find("ac", "a.c"))
nil
```

A pattern cannot contain the character `"\0"`. To match a zero, use `"%z"`:

```
> print(string.gsub("a\0b\0c", "%z", "Z"))
aZbZc   2
```

Matches of Varying Lengths

In the previous section, you could always tell just by looking at a pattern how long its match would be. Many patterns need to match varying quantities of characters. An example of this is *squeezing* whitespace, which turns all runs of one or more whitespace characters into a single space.

Try It Out   **Squeezing Whitespace**

1. Define the following function:

```
-- Squeezes whitespace:
function Squeeze(Str)
  return (string.gsub(Str, "%s+", " "))
end
```

2. Run this test code:

```
TestStrs = {
  "nospaces",
  "alpha bravo charlie",
  "   alpha    bravo    charlie   ",
  "\nalpha\tbravo\tcharlie\na\tb\tc",
  [[
    alpha
    bravo
    charlie]]}
for _, TestStr in ipairs(TestStrs) do
  io.write("UNSQUEEZED: <", TestStr, ">\n")
  io.write("  SQUEEZED: <", Squeeze(TestStr), ">\n\n")
end
```

The output should be as follows:

```
UNSQUEEZED: <nospaces>
  SQUEEZED: <nospaces>

UNSQUEEZED: <alpha bravo charlie>
  SQUEEZED: <alpha bravo charlie>

UNSQUEEZED: <    alpha     bravo     charlie    >
  SQUEEZED: < alpha bravo charlie >

UNSQUEEZED: <
alpha    bravo    charlie
a        b        c>
  SQUEEZED: < alpha bravo charlie a b c>

UNSQUEEZED: <      alpha
    bravo
    charlie>
  SQUEEZED: < alpha bravo charlie>
```

How It Works

The `%s` character class matches a whitespace character (`"\t"`, `"\n"`, `"\v"`, `"\f"`, `"\r"`, and `" "`, plus any other whitespace characters defined by your locale). A character class followed by + (the plus sign) is a single pattern item that matches one or more (as many as possible) of that character class. Therefore, `"%s+"` matches sequences of consecutive whitespace characters in this example:

```
> print(string.find("abc xyz", "%s+"))
4       4
> print(string.find("abc    xyz", "%s+"))
4       6
```

The characters do not all have to be the same, as shown here:

```
> print(string.find("abc\n \txyz", "%s+"))
4       6
```

Squeeze's `string.gsub` call replaces any such sequences with a single space. (The parentheses around the call are there to keep `string.gsub`'s second value from being returned.)

+ works with any character class. For example:

```
> print(string.gsub("aaa bbb aaa ccc", "a+", "X"))
X bbb X ccc     2
> print(string.gsub("aaa bbb aaa ccc", "[ab]+", "X"))
X X X ccc       3
```

Matches never overlap. When `"a+"` grabs all three occurrences of a at the beginning of `"aaa bbb aaa ccc"`, it starts looking for the next match at the fourth character, not the second.

* (the asterisk, or star) is similar to +, except it matches *0 or more* characters. In the following example, `"^[%a_][%w_]*$"` matches Lua identifiers and keywords (%w matches "word" characters, which are letters and numbers):

```
> Strs = {"Str1", "_G", "function", "1st", "splunge?",
>>    "alpha bravo charlie", '"global" substitution'}
> for _, Str in ipairs(Strs) do
>>    print(string.format("%q is %sa valid identifier or keyword",
>>      Str, string.find(Str, "^[%a_][%w_]*$") and "" or "NOT "))
>> end
"Str1" is a valid identifier or keyword
"_G" is a valid identifier or keyword
"function" is a valid identifier or keyword
"1st" is NOT a valid identifier or keyword
"splunge?" is NOT a valid identifier or keyword
"alpha bravo charlie" is NOT a valid identifier or keyword
"\"global\" substitution" is NOT a valid identifier or keyword
```

Figure 5-3 is a diagram of `"^[%a_][%w_]*$"`.

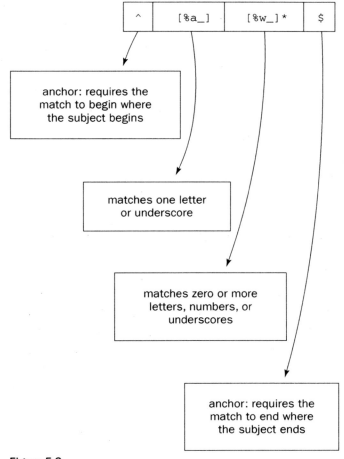

Figure 5-3

Notice that the * only applies to the character class right before it. This is also true of +, and of − and ?, the two other similar magic characters you'll soon learn.

> *If you know what regular expressions are, then you've already figured out that patterns are the Lua equivalent. The limitation on what length modifiers like * can apply to is one of the things that keep Lua patterns from being full-fledged regular expressions, a choice that was made intentionally, to keep the string library small and simple. You can simulate most regular expression features through a clever use of Lua patterns.*

When string.find finds a zero-length match, the start and end positions it returns will be the positions of (respectively) the characters after and before the match. Generally, such a match is at the beginning of the string, so the positions are 1 and 0. Zero-length matches can be confusing. The first of the following string.finds matches "aa", but the second one matches the empty string at the beginning of "aabb":

```
> print(string.find("aabb", "a*"))
1       2
> print(string.find("aabb", "b*"))
1       0
```

This is because searches always start at the beginning of the subject. When the pattern is "a*", Lua tries to find any occurrences of the letter a at the beginning of the subject string. In this example, it finds two. When the pattern is "b*", Lua tries to find any occurrences of b at the beginning of the subject string. In this too, it succeeds, but only by finding zero b's—the empty string.

string.find finds just the first match, so only if Lua fails to find a match at the beginning of the subject does it look for one at the second character. If it fails there, it looks at the third, and so on. A string .gsub can replace multiple matches. Some of them may be empty strings, but none of them will overlap. Of the matches in the following example, all but the second-to-last are empty strings:

```
> print(string.gsub("aabb", "b*", "<match>"))
<match>a<match>a<match><match>   4
```

Sometimes a search finds substrings that look like matches but turn out not to be. For example, this function trims (removes) any whitespace from the end of a string:

```
-- Trims trailing whitespace:
function TrimRight(Str)
  return (string.gsub(Str, "%s+$", ""))
end
```

If given " A B C " (that's two spaces before and after each letter), the example returns " A B C". Here's what string.gsub needs to do behind the scenes for this to work: It grabs as many whitespace characters as it can starting at character 1 of the subject. (This is two whitespace characters.) Then it checks whether it's hit the end of the subject. It hasn't, so it tries grabbing one less whitespace character for a total of one. This of course doesn't get it to the end of the subject either, and because grabbing zero whitespace characters is not an option with +, it gives up on finding a match at character 1 of the subject and goes through the same business at character 2. This doesn't result in a match either, so it moves on to character 3, where it can give up immediately, because character 3 is not a whitespace character. This whole process continues down the subject string until a match is finally found at character 10 (right after the C).

In the previous example, `string.gsub` looks at some characters more than once. Character 2 gets looked at once as a continuation of a potential match at character 1, and again as the beginning of a potential match. This is called *backtracking*.

By comparison, the `Squeeze` function from earlier in this chapter had a `string.gsub` that used the same pattern except without the $ anchor. Given the same subject string, it would grab as many whitespace characters as it could starting at character 1, and because this would be a match, it could immediately jump to character 3. It knows just by looking at each character in the subject whether that character is the start of a match or not, and it also doesn't have to backtrack to see how long the match is.

If a pattern match seems to be a slow spot in your program, try to rewrite it to reduce or eliminate backtracking. The version of `TrimRight` given earlier is fine for short strings, but it will be noticeably slow if used to trim a sufficiently long string (perhaps read in from a file) with lots of runs of consecutive whitespace in it. There are a few ways to write `TrimRight` to avoid backtracking. One is to look at as many characters of the string as necessary, starting at the end and working towards the beginning, like this:

```
-- Trims trailing whitespace:
function TrimRight(Str)
   -- By searching from the end backwards, find the position
   -- of the last nonwhitespace character:
   local I = #Str
   while I > 0 and string.find(string.sub(Str, I, I), "%s") do
      I = I - 1
   end
   return string.sub(Str, 1, I)
end
```

The - (hyphen or minus sign) is just like * except that * matches as many characters as possible, and - matches as few as possible. Both the patterns in the following example match two vertical bar characters and the characters in between them, but the first one finds the biggest match it can, whereas the second finds the smallest it can:

```
> print(string.find("|abc|def|", "%|.*%|"))
1        9
> print(string.find("|abc|def|", "%|.-%|"))
1        5
```

Because * and +match as many characters as possible, they are called *greedy*. In contrast, - is called *nongreedy*.

`string.find` always finds the first match in the subject, no matter whether greedy or nongreedy matching is used. In the following example, both the greedy pattern and the nongreedy matches find `"<lengthy>"`, even though `"<short>"` has less characters:

```
> Str = "blah<lengthy>blah<short>blah"
> print(string.find(Str, "%<%a*%>"))
5        13
> print(string.find(Str, "%<%a-%>"))
5        13
```

Also, the greedy/nongreedy distinction controls *how long* a match will be, but not *whether* a match will be found. If * finds a match, then - will find one too, and vice versa.

A character class followed by ? (a question mark) matches zero or one of that character class. In the following example, this is used to match either "Mr" or "Mr.":

```
> print(string.gsub("Mr. Smith and Mr Smythe", "Mr%.?", "Mister"))
Mister Smith and Mister Smythe  2
```

? is greedy in this example — it matched the dot in "Mr." even though nothing after it forced it to.

*, +, -, and ? are all of the magic characters used to control the length of a match. Here's a summary:

To Match	Do
Exactly one character	Use a character class by itself
Exactly *n* characters	Use *n* character classes in a row
Zero or more characters, as many as possible	Follow the character class with *
One or more characters, as many as possible	Follow the character class with +
Zero or more characters, as few as possible	Follow the character class with –
Zero or one characters, as many as possible	Follow the character class with ?

These magic characters can be combined for other match lengths. For example, "%a%a%a%a?%a?%a?" matches three to six letters, and "%a%a%a%a*" matches three or more letters.

Captures

Selected parts of a match can be *captured*, which means they can be separated from the rest of the match. This allows one pattern to do the work of several.

The FriendlyDate function used in following example takes a date formatted as yyyy-mm-dd; captures that date's year, month, and day; and returns the same date in a more user-friendly format. First, define the FriendlyDate helper function, Ordinal, and FriendlyDate itself, like this:

```
-- Returns the ordinal form of N:
function Ordinal(N)
  N = tonumber(N)
  local Terminator = "th"
  assert(N > 0, "Ordinal only accepts positive numbers")
  assert(math.floor(N) == N, "Ordinal only accepts integers")
  if string.sub(N, -2, -2) ~= "1" then
    local LastDigit = N % 10
    if LastDigit == 1 then
      Terminator = "st"
    elseif LastDigit == 2 then
      Terminator = "nd"
```

```
      elseif LastDigit == 3 then
        Terminator = "rd"
      end
    end
    return N .. Terminator
  end

  -- Returns a user-friendly version of a date string.  (Assumes
  -- its argument is a valid date formatted yyyy-mm-dd.)
  function FriendlyDate(DateStr)
    local Year, Month, Day = string.match(DateStr,
      "^(%d%d%d%d)%-(%d%d)%-(%d%d)$")
    Month = ({"January", "February", "March", "April", "May",
      "June", "July", "August", "September", "October",
      "November", "December"})[tonumber(Month)]
    return Month .. " " .. Ordinal(Day) .. ", " .. Year
  end
```

Then try it out like this:

```
> print(FriendlyDate("1964-02-09"))
February 9th, 1964
> print(FriendlyDate("2007-07-13"))
July 13th, 2007
> -- FriendlyDate assumes its argument is valid.  It complains
> -- about some invalid arguments, but not all of them:
> print(FriendlyDate("9999-99-99"))
stdin:7: attempt to concatenate local 'Month' (a nil value)
stack traceback:
        stdin:7: in function 'FriendlyDate'
        stdin:1: in main chunk
        [C]: ?
> print(FriendlyDate("0000-12-99"))
December 99th, 0000
```

Parentheses within a pattern are used to capture parts of the match. The string.match function returns all captures from the first match it finds, or nil if no match is found:

```
> Pat = "(%a)(%a*)"
> print(string.match("123 alpha bravo charlie", Pat))
a       lpha
> print(string.match("123", Pat))
nil
```

In FriendlyDate, the pattern given to string.match captures the year, month, and day, which will be nil if DateStr is incorrectly formatted, as shown here:

```
  -- Returns a user-friendly version of a date string.  (Assumes
  -- its argument is a valid date formatted yyyy-mm-dd.)
  function FriendlyDate(DateStr)
    local Year, Month, Day = string.match(DateStr,
      "^(%d%d%d%d)%-(%d%d)%-(%d%d)$")
    Month = ({"January", "February", "March", "April", "May",
```

199

```
        "June", "July", "August", "September", "October",
        "November", "December"})[tonumber(Month)]
    return Month .. " " .. Ordinal(Day) .. ", " .. Year
end
```

After the year, month, and day are in hand, it's just a matter of turning the month from a number to a name, and turning the date from, e.g., `"01"` to `"1st"`.

`string.find` also returns any captures, after its first two return values. For example:

```
> print(string.find("123 alpha bravo charlie", "(%a)(%a*)"))
5       9       a       lpha
```

Lua 5.0 didn't have `string.match`. In its place, use `string.find` (ignoring its first two return values).

If `string.match` is given a pattern with no captures, it returns the entire (first) match like this:

```
> print(string.match("123 alpha bravo charlie", "%a+"))
alpha
```

If one capture contains another, they are ordered according to the position of the first parenthesis like this:

```
> print(string.match("abcd", "(((%a)(%a))((%a)(%a)))"))
abcd    ab      a       b       cd      c       d
```

If `()` is used as a capture, then the position in the subject is captured — more specifically, the position of the next character. The position at the end of a pattern is the length of the subject plus one, as shown here:

```
> print(string.match("abcd", "()(%a+)()"))
1       abcd    5
```

A position capture is a number, such as the following:

```
> print(type(string.match("abcd", "ab()cd")))
number
```

All other captures are strings, although they may look like numbers or be empty strings, as shown in the following example:

```
> print(type(string.match("1234", "(%d+)")))
string
> print(string.match("1234", "(%a*)") == "")
true
```

A `*`, `+`, `-`, or `?` character must be directly after its character class, with no intervening capture parentheses. Similarly, a `^` or `$` anchor character must be the very first or last character in its pattern. In the current implementation of Lua, the patterns `"(%a)*"` and `"(^%a)"` are both valid, but they have different meanings then you might expect. `"(%a)*"` means "capture a letter that is followed by a star" in the following example:

```
> print(string.match("ab*cd", "(%a)*"))
b
```

And `"(^%a)"` means "capture a caret and a letter" here:

```
> print(string.match("a^z", "(^%a)"))
^z
```

The equivalent patterns that give the star and the caret their magic meanings are `"(%a*)"` and `"^(%a)"` in the following example::

```
> print(string.match("ab*cd", "(%a*)"))
ab
> print(string.match("a^z", "^(%a)"))
a
```

A percent followed by 1 through 9 represents that capture, so `%1` is the first capture. This means that in the following example, `"(%a+) %1"` matches two consecutive identical words separated by a space (the pattern translates to "match and capture a word, match a space, match the first capture"):

```
> print(string.gsub("Paris in the the spring",
>>   "(%a+) %1", "WORD WORD"))
Paris in WORD WORD spring       1
```

A capture used within the pattern that captured it is said to be *replayed*. You cannot replay a capture inside itself, because this would cause an infinite regress. If you try to do so, you get the following error:

```
> print(string.match("blah", "(%1)"))
stdin:1: invalid capture index
stack traceback:
        [C]: in function 'match'
        stdin:1: in main chunk
        [C]: ?
```

You can also access captures within a `string.gsub` replacement string. For example (`%%` represents a literal percent sign):

```
> Percents = "90 percent, 100 percent, 110 percent"
> print(string.gsub(Percents, "(%d+) percent", "%1%%"))
90%, 100%, 110% 3
```

In a replacement string, `%0` stands for the whole match, as in this example:

```
> Str = "alpha, bravo, charlie"
> print(string.gsub(Str, "%a+", "<%0>"))
<alpha>, <bravo>, <charlie>       3
```

Lua 5.0 didn't understand %0. The whole match, if desired, had to be explicitly captured.

Because percent signs are magic in replacement strings, any replacement string supplied by a user or otherwise generated at run time must be percent-escaped automatically, like so:

```
Str = string.gsub(Str, "%%", "%%%%")
```

Matching Balanced Delimiters

Parentheses, curly braces, and square brackets, as used in Lua, are examples of *delimiters*, because they mark the beginning and end of whatever they surround. You use them in pairs, so that each open delimiter has a corresponding close delimiter. Delimiters that are paired in this way are said to be *balanced*, and Lua offers a pattern item that matches them. This pattern item is four characters long: the first two characters are "%b", and the next two are the open delimiter and the close delimiter. For example, "%b()" matches balanced parentheses, "%b{}" matches balanced curly braces, and "%b[]" matches balanced square brackets. The two characters after %b always represent themselves—any magic meaning they might have is ignored.

Here's an example that converts the two top-level pairs into "balanced":

> *To get at the inner pairs, you'd only need to grab the top-level pairs and run "%b()" on them.*

```
> Str = "((a b) (b c)) ((c d) (e f))"
> print(string.gsub(Str, "%b()", "balanced"))
balanced balanced          2
```

For comparison, here are three attempts to do this without the %b pattern item, where the first would work if there was only one pair of parentheses, and the second two would work if there were no nested pairs:

```
> print(string.gsub(Str, "%(.*%)", "imbalanced"))
imbalanced      1
> print(string.gsub(Str, "%(.-%)", "imbalanced"))
imbalanced imbalanced) imbalanced imbalanced)   4
> print(string.gsub(Str, "%([^()]*%)", "imbalanced"))
(imbalanced imbalanced) (imbalanced imbalanced) 4
```

The %b delimiters can be any characters (other than "\0"). For example, a "%b %" pattern would match delimited strings that begin with a space and end with a percent sign.

A string like '{"a", "}", "z"}' would confuse "%b{}", because it doesn't know not to treat the quoted "}" as a delimiter. If you run into this situation, and you can figure out which delimiter characters should be ignored, then you can use the trick of converting them to characters you know will be unused (such as "\1" and "\2"), doing the %b matching, and then converting them back.

> *It might be easier to just arrange for the string you're looking at to be a valid Lua table constructor. To do this, you can prepend "return" to it, apply loadstring to it, give the resulting function an empty environment with setfenv, and call the function (using pcall to guard against errors, as described in the next chapter). The function's return value will be the table described by the table constructor.*

More on string.find, string.match, and string.gsub

There are a few more features of string.find, string.match, and string.gsub that need to be covered. After you learn them, you'll know everything there is to know about these functions.

`string.find` and `string.match` both take a third argument, which is a number that specifyies which character of the subject to start the search at. Any matches that start before this character will be ignored. For example:

```
> Subj, Pat = "abc <--> xyz", "(%a+)"
> -- Start searching at character 2 ("b"):
> print(string.match(Subj, Pat, 2))
bc
> -- Start searching at character 5 ("<"):
> print(string.match(Subj, Pat, 5))
xyz
```

A caret anchors the pattern at the beginning of the search, not the beginning of the subject, as follows:

```
> Subj, Pat = "aa ab ac", "^(a%a)"
> -- Character 4 is an "a", so this matches:
> print(string.match(Subj, Pat, 4))
ab
> -- Character 5 is not an "a", so this doesn't match:
> print(string.match(Subj, Pat, 5))
nil
```

Returned string positions are reckoned from the beginning of the subject (not the beginning of the search) like this:

```
> Subj = "aa ab ac"
> print(string.find(Subj, "(a%a)", 6))
7       8       ac
> print(string.match(Subj, "()(a%a)()", 6))
7       ac      9
```

If the fourth `string.find` argument is true, it will ignore the magic meanings of characters in its second argument, treating it as a plain old string rather than a pattern:

> *To give a fourth argument, you need to give a third; use 1 if you want the search to start at the beginning of the subject as usual.*

```
> -- Both of these look for a caret, an "a", a percent sign,
> -- and another "a":
> print(string.find("characters: ^a%a", "^a%a", 1, true))
13      16
> print(string.find("ab", "^a%a", 1, true))
nil
```

So far, the `string.gsub` replacement argument (the third argument) has always been a string. That string can include captures, but sometimes that's not enough power to do what you want to do. For smarter replacements, the replacement argument can be a function or a table. If it's a function, it is called on each match with the match's captures as arguments, and the match is replaced with the function's return value. In the following example, the first letter and the rest of the letters of each word are captured, and the first letter is capitalized:

```
> Str = "If it ain't broke, don't fix it."
> Str = string.gsub(Str, "(%a)([%a'-]*)",
>>    function(First, Rest)
>>      return string.upper(First) .. Rest
>>    end)
> print(Str)
If It Ain't Broke, Don't Fix It.
```

If there are no captures, the whole match is passed to the function. If the function returns nil or false, no replacement is done. Both these points are demonstrated by the following example, which turns "cat" into "dog", but makes no change to other words that contain "cat":

```
> Str = "concatenate cathy ducat cat"
> Str = string.gsub(Str, "%a+",
>>    function(Match)
>>      return Match == "cat" and "dog"
>>    end)
> print(Str)
concatenate cathy ducat dog
```

In Lua 5.0, if the replacement function returned nil or false, the match was replaced with the empty string.

If the string.gsub replacement argument is a table, then the first capture — or the whole match, if there are no captures — is used to index the table, and the match is replaced with the value at that index, unless it's nil or false, in which case no replacement is done. Here's an example:

```
> Str = "dog bites man"
> Str = string.gsub(Str, "%a+", {dog = "man", man = "dog"})
> print(Str)
man bites dog
```

In Lua 5.0, the replacement argument could only be a string or a function.

Iterating Through All Matches

There's one more function in the string library: string.gmatch (where gmatch stands for global match). string.match only sees the first match, but string.gmatch lets you get at all the matches. It does this by iterating through the matches — like pairs and ipairs, it's an iterator factory.

The following example of string.gmatch is an HTML *tokenizer*. Most computer languages are composed, at one level, of *tokens*. These are the units in terms of which the language's syntax is defined (Lua tokens include literal strings, keywords, parentheses, commas, and so on.) The example separates a string of HTML (the language used to write web pages) into tokens. Specifically, it returns a table of HTML tags and what's in between those tags. An HTML tag consists of characters delimited by open and close angle brackets (<>), like <this>. (This is a crude tokenizer — an industrial-strength HTML tokenizer would take us too far off topic.)

Here's the example, which defines the `string.gmatch` function:

```
-- Turns a string of HTML into an array of tokens.  (Each
-- token is a tag or a string before or after a tag; literal
-- open angle brackets cannot occur outside of tags, and
-- literal close angle brackets cannot occur inside them.)
function TokenizeHtml(Str)
  local Ret = {}
  -- Chop off any leading nontag text:
  local BeforeFirstTag, Rest = string.match(Str, "^([^<]*)(.*)")
  if BeforeFirstTag ~= "" then
    Ret[1] = BeforeFirstTag
  end
  -- Get all tags and anything in between or after them:
  for Tag, Nontag in
    string.gmatch(Rest, "(%<[^>]*%>)([^<]*)")
  do
    Ret[#Ret + 1] = Tag
    if Nontag ~= "" then
      Ret[#Ret + 1] = Nontag
    end
  end
  return Ret
end
```

Now, try it out:

```
> Html = "<p>Some <i>italicized</i> text.</p>"
> for _, Token in ipairs(TokenizeHtml(Html)) do print(Token) end
<p>
Some
<i>
italicized
</i>
 text.
</p>
```

First, `TokenizeHtml` separates its argument into two parts: the possibly empty string before the first tag (if there is a first tag), and the possibly empty remainder of the string:

```
function TokenizeHtml(Str)
  local Ret = {}
  local BeforeFirstTag, Rest = string.match(Str, "^([^<]*)(.*)")
  if BeforeFirstTag ~= "" then
    Ret[1] = BeforeFirstTag
  end
```

Notice that this match cannot fail, even on an empty string. Also notice that, if there's at least one tag in `Str`, the `BeforeFirstTag` string will be as long as it needs to be to include everything that comes before the tag, because greedy matching is used.

After it saves the data before the first tag (if it's nonempty), `string.gmatch` can loop through the rest of the string. `string.gmatch` takes a subject and a pattern. It returns an iterator that, on each iteration, returns the captures from the pattern's next match in the subject. In this case, the pattern is as follows:

```
"(%<[^>]*%>)([^<]*)"
```

Figure 5-4 shows how this pattern can be diagrammed.

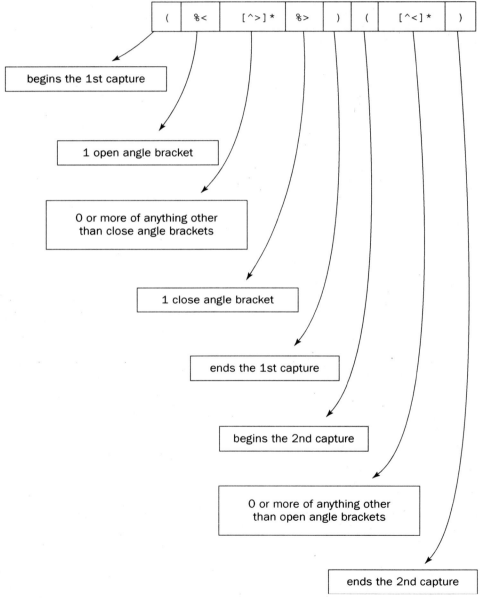

Figure 5-4

The two captures returned by the iterator are given the names Tag and Nontag. In this example, the string.gmatch function specifies that Tag will never be the empty string (at a minimum, it will be "<>"), and if two tags are next to each other, then Nontag will be empty, in which case won't be put into Ret:

```
for Tag, Nontag in
  string.gmatch(Rest, "(%<[^>]*%>)([^<]*)")
do
  Ret[#Ret + 1] = Tag
  if Nontag ~= "" then
    Ret[#Ret + 1] = Nontag
  end
end
```

The loop does an iteration for each match, so if there are no tags to be found, then it will do zero iterations and Ret will have only one or zero elements.

In Lua 5.0, string.gmatch was named string.gfind (but was otherwise identical).

If the pattern given to string.gmatch has no captures, the iterator will return the whole match:

```
> for Letter in string.gmatch("1st 2nd 3rd", "%a") do
>>    print(Letter)
>> end
s
t
n
d
r
d
```

Tricks for the Tricky

Sometimes when you can't write a pattern to match what you want to match, you can get around this by matching a little more than you need to, and then ignoring the match if it's a false positive. This is the approach used in the previous cat-to-dog example:

```
> Str = "concatenate cathy ducat cat"
> Str = string.gsub(Str, "%a+",
>>    function(Match)
>>      return Match == "cat" and "dog"
>>    end)
> print(Str)
concatenate cathy ducat dog
```

This approach would also work for tasks such as the following:

❑   Changing "cat", "dog", and "bird", but not other words, to "animal"

❑   Matching "cat" case-insensitively without using "[Cc][Aa][Tt]"

❑   Matching 3-to-10-letter words

207

Another technique is to use a modified version of the subject. In the following, the pattern `"%Wcat%W"` even finds the word "cat" at the end of the subject, because the concatenated newlines ensure that it can't be at the *very* end (or the very beginning):

```
> Str = "concatenate cathy ducat cat"
> Count = 0
> for _ in string.gmatch("\n" .. Str .. "\n", "%Wcat%W") do
>>    Count = Count + 1
>> end
> io.write("'cat' occurs ", Count, " time(s)\n")
'cat' occurs 1 time(s)
```

Another technique is to capture positions and use them to look around inside the subject, like this:

```
> Str = "concatenate cathy ducat cat"
> Str = string.gsub(Str, "()cat()",
>>    function(Pos1, Pos2)
>>       Pos1 = Pos1 - 1 -- The character before the match.
>>       -- Is the match at the beginning of the string or
>>       -- preceded by a nonword character?
>>       if Pos1 == 0 or string.find(Str, "^%W", Pos1) then
>>          -- Is it also at the end of the string or followed by
>>          -- a nonword character?
>>          if Pos2 > #Str or string.find(Str, "^%W", Pos2) then
>>             return "dog"
>>          end
>>       end
>>    end)
> print(Str)
concatenate cathy ducat dog
```

In the case of matching a whole word, there's yet another technique — the undocumented *frontier* pattern item, which is shown here:

```
> Str = "concatenate cathy ducat cat"
> Str = string.gsub(Str, "%f[%w]cat%f[%W]",
>>    function(Match)
>>       return Match == "cat" and "dog"
>>    end)
> print(Str)
concatenate cathy ducat dog
```

`%f` is followed by a bracket class. It matches an empty string that comes after a character not in the class and before one that is in the class, but the empty string matched can also be at the beginning or end of the subject. The pattern `"%f[a]a"` matches any "a" that isn't preceded by another "a," and the pattern `"a%f[^a]"` matches any "a" that isn't followed by another "a."

The fact that `%f` is undocumented means that it may — without notice — change or disappear altogether in a subsequent release of Lua. It also means that there's no explicit guarantee of its behavior, and it may act unexpectedly when used in unusual situations such as this one:

```
> -- This should find the empty string at the beginning of the
> -- subject, but it doesn't (due to an implementation quirk):
> print(string.find("\0", "%f[%z]"))
nil
```

Magic Characters Chart

Here's a chart of all the magic characters and magic character sequences that patterns can contain:

Character	Description
%	Escapes the magic character that follows it
.	Matches any character
%a	Matches a letter
%c	Matches a control character
%d	Matches a decimal digit
%l	Matches a lowercase letter
%p	Matches a punctuation character
%s	Matches a whitespace character
%u	Matches an uppercase letter
%w	Matches a word character (a letter or a number)
%x	Matches a hexadecimal digit
%z	Matches a "\0" character
%A, %C, %D, etc.	Matches any character not matched by %a, %c, %d, etc.
[abc]	Matches a, b, or c
[A-Ea-e%d]	Matches A through E, a through e, or a digit
[^abc]	Matches any character other than a, b, or c
*	Makes the preceding character class match zero or more characters (greedy)
+	Makes the preceding character class match one or more characters (greedy)
-	Makes the preceding character class match zero or more characters (nongreedy)
?	Makes the preceding character class match zero or one character(s) (greedy)
^	Anchors the pattern at the beginning
$	Anchors the pattern at the end
%1, %2, etc.	Matches the first capture, second capture, etc. (up to 9)
%b(), %b<>, etc.	Matches balanced parentheses, angle brackets, etc.
%f[%a_], %f[^AEIOUaeiou], etc.	Undocumented — matches the empty string ("frontier") at the transition from something not matched by the given bracket class to something matched by it.

Summary

In this chapter, you learned all the functions in the string library (except for `string.dump`, which is covered in Chapter 10), along with a few in the I/O library. Here are the highlights:

❑ You can convert the case of strings with `string.lower` and `string.upper`.

❑ You can obtain substrings with `string.sub`.

❑ You can format strings with `string.format`, whose first argument is a format string with placeholders (which start with a percent sign).

❑ You get more fine-grained control over output with `io.write`, and over standard input with `io.read`.

❑ When you use `io.open` to open a file, it returns a file handle — an object with `read`, `write`, and `close` methods.

❑ You perform pattern matching with magic characters such as %, ^, and *.

❑ Anchoring (which you do with ^ and $) forces a match to be at the beginning and/or end of the subject string (or the searched part of the subject string, if a third argument is given to `string.find` or `string.match`).

❑ Greedy matching ("*", "+", and "?") matches as many characters as possible. Nongreedy matching ("-") matches as few as possible. Either way, each match will be as close to the beginning of the searched part of the subject string as possible.

❑ `string.gsub` does substitution on all matches of a pattern.

❑ `string.find` finds the first match.

❑ `string.match` returns the captures from the first match.

❑ `string.gmatch` returns an iterator that loops through all matches.

At this point, you have all the tools you need to start writing real programs, except that the programs you write may not be very robust. In the next chapter, you'll learn how to prevent errors, or to keep them from stopping your program cold when they do happen. To test your understanding of this chapter, you can do the following exercises (answers are in the appendix).

Exercises

1. Write a function that takes an n-character string and returns an n-element array whose elements are the string's characters (in order).

2. Write the format string `Frmt` so that the following:

```
for _, Name in ipairs({"Lynn", "Jeremy", "Sally"}) do
    io.write(string.format(Frmt, Name))
end
```

will print this:

```
  Lynn
Jeremy
 Sally
```

3. Write a comparison function that allows `table.sort` to sort in "dictionary order." Specifically, case distinctions and any characters other than letters or numbers should be ignored, unless they are the only ways in which two strings differ.

```
> Names = {"Defoe", "Deforest", "Degas", "de Forest"}
> table.sort(Names, DictCmp)
> for _, Name in ipairs(Names) do print(Name) end
Defoe
Deforest
de Forest
Degas
```

4. Write a function that starts up a subinterpreter that prints a prompt, reads a line, and prints the result(s) of evaluating the expression(s) typed onto that line. Typing a line with nothing but the word "quit" should exit the subinterpreter.

```
> ExprInterp()
expression> 2 + 2
4
expression> true, false, nil
true    false   nil
expression> string.gsub("somewhere", "[Ss]", "%0h")
shomewhere      1
expression> quit
>
```

There's no need to check for errors in what is typed (you'll learn how to do this in the next chapter) or to special-case empty lines. (Hint: This exercise doesn't require any pattern matching.)

5. The `TrimRight` function given in this chapter trims off trailing whitespace. Write its counterpart: `TrimLeft`, a function that trims leading whitespace.

6. Does `TrimLeft` ever need to do any backtracking?

7. Write an `Interpolate` function that replaces dollar signs followed by identifiers with the value of the named global variable.

```
> Where, Who, What =
>>   "in xanadu", "kubla khan", "a stately pleasure-dome"
> print(Interpolate("$Where did $Who\n$What decree"))
in xanadu did kubla khan
a stately pleasure-dome decree
> print(Interpolate("string = $string, asdf = $asdf"))
string = table: 0x481dd0, asdf = nil
```

Handling and Avoiding Errors

Program correctness matters on every count, from user acceptance and trust to the downstream consequences of program output. In this chapter, you learn about the following:

❑ The kinds of errors that can occur in your programs

❑ Lua's mechanisms for handling errors

❑ Techniques to avoid program errors

❑ Techniques to locate program errors

Along the way, you'll become familiar with Lua's I/O library, which is included in some of the examples.

Kinds of Errors

Some flaws can turn up before a program is executed. These are compile-time errors, which Lua can find as it converts your source code into executable bytecode. Often these result from simple misspellings or typing slips as you edit your source code. Other flaws are more insidious — Lua recognizes them as syntactically correct so they make their way into the executable bytecode. These errors await discovery at run time, preferably by you during testing rather than by someone who's actually using a product after it's been released with the erroneous code.

Syntax Errors

Syntax refers to the way various language elements are allowed to fit together, completely independent from the meaning of those elements. A programming language like Lua is necessarily fussy about syntax, because source code expressed in it needs to translate unambiguously to bytecode, the instructions that Lua's virtual machine can deal with. During the 1960s (the renaissance era of modern programming languages) computer science practitioners such as Niklaus Wirth understood the importance of specifying syntactic rules that express naturally and simply the intent of a programmer. Lua's syntax falls neatly into this heritage. Take time to study the page in the Lua manual that describes Lua's complete syntax. Doing so can provide much insight into the Lua language and the way the Lua parser operates.

Essentially, it is the job of Lua's parser to recognize syntactically correct Lua programs and, in the case of an incorrect program, to let you know where the problem is. Of course, the program you submit to Lua might have more than one syntax error, but Lua will stop at the first one it encounters and print a message that should allow you to pinpoint the location of the problem. Usually, but not always, you'll instantly recognize the offending construction, make a quick fix, and compile the code again.

Here is an example of a syntax error:

```
a = 1 + + 2
```

This results in an "unexpected symbol near '+'" message.

Here's another example:

```
for do
```

Lua expects a variable name to follow `for`, so it generates a "'<name>' expected near 'do'" message.

And here's an erroneous script example:

```
Str = 'hello, world
```

The result is the message "unfinished string near ''hello, world'". When you run this as a non-interactive Lua script, this error is generated immediately. When you type it in interactively, Lua presents you with a continuation prompt and defers the error until you provide more input. Strings that begin with a single or double quote must end, on the same line, with a matching quote. Lua supports multiline strings, for which you use the [[ ]] notation (or represent each newline with a backslash-escaped n or backslash-escaped newline, as described in Chapter 2).

Now take a look at this example:

```
break
```

By itself, this command results in the message "no loop to break near '<eof>'" (where <eof> refers to "end of file").

Here's a function call example:

```
Fnc
(42)
```

Lua generally allows you to put whitespace, including line endings, wherever you like. As mentioned in Chapter 3, however, calling a function is an exception: The opening parenthesis must occur on the same line as the function expression. The preceding construction leads to the message "ambiguous syntax (function call x new statement) near '('."

Now look at this:

```
Tbl:Fnc 4
```

This results in the message "function arguments expected near '4'." When Lua sets up a method call, it expects the usual function argument specification: a list of zero or more arguments wrapped in parentheses, a single quoted string, or a single table constructor.

In the following example, the vararg expression . . . is used inside a function whose parameter list does not end in . . . :

```
function Fnc() print(...) end
```

This results in the message "cannot use '...' outside a vararg function near '...'." A Lua script, whether it is a single line entered interactively in the Lua interpreter or a complete file that has been loaded noninteractively, has an implicit . . . that contains any arguments with which it is called.

In the case of a single line entered in the Lua interpreter, there can't be any arguments, but still you can see that the following statement is valid:

```
print(...)
```

Unlike named parameters, the . . . expression has limited visibility and cannot be used as an upvalue.

For more on upvalue, see Chapter 3

These are contrived examples—you'll rarely, if ever, see some of these syntax error messages. Or if you do get an error message from Lua, it may not make immediate sense. For example, if you enter the following:

```
string.sub9"Hello", 1, 1)
```

it will return the message "unexpected symbol near ','." You can easily recognize the last problem as a typing mistake in which "9" was typed instead of "(", so what accounts for Lua's error message? Recall that Lua permits the parentheses to be omitted when calling a function with a single string argument. In this case, Lua treats string.sub9 as a global function that, at run time, will be passed the string "Hello". In this context, the comma that follows "Hello" doesn't make sense, and Lua lets you know about it.

Some programming languages require variables to be declared before use. When programs written in these languages are compiled, any reference to an undeclared variable will be reported as an error. This is not the case with Lua. Any variable name that does not match an in-scope local variable name is considered to be one that will be resolved at run time in the global environment.

Some very uncommon compile-time errors have to do with internal limits rather than syntax violations. We've never encountered any of these in practice or heard of them occurring. But, in the spirit of inquiry and with a hammer in hand, give it a try. The following Lua program generates another Lua program, one that contains an impracticably large number of nested do blocks. In the first program, a routine is called recursively to generate a text file that simulates a handwritten Lua script. Here are the contents of the recurse.lua script:

```
function Recurse(Count, Indent)
   Indent = Indent or ""
```

```
    if Count > 0 then
        io.write(Indent, "do\n")
        Recurse(Count - 1, Indent .. "  ")
        io.write(Indent, "end\n")
    end
end

Recurse(299)
```

Now attempt to compile the program that this script generates:

```
lua recurse.lua | lua
```

The pipe directs the output of the first program to the input of the second. Note that, in the spirit of the Unix tool philosophy, the Lua interpreter acts like a filter when its standard input is not a terminal. This results in the following message:

```
stdin:200: chunk has too many syntax levels
```

Notice the line number that seems to indicate that Lua was okay with nesting blocks just up to that limit. In practice, your nested blocks will never exceed even a small fraction of that number. But this limit and other limits involving expression complexity are worth keeping in mind if you ever automatically generate Lua programs.

The Call Stack

When a function is called in Lua, space needs to be set aside to hold local variables and certain bookkeeping information such as where program control should resume when the function returns. Because Lua functions are reentrant (that is, there can be multiple outstanding calls to the same function at a given time), this storage must be bound to a particular function call rather than just to the function itself. When Lua compiles a program, it knows how much space needs to be reserved for a particular function, but the actual contents of that space aren't known until the function is actually called. The simplest solution that meets these requirements is a last-in first-out stack. This is a data structure in which items to be stored are pushed onto the top of the stack, increasing its size, and items to be retrieved are popped from the top of the stack, decreasing its size. When a function is called, its stack frame is pushed onto the call stack, and when it returns, that frame is popped, making the vacated space available for other function calls.

The details of the call stack are hidden from general view. As a Lua programmer, you want to keep in mind that a stack is being used behind the scenes to make sure that function calls work as expected, but in general you won't need to be aware of its implementation or details. For the times when you *do* need a window into your program's internal environment, Lua provides a debugging library. You can use one of its functions, debug.traceback, to generate a list of pending function calls, essentially an overview of the call stack. The debug.traceback function augments the string you pass it with such a list.

```
1   function B()
2       print(debug.traceback("B"))
```

```
 3    end
 4
 5    function A()
 6       print(debug.traceback("A 1"))
 7       B()
 8       print(debug.traceback("A 2"))
 9    end
10
11    A()
```

The output that this program generates has a strong resemblance to the error messages that were shown earlier:

```
A 1
stack traceback:
        trace.lua:6: in function 'A'
        trace.lua:11: in main chunk
        [C]: ?
B
stack traceback:
        trace.lua:2: in function 'B'
        trace.lua:7: in function 'A'
        trace.lua:11: in main chunk
        [C]: ?
A 2
stack traceback:
        trace.lua:8: in function 'A'
        trace.lua:11: in main chunk
        [C]: ?
```

Notice that the traceback doesn't give you a history of function calls. For example, you won't find any reference to the print function. What it does show you is a list of functions that have been called but that have not yet returned. The topmost indented line indicates the location in the Lua script where debug.traceback was called. Each line beneath that shows a pending function and the line number from which it was called. These lines are shown with the most recently called functions first. The bottom line indicates that the first function call originated in a C function for which no line number information is available.

Runtime Errors

When a Lua source file is successfully compiled into bytecode and executed by the interpreter, an error results in a descriptive message followed by a stack traceback. Here's an example:

```
function C()
  print(1 + nil)
end

function B()
  C()
```

```
  end

  function A()
    B()
  end

  A()
```

When this runs, Lua prints the following:

```
lua: err.lua:2: attempt to perform arithmetic on a nil value
stack traceback:
        err.lua:2: in function 'C'
        err.lua:6: in function 'B'
        err.lua:10: in function 'A'
        err.lua:13: in main chunk
        [C]: ?
```

In addition to the message that describes what went wrong during program execution and on which line, there is also a `stack traceback` section. That portion of the output is a snapshot of pending function calls and provides you with the context of the error. It's important to have a good grasp of how call stacks operate in Lua, not only for reading stack tracebacks, but also for writing programs that work well with Lua's error-handling system.

Handling Errors

As you develop a program, there are a number of ways you can deal with the inevitable errors that crop up. Your best course of action will be dictated by the following:

❑   How the program is to be used and its targeted user

❑   Whether the error is surmountable

❑   Whether the error is code-related or data-related

Default Error Behavior

The default behavior of the standalone Lua interpreter when it encounters an error condition is to print a message followed by a stack traceback and then to terminate the program, like this:

```
local function Fnc(A, B, C)
  print(A + B + C)
end

print("Position 1")
Fnc(1, nil, 3)
print("Position 2")
```

The output includes the expected error and also shows that `"Position 2"` was never reached:

```
Position 1
lua: err.lua:2: attempt to perform arithmetic on local 'B' (a nil value)
```

```
stack traceback:
        err.lua:2: in function 'Fnc'
        err.lua:6: in main chunk
        [C]: ?
```

For many quickly written scripts that are intended to be run by the developer, this behavior is acceptable. In these cases, the runtime error can be treated as if it was a syntax error — that is, you can identify the problem, correct it, and run the script again, repeating the process until the program does what you want it to do.

In the context of a program used in the real world, Lua's default response to errors is rather draconian. It is bad form to abruptly terminate a program while a network connection, database connection, or file is still open. Buffers may not have been flushed and system resources may not be freed in a timely or consistent manner. In the case of a program with a user interface, it can be more than annoying to have a program abnormally end. A considerable amount of work may be lost when a program crashes.

Checking Assumptions

When you track down the source of runtime errors, you may find that certain assumptions you made have proved to be invalid. For example, you may have implemented a loop in which you assume the value of some variable will never exceed a certain number, or you may have written a function that requires a string as its first argument. The problem is that the consequences of an invalid assumption might occur far from its source. Sometimes, errors occur with such irregularity that it is hard to even know where to start looking. These can stem from multiple invalid assumptions that by themselves don't cause apparent problems, but wreak havoc in combinations that might occur infrequently. Avoid these oblique issues by testing your assumptions directly. Lua makes this easy for you with the assert function, as shown in this example:

```
local function Quote(Str)
  assert(type(Str) == "string", "Str is not a string")
  return string.format("%q", Str)
end

print(Quote('Huckleberry "Blue" Hound'))
print(Quote(1))
```

This outputs the following:

```
"Huckleberry \"Blue\" Hound"
lua: test.lua:2: Str is not a string
stack traceback:
        [C]: in function 'assert'
        test.lua:2: in function 'Quote'
        test.lua:7: in main chunk
        [C]: ?
```

The idea here is that it is far better to terminate an errant program the moment you know something has gone wrong than to let the problem become clouded by further processing. Keep in mind that this is a development technique that is intended to address problems with program infrastructure — that is, things over which you as the developer have control.

Stack Tracebacks and End Users

Abnormal program termination may occur repeatedly as you develop a script and consequently you can become accustomed to stack tracebacks. However, an end user who encounters a stack traceback won't have a clue what it means and will inevitably lose some trust in your program. Treat stack tracebacks as a symptom of a bug that should not make it past the development stage. To emphasize this, you may want to display stack tracebacks with the header `Programmer error`. Later in this chapter, you'll see how to avoid the conditions that generate stack tracebacks, but first you'll learn a technique to intentionally generate them and the circumstance in which you should.

Code Errors

View your program as comprising code on one hand and data on the other. Code is the fixed deliverable made up of program statements and data is the material your program processes at run time. Calls to assert are an appropriate way of dealing with code errors. The program you deliver should be free of coding errors, and if abnormal endings and stack tracebacks get you closer to eliminating them, then using `assert` is fully warranted.

Data Errors

Data errors are by their nature different than code errors. Essentially, your job here is to make your program respond gracefully when garbage is shoveled into it, because sooner or later, intentionally or not, your program's input domain will be taxed grievously. Your best approach is to mistrust all data that your program reads — the closer to the source, the better.

In the preceding example, you have control over the type of value that you pass to the `Quote` function. You may not, however, have control over the string's value, which may have been entered by the user into a text field. If the string itself needs to conform to certain patterns for the program to function correctly, that should be checked and handled by some user-friendlier means than `assert`. Of course, you may use `assert` to ensure that your string screening logic is working as expected, because if it isn't, you've got some code adjustments to make.

The assert and error Functions

You don't have to leave it up to Lua to issue errors. There may be circumstances in which your program should issue an error itself, and for these cases, Lua provides the `assert` and `error` functions. Use the `assert` function to issue an error if an assumption proves to be invalid at run time. To issue an error unconditionally, no questions asked, use the `error` function.

One or more values are passed to the `assert` function. These values may be passed in directly, but usually they are the results of an expression such as a function call. If the first argument is either `false` or `nil`, `assert` generates an error and prints an error message followed by a stack traceback. If a second argument is present, it is used as the error message; otherwise, the string `"assertion failed!"` is used. If the first argument is neither false nor `nil`, then `assert` returns every argument that was passed in:

```
function Reflect(A)
  return A, 1, 2, 3
```

```
   end

print(assert(Reflect(0)))
print(assert(Reflect(nil)))
```

This displays the following:

```
0        1        2        3
lua: test.lua:6: 1
stack traceback:
        [C]: in function 'assert'
        test.lua:6: in main chunk
        [C]: ?
```

The `assert` function is a wrapper for the more general `error` function, which you can be use to unconditionally generate an error.

Defining Your Own Error Condition

Lua has a well-defined set of conditions under which an error will occur. Using the error function, you can define your own as well. Here's how:

```
function Answer(Question)
  local Res
  if Question == "no bananas" then
    Res = "yes"
  elseif Question == "everything" then
    Res = 42
  elseif Question == "Tuesday" then
    Res = "Belgium"
  else
    error("No answer for " .. tostring(Question))
  end
  return Res
end

print(Answer("this statement is false"))
```

Running this results in the following:

```
lua: answer.lua:10: No answer for this statement is false
stack traceback:
  [C]: in function 'error'
  answer.lua:10: in function 'Answer'
  answer.lua:15: in main chunk
  [C]: ?
```

The same error-handling mechanism is used for user-generated errors as for those originating in the Lua core.

You can pass an integer as an optional second argument to `error`. Passing 0 suppresses line number information in the error message. If you specify the value 1 (the default if the argument is missing), the line number where error was called will be displayed. A higher value tells Lua how far down on the call stack

221

to reach to determine which line number to display. This is useful if you write an error handler that in turn calls error. In this case, you don't want to mislead the programmer by displaying a line in your handler; you want to show the line where the call to your handler was made, so a value of 2 is appropriate.

Anticipating Error Conditions

One way to cope with the problem of runtime errors is to diligently check for the conditions that can lead to an error. For example, a function that prints the sum of its three arguments could be written as follows:

```
local function Fnc(A, B, C)
   A, B, C = tonumber(A), tonumber(B), tonumber(C)
   print(A and B and C and A + B + C
      or "Three numbers expected")
end

print("Position 1")
Fnc(1, "2", 3)
print("Position 2")
Fnc(1, "Lua", 3)
print("Position 3")
```

Here, where the conditions needed to calculate and print the sum of three numbers are not met, an alternative is printed instead:

```
Position 1
6
Position 2
Three numbers expected
Position 3
```

After reaching position 3, the program terminates normally, even though the values passed in the second call to Fnc included a nonnumeric value.

Anticipating an error condition allows you to handle the situation appropriately. For example, in an interactive program you could allow the user to specify an alternate course of action or to repeat an action with different input values. If it is appropriate to terminate the program, at least this can be done gracefully, closing open resources as needed and reporting the condition in an expected fashion.

Working with Return Values

Because the preceding example uses the print function, its use is restricted to programs that can work with the standard output channel. Its output is directed to the user rather than the caller. In all but the simplest cases, you'll want to avoid this kind of restriction by making your functions independent of the kind of program that uses them. This practice enables you build up a library of functions that should be portable to different platforms. The key to this is to have functions and their callers communicate by means of parameter lists and return values. The actual input and output to the system can then be handled at a higher level by the caller of the platform-independent functions.

One of Lua's many distinctive features is that it allows functions to return multiple values. A convention has evolved regarding how functions should indicate success and failure. If a function succeeds, its first return value should be something other than `false` or `nil`. Usually this return value is the principal value the function was called on to produce, like a file handle or string capture. This value can be followed by other pertinent values. If the function fails, its first value should be `nil`. This is followed by something that explains why the error occurred, usually an error message but possibly something else like a table or numeric error code.

The example can be reworked to follow this convention:

```
local function Fnc(A, B, C)
  local Sum, ErrStr
  A, B, C = tonumber(A), tonumber(B), tonumber(C)
  if A and B and C then
    Sum = A + B + C
  else
    ErrStr = "Three numbers expected"
  end
  return Sum, ErrStr
end

print("Position 1")
local Sum, ErrStr = Fnc(1, "2", 3)
print(Sum or ErrStr)
print("Position 2")
local Sum, ErrStr = Fnc(1, nil, 3)
print(Sum or ErrStr)
print("Position 3")
```

The output is like that of the previous example:

```
Position 1
6
Position 2
Three numbers expected
Position 3
```

You'll occasionally see a clever use of `assert` that utilizes Lua's return value convention. For example:

```
Hnd = assert(io.open("index.html", "r"))
```

The `io.open` function returns `nil` followed by an error message if the file cannot be opened; otherwise, it returns the handle to the opened file. In either case, these return values are passed directly to `assert`. In the event that `io.open` fails, the first argument to `assert` will be nil. This causes `assert` to issue a runtime error using as its error value the second argument it receives, namely the error message returned by `io.open`. If, on the other hand, `io.open` succeeds, `assert` receives as its first argument the handle to the open file. Because this value is neither `false` nor `nil`, it simply returns this value and does not issue an error.

The problem with using `assert` is that, in the event of a failed assertion, the default action is to terminate the program. In the case of the example shown here, there may be good reasons why the file `index.html` cannot be opened, and to bring the entire program to a halt just because the file can't be opened is especially heavy-handed. In the next section, you'll learn about structured programming techniques that let you recover gracefully and simply from conditions like this. The assert function is extremely useful for ferreting out wrong assumptions in your code, but it's not the best approach to handle conditions that are beyond the programmer's control.

Another convention has evolved to handle the returns values of a function that is called indirectly through another function. Like all values in Lua, a function is a first class value and can be passed as an argument, something you've already seen with the comparison function that can be optionally passed to table.sort. In some cases, a function's job can simply be to call another function in a modified runtime environment. The pcall and xpcall functions (described later in this chapter) are examples of this. However, the added indirection requires some means to distinguish between errors caused by the function that is called directly and the one that is called indirectly. Typically in this case, the directly-called function returns true if it succeeds; this is followed by the return values of the indirectly-called function whether it succeeds or fails. If the directly-called function fails, it returns false followed by an error message.

Structuring Code

In the examples you've seen so far, the program code has been structured to visually indicate the blocks as Lua sees them. For example, the statements following an if expression are indented to show what gets executed if the expression evaluates to true. The benefit to this structuring is that you can tell at a glance what state the program is in — for example, which files are open and which conditions are currently met.

Following is an example that uses Lua's return value convention with structured programming to generate a file listing with line numbers. It shows how error handling can be integrated with block structuring to handle errors in a predictable and robust way. As you study the example, ask yourself what happens under different scenarios. For example, what happens to the source file handle if the destination file cannot be opened?

```lua
local function FileCopyLineNum(SrcFileStr, DstFileStr)
  local SrcHnd, DstHnd, ErrStr, Line
  SrcHnd, ErrStr = io.open(SrcFileStr, "r")
  if SrcHnd then
    DstHnd, ErrStr = io.open(DstFileStr, "w")
    if DstHnd then
      Line = 0
      for Str in SrcHnd:lines() do
        Line = Line + 1
        DstHnd:write(Line, " ", Str, "\n")
      end
      if Line == 0 then
        ErrStr = SrcFileStr .. ": File is empty"
        Line = nil
      end
      DstHnd:close()
    end
    SrcHnd:close()
  end
  return Line, ErrStr
```

```
    end

    local Count, ErrStr = FileCopyLineNum("index.html", "index.lst")
    io.write(Count and ("OK: count " .. Count) or ErrStr, "\n")
```

If `index.html` does not exist, this script outputs the following:

```
    index.html: No such file or directory
```

If this file exists but is empty, the output is this:

```
    index.html: File is empty
```

If `index.html` exists and has lines in it, and `index.lst` can be opened for writing, the output looks like this:

```
    OK: count 243
```

The general idea behind structuring your code is to place operations in their correct position. For example, an indented block follows the conditional statement that tests whether the source file has been successfully opened. You can bring much clarity to your code by ensuring that this condition remains valid through the entire block, and that the condition is invalid outside of the block. In this example, that's done by closing the source file at the very end of the conditional block. You don't need to check whether the file is currently open and ready to be closed — the block structure guarantees that it is, regardless of what happened inside the block. Whether or not the destination file is successfully opened, you know from the visual representation of the code where the source file is open and where it needs to be closed.

Why would it be a problem to close the source file as soon as its contents have been copied? A glance at the indentation of the code should tell you immediately: the source file would not be properly closed if an error occurred while opening the destination file.

Lua enables you to keep your program clear by declaring local variables only where you need them, that is, to keep their scope at a minimum. Here, the declaration of `DstHnd` could have been deferred to the point after the source file has been opened. However, the declaration of `Line` and `ErrStr` need to be where they are, because they are used as return values. Furthermore, neither should be redeclared in an inner block because this would mask the outer values. Beginners to Lua often wish that variables would be local by default, but doing so would make this powerful form of scope control impossible.

Notice that no assumptions about the user interface are made in the `FileCopyLineNum` function. Communication with this function occur through its parameter list and its return values.

A slight visual problem occurs in the destination file when the number of digits in the line number changes. This can be remedied with string formatting, as described in Chapter 5.

Bigger problems have to do with guarding against unintended input. What if the function is called with nonstring arguments? What if a binary file is specified as the source file? Worse still, what if an important system file is specified as the destination file?

Calling the function with nonstring arguments is a code issue, and in this case you'll learn about the problem when you call `io.open`. Like a syntax error, after you correct the problem, it won't be an issue anymore. If this routine merely stored the arguments for later processing, some assertions might be necessary to ensure that each argument is a string.

As written, the `FileCopyLineNum` function assumes that the source file is a text file. In the copy loop, you could check for the presence of unexpected characters or unexpectedly long source lines. If either of these occurs, you could terminate the loop and proceed appropriately.

The risk of overwriting an important file is more difficult to address. The relevant question is whether this routine is at the right level to implement a safeguard. Clearly, `io.open` isn't making the check, and it could be convincingly argued that `FileCopyLineNum` shouldn't either. If it doesn't, the burden is on the caller to make sure that the destination file is safe to create or overwrite. The important lesson is that you need to consider these issues and strive to cover them at the right place in your code.

Even if the block following a resource test does not itself contain nested indented blocks, it is still a good policy to defer closing the resource until the end of the block, because as you refine the program and possibly add new conditionals, knowing that the resource is open throughout the block is one less thing you have to verify.

Some programmers criticize, sometimes with alarming fervor, this type of code structuring, complaining that indentation levels can become excessive and that even small changes to a routine's logic can necessitate shifting large blocks to the left or right (something that is easy to do in a decent text editor). In practice, deep nesting indicates a need to break blocks into functions. Doing so makes your program more modular and reduces the degree of indentation. The functions in the following example are fictitious and, for simplicity's sake, are called without any arguments and portrayed without error handling:

```
A = ResourceOpen()
if A then
  B = ItemFirst()
  while B do
    C = ResourceOpen()
    if C then
      for D in E() do
        if F then
          DoSomething()
        end
      end
      ResourceClose(C)
    end
    B = ItemNext(B)
  end
  ResourceClose(A)
end
```

This can be rewritten as follows:

```
function Moon(B, C)
  for D in E() do
    if F then
      DoSomething()
```

```
      end
    end
  end

function Sun(B)
  C = ResourceOpen()
  if C then
    Moon(B, C)
    ResourceClose(C)
  end
end

A = ResourceOpen()
if A then
  B = ItemFirst()
  while B do
    Sun(B)
    B = ItemNext(B)
  end
  ResourceClose(A)
end
```

Error-Containment Functions

In the examples you have seen so far, runtime errors result in the termination of the entire program. Fortunately, this can be avoided. Lua provides a mechanism — the protected environment — to contain the damage caused by an error condition. The Lua `pcall` and the `xpcall` functions enable you to suppress the propagation of an error.

The pcall Function

Any Lua function, including Lua scripts loaded from disk and converted to a function by `loadfile`, can be run in a protected environment. You do this by calling `pcall` with the function to be called as its first argument. Additional arguments to `pcall` are passed as arguments to this function. The principal difference between calling a function directly and calling it through `pcall` is the way errors are handled. As you've seen so far, if an error occurs in a function that is called directly, the Lua interpreter responds by displaying the stack traceback and terminating the program. If, on the other hand, an error occurs in a function that has been invoked by `pcall`, the error is reported as one of the return values of `pcall`. You can handle the error in whatever way you consider appropriate.

Try It Out   **Using pcall**

In this Try It Out, you'll see the `pcall` function in action. The following code is a revision of the first example from this chapter adapted to run in a protected environment.

1.   With your text editor, create a new file with the following contents:

```
function C()
  print("C 1")
  print(1 + nil)
  print("C 2")
```

```
   end

function B()
   print("B 1")
   C()
   print("B 2")
end

function A()
   print("A 1")
   B()
   print("A 2")
end

print("Main 1")
local Code, ErrStr = pcall(A)
print("Main 2", Code and "Success" or ErrStr)
```

2. Save this script as **err.lua**.

3. Run the script with the Lua interpreter, like this:

```
lua err.lua
```

The output is as follows:

```
Main 1
A 1
B 1
C 1
Main 2  err.lua:3: attempt to perform arithmetic on a nil value
```

How It Works

The main clue to understanding what happened is the lack of `"C 2"`, `"B 2"`, and `"A 2"` markers. If this gives you the notion that when the error occurred control was transferred directly back to `pcall`, you're entirely correct.

Remember, it is the call stack that allows functions to return properly. In effect, the stack is Lua's only memory regarding where it came from and where it should return to. The `pcall` function effectively marks the current position on the stack and arranges with Lua to return to that mark — the recover point — in the event of an error. Up until the error occurred, the stack functioned as expected. You can follow this in more detail by adding a call to `debug.traceback` in the print statements. For example, replace `print("A 1")` with `print(debug.traceback("A 1"))`.

A protected call will keep your program from sinking after a runtime error, but it may tilt frightfully to starboard. Imagine that the `"A 1"`, `"B 1"`, and `"C 1"` markers indicate positions where resources such as database connections and files are opened, and the markers `"A 2"`, `"B 2"`, and `"C 2"` indicate the positions where the resources are closed. When `pcall` returns with a return code indicating that an error took place, it may be difficult to programmatically determine which resources are in need of closing.

Some resources — in such as userdata resources that have been specially programmed — will close themselves when they are no longer accessible to your program and are consequently collected as garbage. Using Lua's C programming interface, you can create resource handles to behave this way. However, you should not depend on this behavior to close resources. A very large number of open resources may accumulate between garbage collection cycles, and this can have an adverse effect on the operation of your program.

Another method to manage dangling resources is to pass a newly constructed local table to your function by means of pcall. You can use this table to store handles for open resources, among other things. When a resource is opened, its handle is stored in the table. After the resource is closed, its handle is set to nil. This table would be passed as an argument to all functions in the call chain. Unfortunately, this approach couples these functions in a way that may be undesirable. It also means that the caller of the protected function must know, given an assortment of handles, how to close the resources. A variation on this theme would be to store a closure that would close the resource instead of a resource handle.

The caller of a protected function must also, in the event of an error, determine the best subsequent course of action. Should the program clean up and terminate? Should it invoke the protected function again with different arguments? One action your program should definitely not take is to proceed as if nothing happened.

The xpcall Function

You may have noticed that the error message returned by pcall does not have a stack traceback. After pcall returns, all stack levels between pcall and the place where the error occurred are no longer accessible, so no traceback can be constructed. The xpcall function is like pcall, except that you specify as its second argument an error handler that is called before Lua transfers control back to the place where xpcall was called. This handler receives the error message and returns the new error value, usually the same error message after it has been augmented with a stack traceback. The xpcall function differs from the pcall function in two respects:

- ❑ It uses an error handler.
- ❑ It is unable to pass arguments to the function it calls.

Here's an example of its use:

```
function A()
   print(1 + nil)
end

print(xpcall(A, debug.traceback))
```

This outputs the following:

```
false   err.lua:2: attempt to perform arithmetic on a nil value
stack traceback:
      err.lua:2: in function <err.lua:1>
      [C]: in function 'xpcall'
      err.lua:5: in main chunk
      [C]: ?
```

Here, the debug.traceback function was used as a handler, but you can write your own as well. It can return something other than an error string if you want.

User-Written Scripts

Many applications employ Lua so that users can prepare and run their own extension scripts. However, you should run these scripts in protected mode to contain any errors that may occur.

Most users have experienced programs that run fine as long as nothing unexpected occurs, but operate erratically after they attempt to recover from an error. If your application supports the execution of user-provided Lua scripts, you need to guard against destabilizing your entire application as a result of running an errant script. As you learned in Chapter 4, Lua provides sandboxing mechanisms to isolate these user-written scripts from each other and from the host application. In the next chapter, you'll see that Lua supports a way to require that only local variables be created by a script. Doing this helps to ensure that resources are cleaned up properly in the event of an error. Similarly, functions that could pose a risk to the operating environment are easily made unavailable to the user-written scripts.

Locating Errors

The diagnostic message and stack traceback that Lua presents when a runtime error occurs are often sufficient for you to identify exactly what went wrong. However, sometimes an error occurs long after the source of the problem has been executed. For example, an error might indicate that arithmetic was attempted on a nil value, and you are left wondering how a certain variable ever *became* nil. A good approach when you don't have a clue where something like this may have occurred is to use the `print` function or a message box routine to temporarily display important values at various points where you think the problem may have originated. But rather than sprinkling such calls haphazardly throughout your code, you'll usually do better by attempting to repeatedly divide the problem area in half.

Summary

In this chapter, you've learned to do the following:

❑   Look for and correct syntax errors.

❑   Handle runtime errors (both code-based and data-based).

❑   Understand Lua's call stack.

❑   Use `assert` when it's desirable to do so.

❑   Read stack tracebacks.

❑   Structure your code with an emphasis on resource lifespan.

❑   Protect a function call so that the entire application isn't abnormally ended if it causes a runtime error.

Any mechanism that enables you to understand the internal state of your program is valuable in ensuring that it is functioning as expected or in uncovering errors. In the next chapter, you'll learn about Lua modules, and one of the examples shows you how to generate a tree diagram of Lua tables. A rendering like that can provide a lot more information than a simple `print` statement can and is consequently a good tool to have when tracking down program errors.

Exercises

1. In the Lua interpreter, issue the following statement:

```
> print(1 + nil)
```

Why doesn't `print` show up in the resulting stack traceback?

2. How would you add the prefix 'Programmer error' to the stack traceback?

3. The `pcall` function accepts arguments, and the `xpcall` function accepts an error handler. How can you write a protected function caller that accepts both arguments and an error handler?

Using Modules

One of the most important techniques of structured programming is partitioning a program into subprograms that have well-defined interfaces and protected implementations. In this chapter, you learn how to do the following:

❑   Work with interfaces and implementations

❑   Modularize Lua scripts

❑   Use Lua modules from your application scripts

As a working example, you'll explore a Lua value inspection module that should prove useful when you develop Lua programs.

Interfaces and Implementations

An *interface* is the part of a subprogram that is known to callers of the subprogram. The *implementation* refers to the way the subprogram works internally. If a subprogram's interface is clearly defined and its implementation doesn't depend on variables that can be modified by other program parts, then it has the desirable attribute of being reusable. This discipline is often referred to as encapsulation or information hiding or modularization. You've seen already how functions in Lua present an interface behind which local variables are protected from tampering. A function is loosely coupled (and therefore is more easily used in a variety of contexts) to the extent that it minimizes the scope of the variables it uses.

These notions of interface and implementation extend to files containing Lua code. When such a file is loaded, Lua converts it into a function, to which arguments can be passed and from which results can be returned. In this way, a Lua file has its own interface and its own implementation.

A Lua module is simply a file that conforms to certain rules. First, it can be located and loaded at runtime. Second, it receives one argument: the name of the module. And third, it returns at most one result. The use of modules doesn't guarantee reusability, but it certainly promotes this objective by providing a useful level at which to define an interface beneath which the actual workings can be hidden.

Libraries written in C and other low-level languages are conventionally made available through Lua's module mechanism. You can also associate a namespace (a Lua table that contains the module's functions and other fields) with a module. This practice lends clarity to programs and reduces the chance of name clashes.

The require Function

The principal high-level function that implements module conventions in Lua is `require`. The various lower-level functions it uses to actually locate, load, and run modules are all available to Lua programs. `require` simply codifies the way modules are handled to make the business of creating and using modules more uniform across applications.

Newcomers to Lua may confuse `require` with a directive, which is a direction to be heeded at compile-time rather than runtime. In particular, C programmers may initially make the mistake of thinking require acts like #include. Keep in mind that require is a function and that any modules that are required need to be available at runtime. Lua does not have any preprocessor or compiler directives.

Try It Out   **Using Modules**

There are a few interesting and clever subtleties to modules in Lua, but the basic operation is straightforward. Here's an example that illustrates modules at their simplest. It demonstrates how you can package Lua code into a module so that it can be used by other scripts, and how a script makes use of a module.

1.   Add a temporary variable to your shell environment. In Unix-type systems, issue this command:

```
export LUA_PATH='?.luac;?.lua'
```

2.   In Windows, issue this command from a shell prompt:

```
set LUA_PATH=?.luac;?.lua
```

3.   With a text editor, create a new file and add the following lines to it:

```
function ObjectShow(Val, Key, TruncLen)
   print(Key, Val)
end
```

4.   Save this module file as show.lua.

5.   Create another file with these contents:

```
require("show")
ObjectShow("My table", {A = 1})
```

6.   Save this main script file as showtest.lua in the same directory as `show.lua`.

7.   Run the script by executing the following command:

```
lua showtest.lua
```

The response looks something like this:

```
My table      table: 00755610
```

How It Works

Lua's response doesn't appear especially spectacular, but a fair amount of processing occurs behind the scenes.

First, Lua starts up and transfers the contents of the shell environment variable LUA_PATH to its own variable named package.path. Your script can modify this variable, but in this example, you leave it alone.

The script calls Lua's built-in require function with the name of the module you want to import, namely show.

> *(In many cases, the require call is followed by a string without parentheses. Remember that Lua treats a function followed by a literal string the same as if the string had parentheses around it.*

After verifying that the show module has not already been loaded, the require function traverses, in order, the segments of the package.path variable that are delimited by semicolons. In this example, these segments are ?.luac and ?.lua. For each segment, the function performs a simple pattern substitution. It replaces each occurrence of the question mark with the name that was passed to it and checks to see if a file by that name exists. The first substitution results in the show.luac filename. Because the segment does not contain path information, the require function follows the usual shell semantics and looks in the current working directory for the file. It doesn't find this file, so it moves onto the next segment. The second substitution results in the show.lua filename, which it is able to find.

The require function loads show.lua as a chunk and calls it with a single argument, the string "show".

The execution of show.lua results in the formation of a new global variable, an ObjectShow function. Here, show.lua doesn't return any value, but if it did, require would return it to the main script.

Where to Put Modules

You'll want to create a directory to hold Lua extension modules, but you do not want that directory in the operating system's search path, because you want the system to locate lua, and you want lua to locate its modules. Some of the modules are executable libraries that will be loaded and linked at run-time. These libraries are tailored specifically to Lua, and you don't want the operating system to inadvertently load one or to even waste time looking through them.

The following section summarizes what you need to do to assure that Lua can find its modules. First, you create a directory for modules, and then you set an environment variable to be used by Lua to locate modules.

Creating a Module Directory

The locations shown here for Lua module directories are fairly standard among Lua users, but you may change them if you want to or if you lack sufficient system privileges to create them. On Unix-type systems, use a command like this:

```
mkdir -p /usr/local/lib/lua/5.1
```

Some installers of Lua use the directory `/usr/local/share/lua/5.1` for Lua scripts and reserve `/usr/local/lib/lua/5.1` for shared libraries that interface with Lua's C API.

On Windows, issue commands like these to create the module directory:

```
mkdir "c:\program files\lua"
mkdir "c:\program files\lua\5.1"
```

Setting Lua's Environment Variable

The `LUA_PATH` environment variable used in the preceding Try It Out example is rather simple — it doesn't include any directory information. Change that now so that `LUA_PATH` takes into account the new directory you have created. On Unix-type systems, where filenames look like this:

```
/usr/local/lib/lua/5.1/show.lua
```

make the following assignment:

```
export LUA_PATH='?.lua;/usr/local/lib/lua/5.1/?.lua'
```

On Windows, where filenames that look like this:

```
C:\Program Files\lua\5.1\show.lua
```

make the following assignment:

```
set LUA_PATH=?.lua;C:\Program Files\lua\5.1\?.lua
```

If necessary, you can refer to Chapter 1 for instructions on setting environment variables. Note that on Windows, backslashes should not be escaped and names with spaces should not be quoted.

Regardless of the form that filenames take, the simple pattern substitution that Lua uses to locate modules is the same. The particular values for `LUA_PATH` shown previously specify that Lua is to look for Lua modules first in the current directory and then, if that fails, in the designated common directory.

Preserving a Module's Interface

The preceding Try It Out example was trivial, but you will enhance it in the next Try It Out to provide many more details about the passed-in value. The revised module will prove to be very useful when you're developing programs in Lua. In this example, you'll do the revision while preserving the module's interface. That is, although you'll change the implementation of `show.lua` dramatically, you will not change the part that it exposes to the outside world, namely the `ObjectShow` function and its list of parameters. You'll appreciate the importance of this when you realize that you don't have to change `showtest.lua` in the slightest to benefit from the updated implementation of `show.lua`. This kind of encapsulation forms the basis of a well-designed application which is partitioned into a number of general-purpose, reusable modules.

Try It Out   **Extending the show Module**

In this Try It Out, you'll dramatically enhance the show module to display more details about the value to be examined. In doing so, you'll preserve the interface of the previous version.

1.   Replace the contents of show.lua with the following:

```
-- This function conditions a key or value for display

local function LclRenderStr(Obj, TruncLen)
  local TpStr = type(Obj)
  if TpStr == "string" then
    Obj = string.gsub(Obj, "[^%w%p ]", function(Ch)
      return "\\" .. string.format("%03d", string.byte(Ch)) end )
    if TruncLen and TruncLen > 0 and string.len(Obj) > TruncLen + 3 then
      -- This could misleadingly truncate numeric escape value
      Obj = string.sub(Obj, 1, TruncLen) .. "..."
    end
    Obj = '"' .. Obj .. '"'
  elseif TpStr == "boolean" then
    Obj = "boolean: " .. tostring(Obj)
  else
    Obj = tostring(Obj)
  end
  return Obj
end

-- This function replaces ["x"]["y"] stubble with x.y. Keys are assumed to be
-- identifier-compatible.

local function LclShave(Str)
  local Count
  Str, Count = string.gsub(Str, '^%["(.+)%"]$', '%1')
  if Count == 1 then
    Str = string.gsub(Str, '%"]%["', '.')
  end
  return Str
end

local function LclRender(Tbl, Val, KeyStr, TruncLen, Lvl, Visited, KeyPathStr)
  local VtpStr, ValStr
  VtpStr = type(Val)
  if Visited[Val] then
    ValStr = "same as " .. Visited[Val]
  else
    ValStr = LclRenderStr(Val, TruncLen)
    if VtpStr == "function" then -- Display function's environment
      local Env = getfenv(Val)
      Env = Visited[Env] or Env
      ValStr = string.gsub(ValStr, "(function:%s*.*)$", "%1 (env " ..
        string.gsub(tostring(Env), "table: ", "")  .. ")")
    elseif VtpStr == "table" then
      ValStr = ValStr .. string.format(" (n = %d)", #Val)
    end
  end
```

```
    KeyPathStr = KeyPathStr .. "[" .. KeyStr .. "]"
    table.insert(Tbl, { Lvl, string.format('[%s] %s',
      KeyStr, ValStr) })
  if VtpStr == "table" and not Visited[Val] then
    Visited[Val] = LclShave(KeyPathStr)
    local SrtTbl = {}
    for K, V in pairs(Val) do
      table.insert(SrtTbl, { LclRenderStr(K, TruncLen), V, K, type(K) })
    end
    local function LclCmp(A, B)
      local Cmp
      local Ta, Tb = A[4], B[4]
      if Ta == "number" then
        if Tb == "number" then
          Cmp = A[3] < B[3]
        else
          Cmp = true -- Numbers appear first
        end
      else -- A is not a number
        if Tb == "number" then
          Cmp = false -- Numbers appear first
        else
          Cmp = A[1] < B[1]
        end
      end
      return Cmp
    end
    table.sort(SrtTbl, LclCmp)
    for J, Rec in ipairs(SrtTbl) do
      LclRender(Tbl, Rec[2], Rec[1], TruncLen, Lvl + 1, Visited, KeyPathStr)
    end
  end
end

-- This function appends a series of records of the form { level,
-- description_string } to the indexed table specified by Tbl. When this
-- function returns, Tbl can be used to inspect the Lua object specified by
-- Val. Key specifies the name of the object. TruncLen specifies the maximum
-- length of each description string; if this value is zero, no truncation will
-- take place. Keys are sorted natively (that is, numbers are sorted
-- numerically and everything else lexically). String values are displayed with
-- quotes, numbers are unadorned, and all other values have an identifying
-- prefix such as "boolean". Consequently, all keys are displayed within their
-- type partition. This function returns nothing; its only effect is to augment
-- Tbl.

function ObjectDescribe(Tbl, Val, Key, TruncLen)
  LclRender(Tbl, Val, LclRenderStr(Key, TruncLen), TruncLen or 0, 1, {}, "")
end

-- This function prints a hierarchical summary of the object specified by Val
-- to standard out. See ObjectDescribe for more details.

function ObjectShow(Val, Key, TruncLen)
  local Tbl = {}
```

```
   ObjectDescribe(Tbl, Val, Key, TruncLen)
   for J, Rec in ipairs(Tbl) do
      io.write(string.rep("  ", Rec[1] - 1), Rec[2], "\n")
   end
end
```

2. Save the file in the module directory you created earlier. This will be the show module's permanent home.

3. In order to avoid some possible confusion, delete the older version show.lua in your current working directory. Now when you run showtest.lua, you'll be presented with a richer display of the table you pass to ObjectShow.

4. Take a look at the entire Lua global environment as follows:

```
require("show")
ObjectShow(_G, "_G")
```

The output will span more lines than can fit on most screens, so you may want to pipe the output through a paging filter:

```
lua showtest.lua | more
```

On Linux, the wryly named less filter will provide more scrolling and search options.

How It Works

Being able to display data structures this way is indispensable when you're developing scripts. After you have installed show.lua in a location included in the LUA_PATH sequence, other scripts you write can make use of it by simply requiring it.

The Lua interpreter enables you to specify a required module on the command line using the -l switch. For example, you view the global environment from your shell prompt as follows:

```
lua -l show -e "ObjectShow(_G, '_G')" | more
```

This Try It Out illustrates Lua's module location and loading logic. You follow steps that are similar to the previous Try It Out, but now show.lua resides in a "permanent" location where you can put other Lua modules.

This example also illustrates the concept of interface preservation. It can be argued that this particular script's interface could be improved, and you'll soon learn techniques to do so, but the advantage of preserving a module's interface should be clear.

There are some programming techniques that this example demonstrates as well. In particular, show.lua addresses the tree structure of Lua tables. Trees are special because any subtree (any table within a containing table) s a tree itself. A function that processes a tree can be used to process a subtree. This presents a classic application of using functions recursively.

Also note the use of thin wrappers at the bottom of the script. The ObjectShow function in the revised show.lua is simply a wrapper around the ObjectDescribe function. ObjectShow writes to the standard output stream, but ObjectDescribe and the functions it calls do not. This means you can use ObjectDescribe in a wider variety of contexts than ObjectShow. For example, you can call

`ObjectDescribe` by a web page generator or a graph generator. If a wrapper around `ObjectDescribe` required the services of some other module, such as a graphing library, it would make sense to place this wrapper in its own module. Requiring such a module directly in `show.lua` where it isn't generally needed would diminish the reusability of `show.lua`.

Module Bookkeeping

A module can in turn require modules of its own. This sets up the scenario in which the same script might be required more than once. For example, you may require two modules, each of which requires the same third module. How does Lua handle situations like this? As is usual with Lua, a short example can provide all the insight you need to figure things out. With your text editor, create a file named **modload.lua** with the following contents:

```
print(..., package.loaded[...])
Serial = (Serial or 0) + 1
return Serial
```

Notice the use of the three dots (the `vararg` expression) as a placeholder for the module name. Remember that when Lua loads a chunk, it converts the chunk to a function. As with any Lua function, any practical number of arguments of any type can be passed to it. In this case, however, Lua has no way of knowing what arguments might be expected by the embedded chunk, so the arguments are passed in using the `vararg` mechanism. `require` passes only the module name to a module, so the `vararg` expression evaluates to a single string.

In the same directory, create a file named modloadtest.lua with the following contents:

```
local ModStr = "modload"
print("Main, before require", package.loaded[ModStr])
local Val = require(ModStr)
print("Main, after 1st require", package.loaded[ModStr], Val)
Val = require(ModStr)
print("Main, after 2nd require", package.loaded[ModStr], Val)
package.loaded[ModStr] = nil
Val = require(ModStr)
print("Main, after reset", package.loaded[ModStr], Val)
```

Now run the module like this:

```
lua modloadtest.lua
```

The output will look like the following:

```
Main, before require    nil
modload userdata: 6731F6D0
Main, after 1st require 1        1
Main, after 2nd require 1        1
modload userdata: 6731F6D0
Main, after reset       2        2
```

Lua uses the table package.loaded to associate the name of a module with its return value. If the entry for a particular module is nil, it generally means that the module has not yet been loaded. As you can see, it might also mean that the table field has been cleared by your script to force a reload of the module. The userdata is Lua's way of indicating that a module is in the process of being loaded and no return value is available. This enables Lua to recognize a recursive loading loop and raise an error. The use of a userdata for this purpose is quintessential Lua, because it's a value that simply cannot be mistaken for the return value of a module.

Note that the require function did not load the module when it was called a second time. The package.loaded example value indicated that the module was already loaded, so require simply returned the value associated with it. This behavior suggests that you should do no more than define functions and initialize variables when the module chunk is called.

> On systems such as Windows, filenames are case-insensitive. For example, Lib.lua is considered to be the same file as lib.lua. However, the associative table lookup mechanism that Lua uses to detect whether a file has already been loaded is case-sensitive. This can lead to a module being inadvertently loaded twice if somewhere in your application you call require("Lib") and elsewhere you call require("lib").

Experiment with little variations to the modload.lua module to see how Lua responds. For example:

❑   Return nil rather than Serial.

❑   Require modload from within modload.lua.

❑   Make Serial a local variable instead of a global.

Bytecode

In the first Try It Out of this chapter, you saw the extension .luac in the LUA_PATH environment variable. This is the extension conventionally given to Lua bytecode, which is code that has been generated by the Lua compiler for subsequent use in the Lua virtual machine. Lua's script loading mechanism can read both Lua source code and Lua bytecode. When it reads a chunk, it distinguishes between the two forms and in the case of bytecode, it dispenses with the compiling stage. You can use the standalone version of the Lua compiler, named luac or luac.exe depending on your platform, to generate a bytecode file. The topic of bytecode fits into a discussion of modules because a compiled Lua script can be placed in the module directory.

Why would you want to execute bytecode rather than source code? Actually, for fewer reasons than you might at first suppose.

In general, the platform and the Lua version of both the Lua compiler and the Lua interpreter must match for bytecode to be executed properly. The instruction set used by Lua's virtual machine has changed over time. All bets are off when you compile Lua programs on one machine and run the resulting bytecode on another. Even if the two systems are running on similar hardware, it is likely that sooner or later there will be a version discrepancy between the compiler on one machine and the interpreter on another.

Lua has such a fast compiler that, in general practice, little performance is gained by skipping the compiling step. If you need to execute a Lua script repeatedly, it makes sense to load and compile the file once and then repeatedly call the resulting function.

The Lua compiler has a very nice feature that lets you amalgamate more than one Lua script into one bytecode file. To do this, simply specify the source files on the `luac` command line. This cannot be accomplished by using the `require` function, because even with a compiled script a call to `require` occurs at runtime. In fact, if you want to produce a single bytecode file that embeds Lua modules rather than loads them at runtime, you should include the modules on the `luac` command line and comment out calls to `require`.

If you're looking for top-notch performance of Lua programs on the x86 platform, investigate LuaJIT, a beautifully implemented just-in-time compiler for Lua programs created by Mike Pall. The LuaJIT package includes a replacement for `lua` called `luajit` that compiles Lua bytecode into x86 machine code as a program runs. You can find it at `luaforge.net`.

Namespaces

Consider the following `Util.lua` module:

```
function Quote(Str)
   return string.format("%q", Str)
end
```

Now look at the following `UtilTest.lua` test script, which requires `Util.lua`:

```
require("Util")
print(Quote('Natty "Pathfinder" Bumppo'))
```

Some programmers who use the `Util` module would be displeased that the variable `Quote` "pollutes" the global environment. In general, you would do well to model your approach after that used with the Lua libraries, and bundle your variables into a namespace table. For example, the string length function is given the name `len` in the global table named `string`. There are many ways you can implement a module with a namespace. The most common ways will be shown here, each implementing the `Quote` example in a slightly different manner.

Creating and Reusing Namespaces

Usually, a module will create a namespace table and place its functions and other variables in it. Here is the `Quote` example using this technique. The `Util.lua` module script contains the following:

```
Util = {}

function Util.Quote(Str)
   return string.format("%q", Str)
end

return Util
```

The `UtilTest.lua` calling script contains this:

```
require("Util")
print(Util.Quote('Natty "Pathfinder" Bumppo'))
```

In this case, the namespace table `Util` is created as a global variable. By convention, it is also returned from the module. If more than one module is to add fields to the namespace table, it is important not to overwrite it. Find the following line:

```
Util = {}
```

And replace it with this:

```
Util = Util or {}
```

You need to do this in each module that adds fields to the `Util` table.

A module can add one or more fields into a standard library namespace. In this case, there is some merit in conforming to the naming conventions used in the namespace. Here is the `Quote` example applied to the standard `string` table (notice that the function is given an all-lowercase name). The `Util.lua` module script now contains the following:

```
function string.quote(Str)
    return string.format("%q", Str)
end

return string
```

The `UtilTest.lua` test script contains this:

```
require("Util")
print(string.quote('Natty "Pathfinder" Bumppo'))
```

A module does not have to create any global variables. Here is the `Quote` example using a local namespace table. The `Util.lua` module script contains the following:

```
local Util = {}

function Util.Quote(Str)
    return string.format("%q", Str)
end

return Util
```

The `UtilTest.lua` calling script contains this:

```
Utility = require("Util")
print(Utility.Quote('Natty "Pathfinder" Bumppo'))
```

In this case, the namespace table must be returned by the module; otherwise, it would not be accessible to the program which requires it. Of course, nothing prevents the requiring program itself from assigning the namespace table to a global variable.

Avoiding Global Variables

Good modularization technique requires that you channel all access to your module through its interface. Creating global variables in a module exposes a part of its implementation and, because these variables are subject to modification outside the module itself, increases the chance of hard-to-track bugs. What methods can you use to avoid inadvertently creating globals?

Using the strict Module

One technique is to use the `strict.lua` module, which is included in the `etc` directory of the Lua source distribution. Copy this file to the module directory you set up earlier in this chapter so that it can be loaded with a call to `require`. Here's an example of its use:

```
require "strict"

local function Test()
   A = 2
   B = 3
end

A = 1
Test()
```

Running this script results in the following error message:

```
assign to undeclared variable 'B'
```

The assignment to A in function Test was okay, but the assignment to B was not. When using the `strict` module, global variables must be first assigned at the main level of the chunk. This is what the line does, which makes the subsequent reassignment of A in Test work fine:

```
A = 1
```

Reporting All Global Assignments

You can use the Lua compiler to list the virtual machine instructions of your program. Here's an example of how to do this using the `show.lua` script:

```
luac -l -p show.lua
```

This results in a flurry of lines that look like the following:

```
       6       [104]    MOVE          8 2 0
       7       [104]    CALL          4 5 1
       8       [105]    GETGLOBAL     4 1      ; ipairs
       9       [105]    MOVE          5 3 0
      10       [105]    CALL          4 2 5
      11       [105]    TFORPREP      4 11     ; to 23
```

The SETGLOBAL instruction indicates the assignment of a global variable. You can simply filter out everything except these SETGLOBAL instructions using `grep`, like this:

```
luac -l -p show.lua | grep SETGLOBAL
```

On the Windows platform where `grep` isn't available by default, you can try the following command:

```
luac -l -p show.lua | find "SETGLOBAL"
```

This generates the following output, which confirms that there are no global assignments other than the intended ones:

```
       10      [95]    SETGLOBAL      3 0     ; ObjectDescribe
       12      [102]   SETGLOBAL      3 1     ; ObjectShow
```

The module Function

You can modularize a Lua script by calling the `module` function. Calling this function simplifies the process of modularizing your Lua code by creating a namespace table and effectively placing all global variables into this table.

Try It Out   **Using the module Function**

1.   Modify `Util.lua` so that it contains the following:

```
local format = string.format

module(...)

function Quote(Str)
  return format("%q", Str)
end
```

2.   The calling script `UtilTest.lua` contains:

```
require("Util")
print(Util.Quote('Natty "Pathfinder" Bumppo'))
```

3.   Invoke the script in the usual way:

```
lua UtilTest.lua
```

The result is a quoted version of the specified string:

```
"Natty \"Pathfinder\" Bumppo"
```

How It Works

A number of things happen with the `module` function behind the scenes. Here is a summary of how it works:

1.   The `require` function is called with the `"Util"` string.

2.   `require` resolves this by locating and loading `"Util.lua"` as a chunk and calling it with the single `"Util"` argument.

3. The first statement to be executed in the module is the assignment of `string.format` to the local variable `format`. This is needed because the subsequent call to `module` will make all global variables inaccessible. Recall that Lua resolves references to global variables (that is, variables that are not introduced with the `local` keyword) in the global environment. By default, every function and chunk is associated with a common global environment, but you can change this programmatically.

4. `module` is called with the `"Util"` string because, in this context, the vararg expression . . . holds everything that the chunk itself received when it was called by the `require` function.

5. `module` creates a namespace table with the name `Util` in the current global environment.

6. `module` changes the environment of the chunk to this newly created namespace table.

7. After `module` returns, the chunk creates the `Quote` function and gives it the name `Quote` in its global environment. Because of the machinations of module, this is not the original environment — it's the table that has the name `Util` in the original environment.

8. The string formatting function is called. However, Lua is now resolving all global variables in the new namespace table, which doesn't contain `string.format`, so the local variable that points to this function has to be used.

9. `require` returns with the net effect that a new global variable named `Util` has been created.

It would be tedious if, before calling `module`, you needed to make a local copy of every global variable that you were going to access. You could instead make a local copy of the namespaces you were going to use, like this:

```
local string = string
local table = table
```

Lua allows you to take this to the next step, and make a local copy of the entire global environment. To do this, you add the following to the `Util.lua` file:

```
local _G = _G

module(...)

function Quote(Str)
   return _G.string.format("%q", Str)
end
```

Now you can access the members of the original environment within the local table `_G`.

Alternatively, you can dispense with the local copy altogether and arrange to have Lua look for global variables in the original environment by means of a *metatable*. (Metatables and metamethods will be explained in Chapter 11.) The most convenient way to set this up is to pass the function `package.seeall` as a second argument to `module`, like this:

```
module(..., package.seeall)

function Quote(Str)
   return string.format("%q", Str)
end
```

The arguments to `module` can include, after the module name, zero or more functions. After `module` creates the new namespace table, it calls each of these functions in turn with the namespace table as an argument. `package.seeall` creates a metatable for the namespace table that is passed to it, and sets the `index` metamethod to look for missing fields in the global environment. In the previous example, string is missing from the module's global environment, so Lua successfully looks for it in the original environment.

C Modules

Lua modules are not restricted to Lua scripts. One of the defining aspects of Lua is its ability to interoperate smoothly with bindings written in C or some other low-level language. Bindings of this type must be built to conform with platform-dependent library requirements and with Lua's C programming interface. This feature allows Lua to act as an intermediary between the scripts you write and a vast collection of libraries that perform tasks such as network communication, document preparation, and user interface management. This topic is discussed in more detail in Chapters 9 and 13.

If the `require` function fails to locate a matching file using LUA_PATH, it uses a similar approach to locate a compiled library. When searching for a library, `require` employs the same pattern substitution method as before but uses the LUA_CPATH environment variable. If it finds a match, it calls on the operating system to load the library. If this succeeds, it then locates and calls the function with the name formed by prepending `luaopen_` to the name of the module you are requiring. The `require` function has additional nuances which allow you to bundle submodules into a module and to accommodate versioned modules; these techniques are described in the Lua manual.

Summary

In this chapter, you've learned about the following:

❏ Program modularization

❏ The importance of adhering to an established module interface

❏ The possibility of modifying a module's implementation without breaking the programs that use it

❏ Lua's support for modules using the `require` and `module` functions

❏ Lua's method of locating and loading modules

Modules form the basis of a large number of Lua libraries and community libraries, which are discussed in the proceeding chapters. But before you go on, try out the concepts you learned in this chapter in the following exercises.

Exercises

1. In subsequent chapters, the `show` module will be used to provide insight into data structures managed by your programs. Convert the module into one that returns a table with the functions `Describe` and `Show`.

2. Imagine a Lua script named `nomod.lua` with the following contents:

```
error("cannot find module " .. ...)
```

Assuming there is no file named `xyz.lua` in the current directory, what happens when the following script is run?

```
package.path = "?.lua;nomod.lua"

require "xyz"

print("Here in test.lua")
```

Extending Lua's Behavior with Metamethods

You use metatables and metamethods mainly to create what can, loosely speaking, be described as user-defined types. For example, if you have defined a table that represents a number-like value, metamethods let you use arithmetical operators with it as though it really were a number. In this chapter, you learn how to do the following:

- ❏ Use operators with types that they normally don't work with
- ❏ Control what happens when a table is indexed or a table field is assigned to
- ❏ Customize how a value is converted to a string

Using Concatenation and Arithmetical Operators on Tables

If you use tables as operands to the concatenation operator, you get the following error:

```
> A, B = {}, {}
> print(A .. B)
stdin:1: attempt to concatenate global 'A' (a table value)
stack traceback:
        stdin:1: in main chunk
        [C]: ?
```

There's a way to override this, though, so the concatenation operator is handled by a function that you define.

Try It Out   **Splicing Two Arrays with the Concatenation Operator**

1.   Define the function `MakeSpliceArr` and its upvalue `SpliceMeta` as follows (notice that `SpliceMeta`'s field `__concat` starts with two underscores):

```lua
do
  local SpliceMeta -- SpliceMeta needs to be in
    -- SpliceMeta.__concat's scope.
  SpliceMeta = {
    -- Makes a new array by splicing two arrays together:
    __concat = function(ArrA, ArrB)
      assert(type(ArrA) == "table" and type(ArrB) == "table")
      local Ret = setmetatable({}, SpliceMeta)
      for I, Elem in ipairs(ArrA) do
        Ret[I] = Elem
      end
      local LenA = #ArrA
      for I, Elem in ipairs(ArrB) do
        Ret[LenA + I] = Elem
      end
      return Ret
    end}

  -- Takes an array, returns that array after giving it a
  -- metamethod that makes it "spliceable" with the
  -- concatenation operator:
  function MakeSpliceArr(Arr)
    return setmetatable(Arr, SpliceMeta)
  end
end
```

2.   Use it to make two spliceable arrays:

```lua
-- Note -- curly braces, not parentheses:
A = MakeSpliceArr{"alpha", "bravo", "charlie"}
B = MakeSpliceArr{"x-ray", "yankee", "zulu"}
```

3.   Concatenate them and look at the result:

```lua
C = A .. B
for I, Elem in ipairs(C) do
  print(I, Elem)
end
```

You should see the following:

```
1       alpha
2       bravo
3       charlie
4       x-ray
5       yankee
6       zulu
```

How It Works

Every table in Lua (actually every value, but more on that later) can have something called a *metatable*. By default, a table does not have a metatable. The built-in `setmetatable` function gives its first argument a metatable (its second argument), and then returns the first argument. Using `setmetatable`, the `MakeSpliceArr` function sets the `SpliceMeta` table as the metatable of the array given to it:

```
function MakeSpliceArr(Arr)
   return setmetatable(Arr, SpliceMeta)
end
```

A and B therefore both have the same metatable. When Lua sees you concatenating A and B, it checks to see if they are both strings or numbers. Because they aren't, normal string concatenation can't be done, so it looks to see if the first operand has a metatable, and if that metatable has a field called __concat (two underscores), and if that field contains a function. Because this all checks out, it calls __concat with the first and second operands as arguments, and uses __concat's result as the result of the `..` operator.

A metatable's __concat field is an example of a *metamethod*.

The __concat function defined in the example splices the two arrays given to it, creating a new array that has all elements of the first, then the second array, in order. This new array is given the `SpliceMeta` metatable, so that it will have the same behavior with the concatenation operator:

```
> for I, Elem in ipairs(C .. C) do
>>    print(I, Elem)
>> end
1       alpha
2       bravo
3       charlie
4       x-ray
5       yankee
6       zulu
7       alpha
8       bravo
9       charlie
10      x-ray
11      yankee
12      zulu
```

This is why `local SpliceMeta` and the assignment of the table to `SpliceMeta` are separated into two statements. If they were one statement, then `SpliceMeta`'s scope wouldn't begin until the next statement, and the `SpliceMeta` used inside __concat would be global.

Because the first operand's __concat metamethod is used if it has one, the second operand doesn't have to have one. For example:

```
> for I, Elem in ipairs(A .. {"delta", "echo", "foxtrot"}) do
>>    print(I, Elem)
>> end
1       alpha
2       bravo
3       charlie
```

```
4       delta
5       echo
6       foxtrot
```

If the first operand has no __concat metamethod but the second one does, then that metamethod is used (but the left operand is still the metamethod's first argument), as follows:

```
> for I, Elem in ipairs({"uniform", "victor", "whiskey"} .. B) do
>>    print(I, Elem)
>> end
1       uniform
2       victor
3       whiskey
4       x-ray
5       yankee
6       zulu
```

Only if neither operand has a __concat metamethod do you get an error for attempting to concatenate a table.

If more than two tables are concatenated, then (assuming no parentheses are used) at least one of the last two has to have a __concat metamethod. This works because SpliceMeta.__concat's result itself has a __concat metamethod. It depends on the last two operands rather than the first two because concatenation is right associative. Here's an example of multiple concatenated tables:

```
> A, B, C, D = {"a"}, {"b"}, {"c"}, {"d"}
> Test = MakeSpliceArr(A) .. B .. C .. D
stdin:1: attempt to concatenate global 'C' (a table value)
stack traceback:
        stdin:1: in main chunk
        [C]: ?
> Test = A .. MakeSpliceArr(B) .. C .. D
stdin:1: attempt to concatenate global 'C' (a table value)
stack traceback:
        stdin:1: in main chunk
        [C]: ?
> Test = A .. B .. MakeSpliceArr(C) .. D
> Test = A .. B .. C .. MakeSpliceArr(D)
```

To take away a value's metatable, give setmetatable a second argument of nil:

```
> A = MakeSpliceArr{"alpha", "bravo", "charlie"}
> setmetatable(A, nil)
> A2 = A .. A
stdin:1: attempt to concatenate global 'A' (a table value)
stack traceback:
        stdin:1: in main chunk
```

To retrieve a value's metatable, use getmetatable (it returns nil if its argument has no metatable):

```
> A = MakeSpliceArr{"alpha", "bravo", "charlie"}
> SpliceMeta = getmetatable(A)
> for K, V in pairs(SpliceMeta) do print(K, V) end
__concat        function: 0x807ce78
```

Don't make the terminological mistake of saying that a table *is* a metatable when you mean that it *has* a metatable. (For example, `MakeSpliceArr` does not return a metatable — it returns a table that has a metatable.) A table and its metatable are generally two different tables, though there's nothing preventing a table from having itself as a metatable.

There are metamethods for all of Lua's operators except the Boolean ones (`and`, `or`, and `not`). In the next Try It Out, you use arithmetical metamethods to define a simple implementation of *rational* numbers. Unlike the floating-point numbers that Lua normally uses, rational numbers can represent quantities like $f^{1/3}$ and $f^{1/5}$ with perfect accuracy.

Try It Out   Defining Rational Numbers

1. Save the following as rational.lua:

```lua
-- A basic rational number implementation.

-- Returns A and B's greatest common divisor:
local function GetGcd(A, B)
   local Remainder = A % B
   return Remainder == 0 and B or GetGcd(B, Remainder)
end

-- Metamethods:

local function Add(A, B)
   return MakeRat(A.Numer * B.Denom + B.Numer * A.Denom,
     A.Denom * B.Denom)
end

local function Sub(A, B)
   return A + -B
end

local function Mul(A, B)
   return MakeRat(A.Numer * B.Numer, A.Denom * B.Denom)
end

local function Div(A, B)
   assert(B.Numer ~= 0, "Divison by zero")
   return A * MakeRat(B.Denom, B.Numer)
end

local function Unm(A)
   return MakeRat(-A.Numer, A.Denom)
end

local function ToString(Rat)
   return Rat.Numer .. "/" .. Rat.Denom
end

local RatMeta = {
   __add = Add,
   __sub = Sub,
   __mul = Mul,
```

```
      __div = Div,
      __unm = Unm,
      __tostring = ToString,
    }

    -- The three global functions supplied by this library:

    -- Instantiates a rational number:
    function MakeRat(Numer, Denom)
      Numer, Denom = tonumber(Numer), tonumber(Denom)
      assert(Denom ~= 0, "Denominator must be nonzero")
      assert(Numer == math.floor(Numer) and Denom == math.floor(Denom),
        "Numerator and denominator must be integers")
      -- Make sure the denominator is positive:
      if Denom < 0 then
        Numer, Denom = -Numer, -Denom
      end
      -- Reduce the fraction to its lowest terms:
      local Gcd = GetGcd(Numer, Denom)
      local Rat = {
        Numer = Numer / Gcd,
        Denom = Denom / Gcd}
      return setmetatable(Rat, RatMeta)
    end

    -- Instantiates a rational number from a string of the form
    -- "numerator/denominator":
    function r(Str)
      local Numer, Denom = string.match(Str, "^(%-?%d+)%/(%-?%d+)$")
      assert(Numer, "Couldn't parse rational number")
      return MakeRat(Numer, Denom)
    end

    -- Converts a rational to a (floating-point) number:
    function RatToNumber(Rat)
      return Rat.Numer / Rat.Denom
    end
```

2.   Require the file and multiply two rational numbers:

```
> require("rational")
> print(r"2/3" * r"1/10")
1/15
```

3.   Add the floating-point approximation of $f\frac{1}{3}$ to itself 300000 times:

```
> FloatAcc = 0
> for I = 1, 300000 do
>>    FloatAcc = FloatAcc + 1 / 3
>> end
> print(FloatAcc)
99999.999999689
```

4. Add the rational number $f\frac{1}{3}$ to itself 300000 times:

```
> RatAcc = r"0/1"
> OneThird = r"1/3"
> for I = 1, 300000 do
>>    RatAcc = RatAcc + OneThird
>> end
> print(RatAcc)
100000/1
```

5. Verify that the result is exactly 100000:

```
> print(RatToNumber(RatAcc) == 100000)
true
```

6. Print the rational number $f^{15}\!/_{100}$:

```
> Rat = r"15/100"
> print(Rat) -- Will be reduced to lowest terms.
```

7. Print the negative version of the previous rational number:

```
> print(-Rat)
-3/20
```

How It Works

A rational number is just a fraction — a numerator over a denominator. It is represented as a table with `Numer` and `Denom` fields and a metatable with `__add` (addition), `__sub` (subtraction), `__mul` (multiplication), `__div` (division), and `__unm` (unary minus) metamethods. (Like `__concat`, these and all other metamethods start with two underscores.)

In the following part of the Try It Out, `r"2/3"` and `r"1/10"` create the rational numbers two thirds and one tenth:

```
> print(r"2/3" * r"1/10")
1/15
```

The function is called `r` *to minimize the typing needed for rational "literals." Remember also that* `r"2/3"` *means the same thing as* `r("2/3")`.

When these two rational numbers are multiplied, what happens is basically the same as what happened in the previous concatenation example: Lua sees that they are tables (rather than numbers), so it looks for a `__mul` metamethod, finds one in the left operand, and calls it with both operands as arguments. This metamethod returns the result (one fifteenth). As it does with all values, `print` runs this result through `tostring`, which sees the `__tostring` metamethod and uses it to do the conversion. (More on `__tostring` later.)

The `FloatAcc` section of the example initializes an accumulator to 0 and increments it 300000 times by the floating-point approximation of $f\frac{1}{3}$. The inaccuracy snowballs, as shown by the final value of `FloatAcc`:

```
> FloatAcc = 0
> for I = 1, 300000 do
>>    FloatAcc = FloatAcc + 1 / 3
```

```
>> end
> print(FloatAcc)
99999.999999689
```

The `RatAcc` section, on the other hand, shows no loss of accuracy:

```
> RatAcc = r"0/1"
> OneThird = r"1/3"
> for I = 1, 300000 do
>>    RatAcc = RatAcc + OneThird
>> end
> print(RatAcc)
100000/1
> print(RatToNumber(RatAcc) == 100000)
true
```

You may have noticed that the `RatAcc` loop took longer to run than the `FloatAcc` loop. Floating-point numbers will always be faster than rational numbers because your computer includes dedicated hardware to do floating-point math, but in the interest of simplicity, this rational number library makes no special effort to narrow the speed gap.

The __add, __sub, __mul, and __div metamethods all handle binary operators, so they take two arguments. The __unm metamethod handles a unary operator, so it takes one argument:

```
> Rat = r"15/100"
> print(Rat) -- Will be reduced to lowest terms.
3/20
> print(-Rat)
-3/20
```

The __pow, __mod, and __len metamethods define the behavior of the ^ (exponentiation), % (modulo), and # (length) operators. All of these metamethods (the arithmetical ones, __concat, and __len) are not for redefining behavior that already exists, but for adding new behavior. Normally, you can't use a table as an operand to an arithmetical operator or the concatenation operator, so you would use metamethods to define its behavior with these operators. But a table's behavior with the length operator is already defined, so giving a table a __len metamethod has no effect, as shown here:

```
> T = {"one", "two", "three", [1000] = "one thousand"}
> print(table.maxn(T))
1000
> setmetatable(T, {
>>    __len = function(T) return table.maxn(T) end})
> print(#T)
3
```

Lua does pay attention to a __len metamethod if it belongs to a value for which the length operator is not already defined (i.e., something other than a table or string). Giving metatables to values other than tables will be covered later in this chapter.

Relational Metamethods

You can use metamethods to make rational numbers work with equality and inequality operators (== and ~=) and other relational operators (<, >, <=, and >=). To do this, add appropriate __eq (equal) and __lt (less than) metamethods, like this:

```
local function Unm(A)
    return MakeRat(-A.Numer, A.Denom)
end

local function Eq(A, B)
    -- This and Lt work because MakeRat always makes sure the
    -- denominator is positive and reduces to lowest terms:
    return A.Numer == B.Numer and A.Denom == B.Denom
end

local function Lt(A, B)
    local Diff = A - B
    return Diff.Numer < 0
end

local function ToString(Rat)
    return Rat.Numer .. "/" .. Rat.Denom
end

local RatMeta = {
    __add = Add,
    __sub = Sub,
    __mul = Mul,
    __div = Div,
    __unm = Unm,
    __eq = Eq,
    __lt = Lt,
    __tostring = ToString,
}
```

Remember, to see these changes you'll need to set package.loaded.rational *to* nil, *or use* dofile("rational.lua") *instead of* require("rational"), *or restart Lua.*

The __eq (equal) and __lt (less than) metamethods are enough to define all the relational operators. The inequality operator produces the opposite of the __eq result, and the greater-than operator produces the __lt result after swapping the operands. For example:

```
> print(r"20/100" == r"2/10")
true
> print(r"20/100" ~= r"2/10")
false
> print(r"7/16" < r"1/2")
true
> print(r"7/16" > r"1/2")
false
```

The less-than-or-equal and greater-than-or-equal operators are also defined in terms of __lt — for example, A <= B is defined as not (B < A) — *unless* there's an __le (less than or equal) metamethod.

257

Rational numbers have what mathematicians call a *total order*. This means that if two rational numbers are not equal, then one is less than the other. If you want to compare things for which this is not true, you need to define __le in addition to __lt. For example, imagine you're working with values that "represent shapes on a two-dimensional surface. A handy interpretation of <= would be "is contained within," so that A <= B means "is every point in A also in B?" This is not a total order, because if A contains points not in B and B contains points not in A, then both A <= B and B <= A are false. Therefore, such shapes would need __le (is A contained in B), __lt (is A contained in B but not identical with it), and __eq (is A identical with B).

The __eq metamethod is only consulted when the values being compared meet all of these criteria:

❏   They are both tables, or they are both full userdatas (discussed later in this chapter).

❏   They are not the same value

❏   They have the same __eq metamethod.

If any one of these three conditions is not true, then the values are compared as if they had no __eq metamethods.

The rawequal function does a test for equality that bypasses any __eq metamethods that may be present. For example:

```
> Rat1, Rat2 = r"22/7", r"22/7"
> print(Rat1 == Rat2) -- __eq says they're equal,
true
> print(rawequal(Rat1, Rat2)) -- but they're different tables.
false
```

The __lt and __le metamethods are only consulted when the values being compared meet all of these criteria:

❏   They are the same type.

❏   They are neither numbers nor strings.

❏   They have the same __lt (__le) metamethod.

If any one of these three of these conditions is not true, then an error occurs.

> *These conditions (for when __eq, __lt, and __le are used) are stricter than those for the other operator metamethods because the relational operators themselves are stricter. For example, all of the nonrelational binary operators can, even without metamethods, be used with mixed types (strings and numbers), but using <, >, <=, or >= to compare a string and a number is an error.*

Indexing and Call Metamethods

There are metamethods that allow you to control what happens when something is indexed, when it is on the left side of an indexing assignment, or when it is called. In the following Try It Out, you use the indexing and indexing assignment metamethods when defining a table that considers two keys the same if they differ only in case.

Try It Out   Defining Case-Insensitive Tables

1. Define the `MakeIgnoreCase` function, along with its helper functions and metatable, as follows:

```lua
do
  -- Returns Val after (if it's a string) lowercasing it:
  local function Lower(Val)
    if type(Val) == "string" then
      Val = string.lower(Val)
    end
    return Val
  end

  local Meta = {
    __newindex = function(Tbl, Key, Val)
      rawset(Tbl, Lower(Key), Val)
    end,
    __index = function(Tbl, Key)
      return rawget(Tbl, Lower(Key))
    end}

  -- Returns a new table with a metatable that makes its
  -- keys case-insensitive:
  function MakeIgnoreCase()
    return setmetatable({}, Meta)
  end
end
```

2. Make a case-insensitive table, assign a value to its `abc` field, and then verify that the value is accessible from the `ABC`, `Abc`, and `abc` fields:

```lua
> Tbl = MakeIgnoreCase()
> Tbl.abc = 1
> print(Tbl.ABC, Tbl.Abc, Tbl.abc)
1       1       1
```

3. Assign a different value to the table's `Abc` field, and then verify that the new value is accessible from the `ABC`, `Abc`, and `abc` fields:

```lua
> Tbl.Abc = 2
> print(Tbl.ABC, Tbl.Abc, Tbl.abc)
2       2       2
```

4. Assign another value to the table's `ABC` field, and then verify that the new value is accessible from the `ABC`, `Abc`, and `abc` fields:

```lua
> Tbl.ABC = 3
> print(Tbl.ABC, Tbl.Abc, Tbl.abc)
3       3       3
```

5. Loop through the table, verifying that it only has one field, not three:

```lua
> for K, V in pairs(Tbl) do print(K, V) end
abc     3
```

How It Works

The metamethod for indexing assignment (setting a key to a value) is __newindex. When Lua sees Tbl.abc = 1, it checks to see whether Tbl already has an abc field. It doesn't, but it does have a __newindex metamethod, so instead of putting the abc = 1 key-value pair directly into Tbl, Lua calls __newindex with three arguments: Tbl, "abc", and 1. After making sure that "abc" is all lower-case, __newindex needs to set Tbl.abc to 1. It can't do this with a regular indexing assignment (that would cause infinite recursion), so it uses the function rawset, which sets a table's key to a value but bypasses the table's __newindex metamethod (if present).

The metamethod for indexing (getting a key's value) is __index. When Lua sees print(Tbl.ABC), it checks to see whether Tbl already has an ABC field. It doesn't, but it does have an __index metamethod, so instead of giving a result of nil, Lua calls __index with two arguments: Tbl and "ABC". After lower-casing "ABC", __index gets the value of Tbl.abc (using rawget to avoid infinite recursion). This value is what is printed.

The pairs loop shows that even after setting the "abc", "Abc", and "ABC" keys there's only one key in the table:

```
> for K, V in pairs(Tbl) do print(K, V) end
abc     3
```

pairs and ipairs both bypass a table's __index metamethod. That's the desired behavior here, but if you want something different, you can write your own replacements for pairs, next (the iterator used by pairs), and ipairs. There's an example of this later in this chapter.

The __newindex and __index methods are only called when the given key isn't in the table. To demonstrate this, put the following debugging statements into them:

```
local Meta = {
  __newindex = function(Tbl, Key, Val)
    print("__newindex:", Tbl, Key, Val)
    rawset(Tbl, Lower(Key), Val)
  end,
  __index = function(Tbl, Key)
    print("__index:", Tbl, Key)
    return rawget(Tbl, Lower(Key))
  end}
```

Now you can see when the __newindex and __index methods are called:

```
> Tbl = MakeIgnoreCase()
> Tbl.abc = 1 -- Calls __newindex because there's no Tbl.abc.
__newindex:     table: 0x4961e8 abc       1
> Tbl.abc = 2 -- Doesn't call __newindex since Tbl.abc exists.
> print(Tbl.ABC) -- Calls __index because there's no Tbl.ABC.
__index:        table: 0x4961e8 ABC
2
> print(Tbl.abc) -- Doesn't call __index because Tbl.abc exists.
2
```

This is fine for the case-insensitive table, but in other situations, you might want __newindex and __index to always be called. The way to do this is to give the metamethods to a *proxy table*, which is a table that always stays empty. The next example uses this technique. It's a table that remembers the order in which things were put into it.

Try It Out   Employing Ordered Tables

1. Save the following as `orderedtbl.lua`:

```lua
-- "Ordered tables" -- they remember the order in which
-- things are put into them.

local RealTbls = {} -- Keys: proxy tables; values: the real
  -- tables.
local NumToKeys = {} -- Keys: proxy tables; values: arrays
  -- of real tables' keys, in order.
local KeyToNums = {} -- Keys: proxy tables; values: tables
  -- mapping real tables' keys to their (order) numbers.

-- Does the bookkeeping necessary to add a key and its order
-- to the real table (or update/delete a key):
local function __newindex(Proxy, Key, Val)
  local RealTbl = RealTbls[Proxy]
  local NumToKey = NumToKeys[Proxy]
  local KeyToNum = KeyToNums[Proxy]
  if RealTbl[Key] == nil then
    -- This is a new key.  Only add it if the value's
    -- non-nil:
    if Val ~= nil then
      -- Record the value:
      RealTbl[Key] = Val
      -- Record the order:
      NumToKey[#NumToKey + 1] = Key
      KeyToNum[Key] = #NumToKey
    end
  else
    -- This is an already existing key.
    if Val ~= nil then
      -- Record the new value:
      RealTbl[Key] = Val
    else
      -- Delete it:
      RealTbl[Key] = nil
      local Num = KeyToNum[Key]
      KeyToNum[Key] = nil
      -- table.remove will shift down anything in NumToKey
      -- that's higher than Num, but it needs to be done by
      -- hand for KeyToNum:
      if Num < #NumToKey then
        for SomeKey, SomeNum in pairs(KeyToNum) do
          if SomeNum > Num then
            KeyToNum[SomeKey] = SomeNum - 1
          end
        end
      end
      table.remove(NumToKey, Num)
```

```lua
      end
    end
  end

  -- Returns Key's value in the real table:
  local function __index(Proxy, Key)
    return RealTbls[Proxy][Key]
  end

  -- An iterator that iterates through all the real table's
  -- key-value pairs in the correct order:
  local function __next(Proxy, PrevKey)
    assert(type(Proxy) == "table", "bad argument to 'next'")
    local RealTbl = RealTbls[Proxy]
    local NumToKey = NumToKeys[Proxy]
    local KeyToNum = KeyToNums[Proxy]
    -- This will be 0 only if PrevKey is the seed value nil:
    local PrevNum = KeyToNum[PrevKey] or 0
    local Key = NumToKey[PrevNum + 1]
    return Key, RealTbl[Key]
  end

  local RealIpairs = ipairs

  -- Returns an ipairs iterator for the real table:
  local function __ipairs(Proxy)
    return RealIpairs(RealTbls[Proxy])
  end

  -- The metatable:
  local OrderMeta = {__newindex = __newindex, __index = __index,
    __next = __next, __ipairs = __ipairs}

  local RealNext = next

  -- A metatable-aware replacement for next:
  function next(Tbl, Key)
    local Meta = getmetatable(Tbl)
    if Meta and Meta.__next then
      return Meta.__next(Tbl, Key)
    else
      return RealNext(Tbl, Key)
    end
  end

  -- A metatable-aware replacement for pairs:
  function pairs(Tbl)
    -- The real pairs only needs to be replaced because it
    -- returns its own copy of next unaffected by our
    -- replacement.
    assert(type(Tbl) == "table", "bad argument to 'pairs'")
    return next, Tbl, nil
  end

  -- A metatable-aware replacement for ipairs:
```

262

```
function ipairs(Tbl)
  local Meta = getmetatable(Tbl)
  if Meta and Meta.__ipairs then
    return Meta.__ipairs(Tbl)
  else
    return RealIpairs(Tbl)
  end
end


-- Returns a table that remembers the order in which keys
-- are added to it:
function MakeOrderedTbl()
  local RealTbl, Proxy = {}, {}
  RealTbls[Proxy] = RealTbl
  -- The following two tables are two complementary ways of
  -- recording the order that keys are added in:
  NumToKeys[Proxy] = {}
  KeyToNums[Proxy] = {}
  return setmetatable(Proxy, OrderMeta)
end
```

2.   Require the file, make an ordered table, and give it some key-value pairs:

```
> require("orderedtbl")
> Tbl = MakeOrderedTbl()
> Tbl.John = "rhythm guitar"
> Tbl.Paul = "bass guitar"
> Tbl.George = "lead guitar"
> Tbl.Ringo = "drumkit"
```

3.   Verify that the pairs are looped through in the same order in which they were added:

```
> for Name, Instr in pairs(Tbl) do print(Name, Instr) end
John     rhythm guitar
Paul     bass guitar
George   lead guitar
Ringo    drumkit
```

4.   Change one key's value and verify that the pairs are still in the same order:

```
> Tbl.George = "lead guitar, sitar"
> for Name, Instr in pairs(Tbl) do print(Name, Instr) end
John     rhythm guitar
Paul     bass guitar
George   lead guitar, sitar
Ringo    drumkit
```

5.   Remove one key and verify that the remaining pairs are still in the same order:

```
> Tbl.Paul = nil -- I buried Paul.
> for Name, Instr in pairs(Tbl) do print(Name, Instr) end
John     rhythm guitar
George   lead guitar, sitar
Ringo    drumkit
```

263

How It Works

`pairs` iterates through the `Tbl` pairs in the same order as they were added. If you modify a key's value, the order is not changed, and you can delete a key by setting its value to `nil`. Most of the hard work is done by `__newindex`. Because the proxy table is always empty, every attempt to do indexing assignment on it is routed through `__newindex`, which keeps the following three tables for each proxy table:

- ❏ `RealTbls[Proxy]`: The real table that corresponds to the proxy table — it contains all the key-value pairs, in the usual order.

- ❏ `NumToKeys[Proxy]`: An array of the `RealTbls[Proxy]` keys, in order of addition.

- ❏ `KeyToNums[Proxy]`: A mapping of all the keys to their positions in `NumToKeys[Proxy]`.

`RealTbls[Proxy]` is necessary for retrieving a value given its key, `NumToKeys[Proxy]` is necessary for looping through the keys in order, and `KeyToNums[Proxy]` is necessary for finding a given key's position in `NumToKeys[Proxy]` (for iteration, and also for modification or deletion of already existing pairs).

The `__next` metamethod is an iterator that uses these tables to iterate in the desired order. Lua itself knows nothing about a `__next` metamethod — the only thing that knows about it is `orderedtbl.lua`'s replacement for `next` (which, in turn, is what the `pairs` replacement returns). Similarly, Lua itself neither defines nor looks for an `__ipairs` metamethod — the only thing that knows about it is the `ipairs` replacement. (There's nothing that requires `__next` and `__ipairs` to start with two underscores, but it makes it easier to see that they're metamethods.) These `next` and `ipairs` replacements still work with regular tables. If they don't find the metamethods they look for, they use the real `next` and `ipairs` (stored as upvalues).

There's a problem with `orderedtbl.lua`. *The tables* `RealTbls`, `NumToKeys`, *and* `KeyToNums` *get bigger (consuming more memory) every time* `MakeOrderedTbl` *is called, but they never get smaller, even when the table returned by* `MakeOrderedTbl` *is no longer in use. This is called a* memory leak, *and a fix for it, using the* `__mode` *metamethod, is shown in Chapter 10.*

Both `__newindex` and `__index` can be tables. As such, you can use them instead of the table being indexed like this:

```
> TblA, TblB = {}, {}
> setmetatable(TblB, {__newindex = TblA, __index = TblA})
> TblB[1] = "one"
> print(TblB[1])
one
> -- It's not really in TblB:
> print(rawget(TblB, 1))
nil
> -- It's really in TblA:
> print(TblA[1])
one
```

If `__newindex` and/or `__index` are tables that themselves have indexing metamethods, these are used. That means that one table can get some of its values from another table, which gets some of its values from another, and so on. This is called *inheritance* and is illustrated in the following example:

```
> TblA = {"one", "two", "three", "four", "five", "six"}
> TblB = {[3] = "III", [4] = "IV", [5] = "V", [6] = "VI"}
> -- Make TblB inherit from TblA:
```

```
> setmetatable(TblB, {__index = TblA})
> TblC = {[5] = "*****", [6] = "******"}
> -- Make TblC inherit from TblB:
> setmetatable(TblC, {__index = TblB})
> -- TblC thus indirectly inherits from TblA:
> for I = 1, 6 do print(I, TblC[I]) end
1       one
2       two
3       III
4       IV
5       *****
6       ******
```

This can twist and turn through up to 100 tables (or more if you recompile Lua with a higher value for MAXTAGLOOP).

Other than __tostring (and the __next and __ipairs metamethods defined in orderedtbl.lua), all of the metamethods you've seen so far are *syntactical metamethods*, which means they correspond to syntactical constructs (all of the operators, plus indexing and indexing assignment). Another syntactical metamethod yet to be covered is __call. This metamethod controls what happens when something other than a function is called. For instance, if a table has the __call method given in the following example, then calling it (as though it were a function) returns true if all the arguments are keys in it with true values, and false otherwise:

```
> CallMeta = {
>>    -- Are all of the arguments true-valued keys in Tbl?
>>    __call = function(Tbl, ...)
>>      for I = 1, select("#", ...) do
>>        if not Tbl[select(I, ...)] then
>>          return false -- NON-STRUCTURED EXIT: FOUND A KEY
>>            -- WITH A NON-TRUE VALUE.
>>        end
>>      end
>>      return true
>>    end}
> Tbl = {John = "rhythm guitar", Paul = "bass guitar",
>>    George = "lead guitar", Ringo = "drumkit"}
> setmetatable(Tbl, CallMeta)
> -- Same truth-value as (Tbl.Paul and Tbl.John):
> print(Tbl("Paul", "John"))
true
> -- Same truth-value as (Tbl.Ringo and Tbl.Mick and Tbl.Keith):
> print(Tbl("Ringo", "Mick", "Keith"))
false
```

Non-Tables with Metamethods

As mentioned earlier, all datatypes (not just tables) can have metatables. The setmetatable function only works with tables. The metatables of other types must be set either from C or with the function debug.setmetatable. Unlike tables, most other types have per-type metatables. This means that giving a metatable to a number gives it to all numbers. In the following example, a __len metamethod is given to numbers (where making the math.abs argument positive if it's negative is called getting the argument's *absolute value*):

```
> print(#99)
stdin:1: attempt to get length of a number value
stack traceback:
        stdin:1: in main chunk
        [C]: ?
> debug.setmetatable(1, {__len = math.abs})
> print(#99)
99
> print(#-99)
99
```

Unlike setmetatable, debug.setmetatable *returns a Boolean:* true *if it succeeded,* false *otherwise.*

By default, types have no metatable, except for strings, whose __index metamethod is the string table, as shown here:

```
> StringMeta = getmetatable("")
> for Name, Meth in pairs(StringMeta) do print(Name, Meth)
> end
__index table: 0x8066f30
> print(StringMeta.__index == string)
true
```

This means that all the functions of the string library are available from any string. For example:

```
> SomeString = "some string"
> print(SomeString.char(65, 66, 67))
ABC
```

More usefully, it means that any string function that takes a string as its first argument (that's almost all of them) can be used in object-oriented style, with the string as the object and the function as its method. For example:

```
> Greet = "Hello"
> print(Greet:upper())
HELLO
> FrmtStr = '<a href="%s">%s</a>'
> print(FrmtStr:format("http://luaforge.net", "LuaForge"))
<a href="http://luaforge.net">LuaForge</a>
```

A literal string can be used in this way, but only if it's surrounded in parentheses like this:

```
> print(("a"):rep(5))
aaaaa
```

There's one more type whose behavior with metatables needs special clarification. The *userdata* type will be covered in Chapter 13, but it's basically a way of exposing a C datatype (or a datatype of some other language) to Lua. It comes in two varieties: full userdatas and light userdatas. Both varieties are identified by the `type` function as `"userdata"`, but their behavior with metatables is different. Metatable-wise, full userdatas are similar to tables, and light userdatas are similar to nontables:

❑ Each full userdata can have its own metatable.

❑ Giving a metatable to a light userdata gives it to all light userdatas.

In Lua 5.0, only tables and full userdatas could have metatables.

Non-Syntactical Metamethods

As mentioned previously, __tostring is a non-syntactical metamethod, which means that it doesn't control the behavior of an operator or other syntactical construct. Instead, it controls the behavior of the function `tostring`, which will always use a value's __tostring metamethod, if present, to convert that value to a string. In this way, __tostring is no different from __next and __ipairs, except that it is consulted by a built-in Lua function and they are not.

One other metamethod consulted by a built-in function (or two functions, in this case) is __metatable. If `getmetatable` sees that a value has a __metatable metamethod, it returns that metamethod instead of the metatable itself. If `setmetatable` sees that a value has a __metatable metamethod, it triggers an error rather than setting the metatable. A __metatable metamethod can be any type (except `nil`, of course).

This is most commonly used to protect metatables from tampering. Here's an example:

```
> T = setmetatable({}, {__metatable = false})
> print(getmetatable(T))
false
> T = setmetatable(T, nil)
stdin:1: cannot change a protected metatable
stack traceback:
        [C]: in function 'setmetatable'
        stdin:1: in main chunk
        [C]: ?
```

`debug.setmetatable` and `debug.getmetatable` both ignore __metatable.

The two remaining nonsyntactical metamethods defined by Lua both control *garbage-collection*, which is the automatic process of reclaiming no-longer-used memory for reuse.

The __mode metamethod is for tables. It is explained in Chapter 10 (which contains a fix for the problem with `orderedtbl.lua` mentioned earlier).

The __gc metamethod is for full userdatas. It is explained in Chapter 13.

Metamethod Applicability

You have seen a number of cases where metamethods are ignored. The following chart lists all the metamethods defined by Lua's core and its built-in libraries and shows which situations they are applicable in.

Metamethod	Applicability
__add __mod __call __mul __concat __pow __div __sub __len __unm	Only consulted if the syntactical construct they are for doesn't already have a meaning for the given types.
__eq __lt __le	Only consulted if both operands are the same type and have the same metamethod. Additionally, __eq is only consulted if the operands are unequal tables or full userdatas; __lt and __le are only consulted if the operands are not numbers or strings.
__index __newindex	Not consulted if the given key exists.
__tostring __metatable	Consulted by tostring and getmetatable/setmetatable, respectively.
__mode	For tables only ("k", "v", or "kv").
__gc	For full userdatas only.

Summary

In this chapter, you were introduced to the concept of metamethods and to all the metamethods defined by Lua's core and its built-in libraries. Here are some highlights of what you've learned:

❑　You can use metamethods to give new behavior to all of the operators except for the Boolean ones, and to table indexing, indexing assignment, and calls.

❑　Nonrelational binary metamethods are retrieved from the left operand or from the right operand if the left one doesn't have the appropriate metamethod.

❑　You can use proxy tables to increase the power of __newindex and __index.

❑　__newindex and __index can themselves be tables, and they can use their own indexing metamethods (if they exist) to implement inheritance.

❑　You can also use metamethods to control how values are converted to strings and how they are garbage-collected.

❑　Metamethods serve mainly to define new behavior, not to redefine existing behavior. Even the exceptions to that rule are limited, which is why __eq only works with tables or full userdatas, and why __newindex and __index only work with nonexistent keys.

The next chapter explains something new to add to your arsenal of control flow tools (alongside control structures and functions). But before moving on, this chapter concludes with a couple of exercises (answers are in the appendix).

Exercises

1. Write a metamethod that makes the unary minus operator give a reversed copy of an array:

```
> Arr = setmetatable({"one", "two", "three"}, Meta)
> for I, Val in ipairs(-Arr) do print(I, Val) end
1       three
2       two
3       one
```

2. Write a function that makes the table given to it read-only:

```
> Tbl = {"Hello"}
> Protect(Tbl)
> print(Tbl[1])
Hello
> Tbl[2] = "Goodbye"
stdin:14: attempt to assign to a protected table
stack traceback:
        [C]: in function 'error'
        stdin:14: in function <stdin:13>
        stdin:1: in main chunk
        [C]: ?
> Tbl[1] = "Goodbye"
stdin:14: attempt to assign to a protected table
stack traceback:
        [C]: in function 'error'
        stdin:14: in function <stdin:13>
        stdin:1: in main chunk
        [C]: ?
> setmetatable(Tbl, nil)
stdin:1: cannot change a protected metatable
stack traceback:
        [C]: in function 'setmetatable'
        stdin:1: in main chunk
        [C]: ?
```

Handling Events Naturally with Coroutines

When you're implementing an application, you, as a developer, should strive for simplicity and generality. These qualities make a program easy to extend and maintain, and allow it to be reused under a variety of platforms and circumstances. However, real-world requirements often conspire to make these objectives hard to attain. In this chapter, you'll learn how Lua *coroutines* provide you with an elegant and powerful tool that can dramatically simplify certain kinds of problems. For example, you can use coroutines to manage concurrent tasks, such as updating a progress bar and responding appropriately to user input while transferring a file.

You also use coroutines to provide contextual continuity to functions. A routine that is called intermittently as part of a continuing task may need to go to great lengths to reestablish the context of the task — that is, to remember "where it left off." For example, a tokenizing routine may be called from various parts of a parsing application yet must, when it is invoked, pick up right where it left off and return the next available token to the caller.

The event-driven nature of interactive programs can lead to logical discontinuities in the application source code. For example, in the interest of clarity, a program should invoke a window and wait until it is closed in much the same way that it calls a file reading routine. This way, directly after the call to show a window, the program can take the suitable course of action depending on the way the window is closed. However, most GUI development models don't allow a window to block like this. Instead, one or more functions are generally registered that are called in response to events such as the closing of a window. This prevents a sequence of statements from including both the display of a window and the action taken after its closure.

A number of attempts to tame problems such as these have evolved over the years with varying levels of success. These will be discussed briefly and compared with the way you can use coroutines to tackle the same problems.

Coroutines and Program Control

A coroutine is a subroutine-like body into and out of which program control can flow repeatedly.

The essence of Lua coroutines is the way they use a familiar notation on top of a program control mechanism that may appear unfamiliar. In this section, you'll see some examples of coroutines and learn of the special considerations you must make to use them effectively.

Coroutines Are Not Functions

In Chapter 3, you learned about Lua functions: how they are defined, how they are invoked, and how they receive values from and return values to the caller. The general picture from that chapter is that a function receives program control when it is called, and relinquishes control when it returns. When a function is called, local variables and bookkeeping information are pushed onto a call stack for safekeeping. When a function returns, these data are popped off of the call stack. This pattern of a call stack growing and shrinking frame by frame provides a very logical basis for structuring a program. It models to some extent the way people manage certain everyday tasks.

In Chapter 6, you learned about an error handling mechanism that allows this stack pattern to be circumvented, namely the protected call. In this case, the call stack grows and shrinks as usual, but when an error occurs, the stack is truncated to the point where the protected call was made without going through the usual function returns.

A coroutine is another mechanism that doesn't quite fit into the familiar nested nature of function calls. Like ordinary functions, coroutines are invoked with argument values and eventually they return values. But coroutines differ from functions in the following ways:

❑ Unlike a function, a coroutine must be specially prepared, or *instantiated*, before it can be activated. You use the `coroutine.create` function to do this.

❑ When a coroutine is invoked — that is, when it receives program control by means of the `coroutine.resume` function — it operates on its own call stack, not that of its caller. A coroutine's stack serves the usual purpose of keeping track of function calls and local variables. As with an ordinary program, the use of this stack is transparent to the programmer. Although invoking a coroutine seems like calling a function, it is more similar to starting a new program.

❑ In the absence of an error, a coroutine relinquishes control to its invoker either by *yielding* with the `coroutine.yield` function, or by returning (either with a `return` statement or by reaching the end of the coroutine body).

❑ After a coroutine returns control by yielding, it can be resumed — that is, it can be given program control again — with the return of its call to `coroutine.yield`. A coroutine can yield and be resumed repeatedly.

❑ After a coroutine terminates, it cannot be activated again. Returning from the main body of a coroutine is much like returning from the main body of a program.

How Coroutines Are Like Programs

Even though coroutines look a lot like functions (in fact, you can use `coroutine.wrap` to put a function wrapper around a coroutine), it's beneficial to think of a coroutine as a separate program rather than as an enhanced function. All of the operations available to an ordinary Lua program, such as creating variables and calling functions, are available to coroutines. Because each coroutine has its own call stack, its particular statement path, or *thread*, is independent of the program's initial statement path (the *main thread*) and that of other coroutines. One and only one thread is active at any given time during the execution of a program. To a limited extent, a useful analogy is a text editor that can have multiple files open simultaneously. You can switch to any of the open files, but only one can be active. Similarly, a Lua program can have many threads, but only one will be currently running.

The distinctive magic of coroutines centers on the `coroutine.yield` and `coroutine.resume` functions. The `coroutine.yield` function may be used as a coroutine's way of saying to its caller, "I don't know how long I'm going to have to sit around waiting for something interesting to happen, so I'll let you take control. When something happens that I should know about, wake me up from my nap and let me know about it." The `coroutine.resume` function, in this context, is the currently active thread's way of saying, "Hey, sleepy coroutine, wake up. Here's something of interest for you. When you reach another lull, let me know and I'll take over again."

Coroutines Transfer Control

There are alternate uses of coroutines. In another context, perhaps the transfer of a number of files, a coroutine might call `coroutine.yield` as a way of saying, "I'm busy right now, but I know that other threads are in need of some machine cycles too, so I'll relinquish control to let them do some work." In this scenario, a dispatcher may resume a number of coroutines in turn to overlap multiple tasks.

Even though `coroutine.yield` and `coroutine.resume` look like ordinary functions, they map to thread transfer operations that are very unlike ordinary functions. One very nice attribute of coroutines in Lua is that, as a programmer, you can use familiar function notation to switch between threads, exchanging values as you do so.

Wrapping a Coroutine

Coroutine usage can be simplified somewhat with `coroutine.wrap`. This function is used to instantiate a coroutine just as `coroutine.create` does, but instead of returning the new coroutine itself, it returns a function that resumes the coroutine. To resume the wrapped coroutine, either initially or after it has yielded, you simply call the returned function with the arguments you want to pass to it. This function is unprotected, so if an error occurs in the coroutine, the function will not return. By using the `coroutine.running` function, you can identify the wrapped coroutine but, in general, if you need this value, you are better off using unwrapped coroutines.

Coroutines Are Cooperative

Coroutines enable a program to *multitask*, which means it can interleave the execution of more than one task over a period of time. Just like the main body of a program, the body of a coroutine gives every appearance of being in complete control of the machine. However, the programmer of a coroutine knows that other threads require time to execute too, so a coroutine is programmed to yield control at opportune times, knowing that in due course it will receive control again. In the following exercise, you learn how to write a script that enables coroutines to cooperate.

Try It Out   Learning to Cooperate

The following script demonstrates the use of coroutines to volley control back and forth cooperatively.

1.   With your text editor, enter the following script:

```
local function KnightFnc()
  print [[Knight:
The name of the song is called "HADDOCKS' EYES."
```

```
]]
    coroutine.yield()
    print [[Knight, looking a little vexed:
No, you don't understand, that's what the name is CALLED. The
name really IS "THE AGED AGED MAN."
]]
    coroutine.yield()
    print [[Knight:
No, you oughtn't, that's quite another thing! The SONG is
called "WAYS AND MEANS," but that's only what it's CALLED, you
know!
]]
    coroutine.yield()
    print [[Knight:
I was coming to that. The song really IS "A-SITTING ON A GATE",
and the tune's my own invention.
]]
end

local function Alice()
    local Knight = coroutine.create(KnightFnc)

    coroutine.resume(Knight)
    print [[Alice, trying to feel interested:
Oh, that's the name of the song, is it?
]]
    coroutine.resume(Knight)
    print [[Alice:
Then I ought to have said "That's what the SONG is called"?
]]
    coroutine.resume(Knight)
    print [[Alice, completely bewildered:
Well, what IS the song, then?
]]
    coroutine.resume(Knight)
end

Alice()
```

2. Save the file as `looking_glass.lua`.

3. Run the script using the Lua interpreter as follows:

```
lua looking_glass.lua
Knight:
The name of the song is called "HADDOCKS' EYES."

Alice, trying to feel interested:
Oh, that's the name of the song, is it?

Knight, looking a little vexed:
No, you don't understand, that's what the name is CALLED. The
name really IS "THE AGED AGED MAN."

Alice:
```

```
Then I ought to have said "That's what the SONG is called"?

Knight:
No, you oughtn't, that's quite another thing! The SONG is
called "WAYS AND MEANS," but that's only what it's CALLED, you
know!

Alice, completely bewildered:
Well, what IS the song, then?

Knight:
I was coming to that. The song really IS "A-SITTING ON A GATE",
and the tune's my own invention.
```

How It Works

In this dialog taken from Lewis Carroll's *Through the Looking-Glass* (which is, incidentally, a startlingly prescient glimpse into the realm of variable names and indirection), the main thread (`Alice`) and the coroutine thread (`Knight`) cooperate by relinquishing control at appropriate points. Note that each thread proceeds as if it is in charge. In fact, this *is* the case — each thread *does* have program control until it cooperatively gives it up. This happens when the invoking thread, `Alice`, calls `coroutine.resume` and when the coroutine `Knight` calls `coroutine.yield`. Each thread executes statements from a sequence that are interleaved with statements from the other thread's sequence.

When a coroutine is resumed, it is specified explicitly in the call to `coroutine.resume`. However, when a coroutine yields, it always transfers control back to the thread that resumed it.

When a program without coroutines includes a function that produces something and another that consumes it, either the producer function or the consumer function will be in control of the program flow. The other function will be called repeatedly as a service and will run each time from its beginning.

Outside Looking In

An admittedly whimsical way to look at coroutines is to consider an ordinary function call as the placement of program control into an ordinary bottle. When the function terminates, program control flows out of the bottle back to the caller. This analogy emphasizes that no matter how much control a function may have when it is active, it is constrained to eventually run its course and return to its caller. With the inside-out nature of coroutines, the analogy to an ordinary bottle just doesn't "hold water." Instead, when a coroutine yields, it places program control into a Klein bottle, the four dimensional equivalent of a Möbius strip. If you trace the surface of such a bottle, you find the "inside" and "outside" to be one and the same. A yielding coroutine curiously enters not a constrained enclosure, but the rest of the program. This analogy plays on Lua's way of making the transfer of control between coroutines look like function calls. If you find yourself getting confused about coroutines, focus on `coroutine.resume` and `coroutine.yield` as control transfer points rather than as functions.

The following Try It Out puts these ideas on a more familiar footing by using a classic application of coroutines: the interaction of a producer and a consumer. In particular, pay attention to how the producer's call to `coroutine.yield` looks like an ordinary function call, but in fact, it is the mechanism by which program control is transferred back to the consumer. Unlike a called function, the consumer can run its course without ever transferring control back to the producer.

A Word About Preemptive Multitasking

The cooperative nature of multitasking with coroutines distinguishes it from *preemptive multitasking*, in which the operating system decides when control is transferred from one thread to another, usually based on time slices. In the discussion that follows, threads in a preemptive multitasking environment will be referred to as *system threads*. Like a coroutine, a system thread has its own stack, so it is free to manipulate local variables and call and return from functions. However, a system thread must handle the following issues, which a coroutine does not:

❑ Explicit arrangement with the operating system needs to be made to keep certain blocks of code, such as a series of file writes that need to remain synchronized, from being interrupted.

❑ Access to globally shared resources must be properly synchronized to avoid corruption by different system threads.

❑ The termination of a system thread often needs to be specially coordinated with other system threads. Sometimes, a system thread's sole purpose is to coordinate the termination of other threads.

In practice, system threads can be messy. The simplest of programs take on a whole new level of complexity when preemptive multitasking is introduced. This occurs primarily because of the need to avoid *race* conditions in which statements are executed by system threads in an order that is incorrect and unexpected. Even if system threads don't have control over when they are preempted, they nevertheless need to exhibit a high degree of cooperation with other system threads to manage global resource access and proper termination issues. In light of the long history of coroutines, you may understandably wonder why they have been overshadowed by preemptive solutions in recent decades.

A Lua universe is the reentrant C data structure that all Lua programs are based on. Lua supports preemptive multitasking if special care is taken to protect this structure. To do so, follow these guidelines:

❑ If multiple system threads interact with a single Lua universe, they must be properly regulated with locks. Lua allows you to provide a locking function and an unlocking function that will be called by Lua when, respectively, it enters and leaves a block of code that must not be interrupted. These functions are not implemented within the Lua core because they in turn call operating system-dependent functions. This solution comes with a performance penalty due to locking overhead.

❑ More than one Lua universe can be active in a C program that embeds Lua. You can avoid locking requirements by arranging to have each Lua universe accessible to only one system thread. This avoids locking overhead, but requires you to provide a system thread-safe mechanism to transfer data from one Lua universe to another.

Preemptive multitasking is not covered any further in this book.

Try It Out   Sharing Control

Coroutines provide a framework that puts the consumer and producer on similar footing. The script that follows demonstrates this. In it, the producer thread generates simulated input events. The consumer thread simply displays these events in text form.

1.   Using your text editor, create a new document with the following contents:

```lua
local function LclProducer()
  print("Producer: initialize")
  -- Simulate event generation
  local List = {"mouse", "keyboard", "keyboard", "mouse"}
  for J, Val in ipairs(List) do
    local Evt = string.format("Event %d (%s)", J, Val)
    print("Producer: " .. Evt)
    coroutine.yield(Evt)
  end
  print("Producer: finalize")
  return "end"
end

local function LclConsumer()
  local GetEvent = coroutine.wrap(LclProducer)
  local Evt
  print("Consumer: initialize")
  while Evt ~= "end" do
    Evt = GetEvent()
    print("Consumer: " .. Evt)
  end
  print("Consumer: finalize")
end

LclConsumer()
```

2.   Save the file as `producer_consumer.lua`.

3.   Run the script with the Lua interpreter as follows:

```
lua producer_consumer.lua
Consumer: initialize
Producer: initialize
Producer: Event 1 (mouse)
Consumer: Event 1 (mouse)
Producer: Event 2 (keyboard)
Consumer: Event 2 (keyboard)
Producer: Event 3 (keyboard)
Consumer: Event 3 (keyboard)
Producer: Event 4 (mouse)
Consumer: Event 4 (mouse)
Producer: finalize
Consumer: end
Consumer: finalize
```

How It Works

In this script, LclConsumer runs in the main thread, and LclProducer runs in its own coroutine thread. Notice that coroutine.resume is not called explicitly in the code. That's because the GetEvent function (the product of coroutine.wrap) does this implicitly whenever it is called. The aspect of this script that warrants attention is how each thread transfer (GetEvent in LclConsumer and coroutine.yield in LclProducer) occurs within a loop. This is an indication that each thread has control. Local variables that are within the scope in the loop are preserved in the same way as if the resume and yield calls were ordinary function calls. Writing routines from this vantage is generally more natural than writing a routine that runs to completion each time it is called.

Had this example been used in a real event-driven environment, the loop in which LclProducer visits each array element would be replaced by a loop in which successive events are retrieved from the operating system. The fact that these events could arrive sporadically wouldn't change the way the two threads interact.

Coroutines Have Status

You've seen that a coroutine is instantiated with a call to coroutine.create. From that point on, a coroutine always has an operational status. If you're unsure what state a coroutine is in, you can call coroutine.status to find out. That function returns a string with one of the following values:

Status	Description
"suspended"	The specified coroutine is resumable.
"running"	The specified coroutine is currently running.
"normal"	The specified coroutine has resumed another coroutine.
"dead"	The specified coroutine has returned normally or in error.

Try It Out **Examining the Status of Coroutines**

1. Using your text editor, create a new file with the following contents:

```
local A, B, C

local function Status(Str)
  io.write(string.format("%-8s A is %-10s C is %-10s (%s)\n",
    Str, coroutine.status(A), coroutine.status(C),
    tostring(coroutine.running() or "main thread")))
end

function A()
  Status("A")
end

function B()
  Status("B")
end

function C()
```

```
      Status("C 1")
      coroutine.resume(A)
      Status("C 2")
      B()
      Status("C 3")
      coroutine.yield()
      Status("C 4")
   end

   A = coroutine.create(A)
   B = coroutine.wrap(B)
   C = coroutine.create(C)
   Status("Main 1")
   coroutine.resume(C)
   Status("Main 2")
   coroutine.resume(C)
   Status("Main 3")
```

2. Save this file as `status.lua`.

3. Run the script using the Lua interpreter as follows:

```
lua status.lua
Main 1    A is suspended   C is suspended   (main thread)
C 1       A is suspended   C is running     (thread: 00767F80)
A         A is running     C is normal      (thread: 007659C0)
C 2       A is dead        C is running     (thread: 00767F80)
B         A is dead        C is normal      (thread: 00766BD0)
C 3       A is dead        C is running     (thread: 00767F80)
Main 2    A is dead        C is suspended   (main thread)
C 4       A is dead        C is running     (thread: 00767F80)
Main 3    A is dead        C is dead        (main thread)
```

How It Works

In the course of this script, coroutine C assumes each possible status. Coroutine A never assumes the `"normal"` status, because it never resumes another coroutine.

The return value of `coroutine.wrap` is a function wrapper around a coroutine, not a coroutine, so it is not a suitable as an argument to `coroutine.status`. However, when B is called, its wrapped coroutine assumes the `"running"` status, in this case temporarily taking that status away from C.

Rules of Conduct

The care and feeding of coroutines is quite modest in return for the coolness they lend to a program. Here are some requirements you need to consider when welcoming coroutines into your application.

Work Shoulder-to-Shoulder

A running coroutine must explicitly yield control in a timely manner. A coroutine that runs too long without yielding deprives other threads of the chance to execute. Selecting a point at which to yield is usually straightforward. If the coroutine has produced one or more values to be delivered, it can yield with them as arguments and they will be delivered as return values of the invoking thread's `resume` call.

If the time needed to produce these values is long, the task can sometimes be partitioned into smaller pieces. In this case, the coroutine enters a loop in which parts of the product are yielded and the resuming thread reassembles them into the complete value. The resuming thread can cycle through a number of coroutines, resuming each in turn.

Trust the Dispatcher

Another time a coroutine should yield is when it begins waiting an indeterminate time for something to occur. The problem is that the only way a yielding coroutine will regain control is if it is resumed, so there must be some way for the resumer to know when the coroutine's wait is complete. This is usually possible with message-based applications in which notifications are pulled from an event queue. In this case, a thread (which is often the main thread) can be dedicated to dispatching these events by executing a loop in which it repeatedly collects an event and resumes the appropriate coroutine.

Expect the Best, Prepare for the Worst

A yielding coroutine generally has no control over which other threads will be activated, or in what order, before it is resumed. Consequently, you must pay some attention to the points at which a coroutine yields to prevent the possibility of unexpected modification of shared resources. For this reason, it pays to limit the scope of variables as much as possible. Avoid yielding in critical sequences of code. For example, if an external file and an internal Lua table need to remain synchronized, don't yield between the points where the update begins and where it ends.

Play on Your Side of the Fence

Coroutines face some restrictions where the C runtime stack is involved. A Lua function that is called from a library that uses Lua's C interface utilizes stacks on both sides of this interface. Coroutines run properly in this circumstance, but they cannot yield across the C interface because this would cause problems with the single stack that is used in the C code. This restriction applies to certain Lua functions such as `dofile` and `pcall`. Consider the following script:

```
local function A()
   coroutine.yield()
end

local function B()
   print(pcall(A))
end

coroutine.wrap(B)()
```

This generates the following output:

```
false    attempt to yield across metamethod/C-call boundary
```

In general, yields across the C interface can usually be worked around. If you encounter a situation where they are required, investigate Coco, a Lua patchset created by Mike Pall and located on the LuaForge site. This extension creates a C stack for each coroutine. It runs on POSIX and Windows (including Windows 98 and above).

Avoid the Deep End

The Lua distribution comes with a file named `sieve.lua` located in the `test` subdirectory. This script generates prime numbers up to a specified value (1000 by default) using, with coroutines, an algorithm created by the brilliant Hellenistic mathematician Eratosthenes. As shown by this program, coroutines and recursion appear to be a natural fit. Unfortunately, a known issue with Lua coroutines keeps the C runtime stack (yes, it keeps showing up in these problem areas) from being protected against an overflow condition. Unless you can be sure the C runtime stack is sufficiently large to handle your particular case, you'll want to avoid deeply recursive coroutines. Note also that the problem, because it pertains to the C stack, cannot be bounded with a protected call.

Managing Concurrent Tasks

You can multitask with coroutines to partition long jobs into smaller segments. If your program has some way of detecting user input without blocking (which is not possible with ANSI C and, consequently, standard Lua), then you can use this feature to interrupt or otherwise modify the course of these jobs.

Try It Out   Partitioning Longs Jobs with Coroutines

1. Using your text editor, create a new file with the following script:

```lua
local function Multitask()

    local function LclWork(Id, Count) -- Simulate some work
        for J = 1, Count do
            io.write(Id)
            io.flush()
            local Stop = os.time() + 1
            while os.time() < Stop do end
            coroutine.yield()
        end
    end

    local function LclContinue() -- Simulate check for user cancellation
        return math.random(12) > 1
    end

    local WorkA = coroutine.create(function () LclWork('A', 2) end)
    local WorkB = coroutine.create(function () LclWork('B', 4) end)
    math.randomseed(os.time())
    local A, B, Ok = true, true, true

    while (A or B) and Ok do
        Ok = LclContinue()
        if Ok and A then
            A = coroutine.resume(WorkA)
        end
        Ok = LclContinue()
        if Ok and B then
            B = coroutine.resume(WorkB)
        end
    end
```

```
      io.write(Ok and " done" or " cancel", "\n")

end

Multitask()
```

2.   Save this file as `multitask.lua`.

3.   Run through the following invocations using the Lua interpreter (because user cancellation is simulated randomly, the output you see will likely be different from what is shown here):

```
lua multitask.lua
ABABBB done

lua multitask.lua
ABA cancel

lua multitask.lua
AB cancel
```

How It Works

This example uses a number of simulations to demonstrate multitasking. For one, a bunch of cycles are consumed repeatedly calling `os.time` to simulate a segment of work. In a real application, arrange to have work performed in a coroutine, yielding after a segment of it has been completed. If user input is needed, it must be retrieved in a nonblocking manner. That is, some mechanism like an event queue or keypress buffer must be available for examination without actually waiting for user input.

The example presented here is just one of many variations you can use to repeatedly resume active coroutines. A common construction is to use an array to hold a number of coroutines.

Retaining State

When you programmatically open a file, you obtain a handle that is used for subsequent operations such as writing to the file and closing it. The handle is *opaque*, which means that information about the file's state (such as its buffers and file position and other internal details) is hidden from view. Within the file routines themselves, the handle is mapped to a data structure that allows the internal state to be accessed during an operation and retained between operations. The discipline of object orientation extends this notion by bundling fields and methods while restricting access to internal data. Each approach has been used extensively and successfully.

A Lua coroutine retains state through its dedicated stack. As you saw in the consumer and producer example, thread transfers don't affect the local variables in these stacks. Because of these stacks, a Lua coroutine can yield from a function other than its main body.

Exercising a Coroutine's Memory

One example of a body of code that must maintain its internal state is a *tokenizer*, a routine whose job is to deliver on demand the next lexical unit in a sequence. The following Try It Out shows how a coroutine can be used to let a tokenizer keep track of its internal state.

Try It Out   **Creating a Tokenizing Coroutine**

Expression analysis benefits from the use of a coroutine to collect tokens. Here, you'll see how naturally a coroutine-based tokenizer fits into a larger program.

1.   Using your text editor, create a new file with the following contents:

```
local Token, Pos

local function LclToken(ExpStr)
  local Len, PosStart, PosEnd, Allow
  Allow = "factor"
  Len = string.len(ExpStr)
  Pos = 1
  while Pos <= Len do
    if Allow == "factor" then
      PosStart, PosEnd, Token = string.find(ExpStr,
        "^%s*([%+%-]?%d+%.?%d*)%s*", Pos)
      if PosStart then
        Token = tonumber(Token)
      else
        PosStart, PosEnd, Token = string.find(ExpStr,
          "^%s*(%()%s*", Pos)
        if not PosStart then
          error("expected number or '(' at position " .. Pos)
        end
      end
    else -- "op"
      PosStart, PosEnd, Token = string.find(ExpStr,
        "^%s*([%)%+%-%*%/])%s*", Pos)
      if not PosStart then
        error("expected operator at position " .. Pos)
      end
    end
    Allow = coroutine.yield()
    Pos = PosEnd + 1
  end
  Token = "end"
  coroutine.yield()
  error("end of expression overreached")
end

local LclExpression

local function LclFactor()
  local Val = 0
  if type(Token) == "number" then
    Val = Token
    LclToken("op")
  elseif Token == "(" then
    LclToken("factor")
    Val = LclExpression()
    if Token == ")" then
      LclToken("op")
    else
      error("missing ')' at position " .. Pos)
```

```lua
      end
    else
      error("expecting number or '(' at position " .. Pos)
    end
    return Val
  end

  local function LclTerm()
    local Val = LclFactor()
    while Token == '*' or Token == '/' do
      if Token == '*' then
        LclToken("factor")
        Val = Val * LclFactor()
      else
        LclToken("factor")
        Val = Val / LclFactor()
      end
    end
    return Val
  end

  function LclExpression()
    local Val = LclTerm()
    while Token == '+' or Token == '-' do
      if Token == '+' then
        LclToken("factor")
        Val = Val + LclTerm()
      else
        LclToken("factor")
        Val = Val - LclTerm()
      end
    end
    return Val
  end

  local function LclEvaluate(ExpStr)
    LclToken = coroutine.wrap(LclToken)
    LclToken(ExpStr)
    local Val = LclExpression()
    if Token ~= "end" then
      error("unexpected token at position " .. Pos)
    end
    return Val
  end

  -- Evaluates the specified expression. If successful, returns result of
  -- expression. If the expression can't be evaluated, (nil, error message, error
  -- position) is returned.

  function Evaluate(ExpStr)
    local ErrPos
    local Code, Val = pcall(LclEvaluate, ExpStr)
    if Code then
      Code, Val = Val, nil
```

```
      else
        Code, ErrPos = nil, Pos
      end
      return Code, Val, ErrPos
    end

    local ExpStr = arg[1] or "1 + 1"
    local Result, ErrStr, ErrPos = Evaluate(ExpStr)
    io.write("Expression: ", ExpStr, "\n")
    if Result then
      io.write("Result: ", Result, "\n")
    else
      io.write(string.rep(' ', ErrPos + 11), "^\n")
      io.write("Error: ", ErrStr, "\n")
    end
```

2. Save the file as expr.lua.

3. Using the Lua interpreter, try the evaluator out with the following expressions:

```
lua expr.lua "1 + 2 * 3 / 4 * 5 - 6"
Expression: 1 + 2 * 3 / 4 * 5 - 6
Result: 2.5

lua expr.lua "(1 + 2) * 3 / 4 * (5 - 6)"
Expression: (1 + 2) * 3 / 4 * (5 - 6)
Result: -2.25

lua expr.lua "1+1"
Expression: 1+1
Result: 2

lua expr.lua "1++1"
Expression: 1++1
Result: 2

lua expr.lua "1+++1"
Expression: 1+++1
              ^
Error: expr.lua:75: expr.lua:18: expected number or '(' at position 3

lua expr.lua "1 1"
Expression: 1 1
              ^
Error: expr.lua:42: expr.lua:25: expected operator at position 3

lua expr.lua "1 % 2"
Expression: 1 % 2
              ^
Error: expr.lua:42: expr.lua:25: expected operator at position 3

lua expr.lua "1 + 1 )"
Expression: 1 + 1 )
                  ^
```

```
Error: expr.lua:90: unexpected token at position 7

lua expr.lua "( 1 + 1
Expression: ( 1 + 1
                  ^

Error: expr.lua:49: missing ')' at position 8

lua expr.lua "(((1)))"
Expression: (((1)))
Result: 1
```

How It Works

A parser's job is to analyze the elements of an expression. In the four-function expression evaluator presented here, the method of *recursive descent* is used. The idea is to treat an expression as a series of terms to be added or subtracted. Each term is treated similarly as a series of factors to be multiplied or divided. And each factor is treated as either a number or as a parenthesized expression. In the last case, the same function used to analyze the outermost expression can be called recursively to analyze the subexpression. This can be repeated to any practical depth. With this method, the precedence of the various operators is built into the structure of the parser.

The task of parsing requires the services of a tokenizer, a routine that identifies constituent elements. The tokenizer is called from various parts of the parser, and it must keep track of where it's been so that it can effectively collect the next available token. Additionally, the tokenizer is called in a context-sensitive manner. Based on where in the parser the request for a token is made, either a factor (a number or opening parenthesis) or an operator (+, -, *, /, closing parenthesis, or end of expression) is requested. This prevents a simple loop from simply collecting all tokens and placing them into a table prior to calling the parser. The context-sensitivity is required; for example, to recognize -3 as a number in one case, and as the subtraction operator followed by a number in another.

Here are some aspects of this program that warrant special note:

❑ The combination of `pcall` and coroutines doesn't present any problems here. The `LclToken` coroutine yields repeatedly as it generates tokens, but always to a thread running in the same protected call. Note also that there are no open resources such as files that are left unclosed when an expression error is encountered.

❑ The `coroutine.wrap` is used to convert `LclToken` from a variable that references an ordinary function to one that references a coroutine that can be invoked like a function — without explicitly using `coroutine.resume`.

❑ The body of `LclToken` is not intended to return. If `LclToken` is called after the "end" token (indicating the end of the expression) has been retrieved, a descriptive error is issued. Had `LclToken` returned rather than yielded after setting the "end" token, and if the coroutine was resumed, the less helpful "cannot resume dead coroutine" message would have been displayed.

Iterating with Coroutines

In Chapter 4, you learned how to create an iterator, a mechanism that encapsulates many details of looping through sequences. Recall that behind the scenes, Lua calls your iterator function repeatedly to produce successive return values. Coroutines are useful in this context because they don't have to be run from their beginning at each call.

Try It Out **Looping Backwards with a Coroutine Iterator**

In this Try It Out, you'll write a new version of the `ReverseIPairs` iterator factory that you first saw in Chapter 4. This one will use a coroutine to achieve the same goal of iterating through an array in reverse order.

1. Create a new file with your text editor and include the follow script:

```
local function ReverseIPairs(Arr)
  local function Iter()
    for J = #Arr, 1, -1 do
      coroutine.yield(J, Arr[J])
    end
  end
  return coroutine.wrap(Iter)
end

for J, Str in ReverseIPairs({"one", "two", "three"}) do
  print(J, Str)
end
```

2. Save the file as `co_iter.lua`.

3. Run the script using the Lua interpreter as follows:

```
lua co_iter.lua
3       three
2       two
1       one
```

How It Works

The `ReverseIPairs` iterator factory returns only one value, a function that wraps `Iter` as a coroutine body. No state information needs to be returned; that's all contained in the coroutine itself. When the loop within `Iter` is complete, `nil` is implicitly returned. This signals the end of the generic `for` loop to Lua, and the iterator function is not called anymore.

Handling Events Simply

In the era of dumb terminals, timesharing servers and near-total disregard for user-friendliness (veteran programmers refer to this time period as the "good old days"), interactive programs were *modal*—all user input was channeled into one screen at a time. In the middle of one screen, a user simply couldn't access another. The advantages were all with the software developer. Programming modal screens was easy and promoted clear code that was straightforward to follow because screen functions blocked the way a call to open a file blocked—they simply didn't return until the screen was either approved or cancelled. The ease that programmers had with this model was paid for with user frustration. The limitations of this kind of program became apparent even before the era of GUIs. The solution was for all application input events to be centrally queued and dispatched to appropriate handlers. This new paradigm allowed users to switch between open screens at the cost of complicated program code. Given the constraint of a single application call stack, the event-driven approach led to a programming model that is still pervasive. The following sections describe how this model works, with the focus on the call stack.

The Event Loop

When an event-driven application starts, it typically takes care of some initialization work. The function calls that take place here result in some stack activity.

At some point, usually right after a window or some other *event sink* is created, the application begins a loop in which events are requested by calling a system function. In the X Window System, this is the `XNextEvent` function; in Windows, it is the `GetMessage` function. The height of the stack at this point indicates a "low watermark." Until the event retrieval loop is terminated prior to the end of the program, the call stack will not shrink below this level. It will, however, be quite active above this level as various functions are called in response to particular events, such as keyboard presses, mouse actions, and window-drawing requests. In a well-functioning application, the processing of any event should take no longer than a tenth of a second or so to avoid choppy window refreshes and sluggish response times.

The event retrieval function is a *blocking* function — it does not return until an event occurs. It is where an interactive application yields control to the system and generally spends most its time waiting. After handling an event, program control has to return to the event loop to retrieve the next event. This implies that the application call stack has to return to its low watermark, meaning that the various event handlers that are called must find some other means than local variables to retain the state needed for continuity. Because of their integrated approach to methods and fields, object-oriented solutions abound in event-driven systems. For example, a window object can store fields such as list contents and control properties that persist between event notifications.

Modal windows are supported in this single call stack model, but they have the unfortunate consequence of disabling other active windows, preventing users from switching from one window to another within the application. The window created with a blocking call to `DialogBox` in the Windows API is an example of a modal window. In order to block, such a window is implemented with its own event loop. The modal window's event loop allows other windows to be redrawn when needed, but only the modal window itself is permitted to receive user input. The disabling of other windows prevents problems with variables maintained in the stack between the low watermark and the point at which the modal event loop is implemented. After the modal window is dismissed, you wouldn't want references to other windows that may have been closed or altered. Any practical number of modal windows can be stacked in a chain, but the limitation of only one window that can receive user input makes this technique suitable only for small dialog boxes that can be cancelled without hardship if the user needs to work in another window. In other words, a modal window is easy for the programmer and frustrating for the user.

If you have reached the conclusion that it is the single stack model that prevents switchable, blocking windows, you are correct. What is needed is a window event handler that has its own stack. The solution is to implement this handler as a coroutine. Giving users the flexibility of switching between windows while implementing them, behind the scenes, as blocking windows is a remarkable capability of coroutines. It dramatically simplifies the development of event-driven programs.

Try It Out   Handling Events with Coroutines

In order to focus on the essential structure of a coroutine-based event handling module, the following program uses the command line shell to simulate how windows would behave in a GUI. This not only keeps the code free of a lot of low-level windowing code, it allows you to test it in a pure, platform-independent Lua environment.

1. With your text editor, create a new file with the following contents:

As you can see, there is a lot of code here, so this is a good place to remind you that this and every other script in this book is available from wrox.com.

```
local Window, Lcl = {}, {}

-- Queue of posted event messages

Lcl.MsgQueue = {}

-- Window structure
--    Parent: window object of parent
--    Id: string identifier, e.g. 1.2.5 for 5th child of 2nd child of window 1
--    Co: coroutine(Fnc) blocks until terminating event
--    ChildCount: number of active children
--    ChildSerial: used for naming new children
--    ChildList: associative array keyed by child window objects
--    Close: assigned the terminating message (usually "cancel" or "ok")
--    User: table passed to handler to hold data that must persist from event to
--       event

-- List of window structures keyed by Id

Lcl.WindowList = {}

-- Currently active window

Lcl.WindowActive = nil

-- Value of message to indicate that associated window should be unblocked

Lcl.MsgReturn = "\000"

-- Display all active windows

function Lcl.Show()
  local List = {}
  for Id, Wnd in pairs(Lcl.WindowList) do
    table.insert(List, Wnd.Close and (Id .. " (pending closure)") or Id)
  end
  table.sort(List)
  for J, Id in ipairs(List) do
    io.write(Id, "\n")
  end
end

-- This function is called when an event occurs that could result in the return
-- of a window call.

function Lcl.Destroy(Wnd)
  if Wnd.Close and Wnd.ChildCount == 0 then
    io.write("Unblocking window ", Wnd.Id, "\n")
    table.insert(Lcl.MsgQueue, {Wnd, Lcl.MsgReturn})
  end
```

```
end

-- Show some help text

function Lcl.Help()
  io.write("Type 'show' to see all active windows\n")
  io.write("Type 'window_id msg' to send message to window\n")
  io.write("Standard messages are 'create', 'ok' and 'cancel'\n")
end

-- Simulate the generation of a window event. For a windowed application, this
-- would typically originate with the graphical shell (Windows: GetMessage,
-- XLib: XNextEvent. No coroutine yielding occurs here, so this can be a
-- binding to C.

function Lcl.EventGet()
  local Wnd, Msg
  if Lcl.MsgQueue[1] then -- If event is queued, retrieve the first one in
    local Rec = table.remove(Lcl.MsgQueue, 1)
    Wnd, Msg = Rec[1], Rec[2]
  else -- Wait for event from user
    while not Msg do
      io.write("Cmd> ")
      local Str = io.read()
      Str = string.gsub(Str, "^ *(.-) *$", "%1")
      Str = string.lower(Str)
      if Str == "help" or Str == "?" then
        Lcl.Help()
      elseif Str == "show" then
        Lcl.Show()
      else -- Pass message along to designated window
        local IdStr, MsgStr = string.match(Str, "(%S+)%s+(%S+)")
        if IdStr then
          Wnd = Lcl.WindowList[IdStr]
          if Wnd then
            if not Wnd.Close then
              Msg = MsgStr
            else
              io.write("Window ", IdStr, " is inactive\n")
            end
          else
            io.write("Unknown window: ", IdStr, "\n")
          end
        else
          io.write("Expecting 'help', 'show' or 'window_id msg'\n")
        end
      end
    end
  end
  return Wnd, Msg
end

-- Main event loop. All coroutines are resumed from this function and yield
-- back to it.

function Lcl.EventLoop()
```

```lua
        local Wnd, Msg
        local Loop = true
        while Loop do
          Wnd, Msg = Lcl.EventGet()
          if Wnd then
            Lcl.WindowActive = Wnd
            if Msg == Lcl.MsgReturn then
              -- Resume blocking window call
              if Wnd.Co then
                coroutine.resume(Wnd.Co, Wnd.Close)
              else
                Loop = false
                Msg = Wnd.Close
              end
            else
              -- Non-terminating message was received. Notify window in new coroutine
              -- rather than direct function call because a new blocking window may
              -- be raised.
              local Co = coroutine.create(Wnd.Fnc)
              coroutine.resume(Co, Wnd.User, Msg)
            end
          end
        end
        return Msg
    end

    function Window.Show(Fnc)
        local Parent = Lcl.WindowActive -- Nil for first window shown
        local Msg, Id
        if Parent then
          Parent.ChildSerial = Parent.ChildSerial + 1
          Id = Parent.Id .. "." .. Parent.ChildSerial
        else -- First window
          Lcl.Help()
          Id = "1"
        end
        local Co = coroutine.running()
        local Wnd = {Parent = Parent, Co = Co, Id = Id, Fnc = Fnc,
          ChildCount = 0, ChildSerial = 0, ChildList = {}, User = {Id = Id}}
        io.write("Creating window ", Wnd.Id, "\n")
        table.insert(Lcl.MsgQueue, {Wnd, "create"})
        Lcl.WindowList[Id] = Wnd
        if Parent then
          assert(Co)
          Parent.ChildList[Wnd] = true
          Parent.ChildCount = Parent.ChildCount + 1
          -- We're running in a coroutine; yield back to event loop. The current
          -- coroutine will not be resumed until the newly created window and all of
          -- its descendent windows have been destroyed. This happens when a
          -- Lcl.MsgReturn is posted for this window.
          Msg = coroutine.yield()
          Parent.ChildCount = Parent.ChildCount - 1
          Parent.ChildList[Wnd] = nil
          -- Close parent if it's in pending state
          Lcl.Destroy(Parent)
        else
```

```
      assert(not Co)
      -- We're running in main thread; call event loop and don't return
      -- until the loop ends
      Msg = Lcl.EventLoop()
    end
    Lcl.WindowList[Id] = nil
    return Msg
  end

  function Window.Close(Msg)
    local Wnd = Lcl.WindowActive
    Wnd.Close = Msg or "destroy"
    Lcl.Destroy(Wnd)
  end

  return Window
```

2. Save this file as `window.lua`.

3. Create another new file with the following contents:

```
local Window = require("window")

-- Sample window message handler.

local function SampleWindow(Wnd, Msg)
  Wnd.Serial = (Wnd.Serial or 0) + 1
  io.write("Window ", Wnd.Id, ", message ", Msg, ", serial ", Wnd.Serial, "\n")
  if Msg == "ok" or Msg == "cancel" then
    io.write("Calling Window.Close on ", Wnd.Id, "\n")
    Window.Close(Msg)
    io.write("Called Window.Close on ", Wnd.Id, "\n")
  elseif Msg == "button" or Msg == "new" then
    local Time = os.date("%X")
    io.write("Calling Window.Show from ", Wnd.Id, " (", Time, ")\n")
    local Status = Window.Show(SampleWindow)
    io.write("Called Window.Show from ", Wnd.Id, ", child returned ",
      Status, " (", Time, ")\n")
  end
end

-- Main statements

io.write("Application: starting\n")
local Status = Window.Show(SampleWindow)
io.write("Window returned ", Status, "\n")
io.write("Application: ending\n")
```

4. Save this script as `window_app.lua`.

5. Make sure that `?.lua` is specified in your LUA_PATH environment variable. Invoke the `window_app.lua` script and simulate a simple session in which a main window and a child window are created and, in reverse order, closed:

```
lua window_app.lua
Application: starting
Type 'show' to see all active windows
```

```
Type 'window_id msg' to send message to window
Standard messages are 'create', 'ok' and 'cancel'
Creating window 1
Window 1, message create, serial 1
Cmd> 1 mouse
Window 1, message mouse, serial 2
Cmd> 1 keypress
Window 1, message keypress, serial 3
Cmd> 1 new
Window 1, message new, serial 4
Calling Window.Show from 1 (09:11:25)
Creating window 1.1
Window 1.1, message create, serial 1
Cmd> show
1
1.1
Cmd> 1.1 ok
Window 1.1, message ok, serial 2
Calling Window.Close on 1.1
Unblocking window 1.1
Called Window.Close on 1.1
Called Window.Show from 1, child returned ok (09:11:25)
Cmd> 1 mouse
Window 1, message mouse, serial 5
Cmd> 1 ok
Window 1, message ok, serial 6
Calling Window.Close on 1
Unblocking window 1
Called Window.Close on 1
Window returned ok
Application: ending
```

6. Invoke the script again. This time, build up a window tree and experiment with closing the windows in something other than reverse order, like this:

```
lua window_app.lua
Application: starting
Type 'show' to see all active windows
Type 'window_id msg' to send message to window
Standard messages are 'create', 'ok' and 'cancel'
Creating window 1
Window 1, message create, serial 1
Cmd> 1 new
Window 1, message new, serial 2
Calling Window.Show from 1 (09:03:18)
Creating window 1.1
Window 1.1, message create, serial 1
Cmd> 1 new
Window 1, message new, serial 3
Calling Window.Show from 1 (09:03:20)
Creating window 1.2
Window 1.2, message create, serial 1
Cmd> 1 new
Window 1, message new, serial 4
```

```
Calling Window.Show from 1 (09:03:21)
Creating window 1.3
Window 1.3, message create, serial 1
Cmd> 1.1 new
Window 1.1, message new, serial 2
Calling Window.Show from 1.1 (09:03:28)
Creating window 1.1.1
Window 1.1.1, message create, serial 1
Cmd> 1.2 new
Window 1.2, message new, serial 2
Calling Window.Show from 1.2 (09:03:31)
Creating window 1.2.1
Window 1.2.1, message create, serial 1
Cmd> 1.2 new
Window 1.2, message new, serial 3
Calling Window.Show from 1.2 (09:03:33)
Creating window 1.2.2
Window 1.2.2, message create, serial 1
Cmd> 1.2.2 new
Window 1.2.2, message new, serial 2
Calling Window.Show from 1.2.2 (09:03:39)
Creating window 1.2.2.1
Window 1.2.2.1, message create, serial 1
Cmd> show
1
1.1
1.1.1
1.2
1.2.1
1.2.2
1.2.2.1
1.3
Cmd> 1.2.1 ok
Window 1.2.1, message ok, serial 2
Calling Window.Close on 1.2.1
Unblocking window 1.2.1
Called Window.Close on 1.2.1
Called Window.Show from 1.2, child returned ok (09:03:31)
Cmd> 1.3 ok
Window 1.3, message ok, serial 2
Calling Window.Close on 1.3
Unblocking window 1.3
Called Window.Close on 1.3
Called Window.Show from 1, child returned ok (09:03:21)
Cmd> show
1
1.1
1.1.1
1.2
1.2.2
1.2.2.1
Cmd> 1 ok
Window 1, message ok, serial 5
Calling Window.Close on 1
```

```
Called Window.Close on 1
Cmd> 1.1 ok
Window 1.1, message ok, serial 3
Calling Window.Close on 1.1
Called Window.Close on 1.1
Cmd> show
1 (pending closure)
1.1 (pending closure)
1.1.1
1.2
1.2.2
1.2.2.1
Cmd> 1.2.2 ok
Window 1.2.2, message ok, serial 3
Calling Window.Close on 1.2.2
Called Window.Close on 1.2.2
Cmd> show
1 (pending closure)
1.1 (pending closure)
1.1.1
1.2
1.2.2 (pending closure)
1.2.2.1
Cmd> 1.2.2.1 ok
Window 1.2.2.1, message ok, serial 2
Calling Window.Close on 1.2.2.1
Unblocking window 1.2.2.1
Called Window.Close on 1.2.2.1
Unblocking window 1.2.2
Called Window.Show from 1.2.2, child returned ok (09:03:39)
Called Window.Show from 1.2, child returned ok (09:03:33)
Cmd> show
1 (pending closure)
1.1 (pending closure)
1.1.1
1.2
Cmd> 1.2 ok
Window 1.2, message ok, serial 4
Calling Window.Close on 1.2
Unblocking window 1.2
Called Window.Close on 1.2
Called Window.Show from 1, child returned ok (09:03:20)
Cmd> 1.1.1 ok
Window 1.1.1, message ok, serial 2
Calling Window.Close on 1.1.1
Unblocking window 1.1.1
Called Window.Close on 1.1.1
Unblocking window 1.1
Called Window.Show from 1.1, child returned ok (09:03:28)
Unblocking window 1
Called Window.Show from 1, child returned ok (09:03:18)
Window returned ok
Application: ending
```

How It Works

There are two functions exported from the window module: `Window.Show` and `Window.Close`. The first is used to raise a window, and the second is used to signal its closure. In a full-featured window library, some sort of descriptive data structure would typically be passed to `Window.Show` that describes the controls and parameters of the window to be displayed.

When a window is raised, it is associated with a function that acts as its event handler. For simplicity in this example, the function `SampleWindow` is used for all windows, but typically you would have one handler for each unique window. Any event message that pertains to a specific window will be sent to its event handler. Here, the only messages that `SampleWindow` responds to are `ok`, `cancel`, `button`, and `new`. In an actual event-driven application, messages would be more generic (for example, `button click` rather than `ok`), and they would be accompanied by parameters that would provide additional details about the message.

Each event notification in this library is sent to the handler in a new thread. That is, with each new event, the event handler is instantiated as a coroutine and resumed with the event passed as an argument. This is done because the event dispatcher can't know which, if any, event will result in the application blocking in another call to `Window.Show`. Otherwise, it could call the event handler as a function for each event that it knew would not block because control would return promptly and it could return to the business of dispatching events.

A consequence of this model is that variables local to the handler are not shared between invocations. Here is a clarification of the tradeoff that is made:

❑ On one hand, a coroutine can repeatedly yield and be resumed. In this case, local variables are retained. The consumer-producer and expression evaluation programs are examples of this. In this type of arrangement, an event processing loop is placed in the scope of local variables that will be retained between yields.

❑ On the other hand, a coroutine can yield and not be resumed until a particular event occurs — in this case, the window closure event. To allow a window event handler to behave this way, a new coroutine needs to be created using the handler as a body for each event notification. This approach gives you the advantage of blocking window calls, but requires you to find another place to store persistent data. In the window example, you can simply store persistent fields in the `Wnd` table argument that is passed to the handler for just this purpose.

The important aspect to note as you run this program is that the calls to `Window.Show` are blocking calls. Even if `Window.Close` is called on a window, it will not return until all of its descendents are closed. (Incidentally, it would be a simple matter to adjust this behavior so that, when a window is closed, all of its active descendents are forced to close.) The capability to sequentially raise a window and wait for it to terminate frees your application code from much of the complexity often associated with interactive, event-driven programs.

Yielding to Another Coroutine

A coroutine in Lua always yields back to the thread that resumed it. If you would rather specify a coroutine to which to yield, the function `Lcl.EventLoop` in the previous example gives you the first of two required steps. These steps are:

1. Implement a dispatcher that handles all resuming of coroutines.

2. When yielding, provide the dispatcher with enough information to resume the desired coroutine.

In this framework, it will be the dispatcher thread to which all coroutines yield. If an argument of the yield, say the first, always specifies the desired coroutine to resume, the dispatcher can do this transparently on behalf of the yielding coroutine.

Summary

In this chapter, you learned how to use Lua coroutines in a variety of situations to implement solutions that would otherwise be cumbersome. These include the following:

- ❑ Sequentially running multiple jobs
- ❑ Retaining state as with an expression tokenizer
- ❑ Implementing an iterator
- ❑ Blocking on a call that returns an event

You also learned the following coroutine concepts:

- ❑ Their capabilities derive from transferring control between threads that each have a dedicated call stack.
- ❑ Only one thread is active at a time>
- ❑ The transfer of control between threads is done with a natural function-like mechanism, namely `coroutine.yield` and `coroutine.resume`, that permits the exchange of values.

In the next chapter, you'll dust off your software development kit and learn how to extend Lua with routines that you'll program in C. In the meantime, try your hand at the following exercises.

Exercises

1. Without actually running it, determine what the following script prints.

```
local function F()
   local J, K = 0, 1
   coroutine.yield(J)
   coroutine.yield(K)
   while true do
      J, K = K, J + K
      coroutine.yield(K)
   end
end

F = coroutine.wrap(F)

for J = 1, 8 do
   print(F())
end
```

2. Write a coroutine-based iterator named `JoinPairs` that pairs elements from parallel lists. For example, the following loop:

```
for Name, Number in JoinPairs({"Sally", "Mary", "James"}, {12, 32, 7}) do
   print(Name, Number)
end
```

should generate the following output:

```
Sally    12
Mary     32
James    7
```

3. In the producer-consumer example, the consumer thread resumes the producer thread. Modify the example so that this is turned around; that is, execute the producer function in the main thread and run the consumer as a coroutine.

Looking Under the Hood

This chapter covers various ways of looking at the inner workings of Lua. To continue the automotive metaphor of the title, you can write many useful programs without knowing the things in this chapter, just as you can drive a car without knowing how to change the oil. However, the knowledge and techniques in this chapter will help you find bugs, and let you do things with Lua that otherwise wouldn't be possible. You'll learn about the following:

❑   Using bytecode

❑   Controlling Lua's memory management

❑   Understanding the implementation of tables and strings

❑   Looking directly inside functions to see and alter their local variables

❑   Tracing the execution of your code on a call-by-call, line-by-line, or instruction-by-instruction basis

Bytecode and luac

As mentioned in Chapter 3, before Lua can execute source code, it needs to compile it into bytecode, which is then interpreted by the bytecode interpreter. Another name for the bytecode interpreter is the *virtual machine*, because it's kind of like an imaginary computer (imaginary in the sense that no one has ever built one out of silicon — it's just simulated by your real computer). Lua comes with two programs: the command-line interpreter lua, and the bytecode compiler luac. The main purpose of luac is to compile Lua source code to bytecode and save that bytecode to a file (so it can be run later), but it can also output a human-readable listing of the bytecode.

Try It Out   Reading Bytecode with luac

1.   Save the following as test.lua:

```
-- A short script (for use as a luac test).

function Greet(Name)
  print("Hello, " .. Name .. ".")
```

```
      end

      Greet("whoever you are")
```

2. Run `luac` as follows:

```
luac -p -l test.lua
```

The output should look something like this:

```
main <test.lua:0,0> (6 instructions, 24 bytes at 0x471410)
0+ params, 2 slots, 0 upvalues, 0 locals, 2 constants, 1 function
         1       [5]     CLOSURE       0 0      ; 0x471560
         2       [3]     SETGLOBAL     0 -1     ; Greet
         3       [7]     GETGLOBAL     0 -1     ; Greet
         4       [7]     LOADK         1 -2     ; "whoever you are"
         5       [7]     CALL          0 2 1
         6       [7]     RETURN        0 1

function <test.lua:3,5> (7 instructions, 28 bytes at 0x471560)
1 param, 5 slots, 0 upvalues, 1 local, 3 constants, 0 functions
         1       [4]     GETGLOBAL     1 -1     ; print
         2       [4]     LOADK         2 -2     ; "Hello, "
         3       [4]     MOVE          3 0
         4       [4]     LOADK         4 -3     ; "."
         5       [4]     CONCAT        2 2 4
         6       [4]     CALL          1 2 1
         7       [5]     RETURN        0 1
```

How It Works

The `-p` option tells `luac` to only *parse* the file (check it for syntactical correctness) rather than actually outputting any bytecode. The `-l` option tells it to print a bytecode listing. The last argument, `test.lua`, names the file to be used as source code. (This filename has to be the last argument; no options can follow it.)

The bytecode listing itself has two sections: one for the main chunk (the whole file `test.lua`) and one for the `Greet` function definition. This chapter isn't big enough to give anywhere close to a comprehensive description of the virtual-machine instructions that bytecode is composed of, but a line-by-line breakdown will give you at least an impression of how bytecode works.

First, the following lines give information about the main chunk (more on this in a moment):

```
main <test.lua:0,0> (6 instructions, 24 bytes at 0x471410)
0+ params, 2 slots, 0 upvalues, 0 locals, 2 constants, 1 function
```

Then the `CLOSURE` instruction creates a function, using the definition at `0x471560` where the `[5]` means that this corresponds to line 5 of the source code (the end of `Greet`'s function definition):

```
         1       [5]     CLOSURE       0 0      ; 0x471560
```

This instruction assigns the function to the global variable `Greet`:

```
         2       [3]     SETGLOBAL     0 -1     ; Greet
```

This instruction gets the value (a function) of the global variable `Greet`:

```
3        [7]      GETGLOBAL       0 -1     ; Greet
```

This instruction loads one of the main chunk's constants (`"whoever you are"`) into register 1:

```
4        [7]      LOADK           1 -2     ; "whoever you are"
```

The Lua virtual machine has up to 250 *registers*, or temporary storage locations. Here, a register is being used to store `"whoever you are"` until it is passed to a function. Registers are also used to store arguments and other local variables. In the example's output, where the second line says 2 slots, that means that the main chunk uses 2 registers. Registers reside on the call stack, so each function call gets a fresh set.

```
Continuing with the line-by-line breakdown of the example, the following
instruction calls register 0 (the Greet function) with 1 argument and 0 return
values (subtract 1 from both the 2 and the 1 to get these values):        5
[7]     CALL            0 2 1
```

Then this instruction returns from the main chunk, thereby ending the script:

```
6        [7]      RETURN          0 1
```

These lines give information about the `Greet` function definition — it resides at 0x471560, has one argument (parameter) and three constants, and uses five registers:

```
function <test.lua:3,5> (7 instructions, 28 bytes at 0x471560)
1 param, 5 slots, 0 upvalues, 1 local, 3 constants, 0 functions
```

This instruction gets the value (a function) of the global variable `print`:

```
1        [4]      GETGLOBAL       1 -1     ; print
```

These instructions put the constant `"Hello, "`, the function's argument, and the constant `"."` into registers 2, 3, and 4:

```
2        [4]      LOADK           2 -2     ; "Hello, "
3        [4]      MOVE            3 0
4        [4]      LOADK           4 -3     ; "."
```

And finally, these instructions concatenate registers 2 through 4, call `print`, and return from `Greet`:

```
5        [4]      CONCAT          2 2 4
6        [4]      CALL            1 2 1
7        [5]      RETURN          0 1
```

If you want to know more about the Lua virtual machine, check out Kein-Hong Man's "A No-Frills Introduction to Lua 5.1 VM Instructions." It's available at `luaforge.net`, along with his ChunkSpy program, which is a tool for analyzing bytecode.

You can use bytecode listings to find certain kinds of bugs, troubleshoot efficiency issues, and understand the meaning of particularly hairy pieces of source code. To create a bytecode file, get rid of the -p option (and the -l option) and supply the output filename with the -o option, or don't supply it and look for the output in the file luac.out. A common convention is to end bytecode files in .luac, but (as with .lua files), you can name them anything you want and Lua won't care. For example, this line creates a test.luac file:

```
luac -o test.luac test.lua
```

You can run this like a regular Lua file, by typing the following:

```
lua test.luac
```

The output is this:

```
Hello, whoever you are.
```

Lua can tell the difference between bytecode and source code by looking at the first byte of the file. If it's the character "\27", then the file is treated as bytecode; otherwise it's treated as normal source code. This applies not only to the command-line interpreter, but also to loadstring and its cousins load, loadfile, and dofile, all of which can accept either source code or bytecode.

The string.dump function converts from a Lua function to bytecode as follows:

```
> function Greet(Name)
>>    print("Hello, " .. Name .. ".")
>> end
>
> -- Convert Greet to bytecode:
> Bytecode = string.dump(Greet)
> -- Convert it back to a function and call it:
> (loadstring(Bytecode))("Insert name here")
Hello, Insert name here.
```

According to the Lua reference manual, the function given to string.dump cannot have upvalues. An undocumented feature (which therefore may change without notice in a future version) is that a function with upvalues may be dumped, but in the dumped version, all the upvalues will be private to the function (even if the original shared them with another function) and they'll be nil until assigned to from within the function. (In Lua 5.0, string.dump triggered an error if given a function with upvalues.)

luac is necessary less often than you might think. For example, you can use luac to do the following:

❑   Save the time you would otherwise spend to compile a source code file before running it. Because Lua's bytecode compiler is so fast, this is very seldom a big enough time saver to be worth the hassle.

❑   Hide scripts from snooping eyes and fiddling fingers. Other than constant strings, a .luac file looks like gobbledygook in a text editor, and this is enough to protect it from casual exploration, but a determined person (armed with the aforementioned ChunkSpy, for example) can still read and modify it.

❑   Save space. Because .luac files are not necessarily much smaller (or any smaller) than the corresponding .lua files, this is also seldom worth the hassle. One case where it can be worthwhile is in embedded systems, where space is at a premium. (If source code is never used on the embedded device itself, then the bytecode-compiler component of Lua doesn't need to be present, which saves more space.)

❑ Check syntax. The -p option allows you to check files for syntax errors without actually running them.

❑ Generate bytecode listings (as discussed previously) for debugging purposes.

These last two uses are the domain of lint-type program checkers. For example, a program to find unintentional global variables could create a list of all globals by looking at GETGLOBAL and SETGLOBAL instructions in a bytecode listing.

Bytecode is not portable. A bytecode file generated on one machine can only be used on another if the second machine has the same byte order (little-endian versus big-endian) and word size (32-bit versus 64-bit, for example). *Byte order* just refers to the order in which multiple-byte numbers are laid out in memory.

Also, because the virtual machine is nothing more than a means of implementing Lua, bytecode is not portable between different versions. Therefore, Lua 5.0 bytecode won't work on Lua 5.1 or vice versa.

The following table lists the luac options and what they do.

Option	Action
-l	Prints a bytecode listing.
-o	Uses the following command-line argument as the name of the output file. (The default is luac.out.)
-p	Only parses the source code — doesn't output any bytecode.
-s	Strips debugging information (making the output file smaller, but losing things like the line numbers used in error messages).
-v	Prints version information.
--	Stops handling options (this is useful if you want to compile a script whose name starts with -).
-	Treats standard luac input as source code (otherwise, the file named by the last luac argument is used as source code).

Garbage Collection

If a value is of a type that uses a variable amount of space (such as a string, table, or function) or if it's used as an upvalue and hence may outlive its stack frame, Lua automatically sets aside the necessary space for it in memory. If Lua subsequently notices that this value is no longer either pointed to by a variable or is used as a key or value in a table, it marks that value's memory as no longer occupied so that it can be reused. This process is called *garbage collection*.

In the following Try It Out, you print bar charts to show how memory usage varies as strings are created and garbage-collected.

Measuring Memory Usage

1. Type the following function into the interpreter:

```
function GarbageTest(Len)
  -- Clean up any garbage:
  collectgarbage("collect")
  for I = 0, 9 do
    -- Create a Len-character string and put it in a variable
    -- that will go out of scope at the end of this iteration:
    local Junk = string.rep(I, Len)
    -- Print a line of a bar chart showing memory usage:
    print(string.rep("#", collectgarbage("count"))) -- This use
      -- of string.rep increases memory usage a bit too, but
      -- that can be ignored.
  end
end
```

2. Call `GarbageTest` with an argument of `200`. The output should look something like this:

```
####################
####################
####################
####################
####################
####################
####################
#####################
#####################
#####################
```

3. Call `GarbageTest` with an argument of `3000`. The output should look something like this:

```
##########################
###############################
####################################
#########################################
##############################################
#############################
##################################
######################################
###########################################
#################################################
```

How It Works

The `collectgarbage` function does various things related to garbage collection, depending on the option string given as its first argument. At the beginning of `GarbageTest`, it's called with the `"collect"` option, which makes Lua run a garbage-collection cycle (so that `GarbageTest` can run with a clean slate). On every iteration of the loop, a new string is created, then `collectgarbage` is used with the `"count"` option that makes it return the current memory usage (in kilobytes), and this number is printed in bar chart form. Because `Junk` is local, a string created on one iteration is not accessible from the next iteration, which means it's eligible for garbage collection. When the strings are only 200 characters long, you can see memory usage slowly ramp up, but when they are 3000 characters long, memory usage ramps up more quickly, until the garbage collector kicks in and frees up the memory used by strings from previous iterations. That's why the second bar chart has a sawtooth shape.

Any code that creates a lot of large strings (or other collectable objects such as tables) that immediately become inaccessible is said to *churn* the memory pool. Memory churn causes the garbage collector to kick in often and can hence slow down your program. The previous example causes memory churn on purpose, but here are two rules of thumb for avoiding churn caused by strings:

❑ Don't do in several `string.gsub` strings what can be done in one string.

❑ Instead of building up a string piece by piece by concatenating onto the end of it on every iteration of a loop, put the pieces into an array and concatenate it all at once with `table.concat`.

These are important mainly when the strings are long; otherwise the churn is not noticeable.

`collectgarbage` has other options that enable you to stop and restart the garbage collector and tweak how often it kicks in automatically and how fast it runs. These options are summarized in Chapter 11. For more details, see the Lua reference manual.

> `collectgarbage` *did not take the same arguments in Lua 5.0 as it does in Lua 5.1, and it didn't have as many uses. Some of the slack was picked up by the* `gcinfo` *function.*

If a table has a metatable whose __mode field is a string containing the letter `"k"`, and the garbage collector sees a key in that table that, if it weren't a key in that table, would be inaccessible, then the garbage collector will remove that key-value pair. (This doesn't happen if the key is a string, number, or Boolean.) For example:

```
> F1 = function() end
> F2 = function() end
> F3 = function() end
> WeakKeyedTbl = {[F1] = 1, [F2] = 2, [F3] = 3}
> setmetatable(WeakKeyedTbl, {__mode = "k"})
> -- Make function F2 inaccessible except via WeakKeyedTbl:
> F2 = nil
> collectgarbage("collect")
> -- The key-value pair [F2] = 2 is no longer in WeakKeyedTbl:
> for F, N in pairs(WeakKeyedTbl) do
>>    print(F, N)
>> end
function: 0x493890     1
function: 0x493e10     3
```

Such a table is said to have *weak keys*.

Similarly, if the letter `"v"` is contained in the string in the __mode field of a table, and the garbage collector sees a value in that table that, if it weren't a value in that table, would be inaccessible, then the garbage collector will remove that key-value pair (again, only if the value is not a string, number, or Boolean). For example:

```
> F1 = function() end
> F2 = function() end
> F3 = function() end
> WeakValuedTbl = {F1, F2, F3}
> setmetatable(WeakValuedTbl, {__mode = "v"})
> -- Make function F2 inaccessible except via WeakValuedTbl:
```

```
> F2 = nil
> collectgarbage("collect")
> -- The key-value pair [2] = F2 is no longer in WeakValuedTbl:
> print(WeakValuedTbl[1], WeakValuedTbl[2], WeakValuedTbl[3])
function: 0x493890      nil      function: 0x493e10
```

Such a table is said to have *weak values*.

> *The reason this doesn't apply to strings, numbers, and Booleans is that they are never truly inaccessible. For example, if the string* "ab" *doesn't happen to already be in a variable or a table, it can still be obtained by concatenating* "a" *and* "b".

Weak keys and values are useful when you want to make an association between a function, table, thread (coroutine), or userdata and some second value, and it's impossible or inconvenient to make that second value part of the first value, but you don't want the association to stick around when you're done with the first value. For instance, a weak-keyed table could have functions as keys and descriptions of those functions as values. When no other variable or table contained a particular function, it and its description would automatically disappear from the table.

The memory leak in orderedtbl.lua that was pointed out in Chapter 8 can be fixed by giving the three tables responsible for the leak weak keys this:

```
local RealTbls = {} -- Keys: proxy tables; values: the real
   -- tables.
local NumToKeys = {} -- Keys: proxy tables; values: arrays
   -- of real tables' keys, in order.
local KeyToNums = {} -- Keys: proxy tables; values: tables
   -- mapping real tables' keys to their (order) numbers.
-- Prevent leakage by giving all of the above tables weak keys:
local ModeMeta = {__mode = "k"}
setmetatable(RealTbls, ModeMeta)
setmetatable(NumToKeys, ModeMeta)
setmetatable(KeyToNums, ModeMeta)

-- Does the bookkeeping necessary to add a key and its order
-- to the real table (or update/delete a key):
local function __newindex(Proxy, Key, Val)
```

The __mode string can contain both "k" and "v" (as in "kv"), in which case both the keys and the values of that table are weak. (Any other characters that might also be in the string are ignored.)

Don't change a metatable's __mode field after it has been used as a metatable; otherwise you'll get unpredictable results (because Lua caches this field).

One other metamethod that has to do with garbage collection is specific to userdata. The userdata type will be covered in Chapter 13, but it's basically a way of exposing a C datatype (or a datatype of some other language) to Lua. When userdata that has a metatable with a __gc field is up for garbage collection, then the value of that field is called with the userdata as an argument. The __gc function should free any memory or other resources (such as open files or network connections) that were allocated outside of Lua when the userdata was created. In this way, languages that are not garbage collected (such as C) can reap the benefits of garbage collection when interfaced with Lua. (This rationale explains why __gc has no effect on tables, which already reap said benefits.)

The Implementation of Tables and Strings

Tables and strings are both implemented using a technique called *hashing*. Imagine that you had a formula for converting a person's name into a number between one and a thousand. If this formula gives a result of 719 for the name John Smith, then 719 is said to be the *hash* of John Smith. Now imagine a thousand-page phone book organized by hash. Assume that there aren't too many people in the phone book, and assume that the hash formula is such that they are distributed more or less randomly throughout the book (so that all the people whose last names start with S aren't clumped together, for example). Given these assumptions, if you turn to page 719, you'll have only one or at most a handful of names to look through to find John Smith.

This would be pretty impractical for a phone book meant for humans, but it turns out to be an efficient way for a computer to store things and retrieve them. A table index like `Tbl.Xyz` tells Lua to hash `"Xyz"` and look for its value in the same place as the other keys (if any) with the same hash.

Hashing is a good way to store key-value pairs if the keys can be any type at all. But for keys that are consecutive integers, nothing beats storing only the values in memory one right after the other, in order by key. Finding a particular key's value is then just a matter of adding that key to the memory address right before where the values start, which avoids the overhead of computing the hash and possibly searching through other keys with the same hash. If Lua notices that an array has consecutive integer keys starting at `1`, then it lays their values out this way, in what is called the *array part* of the table. The rest of the table is kept in the *hash part*.

This makes Lua tables more efficient for common uses, but it's just an implementation detail — it doesn't alter a table's behavior as far as what key-value pairs that table contains. For example, `ipairs` goes through all consecutive integer keys whether they're in the array part or the hash part of the table. (The distinction between a table's array part and hash part explains some aspects of Lua's behavior that are explicitly undefined, such as the unpredictable length of an array with gaps.)

Lua strings are said to be *interned*. This means that a new string is only created if a string does not already exist with the same sequence of characters. On the second line of the following example, when `"X"` and `"YZ"` are concatenated to form `"XYZ"`, Lua asks itself, "do I already have a string that has this sequence of characters?" (This is the part of strings' implementation that uses hashing, so that answering this question doesn't require a search through every single currently existing string.)

```
A = "XYZ"
B = "X" .. "YZ"
```

In this case, the answer is yes, so rather than setting aside a new hunk of memory to store the string, it just assigns the string that's already in A to B. This is why Lua strings are immutable — otherwise A would change if B were changed. The main advantages of interning are that determining whether two strings are equal is very quick, and it takes the same amount of time even if the strings are very long. Another advantage is that storing lots of identical strings takes much less memory.

A disadvantage of interning is that even strings that are used only briefly need to go through the overhead of being hashed and then being interned (if they're not already equal to a previously interned string). This is why the `GarbageTest` example caused memory churn: On every iteration, a new string was interned, but at the end of every iteration, the just-interned string became eligible for garbage collection. The rules of thumb given for avoiding memory churn work because they avoid unnecessarily interning long but short-lived strings.

The Debug Library

The debug library includes various functions for looking under the hood of Lua code. These functions are available in the table `debug`.

Use the debug library with caution. Its functions violate the normal rules of what values and variables are accessible from where. These functions can also be slow. Unless you are writing a debugging tool or something else that needs to poke around in Lua's guts, you probably don't want to use the debug library.

All of the functionality described in this section is also available from C. In cases where speed is important, you may want to work from C rather than Lua.

Inspecting and Manipulating Running Code

Some of the debug library's functions enable you to look at and alter running functions and their variables. In the following Try It Out, you use these functions to access local variables that are not in scope.

Try It Out **Accessing Out-of-Scope Locals**

1. Type the following into the interpreter:

```
I = "global"

function Inner()
   local I = "inside Inner, outside loop"
   for I = 1, 10 do
     if I == 5 then
        debug.debug()
     end
     print("I (inside loop): " .. I)
   end
end

function Outer()
   local I = "inside Outer"
   Inner()
end
```

2. Call `Outer`. You'll see the following:

```
> Outer()
I (inside loop): 1
I (inside loop): 2
I (inside loop): 3
I (inside loop): 4
lua_debug>
```

3. The last line ("`lua_debug>`") is a debugging prompt. It's similar to the prompt you're already familiar with, but less full-featured. In particular, it doesn't accept input spread between multiple lines, and you might also find that line-editing keys such as backspace don't work with it, so type the following carefully:

```
lua_debug> print(I)
global
lua_debug> local I = "this chunk"; print(debug.getlocal(1, 1))
I       this chunk
lua_debug> print(debug.getlocal(2, 1))
nil
lua_debug> print(debug.getlocal(3, 1))
I        inside Inner, outside loop
lua_debug> print(debug.getlocal(3, 2))
(for index)     5
lua_debug> print(debug.getlocal(3, 3))
(for limit)     10
lua_debug> print(debug.getlocal(3, 4))
(for step)      1
lua_debug> print(debug.getlocal(3, 5))
I       5
lua_debug> print(debug.getlocal(3, 6))
nil
lua_debug> print(debug.getlocal(4, 1))
I        inside Outer
lua_debug> print(debug.setlocal(3, 5, "Kilroy was here!"))
I
lua_debug> cont
I (inside loop): Kilroy was here!
I (inside loop): 6
I (inside loop): 7
I (inside loop): 8
I (inside loop): 9
I (inside loop): 10
```

How It Works

The debug.debug function opens an "interpreter within the interpreter" — an interpreter that runs while something else (in this case, the for loop inside of Inner) is still running. There is nothing magical about this — you could write it yourself using io.read, loadstring, and io.stderr:write. Because each line you type is a separate chunk, you can't access variables local to Inner and Outer in the normal way shown here:

```
lua_debug> print(I)
global
```

Instead, you can use the debug.getlocal function, which can access variables even if they're out of scope. This function takes two arguments, both numbers. You use the first argument to specify which stack frame you want to look in. In the second argument, you specify which local within that stack frame you want. debug.getlocal itself is considered to be at stack frame 0, and the function calling debug .getlocal is considered to be at stack frame 1, so the following means "get the first local variable in the current function" (the current function being the chunk typed at the prompt):

```
lua_debug> local I = "this chunk"; print(debug.getlocal(1, 1))
I       this chunk
```

debug.getlocal returns both the variable's name and its value.

Local variables are numbered consecutively, starting at 1. In the following snippet, `debug.getlocal` is asked for the first local variable in stack frame 2, which is the `debug.debug` function itself. `debug.debug` has no local variables, so `debug.getlocal` returns `nil`:

```
lua_debug> print(debug.getlocal(2, 1))
nil
```

Because `debug.debug` is at stack frame 2, the function that called it (`Inner`) must be at stack frame 3. Not only can `debug.getlocal` see both of `Inner`'s local variables named `I`, but it can also see the hidden variables that Lua uses to keep track of the loop. These are the ones whose names start with an open parenthesis:

```
lua_debug> print(debug.getlocal(3, 1))
I           inside Inner, outside loop
lua_debug> print(debug.getlocal(3, 2))
(for index)     5
lua_debug> print(debug.getlocal(3, 3))
(for limit)     10
lua_debug> print(debug.getlocal(3, 4))
(for step)      1
lua_debug> print(debug.getlocal(3, 5))
I       5
lua_debug> print(debug.getlocal(3, 6))
nil
```

`debug.getlocal` can also see inside `Outer` as follows:

```
lua_debug> print(debug.getlocal(4, 1))
I           inside Outer
```

The `debug.setlocal` function is similar to `debug.getlocal`, except it assigns a value to the specified local (and returns the local's name). If the debugging prompt sees a line with nothing but the magic word `cont` on it, then `debug.debug` returns and the code that called it continues. In this case, the loop continues where it left off, except `I` has received a new value:

```
lua_debug> print(debug.setlocal(3, 5, "Kilroy was here!"))
I
lua_debug> cont
I (inside loop): Kilroy was here!
I (inside loop): 6
I (inside loop): 7
I (inside loop): 8
I (inside loop): 9
I (inside loop): 10
```

Rather than figuring out in your head what functions are at what stack frames, you can use the `debug.traceback` function (introduced in Chapter 6) as shown in this example:

```
> Outer()
I (inside loop): 1
I (inside loop): 2
I (inside loop): 3
```

```
I (inside loop): 4
lua_debug> print(debug.traceback())
stack traceback:
        (debug command):1: in main chunk
        [C]: in function 'debug'
        stdin:5: in function 'Inner'
        stdin:3: in function 'Outer'
        stdin:1: in main chunk
        [C]: ?
```

For more detail about a given stack frame and the function running at that stack frame, use the function debug.getinfo, which returns either an associative table or nil if there is no frame at the requested stack level. The table's fields will be explained in a moment, but you can see the correspondence between each stack frame's short_src, currentline, and name fields in the following example and that stack frame's line in the previous traceback:

```
lua_debug> for K, V in pairs(debug.getinfo(1)) do print(K, V) end
nups     0
what     main
func     function: 0x495e40
lastlinedefined 0
source   =(debug command)
currentline     1
namewhat
linedefined      0
short_src       (debug command)
lua_debug> for K, V in pairs(debug.getinfo(2)) do print(K, V) end
source   =[C]
what     C
func     function: 0x485730
nups     0
short_src       [C]
name     debug
currentline     -1
namewhat        field
linedefined     -1
lastlinedefined -1
lua_debug> for K, V in pairs(debug.getinfo(3)) do print(K, V) end
source   =stdin
what     Lua
func     function: 0x495918
nups     0
short_src       stdin
name     Inner
currentline     5
namewhat        global
linedefined     1
lastlinedefined 9
lua_debug> for K, V in pairs(debug.getinfo(4)) do print(K, V) end
source   =stdin
what     Lua
func     function: 0x496cc8
nups     0
short_src       stdin
```

```
name      Outer
currentline     3
namewhat        global
linedefined     1
lastlinedefined 4
lua_debug> for K, V in pairs(debug.getinfo(5)) do print(K, V) end
nups   0
what   main
func      function: 0x495240
lastlinedefined 0
source   =stdin
currentline     1
namewhat
linedefined     0
short_src       stdin
lua_debug> for K, V in pairs(debug.getinfo(6)) do print(K, V) end
nups   0
what   C
func      function: 0x480d78
lastlinedefined -1
source   =[C]
currentline     -1
namewhat
linedefined     -1
short_src       [C]
lua_debug> print(debug.getinfo(7))
nil
```

If no second argument is given, the contents of the table default to the fields shown in the previous output. If the second argument is a string, the characters in it are treated as code letters that specify which fields to include. The following table gives the meanings of the fields. All line numbers are line numbers of the chunk the function was defined in or -1 if no line number is available. Some of the code letters select multiple fields.

Field name	Meaning	Code Letter
activelines	A table whose indexes are the line numbers of those lines in this stack frame's function that have code on them. Empty lines and lines with nothing but comments don't count, nor do lines where nothing actually happens on the bytecode level (such as lines with end keywords). This is the only field not returned if no second argument is given.	L
currentline	The line number of the currently running line in the selected stack frame.	l (lowercase)
func	This stack frame's function.	f
lastlinedefined	The line number of the last line of the function's definition.	S (uppercase)

Field name	Meaning	Code Letter
`linedefined`	The line number of the first line of the function's definition.	`S` (uppercase)
`name`	The function's name, or `nil` if Lua can't figure out a meaningful name (because the function is anonymous, for example). If the function did a tail call, this will be the empty string.	`n`
`namewhat`	What type of name the `name` field is. This can be `"field"`, `"global"`, `"local"`, `"method"`, `"upvalue"`, or (if no `name` was found) `""`.	`n`
`nups`	The number of upvalues the function has.	`u` (lowercase)
`short_src`	An abbreviated version of `source` (convenient for use in error messages).	`S` (uppercase)
`source`	If the chunk in which the function was defined was a file, then the `source` field is the character `@` followed by the filename. If the chunk was just a string, `source` is that string, or the string's chunk name if one was given (as the second argument to `loadstring`, for example). If the function is a C function, `source` is `"=[C]"`. If the stack frame has been reused by a tail call, then `source` is `"=(tail call)"`.	`S` (uppercase)
`what`	If the function did a tail call (and its stack frame has therefore been overwritten), `what` is `"tail"`. Otherwise, if the function is an entire chunk, `what` is `"main"`; or if it's a regular Lua function or a C function, `what` is `"Lua"` or `"C"`. A function written in a language other than Lua or C is considered a C function, because its Lua binding is in C.	`S` (uppercase)

When you're figuring out the number to give functions like `debug.getlocal` and `debug.getinfo` to specify a stack frame, you should include tail calls in your reckoning, even though they don't really get their own stack frames. Because tail calls reuse their callers' stack frames, no other information is available about a function that did a tail call. For example:

```
> return (function() -- This whole chunk is a function that
>>    -- does a tail call to an anonymous function.  This
>>    -- anonymous function can get its caller's info, but
>>    -- there's not much there:
>>    for K, V in pairs(debug.getinfo(2)) do
>>      print(K, V)
>>    end
>> end)()
source  =(tail call)
what    tail
```

```
nups        0
short_src        (tail call)
name
currentline      -1
namewhat
linedefined      -1
lastlinedefined -1
```

The first argument to debug.getinfo can be a function rather than a stack level. For example:

```
> function Greet(Name)
>>    print("Hello, " .. Name .. ".")
>> end
>
> for K, V in pairs(debug.getinfo(Greet)) do
>>    print(K, V)
>> end
nups        0
what        Lua
func        function: 0x494078
lastlinedefined 3
source      =stdin
currentline      -1
namewhat
linedefined      1
short_src        stdin
```

Notice that currentline is –1 because debug.getinfo doesn't know whether the function passed to it is even running, or, if it is, what stack levels it's running on. Also notice that name is not included. That's because as far as debug.getinfo is concerned, the function passed to it is just a value (it doesn't know that you got it from the global variable Greet).

The debug.getupvalue and debug.setupvalue functions are similar to debug.getlocal and debug.setlocal, except that they are for upvalues, whereas the latter functions are only for locals whose scope begins (and ends) within the function at the given stack frame. Also, instead of taking a stack frame as their first argument, debug.getupvalue and debug.setupvalue can only take a function, as specified here:

```
> do
>>    local N = 0
>>
>>    -- Returns a number one higher than the last every time
>>    -- it's called:
>>    function Counter()
>>      N = N + 1
>>      return N
>>    end
>> end
> -- Print Counter's first upvalue's name and value:
> print(debug.getupvalue(Counter, 1))
N        0
```

```
> -- Counter only has one upvalue; trying to get the second
> -- returns nothing:
> print(debug.getupvalue(Counter, 2))

> print(Counter())
1
> print(Counter())
2
> print(debug.getupvalue(Counter, 1))
N        2
> -- Set the upvalue to -100; Counter will add one to this
> -- before returning it:
> debug.setupvalue(Counter, 1, -100)
> print(Counter())
-99
```

Because of Lua's scoping rules, two locals in the same stack frame can have the same name, but two upvalues in the same function cannot.

Separate threads of execution have separate stacks. debug.getinfo, debug.getlocal, debug.setlocal, and debug.traceback work by default on the currently running thread, but take an optional first argument of the thread to be used (shifting any other arguments over to compensate). For example:

```
> function FncA()
>>    FncB()
>> end
>
> function FncB()
>>    coroutine.yield()
>> end
>
> Thread = coroutine.create(FncA)
> coroutine.resume(Thread)
> print(debug.traceback(Thread, "Inside another thread"))
Inside another thread
stack traceback:
        [C]: in function 'yield'
        stdin:2: in function 'FncB'
        stdin:2: in function <stdin:1>
```

None of Lua 5.0's debug functions took this optional first argument.

Hooks

The debug library enables you to use *hooks*, which are functions that Lua calls automatically as other code is running. These are useful for debugging, and you can also use them to *profile* code (to find out how much time is spent in which parts of a program, for example).

In the following Try It Out, you define a hook that prints information about function calls and returns as they happen.

1.   Save the following as `calltrace.lua`:

```lua
-- Creates two global functions: a function that traces function calls
-- and returns, and another function to turn it off.
--
-- Usage:
--   require("calltrace")
--   Trace() -- Turns on tracing.
--   Untrace() -- Turns off tracing.

-- The current depth of the stack (nil when not tracing):
local Depth

-- Returns a string naming the function at StackLvl; this string will
-- include the function's current line number if WithLineNum is true.  A
-- sensible string will be returned even if a name or line numbers
-- can't be found.
local function GetInfo(StackLvl, WithLineNum)
  -- StackLvl is reckoned from the caller's level:
  StackLvl = StackLvl + 1
  local Ret
  local Info = debug.getinfo(StackLvl, "nlS")
  if Info then
    local Name, What, LineNum, ShortSrc =
      Info.name, Info.what, Info.currentline, Info.short_src
    if What == "tail" then
      Ret = "overwritten stack frame"
    else
      if not Name then
        if What == "main" then
          Name = "chunk"
        else
          Name = What .. " function"
        end
      end
      if Name == "C function" then
        Ret = Name
      else
        -- Only use real line numbers:
        LineNum = LineNum >= 1 and LineNum
        if WithLineNum and LineNum then
          Ret = Name .. " (" .. ShortSrc .. ", line " .. LineNum
            .. ")"
        else
          Ret = Name .. " (" .. ShortSrc .. ")"
        end
      end
    end
  else
    -- Below the bottom of the stack:
    Ret = "nowhere"
  end
  return Ret
```

```lua
  end

-- Returns a string of N spaces:
local function Indent(N)
  return string.rep(" ", N)
end

-- The hook function set by Trace:
local function Hook(Event)
  -- Info for the running function being called or returned from:
  local Running = GetInfo(2)
  -- Info for the function that called that function:
  local Caller = GetInfo(3, true)
  if Event == "call" then
    Depth = Depth + 1
    io.stderr:write(Indent(Depth), "calling ", Running, " from ",
      Caller, "\n")
  else
    local RetType
    if Event == "return" then
      RetType = "returning from "
    elseif Event == "tail return" then
      RetType = "tail-returning from "
    end
    io.stderr:write(Indent(Depth), RetType, Running, " to ", Caller,
      "\n")
    Depth = Depth - 1
  end
end

-- Sets a hook function that prints (to stderr) a trace of function
-- calls and returns:
function Trace()
  if not Depth then
    -- Before setting the hook, make an iterator that calls
    -- debug.getinfo repeatedly in search of the bottom of the stack:
    Depth = 1
    for Info in
      function()
        return debug.getinfo(Depth, "n")
      end
    do
      Depth = Depth + 1
    end
    -- Don't count the iterator itself or the empty frame counted at
    -- the end of the loop:
    Depth = Depth - 2
    debug.sethook(Hook, "cr")
  else
    -- Do nothing if Trace() is called twice.
  end
end

-- Unsets the hook function set by Trace:
```

```
function Untrace()
  debug.sethook()
  Depth = nil
end
```

2. Type the following into the interpreter:

```
require("calltrace")

function FncA()
  FncB()
end

function FncB()
  FncC()
end

function FncC()
  print("Inside FncC")
end

Trace()
FncA()
Untrace()
```

3. Starting from where you typed `Trace()`, the output should look like this:

```
> Trace()
    returning from sethook ([C]) to Trace (./calltrace.lua, line 99)
    returning from Trace (./calltrace.lua) to chunk (stdin, line 1)
  returning from chunk (stdin) to C function
> FncA()
  calling chunk (stdin) from C function
    calling FncA (stdin) from chunk (stdin, line 1)
      calling FncB (stdin) from FncA (stdin, line 2)
        calling FncC (stdin) from FncB (stdin, line 2)
          calling print ([C]) from FncC (stdin, line 2)
            calling C function from print ([C])
            returning from C function to print ([C])
Inside FncC
          returning from print ([C]) to FncC (stdin, line 2)
        returning from FncC (stdin) to FncB (stdin, line 2)
      returning from FncB (stdin) to FncA (stdin, line 2)
    returning from FncA (stdin) to chunk (stdin, line 1)
  returning from chunk (stdin) to C function
> Untrace()
  calling chunk (stdin) from C function
    calling Untrace (./calltrace.lua) from chunk (stdin, line 1)
      calling sethook ([C]) from Untrace (./calltrace.lua, line 107)
>
```

How It Works

When `Trace` is called, it measures the current depth of the stack (by calling `debug.getinfo` with deeper and deeper stack levels until it returns `nil`), and then it uses `debug.sethook(Hook, "cr")` to

set `Hook` as a hook to be called whenever a function is called (the `c` in `"cr"`) and whenever a function returns (the `r`). The hook itself is called with an argument of `"call"`, `"return"`, or `"tail return"`, depending on why it was called. It runs on top of the stack, which means it can get information about the function that was running when the hook was called by using 2 as an argument to `debug.getinfo`, and information about the function that called that one by using 3. The retrieval of this information is hidden in the `GetInfo` function (which therefore needs to add 1 to its argument before calling `debug`
`.getinfo`). The hook prints this information, indenting it by one column per stack frame.

As soon as the hook is set, it starts tracing. These lines show control returning from `debug.sethook`, through `Trace` and the interpreted chunk, back to the interpreter itself:

```
returning from sethook ([C]) to Trace (./calltrace.lua, line 99)
returning from Trace (./calltrace.lua) to chunk (stdin, line 1)
returning from chunk (stdin) to C function
```

Then when `FncA` is called, it calls `FncB`, which calls `FncC`, which calls `print`, which calls a C function (`tostring`, if you're curious). This C function returns, and then `print` prints the message given to it by `FncC`:

```
calling chunk (stdin) from C function
 calling FncA (stdin) from chunk (stdin, line 1)
  calling FncB (stdin) from FncA (stdin, line 2)
   calling FncC (stdin) from FncB (stdin, line 2)
    calling print ([C]) from FncC (stdin, line 2)
     calling C function from print ([C])
     returning from C function to print ([C])
Inside FncC
```

Control then returns back to the main loop of the interpreter through `FncC`, `FncB`, `FncA`, and the chunk where `FncA` was called:

```
     returning from print ([C]) to FncC (stdin, line 2)
    returning from FncC (stdin) to FncB (stdin, line 2)
   returning from FncB (stdin) to FncA (stdin, line 2)
  returning from FncA (stdin) to chunk (stdin, line 1)
 returning from chunk (stdin) to C function
```

In this example, the `Inside FncC` message was right where you'd expect it to be, just before `print` returned. Because that message was printed to standard output and the call trace was printed to standard error, your system may not output them in the right order, particularly if you use your shell's redirection operators to send the program's output to files or other programs.

A hook is not called again until after it has returned. That's why `Hook`'s call to `GetInfo` is not traced. (If it were, there'd be an infinite regress and the rest of the program would never be reached.)

`Untrace` unsets the hook by calling `debug.sethook` with no arguments. (It also `nil`s out `Depth` so that future calls to `Trace` from different stack levels will work.)

Tail calls are indented as though they grew the stack, like this:

```
do -- local scope for Count.
   local Count = 5

   -- Keeps tail-calling itself until Count is 0:
   function Tail()
     if Count == 0 then
       return
     else
       Count = Count - 1
       return Tail()
     end
   end
end
```

The function's call trace looks like this:

```
calling chunk (stdin) from C function
 calling Tail (stdin) from chunk (stdin, line 1)
  calling Tail (stdin) from Tail (stdin, line 10)
   calling Tail (stdin) from Lua function (stdin, line 10)
    calling Tail (stdin) from Lua function (stdin, line 10)
     calling Tail (stdin) from Lua function (stdin, line 10)
      calling Tail (stdin) from Lua function (stdin, line 10)
      returning from Lua function (stdin) to overwritten stack frame
     tail-returning from Lua function (stdin) to overwritten stack frame
    tail-returning from Lua function (stdin) to overwritten stack frame
   tail-returning from Lua function (stdin) to overwritten stack frame
  tail-returning from Lua function (stdin) to overwritten stack frame
 tail-returning from Tail (stdin) to chunk (stdin, line 1)
returning from chunk (stdin) to C function
```

Notice that a *tail return* is *not* a return from a tail call. It's a return from a function that did a tail call.

It's possible to write a version of `Trace` that takes a list of functions and only traces those functions. The hook would still be called on every call and return, but it would check the list before printing anything. Depending on what information you wanted to print about returns from tail calls, you might need to manage your own stack that would grow even on tail calls.

If you use an end-of-file to exit the interpreter while calls are still being traced, you'll see the trace hit the left margin like this:

```
> ^D
returning from C function to nowhere
```

Because the second argument to `debug.sethook` was `"cr"`, the hook was called on calls and returns. If that argument includes the letter `"l"`, the hook will be called on every line of code, not counting lines where nothing happens (lines not counted by the `activelines` field of `debug.getinfo`'s return value). The hook will be called with two arguments: the string `"line"`, and the line number.

If `debug.sethook` has a nonzero third argument (called the *hook count*), the hook will be called every time that many bytecode instructions have been executed. It will receive the `"count"` string as an argument.

The debug.gethook function returns three values: the current hook function, the current *hook mask* (the string containing zero or more of "c", "l", and "r"), and the current hook count. For example, if there's no hook set, then the following:

```
HookFnc, HookMask, HookCount = debug.gethook()
print("HookFnc: " .. tostring(HookFnc) .. "; HookMask: '"
  .. HookMask .. "'; HookCount: " .. HookCount)
```

will print this:

```
HookFnc: nil; HookMask: ''; HookCount: 0
```

If the calltrace.lua hook is set, then it will print this:

```
HookFnc: function: 0x495e58; HookMask: 'cr'; HookCount: 0
```

Hooks are a per-thread setting. When you set a hook, it only gets set (and then called) in one thread. Like debug.getinfo, debug.getlocal, debug.setlocal, and debug.traceback, debug.sethook and debug.gethook work by default on the currently running thread, but take the thread to be used as an optional first argument. In debug.sethook, its other arguments are shifted over to compensate.

The Lua 5.0 versions didn't take this optional argument.

Other Functions in the Debug Library

debug.getfenv and debug.setfenv are just like getfenv and setfenv, except that they work with both Lua and C functions, as well as userdata and threads. (getfenv and setfenv only work with Lua functions.)

Similarly, debug.getmetatable and debug.setmetatable are like getmetatable and setmetatable except that they work with all values, not just tables.

debug.getregistry returns the *registry table*, a table that C code can use as a storage area. (See Chapter 13.)

Lua 5.0 did not include any of these five functions.

Summary

In this chapter you learned the following:

❑   You can use the luac command-line program to compile source code to bytecode, or to print a human-readable bytecode listing.

❑   Memory that is no longer used is reclaimed by the garbage collector. You can control the garbage collector's behavior with the collectgarbage function.

❑   You can use a technique called hashing to implement tables. If Lua thinks that part of a table is being used as an array, it lays that part out sequentially in memory, which is more efficient than hashing for array use.

❑ You can also implement strings with hashing. These strings are interned: two strings with the same contents are the same string, and their contents are at the same memory location.

❑ The debug library enables you to examine local variables and altered them even if they're out of scope.

❑ The debug library also enables you set a hook that will be called on every function call, function return, or line of source code, or every so many bytecode instructions.

The next chapter will complete this book's treatment of the Lua language itself, by summarizing Lua's built-in library functions. The chapter after that discusses libraries written by members of the Lua community, then there's a chapter on the C side of Lua, and then the rest of the book is about doing various things in Lua (such as using databases, web programming, and more).

But first, here are a couple of exercises (with answers in the appendix) to enhance what you've learned in this chapter.

Exercises

1. Imagine you have a file of Lua source code (not bytecode) that the Lua interpreter refuses to run, giving instead the error message "bad header in precompiled chunk." What must be wrong with the file to cause this message? (The hint here is the word "precompiled.")

2. Write a GetVar function that takes a variable name and returns the value of the variable in the scope where it was called. It should follow the same scoping rules as Lua itself (locals, then upvalues, then globals) except that it doesn't need to find external locals that aren't actually upvalues (because of not being referred to as variables anywhere in the function being searched).

   The variable D in the following test code is an example of this. According to Lua's scoping rules, the value of D in InnerFnc should be "upvalue" *and not* "global"*, but finding would-be upvalues like D is actually impossible to do except in special cases.*

   To test your function, run the following code:

```
G1 = "global"
Up = "upvalue"
L = "local"
OL = "outer local"
IL = "inner local"
A, B, C, D, E = G1, G1, G1, G1, G1

function OuterFnc()
  local A, B, C, D = Up, Up, Up, Up

  local function InnerFnc(A)
    local A = IL
    local B = L
    local _ = C -- Without this, C, like D, would not be an
      -- upvalue of InnerFnc.
    for _, Name in ipairs({"A", "B", "C", "D", "E"}) do
      print(Name, GetVar(Name))
```

```
        end
    end

    InnerFnc(OL)
end

OuterFnc()
```

It should print the following:

```
A        inner local
B        local
C        upvalue
D        global
E        global
```

Exploring Lua's Libraries

Up to this point in the book you've been learning about the fundamentals of Lua, occasionally using some of its library functions. In this chapter, all of Lua's standard library functions are briefly summarized to remind you of their basic usage. Practically every function has many more features than can be covered in detail within the scope of this book, and the examples that are included here are mostly contrived for brevity. (For the definitive documentation of these features, see the *Lua Reference Manual*.)

In this chapter, you'll find summaries of the following:

- ❑ General-purpose functions in the core library
- ❑ Functions that manage coroutines
- ❑ Package functions that implement Lua's module system
- ❑ String conversion and pattern matching functions
- ❑ Functions that help with using tables as arrays
- ❑ Bindings to the C runtime library's math functions
- ❑ Functions for reading from and writing to files and streams
- ❑ Operating system functions
- ❑ Functions to help with debugging your Lua programs

An example is provided for each function or group of functions.

Core Library

The core library functions reside in the global environment. They have no containing namespace table.

Environment Functions

The following functions let you set and retrieve a function's environment—the table that Lua uses to resolve global references—and get or set the global environment of the running thread when given a stack level of 0:

❏ getfenv (*optional function or stack level*): Returns the environment table of the given function, or the function running at the given stack level. The argument defaults to 1, which is the stack level of the current function (the one calling getfenv).

❏ setfenv (*function or stack level, environment table*): Gives an environment table to the given function or the function at the given stack level, and returns the function.

This example demonstrates how you can set a global environment for a particular function:

```
Str = "Global"

function Sandbox()
  print(getfenv(), Str)
end

setfenv(Sandbox, {print = print, getfenv = getfenv, Str = "Sandbox"})
Sandbox()
print(getfenv(), Str)
```

The output generated by the example shows how the value of the global variable Str depends on the environment:

```
table: 00765740 Sandbox
table: 00760300 Global
```

Metatable Functions

These functions let you set, retrieve, and circumvent metatables, the mechanism by which you can modify the default behavior for various operations:

❏ getmetatable (*value*): Returns its argument's __metatable metamethod, its argument's metatable if there is no __metatable metamethod, or nil if there is no metatable.

❏ setmetatable (*table, metatable*): Gives a metatable to a table. An error will be triggered if the table has a __metatable metamethod.

❏ rawequal (*first value, second value*): Returns true if the two values are equal, bypassing any metamethods.

❏ rawget (*table, index*): Retrieves *table*[*index*], bypassing any metamethods.

❏ rawset (*table, index, value*): Assigns a value to *table*[*index*], bypassing any metamethods.

This example shows how you can use the __eq metamethod to modify the way that the equality operator works for tables:

```
MtTbl = {__eq = function(T1, T2) return T1.Val == T2.Val end}
A = {Val = 10}
setmetatable(A, MtTbl)
B = {Val = 10}
setmetatable(B, MtTbl)
C = {Val = 12}
setmetatable(C, MtTbl)
print(MtTbl, getmetatable(A), getmetatable(B), getmetatable(C))
print("A == B", A == B)
print("A == C", A == C)
print("rawequal(A, B)", rawequal(A, B))
print("rawequal(A, C)", rawequal(A, C))
```

The example generates the following output, demonstrating that the __eq metamethod is engaged by the equality operator and bypassed with the rawequal function:

```
table: 00765530 table: 00765530 table: 00765530 table: 00765530
A == B  true
A == C  false
rawequal(A, B)  false
rawequal(A, C)  false
```

This example illustrates how extra functionality can be attached to the assignment and retrieval of a table's field.

```
local function WindowCreate(TitleStr)

  local function WindowTextGet()
    -- Simulate GUI call
    io.write("  Retrieving ", TitleStr, "\n")
    return TitleStr
  end

  local function WindowTextSet(Str)
    -- Simulate GUI call
    local OldTitleStr = TitleStr
    io.write("  Setting ", Str, "\n")
    TitleStr = Str
    return OldTitleStr
  end

  local function MtIndex(Tbl, Key)
    return Key == "Title" and WindowTextGet() or Tbl[Key]
  end

  local function MtNewIndex(Tbl, Key, Val)
    if Key == "Title" then
      WindowTextSet(Val)
    else
      Tbl[Key] = Val
    end
  end
```

```
    local Wnd, MtTbl = {}, {__index = MtIndex, __newindex = MtNewIndex}

    setmetatable(Wnd, MtTbl)

    return Wnd

end

local Wnd = WindowCreate("Title 1")
local Str = Wnd.Title
io.write("1 ", Str, "\n")
Wnd.Title = "Title 2"
Str = Wnd.Title
io.write("2 ", Str, "\n")
rawset(Wnd, "Title", "Title 3")
Str = rawget(Wnd, "Title")
io.write("3 ", Str, "\n")
Wnd.Title = "Title 4" -- No metamethod
Str = Wnd.Title -- No metamethod
io.write("4 ", Str, "\n")
```

The output of the example shows how metamethods can define new behavior for indexing and assignments operations. Note that the use of rawset creates a field named Title in the Wnd table, effectively disabling the use of metamethods for subsequent indexing and assignments:

```
    Retrieving Title 1
1 Title 1
    Setting Title 2
    Retrieving Title 2
2 Title 2
3 Title 3
4 Title 4
```

Chunk-Loading Functions

The chunk-loading functions generate a function from a Lua chunk. The chunk can be in either source or precompiled form. Specifically, each of these functions does the following:

❑   dofile (*optional name of file*) : Executes the specified Lua script, or standard input if the filename is missing.

❑   load (*loader function, optional chunk name*) : Repeatedly calls the loader function to build up a Lua chunk. Each time the loader function is called it returns the next portion of the Lua script in the form of a string. When the entire script has been loaded, the loader function must return nil, at which point load compiles the chunk and returns the function without running it.

❑   loadfile (*optional name of file*) : Loads the specified file as a Lua chunk and returns the compiled function without running it.

❑   loadstring (*script string, optional name*) : Loads the specified string as a Lua chunk and returns the compiled function without running it.

The following example demonstrates the preceding functions with a simple Lua chunk that simply prints the arguments that are passed to it. The first iteration of the loop loads the chuck in source form, the second in precompiled form:

```lua
local FileStr = "test.lua"

for J = 1, 2 do
  local LuaStr
  if J == 1 then
    io.write("=== Source chunk ===\n")
    LuaStr = "print('source', ...)"
  else
    io.write("=== Compiled chunk ===\n")
    LuaStr = string.dump(function(...) print('compiled', ...) end)
  end
  local Hnd = io.open(FileStr, "wb")
  if Hnd then
    Hnd:write(LuaStr)
    Hnd:close()
    io.write("[dofile]      ")
    dofile(FileStr)
    io.write("[loadfile]    ")
    local Fnc, ErrStr = loadfile(FileStr)
    if Fnc then
      Fnc(1, 2, 3)
      io.write("[loadstring] ")
      Fnc, ErrStr = loadstring(LuaStr)
      if Fnc then
        Fnc(1, 2, 3)
        io.write("[load]        ")
        local RetStr = LuaStr
        local function Loader()
          local Ret = RetStr
          RetStr = nil
          return Ret
        end
        Fnc, ErrStr = load(Loader)
        if Fnc then
          Fnc(1, 2, 3)
        else
          io.write(ErrStr, "\n")
        end
      else
        io.write(ErrStr, "\n")
      end
    else
      io.write(ErrStr, "\n")
    end
  else
    io.write("Error opening ", FileStr, " for writing\n")
  end
end
os.remove(FileStr)
```

The example generates the following output:

```
=== Source chunk ===
[dofile]      source
[loadfile]    source     1        2        3
[loadstring]  source     1        2        3
[load]        source     1        2        3
=== Compiled chunk ===
[dofile]      compiled
[loadfile]    compiled   1        2        3
[loadstring]  compiled   1        2        3
[load]        compiled   1        2        3
```

Note that chunks executed with dofile can't accept arguments. Note also that all of the functions handle source chunks and precompiled chunks correctly.

Error-Containment Functions

These functions are used to keep runtime errors from propagating toward the host program:

❑   pcall (*function, optional arguments*): The specified function is called with the specified arguments. In the event of an error, a one-line message is generated.

❑   xpcall (*function, error handler*): The specified function is called. In the event of an error, the specified error handler is invoked before the stack is reset, allowing a stack traceback to be constructed. The handler is passed an error string and returns an augmented error string.

If the specified function runs without errors, both pcall and xpcall return true followed by the function's own return values. If an error occurs, false is returned followed by the error message.

This example shows how a runtime error can be caught and managed within a Lua program.

```
io.write("Start of tests\n")
io.write("-- pcall --\n")
local BadLuaStr = "print('Intentional error ahead', ...) error('crash')"
Fnc, ErrStr = loadstring(BadLuaStr, "Demonstration")
if Fnc then
  local Code, ErrStr = pcall(Fnc, "pcall")
  if not Code then
    io.write("[pcall error] ", ErrStr, "\n")
  end
  io.write("-- xpcall --\n")
  local Code, ErrStr = xpcall(Fnc, debug.traceback)
  if not Code then
    io.write("[xpcall error] ", ErrStr, "\n")
  end
else
  io.write("[loadstring error] ", ErrStr, "\n")
end
io.write("End of tests\n")
```

The example generates the following output, showing that the script recovers from both errors:

```
Start of tests
-- pcall --
Intentional error ahead pcall
[pcall error] [string "Demonstration"]:1: crash
-- xpcall --
Intentional error ahead
[xpcall error] [string "Demonstration"]:1: crash
stack traceback:
        [C]: in function 'error'
        [string "Demonstration"]:1: in main chunk
        [C]: in function 'xpcall'
        test.lua:11: in main chunk
        [C]: ?
End of tests
```

Module Functions

These functions are Lua's means to modularize your programs:

❑   module (*module name, zero or more preparation functions*): Modularizes a script, storing all new global variables in a namespace table. This table will be assigned to a global variable with the specified module name. Any functions that are specified are called in turn with the namespace table as an argument. The package.seeall function is commonly used in this capacity.

❑   require (*module name*): Loads and executes the specified Lua file following a well-defined protocol.

See the package *library functions for related functions.*

The following example generates a little module that simply assigns a greeting to a string, and then loads the module using Lua's module system:

```
io.output("testmod.lua")
io.write [[module(...)

Str = "Hello from " .. (...)
]]

io.close()
io.output(io.stdout)
package.path = "?.lua"
require("testmod")
io.write(testmod.Str, "\n")
```

The following output from the example shows that the module is successfully loaded:

```
Hello from testmod
```

The Garbage-Collection Function

Garbage collection refers to the automatic reclamation of memory used by Lua values that can no longer be accessed by your program. It has one function:

```
collectgarbage("collect" or "count" or "restart" or "setpause" or "setstepmul"
or "step" or "stop", optional extra argument)
```

This function performs one of actions described in the following table based on the value of the first argument.

Action	Description
`"collect"`	Forces a garbage-collection cycle.
`"count"`	Returns the amount (in kilobytes) of memory in use.
`"restart"`	Restarts garbage collection (if it has been stopped).
`"setpause"`	Sets the garbage-collection pause to the extra argument divided by 100.
`"setstepmul"`	Sets the garbage-collection step multiplier to the extra argument divided by 100.
`"step"`	Runs one step of garbage collection. The bigger the extra argument is, the bigger this step will be. (The exact relationship between the extra argument and the step size is undefined.) `collectgarbage` will return `true` if the triggered step was the last step of a garbage-collection cycle.
`"stop"`	Stops garbage collection.

The following example shows the effect of collecting garbage after creating and then releasing a large string:

```
local function KbUsed(Seq)
   io.write(string.format("%2d %8.2f KB\n", Seq, collectgarbage("count")))
end
KbUsed(1)
Str = string.rep("*", 1e5)
KbUsed(2)
Str = nil
collectgarbage("collect")
KbUsed(3)
collectgarbage("collect")
KbUsed(4)
collectgarbage("collect")
KbUsed(5)
```

The example prints the following lines, showing how successive garbage collection cycles reclaim memory:

```
1    21.15 KB
2   324.48 KB
3    44.19 KB
4    25.88 KB
5    21.30 KB
```

Type and Conversion Functions

These functions let you identify types and convert between them:

- ❑ `tonumber` (*value, optional numeric base from 2 to 36*) : Converts the specified value to a number using the specified base. The value must represent an unsigned integer if the base is other than 10. For base 10, the default, the value can represent a floating point number.

- ❑ `tostring` (*value*) : Returns a string representation of the specified value, using the `__tostring` metamethod if one is registered.

- ❑ `type` (*value*) : Returns a string representation of the specified value's type. This will be `"nil"`, `"boolean"`, `"number"`, `"string"`, `"table"`, `"function"`, `"thread"` or `"userdata"`.

The following example demonstrates the conversion of a binary number to decimal:

```
BinStr = "101010"
Num = tonumber(BinStr, 2)
DecStr = tostring(Num)
io.write(BinStr, " (", type(BinStr), "), ", Num, " (", type(Num), "), ",
  DecStr, " (", type(DecStr), ")\n")
```

The example prints the following:

```
101010 (string), 42 (number), 42 (string)
```

Basic Output

This category provides a quick way for Lua programs to print values to standard output. The `print` (*zero or more values*) function writes the string equivalent of each argument to standard output. A tab is written after each argument except the last in which case a newline is written.

This example prints an assortment of values to the standard output stream:

```
print(nil, 1 == 1, 1 + 1, "one", function() end, {})
```

The output shows how various values are rendered by the `print` function:

```
nil     true    2       one     function: 003D9490      table: 003DA478
```

Error-Condition Functions

These functions conditionally or unconditionally cause an error to propagate toward the host program at runtime. The most recent protected call will contain the error and prevent it from propagating further.

Here are the error-condition functions and examples of each:

- ❑ `assert` (*test expression, optional error message*) : If the test expression evaluates to `false` or `nil`, an error is raised with the specified error message or, if it is missing, with the text `assertion failed!` For example, the following tests the assumption of a value's type:

```
Val = 12
assert(type(Val) == "boolean", "Expecting boolean value")
```

This outputs the following stack traceback when the assertion expression evaluates to false:

```
lua: assert.lua:2: Expecting boolean value
stack traceback:
        [C]: in function 'assert'
        assert.lua:2: in main chunk
        [C]: ?
```

❑   error (*error message, optional "skip" level*) : Unconditionally causes an error using the specified message. The second argument specifies the number of stack frames to skip when reporting the error's origin. This is useful when writing a custom error handler. This example issues an error:

```
error("Printer on fire.")
```

The output of the example uses the Lua interpreter's default error handler:

```
lua: err.lua:1: Printer on fire.
stack traceback:
        [C]: in function 'error'
        error.lua:1: in main chunk
        [C]: ?
```

Table Traversal Functions

These functions let you visit each key-value pair in a table:

❑   ipairs (*array*): Can be used in a generic for loop to visit all array fields in the specified table. These are values whose keys are contiguous integers beginning with 1.

❑   next (*table, optional seed key*) : Returns the next key-value pair from the table's internally ordered sequence. The first key and value from this sequence are returned when the key argument is omitted. The value nil is returned when the last key in the sequence is specified.

❑   pairs (*table*) : Can be used in a generic for loop to iterate over all key-value pairs in the table.

This example initializes a table with indexed and associative elements and iterates through the table using the table traversal functions:

```
Tbl = {[0] = "zero", "one", "two", Id = 100, Name = "Alexander Botts",
  "three", [10] = "ten"}

io.write("--- ipairs ---\n")
for J, Val in ipairs(Tbl) do
  io.write(J, ": ", tostring(Val), "\n")
end

io.write("--- pairs ---\n")
for Key, Val in pairs(Tbl) do
  io.write(tostring(Key), ": ", tostring(Val), "\n")
```

```
  end

io.write("--- next ---\n")
local Key, Val = next(Tbl)
while Key do
  io.write(tostring(Key), ": ", tostring(Val), "\n")
  Key, Val = next(Tbl, Key)
end
```

The example's output show how `pairs` and `next` can be used to visit all key-value pairs in a table, but `ipairs` traverses only array elements:

```
--- ipairs ---
1: one
2: two
3: three
--- pairs ---
1: one
2: two
3: three
0: zero
10: ten
Name: Alexander Botts
Id: 100
--- next ---
1: one
2: two
3: three
0: zero
10: ten
Name: Alexander Botts
Id: 100
```

Vararg-Related Functions

The following two functions are useful for working with vararg expressions (. . .), vararg functions, functions that return multiple values, and multiple assignment:

❑   select (*position or* "#", *zero or more extra arguments*) : When the first argument is "#", this function returns the number of extra arguments. When the first argument is an integer, it returns the extra argument specified by that integer, and all of the following extra arguments.

❑   unpack (*array, optional start position, optional end position*) : Returns the values (in order) in the given array. The start and end positions default (respectively) to 1 and the length of the array.

The following example demonstrates the use of `select` and `unpack`:

```
function Test(...)
  io.write("*** Entering Test ***\n")
  for J = 1, select("#", ...) do
    io.write(select(J, ...))
    io.write("\n")
```

```
      end
   end

   List = {"One", "Two", "Three"}
   Test(unpack(List))
   Test(unpack(List, 1, 2))
   Test(unpack(List, 2))
```

The example's output shows how `unpack` can be used to return a contiguous range of arrayed values, and how `select` can be used to obtain the elements in a vararg expression and their number:

```
*** Entering Test ***
OneTwoThree
TwoThree
Three
*** Entering Test ***
OneTwo
Two
*** Entering Test ***
TwoThree
Three
```

Coroutine Library

The following coroutine functions are used to cooperatively manage multiple threads in a Lua program:

❑   `coroutine.create`(*function*): Creates a coroutine from the specified function. The returned value is of type `thread`.

❑   `coroutine.resume`(*coroutine, optional values*): Activates a coroutine with any practical number and type of arguments. The values following the coroutine in the argument list are passed to the coroutine as follows. When the coroutine is initially activated, the arguments are conveyed in the coroutine body's argument list. When the coroutine is subsequently resumed, these arguments appear as return values from `coroutine.yield`. This function returns the values that are passed to `coroutine.yield` or are explicitly returned when the coroutine ends.

❑   `coroutine.running`(): Returns the currently running coroutine, or `nil` if the main thread is running.

❑   `coroutine.status`(*coroutine*): Returns a string with the value `"running"`, `"suspended"`, `"normal"` or `"dead"`.

❑   `coroutine.wrap`(*function*): Creates a coroutine from the specified function and returns a function wrapper to it. The coroutine is resumed by calling the returned function directly. This can make activating the coroutine simpler; however, runtime errors are not contained.

❑   `coroutine.yield`(*zero or more values*): Transfers control back to the caller of `coroutine.resume` that activated the current coroutine. The arguments are conveyed to the caller in the form of return values from `coroutine.resume`.

The following example shows how coroutines can be used to retain the state needed to generate a running average of numbers. Both the wrapped and unwrapped varieties of coroutines are demonstrated:

```lua
local function Average()
  local Co = coroutine.running()
  Val = coroutine.yield(tostring(Co) .. " is " .. coroutine.status(Co))
  local Count, Sum = 1, Val
  while true do
    Sum = Sum + coroutine.yield(Sum, Sum / Count)
    Count = Count + 1
  end
end

local CoAve = coroutine.create(Average)
local Code, Str = coroutine.resume(CoAve)
if Code then
  io.write(Str, "\n")
  local Ave = coroutine.wrap(Average)
  io.write(Ave(), "\n\n")
  io.write("Val A  Sum A  Ave A    Val B  Sum B  Ave B\n")
  io.write("-----  -----  -----    -----  -----  -----\n")
  math.random() -- On some systems that shall remain nameless, the
    -- first call to math.random is easy enough to predict that it
    -- destroys the illusion of randomness; throw it away.
  for J = 1, 6 do
    local Code, ValA, SumA, AveA, ValB, SumB, AveB
    ValA = math.random(0, 100)
    Code, SumA, AveA = coroutine.resume(CoAve, ValA)
    if Code then
      ValB = math.random(0, 100)
      SumB, AveB = Ave(ValB)
      io.write(string.format("%5d  %5d  %5.2f    %5d  %5d  %5.2f\n",
        ValA, SumA, AveA, ValB, SumB, AveB))
    end
  end
end
```

The example's output shows identical results calculated for identical input to the averaging coroutines:

```
thread: 003DAD60 is running
thread: 003DB3B0 is running

Val A  Sum A  Ave A    Val B  Sum B  Ave B
-----  -----  -----    -----  -----  -----
   56     56  56.00       19     19  19.00
   81    137  68.50       59     78  39.00
   48    185  61.67       35    113  37.67
   90    275  68.75       83    196  49.00
   75    350  70.00       17    213  42.60
   86    436  72.67       71    284  47.33
```

Package Library

The following functions, strings, and tables in this library are used with or by `module` and `require` to implement Lua's package system:

- ❑ `package.loadlib`(*library name, function name*): Loads the specified library and returns a function bound to the specified C function in the library. Because ANSI C doesn't provide for loading libraries dynamically, this function is implemented in a platform-specific manner and is available only on mainstream systems. The following example demonstrates the direct loading of a shared library:

  Usually a Lua program uses the `require` function instead of `loadlib` to take advantage of Lua's package searching and caching conventions.

  ```
  Fnc, ErrStr = package.loadlib("./luabogo.so", "luaopen_bogo")
  if Fnc then
    Fnc("bogo")
  else
    io.write(ErrStr, "\n")
  end
  ```

- ❑ `package.seeall`(*namespace table*): Sets the metatable for a module namespace so that values in the global environment can be accessed. This is used as a preparation function with the `module` function. For example, the following creates a small module that specifies `package.seeall` as an argument to `module` so that it can access to the global environment. Note that `package.path` is modified so that the script looks for the module in the current directory:

  ```
  io.output("testmod.lua")
  io.write [[module(..., package.seeall)
  local ModStr = (...)

  function Hello()
    io.write("Hello from ", ModStr, "\n")
  end
  ]]

  io.close()
  io.output(io.stdout)
  package.path = "?.lua"
  require("testmod")
  testmod.Hello()
  ```

  The example's output shows how the module is able to call `io.write` as a result of using `package.seeall`:

  ```
  Hello from testmod
  ```

- ❑ `package.preload`: Each key in this table is the name of a module, and the corresponding value is a function that is called to load the module. Lua's package mechanism checks this table for a module loading function before it searches for a file-based module.

❑ `package.loaded`: Each key in this table is the name of a loaded module, and the corresponding value is the value that was returned by the module's loading function. Lua's package mechanism checks this table when `require` is called to see if the module has already been loaded. If it has, the corresponding value is returned rather than loading the module again.

❑ `package.path`: This string consists of semicolon-separated segments that are used to locate a Lua module file. It is initially assigned the value of the environment variable LUA_PATH (or a default value from `luaconf.h`, if LUA_PATH is not defined). When searching for a module file, Lua replaces each question mark with the name passed to `require`.

❑ `package.cpath`: This string consists of semicolon-separated segments that are used to locate a compiled library. It is initially assigned the value of the environment variable LUA_CPATH (or a default value from `luaconf.h`, if LUA_CPATH is not defined). When searching for a library, Lua replaces each question mark with the name passed to `require`.

The following example demonstrates the use of the `package.loaded` and `package.preloaded` tables:

```
io.output("a.lua")
io.write('return {Str = "Module a (file)."}')
io.close()
io.output("b.lua")
io.write('return {Str = "Module b (file)."}')
io.close()
io.output("c.lua")
io.write('return {Str = "Module c (file)."}')
io.close()
io.output(io.stdout)

package.cpath = ""
package.path = "./?.lua"

function package.preload.a()
  return {Str = "Module a."}
end

package.loaded.b = {Str = "Module b."}

local function Report(ModStr)
  io.write('package.loaded["', ModStr, '"] = ',
    tostring(package.loaded[ModStr]), '\n')
end

Report("a")
Report("b")
Report("c")
local A = require("a")
local B = require("b")
local C = require("c")
io.write("A: ", A.Str, "\nB: ", B.Str, "\nC: ", C.Str, "\n")
Report("a")
Report("b")
Report("c")
```

Three file-based modules are created, and `package.cpath` and `package.path` are set so that Lua will look for Lua modules only in the current working directory, and will not look for compiled libraries at all. A loader function is associated with `"a"` in the `package.preload` table. When the `"a"` module is required, Lua will call this function and return the value that it returns. A table is associated with `"b"` in the `package.loaded` table. When the `"b"` module is required, Lua returns this value directly. Because the `"c"` module doesn't have an entry in either of these tables, Lua searches for a file module. It does this by stepping through each semicolon-separated segment in `package.path`, replacing each ? with the name of the module. In this example, the one segment in `package.path` forms the name `./c.lua`, and Lua successfully opens this file as a Lua chunk. The example outputs the following lines:

```
package.loaded["a"] = nil
package.loaded["b"] = table: 003DA7E8
package.loaded["c"] = nil
A: Module a.
B: Module b.
C: Module c (file).
package.loaded["a"] = table: 003DAEC8
package.loaded["b"] = table: 003DA7E8
package.loaded["c"] = table: 003DAFF0
```

String Library

The string library provides a versatile set of functions for manipulating text in Lua programs. Character positions may be positive or negative integers. A positive value indicates a position counted from the beginning of the string with the first character at position 1. A negative value indicates a position counted backwards from the end of the string, with the last character at position -1.

Pattern-Based String Functions

The following string functions use Lua's pattern matching facility to locate and extract character sequences in a string (see "Pattern Matching" in Chapter 5 for details about matching text):

❑   `string.find`(*subject string, pattern string, optional start position, optional plain flag*): Looks for a pattern in the specified subject string. The search is done with Lua's pattern-matching rules unless the optional plain flag is true, in which case a character-for-character search is done, with none of the characters in the pattern string having their magic meaning. The search begins at the beginning of the subject unless a start position is specified. If a match is found, the start and end positions are returned followed by any captures that are specified in the pattern string. For example, the following demonstrates the use of `string.find` with an incremented starting position to extract all alphanumeric sequences from a string:

```lua
local Str = "/var/local/www"
local PosStart, PosEnd, MatchStr = 1
while PosStart do
  PosStart, PosEnd, MatchStr = string.find(Str, "(%w+)", PosStart)
  if PosStart then
    io.write(MatchStr, "\n")
    PosStart = PosEnd + 1
  end
end
```

The example prints the following lines.

```
var
local
www
```

❑ `string.gmatch`(*subject string, pattern string*): Iterator factory for looping through pattern matches in the subject string using a generic `for` loop. For example, the following is a more convenient method than the one in the previous example that you can use to extract matching character sequences from a string:

```
for Str in string.gmatch("CamelbackName", "%u%l+") do
  io.write(Str, "\n")
end
The example prints the following string captures.Camelback
Name
```

❑ `string.gsub`(*subject string, pattern string, replacement string or function or table, optional limit count*): Substitutes each pattern match found in the subject string with a replacement. The replacement argument can be a string (which can contain captures such as `"%1"`), or a function that is called for each match (with captures passed as arguments), or a table in which the value given by a matching key is used for the replacement. The number of replacements can be limited by specifying a numeric fourth argument. The following example shows how `string.gsub` can be used to modify the contents of a string:

```
-- Generate list of month names in current locale
local Dt = os.date("*t")
Dt.day = 1
local MonthList = {}
for Month = 1, 12 do
  Dt.month = Month
  MonthList[Month] = os.date("%B", os.time(Dt))
end

function ExpandDate(Month, Day, Sep)
  return (MonthList[tonumber(Month)] or "---") .. " " ..
    tonumber(Day) .. (Sep == "," and ", " or "")
end

local Str = "0117,0211,0818"
io.write("Before: ", Str, "\n")
Str = string.gsub(Str, "(%d%d)(%d%d)(%,?)", ExpandDate)
io.write("After:  ", Str, "\n")
```

The example prints the following lines.

```
Before: 0117,0211,0818
After:  January 17, February 11, August 18
```

❑ `string.match`(*subject string, pattern string, optional start position*): Returns the captures of the first match found in the subject. If no match is found, `nil` is returned. If a match is found but no captures are specified, the entire match is returned. For example, the following extracts the red, green and blue hexadecimal components of a color identifier:

```
local ClrStr = "#C6EFF7"
local Red, Green, Blue = string.match(ClrStr, "%#(%x%x)(%x%x)(%x%x)")
if Red then
  io.write("Red: ", tonumber(Red, 16), ", Green: ", tonumber(Green, 16),
    ", Blue: ", tonumber(Blue, 16), "\n")
end
```

The following line is printed by the example:

```
Red: 198, Green: 239, Blue: 247
```

String-Conversion Functions

Lua's string-conversion functions return one or more values pertaining to the specified string or sub-string, as follows:

❑ string.byte *(string, optional start position, optional end position)*: Returns the platform-dependent byte values associated with a range of text characters. If the start position is missing, 1 is used. If the end position is missing, the start position is used. For example, the following returns the byte values of the letters L, u and a:

```
print(string.byte("Lua", 1, 3))
```

The following values are printed by the example:

```
76      117     97
```

❑ string.char *(zero or more integers)*: Constructs and returns a string comprising the characters associated with the platform-dependent argument values. For example, the following converts the specified numeric values to a string:

```
print(string.char(76, 117, 97))
```

The example prints the following string:

```
Lua
```

❑ string.dump *(function)*: Returns a copy of the function converted to binary string form for storage or transmission. It can be restored with one of the load functions. (Officially, the function cannot have upvalues, but Chapter 10 describes what happens if it does.) The following example converts a simple Lua function to string form, and then creates a new function from the string and executes it with a number of arguments:

```
Str = string.dump(function(...) print(...) end)
print(string.gsub(Str, "%A+", "..."))
loadstring(Str)(1, 2, 3)
```

The example prints the following lines (the actual values shown in the first line may vary between platforms):

```
...LuaQ...sb...lua...E...print...arg... 7
1       2       3
```

❑ string.format *(format string, zero or more values)*: Returns a single formatted string. The format string specifies how the arguments that follow it are to be formatted, following conventions close to those used by the `printf` function in the standard C library. For example, you could use `string.format` to generate a hexadecimal color identifier like this:

```
io.write(string.format("Color: #%02X%02X%02X\n", 198, 239, 247))
```

The following line is printed by the example:

```
Color: #C6EFF7
```

❑   `string.len` (*string*): Returns the number of bytes in the specified string, including non-text characters such as `"\0"`.

❑   `string.lower` (*string*): Returns a copy of the specified string in which all uppercase letters are transformed to their lowercase values.

❑   `string.rep` (*string, repeat count*): Returns a string made up of the specified string repeated the specified number of times.

❑   `string.reverse` (*string*): Returns a copy of the specified string in which the sequence of the characters is reversed.

❑   `string.sub` (*string, start position, optional end position*): Returns the portion of the specified string indicated by the start and end positions.

❑   `string.upper` (*string*): Returns a copy of the specified string in which all lower case letters are transformed to their upper case values.

This example demonstrates a number of conversions in which the returned string is a modification of the passed-in string:

```
local Str = "Lua"
io.write(string.format("Normal: '%s', reversed: '%s', " ..
  "lower: '%s', upper: '%s'\n\n",
  Str, string.reverse(Str), string.lower(Str), string.upper(Str)))
for J, TblStr in ipairs{"coroutine", "debug", "io", "math",
  "os", "package", "string", "table"} do
  local Count = 0
  for FldStr in pairs(_G[TblStr]) do
    Count = Count + 1
  end
  io.write(string.format("%s%s%d\n", TblStr, string.rep(".",
    14 - string.len(TblStr) - string.len(Count)), Count))
end
```

The example prints the following lines:

```
Normal: 'Lua', reversed: 'auL', lower: 'lua', upper: 'LUA'

coroutine....6
debug.......14
io.........14
math.......31
os.........11
package......8
string......15
table........9
```

Table Library

The table functions provide a means to work with tables as arrays (that is, tables with contiguous integer indexes beginning with 1). The table library contains the following functions:

❏   `table.concat` (*array, optional separator string, optional start position, optional end position*) : Returns a single string made up of the elements in the specified table, which must be strings or numbers. If a separator is specified, it will be used to delimit the elements. A range of elements can be specified using the start and end positions.

❏   `table.insert` (*array, optional position, value*) : Inserts a value into the specified table. If the position is missing, the value is added to the end of the array, otherwise it's added to the indicated position. In either case, the number of values in the array is increased by one. If the insertion is into before the last position, elements are moved up to make room.

❏   `table.maxn` (*array*) : Effectively performs a `pairs` loop to determine the largest positive numeric key in the specified table. The returned number may be larger than the value an `ipairs` loop would reach, and the number may be a noninteger. If there are no positive keys, 0 is returned.

❏   `table.remove` (*array, optional position*) : Removes the table element associated with the specified position and returns its value. If the position is missing, the last element in the array is removed. Elements are moved down to fill the vacated position.

❏   `table.sort` (*array, optional comparison function*) : Sorts the elements in the specified array. If a comparison function is specified, it will be called as needed with two table elements as arguments. It should return `true` if the first element is less than the second and `false` otherwise. If this function is not specified, < will be used to compare elements.

This example demonstrates the manipulation of a table:

```
Tbl = {"This is line 4", "This line is out of place", "This is line 2"}
table.insert(Tbl, "This is line 1")
table.remove(Tbl, 2)
table.insert(Tbl, "This is line 3")
table.insert(Tbl, "This is line " .. table.maxn(Tbl) + 1)
table.sort(Tbl)
io.write(table.concat(Tbl, "\n"), "\n")
```

The example prints the following lines:

```
This is line 1
This is line 2
This is line 3
This is line 4
This is line 5
```

Math Library

The functions in the math library are closely bound to functions of the same name in the standard C library. Plots of some of the functions are shown here—these were generated with Lua using the GD library (which you'll get a chance to experiment with in the "Producing a Function Plot" Try It Out in Chapter 12).

Trigonometric Functions

These functions return a numeric value corresponding to right triangle side ratios. A circle of radius 1 is defined by the points (cos(*angle*), sin(*angle*)) for angles ranging from 0 to 2 * pi radians.

The trigonometric functions are as follows:

❑ `math.sin`(*angle in radians*): Returns the sine of the specified angle. See Figure 11-1 for a plot of this function.

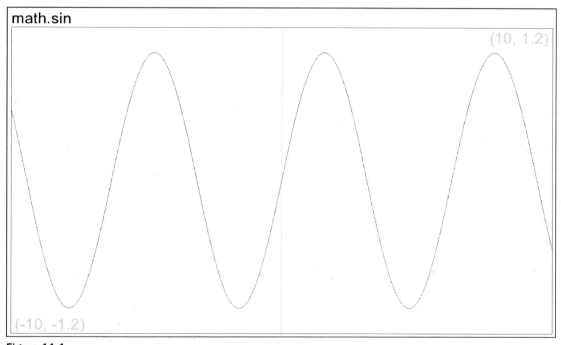

Figure 11-1

❑   `math.cos` (*angle in radians*) : Returns the cosine of the specified angle. See Figure 11-2 for a plot of this function.

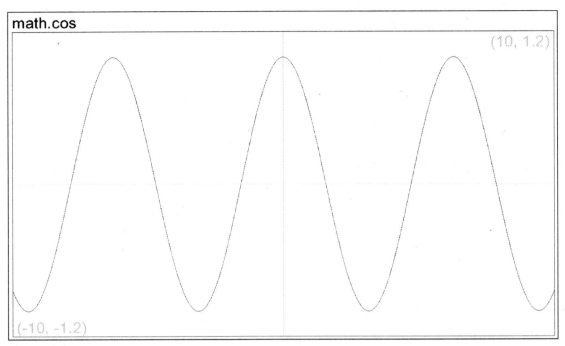

Figure 11-2

❑   math.tan(*angle in radians*): Returns the tangent of the specified angle. See Figure 11-3 for a plot of this function.

math.tan

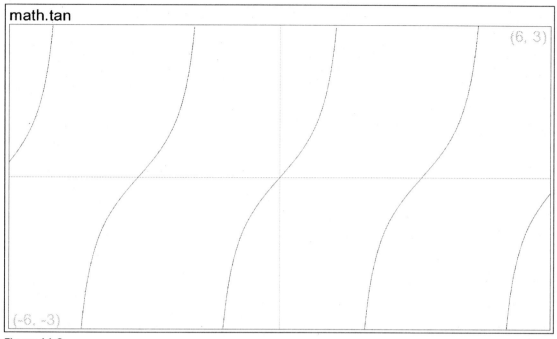

Figure 11-3

Inverse Trigonometric Functions

These functions return a numeric angle in radians that corresponds to a sine, cosine or tangent value. Because cosine and sine values range between -1 and 1, the arcsine and arccosine functions are defined only for arguments in this range.

The inverse trigonometric functions are as follows:

❏   math.asin (*value from -1 to 1*): Returns the angle in radians whose sine is specified. See Figure 11-4 for a plot of this function.

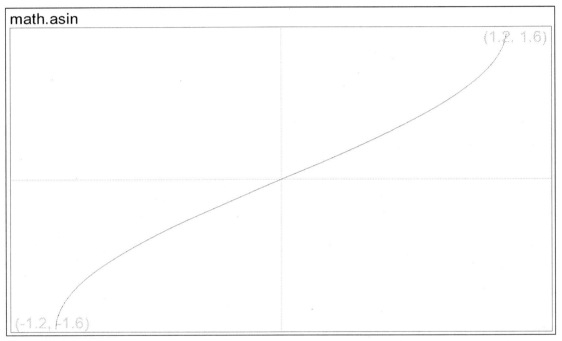

math.asin

(1.2, 1.6)

(-1.2, -1.6)

Figure 11-4

❏   math.acos (*value from -1 to 1*): Returns the angle in radians whose cosine is specified. See Figure 11-5 for a plot of this function.

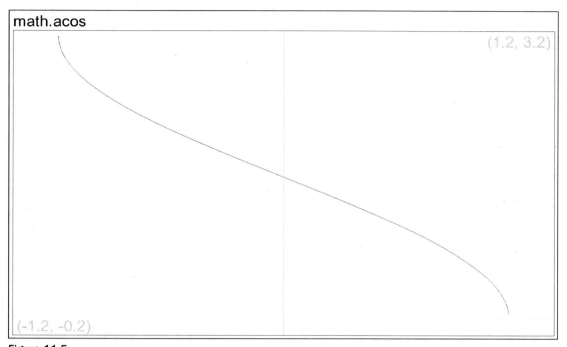

Figure 11-5

❑ `math.atan` (*value*): Returns the angle in radians whose tangent is specified. See Figure 11-6 for a plot of this function.

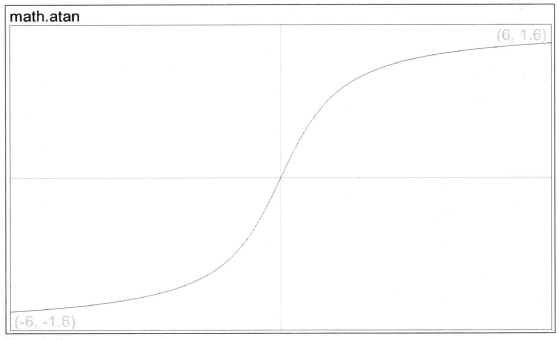

math.atan

(6, 1.6)

(-6, -1.6)

Figure 11-6

❑ `math.atan2` (*numerator, denominator*): Returns the angle of a bidimensional vector (numerator, denominator). The denominator may be zero.

This example runs through a range of numerators and denominators for the arctangent function:

```
for Y = -3, 3 do
  for X = -3, 3 do
     io.write(string.format("%5.2f ", math.atan2(Y, X) / math.pi))
  end
  io.write("\n")
end
```

The example prints the following lines:

```
-0.75 -0.69 -0.60 -0.50 -0.40 -0.31 -0.25
-0.81 -0.75 -0.65 -0.50 -0.35 -0.25 -0.19
-0.90 -0.85 -0.75 -0.50 -0.25 -0.15 -0.10
 1.00  1.00  1.00  0.00  0.00  0.00  0.00
 0.90  0.85  0.75  0.50  0.25  0.15  0.10
 0.81  0.75  0.65  0.50  0.35  0.25  0.19
 0.75  0.69  0.60  0.50  0.40  0.31  0.25
```

Hyperbolic Functions

These functions are to the hyperbola what the trigonometric functions are to the circle. The right half of the equilateral hyperbola is defined by the points (cosh(*hyperbolic angle*), sinh(*hyperbolic angle*)).

The hyperbolic functions are as follows:

❑ `math.sinh`(*hyperbolic angle*): Returns the hyperbolic sine of the specified value. See Figure 11-7 for a plot of this function.

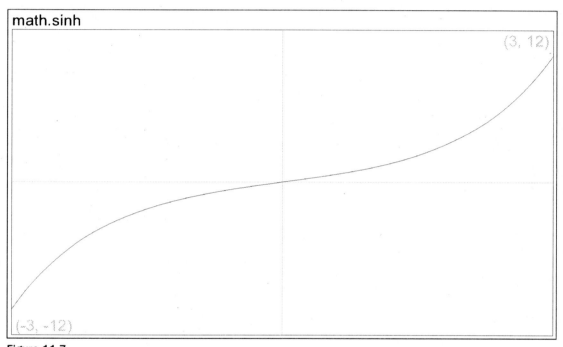

Figure 11-7

❑   math.cosh (*hyperbolic angle*): Returns the hyperbolic cosine of the specified value. See Figure 11-8 for a plot of this function.

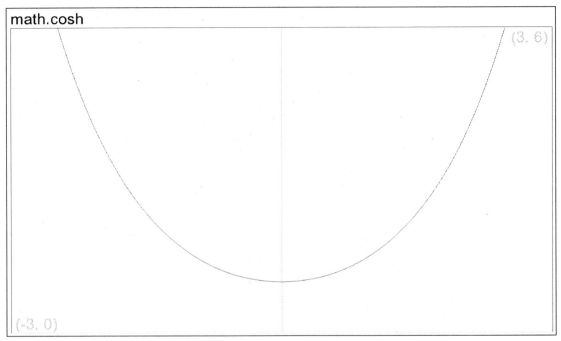

Figure 11-8

❑ math.tanh(*hyperbolic angle*): Returns the hyperbolic tangent of the specified value. See Figure 11-9 for a plot of this function.

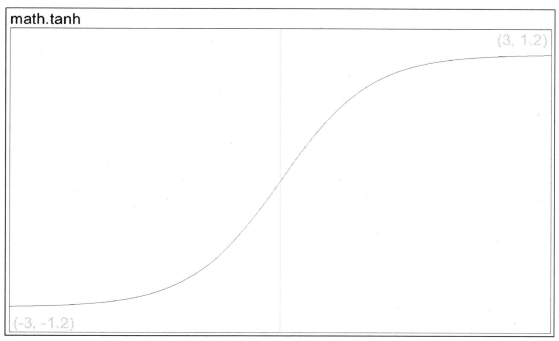

math.tanh

(3, 1.2)

(-3, -1.2)

Figure 11-9

Exponent Functions

These functions return the value of a number raised to another:

❑   math.exp (*natural exponent*): Returns the value of *e* raised to the specified exponent. See Figure 11-10 for a plot of this function.

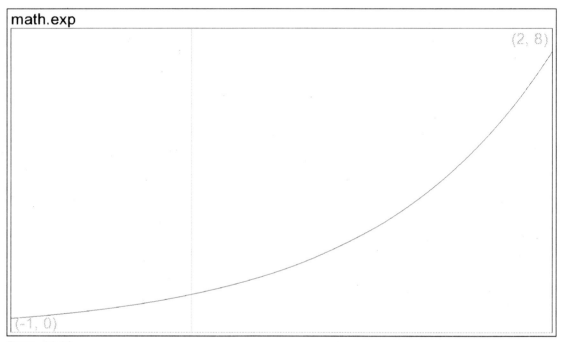

Figure 11-10

❏ math.pow(*base, exponent*): Returns the specified base raised to the specified exponent. The following example demonstrates this function:

```
local Base, Exp = 0, 10
local Pow = math.pow(Base, Exp)
io.write(Base, " ^ ", Exp, " = ", Pow == 0 and "nothing at all" or Pow, "\n")
-- With a friendly tip of the hat to Ian Anderson
```

The following line is printed by the example:

```
0 ^ 10 = nothing at all
```

❏ math.sqrt(*number*): Returns the square root of the specified number. See Figure 11-11 for a plot of this function.

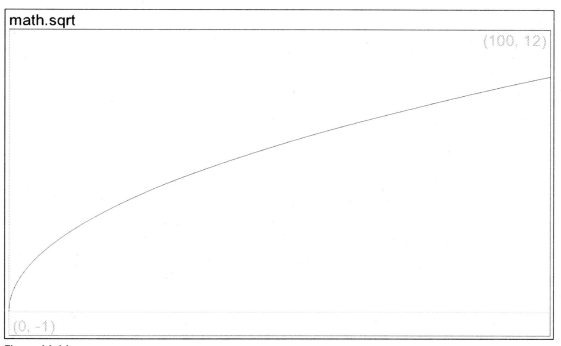

Figure 11-11

Logarithm Functions

These functions are the inverse of the exponent functions:

❑   math.log (*positive number*): Returns the natural (base-*e*) logarithm of the specified number. The number *e* raised to the return value equals the specified argument. See Figure 11-12 for a plot of this function.

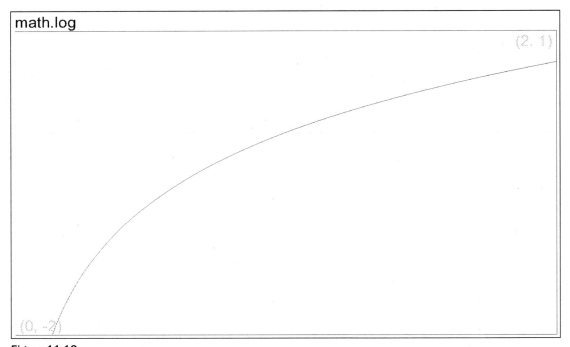

Figure 11-12

❑   `math.log10(`*number*`)`: Returns the base-10 logarithm of the specified number. The number 10 raised to the return value equals the specified argument. See Figure 11-13 for a plot of this function.

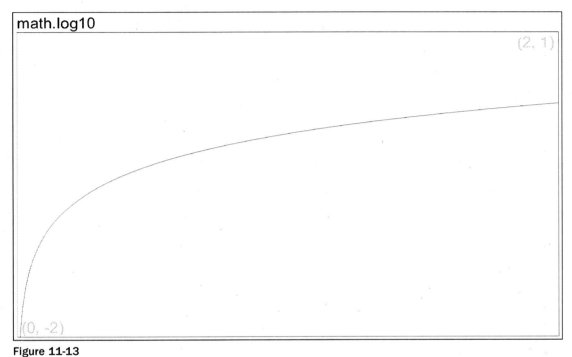

Figure 11-13

Adjustment Functions

These functions adjust the specified value by sign or value:

❏   math.abs(*number*): Returns the absolute value of the specified number; a non-numeric argument causes an error. See Figure 11-14 for a plot of this function.

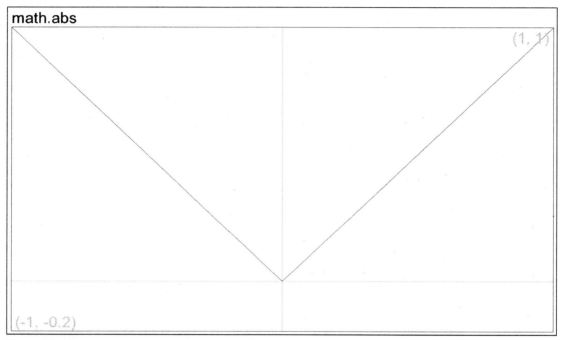

Figure 11-14

❑   `math.ceil(`*number*`)`: Returns the smallest integer greater than or equal to the specified numeric argument. See Figure 11-15 for a plot of this function.

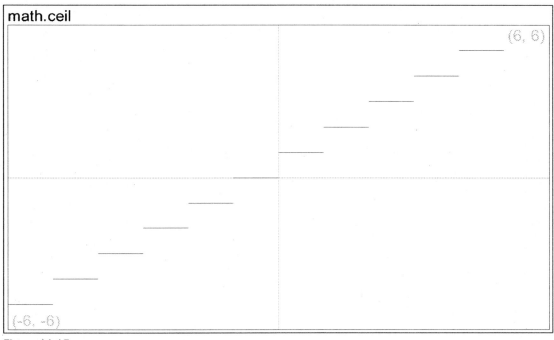

Figure 11-15

❑ `math.floor(number)`: Returns the greatest integer less than or equal to the specified numeric argument. See Figure 11-16 for a plot of this function.

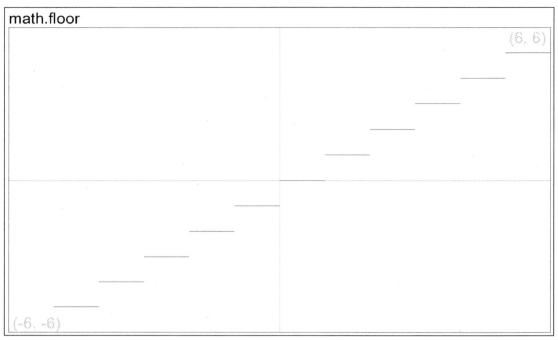

Figure 11-16

Floating Point Representation

These functions are used in the representation of floating point numbers as the product of a mantissa and two raised to an integer exponent:

❑ `math.frexp(number)`: Returns the mantissa and integer exponent of the specified number. The returned values are adjusted so that the absolute value of the mantissa is greater than or equal to 0.5 and less than 1.0, except where the specified number is 0, in which case both return values are 0.

❑ `math.ldexp(mantissa, integer exponent)`: Returns the product of the specified mantissa and two raised to the specified exponent.

This example breaks the value pi into a mantissa and exponent and then recombines them:

```
local Mantissa, Exp = math.frexp(math.pi)
io.write("Pi: ", Mantissa, " * 2 ^ ", Exp, " = ",
  math.ldexp(Mantissa, Exp), "\n")
```

The following line is printed by the example:

```
Pi: 0.78539816339745 * 2 ^ 2 = 3.1415926535898
```

Angle Conversion Functions

These helper functions convert angle values between degrees and radians:

❑ `math.deg` (*angle in radians*): Returns the number of degrees in the specified number of radians. For example, this converts some radian values to degrees:

```
io.write("Radians  Degrees\n")
io.write("-------  -------\n")
for Step = 0, 2, 0.25 do
   local Degree = math.deg(math.pi * Step)
   io.write(string.format("%4.2f pi  %7.1f\n", Step, Degree))
end
```

The example prints the following table:

```
Radians  Degrees
-------  -------
0.00 pi      0.0
0.25 pi     45.0
0.50 pi     90.0
0.75 pi    135.0
1.00 pi    180.0
1.25 pi    225.0
1.50 pi    270.0
1.75 pi    315.0
2.00 pi    360.0
```

❑ `math.rad` (*angle in degrees*): Returns the number of radians in the specified number of degrees. For example, this redefines `math.sin` to accept its angle argument in degrees rather than radians:

```
math._sin = math.sin

-- Redefine math.sin to accept angle in degrees

math.sin = function(degrees)
   return math._sin(math.rad(degrees))
end

io.write("  x   sin(x)\n")
io.write("---   ------\n")
for Deg = 0, 360, 90 do
   io.write(string.format("%3d  %6.2f\n", Deg, math.sin(Deg)))
end
```

The example prints the following table:

```
  x   sin(x)
---   ------
  0    0.00
 90    1.00
180    0.00
270   -1.00
360   -0.00
```

Pseudo-Random Number Functions

These functions are used to generate pseudo-random numbers:

- ❏   `math.randomseed(`*number*`)`: Seeds the pseudo-random number generator. You can obtain identical sequences of pseudo-random numbers by calling this function with the same value.

- ❏   `math.random(`*optional bound, optional bound*`)`: Returns a pseudo-random number in one of three ways. If no argument is specified, the return value is greater than or equal to 0 and less than 1. If one number is specified, the return value is an integer greater than or equal to 1 and less than or equal to the specified argument. If two numbers are specified, the return value is an integer greater than or equal to the first argument and less than or equal to the second.

This example shows how you can obtain identical sequences of pseudo-random numbers by seeding the generator with the same value:

```
local Seed = os.clock()
for J = 1, 2 do
  math.randomseed(Seed)
  math.random() -- On some systems that shall remain nameless, the
    -- first call to math.random is easy enough to predict that it
    -- destroys the illusion of randomness; throw it away.
  for J = 1, 10 do
    io.write(math.random(100, 200), " ")
  end
  io.write("\n")
end
```

The example prints identical sequences of numbers (the particular values depend on the seed value returned from `os.clock`):

```
123 165 107 127 136 125 199 132 194 118
123 165 107 127 136 125 199 132 194 118
```

Modulus Functions

These functions return the remainder of a division or the fractional part of an expression:

- ❏   `math.modf(`*number*`)`: Returns the integer and fractional portions of the specified number. Both of the return values carry the same sign as the argument.

- ❏   `math.fmod(`*numerator, denominator*`)`: Returns the remainder of the numerator divided by the denominator. The return value is undefined for a denominator equal to 0.

This example shows various manipulations of rational numbers:

```
local function Rational(Num, Den)
  local Whole, Frac = math.modf(Num / Den)
  io.write(Num, " / ", Den, " = ", Whole, " + ", Frac, "\n")
  io.write(Num, " / ", Den, " = ", Whole, " + ",
    math.fmod(Num, Den), " / ", Den, "\n")
end
```

```
Rational(5, 3)
Rational(-5, 3)
Rational(5.2, math.pi)
```

The example prints the following lines:

```
5 / 3 = 1 + 0.66666666666667
5 / 3 = 1 + 2 / 3
-5 / 3 = -1 + -0.66666666666667
-5 / 3 = -1 + -2 / 3
5.2 / 3.1415926535898 = 1 + 0.65521140815571
5.2 / 3.1415926535898 = 1 + 2.0584073464102 / 3.1415926535898
```

Minimum and Maximum Functions

These functions return the minimum or maximum value in a list of values:

❑   math.max(*one or more numbers*): Returns the greatest value in the specified list.

❑   math.min(*one or more numbers*): Returns the smallest value in the specified list.

This example returns the minimum and maximum values from an array:

```
local function Range(...)
   io.write("Count: ", select("#", ...), ", Min: ", math.min(...),
      ", Max: ", math.max(...), "\n")
end

Range(3, 1, 72, 5.4, math.pi)
```

The following line is printed by the example:

```
Count: 5, Min: 1, Max: 72
```

Constants

These are not functions, but numbers that may be useful in certain calculations:

❑   math.huge: A number greater than or equal to any other number. This is positive infinity on systems that have a representation for infinity. The following example multiplies each number from NumListA with its counterpart in NumListB and prints the highest product obtained. Max is initialized to -math.huge (note the unary minus), which is guaranteed not to be greater than any of the actual maximum products.

```
NumListA = {2, 5, 3}
NumListB = {5, 3, 2}
local Max = -math.huge
for I, NumA in ipairs(NumListA) do
   local NumB = NumListB[I]
   Max = math.max(Max, NumA * NumB)
end
io.write("The maximum product was ", Max, ".\n")
```

The example prints the following:

```
The maximum product was 15.
```

❏   math.pi: The ratio of a circle's circumference to its diameter. For example, this computes a circle's area from its radius:

```
function CircleArea(Radius)
  return math.pi * Radius ^ 2
end

Radius = 5
io.write("radius: ", Radius, " feet; area: ",
  CircleArea(Radius), " square feet\n")
```

The example prints the following:

```
radius: 5 feet; area: 78.539816339745 square feet
```

Input/Output Library

The functions in the input/output (I/O) library enable your program to read from and write to files and the standard input/output streams.

By default, the io.read and io.write functions read from and write to standard input and standard output respectively. You can change this behavior with the io.input and io.output functions.

When working with multiple files, it is usually more convenient to obtain file handles and use their associated methods for reading, writing and performing other file operations.

Here are all the functions in the I/O library:

❏   io.close (*optional file*): Closes the default output file if no argument is specified; otherwise it closes the specified file. (See also the file handle close method.)

❏   io.flush (): Commits the default output buffer.

❏   io.input (*optional file or name of file*): Returns the default input file handle if called without an argument. If it is called with a handle to an open file, the file becomes the new default input file so that calls to io.read read from it. If the function is called with the name of a file, the file is opened in text mode and becomes the new default input file.

❏   io.lines (*optional name of file*): Returns an iterator for use in a generic for loop. If a filename is specified, the file is opened in text mode. When all lines have been read, the file is closed. If no argument is specified, the for loop reads lines from the default input file. In this case, the file is not closed after all lines have been read.

❏   io.open (*name of file, optional open mode*): Opens the specified file and returns a handle to it. (The returned file handle's methods are discussed later in this section.) If an error occurs, it returns nil followed by an error message. If the open mode is missing, the file is opened in text mode for reading. The following table lists the supported modes.

On platforms such as Windows, you can disable the control code processing done for text files by appending "b" to the open mode, which opens the file in binary mode.

Mode	Description
"r"	Opens an existing file for reading
"w"	Overwrites an existing file, or creates a new file, for writing
"a"	Opens an existing file, or creates a new file, for appending
"r+"	Opens an existing file for reading and writing
"w+"	Overwrites an existing file, or creates a new file, for reading and writing
"a+"	Opens an existing file, or creates a new file, for reading and appending

❏ io.output (*optional file or name of file*): Returns the default output file handle if called without an argument. If it is called with a handle to an open file, the file becomes the new default output file so that calls to io.write write to it. If the function is called with the name of a file, the file is opened in "w" mode (that is, it is overwritten if it exists, or created if it doesn't) and becomes the new default output file.

❏ io.read (*zero or more of* "*a" *or* "*n" *or* "*l" *or number*): Returns the next line from the default input file if no argument is specified. The argument specifies what kind and how much data is to be read. Its meaning is summarized in the following table.

If data corresponding to the specified format cannot be read, nil is returned (but is not followed with an error message).

Format	Description
"*n"	Reads and returns a number
"*a"	Reads the complete remainder of file
"*l"	Reads the next line, and removes the end-of-line marker
number	Reads the specified number of bytes

❏ io.tmpfile(): Opens a temporary file for reading and writing and returns a handle to it. When the program ends normally, this file will be deleted.

❏ io.type (*file*): Returns "file", "closed file", or nil depending on the argument.

❏ io.write (*zero or more strings or numbers*): Writes each of its arguments to the default output file, and returns true if the write is successful. An error is issued if the default output file is closed or a value other than a string or number is written. In certain cases (for example, if the full disk is full), nil followed by an error message is returned.

❑ `io.popen` (*shell command, optional mode*): Launches the specified command and returns a handle. If the mode is `"r"` or not given, this handle can be used as a file handle to read the standard output of the command. If it is `"w"`, the handle can be used to write to the command's standard input. This function is not available on all platforms.

This example demonstrates the execution of a command and the capturing of its output:

```
Hnd, ErrStr = io.popen("lua -h")
if Hnd then
   for Str in Hnd:lines() do
     io.write(Str, "\n")
   end
   Hnd:close()
else
   io.write(ErrStr, "\n")
end
```

The example produces the following output:

```
usage: lua [options] [script [args]].
Available options are:
  -e stat   execute string 'stat'
  -l name   require library 'name'
  -i        enter interactive mode after executing 'script'
  -v        show version information
  --        stop handling options
  -         execute stdin and stop handling options
```

The following functions are all the methods of file handles:

❑ *file handle*:`close()`: Closes the file.

❑ *file handle*:`flush()`: Commits the file's output buffer.

❑ *file handle*:`lines()`: Like `io.lines`, this returns an iterator for use in a generic `for` loop using the specified file for input. Unlike `io.lines`, it does not close file associated file after the traversal.

❑ *file handle*:`read` (*zero or more of* `"*a"` *or* `"*n"` *or* `"*l"` *or number*): Like `io.read`, this reads data from the specified file.

❑ *file handle*:`seek` (*optional* `"set"` *or* `"cur"` *or* `"end"`, *optional offset*): Sets the file pointer in the specified file and returns the new position measured from the beginning of the file. Unlike most Lua index values, the offsets to this function are zero-based. The offset is measured from the beginning of the file if the first argument is `"set"`; from the current position in the file if it's `"cur"`; or from the end of the file if it's `"end"`. The default argument values are `"cur"` and 0, so the current file position can be obtained by calling this function without arguments.

❑ file handle:`setvbuf` (`"no"` *or* `"full"` *or* `"line"`, *optional size*): Configures the buffering used by the specified file. The size argument specifies the size of the buffer in bytes. This function returns `true` on success, or `nil` followed by an error message on failure. The following table describes the buffering modes. (For more detail on this function, consult the documentation for the C function `setvbuf`.)

Mode	Description
"no"	Writes are committed without buffering.
"full"	Writes are committed only when buffer is full or explicitly flushed.
"line"	Writes are committed when a newline is encountered, when the buffer is explicitly flushed, or when input from a special device is detected.

❑ *file handle*: write (*zero or more strings or numbers*): Writes each of its arguments to the file. An error is issued if the file is closed or a value other than a string or number is written. In certain cases (for example, if the disk is full), this function returns nil followed by an error message.

This example demonstrates full buffering with a file so that only a full buffer or explicit flush commits the written data to the file, as well as file pointer positioning:

```
FileStr = "test.txt"
Hnd, ErrStr = io.open(FileStr, "w")
if Hnd then
  Hnd:setvbuf("full", 1024)
  for K = 1, 4 do
    if K == 3 then
      Pos = Hnd:seek("cur", 0)
      Hnd:write("Special line\n")
    end
    Hnd:write(string.format("Line %02d\n", K))
  end
  Hnd:flush()
  Hnd:close()
  Hnd, ErrStr = io.open(FileStr, "r")
  if Hnd then
    for Str in Hnd:lines() do
      io.write(Str, "\n")
    end
    Hnd:seek("set", Pos)
    Str = Hnd:read("*l")
    io.write(Str, "\n")
    Hnd:close()
  else
    io.write(ErrStr)
  end
else
  io.write(ErrStr)
end
```

The example prints the following lines:

```
Line 01
Line 02
Special line
Line 03
Line 04
Special line
```

Operating System Library

These functions provide access to the operating system's time, date, shell, and file management services.

CPU Timing

Identifying bottlenecks is sometimes as simple as monitoring the amount of time the central processing unit spends on various parts of a Lua program. In general, you should repeat the code you want to examine a sufficient number of times with a loop so that you have figures well above the noise level.

The operating system library includes the os.clock() timing function, which returns the approximate number of CPU time measured in seconds used by the current program. For example, this gives a benchmark for adding elements to an array:

```
local Count = 1e7
local Tbl = {}
local Tm = os.clock()
for J = 1, Count do
   table.insert(Tbl, J)
end
io.write("table.insert: ", os.clock() - Tm, " sec\n")
Tbl = {}
Tm = os.clock()
for J = 1, Count do
   Tbl[#Tbl + 1] = J
end
io.write("Indexed insert: ", os.clock() - Tm, " sec\n")
```

The example prints the following lines:

```
table.insert: 5.328 sec
Indexed insert: 3.906 sec
```

Time and Date Functions

The functions in the time and date category are flexible enough to handle a wide spectrum of applications:

❑ os.date(*optional format string, optional time value*): Returns the current time or the specified time either as a string or as an associative table. A table is returned if the format string is "*t"; otherwise it uses the same format specification as strftime in the standard C library. To return the time in Universal Coordinated Time format, prepend the format specifier with "!". If you don't specify a time value, the current time is used. If you do specify it, use the format returned by os.time.

❑ os.difftime(*high time, low time*): The difference is seconds between the two time arguments is returned. Use the format returned by os.time for the arguments.

❑ os.time(*optional time table*): Returns the specified time as a scalar value, often the number of seconds that have passed in a standard epoch. If you do not specify the time argument, the current time is used. If you do specify it, do so with a table that contains the year, month and day fields. You can include hour, min, sec and isdst in the table as well.

The following example calculates the number of seconds from a given moment:

```
TmStart = os.time{year = 2001, month = 1, day = 1, hour = 0}
TmNow = os.time()
io.write(os.difftime(TmNow, TmStart), " seconds have passed since ",
   os.date("%d %B %Y", TmStart), "\n")
```

The following line is printed by the example:

```
180787215 seconds have passed since 01 January 2001
```

Filesystem Functions

In addition to the I/O functions, the standard C library provides paltry support for managing files. (A number of modules for Lua remedy this deficiency.)

The filesystem functions are as follows:

❑ os.remove (*name of file*): Removes the specified file. If successful, this returns true; otherwise it returns nil followed by an error message. On Unix-type systems, you can use this function to remove an empty directory.

❑ os.rename (*old name of file, new name of file*): Renames a file or directory.

❑ os.tmpname (): Returns a name that can you can use to create a temporary file or directory.

This example demonstrates how a temporary file is created, written to, closed, and then read from:

```
FileStr = os.tmpname()
Hnd = io.open(FileStr, "w")
if Hnd then
   io.write("Opened temporary file ", FileStr, " for writing\n")
   Hnd:write("Line 1\nLine 2\nLine 3\n")
   Hnd:close()
   for Str in io.lines(FileStr) do
     io.write(Str, "\n")
   end
   os.remove(FileStr)
else
   io.write("Error opening ", FileStr, " for writing\n")
end
```

The following lines are printed by the example:

```
Opened temporary file /tmp/lua_a05eSj for writing
Line 1
Line 2
Line 3
```

Other Operating System Functions

The remaining functions in the os table let your Lua script interact with the operating shell and its environment variables, and use locale settings to control language- and country-specific behavior:

❑   os.execute(*optional shell command string*): The specified command is passed to the shell for execution. The code returned from the shell is in turn returned by this function. If the command is missing, this function checks for the existence of the shell, returning a non-zero value if it is available and zero if it is not.

❑   os.exit(*optional integer code*): Terminates the host program. If the exit code is missing, the library will provide the code that indicates success for the platform on which the host is running; this is usually zero.

❑   os.getenv(*variable name string*): Retrieves the value associated with the argument in the environment of the current process. If the name doesn't exist in the environment, nil is returned.

❑   os.setlocale(*locale string, optional* "all" *or* "collate" *or* "ctype" *or* "monetary" *or* "numeric" *or* "time"): Queries or sets locale information for the current program. To perform a query, specify nil as the first argument. To set the locale information, specify a locale string such as "pt_BR" or "en_US". The supported categories are "all", "collate", "ctype", "monetary", "numeric", and "time". If the category is missing, "all" is assumed.

Here is an example of os.execute, os.getenv, os.setlocale, and os.exit in action:

```
print("os.execute returned:", os.execute("ls -sh")) -- "ls" is a
    -- directory listing program available on Unix-like systems.
print("HOME environment variable:", os.getenv("HOME"))
assert(os.setlocale("pt_BR", "numeric"))
print(math.pi) -- Prints with a comma!
os.exit()
print("This will never get printed!")
```

The example's output is as follows:

```
total 8.0K
4.0K calltrace.lua
4.0K test.lua
os.execute returned:     0
HOME environment variable:       /home/wthrall
3,1415926535898
```

Debugging Library

The functions in the debug namespace table are not for normal use, but for writing error handlers, debuggers, profilers, and other things that need to do introspection (the inspection of running code). For a more detailed discussion of these functions, see Chapter 10.

Some of these functions take an optional thread argument. Those functions work on the given thread, or (by default) on the currently running thread. Even if the thread argument is omitted, you can specify other arguments by shifting their positions to the left. For example, you can use the debug.getinfo function or stack level argument as either its first or second argument, depending on whether the optional thread argument was given. Arguments that are stack levels, local indexes, or upvalue indexes are positive integers, with 1 representing the top of the stack, the first local variable, or the first upvalue.

The following functions are in the debugging library:

❏ `debug.debug()`: Reads and interprets lines from standard input, and returns when it reads a line consisting of the word "cont". Local variables visible in the scope where `debug.debug` is called are only accessible using `debug.getlocal`, `debug.setlocal`, `debug.getupvalue`, and `debug.setupvalue`.

❏ `debug.getfenv` (*function or thread or userdata*): Returns its argument's environment table.

❏ `debug.gethook` (*optional thread*): Returns the current hook function, the current hook mask (a string containing zero or more of "c", "l", and "r"), and the current hook count.

❏ `debug.getinfo` (*optional thread, function or stack level, optional flag string*): If a function is given, this returns an associative table of information about that function; if a stack level is given, it returns an associative table of information about the function running at that stack level, or `nil` if the stack level is invalid. By default, the returned table includes the fields `currentline`, `func`, `lastlinedefined`, `linedefined`, `name`, `namewhat`, `nups`, `short_src`, `source`, and `what`. The letters in the flag string control which fields the table contains. For example, if the flag string contains an "L", then the table will include an `activelines` field. (For more details, see the table in Chapter 10.)

❏ `debug.getlocal` (*optional thread, stack level, local index*): Returns the name and value of the numerically specified local variable at the specified stack level. If the local index is higher than the amount of local variables at the specified stack level, `nil` is returned. If the stack level is higher than the amount of active stack levels, an error occurs.

❏ `debug.getmetatable` (*value*): Returns its argument's metatable if one is present; otherwise it returns `nil`. This function bypasses its argument's __metatable metamethod if one is present.

❏ `debug.getregistry()`: Returns the *registry table*, a table that C code can use as a storage area.

❏ `debug.getupvalue` (*function, upvalue index*): Returns the name and value of the numerically specified upvalue of the given function. If the upvalue index is higher than the function's amount of upvalues, `nil` is returned.

❏ `debug.setfenv` (*function or thread or userdata, environment table*): Gives an environment table to a function, thread, or userdata.

❏ `debug.sethook` (*optional thread, hook function, hook mask string with "c" and/or "r" and/or "l", optional instruction count*): Makes the given function the *hook* (a function that is called by Lua when certain events happen). The hook mask (a string) and the instruction count determine which events trigger the hook. If the hook mask contains "c", then on every function call (including tail calls), the hook will be called with the "call" argument. If the hook mask contains "r", then on every return (including tail returns) the hook will be called with the "return" or "tail-return" argument. If the hook mask contains "l", then on every source code line (except for lines where nothing happens) the hook will be called with the "line" and the line number arguments. If there is a nonzero instruction count, then every time that many bytecode instructions have been executed, the hook will be called with the "count" argument. If `nil` is given instead of a function, then any function that is currently set as the hook is removed.

❏ debug.setlocal (*optional thread, stack level, local index, value*): Assigns the given value to the numerically specified local variable at the specified stack level, and returns the local variable's name. If the local index is higher than the amount of local variables at the specified stack level, nil is returned; if the stack level is higher than the amount of active stack levels, an error occurs.

❏ debug.setmetatable (*value, metatable*): Gives a metatable to the given value, even if that value has a __metatable metamethod.

❏ debug.setupvalue (*function, upvalue index, value*): Assigns the given value to the numerically specified upvalue of the given function, and returns the upvalue's name. If the upvalue index is higher than the function's amount of upvalues, nil is returned.

❏ debug.traceback (*optional thread, optional message string, optional level argument*): Returns a string containing the message string followed by a stack traceback. The level argument specifies which stack frame to start the traceback from, with 1 (the default) being the function that called debug.traceback, 2 being the function that called that function, 3 being the function that called *that* function, and so on.

This example sets a hook that is called on every line and every function call and return, which then prints information about the current line, call, or return:

```lua
function Hook(Event, LineNum)
  -- Info for the currently running function (not counting this hook):
  local Info = debug.getinfo(2)
  if Event == "call" then
    io.write("'", Info.name or "???", "' is being called; ")
    if Info.nups == 0 then
      io.write("it has no upvalues.\n")
    else
      io.write("its upvalues are:\n")
      for I = 1, Info.nups do
        local Name, Val = debug.getupvalue(Info.func, I)
        io.write("  ", Name, "\t", tostring(Val), "\n")
      end
    end
  elseif Event == "return" or Event == "tail return" then
    io.write("'", Info.name or "???", "' is being returned from.\n")
  elseif Event == "line" then
    local LclCount = 0

    -- An iterator that returns the names and values of the current
    -- function's local variables:
    local function Locals()
      LclCount = LclCount + 1
      return debug.getlocal(3, LclCount)
    end

    local Lcls = {}
    for LclName, LclVal in Locals do
      -- Ignore temporary locals used by the Lua virtual machine:
      if string.sub(LclName, 1, 1) ~= "(" then
        Lcls[#Lcls + 1] = LclName .. " (" .. tostring(LclVal) .. ")"
      end
    end
    io.write("line ", LineNum, "; ")
```

```
      if #Lcls > 0 then
        -- This doesn't include upvalues:
        io.write("in-scope local(s): ", table.concat(Lcls, ", "),
          "\n")
      else
        io.write("no in-scope locals.\n")
      end
    end
end

local Fruit1, Fruit2 = "banana", "kiwi"

function FncB()
  return Fruit1 .. "/" .. Fruit2 -- Line 48.
end

function FncA(Fruit)
  local Fruits = FncB() -- Line 52.
  return Fruit .. "/" .. Fruits -- Line 53.
end

debug.sethook(Hook, "crl")
print("### " .. FncA("apple")) -- Line 57.
debug.sethook(nil) -- Line 58.
```

The example gives the following output:

```
'sethook' is being returned from.
line 57; in-scope local(s): Fruit1 (banana), Fruit2 (kiwi)
'FncA' is being called; it has no upvalues.
line 52; in-scope local(s): Fruit (apple)
'FncB' is being called; its upvalues are:
   Fruit1        banana
   Fruit2        kiwi
line 48; no in-scope locals.
'FncB' is being returned from.
line 53; in-scope local(s): Fruit (apple), Fruits (banana/kiwi)
'FncA' is being returned from.
'print' is being called; it has no upvalues.
'???' is being called; it has no upvalues.
'???' is being returned from.
### apple/banana/kiwi
'print' is being returned from.
line 58; in-scope local(s): Fruit1 (banana), Fruit2 (kiwi)
'sethook' is being called; it has no upvalues.
```

Summary

In this chapter, you've reviewed some of the library functions from earlier in the book, and learned about others. Prior to this chapter, you learned about the Lua language. From this point on, you'll be exploring how Lua can serve as an integral component in real-world applications. The next chapter starts this off with a small survey of open-source libraries that work well with Lua.

Using Community Libraries

In Chapter 7, you learned how to modularize your Lua programs and why it's a good practice to do so. At the end of that chapter, you saw that you can write modules in languages like C as well as Lua. Throughout the remaining chapters of this book, the term *library* will refer to a collection of one or more routines that have been compiled from a lower-level language like C, C++ or Pascal. Depending on the context, a library may or may not have anything to do with Lua. A library that acts as an intermediary between Lua and another library is often called a *binding*.

This chapter extends the topic of libraries and how they interact with Lua. In it, you will become familiar with some libraries and bindings that have been made available to the open source community. The bindings cover a small cross-section of the many ways you can enhance Lua, including the following:

- ❑ Structuring binary data
- ❑ Constructing dynamic graphics
- ❑ Transferring files with various Internet protocols
- ❑ Interfacing with a relational database

Seeing how these libraries work with Lua should allow you to make use of a large number of other libraries. Plan on visiting the LuaForge site to see what's available. Chapter 13 will extend this topic to applications and libraries that you write yourself.

Library Overview

A *library* is a collection of routines and variables that can be linked to an executable program such as a web browser or the Lua interpreter. By providing a well-established interface to common functionality, the use of libraries helps to modularize and standardize an application. For example, the standard C runtime library used by many programs (not just those written in C) implements a wide range of application tasks, including dynamic memory management, file handling, and string operations.

Most libraries can be linked to an application either *statically*, in which portions of a library are directly embedded, or *dynamically*, in which portions of a library are shared concurrently among applications. An application that is statically linked to its libraries is operationally simpler, and consequently easier to deploy, than its dynamically linked counterpart. Such an application is also larger and needs to be relinked if it is to take advantage of updates to any of its libraries.

However, any system like Lua that uses modules loaded at runtime has its own problems with static libraries. The problem has to do with multiple copies of certain library functions linked to the main application and one or more of its loaded modules. In many cases, multiple copies of a statically linked function simply waste space, but with functions that share some internal state, like dynamic memory management functions, it is possible that synchronization problems will occur. For example, if memory is allocated using one copy of the C library and freed using another copy, it is inevitable that unpleasant memory bugs will result.

The solution is to make sure that only one copy of each library is used throughout an application and its loaded modules. This is best managed though libraries that are linked dynamically.

Dynamically Linked Libraries

Modern operating systems support libraries that can be linked to multiple running processes. On Unix-like systems, these are generally known as *shared libraries*; on Windows, these are usually referred to as *dynamic-link libraries*. A common abbreviation for dynamic-link library is DLL.

Resolving External References

The source code in a particular file typically contains references to functions and variables that are defined externally, such as in some other application file or in a library. It is one of the compiler's jobs to create object code that handles these references properly. For example, it sets up calls to external functions using the correct calling convention and arguments. One thing the compiler doesn't know, however, is where in memory these functions will actually reside when the application is executed. When source code is compiled into an object module, enough information to resolve these unknown addresses is provided by the compiler. It is the linker's job to knit the related object modules and any statically linked libraries together into a single application. While doing this, it resolves the addresses that it knows about. However, at this stage, the linker doesn't know the addresses of functions and variables that are part of dynamic-link libraries.

An application can be configured to have dynamic-link addresses resolved when it is loaded by the operating system. Alternatively, an application can explicitly assign dynamic-link addresses to variables using a system-provided function. The first approach is used by Lua for functions such as `sprintf` from the C library. The second approach is used by Lua when loading modules dynamically.

Configuration Options

You can configure the Lua interpreter (or any program that embeds it) in one of two ways so that only one copy of a library is present when running. In the proceeding figures, the application is represented with a bold rectangle and each dynamic-link library with a thin rectangle. Figure 12-1 shows a configuration in which Lua's core functionality is part of the application's main file. The application reaches into the module to run its initialization function (for example, `luaopen_pack`), represented here with the right-pointing arrow. The left pointing arrow indicates that the module reaches into the application to make use of Lua's C interface.

Figure 12-1

By default, Lua is built this way on Unix-like systems. The advantage is that Lua's executable program file (usually named lua) is never separated from its core functionality. Windows supports this scheme, but it has been reported that some software development kits don't implement it well. Figure 12-2 shows the typical configuration for Windows.

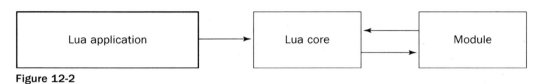

Figure 12-2

Here, Lua's core functionality is placed into its own dynamic-link library and shared by both the application and its modules.

Libraries Built from Source Code

If the operating system you use is mainstream, you'll find many libraries that work very well on it. Due to the large number of platforms that Lua runs on, libraries are typically provided in the form of source code. As you saw in Chapter 1, this approach enables you to compile applications and libraries that are tailor-made to your operating system and its particular configuration.

If you want to press ahead with Lua libraries, refer to Chapter 1 for instructions on setting up development tools for your operating system. Start by following the instructions in that chapter to build Lua itself. In general, doing this will be easier than compiling libraries and will verify that your tools are properly configured.

In the overviews in this chapter, it will be assumed that you're familiar with the basic tasks of compiling an application or library. This includes downloading source packages, extracting the contents of tarballs and zip files, invoking a compiler and linker, and copying files from one location to another. Chapter 1 covers these operations in enough detail to enable you to build the libraries discussed in this chapter.

Some of the commands shown in the proceeding sections require that your system environment have certain variables assigned. A helpful diagnostic to make sure these commands are doing what you expect them to is to precede them with echo. For example, on Unix-like systems, do this:

```
echo cp *.so $LUA_DIR/
```

Or, if you're on Windows, do this:

```
echo xcopy *.dll "%LUA_DIR%\*.*"
```

If the resulting output shows that the environment variable has been properly replaced, you can recall the command, remove the `echo` portion, and execute the revised command. Most shells will let you recall a command by pressing the up arrow key.

Building Libraries on Unix-Like Systems

In general, the makefiles used to build many libraries that interface with Lua will reflect a bias toward Unix-style systems. These makefile scripts often work with little or no fuss. Most source packages include text files named README and INSTALL that contain essential information. Modifications to makefiles should be minimal, although you may need to change pathnames such as the one that identifies the location of the Lua header files. It is prudent to save a copy of any script that you modify.

The proceeding instructions assume the following:

❑   The `LUA_DIR` environment variable specifies the location where you put Lua modules, whether they are Lua scripts or compiled libraries.

❑   The `LUA_PATH` environment variable has the value `?.lua;$LUA_DIR/?.lua`.

❑   The `LUA_CPATH` environment variable has the value `?.so;$LUA_DIR/?.so`.

Building Libraries on Windows

The instructions in this chapter assume you are using version 6 of Microsoft's Visual C++ software development kit. Other mainstream C compiler kits usually work well, too, but note the following caveats:

❑   Make sure the SDK you use can link properly with the standard Windows library MSVCRT.DLL that some prebuilt libraries use.

❑   You may need to adjust some of the compiler and linker commands shown here.

Unfortunately, the small TCC compiler that builds Lua so well is harder to use for compiling libraries because of limitations with this development kit's header file collection.

The proceeding instructions assume the following:

❑   Whatever SDK you use, it is assumed that its installation directory contains the standard `bin`, `lib`, and `include` subdirectories.

❑   The `SDK_DIR` environment variable specifies the location of your software development kit.

❑   The `LIB` environment variable has the value `%SDK_DIR%\lib;%SDK_DIR%\lib\usr`.

❑   The `INCLUDE` environment variable has the value `%SDK_DIR%\include;%SDK_DIR%\include\usr`.

❑   The import library for the Lua DLL, `lua5.1.lib`, has been copied to `%SDK_DIR%\lib\usr`.

❑   The public header files for Lua — `lua.h`, `luaconf.h`, `lualib.h`, and `lauxlib.h` — have been copied to `%SDK_DIR%\include\usr`.

❑   The `LUA_DIR` environment variable specifies the location where you put Lua modules, whether they are Lua scripts or compiled libraries.

❑   The `LUA_PATH` environment variable has the value `?.lua;%LUA_DIR%\?.lua`.

❏ The `LUA_CPATH` environment variable has the value `?.dll;%LUA_DIR%\?.dll`.

❏ The `UTIL_DIR` environment variable specifies the location where you keep certain applications and dynamic-link libraries, including `lua.exe`, `lua5.1.dll`, and `luac.exe`.

❏ The search path includes `%SDK_DIR%\bin` and `%UTIL_DIR%`.

The commands you use to build a library in Windows include one for linking various object files. The link command contains a `/base` option followed by a hexadecimal number. This number specifies the location in the virtual address space of a process where the operating system will attempt to load the library when it is dynamically linked. By providing a unique address to each dynamic-link library that will be loaded together, Windows avoids address corrections when the library is loaded and paging inefficiencies when the program is executed. Several *rebasing* utilities are available that will optimally assign base addresses to dynamic-link libraries after they have been compiled. The approach shown in this book is to explicitly assign them when a library is built, selecting unique addresses at one megabyte boundaries. Avoid using base addresses that interfere with libraries that are larger than one megabyte.

Limits to Portability

Libraries are generally written to be as portable as possible, but sometimes there are system-imposed limits to this. For example, some operating systems do not support signals or file system links, so they consequently can't support a library dealing with these features. A case in point is the lack of support for POSIX libraries on older versions of Windows.

Additionally, some libraries, especially small ones or ones with limited distribution, may require some modifications to build properly on platforms other than the one on which they were developed. You'll learn some of the things you may need to watch for in the following parts of this chapter.

How Lua Interacts with Libraries

You're familiar with using functions like `print`, `string.gsub` and `io.open`. These and Lua's other functions are implemented in C and made available to Lua scripts by means of a program interface. To understand how your Lua script can call these functions, first you need to know how the functions make it into your script's environment (the registration process), and second what happens when a call to a C function is actually made.

The Variable Registration Process

When the standard Lua interpreter starts, it calls a function named `lua_open` that allocates and initializes a state structure (sometimes called an *instance* or *universe*). A pointer to this structure is passed as the first argument to all other functions in the Lua C interface (usually called the *application program interface*, or *API*). Everything that pertains to your Lua script has its basis in this structure. It serves as a liaison that allows a C program to manipulate a script's environment, to be called by a script, and to call into a script. In fact, one of the first things an application does after receiving a pointer to this structure is to modify the initial (and, in practice, often the only) environment by placing functions and other variables (such as `print`, `string.rep` and `_VERSION`) into it. This is done by calling functions with names like `luaopen_base` and `luaopen_string`. These in turn call lower-level API functions that manipulate tables and the Lua call stack.

In the context of libraries, there are a couple of things to note here:

❑ It doesn't matter if functions like `luaopen_string` are embedded statically into the application or are located in an external dynamic-link library, as long as only one copy is accessible during execution and they are properly exported so that Lua bindings can call them.

❑ There is no difference between the way the base and standard libraries are loaded and the way external modules written in C or some other low-level language are loaded. For example, you could compile a Lua interpreter that doesn't load the math library by default. The math library could be built (with no changes to the source code) as a dynamic-link library. In this way, Lua scripts could use the math library by simply including the following line:

```
require("math")
```

Conversely, if you have a module that you want to be loaded by default in your Lua interpreter, you could load it the same way the standard libraries are usually loaded. Keep in mind that these kinds of alterations to Lua's default configuration can diminish the portability of Lua scripts. Unless you are building Lua for a special application where the benefits of these changes outweigh the portability costs, it's probably best to stay with the standard configuration.

Calling a C Function from Lua

When you call a function from a Lua script, you don't need to know whether it is implemented in Lua or in a lower-level language behind the Lua API. In fact, the bytecode that Lua generates for a function call doesn't distinguish between these two kinds of function calls. For example, if you redefine `string.format` in Lua, calls to the new function appear identical to calls to the original function, right down to the generated bytecode.

The following Try It Out illustrates how you can use Lua to call a function written in a language like C.

Try It Out   Building a Diminutive Lua

In this exercise, you'll build an interpreter that includes Lua's core functionality, but excludes its standard libraries. The small size of the source code makes it a great introduction to embedding and extending Lua in your own applications. (These topics are discussed in more detail in Chapter 13.)

The Lua distribution includes a file called `min.c` in the `etc` directory. This file provides an excellent introduction to the way you can embed Lua into your own application and how you can create functions in C that can be called from Lua. Do one of the following, depending on the type of system you're using.

The makefile entry for this program is clearly oriented toward Unix-like platforms. However, instructions are given here for both Unix-like system users and Windows users.

If you've got a Unix-like system and have already built Lua successfully, follow these steps:

1. Navigate to the distribution's `etc` directory and execute the following command:

```
make min
```

This will result in the following three lines:

```
gcc -O2 -Wall -I../src min.c -L../src -llua -lm
echo 'print"Hello there!"' | ./a.out
Hello there!
```

2. Verify that this handles computations and errors correctly by typing the following commands shown in bold:

The # symbol is the shell prompt; it may appear differently on your system.

```
# echo 'print(1+2*3^4)' | ./a.out
163
# echo 'print(1++2)' | ./a.out
stdin:1: unexpected symbol near '+'
```

If you are using version 6 of the Visual C++ toolkit on the Windows platform, follow these steps:

1. Build `min.exe` by navigating to the `etc` subdirectory of the Lua source distribution and executing the following commands:

```
cl /MD /O2 /W3 /c /DLUA_BUILD_AS_DLL min.c
link /OUT:min.exe min.obj lua5.1.lib
```

2. Test the new scaled-down Lua interpreter by typing in the following commands shown in bold:

The > symbol is the shell prompt; it may appear differently on your system.

```
> echo print('Hello there!') | min.exe
Hello there!
> echo print(1+2*3/4) | min.exe
2.5
> echo print(1++2) | min.exe
stdin:1: unexpected symbol near '+'
```

If you encounter any problems building this program, be sure that the assumptions listed previously for application development on your system have been met.

How It Works

Examine the source code of `min.c`. At the top, the C library `stdio.h` header file is included to provide a prototype for `printf`. After this, the main Lua `lua.h` header file is included. It contains all of the information (including prototypes and definitions) that the C compiler needs to interface with Lua's core C API. Header information for Lua's auxiliary helper library is pulled in by including `lauxlib.h`. Double quotes are used to tell the preprocessor to look for the Lua header files first in the C file's directory and, failing this, in the standard header locations. The angle brackets indicate that the specified header file will be found in a standard location.

Skip to the function `main` at the bottom of `min.c`. The interaction with the Lua core begins with the call to `lua_open`. This function returns a pointer to an initialized record of type `lua_State`. This state pointer is used in all subsequent calls to the Lua core. The call to `lua_open` is balanced with a call to `lua_close` at the end of the program.

The `print` function defined in the middle of `min.c` is made available to Lua scripts with a call to `lua_register`:

```
lua_register(L,"print",print);
```

The arguments for this function, in the specified order, are as follows:

❑ The Lua state pointer originally returned by `lua_open`

❑ The name of the global variable that will be assigned the function

❑ The C function itself

In this case, the C function has the same name as its Lua counterpart, but this is not required.

The line below this contains the following statement:

```
luaL_dofile(L,NULL)
```

This auxiliary function loads the specified file and runs it in a protected environment. Here, the NULL argument specifies the standard input, which is why in this exercise, you piped the Lua scripts to the minimal interpreter.

Turn your attention to the `print` function in the middle of `min.c`. Its prototype is as follows:

```
static int print(lua_State *L)
```

Every function that you write in C to be called from Lua will look like this. It will receive a single argument — the Lua state pointer — and return an integer.

Given such a minimal argument list, how can a function know what was passed to it from Lua? How can it return values to Lua? The answer in both cases has to do with the Lua state pointer. With it, you can manipulate the Lua stack frame to find the arguments with which the function was called and to place values that will be returned to the caller.

Lua uses its own call stack to transfer values to and from functions, and to hold values for safekeeping during nested function calls. When a call to a C function is made from Lua, each argument in turn, from left to right, is placed on the stack and the stack count is incremented. This combination of stack operations is known as a *push*. A *pop* undoes the effect of a push — the topmost stack element is copied and the stack count is decremented.

The purpose of `print` in this minimal interpreter is much like it is in the full-featured Lua interpreter: to output a tab-delimited sequence of its arguments in textual form. It does this by first finding out the number of arguments passed to it, like this:

```
int n=lua_gettop(L);
```

This stack is one-based, so each argument can be visited in turn with an indexed loop ranging from 1 to the number n. Functions with names like `lua_isstring` and `lua_isboolean` are used to classify the arguments.

Throughout the loop, each argument is printed in turn. After the first, each argument is preceded with a tab character. After the loop, a newline is emitted.

Finally, print returns the value 0. This is the quantity of values that is returned to the caller of the print function. In addition to querying the stack for values, you can remove, add, and move elements. Values are returned by placing them at the top of the Lua stack and returning their quantity.

The pack Binary Structuring Library

Lua handles text as deftly as it handles numbers. Because strings can contain any byte value (which makes Lua what is known as *8-bit clean*), they can be safely used to hold binary data. You can use the string.byte and string.char functions to work with string elements at the byte level. However, many of the binary blocks that you work with comprise elements that are larger than a byte. Moreover, the way the bytes within these elements are ordered may not correspond to the way your computing hardware orders them. This is the so-called *endian* issue that has its roots in machine architecture. Sometimes binary blocks contain embedded strings. The length of a string might be fixed or variable, and if variable, the length might be placed as a byte or an integer value preceding the string, or the string might be terminated with a null byte. Some binary structures are relatively straightforward, while others may have optional or repeating components and subcomponents.

One of Lua's three authors, Luiz Henrique de Figueiredo, has written and released a number of libraries that extend Lua in many useful ways. One of these libraries, pack, enables you to read and write binary structures from within Lua scripts. To obtain the source code for this library, visit Luiz Henrique's homepage (www.tecgraf.puc-rio.br/~lhf/) and follow the link to his libraries. An informative page explaining how to build, install, and use his libraries is available. Download the package lpack.tar.gz for Lua 5 and place it in the location where you want to build it.

Many of the libraries in Luiz Henrique's collections are bindings that connect Lua to other libraries. For example, the PDF binding allows Lua to interface with PDFLib, a well-known library that is used to generate files in portable document format (PDF). The pack library, however, is a standalone module. All of its functionality is expressed in the lpack.c file.

Building the pack Library on Unix-type Systems

Follow these steps to build the pack module for Unix-type systems:

Skip ahead if you're working on the Windows platform.

1. Extract the tarball as follows:

```
tar xzvf lpack.tar.gz
```

2. Drop into the pack directory with the following command:

```
cd pack
```

3. Build the shared library with the following command:

This command assumes that you have built Lua and installed it using the makefile provided with Lua.

```
cc -ansi -pedantic -Wall -O2 -o pack.so -shared lpack.c
```

The compiler toolkit will locate the necessary header files and libraries in a standard location.

Building and Installing the pack Library on Windows

In this section, you'll compile the pack module for the Windows platform. Some of the steps are on the long side. As elsewhere in this book, if you see ⟲ symbol, it means that the line has been broken to fit on the page. However, when you type in a command that has been broken like this, you should join the fragments together on one line.

Follow these steps:

1. Extract the tarball as follows:

```
7z x lpack.tar.gz
7z x lpack.tar
del lpack.tar
```

2. Drop into the pack directory with the following command:

```
cd pack
```

3. Build the shared library with the following commands:

```
cl /c /W1 /Z1 /Zd /Yd /MD /DWIN32 lpack.c
link /dll /out:pack.dll /base:0x67400000 /machine:ix86 ⟲
/export:luaopen_pack lpack.obj lua5.1.lib msvcrt.lib
```

Testing the pack Library

After building a library, it's good policy to test it before installing it. You'll do that now, but there is one small wrinkle to explain. The pack library has been written so that it can be loaded directly without an intermediate .lua file. The commands used to build the pack library make use of this fact by making the base name of the shared library pack rather than lpack. Because of this, the loading script pack.lua that comes with the library is rendered unnecessary. To prevent it from being inadvertently loaded, rename this file from pack.lua to pack.lua.0 as follows:

1. On Unix-type systems, execute the following:

```
mv pack.lua pack.lua.0
```

Or on Windows, execute following:

```
ren pack.lua pack.lua.0
```

2. Override the value of `package.cpath` in the test command so that shared libraries are sought only in the current directory. On Unix-type systems, test the library as follows:

```
lua -e 'package.cpath="./?.so" require "pack" ⤵
print(string.pack("b3", 76, 117, 97))'
```

On Windows, run this command:

```
lua -e "package.cpath='./?.dll' require 'pack' ⤵
print(string.pack('b3', 76, 117, 97))"
```

If the library has been successfully built, the output should be as follows:

```
Lua
```

Installing the pack Library

To make the `pack` library accessible to Lua scripts on your system, copy `pack.so` or `pack.dll` to the Lua library directory as specified by the environment variable `LUA_DIR`. On Unix-like systems, execute the following:

```
cp pack.so $LUA_DIR/
```

On Windows, use this:

```
xcopy pack.dll "%LUA_DIR%\*.*"
```

Using the pack Library

The `pack` library is made available to your Lua script with the following line:

```
require("pack")
```

This introduces the new functions `string.pack` and `string.unpack`.

If the symbol `USE_GLOBALS` was defined when you compiled `lpack.c`, the global functions `bpack` and `bunpack` will be introduced instead. In this case, make the appropriate replacements to the examples that follow.

The `string.pack` function lets you construct a structured record from one or more elements. Its usage is as follows:

```
string.pack(format string, one or more arguments)
```

This returns a binary record, in the form of a Lua string, based on the format specifier and the string and number arguments that you pass it.

The `string.pack` function examines each character in the format specifier and takes the appropriate action. These actions fall into three categories:

❑ If the character is >, <, or =, the numeric conversions are set to big-endian, little-endian, or native-endian mode respectively. Examples of big-endian machines, in which the most significant byte is lower in memory, are Motorola 68K, Power PC, and Sparc. Network protocols typically require numbers to be big-endian. An example of a little-endian machine is the ubiquitous Intel x86, in which the least significant byte is lower in memory. The = character sets native-endian mode. This character is used to reset the numeric conversion mode back to its default in which a Lua number is converted to a form that is compatible with the underlying hardware. The conversion mode set by any of these three characters persists until another one of them occurs in the format specifier. The default is native-endian mode.

❑ If the character is A, a, b, c, d, f, h, H, i, I, l, L, n, p, P, or z, the next argument in the argument list is appended to the result string in a form that is specified by the letter. See the following table for the nature of the conversion for each of these characters. In general, the position of a letter in the format specifier corresponds to the position of the corresponding argument after the format specifier.

❑ If the character is a digit from 0 through 9, it and any digits after it are converted to an integer and applied as a repetition count for the preceding conversion code. For example, the H2b4 sequence" in a format specifier is equivalent to HHbbbb. A format specifier like this would be followed by six Lua numbers. The first two would be formatted as unsigned shorts and the remaining four would be formatted as bytes.

Format Code	Data Element Type
z	Null-(zero-)-terminated string
p	Byte-prefixed string
P	Word-prefixed string
a	size_t-prefixed string
A	String
f	Float
d	Double
n	Lua number
c	Character
b	Byte (unsigned char)
h	Short
H	Unsigned short
i	Integer
I	Unsigned integer
L	Long
L	Unsigned long

The string that `string.pack` returns is of little use within Lua. Generally, it is written to a file where it is to be used by some other application that understands its format. When you do write it to a file, make sure that the file is opened for writing in binary mode. This is neither required nor harmful on Unix-like systems, but it is imperative in Windows.

The function lets you deconstruct a structured binary record into one or more Lua strings and numbers. Its usage is as follows:

```
string.unpack(structure, format string, optional start position)
```

This returns the position just beyond the last byte read followed by the strings and numbers extracted from the specified structure.

Here is how the `string.unpack` function works. You first pass the binary structure (a Lua string from which primary elements are to be extracted) to it. Such a string will typically come from a file, and the usual caveats about reading the file in binary mode apply. Next, you include a format specifier string that, except for one small difference, is identical to the one used in `string.pack`. The difference is the meaning of an integer that follows the A code. Such a value indicates the length of the string to unpack rather than a repetition count. After this format specifier, you can then include a 1-based starting position. This is optional and is used to specify a position in the structure at which to start unpacking.

The `string.unpack` function returns a position followed by Lua strings and numbers that correspond positionally to codes in the format specifier. The first return value indicates the position just beyond the last byte read — the position at which the next call to `string.unpack` should start. This value turns out to be very useful in unpacking complex structures that contain repeating substructures. The remaining return values are structure elements that have been converted to Lua values.

Try It Out Unpacking the Lua Icon Header

The Lua source distribution comes with an icon file that contains small images of the Lua logo. It is located in the `etc` subdirectory and is named `lua.ico`. The icon file format contains little-endian numbers of various sizes and a repeating substructure, so it is a useful file for exercising the capabilities of `string.unpack`.

1. Save the following code to a file named `icotest.lua`. This script uses the `show` module you created in Chapter 7. If you use the version of `show` that was revised in an exercise at the end of that chapter to include a namespace, you need to change `ObjectShow` to `Object.Show`.

```
require "pack"
require "show"

local function LclFileGet(FileStr)
  local Str
  local Hnd, ErrStr = io.open(FileStr, "rb")
  if Hnd then
    Str = Hnd:read("*all")
    Hnd:close()
  end
  return Str, ErrStr
end
```

```
local FileStr = arg[1] or "../lua-5.1.1/etc/lua.ico"
local IcoStr, ErrStr = LclFileGet(FileStr)
if IcoStr then
  local Ico = {}
  local Pos
  Pos, Ico.Reserved, Ico.Type, Ico.Count = string.unpack(IcoStr, "<H3")
  Ico.List = {}
  for J = 1, Ico.Count do
    local Item = {}
    Pos, Item.Width, Item.Height, Item.ColorCount, Item.Reserved,
      Item.Planes, Item.BitCount, Item.Size, Item.Offset =
      string.unpack(IcoStr, "<b4H2L2", Pos)
    table.insert(Ico.List, Item)
  end
  Pos, Ico.HdrSize, Ico.Width, Ico.Height, Ico.Planes, Ico.Bitcount,
    Ico.Compression, Ico.ImageSize, Ico.XPixelsPerM, Ico.YPixelsPerM,
    Ico.ColorsUsed, Ico.ColorsImportant = string.unpack(IcoStr, "<L3H2L6", Pos)
  ObjectShow(Ico, "Ico")
else
  io.write(ErrStr, "\n")
end
```

2. As you can see by the `require("show")` line near the top, the script makes use of the `show` module introduced in Chapter 7. Invoke the script with the pathname of the icon file as an argument. For example, on a Unix-like system, execute the following command, adjusting the icon path if necessary:

```
lua icotest.lua /usr/local/src/lua-5.1.1/etc/lua.ico
```

This results in a display of the icon's header that looks like this:

```
["Ico"] table: 0x8070ee0 (n = 0)
  ["Bitcount"] 4
  ["ColorsImportant"] 0
  ["ColorsUsed"] 0
  ["Compression"] 0
  ["Count"] 2
  ["HdrSize"] 40
  ["Height"] 64
  ["ImageSize"] 512
  ["List"] table: 0x8070d88 (n = 2)
    [1] table: 0x8070f48 (n = 0)
      ["BitCount"] 0
      ["ColorCount"] 16
      ["Height"] 32
      ["Offset"] 38
      ["Planes"] 0
      ["Reserved"] 0
      ["Size"] 744
      ["Width"] 32
    [2] table: 0x8070f70 (n = 0)
      ["BitCount"] 0
      ["ColorCount"] 16
      ["Height"] 16
      ["Offset"] 782
```

```
        ["Planes"] 0
        ["Reserved"] 0
        ["Size"] 296
        ["Width"] 16
    ["Planes"] 1
    ["Reserved"] 0
    ["Type"] 1
    ["Width"] 32
    ["XPixelsPerM"] 0
    ["YPixelsPerM"] 0
```

How It Works

You can retrieve the details of the icon format from various sites on the Web. From a layout that identifies record elements and their data types and purpose, you have enough information to construct the format specifier and to give meaningful names to the result values. For example, the following line indicates that the first three elements are little-endian unsigned shorts:

```
Pos, Ico.Reserved, Ico.Type, Ico.Count = string.unpack(IcoStr, "<H3")
```

The first field is reserved, the second is an icon type code, and the third is the number of icons contained in the file. Notice that the results are assigned directly to associative table fields. This is generally a convenient way to keep the structure elements organized and accessible. Because there is no inherent order to associative table fields, however, any display of the contents will in general not match the order of the elements in the original data structure. Subsequent calls to `string.unpack` use the most recently returned position as the third argument. Doing so eliminates the need to manually count bytes in the structure.

If you use Lua to work with binary data of any kind, the `pack` library definitely belongs in your toolkit. Like Lua's regular expression functions that break apart plain text data, the use of `string.pack` and `string.unpack` becomes quite natural with a little familiarity.

The cURL File Transfer Library

The command line program cURL (a contraction of Client for URLs) is an extremely popular and portable tool for moving files around on the Internet using protocols such as http, https, ftp, and ftps. It hails from Sweden and is the work of hundreds of contributors, with Daniel Stenberg at the helm. One very nice feature of this program is that its core functionality is factored into a library that can be used by other applications as well. Additionally, the library has an interface that makes it conducive for use by scripting languages like Lua. Visit `curl.haxx.se` for more information on cURL.

Building libcurl

To use cURL from a Lua script, include the following line:

```
require("luacurl")
```

The `luacurl` module binds Lua to the main cURL library. This common arrangement involves a main library (`libcurl.dll` or `libcurl.so`) that provides functionality and a binding (which in this case is `luacurl.dll` or `luacurl.so`) that connects `lua` to the main library.

The cURL application and library are very popular, and it is quite possible that they are already installed on your system. You can check this by issuing the following command:

```
which curl
```

If `curl` is not found, you may be able to download it in the form of a package tailored to your particular platform. Doing so saves you the trouble of building cURL.

If you're going to build cURL, the first step is to make sure you've got a properly installed and up-to-date cURL library. One decision you'll need to make is whether you want support for file transfer protocols based on the secure sockets layer (SSL). Including SSL allows you to use the https and ftps protocols at the expense of more library dependencies and certificate management. The introduction in this chapter will not support SSL.

The `libcurl` library can use the OpenSSL, zlib, and OpenLDAP libraries if they are available. The cURL website can guide you to the websites where you can download these libraries if they are not already installed on your system.

Building libcurl on Unix-Like Systems

As is the case with many libraries, `libcurl` builds like a dream on Linux and friends. Obtain the tarball (`curl-7.15.4.tar.gz` is used here, but you'll want the most recent version if it has been updated) from `curl.haxx.se/download.html` and move it to the location where you want to build it. Then follow these steps:

1. Unpack it with the following command:

```
tar xzvf curl-7.15.4.tar.gz
```

Or if you are unpacking the bzipped package (with the extension `tar.bz2` instead of `tar.gz`), unpack it as follows:

```
tar xjvf curl-7.15.4.tar.gz
```

2. Drop down into the newly created directory:

```
cd curl-7.15.4
```

3. Build the makefiles with the following command:

```
./configure
```

4. Make the entire package with the following command"

```
make
```

5. As root, install the package as follows:

```
make install
```

6. Test the build with the following command:

```
curl -V
```

This should result in a short version and features report.

Building libcurl on Windows

Follow these steps to compile the cURL library:

An alternative that saves you the trouble of building the library is to download a precompiled package.

1. After downloading the most recent version of the cURL source package from `curl.haxx.se/download.html`, move it to the location where you will build it. If you are using the 7-zip utility, extract it as follows, adjusting the tarball name if you have a more recent version:

```
7z x curl-7.15.4.tar.gz
7z x curl-7.15.4.tar
```

The `.tar.gz` and `.tar` files may be deleted.

2. Navigate to the library source directory:

```
cd curl-7.15.4\lib
```

3. If you are using version 6 of Microsoft's Visual C++ software development kit, the makefile of interest is `Makefile.vc6` located in the `lib` subdirectory. Some small adjustments may need to be made to this file on your system. Look for the definition of `CFLAGS` and add the following text to the end of the line:

```
/Dsocklen_t=int
```

4. Locate the section that begins with the line:

```
# release-dll
```

5. A few lines below this, on the line that begins with `LNK`, remove the occurrence of `$(RTLIB)`. One line below this, on the line that begins with `CC`, add a space and `$(RTLIB)` following `$(CCNODBG)`.

6. Execute the following to build the dynamic-link library:

```
nmake -f Makefile.vc6 CFG=release-dll
```

This generates the dynamic-link library libcurl.dll and its associated `libcurl_imp.lib` import library. The library should compile without warnings except for a few messages like this after the link step:

```
File not found - libcurl.lib
0 File(s) copied
```

These may be safely ignored.

7. Issue the following command to copy `libcurl.dll` to a standard location where it will be found by Windows when needed:

```
xcopy libcurl.dll "%UTIL_DIR%\*.*"
```

8. Use the following command to copy the import library to a standard development directory where the linker will be able to find it:

```
xcopy libcurl_imp.lib "%SDK_DIR%\lib\usr\*.*"
```

9. Use the following command to copy the cURL header to a standard development directory where the compiler can find them:

```
xcopy ..\include\curl\*.h "%SDK_DIR%\include\usr\curl\*.*"
```

10. Buildthe command line cURL program, curl.exe, as follows:

```
cd ..\src
nmake -f Makefile.vc6 CFG=release-dll
```

11. Test the build with the following command:

```
.\curl -V
```

This should result in the following output:

```
curl 7.15.4 (i386-pc-win32) libcurl/7.15.4
Protocols: tftp ftp telnet dict ldap http file
Features: Largefile
```

12. Copy curl.exe to your utility directory as follows:

```
xcopy curl.exe "%UTIL_DIR%\*.*"
```

Building luacurl

The luacurl library is a binding that joins Lua to libcurl. It was created by Alexander Marinov and is available at the LuaForge website at luaforge.net.

Download the latest version of the luacurl source package and place it in the location where you intend to build it. The example shown here is for version 1.1 of the binding, so you'll need to make the changes to its name in the following instructions if you are building an updated version.

Building luacurl on Unix-Like Systems

Follow these steps:

1. Extract the zip file in the location where you will build it:

```
unzip luacurl-1.1.zip
```

2. Drop into the luacurl directory:

```
cd luacurl-1.1
```

3. Compile the library was follows:

```
cc -ansi -pedantic -Wall -O2 -o luacurl.so -shared luacurl.c -lcurl
```

4. Execute the following command to test whether the library can be loaded:

```
lua -e 'package.cpath="./?.so" require "luacurl" print(curl)'
```

5. The curl table identifier should be reported. If it is, copy luacurl.so to your Lua library directory:

```
cp luacurl.so $LUA_DIR/
```

Building luacurl on Windows

Follow these steps:

1. Extract the zip file in the location where you will build it:

```
7z x luacurl-1.1.zip
```

2. Drop into the `luacurl` directory:

```
cd luacurl-1.1
```

3. Compile the library as follows. These instructions will work if you are using Microsoft Visual C++ 6.0. Join the line ending with ⊃ with the fragment that follows it.

```
cl /c /W1 /Z1 /Zd /Yd /MD /DWIN32 luacurl.c
link /dll /base:0x68000000 /machine:ix86 /export:luaopen_luacurl ⊃
luacurl.obj lua5.1.lib msvcrt.lib libcurl_imp.lib
```

4. Execute the following command to make sure the library can be loaded:

```
lua -e "package.cpath='./?.dll' require 'luacurl' print(curl)"
```

5. The `curl` table identifier should be reported. If it is, copy `luacurl.dll` to your Lua library directory:

```
xcopy luacurl.dll "%LUA_DIR%\*.*"
```

Using luacurl

The `luacurl` binding provides file transfer capabilities to your Lua scripts by exposing functions from the cURL library. The documentation for `luacurl` is included in the source package as `luacurl.html`. Most of the library's functionality is encapsulated in the object that is returned from a call to `curl.new`. With this object, various options are set using the `setopt` method. These options specify details of the request. The documentation for cURL itself, located in the `docs` subdirectory of the `curl` source tree, has more information about these options. When these options are set, the actual request is made using the `perform` method.

Try It Out   **Retrieving a Web Document**

In this exercise, you will use `luacurl` to programmatically request a resource on the Web.

1. Save the following listing as `curltest.lua`:

```lua
require "luacurl"
require "show"

local FileStr = "test"
local SiteStr = "http://www.lua.org/"

local function LclWrite(FileHnd, BufStr)
  FileHnd:write(BufStr)
  return string.len(BufStr)
end
```

```
local function LclProgress(UserPrm, DownTotal, DownNow, UpTotal, UpNow)
    print(DownTotal, DownNow, UpTotal, UpNow)
end

local Hnd = curl.new()
if Hnd then
  local FileHnd = io.open(FileStr, "wb")
  if FileHnd then
    Hnd:setopt(curl.OPT_WRITEFUNCTION, LclWrite)
    Hnd:setopt(curl.OPT_WRITEDATA, FileHnd)
    Hnd:setopt(curl.OPT_PROGRESSFUNCTION, LclProgress)
    Hnd:setopt(curl.OPT_NOPROGRESS, false)
    Hnd:setopt(curl.OPT_BUFFERSIZE, 5000)
    Hnd:setopt(curl.OPT_HTTPHEADER, "Connection: Keep-Alive",
      "Accept-Language: en-us")
    Hnd:setopt(curl.OPT_URL, SiteStr)
    Hnd:setopt(curl.OPT_CONNECTTIMEOUT, 15)
    local R = { Hnd:perform() }
    ObjectShow(R, "perform")
    local Ok, ErrStr, RetCode = Hnd:perform()
    if Ok then
      io.write("Resource successfully saved as ", FileStr, "\n")
    else
      io.write("Error: ", ErrStr, " (", RetCode, ")\n")
    end
    FileHnd:close()
  else
    io.write("Error opening ", FileStr, "\n")
  end
  Hnd:close()
else
  io.write("Error instantiating curl object.\n")
end
```

2. Run the script with the Lua interpreter:

```
lua curltest.lua
```

This should result in the periodic printing of progress lines indicating the total size of the transfer and how much of it has been downloaded. Because the time needed to resolve the name of the web server is included in this progress, the first few notifications may indicate no transfer of content. The progress notification is done in a callback that could be used to drive a progress bar in an application.

How It Works

After requiring the `luacurl` module, some local variables are declared that identify the resource to be retrieved and the name with which to save it. Placing values like this near the top of a script can help make it a bit more convenient to modify later.

The `LclWrite` function is used as a *callback*, which is a function that is called by the library back into the script. In this case, it is called by `luacurl` when there is retrieved data to be written.

Beneath this is another callback. This one is called at intervals with arguments that indicate the number of bytes transferred and the number of bytes to be transferred.

This is followed by a call to `curl.new`, which is the function that creates a new transaction handle. If this succeeds, the returned value will not be `nil` and a new block is entered. Here, a file is opened in binary mode to save the resource to be downloaded. If the file is successfully opened, a number of options are set which modify how the request is to be made and handled. In this case, the two callbacks are registered. The `curl.OPT_WRITEDATA` option specifies the first parameter to the write callback. Here, the handle to the open file is passed. The cURL library merely passes this parameter back to the calling script without acting on it. This feature makes it easier to avoid global variables or the need to make a closure.

You can use the `curl.OPT_PROXY` option to make a web request through a proxy server. It should receive a string of the form `"http://proxyserver:8888"` where `proxyserver` and `8888` is the name and address of your proxy server and its port, respectively.

Even the address of the desired resource is conveyed to the cURL library by means of an option, in this case, `curl.OPT_URL`. There are dozens of other options, including timeout value, buffer size, and additional headers.

When all options have been set up, the actual request is made with a call to the `perform` method. This method returns `true` if the request succeeds, or `false` followed by a message and a result code if the request fails. Note that cURL considers the transaction a success if everything sent by the server is received. The returned page might, however, be a notification page indicating that the requested page could not be found or that some other error occurred at the server. You must examine the headers of the returned resource to determine that.

The cURL website, `curl.haxx.se`, contains a wealth of information on how the library can be used. In Chapter 16 you'll become familiar with LuaSocket, an alterative and more general package for network communication that was designed from the ground up to work with Lua.

The gd Graphics Library

The `gd` graphics library enables programs to noninteractively construct images in a number of formats. It has become a fixture on web servers around the world for dynamically generating web content at runtime, an example of which you will encounter in Chapter 15. The library was created by Thomas Boutell and is available from `www.boutell.com/gd`.

The notion of a graphics library that is entirely driven by program commands rather than through interactive use is a powerful one. As a programmer, you are accustomed to specifying in exact terms the steps needed to accomplish some goal. When applied to graphic generation, this skill can be leveraged to produce precise images repeatedly and automatically.

Building gd

The `gd` library makes use of a number of libraries for image formatting, font specification, and data compression. Meeting these library requirements on Unix-like systems is nothing out of the ordinary, but it can be a hardship on Windows. Consequently, the documentation for `gd` encourages developers on Windows to use the precompiled DLL and the related files it comes packaged with. That's the approach taken here.

Building gd on Unix-Like Systems

Before building gd, you should check to see if your system already has it. You can do this with the following command:

```
find / -name "libgd.*"
```

If you see lines like this, you've already got the gd library installed, and you can skip the building step:

```
/usr/local/lib/libgd.so.2.0.0
```

Even if the gd library is not present on your system, you may be able to install it as a package tailored for your platform.

Follow these steps to build gd:

1. Acquire gd-2.0.33.tar.gz from www.boutell.com/gd and place it in the location where you'll build it. Unpackage it with this:

```
tar xzvf gd-2.0.33.tar.gz
```

2. Drop into the newly-created directory like this:

```
cd gd-2.0.33
```

3. Take time to read the files README.TXT and INSTALL that are in this directory. They're short and explain library dependencies that may be relevant to your system. Assuming you've got the libraries you need, run the configure script as follows:

```
./configure
```

4. Compile and link the library by running this:

```
make
```

5. As root, install the library by running this:

```
make install
```

Installing gd on Windows

To install gd on Windows, follow these steps:

1. Download gdwin32.zip from www.boutell.com/gd and place it in the location where you'll unzip it. If you're using 7-zip, unpackage it as follows:

```
7z x gdwin32.zip
```

This extracts the zipfile's contents into a directory named gdwin32. Drop into that directory now by issuing this command:

```
cd gdwin32
```

The gd library is implemented in the bgd.dll file.

2. Copy that file to your utility directory like this:

```
xcopy bgd.dll "%UTIL_DIR%\*.*"
```

3. Assuming you're using version 6 of the Microsoft Visual C++ development kit, create and install the import library for this DLL as follows:

```
lib /machine:i386 /def:bgd.def
xcopy bgd.lib "%SDK_DIR%\lib\usr\*.*"
```

4. Install the header files as follows:

```
xcopy *.h "%SDK_DIR%\include\usr\*.*"
```

Building lua-gd

Alexandre Erwin Ittner has written a binding that allows the gd library to be used from Lua scripts. The following instructions use lua-gd-2.0.33r2.tar.gz. In the package name, the number to the left of the r corresponds to the gd library version, and the number to the right indicates the binding release version. If you are using an updated version, make sure it conforms to the gd library version you have installed.

Download the source tarball from lua-gd.luaforge.net and move it to location where you will build the library.

Building lua-gd on Unix-Like Systems

To build lua-gd on Unix-like systems, follow these steps:

1. Extract the package's contents as follows:

```
tar xzvf lua-gd-2.0.33r2.tar.gz
```

2. Change the working directory to this newly-created directory like this:

```
cd lua-gd-2.0.33r2
```

3. The luagd is built to match the functionality of the gd library. For example, if the gd library supports JPEG operations but not XPM operations, then the luagd library will provide bindings for JPEG but not XPM. In order to find out what libraries gd supports, run that library's configuration reporter, as follows:

```
gdlib-config --features --version
```

This should result in a report like this:

```
GD_JPEG GD_FREETYPE GD_PNG GD_GIF
2.0.33
```

4. Compile luagd as follows:

You may need to modify the symbol definitions to match the features of the gd library. Every feature shown in the previous output should be defined using the -D switch.

```
cc -ansi -pedantic -Wall -O2 -DGD_JPEG -DGD_PNG -DGD_FREETYPE ⤶
-DGD_GIF -o gd.so -lgd -shared luagd.c
```

5. Test the new library as follows:

```
lua -e 'package.cpath="./?.so"' test_features.lua
```

A report like this should be generated:

```
Lua-GD version: lua-gd 2.0.33r2
Lua-GD features:
    PNG support .................... Enabled
    GIF support .................... Enabled
    JPEG support ................... Enabled
    XPM/XBM support ................ Disabled
    FreeType support ............... Enabled
    Fontconfig support ............. Disabled
```

6. Copy gd.so to the Lua module directory with this command:

```
cp gd.so $LUA_DIR/
```

Building lua-gd on Windows

To build lua-gd on Windows, follow these steps:

1. Extract the package's contents as follows:

```
7z x lua-gd-2.0.33r2.tar.gz
7z x lua-gd-2.0.33r2.tar
```

You can now delete these files.

2. Jump into the newly created directory as follows:

```
cd lua-gd-2.0.33r2
```

3. Compile the library as follows:

```
cl /c /W1 /Z1 /Zd /Yd /MD /DWIN32 /DGD_PNG /DGD_GIF /DGD_FREETYPE ⊃
/DGD_JPEG /DGD_XPM /DGD_FONTCONFIG luagd.c

link /dll /out:gd.dll /base:0x67500000 /machine:ix86 ⊃
/export:luaopen_gd luagd.obj lua5.1.lib msvcrt.lib bgd.lib
```

4. Test the luagd library with the following command:

```
lua -e "package.cpath='./?.dll'" test_features.lua
```

The following report should be displayed:

```
Lua-GD version: lua-gd 2.0.33r2
Lua-GD features:
    PNG support .................... Enabled
    GIF support .................... Enabled
    JPEG support ................... Enabled
    XPM/XBM support ................ Enabled
    FreeType support ............... Enabled
    Fontconfig support ............. Enabled
```

5. If this test succeeds, install `luagd` as follows:

```
xcopy gd.dll "%LUA_DIR%\*.*"
```

Using lua-gd

The `demos` subdirectory of the `luagd` source package has an abundance of sample scripts that demonstrate the capabilities of the `gd` library and `luagd` binding. Most of the scripts end with a construction something like this:

```
im:png("out.png")
os.execute("display out.png")
```

That is, the `gd` library is called to create an image file, and then the system is called to display it. If this is appropriate for your system, no changes need to be made to the scripts. On Windows, however, you will likely need to modify the command submitted to `os.execute`. If you have a visual display program like IrfanView that is registered to display PNG files, then changing `display` to `start` is sufficient.

Now that you've installed the `gd` library and `luagd` module on your system, you'll use it in the following Try It Out to programmatically generate the Lua logo.

Try It Out　　Generating the Lua Logo

The Lua logo would have delighted Euclid. The center of the moon element is positioned at the corner of the bounding square of the planet, and its radius is based on metrics of this bounding square. The instructions to construct the logo are adapted from a sample script in Luiz Henrique de Figueiredo's PDF binding, with a friendly tip of the hat to its author and to Alexandre Nakonechnyj, the designer of the Lua logo.

1. Copy the following contents to a script named `lua-logo.lua`:

```
require "gd"

local Lcl = {}

local function LclWriteCtr(Hnd, X, Y, Clr, FontStr, PtSize, TextStr)
  local Ext = {gd.stringFT(nil, Clr, FontStr, PtSize, 0, 0, 0, TextStr)}
  Hnd:stringFT(Clr, FontStr, PtSize, 0, X - (Ext[3] - Ext[1]) / 2,
    Y + (Ext[4] - Ext[6]) / 2, TextStr)
end

Lcl.Size = 256
--Lcl.FontStr = "c:/windows/fonts/arial.ttf" -- Windows
Lcl.FontStr = "vera " -- Linux and friends
Lcl.Scale = 1 - math.sqrt(2) / 2
Lcl.RadiusLg = Lcl.Size / 3
Lcl.DiameterLg = 2 * Lcl.RadiusLg
Lcl.RadiusSm = Lcl.Scale * Lcl.RadiusLg
Lcl.DiameterSm = 2 * Lcl.RadiusSm
Lcl.CenterX = (Lcl.Size - Lcl.RadiusSm / 2) / 2
Lcl.CenterY = (Lcl.Size + Lcl.RadiusSm / 2) / 2
```

```
Hnd = gd.createTrueColor(Lcl.Size, Lcl.Size)
Lcl.White = Hnd:colorAllocate(255, 255, 255)
Lcl.Blue = Hnd:colorAllocate(32, 32, 128)
Lcl.Gray = Hnd:colorAllocate(192, 192, 192)
Lcl.Black = Hnd:colorAllocate(0, 0, 0)
Hnd:setAntiAliased(Lcl.Blue)
Hnd:filledRectangle(0, 0, Lcl.Size - 1, Lcl.Size - 1, Lcl.White)
-- Planet
Hnd:filledArc(Lcl.CenterX, Lcl.CenterY, Lcl.DiameterLg, Lcl.DiameterLg,
   0, 360, gd.ANTI_ALIASED, gd.ARC)
-- Moon
Hnd:filledArc(Lcl.CenterX + Lcl.RadiusLg, Lcl.CenterY - Lcl.RadiusLg,
   Lcl.DiameterSm, Lcl.DiameterSm, 0, 360, gd.ANTI_ALIASED, gd.ARC)
-- Moonshadow
Hnd:setAntiAliased(Lcl.White)
Hnd:filledArc(Lcl.CenterX + Lcl.RadiusLg - Lcl.DiameterSm,
   Lcl.CenterY - Lcl.RadiusLg + Lcl.DiameterSm,
   Lcl.DiameterSm, Lcl.DiameterSm, 0, 360, gd.ANTI_ALIASED, gd.ARC)
-- Orbit
Hnd:setAntiAliased(Lcl.Gray)
Hnd:arc(Lcl.CenterX, Lcl.CenterY,
   Lcl.DiameterLg + Lcl.DiameterSm, Lcl.DiameterLg + Lcl.DiameterSm, 0, 300,
   gd.ANTI_ALIASED, gd.ARC)
Hnd:arc(Lcl.CenterX, Lcl.CenterY,
   Lcl.DiameterLg + Lcl.DiameterSm, Lcl.DiameterLg + Lcl.DiameterSm, 330, 360,
   gd.ANTI_ALIASED, gd.ARC)
-- Text
LclWriteCtr(Hnd, Lcl.CenterX, Lcl.CenterY + Lcl.RadiusSm, Lcl.White,
   Lcl.FontStr, 48, "Lua")
Hnd:png("logo.png")
Hnd:gif("logo.gif")
Hnd:jpeg("logo.jpg", 90)
os.execute("start logo.png")
```

2. The font specification may need some adjustment on your system. On Windows, the full path of the Arial font is specified; on systems with Helvetica, use that instead. The gd library is generally successful in finding fonts without path information on Unix-type systems Also, depending on how you view PNG images, you may need to adjust the final line or remove it entirely.

3. To generate the logo, run the script with the Lua interpreter as follows:

```
lua lua-logo.lua
```

This will generate the file logo.png, which should look like Figure 12-3.

Figure 12-3

How It Works

Requiring the lua-gd module introduces the gd namespace to your script. A blank image is created by passing the width and height in pixels to the gd.createTrueColor function or the gd.createPalette function. These functions return an object that is used for subsequent image construction.

The origin for subsequent operations is the upper-left corner. X values increase to the right; Y values increase to the bottom. Units are measured in pixels. Arcs are drawn clockwise starting from the 3 o'clock position using degrees.

Colors need to be allocated using red, green and blue values ranging from 0 to 255. In the case of a palette image, the first color allocated becomes the background color. The stairstep appearance of nonvertical and nonhorizontal lines in the image can be mitigated by anti-aliasing, a technique which blends the boundary between different colors with appropriate shades. This feature is available only with truecolor images. To use it, call the setAntiAliased method with the color you will be using. Then, instead of specifying this color for a drawing operation, specify gd.ANTI_ALIASED.

The extent of a string is obtained using the same function used to render it on an image, namely the stringFT method. Instead of calling it as a method, however, it is called as an ordinary namespace function with the value nil instead of an image object. In this case, the coordinates of the bound rectangle are returned. Both the extent retrieval and text rendering are combined into a helper function named LclWriteCtr in this script.

The graphical drawing in this script is done with the filledRectangle, filledArc, and arc methods.

The gd library constructs the image using its own internal format. The actual file generation occurs with a call to png, pngEx, jpeg, gif, or gd2. These methods are not mutually exclusive — more than one can be called to generate copies in various destination formats. The last image type is the internal format of gd — it is not intended for use by other programs, but it can be useful when images will be subsequently processed by the gd library.

The gd library and lua-gd binding are well suited to many kinds of image production. In the next Try It Out, you use them to generate a graphical representation of a function's output.

Try It Out   Producing a Function Plot

In Chapter 11, a number of the math function summaries were accompanied by a graphical plot that was generated using gd and lua-gd. In this exercise, you specify a function that accepts a number and returns a correlated number. The Lua script creates and initializes a graphic object and uses it to plot the specified function over a range of values. The diagram is then saved as a PNG image.

1. With your text editor, create a new file with the following contents:

Depending on your platform, you may need to adjust the value of the FontStr field near the top of the script. In particular, you need to specify the full path of the directory in which fonts are stored.

```
require "gd"

local Cn = {
  -- FontStr = "c:/windows/fonts/arial.ttf",
  FontStr = "vera",
  Height = 1024,
  Margin = 12,
  PointSize = 36,
}

local function ImgInit()
  local Img = {}
  Img.Height = Cn.Height
  Img.Width = Img.Height * (1 + math.sqrt(5)) / 2
  Img.Hnd = gd.createTrueColor(Img.Width, Img.Height)
  Img.White = Img.Hnd:colorAllocate(255, 255, 255)
  Img.Black = Img.Hnd:colorAllocate(0, 0, 0)
  Img.Gray = Img.Hnd:colorAllocate(192, 192, 192)
  local Ext = {gd.stringFT(nil, Img.White,
    Cn.FontStr, Cn.PointSize, 0, Cn.Margin, Cn.Margin, "X")}
  Img.ChHt = Ext[2] - Ext[8]
  Img.Left = Cn.Margin
  Img.Right = Img.Width - Img.Left - 1
  Img.Top = Cn.Margin + Img.ChHt + Cn.Margin
  Img.Bottom = Img.Height - Img.Left - 1
  Img.Hnd:setAntiAliased(Img.Black)
  Img.Hnd:filledRectangle(0, 0, Img.Width - 1, Img.Height - 1, Img.White)
  Img.Hnd:rectangle(Img.Left, Img.Top, Img.Right, Img.Bottom, Img.Black)
  return Img
end

-- Write antialiased text. XAlign is "left", "center", or "right" and qualifies
-- X. YAlign is "top", "middle", or "bottom" and qualifies Y.

local function LclWrite(Img, X, XAlign, Y, YAlign, Clr, TextStr)
  local Lf, Bt, Rt, _, _, Tp = gd.stringFT(nil, Clr, Cn.FontStr,
    Cn.PointSize, 0, 0, 0, TextStr)
  local Wd = Rt - Lf
  X = XAlign == "center" and X - Wd / 2 or XAlign == "right" and X - Wd or X
  Y = YAlign == "middle" and Y + Img.ChHt / 2 or
```

```
        YAlign == "top" and Y + Img.ChHt or Y
    Img.Hnd:stringFT(Clr, Cn.FontStr, Cn.PointSize, 0, X, Y, TextStr)
end


-- Plot Y = Fnc(X) from X1 to X2. Disjoint is true if change in Y lifts pen.

local function Plot(Img, X1, Y1, X2, Y2, Fnc, TitleStr, Disjoint)
    -- Mapping functions
    -- X = Xm * H + Xb where H is horizontal pixel unit
    -- H = Hm * X + Hb
    -- Y = Fnc(X)
    -- V = Vm * Y + Vb where V is vertical pixel unit
    local Lift, X, Xm, Xb, V, Vm, Vb, Y, H, HPrv, VPrv, Ht, Wd,
        Hm, Hb, YPrv, BadVal
    Ht = Img.Bottom - Img.Top
    Wd = Img.Right - Img.Left
    Xm = (X2 - X1) / Wd
    Xb = X2 - Xm * Img.Right
    Hm = Wd / (X2 - X1)
    Hb = Img.Left - Hm * X1
    Vm = Ht / (Y1 - Y2)
    Vb = Img.Bottom - Vm * Y1

    LclWrite(Img, Cn.Margin, "left", Cn.Margin, "top", Img.Black, TitleStr)
    Img.Hnd:setClip(Img.Left, Img.Top, Img.Right, Img.Bottom)
    Img.Hnd:line(Img.Left + 1, Vb, Img.Right - 1, Vb, Img.Gray) -- Y = 0
    Img.Hnd:line(Hb, Img.Top + 1, Hb, Img.Bottom - 1, Img.Gray) -- X = 0
    BadVal = tostring(math.asin(2))
    Lift = true
    for H = Img.Left, Img.Right do
      X = Xm * H + Xb
      X = X < X1 and X1 or X > X2 and X2 or X -- Constrain sign at boundaries
      Y = Fnc(X)
      if tostring(Y) ~= BadVal then
        if Disjoint and Y ~= YPrv then
          Lift = true
        end
        YPrv = Y
        V = Vm * Y + Vb
        if Lift then
          Lift = false
        else
          if Y >= Y1 and Y <= Y2 then
            Img.Hnd:line(HPrv, VPrv, H, V, Img.Hnd.ANTI_ALIASED)
          end
        end
        VPrv = V
        HPrv = H
      end
    end
    LclWrite(Img, Img.Left + Cn.Margin, "left", Img.Bottom - Cn.Margin, "bottom",
      Img.Gray, "(" .. X1 .. ", " .. Y1 .. ")")
    LclWrite(Img, Img.Right - Cn.Margin, "right", Img.Top + Cn.Margin, "top",
      Img.Gray, "(" .. X2 .. ", " .. Y2 .. ")")
end
```

```
function Waveform(X)
   return math.sin(3*X) * math.sin(X/3)
end

local Img = ImgInit()
Plot(Img, -12, -1.2,  12, 1.2, Waveform, "Waveform")
Img.Hnd:png("waveform.png")
```

2. Save this file as plot.lua.

3. Run the script as follows:

```
lua plot.lua
```

An image file in PNG format named waveform.png will be generated, which is shown in Figure 12-4.

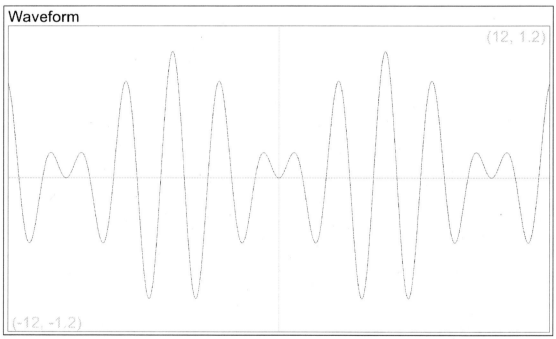

Figure 12-4

How It Works

The local table named Cn near the top of the script holds various constants that the script uses. Placing these values in one place makes it easier to make adjustments later if you need to modify the script's behavior.

The ImgInit function instantiates a graphic object using some of the specified constants. This is a general purpose routine that isn't bound to the plotting function called later in the script.

The `LclWrite` function is another general purpose routine. This one positions text in relation to a specified point. For example, you can render text so that it is centered horizontally on a point and positioned vertically just beneath the point.

The main function in the script is `Plot`. This function takes care of all the scaling and iterating needed to plot the function that you specify with an image object. As arguments, you specify the *domain* of the function (the allowable input values) and the *range* of the function (its output values). These are passed as endpoints. For example, in this script, the value for X1 indicates the low point at which the function is evaluated, and X2 indicates the high point. The main iteration begins with the following line:

```
for H = Img.Left, Img.Right do
```

This loop steps through the drawing region from the left side to the right. The block of the loop determines the input value that corresponds with the position and calls the passed-in function with this value. The value returned from the passed-in function is mapped to a vertical position, and a line is drawn to the previous point.

The `Waveform` function is a custom function that you pass to the `Plot` function for rendering. Experiment with different replacement functions, adjusting the values for X1, X2, Y1, and Y2 as needed.

The SQLite Database Library

There are Lua bindings to many relational databases systems. The one discussed here binds to SQLite, a fast and remarkably compact embeddable database engine that implements much of the SQL92 standard. SQLite is a trouble-free, dependable database system suitable for a wide spectrum of applications. It was created by D. Richard Hipp to fill a niche left vacant by large-scale relational database management systems, such as the need for serverless data management in which an application and its data can be moved together. Relational databases will be explored in more detail in Chapter 14.

Building SQLite3

The SQLite documentation, changelogs, source code comments, and rational version numbering all indicate an exemplary development environment. It is no surprise that SQLite compiles very nicely on a large number of platforms. The version covered here is 3.3.6 — if you're using an updated version, make the appropriate changes to these instructions.

Building SQLite3 on Unix-Like Systems

SQLite is a very popular system, and there is a good chance that it is already installed on your Unix-like system or that a package has been prepared for your platform that will expedite its installation. To see if it is already installed, issue the following command:

```
which sqlite3
```

If this results in a line that looks like the following, then SQLite is installed and you can dispense with the following building procedure:

```
/usr/local/bin/sqlite3
```

If SQLite is not installed, or you have an outdated version of SQLite, you should check to see if a package is available for your platform.

If you are going to build SQLite, start by downloading `sqlite-3.3.6.tar.gz` from `www.sqlite.org` and placing it in your source code development directory. Then do the following:

1. Extract it with the following command:

```
tar xzvf sqlite-3.3.6.tar.gz
```

2. Make the newly created directory your working directory as follows:

```
cd sqlite-3.3.6
```

3. Configure the makefiles as follows:

```
./configure
```

4. Compile the library and database shell like this:

```
make
```

5. As root, install SQLite as follows:

```
make install
```

Building SQLite3 on Windows

Developers on the Windows platform are provided a zip file called `sqlite-source-3_3_6.zip`, which contains preconfigured source code that simplifies the process of building SQLite. Download this zip file and then follow these steps:

1. Create a directory for building the package as follows:

```
mkdir sqlite-3.3.6
cd sqlite-3.3.6
```

2. Extract the contents of the zip file into this directory, replacing `path\to` with the directory where the zip file is located, as follows:

```
7z x path\to\sqlite-source-3_3_6.zip
```

3. Some files can be effectively removed from the build. Do this by renaming them like this:

```
ren os_os2.c os_os2.c0
ren os_unix.c os_unix.c0
ren tclsqlite.c tclsqlite.c0
```

4. A small modification to the SQLite shell source file needs to be made to address Microsoft's naming conventions. Open `shell.c` with your editor and locate the following line:

```
extern int isatty();
```

5. Above this line, insert the following preprocessor definitions:

```
#define isatty _isatty
#define fileno _fileno
#define access _access
```

Unfortunately, these definitions can't be made on the compiler command line because they would interfere with definitions in the header files.

6. Compile the files as follows:

```
cl /c /nologo /I. /Zl /Zd /Yd /MD /W0 *.c
```

7. Exclude `shell.obj` from being pulled into the SQLite DLL by renaming it like this:

```
ren shell.obj shell.o
```

8. Create the DLL and its import library as follows:

```
link /DLL /OUT:sqlite3.dll /BASE:0x66000000 /DEF:sqlite3.def *.obj msvcrt.lib
```

9. Install these products and the SQLite header file as follows:

```
xcopy sqlite3.dll "%UTIL_DIR%\*.*"
xcopy sqlite3.lib "%SDK_DIR%\lib\usr\*.*"
xcopy sqlite3.h "%SDK_DIR%\include\usr\*.*"
```

10. Build the SQLite shell like this:

```
link shell.o /OUT:sqlite3.exe sqlite3.lib msvcrt.lib
```

> The export definition file `sqlite3.def` **has been problematic in recent releases of the SQLite source package for Windows. In version 3.3.7, you need to add the** `sqlite3_enable_load_extension` **and** `sqlite3_load_extension` **symbols to the file before the DLL can be linked properly. In version 3.3.8, the export definition file is missing completely.**

11. Install the shell to your utility directory as follows:

```
xcopy sqlite3.exe "%UTIL_DIR%\*.*"
```

Building lua-sqlite3

Michael Roth has written a two-layer Lua binding to SQLite3. One layer, the backend, is written in C and serves as a *thin* binding to the SQLite API. This binding is thin in the sense that it doesn't add a lot of functionality to what is provided by SQLite. On top of this is the front-end layer. This is written in Lua and provides an interface that uses natural Lua expressions and capabilities. It permits query results to be read in a `for` loop, supports coroutines, and allows handlers to augment database operations.

Download `lua-sqlite3-0.4.1.tar.bz2` from the LuaForge site to the location where you will build it.

Building lua-sqlite3 on Unix-Like Systems

Follow these steps:

1. Extract the source package as follows:

```
tar xjvf lua-sqlite3-0.4.1.tar.bz2
```

2. Drop into the source directory like this:

```
cd lua-sqlite3-0.4.1
```

3. Configure the build process as follows:

```
./configure
```

4. Compile the shared library as follows:

```
make
```

5. Open the file `libluasqlite3-loader.lua` with a text editor, and locate the line that begins with the following:

```
local shared_lib_path =
```

6. Modify the line so that it points to the directory where you place Lua shared libraries. For example, if this directory is `/usr/local/lib/lua/5.1`, then change the line to the following:

```
local shared_lib_path = "/usr/local/lib/lua/5.1"
```

7. Save the file and exit the editor.

8. Install the package as follows:

```
cp *.so $LUA_DIR/
cp libluasqlite3-loader.lua $LUA_DIR/
cp sqlite3.lua $LUA_DIR/
```

Building lua-sqlite3 on Windows

1. Extract the source package as follows:

```
7z x lua-sqlite3-0.4.1.tar.bz2
7z x lua-sqlite3-0.4.1.tar
del lua-sqlite3-0.4.1.tar
```

2. Make the source directory the default working directory like this:

```
cd lua-sqlite3-0.4.1
```

3. Compile the dynamic-link library as follows:

```
cl /c /Z1 /Zd /Yd /MD /DWIN32 libluasqlite3.c

link /dll /base:0x67A00000 /machine:ix86 /export:luaopen_sqlite3 ↪
libluasqlite3.obj lua5.1.lib msvcrt.lib sqlite3.lib
```

4. Create a new file with the following contents. If the directory in which you place your Lua bindings is different from that shown, make the appropriate change.

The value of LibStr *is quoted using double brackets to ensure that the Microsoft-style path delimiters are treated literally.*

```
local LibStr = [[c:\program files\lua\5.1\libluasqlite3.dll]]
load_libluasqlite3 = assert(package.loadlib(LibStr, "luaopen_sqlite3"))
```

5.   Save this file as `libluasqlite3-loader.lua`.

6.   Install the package as follows:

```
xcopy *.dll "%LUA_DIR%\*.*"
xcopy libluasqlite3-loader.lua "%LUA_DIR%\*.*"
xcopy sqlite3.lua "%LUA_DIR%\*.*"
```

Using lua-sqlite3

The documentation for `lua-sqlite3` is named `documentation.html` and is located in the main directory of the source package. The documentation for SQLite, found at www.sqlite.org, is a very helpful source of information. Its pages on SQL language support, keywords, and *pragmas* provide a good introduction to using this database library. Pragmas are SQLite-specific commands that allow you to examine the details of a database and control the way SQLite operates.

If you are new to SQLite and `lua-sqlite3`, you'll find it helpful to initially include the `show` module that was developed in Chapter 7 in your scripts. The `ObjectShow` function can give you a thorough view of a function's return value. This can help you get your bearings when looking at query results.

Try It Out   **Providing a Database Standard Deviation Function**

The `lua-sqlite3` library lets you write functions that can be called from within SQL commands, including an *aggregate* function that returns one value for an entire series of database rows. The way that an aggregate function is registered to `lua-sqlite3` is elegant Lua. You register a function that itself returns two functions: a row-by-row function and a wrapup function. The advantage of this is that any variables that need to be shared between the two generated functions can do so by means of upvalues. This limits the scope of these variables to exactly the parties that need to access them.

As of version 3.3.6, SQLite doesn't have a built-in function to calculate the standard deviation of a series of numbers. This example fills that gap.

1.   Copy the following script to a file named `sqlstddev.lua`:

```
require "sqlite3"

local Cn = {}
Cn.DbStr = "test.db"
Cn.InitStr = [[
  BEGIN TRANSACTION;
  DROP TABLE IF EXISTS T3;
  CREATE TABLE T3(A);
  INSERT INTO T3 VALUES (12);
  INSERT INTO T3 VALUES (27);
  INSERT INTO T3 VALUES (32);
  INSERT INTO T3 VALUES (91);
  INSERT INTO T3 VALUES (79);
  INSERT INTO T3 VALUES (66);
  INSERT INTO T3 VALUES (40);
  INSERT INTO T3 VALUES ( 5);
  INSERT INTO T3 VALUES (53);
  END TRANSACTION;
]]
```

```
local function LclStdDev()
  local Sum, List = 0, {}

  local function LclStep(Val)
    if type(Val) == "number" then
      table.insert(List, Val)
      Sum = Sum + Val
    end
  end

  local function LclFinal(Count)
    local StdDev = 0
    Count = #List
    if Count > 1 then
      local SumDevSq = 0
      local Mean = Sum / Count
      for J, Val in ipairs(List) do
        local Dev = Val - Mean
        SumDevSq = SumDevSq + Dev * Dev
      end
      StdDev = math.sqrt(SumDevSq / (Count - 1))
    end
    return StdDev
  end

  return LclStep, LclFinal
end

local DbHnd, ErrStr = sqlite3.open(Cn.DbStr)
if DbHnd then
  if DbHnd:exec(Cn.InitStr) then
    DbHnd:set_aggregate("stddev", 1, LclStdDev)
    print(DbHnd:first_cols("SELECT STDDEV(A) FROM T3"))
  else
    io.write("Error initializing ", Cn.DbStr, "\n")
  end
  DbHnd:close()
else
  io.write("Error opening ", Cn.DbStr, ": ", tostring(ErrStr), "\n")
end
```

2. Run the script as follows:

```
lua sqlstddev.lua
```

This displays the following standard deviation:

```
29.546573405388
```

How It Works

This script initializes a table in the test.db database file. The file is created if it doesn't already exist. The T3 table is created, or effectively overwritten if it already exists, and is populated with a series of numbers.

The `LclStdDev` function is the *factory* function that produces the row-by-row function (`LclStep`) and the wrapup function (`LclFinal`). These two closures share a Lua table that holds each value submitted to `LclStep`. Also shared is a variable that holds the running sum of the values.

When all rows have been visited, the wrapup function is called. Here, the mean is calculated and, for each value in the series, the square of the deviation from this mean is summed. The variance is calculated by dividing this sum by the degrees of freedom in the sample. Finally, the square root of the variance, the standard deviation, is calculated and returned.

The `set_aggregate` method is used to register the aggregate function with the database instance. The first argument is the name of the function to be used case-insensitively in a query. The next argument specifies the number of arguments the row-by-row function is to be called with. The last argument is the factory function that generates the two closures. This function is not called with any arguments.

User functions can extend SQLite in many useful ways. If you find that you use certain extensions frequently, you can modularize them to promote their reusability and limit their scope. In this case, only a registration function that receives an open database handle need be exported from the module; everything else could be hidden inside it. The module would include the `LclStdDev` function and a line like the following, which registers the function with the specified database handle:

```
DbHnd:set_aggregate("stddev", 1, LclStdDev)
```

Summary

In this chapter, you learned about interfacing Lua with open source libraries. These libraries can be categorized as follows:

❑   Libraries that have nothing to do with Lua and everything to do with a particular functionality, such as the cURL, SQLite, and gd libraries.

❑   Libraries that provide a binding between Lua and another library, such as the `luacurl`, `lua-sqlite3`, and `lua-gd` libraries.

❑   Libraries that combine functionality with a Lua interface, such as the `pack` library.

You saw how a binding can expose a library's C API closely or, at the other end of the spectrum, through a layer of expressive Lua mechanisms such as iterators and objects.

By compiling and installing a small cross-section of libraries, you learned some techniques that can be applied to a large number of other open source libraries. Try your hand at the exercises that follow to stretch these techniques a bit.

If learning about how Lua can be extended with community libraries has stirred an interest in writing your own extensions in C, the next chapter will provide an introduction.

Exercises

1. The `lua-sqlite3` binding lets you register a function, including one that can receive multiple arguments that can be called within a database query. Use this feature to provide a format function for SQLite results. Name the function `format`. It should receive a format string followed by a variable number of arguments to be formatted, very much like `string.format` (hint, hint). And just like `string.format` (hint, hint), it should return one value, the formatted string. An example of its usage is as follows:

    ```
    print(DbHnd:first_cols("SELECT FORMAT('%05d %05d', 12, 34)"))
    ```

    This should return the following:

    ```
    00012 00034
    ```

    The example shows FORMAT receiving fixed arguments, but ordinary database expressions are supported too. Note that the second argument to the `set_function` method can be -1 to indicate that the registered function can receive multiple arguments.

2. A PNG image file is made up of a signature string followed by a *chunk*, which is a variable length data structure that follows a relatively simple format. All numbers in a PNG file are big-endian. The signature is made up of the following eight bytes, shown here in decimal:

    ```
    137, 80, 78, 71, 13, 10, 26, 10
    ```

    The `string.char` function is useful for constructing strings from lists like this one.

    Each chunk has the following layout:

    ```
    Data length: unsigned long integer
    Chunk header: four character string
    Data: <Data length> bytes
    CRC: unsigned long integer
    ```

    CRC stands for Cyclic Redundancy Check, a standard hash checksum of data. In this case, it covers the chunk header and data, but not the data length field.

    Chunks can come in any order, except that chunks with the IHDR and IEND headers are first and last respectively.

    Write a script that steps through each chunk of a PNG file and prints a listing that shows the header, data length and CRC values. A chunk summary for the Lua logo that was constructed in the `gd` library discussion looks like this:

    ```
    Header Length  CRC
    ------ ------  ----------
    IHDR       13  0xD3103F31
    IDAT     4867  0xF5459E04
    IEND        0  0xAE426082
    ```

    Remember to open the PNG file in binary mode to prevent problems on Windows.

    Because the data length field does not immediately precede the data field, you will need to make two calls to `string.unpack` for every chunk. The first will pick up the chunk's data length and header fields, and the second will pick up the CRC field. You don't need to read the data field for the purposes of this exercise.

Interfacing Lua with Other Languages

Lua has a flexible mechanism for binding to program elements written in languages other than Lua. As you saw in the preceding chapter, functions in libraries written in C can be made available to your Lua programs through Lua's C application programming interface (C API or simply API). In this chapter, you delve a little deeper into this interface and learn the basics of writing routines in C that can be used in conjunction with Lua. This includes the following:

- ❏ Embedding Lua in an application
- ❏ Extending Lua with C functions
- ❏ Manipulating the virtual stack in C
- ❏ Passing values between Lua and C
- ❏ Storing Lua values in C
- ❏ Guarding against errors in your C code
- ❏ Structuring the binding layer

Although the focus in this chapter is the C programming language, most mainstream implementations of compiled languages like C++ and Pascal are compatible with the C calling convention — these languages work fine with Lua. In this chapter, references to C programs and libraries are intended to include those that are written in other compatible languages as well.

If you are unfamiliar with C, take a moment to skim through some of the C examples. It should provide ample grounds for appreciating the clean, readable syntax of Lua.

How C Programs Use Lua

Lua's C API can be used both by a host application that *embeds* Lua and by libraries that *extend* Lua. The distinction between these two ways of using Lua can be blurred somewhat because a host application often provides its own functions to extend Lua, and extension libraries can contain their own independent Lua instances. Nevertheless, understanding the distinction can help you make the right design decisions when developing your applications.

Embedding Lua

Lua is packaged as a library. It doesn't include a `main` function (the entry point of a C application) and can't run apart from a host application. The standalone Lua interpreter that you use throughout this book is one such host application. It has a relatively small main source file that uses Lua's API but doesn't itself add anything to the Lua core. In this way, it embeds Lua. Its job is to manage the way scripts are submitted to Lua — either interactively or noninteractively — and the way Lua's output is delivered.

The distinguishing hallmark of an embedding application is that it calls `lua_open` to create and initialize a Lua state. If this function succeeds, it returns a pointer to the newly created state structure. This pointer is used as the first argument to all other functions in the API. When an embedding application is finished running Lua scripts with a particular state, it finalizes and destroys the state by calling `lua_close`.

Extending Lua

The Lua API supports the extension of a Lua state by allowing C functions to be called from scripts. There are two basic ways this can happen:

❑   An embedding application can register extension functions directly.

❑   A running script can, usually with a call to `require`, load and transfer control to a C library that in turn registers its extension functions.

In both cases, the Lua state that is extended is already active in the context of a host application.

Embedding or Extending: Which Is Best?

If you're developing a library that will perform services for an application, you'll be extending Lua. If, however, you're developing an application, you've got a choice between embedding Lua and extending it. A number of factors have a bearing on which path you choose, including the following:

❑   Will your program use Lua only intermittently, for example, to run user-provided helper scripts or to interpret a configuration script?

❑   Does your application need to modify the behavior of the standalone Lua interpreter, for example, to specify which libraries are loaded or which functions are present within a library?

❑   Does your application run in a special environment, such as one that doesn't support dynamic linking of libraries?

If none of these characteristics apply to your application, there are compelling reasons for you to configure it as an extension library. Doing so preserves Lua's flexibility and modularity to the greatest extent, which often leads to serendipitous opportunities for your program to interoperate with other libraries, and will conform to standard usage patterns that developers expect when working with your application. Designing, or redesigning, your application as a library can require a fair amount of effort up front, especially with regard to initialization and finalization sequences and event handling. But after the initial work is done, libraries are generally no harder to maintain than an embedding application.

The standalone Lua interpreter needs to be modified to work well with some platforms. For example, programs that use the Windows graphical user interface don't have a main function and don't, by default, handle standard streams in the expected manner. If you develop for a platform like this, your best choice may be to write your own embedding application, but preserve the behavior of the standalone Lua interpreter as much as possible. Resist the temptation to put application-specific code into the interpreter — usually, this is best placed in a library.

A case for embedding Lua applies to programs like the Zeus programmer's editor. Here, Zeus is an already self-contained application and Lua is used to run scripts provided by end users to automate tasks. Another case is the Plua application for Palm devices, which you will explore in Chapter 18. The Palm OS has certain restrictions that prevent a standard Lua interpreter from being installed.

Communicating Between Lua and C

In the previous chapter, you compiled a minimal interpreter from min.c found in the etc subdirectory of the Lua source package. When doing that, you saw that a C function needs to conform to a certain prototype to be callable from Lua. This prototype is specified in the following declaration within Lua's principal header file, lua.h:

```
typedef int (*lua_CFunction) (lua_State *L);
```

.A C function of type lua_CFunction can be either of the following:

❑   A *loader function*, which is exported from a library and called by Lua when the library is loaded

❑   An *extension function*, which is registered with a Lua state so that it can be called like any other Lua function

After an extension function is registered, the function can be called from a Lua program or, using the Lua API, from within C. Within the Lua program, the function is indistinguishable from one written completely in Lua.

In Chapter 3, you became familiar with the call stack used by Lua. A C extension or loader function has a similar runtime structure — the virtual stack — available to it through the Lua API. When the C function is first called, this stack is empty except for any arguments that were passed to the function from Lua. The leftmost argument passed occupies position one in the stack. This stack can contain values of any Lua type, including nil. It is used to manage operations such as setting up Lua function calls, accessing and manipulating tables, and returning values to the caller.

The proper use of the virtual stack is one of the keys to writing a Lua extension in C. The stack is of limited size, so when you're using deeply recursive routines, you may need to lengthen it with the lua_checkstack function. More typically, you need to take care not to inadvertently fill up the stack with temporary values that should have been removed after use.

High-level programming languages like Lua and C handle stack operations transparently. When it comes to interfacing Lua and C, however, you'll have to be aware of the virtual stack and what it looks like at each statement. You should get in the habit of writing stack snapshots in the form of single-line comments. For example, the following comment indicates that you expect a table and a string to occupy positions one and two of the stack:

```
// Stk: Tbl? Str?
```

When a verification has been made, for example with the `lua_istable` function, the question mark of the verified value can be removed as follows:

```
// Stk: Tbl Str?
```

Often, you'll have a deeply occupied stack, or will write a helper function, and will be concerned only with the top of the stack. Lua facilitates stack access in these situations by letting you use a negative index to effectively count from the top of the stack. When using negative indexes, index -1 refers to the topmost item, index -2 the second from top item, and so on. Three consecutive dots can be used in a stack diagram to denote the presence of zero or more stack items that will be preserved in the current set of statements. Here's an example:

```
// Stk: ... TitleStr MsgStr
```

In this example, index -1 refers to the message string, and index -2 refers to the title string. The objective of these diagrams is to help the programmer keep the stack in balance and to keep track of positions. Some operations such as manipulating table fields in a loop can generate quite a lot of stack activity, and in these cases, any technique that helps you monitor where values are on the stack is of some value.

Returning values to the caller occurs with the virtual stack. You use the Lua API to place the return values at the top of the stack, with the rightmost value occupying the top position. You do not need to clear the stack before setting this up. Lua handles all items beneath the return values on the stack properly. The integer value that is returned by the C extension function is used by Lua to determine the number of Lua values to return to the caller. For example, suppose you want to return two values — nil and an error message — to the caller of your extension function. Assume that the stack already contains a number and a table in its topmost positions. The following code fragment accomplishes this:

```
// Stk: Id NameTbl
lua_pushnil(L);
// Stk: Id NameTbl nil
lua_pushfstring(L, "Error locating user %d", Id);
// Stk: Id NameTbl nil ErrStr
return 2;
```

Stack diagrams make handling multiple return values properly somewhat easier. This is especially the case when different sets of values are conditionally returned.

In addition to the customary push and pop functions, Lua provides functions for removing, replacing, inserting, copying, and retrieving values on the stack at any valid position.

You may want to explore the use of tools that can automatically generate bindings from specially marked up C or C++. For example, SWIG (www.swig.org) processes a specially prepared interface file and generates a source file that is linked to your application.

Try It Out   **Stacking Gymnastics**

In this exercise, you create a C extension function that does the following:

❑   Receives zero or more integers as arguments

❑   Verifies that each argument is an integer

❑   Juggles some of these values using the Lua API and, after each maneuver, prints a diagram of
     the stack

❑   Returns some values

In addition to exploring various stack operations, this library illustrates the essential framework of an
extension module written in C.

1.   Create a new C file with the following contents:

```
#include "lua.h"
#include "lualib.h"
#include "lauxlib.h"
#include <stdio.h>

#define STACKOP(Code) (Code), LclStackPrint(L, #Code)

/* * */

static void LclStackPrint(
   lua_State *L,
   const char * Str)

{ // LclStackPrint
   int J, Top;

   printf("%-26s [", Str);
   Top = lua_gettop(L);
   for (J = 1; J <= Top; J++) {
     if (lua_isnil(L, J)) printf(" - ");
     else printf(" %d ", lua_tointeger(L, J));
   } // J
   printf("]\n");
} // LclStackPrint

/* * */

static int LclStackLook(
   lua_State *L)

   // three integers <- stack.look(zero or more integers)

{ // LclStackLook
   int J, Top;

   for (J = 1, Top = lua_gettop(L); J <= Top; J++)
```

```
            luaL_checkinteger(L, J);
       LclStackPrint(L, "Initial stack");
       STACKOP(lua_settop(L, 3));
       STACKOP(lua_settop(L, 5));
       STACKOP(lua_pushinteger(L, 5));
       STACKOP(lua_pushinteger(L, 4));
       STACKOP(lua_replace(L, -4));
       STACKOP(lua_replace(L, 5));
       STACKOP(lua_remove(L, 3));
       STACKOP(lua_pushinteger(L, 3));
       STACKOP(lua_insert(L, -3));
       STACKOP(lua_pushvalue(L, 2));
       STACKOP(lua_pop(L, 1));
       return 3;
     } // LclStackLook


     /* * */

     int luaopen_stacklook(
       lua_State *L)

     { // luaopen_stacklook
       static const luaL_reg Map[] = {
          {"look",  LclStackLook},
          {NULL, NULL}
       };

       luaL_register(L, "stack", Map);
       return 1;
     } // luaopen_stacklook
```

2. Save the file as `stacklook.c`.

3. Compile the file into a shared library. On Linux and other Unix-type systems, run the following:

```
cc -o stacklook.so -shared -Wall stacklook.c
```

On Windows, run the following:

```
cl /c /Z1 /Zd /Yd /MD /W4 /DWIN32 stacklook.c
link /dll /out:stacklook.dll /base:0x68100000 /machine:ix86 ⤶
  /export:luaopen_stacklook stacklook.obj msvcrt.lib lua5.1.lib
```

4. With your editor, create a new Lua file with the following contents:

```
package.cpath = "./?.so;./?.dll"
require "stacklook"

print("stack.look", stack.look(1, 2, 3, 4, 5, 6, 7))
```

5. Save it as `look.lua`.

6. Run this script with the standalone Lua interpreter, as follows:

```
lua look.lua
```

The output is this:

```
Initial stack              [ 1  2  3  4  5  6  7 ]
lua_settop(L, 3)           [ 1  2  3 ]
lua_settop(L, 5)           [ 1  2  3  -  - ]
lua_pushinteger(L, 5)      [ 1  2  3  -  -  5 ]
lua_pushinteger(L, 4)      [ 1  2  3  -  -  5  4 ]
lua_replace(L, -4)         [ 1  2  3  4  -  5 ]
lua_replace(L, 5)          [ 1  2  3  4  5 ]
lua_remove(L, 3)           [ 1  2  4  5 ]
lua_pushinteger(L, 3)      [ 1  2  4  5  3 ]
lua_insert(L, -3)          [ 1  2  3  4  5 ]
lua_pushvalue(L, 2)        [ 1  2  3  4  5  2 ]
lua_pop(L, 1)              [ 1  2  3  4  5 ]
stack.look        3        4        5
```

How It Works

The sequence of steps taken when this script is run follows a pattern that is common to many extension libraries.

This is the first line to be executed in the script:

```
package.cpath = "./?.so;./?.dll"
```

It restricts Lua's search for C libraries to the current directory. This is appropriate here because, as a demonstration, the stacklook library won't be copied to the Lua library directory.

The next line engages Lua's package system to search for and load the stacklook module:

```
require "stacklook"
```

The steps taken here are summarized in Chapter 7.

Lua joins the string luaopen_ with the name of the module and calls the function with that name in the loaded library, passing it a pointer to the active Lua state. Here, the function luaopen_stacklook is called. That function must be visible to Lua when it links with the library. When linking the dynamic link library on Windows, the following switch is used to satisfy this requirement:

```
/export:luaopen_stacklook
```

Notice that luaopen_stacklook receives only the state pointer as an argument. When a C function is called by Lua (either a loader function like this one, or a C extension function), it receives arguments that were passed to it on the virtual stack.

The luaopen_stacklook function is where the extension function LclStackLook is registered with Lua. This can be done in a number of ways, but a standard way of doing it is to use luaL_register. This function places the extension functions you specify into a namespace table and associates them with the names you want them to have in Lua. The current program uses it as follows:

```
luaL_register(L, "stack", Map);
```

As always with Lua API functions other than lua_open, the Lua state pointer is passed as the first argument. The convention of naming this pointer L is used here. The second argument is the name of the table to use as a namespace. In this case, stack is used. If a name is specified that doesn't identify a table and isn't a key in the package.loaded table, a new table with the specified name will be created. Alternatively, you can arrange to place a table at the top of the stack using the Lua API and specify NULL for this argument, in which case the table will be used. The third and last argument is the address of an array of records of type luaL_Reg. Records of this type pair a name with an extension function. The last element in this array must contain NULL values to mark the end of the array. In this case, the array is named Map and contains only two elements: the record that pairs the function LclStackLook with the name "look", and the terminating record. The call to luaL_register associates stack.look with the C function LclStackLook and leaves the stack table at the top of the stack.

The following line indicates that luaopen_stacklook is to return the virtual stack's topmost value, that is, the stack table, as the return value from require:

```
return 1;
```

If luaopen_stacklook returned 0 instead, then require would have returned nothing.

After luaopen_stacklook returns, control is transferred back to look.lua. The next line to be executed is as follows:

```
print("stack.look", stack.look(1, 2, 3, 4, 5, 6, 7))
```

This function calls stack.look with a number of integer arguments and prints the values that this function returns. Nothing in this setup makes a distinction between a C function and a Lua function — that's a detail that the Lua engine takes care of. Like every C extension function, LclStackLook is called with the single state pointer argument and a new virtual stack containing the passed arguments.

When stack.look is called, control is transferred back to the C library, this time to the function LclStackLook. The first operation it performs is to verify the passed-in arguments:

```
for (J = 1, Top = lua_gettop(L); J <= Top; J++)
   luaL_checkinteger(L, J);
```

Like all Lua functions that begin with luaL_, the luaL_checkinteger function is an auxiliary function — it is not part of the formal API but a helper function that uses API functions. And like all Lua functions that begin with luaL_check, this function verifies some characteristic about the virtual stack. In this particular case, a check is made to verify that each argument is an integer. If it is, the integer is returned (and ignored in this case); otherwise, an error is generated.

The effect of the various stack functions should be clear from the program output. The lua_settop function lets you specify the number of values on the stack. As shown in the first two lua_settop calls, reducing the stack top effectively clears the truncated values. These can't be recovered by increasing the stack top. The functions beginning with lua_push increase the top position by one and place the specified value in that location. The lua_replace function moves the top value to another position, overwriting the value currently in that location. The lua_insert function is similar, except that room for the moved value is made by moving every item above it up by one. To remove one or more items from the top of the stack, call lua_pop. To remove an item from a specified location in the stack, call lua_remove.

The following line indicates that three values are to be returned from `stack.look`, with the topmost value on the stack corresponding to the rightmost value returned:

```
return 3;
```

Just like the loader function, an extension function returns values to Lua on the virtual stack. The integer return value of the C function indicates the number of items at the top of the stack that will be transferred as return values to the Lua function.

Calling Lua from C

A function written in Lua or one written in C and registered with a Lua state is a Lua value of type *function*. As such, it can be managed on the stack like any other Lua value.

Obtaining a Lua Function

You can place a function value on the virtual stack in a number of ways, including the following:

- ❑ Pass a function as an argument to a C function
- ❑ Retrieve a function from a global variable or namespace table
- ❑ Create a function from C code using the `lua_pushcfunction` or `lua_pushcclosure` functions
- ❑ Load some Lua code as a chunk using the `lua_load`, `luaL_loadstring` or `luaL_loadfile` functions

Calling a Lua Function

To call a Lua function, do the following:

1. Push the function on the stack.

2. Push the arguments to the function, left to right, on the stack.

3. Call `lua_call` with the state pointer, the number of arguments you have just pushed, and the number of results to receive from the called function.

The following example assumes that a function like the following is located at position 1 on the stack:

```
local function MouseClick(X, Y, Button)
  print("Mouse click", X, Y, Button)
end
```

This would be the case if, for example, the function was passed as the first argument to a C function. For example:

```
// Stk: ...
lua_pushvalue(L, 1);
// Stk: ... Fnc
lua_pushinteger(L, X);
```

```
// Stk: ... Fnc X
lua_pushinteger(L, Y);
// Stk: ... Fnc X Y
lua_pushstring(L, Btn == 1 ? "left" : Btn == 2 ? "right" : "middle");
// Stk: ... Fnc X Y BtnStr
lua_call(L, 3, 0);
// Stk: ...
```

When `lua_call` is called, the arguments and the function are popped from the stack. Any values that are returned from the function are adjusted to the specified result count and pushed on the stack. In this example, the result count is zero, so any values that the called function returns will be thrown away. If a result count is specified that is greater than the number of values actually returned, `nils` are pushed to take up the slack. If you want to receive as many values as the function returns, specify `LUA_MULTRET` for the result count. If you do this, you'll want to call `lua_gettop` before you push the function and again after the function returns to ascertain the number actually returned.

Protected Calls

You can call a Lua function in protected mode — in other words, call the function and handle the error if one is generated. For this, use the `lua_pcall` function. This function is like `lua_call` except that it returns a status code and has an additional argument: the location on the stack of an error handler. The return code is zero if the function succeeds. In this case, the return values will be pushed just as `lua_call` would do. If an error occurs, `LUA_ERRRUN`, `LUA_ERRMEM`, or `LUA_ERRERR` will be returned, and only a single error message will be pushed on the stack, regardless of the value specified for the result count.

The error handler is a function that will be called when an error occurs, before the stack has been truncated to its state as of the call to `lua_pcall`. It receives as its single argument an error message, and returns a single value: the revised error message. Typically, an error handler will call on the services of `debug.traceback` to augment the error message with stack information. To avoid having an error handler called, specify 0 for its stack location. Otherwise, you need to arrange to have the error handler placed on the stack so you can specify its position when calling `lua_pcall`.

Here's an example of making a protected call. It is assumed that the function to call is located at position 1, and that `debug.traceback` has been placed in position 2.

```
// Stk: ...
lua_pushvalue(L, 1);
// Stk: ... Fnc
lua_pushinteger(L, X);
// Stk: ... Fnc X
lua_pushinteger(L, Y);
// Stk: ... Fnc X Y
lua_pushstring(L, Btn == 1 ? "left" : Btn == 2 ? "right" : "middle");
// Stk: ... Fnc X Y BtnStr
Code = lua_pcall(L, 3, 0, 2);
if (Code) {
  // Stk: ... ErrStr
  printf("%s occurred.\n%s\n",
    Code == LUA_ERRRUN ? "A runtime error" :
    Code == LUA_ERRMEM ? "A memory error" : "An error handling error",
```

```
      lua_tostring(L, -1));
    lua_pop(L, 1);
    // Stk: ...
  } // if
  // Stk: ...
```

Now, when the following Lua function from the preceding example is called:

```
local function MouseClick(X, Y, Button)
  print("Mouse click", X, Y, Button)
  error("Intentionally generated error")
end
```

it produces output like this:

```
Mouse click  245  168  right
A runtime error occurred.
test.lua:7: Intentionally generated error
stack traceback:
  [C]: in function 'error'
  test.lua:7: in function <test.lua:5>
  [C]: in function 'run'
  test.lua:11: in main chunk
  [C]: ?
```

Lua takes care of cleaning up items on the stack left after an error, just as it does when no errors occur.

Working with Userdata

The *userdata* basic type maps to memory that is only accessible in C. In fact, unless the userdata has been extended with metatables, all a Lua script can do with one is to assign it to a variable and to check whether it is identical to another variable. From within C, the lua_touserdata function is used to retrieve the pointer associated with the userdata.

Userdata comes in two varieties: light and full. A low-calorie userdata is created with the lua_push lightuserdata function. It simply maps the new userdata to a pointer that you provide to the API — Lua does not allocate any memory for it and won't allow you to extend it with metatables. A full userdata is much more useful for the purposes of an extension library. You create it with a call to lua_newuserdata, passing it the obligatory state pointer and the size of the memory you want to have allocated. Always use the C program's sizeof operator to specify the size of the record you'll associate with the userdata. The calling C program receives the address of the full userdata, and the userdata value is pushed on the virtual stack.

Metatables are used both to define operations for a userdata and to classify it as an instance of a particular user-defined type. For example, if you use a full userdata to encapsulate a printer connection, you'll want to provide relevant methods that can be called from Lua. Furthermore, you don't want to confuse a printer userdata with a database userdata. Lua's auxiliary library helps by letting you give a name to the user-defined type, such as printer. You can create a metatable for this purpose with the luaL_newmetatable function. A good place to create a metatable is in an extension library's loader function. It's also convenient to set the metatable's __index metamethod to the metatable itself. This way, you can use luaL_register to register any methods you want to associate with the user-defined type directly in the metatable.

The __gc garbage collection metamethod is a particularly useful mechanism for cleaning up the resources that a userdata may have open in C. Where appropriate, it is good practice to provide a close method for your userdata types. However, the close method may not have been called when the userdata is collected as garbage. You can check for this condition in the __gc metamethod and finalize resources if necessary.

Try It Out   The Life and Times of a Userdata

This exercise implements some of a userdata's rites of passage from cradle to grave, including its creation, association with a metatable, access from Lua, and destruction.

1. Create a new C file with the following contents:

```c
#include "lua.h"
#include "lualib.h"
#include "lauxlib.h"
#include <stdio.h>

#define CnExampleStr "example"

typedef struct {
    int Val;
    int Open;
} ExampleType, * ExamplePtrType;

/* * */

static ExamplePtrType LclExamplePtrGet(
    lua_State *L,
    int StkPos)

    /* Returns example pointer if value at position StkPos is valid and open,
    otherwise an error is generated. */

{ // LclExamplePtrGet
    ExamplePtrType ExamplePtr = luaL_checkudata(L, StkPos, CnExampleStr);
    if (! ExamplePtr->Open)
        luaL_error(L, "attempt to use a closed " CnExampleStr);
    return ExamplePtr;
} // LclExamplePtrGet

/* * */

static int LclExampleStr(
    lua_State *L)

    // "example" <- tostring(ExampleHnd)

{ // LclExampleStr
    ExamplePtrType ExamplePtr;
```

```
  // Stk: ExampleHnd?
  ExamplePtr = luaL_checkudata(L, 1, CnExampleStr);
  if (ExamplePtr->Open)
    lua_pushfstring(L, CnExampleStr " (%d)", ExamplePtr->Val);
  else lua_pushfstring(L, CnExampleStr " (%d, closed)", ExamplePtr->Val);
  // Stk: ExampleHnd IdStr
  return 1;
} // LclExampleStr

/* * */

static int LclExampleGet(
  lua_State *L)

  // Val <- ExampleHnd:get()

{ // LclExampleGet
  ExamplePtrType ExamplePtr = LclExamplePtrGet(L, 1);
  // Stk: ExampleHnd
  lua_pushnumber(L, ExamplePtr->Val);
  printf("Retrieving value of " CnExampleStr " (%d)\n", ExamplePtr->Val);
  // Stk: ExampleHnd Val
  return 1;
} // LclExampleGet

/* * */

static int LclExampleSet(
  lua_State *L)

  // OldVal <- ExampleHnd:set(NewVal)

{ // LclExampleSet
  int Val;
  // Stk: ExampleHnd? NewVal?
  ExamplePtrType ExamplePtr = LclExamplePtrGet(L, 1);
  // Stk: ExampleHnd NewVal?
  Val = luaL_checkint(L, 2);
  // Stk: ExampleHnd NewVal
  printf("Setting value of " CnExampleStr " from %d to %d\n",
    ExamplePtr->Val, Val);
  lua_pushnumber(L, ExamplePtr->Val);
  // Stk: ExampleHnd NewVal OldVal
  ExamplePtr->Val = Val;
  return 1;
} // LclExampleSet

/* * */

static int LclExampleClose(
  lua_State *L)

  // ExampleHnd:close()

{ // LclExampleClose
```

```
    ExamplePtrType ExamplePtr = LclExamplePtrGet(L, 1);
    printf("Closing " CnExampleStr " (%d) explicitly\n", ExamplePtr->Val);
    ExamplePtr->Open = 0;
    return 0;
} // LclExampleClose

/* * */

static int LclExampleGc(
  lua_State *L)

  // metatable(ExampleHnd).__gc(ExampleHnd)

{ // LclExampleGc
  ExamplePtrType ExamplePtr = luaL_checkudata(L, 1, CnExampleStr);
  if (ExamplePtr->Open) {
    printf("Collecting and closing " CnExampleStr " (%d)\n",
      ExamplePtr->Val);
    ExamplePtr->Open = 0;
  } // if
  else printf("Collecting " CnExampleStr " (%d), already closed\n",
    ExamplePtr->Val);
  return 0;
} // LclExampleGc

/* * */

static int LclExampleOpen(
  lua_State *L)

  // ExampleHnd <- example.open(PosNum)

{ // LclExampleOpen
  int Val;
  ExamplePtrType ExamplePtr;

  // Stk: Val?
  Val = luaL_checkint(L, 1);
  // Stk: Val
  ExamplePtr = lua_newuserdata(L, sizeof(ExampleType));
  printf("Opening " CnExampleStr " (%d)\n", Val);
  // Stk: Val ExampleHnd
  ExamplePtr->Val = Val;
  ExamplePtr->Open = 1;
  luaL_getmetatable(L, CnExampleStr);
  // Stk: Val ExampleHnd metatable
  lua_setmetatable(L, -2);
  // Stk: Val ExampleHnd
  return 1;
} // LclExampleOpen

/* * */

int luaopen_ud_example(
  lua_State *L)
```

```
{ // luaopen_ud_example

   static const luaL_reg MetaMap[] = {
      {"close", LclExampleClose},
      {"get", LclExampleGet},
      {"set", LclExampleSet},
      {"__tostring", LclExampleStr},
      {"__gc", LclExampleGc},
      {NULL, NULL}
   }; // MetaMap

   static const luaL_reg Map[] = {
      {"open", LclExampleOpen},
      {NULL, NULL}
   }; // Map

   // Stk: ModuleStr
   // Create metatable for handles of type "example"
   luaL_newmetatable(L, CnExampleStr);
   // Stk: ModuleStr Meta
   // Push copy of metatable
   lua_pushvalue(L, -1);
   // Stk: ModuleStr Meta Meta
   // Retrieve indexed fields from metatable itself
   lua_setfield(L, -2, "__index");
   // Stk: ModuleStr Meta
   // Register functions in metatable at top of stack
   luaL_register(L, NULL, MetaMap);
   // Stk: ModuleStr Meta
   luaL_register(L, "ud_example", Map);
   // Stk: ModuleStr Meta Namespace
   return 1;
} // luaopen_ud_example
```

2. Save the file as `ud_example.c`.

3. Compile this extension into a shared library. On Linux and other Unix-type systems, run this command:

```
cc -o ud_example.so -shared -Wall ud_example.c
```

On the Windows platform, compile the extension as follows:

```
cl /c /Zl /Zd /Yd /MD /W4 ud_example.c
link /dll /out:ud_example.dll /base:0x68200000 /machine:ix86 ⤶
   /export:luaopen_ud_example ud_example.obj msvcrt.lib lua5.1.lib
```

4. Create a new Lua file with the following contents:

```
package.cpath = "./?.so;./?.dll"
require "ud_example"

local HndA = ud_example.open(1)
local HndB = ud_example.open(2)
do -- local block
   local HndC = ud_example.open(3)
```

```
    io.write(tostring(HndA), ", ", tostring(HndB), ", ", tostring(HndC), "\n")
    HndA:set(4)
    HndA:set(1)
    HndA:close()
    io.write("End of local block\n")
  end
  collectgarbage("collect")
  io.write("End of script\n")
```

5. Save this file as ud.lua.

6. Run this script from a command shell:

```
lua ud.lua
```

The script generates this output:

```
Opening example (1)
Opening example (2)
Opening example (3)
example (1), example (2), example (3)
Setting value of example from 1 to 4
Setting value of example from 4 to 1
Closing example (1) explicitly
End of local block
Collecting and closing example (3)
End of script
Collecting and closing example (2)
Collecting example (1), already closed
```

How It Works

This example implements a simple userdata whose only job is to store an integer and, on demand, return it. But the essential framework is the same as the implementation of more practical user-defined types. The important aspects of this are as follows:

❏ The association of a userdata with a metatable to both extend its functionality and to identify it as a particular user-defined type

❏ The access of userdata memory in C

❏ The registration of the __gc metamethod so that a userdata will be eventually closed by the garbage collector if it isn't closed explicitly in a Lua script

The script and the library follow a number of steps. Like the preceding Try It Out, this example is a demonstration that really doesn't belong in a standard Lua location, so the library search is restricted to the current directory. This is done with the following line:

```
package.cpath = "./?.so;./?.dll"
```

The following line loads the extension library and calls luaopen_ud_example:

```
require "ud_example"
```

This function calls `luaL_newmetatable` to create a metatable that will be shared by all userdata instances created in ud_example extension. The new metatable is associated with the name (which in this case is `example`) by which it can be retrieved later.

A userdata can't contain key/value pairs directly the way a Lua table can, but it can implement this behavior using the __index metamethod. For example, when a userdata is indexed in the following line, the __index metamethod that resolves the `get` method:

```
Hnd:get()
```

Here, the metatable itself is associated with the `"__index"` key, so that is where values are looked for by name.

The ordinary methods `close`, `get`, and `set` and the metamethods __tostring and __gc are placed into the metatable with the following line:

```
luaL_register(L, NULL, MetaMap);
```

Notice that the second argument to this function, the library name, is specified as NULL. This instructs the function to place the specified functions into the table that resides at the top of the stack, which in this case is the metatable.

The registration of the userdata methods is followed by the registration of the ud_example library's only function: `open`.

The return value of 1 indicates that the stack's topmost value, namely the namespace table containing the `open` function, is to be returned from the call to `require`.

Back in the ud.lua script, three example handles are created with calls to ud_example.open. To test the __gc metamethod, the third handle is created in a local block where it will be allowed to go out of scope without being explicitly closed.

The `LclExampleOpen` C function manages the opening of these example handles. After verifying that the passed argument is indeed an integer, the userdata is created with a call to `lua_newuserdata`. In this extension library, the returned userdata memory is mapped to a structure of ExampleType. The fields of this structure are initialized; the `Val` field receives the value of the passed-in argument, and the `Open` field is set to a non-zero value. These operations are just placeholders for what could be, in a library having more features, the initialization of resources such as database connections.

As a last step before returning the handle to the caller, the metatable is retrieved and assigned to the new userdata. The metatable that was created in the loader function is retrieved by name in the following line:

```
luaL_getmetatable(L, CnExampleStr);
```

The same metatable will be shared by all userdatas created by ud_example.open. The stack's topmost value, the new userdata, is returned by specifying a return value of 1.

After receiving a handle to the new userdata, the Lua script can interact with it by calling its various methods. When a method such as `set` is called, the invoked C function calls on the helper function `LclExamplePtrGet` to retrieve a pointer to the structure associated with the userdata. This helper function first verifies that the specified argument is a userdata of the right type. It does this in the following line:

```
ExamplePtrType ExamplePtr = luaL_checkudata(L, StkPos, CnExampleStr);
```

This auxiliary function checks to make sure the value is a userdata and that its metatable is the one associated with the specified name (which in this example is CnExampleStr). If these criteria are met, luaL_checkudata returns a pointer to the memory structure associated with the userdata. If they aren't, an error is generated. The returned structure is then checked to verify that the handle is still open. This is strictly an extension issue — Lua doesn't know anything about the resources that you manage in the memory structure. If everything is as expected, LclExamplePtrGet returns the structure pointer to the caller; if not, an error is generated.

In the ud.lua script, the third handle is allowed to fall out of scope while it is still open. It can't be accessed by the Lua script and, because no copy of the userdata was stored in the C code, it can't be accessed by C. Lua consequently is able to classify the userdata as garbage. Lua calls the __gc metamethods of collectable userdata in the reverse order of their creation. When it is invoked in this library, the LclExampleGc C function has the chance to close its open resources.

Of the two remaining handles, one is closed explicitly and the other is left dangling when the script ends. Because the script ends normally, Lua's garbage collector is run one last time, and this is where the remaining open handle is closed.

Although a userdata's __gc metamethod is a good place to make sure resources have been finalized, garbage collection cycles may occur somewhat sporadically. It's usually prudent to include and document a close method in your library's interface so the Lua script can avoid taxing the system with too many open resources or situations where a resource needs to be closed for further processing.

Unlike Unix-type systems, Windows performs some character processing when it reads from and writes to text files. For example, when a linefeed control character (decimal value 10) is written in text mode, it is converted to a carriage return/linefeed pair (decimal values 13 and 10). The reverse is done when reading in text mode. Additionally, the Ctrl+Z control character (decimal value 26) is interpreted as the end of a file. Whatever arguments can be made for or against this type of character translation, programs that work with Windows need to deal with it. (Unix-like systems don't distinguish text files from other types of files.) Fortunately, when you're explicitly opening a file in Lua or C, you've got control over the mode it will be opened in, and you can avoid the consequences of having character translation occur on the wrong type of file by opening it in binary mode. Unfortunately, when Windows launches a program, it sets up the standard input, output and error file handles in text mode. This effectively prevents Windows programs from reading and writing binary data using the standard input and output streams in the default case.

In the following Try It Out, you extend the io library by working with the file userdata.

Try It Out   Setting the Mode of Files

Here, you extend Lua so that the mode of a file can be changed after it has been opened. You do it in such a way that it intentionally has no effect on Unix-like systems. Before proceeding, make sure your development system is set up as recommended in Chapter 1.

1. Using your text editor, create a new file with the following C program:

```
#include "lua.h"
#include "lualib.h"
#include "lauxlib.h"
#include <string.h>
#ifdef WIN32
#include <io.h>
#include <fcntl.h>
#endif

/* * */

static int LclIoModeSet(
  lua_State *L)

{ // LclIoModeSet
  FILE **StrmPtr = (FILE **) luaL_checkudata(L, 1, LUA_FILEHANDLE);
  if (*StrmPtr) {
    int Bin = 0;
    const char *ModeStr = luaL_checkstring(L, 2);
    if (0 == strcmp("binary", ModeStr)) Bin = 1;
    else if (0 != strcmp("text", ModeStr)) luaL_error(L, "expecting either "
      LUA_QL("binary") " or " LUA_QL("text") " mode");
#ifdef WIN32
    _setmode(_fileno(*StrmPtr), Bin ? _O_BINARY : _O_TEXT);
#endif
  } // if
  else luaL_error(L, "attempt to access a closed file");
  return 0;
} // LclIoModeSet

/* * */

int luaopen_iomode(
  lua_State *L)

{ // luaopen_iomode
  static const luaL_reg Map[] = {
    {"modeset",  LclIoModeSet},
    {NULL, NULL}
  };

  luaL_register(L, LUA_IOLIBNAME, Map);
  return 1;
} // luaopen_iomode
```

2. Save this file as `iomode.c`.

3. Compile this extension into a shared library. On Linux and other Unix-type systems, run this command:

```
cc -o iomode.so -shared -Wall iomode.c
```

On the Windows platform, compile the extension as follows:

```
cl /c /Z1 /Zd /Yd /MD /W4 /DWIN32 iomode.c
link /dll /out:iomode.dll /base:0x67900000 /machine:ix86 ⤵
  /export:luaopen_iomode iomode.obj msvcrt.lib lua5.1.lib
```

4. Copy the generated module to your designated Lua library directory. On Unix-type systems, run this:

```
cp iomode.so $LUA_DIR/
```

On Windows, run this:

```
xcopy iomode.dll "%LUA_DIR%\*.*"
```

5. Create a new file with the following contents:

```
local Arg = string.lower(arg[1] or "")
local Read = string.match(Arg, "r")
local Mode = string.match(Arg, "b") and "binary" or "text"

require "iomode"

io.modeset(io.stdout, Mode)
io.modeset(io.stdin, Mode)

if Read then
  local Str = io.read("*all")
  for J = 1, #Str do
    local Val = string.byte(Str, J, J)
    if Val >= 32 then
      io.write("'", string.sub(Str, J, J), "' ")
    else
      io.write(string.format("0x%02x ", Val))
    end
  end
  io.write("\n")
else -- Write
  io.write("1\0132\0103\0264")
end
```

6. Save this file as `iotest.lua`.

7. Test the library as follows:

Depending on your platform, the generated output you get may not look the same as shown here; that will be discussed shortly.

```
lua iotest.lua w | lua iotest.lua r
'1' 0x0d '2' 0x0a '3'

lua iotest.lua wb | lua iotest.lua r
'1' 0x0d '2' 0x0a '3'

lua iotest.lua w | lua iotest.lua rb
'1' 0x0d '2' 0x0d 0x0a '3' 0x1a '4'

lua iotest.lua wb | lua iotest.lua rb
'1' 0x0d '2' 0x0a '3' 0x1a '4'
```

How It Works

Like the preceding examples, this one shows you the basic framework of an extension module written in C. It may seem like a lot of code to wrap around the _setmode and _fileno functions. But much of this is boilerplate code that is relatively unchanged from extension to extension. Additionally, you'll likely write helper functions to consolidate common statement sequences.

When the test script `iotest.lua` is run, the first three lines of the script examine the command line argument:

```
local Arg = string.lower(arg[1] or "")
local Read = string.match(Arg, "r")
local Mode = string.match(Arg, "b") and "binary" or "text"
```

If r or R is present, data is read from the standard input stream. If not, a series of bytes is written to the standard output stream. If b or B is present, binary mode is used; otherwise, text mode is used.

The next line of the test script handles the search for and loading of a Lua module:

```
require "iomode"
```

In this case, the dynamic link library `iomode.dll` or `iomode.so` is found and loaded.

The `luaopen_iomode` calls `luaL_register` to register `LclIoModeSet`. In this case, note that the name of an existing table is used for the LUA_IOLIBNAME namespace — this is Lua's symbolic name for the io table.

After `luaopen_iomode` returns, control is transferred back to `iotest.lua`. The next line to be executed is as follows:

```
io.modeset(io.stdout, Mode)
```

This function will set the mode of the standard output stream to either binary or text, depending on the argument passed to the script.

When `io.modeset` is called, control is transferred back to the C library, this time to the function `LclIoModeSet`. The first line it executes is this:

```
FILE **StrmPtr = (FILE **) luaL_checkudata(L, 1, LUA_FILEHANDLE);
```

This line verifies that the value at position one on the call stack (corresponding to the first argument passed to `io.modeset`) is in fact a file. If it is, the file (actually, a doubly indirected stream) is returned; otherwise an error is generated.

The userdata returned by `luaL_checkudata` is a pointer to a stream pointer. If the stream pointer is NULL, the file has been closed and an error with an appropriate message is generated. Otherwise, the `luaL_checkstring` function is used to verify that the second argument is a string. If it is, this function will return the string; otherwise, it will generate an error with a descriptive message.

It is extremely important that you do not modify string buffers that are held by Lua. Doing so would disrupt Lua's string interning mechanism with dire consequences for your program. Furthermore, any string pointer you obtain should be assumed valid only until control is returned to Lua.

About the File Value

At the shell prompt, if you execute the following:

```
lua -e "print(io.stdin)"
```

you see something like this:

```
file (0x401d76e0)
```

Lua has eight basic types and `file` isn't one of them. In fact, `io.stdin` is of type `userdata`. It is rendered by `tostring` (used by `print`) as `file` because of its particular metatable.

Usually, a C library defines its own userdatas. In this case, however, a userdata defined in the `io` library (the file `liolib.c` in the Lua source distribution) is used, because the function `LclIoModeSet` needs to operate on the underlying stream.

If the second argument is the binary or text string, a mode value is set accordingly; otherwise, an error is generated. Note that the error message uses the macro LUA_QL to provide standard quotes. This gives error messages a uniform appearance throughout Lua. The actual setting of the file mode takes place with the following lines:

```
#ifdef WIN32
  _setmode(_fileno(*StrmPtr), Bin ? _O_BINARY : _O_TEXT);
#endif
```

The fact that the real work of this binding occurs only on the Windows platform suggests that a Lua-only module could be implemented for Unix-like systems that could replace the `iomode` C library. At its simplest, it could consist of the following lines:

```
function io.modeset(Hnd, Mode) end
return io
```

Additional argument checking could be done to increase compatibility with the Windows library.

The following line indicates that no value is to be returned from `io.modeset`:

```
return 0;
```

The next line to be executed in the script is this:

```
io.modeset(io.stdin, Mode)
```

It follows the same sequence as the one preceding it in the script, except that it is the standard input stream that is modified.

The remainder of the script serves as a test of the `io.modeset` extension. If the script is to read the standard input stream (`r` or `R` is included as a command line argument to the script), the following code is run:

```
local Str = io.read("*all")
for J = 1, #Str do
  local Val = string.byte(Str, J, J)
  if Val >= 32 then
    io.write("'", string.sub(Str, J, J), "' ")
  else
    io.write(string.format("0x%02x ", Val))
  end
end
io.write("\n")
```

Everything in the stream is read into a string, and each character in this string is visited in a loop. If the character is printable, it is displayed in quotes; otherwise, its value is displayed in hexadecimal.

If the script is to write a sequence to standard output (a w or W is included in the command line argument to the script), the following line is run:

```
io.write("1\0132\0103\0264")
```

This writes the following seven characters:

1 *carriage return* 2 *linefeed* 3 *Ctrl+Z* 4

You specify the control characters using Lua's standard escape sequence in which a one-, two-, or three-digit decimal value follows a backslash. (Three digits are required if a decimal digit follows the sequence, as it does in each of the previous cases.)

To test the behavior of the extension library from a Windows command shell, the script is invoked in write mode, and its output is piped to the same script invoked in read mode. The four permutations of text and binary mode (text-text, binary-text, text-binary, and binary-binary) reveal how Windows translates certain characters, and how the iomode module can be used to enable binary data transfers through the standard streams.

Take a look at the output of the following commands:

```
lua iotest.lua w | lua iotest.lua r
'1' 0x0d '2' 0x0a '3'

lua iotest.lua wb | lua iotest.lua r
'1' 0x0d '2' 0x0a '3'

lua iotest.lua w | lua iotest.lua rb
'1' 0x0d '2' 0x0d 0x0a '3' 0x1a '4'

lua iotest.lua wb | lua iotest.lua rb
'1' 0x0d '2' 0x0a '3' 0x1a '4'
```

This output illustrates the following:

❑   When writing in text mode, a single linefeed is translated as a carriage return/linefeed pair. A single carriage return or Ctrl+Z is not translated.

❑   When reading in text mode, a carriage return/linefeed pair is translated to a single linefeed. A single carriage return is not translated. The Ctrl+Z character is processed as the end of the stream contents.

❑   Reading and writing in binary mode disables character processing; everything written in this mode can be read again intact. This is the standard behavior in Linux and other Unix-like systems.

Indexing Values in C

Manipulating tables is as important and pervasive in C as it is in Lua. The API gives you a number of ways to access tables and, by means of metamethods, other indexed values.

Retrieving Indexed Values

The `lua_gettable` function is used in C to perform the operation that performs in Lua:

```
Val = Tbl[Key]
```

The __index metamethod can make this operation valid for values of Tbl other than a table, or for a table that doesn't contain Key. This same metamethod behavior applies in C, so whether Tbl is a table or some other value that has an associated __index metamethod, the way to retrieve a value by key is as follows:

1.   Place Tbl on the stack at some known position.

2.   Arrange to have Key placed at the top of the stack using one of the functions that begin with lua_push, such as lua_pushvalue or lua_pushstring.

3.   Call lua_gettable with the Lua state pointer as the first argument and the stack position of Tbl as the second. For example, if Tbl occupies the fourth position from the top of the stack, you could call the following

```
lua_gettable(L, -4);
```

4.   Replace the key at the top of the stack with Tbl[Key]. This value may be nil. In either case, the stack's top position does not change.

In the event that you want to retrieve a value from a table without invoking __index if the key is missing, you can use the lua_rawget function. This does in C what rawget does in Lua. lua_rawget and lua_gettable are similar in that the key is pushed on the stack and the table's position on the stack is specified as the second argument. The function replaces the key with the key's associated value.

When you want to retrieve a value associated with an integer key, you can omit the step where you push the key by using the lua_rawgeti function. For example, if you want to retrieve Tbl[7] and Tbl resides in position 3 of the stack, you would call the function as follows:

```
lua_rawgeti(L, 3, 7);
```

The value of Tbl[7] is pushed on the stack. Like lua_rawget, this function bypasses the metamethod mechanism.

In the absence of metamethods, only tables can be indexed, so `lua_rawget` and `lua_rawgeti` operate only on tables. This restriction can be used to point out an important distinction between programming in Lua and programming in C. If you try the following in Lua:

```
local J = 42
print(J[3])
```

you'll be presented with this Lua error message:

```
attempt to index local 'J' (a number value)
```

Using a protected call, you can recover from an error like this. If you try something similar in C, such as the following:

```
// Stk: ...
lua_pushinteger(L, 42);
// Stk: ... 42
lua_rawgeti(L, -1, 3);
// Stk: ... 42[3]
```

you're in for this less-pleasant response:

```
Segmentation fault
```

A protected call can't prevent the host from abnormally terminating like this. When you're programming with Lua's C API, all of the sharp edges are exposed.

Setting Indexed Values

Each of the API functions for retrieving an indexed value has a complement for setting an indexed value. For example, use the `lua_settable` function in C to perform what the following line does in Lua:

```
Tbl[Key] = Val
```

For example, to make the following assignment in C:

```
Tbl.Name = "Don Quixote"
```

you would use the following sequence:

```
// Stk: ...
lua_newtable(L);
// Stk: ... Tbl
lua_pushstring(L, "Name");
// Stk: ... Tbl "Name"
lua_pushstring(L, "Don Quixote");
// Stk: ... Tbl "Name" NameStr
lua_settable(L, -3);
// Stk: ... Tbl
```

In this case, a new table is created but, because `lua_settable` will invoke the `__newindex` metamethod if needed, any indexable value could be used instead. The sequence shows how the topmost value on the stack must be the value to be assigned, and the value just below it must be the key.

If `Tbl` is a table and you want to avoid any use of metamethods, you can use the `lua_rawset` function as a drop-in replacement for `lua_settable`.

If you're making an assignment to a table with an integer key and want to avoid the use of metamethods, a shortcut is to use the `lua_rawseti` function. For example, you would perform the following Lua function:

```
Tbl[42] = "Hello, world"
```

with the following C code:

```
// Stk: ...
lua_newtable(L);
// Stk: ... Tbl
lua_pushstring(L, "Hello, world");
// Stk: ... Tbl Str
lua_rawseti(L, -2, 42);
// Stk: ... Tbl
```

Retaining Values in C

Userdata can be used by a C library to retain contextual information. No provision needs to be made in the C code to store and retrieve its state information — it simply gets passed in from Lua when needed. But Lua is nothing if not flexible, so it gives you some other choices for storing persistent values. As you've seen so far in this chapter, when you extend Lua with C, you've got to manage many details that are taken care of transparently when working strictly in Lua. For example, the Lua compiler will recognize whether a variable referenced in a Lua script is a local variable or upvalue or one that will need to be looked for in the global environment. In C, the only way to retrieve Lua variables will be to know in advance where they are stored. This applies to the following storage mechanisms.

The Registry

Every Lua state has a table referred to as the registry for storing Lua values. Any C code that has access to the Lua state pointer has access to the registry. Lua code, by design, does not. The shared nature of the registry makes it suitable for some purposes and not for others. As with any table, you need to choose keys well to avoid inadvertent duplicates. This is especially important with the registry, because you can't know what other C libraries will be loaded along with yours. One technique is to use light userdata initialized with the addresses of static variables in the C code. Within an application, each static variable will have a unique address.

The registry is just a table, so it would be a shame to have to provide a bunch of API functions to manipulate it when there are already functions available for table access. Lua's elegant solution is to make the registry table available on the stack at a special position that can't be used for other purposes. Lua gives the symbolic name `LUA_REGISTRYINDEX` to the *pseudo-index* (an index that is treated specially by Lua) that refers to the registry. To access the registry, use any of the table indexing methods you already know about and specify `LUA_REGISTRYINDEX` as the table's stack position.

C Function Environments

Every registered C function is associated with a table known as its environment. When a C function is registered, it inherits the current environment. This can later be changed by means of the `lua_replace` function. This table is accessed, in C only, with the pseudo-index `LUA_ENVIRONINDEX` the same way the registry is. The difference is that the table referenced by `LUA_ENVIRONINDEX` by one function may be different than the one similarly referenced in another function, and the table referenced by `LUA_REG ISTRYINDEX` will always be the same.

It's easy to create an environment that will be shared by all registered functions in a library and by no others. Prior to calling `luaL_register` to register one or more C functions, create a new table and replace the current environment with it. Here is some sample code:

```c
int luaopen_sample(
   lua_State *L)

{ // luaopen_sample
   static const luaL_reg Map[] = {
      {"run", LclRun},
      {NULL, NULL}
   }; // Map

   // Stk: ModuleStr
   lua_newtable(L);
   // Stk: ModuleStr Tbl
   lua_replace(L, LUA_ENVIRONINDEX);
   // Stk: ModuleStr
   luaL_register(L, "sample", Map);
   // Stk: ModuleStr Namespace
   return 1;
} // luaopen_sample
```

Upvalues in C

So far in this chapter, you have called `luaL_register` to register one or more C functions so that they can be called from Lua. The pattern has been to call this function in a library's loader function, but this is not a requirement. Lua provides a lower level function named `lua_pushcclosure` that lets you push a function of type `lua_CFunction` on the stack. This is the critical step that creates a value of type `function` from a C function. For example, in the following C code, the value that `lua_pushcclosure` pushes at the top of stack can be made available to a Lua script and called from there:

```c
// Stk: ...
lua_pushcclosure(L, LclRun, 0);
// Stk: Fnc
```

The functions `lua_isfunction` and `lua_iscfunction` will both return 1 on this value. (When a function is written in Lua, the former function returns 1 and the latter function returns 0.) From its position on the stack, it can be treated like any other Lua value. For example, it can be assigned to a global variable, associated with a key in a table, kept on the stack as a return value or, because it is a function, called in place.

The third argument to `lua_pushcclosure` indicates the number of upvalues to associate with the new Lua function. These values should be at the top of the stack when `lua_pushcclosure` is called. Here's an example:

```
// Stk: ...
lua_pushstring(L, "First upvalue");
// Stk: ... Str
lua_pushinteger(L, 42);
// Stk: ... Str Num
lua_newtable(L);
// Stk: ... Str Num Tbl
lua_pushcclosure(L, LclRun, 3);
// Stk: ... LclRun
```

These values are bound to the *closure* function and are available to it whenever it is called. The function accesses its upvalues as if they resided on the stack. The stack position to use is calculated by the `lua_upvalueindex` macro defined in `lua.h`. This macro maps the position of the upvalue to a pseudo-index value. For example, here is how the first two upvalues (the string and the integer) in the preceding example would be retrieved:

```
Str = lua_tostring(L, lua_upvalueindex(1));
Pos = lua_tointeger(L, lua_upvalueindex(2));
```

You can treat the pseudo-index that `lua_upvalueindex` returns as an ordinary stack position. With this index, you can retrieve upvalues and assign new values to them.

Upvalues in C are private to the function to which they are bound. But the third upvalue in the example is a Lua table, and the values in that table can be shared by using that table as an upvalue for different functions. In this way, you have a lot of control over what information is shared between select functions.

Referencing Values

Lua's auxiliary library has some referencing functions that help you keep track of Lua values in your C code. When given a table, the `luaL_ref` function will do the following:

1. Generate a unique integer key to be used in the specified table.

2. Associate the stack's topmost value with the new integer key in the specified table.

3. Pop the value off of the stack.

4. Return the integer key.

To retrieve the referenced value, use the `lua_rawgeti` function. To remove the stored value from the table, and to make the reference identifier available for reuse, call `luaL_unref`.

Because integers are so easily stored in C, the reference system is a convenient way to have access to Lua values in your library. Any table can be used with the reference system, but it is important that you not subvert the system by using your own numeric keys in it. The registry and C function environment tables are particularly well-suited to the reference mechanism because you don't need to worry about key clashes. Here's an example of using the reference functions to store, retrieve, and release a string value in the registry:

```
int Ref = LUA_NOREF;

// Stk: ...
lua_pushstring(L, "Hello, world");
```

```
// Stk: ... Str
Ref = luaL_ref(L, LUA_REGISTRYINDEX);
// Stk: ...
lua_rawgeti(L, LUA_REGISTRYINDEX, Ref);
// Stk: ... Str
printf("Retrieved string: %s\n", lua_tostring(L, -1));
luaL_unref(L, LUA_REGISTRYINDEX, Ref);
Ref = LUA_NOREF;
// Stk: ... Str
lua_pop(L, 1);
// Stk: ...
```

The `LUA_NOREF` symbolic constant is an integer value that Lua will never return as a valid reference. It is useful to assign this value to a reference identifier before and after use to mark it as inactive. This way, you won't inadvertently try to dereference or release it.

The Thread Environment

Global variables are held in a table known as the thread environment. As with the registry and C function environments, a pseudo-index is used to access the table, which in this case is `LUA_GLOBALSINDEX`. The `lua_getglobal` and `lua_setglobal` macros retrieve and set values in this table by using this pseudo-index. Here's an example that sets a global variable in the thread environment:

```
// Stk: ...
lua_pushstring(L, "0.4.8");
// Stk: ... VerStr
lua_setglobal(L, "APP_VERSION");
// Stk: ...
```

Values stored in this table are accessible in both Lua and C code.

Layering Your Extension Library

The `iomode` extension library is made up of a single C module, and its loader function is called directly by the `require` mechanism. Another approach is to provide a Lua script that acts as the principal module; this script in turn loads a C extension library. This combination gives you the opportunity to leverage Lua and C in the places where they work best: C for low-level primitives and linking to third-party libraries and Lua for everything else.

Sometimes it is worthwhile to distinguish the C code that is aware of Lua from the C code that isn't. If you find that large amounts of C code are sprinkled with only a few calls into the Lua API, it may be beneficial to redesign the interface and place the code that isn't aware of Lua into its own library. This library is then more widely usable, and the Lua-aware code acts as a binding layer between it and Lua.

Try It Out   **Creating a Layered-Extension Library for CSV Records**

A fairly common way to package row and column information is to place it in CSV (comma-separated value) format. Each row occupies one line of text, and each field within a row is delimited with a comma. There are variations in how to handle a field that includes one or more literal commas. One peculiar but pervasive convention is to enclose such a field in double quotes, and to interpret each occurrence of two adjacent double quotes within a quoted field as one double quote. These rules make it difficult to handle CSV records in pure Lua.

This exercise demonstrates a layered extension library to facilitate the reading and writing of CSV records. It handles the low-level parsing in C, and the higher-level functions in Lua.

1. Using your text editor, create a new file and include the following C contents:

```
#include "lua.h"
#include "lualib.h"
#include "lauxlib.h"
#include <string.h>

/* * */

static const char * LclCsv(
  const char * Str,
  luaL_Buffer * BufPtr)

  /* This function parses the comma separated value (CSV) segment beginning at
  the start of Str. In CSV format

    * commas delimit text segments

    * double quotes which surround text are not copied

    * commas occurring within double quoted text are copied verbatim

    * each occurrence of two consecutive double quotes within double quoted
      text are copied as one double quote

  Examples

    abc                  -> |abc|
    "abc"                -> |abc|
    "abc, def"           -> |abc, def|
    "abc ""def"" ghi"    -> |abc "def" ghi|

  */

{ // LclCsv

  typedef enum {CnaIgnore = 0, CnaCopy = 1, CnaInc = 2, CnaQuit = 4} ActionType;

  typedef enum {CnsStart, CnsText, CnsQuoted, CnsHyperQuoted} StateType;

  typedef enum {CncComma, CncQuote, CncChar, CncNull} CatType;

  typedef struct {
    ActionType A;
    StateType S;
  } ContextType;

  static ContextType ContextList[CnsHyperQuoted + 1][CncNull + 1] = {
```

```
      { // CnsStart
        {CnaInc, CnsStart}, // CncComma
        {CnaIgnore, CnsQuoted}, // CncQuote
        {CnaCopy, CnsText}, // CncChar
        {CnaQuit, CnsStart}}, // CncNull

      { // CnsText
        {CnaInc, CnsStart}, // CncComma
        {CnaIgnore, CnsQuoted}, // CncQuote
        {CnaCopy, CnsText}, // CncChar
        {CnaInc | CnaQuit, CnsText}}, // CncNull

      { // CnsQuoted
        {CnaCopy, CnsQuoted}, // CncComma
        {CnaIgnore, CnsHyperQuoted}, // CncQuote
        {CnaCopy, CnsQuoted}, // CncChar
        {CnaInc | CnaQuit, CnsQuoted}}, // CncNull

      { // CnsHyperQuoted
        {CnaInc, CnsStart}, // CncComma
        {CnaCopy, CnsQuoted}, // CncQuote
        {CnaCopy, CnsText}, // CncChar
        {CnaInc | CnaQuit, CnsHyperQuoted}}}; // CncNull

  char Ch;
  ContextType Context;
  CatType Cat;

  Context.S = CnsStart;
  do {
    Ch = *(Str++);
    if (! Ch) Cat = CncNull;
    else if (Ch == 34) Cat = CncQuote;
    else if (Ch == ',') Cat = CncComma;
    else {
      Cat = CncChar;
      if (Ch < ' ') Ch = ' ';
    } // else
    Context = ContextList[Context.S][Cat];
    if (CnaCopy & Context.A) luaL_addchar(BufPtr, Ch);
    if (CnaInc & Context.A) Ch = 0;
  } while (Ch);
  return Str;
} // LclCsv

/* * */

static int LclCsvParse(
  lua_State *L)

  // str_segment, pos <- csv.parse(str [, pos])

{ // LclCsvParse
  const char *Str, *EndStr;
  int Len, Pos;
```

```
      luaL_Buffer Buf;

      Str = luaL_checkstring(L, 1);
      if (lua_isnil(L, 2)) Pos = 1;
      else Pos = luaL_checkinteger(L, 2);
      Len = strlen(Str);
      if ((Pos >= 1) && (Pos <= Len)) {
        luaL_buffinit(L, &Buf);
        EndStr = LclCsv(Str + Pos - 1, &Buf);
        luaL_pushresult(&Buf);
        Pos = EndStr - Str;
        Pos = Pos > Len ? -1 : Pos + 1;
        lua_pushinteger(L, Pos);
      } // if
      else luaL_error(L, "pos is out of range");
      return 2;
    } // LclCsvParse

    /* * */

    int luaopen_csvparse(
      lua_State *L)

    { // luaopen_csvparse
      static const luaL_reg Map[] = {
        {"parse",  LclCsvParse},
        {NULL, NULL}
      };

      luaL_register(L, "csv", Map);
      return 1;
    } // luaopen_csvparse
```

2. Save the file as `csvparse.c`.

3. Compile this extension into a shared library. On Linux and other Unix-type systems, run this command:

```
cc -o csvparse.so -shared -Wall csvparse.c
```

On the Windows platform, compile the extension as follows:

```
cl /c /Z1 /Zd /Yd /MD /W4 /DWIN32 csvparse.c
link /dll /out:csvparse.dll /base:0x67C00000 /machine:ix86 ⊃
  /export:luaopen_csvparse csvparse.obj msvcrt.lib lua5.1.lib
```

4. Copy the generated module to your designated Lua library directory. On Unix-type systems, run this:

```
cp csvparse.so $LUA_DIR/
```

On Windows, run this:

```
xcopy csvparse.dll "%LUA_DIR%\*.*"
```

5. Create another new file with the following Lua contents:

```
require "csvparse"

-- Return a string which has been properly quoted for inclusion in a
-- comma-separated value file.

function csv.escape(str)
  local wrap = ""
  str = tostring(str)
  if string.find(str, '"') then
    str = string.gsub(str, '"', '""')
    wrap = '"'
  end
  if string.find(str, ',') then
    wrap = '"'
  end
  return wrap .. str .. wrap
end

-- Iterator to allow traversal of CSV cells

function csv.cells(str)
  local pos = 1
  local function nextcell()
    local cellstr
    if pos > 0 then
      cellstr, pos = csv.parse(str, pos)
    else
      cellstr = nil
    end
    return cellstr
  end
  return nextcell
end
```

6. Save this file as `csv.lua`.

7. Copy this module to your designated Lua library directory. On Unix-type systems, run this:

```
cp csv.lua $LUA_DIR/
```

On Windows, run this:

```
xcopy csv.lua "%LUA_DIR%\*.*"
```

8. Create another new Lua file with these contents:

```
require "csv"

local Str = 'Natty Bumppo,"Natty Bumppo, Pathfinder","Natty ""Hawkeye"" Bumppo"'

local SubStr, Pos

io.write("--- csv.parse ---\n")
Pos = 1
io.write(Str, "\n")
for J = 1, 10 do
```

```
    if Pos > 0 then
       SubStr, Pos = csv.parse(Str, Pos)
       io.write(string.format("Pos %3d, field [%s], escaped [%s]\n", Pos, SubStr,
          csv.escape(SubStr)))
    end
 end

 io.write("--- csv.cells ---\n")
 for CellStr in csv.cells(Str) do
    io.write(CellStr, "\n")
 end
```

9. Save this file as `csvtest.lua`.

10. From a command shell, run the test script as follows:

```
lua csvtest.lua
--- csv.parse ---
Natty Bumppo,"Natty Bumppo, Pathfinder","Natty ""Hawkeye"" Bumppo"
Pos  14, field [Natty Bumppo], escaped [Natty Bumppo]
Pos  41, field [Natty Bumppo, Pathfinder], escaped ["Natty Bumppo, Pathfinder"]
Pos  -1, field [Natty "Hawkeye" Bumppo], escaped ["Natty ""Hawkeye"" Bumppo"]
--- csv.cells ---
Natty Bumppo
Natty Bumppo, Pathfinder
Natty "Hawkeye" Bumppo
```

How It Works

This extension processes CSV rows and leaves the matter of reading and writing those lines to the `io` library. It comprises two layers: the low level parsing component in C, and the escaping and iterator routines in Lua.

The format of `csvparse.c` is similar to that of `iomode.c`. The loader function `luaopen_csvparse` is called by Lua's package system. It calls `luaL_register` to create (or reuse, if it already exists) the `csv` namespace table and to place into it the `LclCsvParse` extension function keyed with the string "parse".

The extension function uses Lua's string buffering routines. This mechanism lets you construct a string in stages without having to worry about memory issues. You have to pay attention to the virtual stack, however. Here's how string buffering works:

1. The following line initializes `Buf` (of type `luaL_Buffer`) in preparation to building up a CSV field string:

```
luaL_buffinit(L, &Buf);
```

2. Characters are added to the string in the following line:

```
if (CnaCopy & Context.A) luaL_addchar(BufPtr, Ch);
```

The function `luaL_addchar` appends the specified character to the string buffer. When called, it and the other string buffer functions except `luaL_addvalue` expect to find the stack as it was left after the previous string buffer call. (In the case of `luaL_addvalue`, the stack should be the same except that an additional value should be pushed on the top.) In between string buffer calls, you are able to perform operations that manipulate the stack. You just need to make sure the stack is returned to the expected level before calling a string buffer function again.

3. The completed string is pushed on the stack with the following line:

```
luaL_pushresult(&Buf);
```

The `csv.parse` function is called with a string to process and, optionally, a one-based position that indicates where in the string to begin parsing. The arguments are obtained and validated with the following lines:

```
Str = luaL_checkstring(L, 1);
if (lua_isnil(L, 2)) Pos = 1;
else Pos = luaL_checkinteger(L, 2);
```

If the second argument is missing, `Pos` is assigned a default value of one indicating the beginning of the string. If it's an integer, its value is assigned to `Pos`. If it is neither of these, an error is generated. The value of `Pos` is checked to be sure it points to a valid position in `Str`.

The `csv.parse` function is intended to be called repeatedly, each time returning the next field. It does this by returning, in addition to the field string, the position of the next field. When the last field of the CSV row is returned, the value of this position is set to `-1`. A scheme like this is efficient because parsing takes place only as needed and, using Lua's string buffer mechanism, no overhead is spent on transient, partial strings during string construction. If the function succeeds, the call to `luaL_pushresult` pushes the field string on the stack, and the call to `lua_pushinteger` pushes the next position or `-1`. The return value of 2 indicates to Lua that these two values are to be returned, in the order they were pushed, to the caller of `csv.parse`.

The Lua layer of this extension library, `csv.lua`, includes routines to help with reading and writing CSV fields. The `csv.cells` function is an iterator generator that wraps `csv.parse`, allowing the fields of a CSV record to be read in a generic for loop. The `csv.escape` function applies the quoting rules to a single field, helping with the construction of a CSV record.

Summary

The C API is a substantial part of Lua, and this chapter has glossed or outright skipped over some of its features. But, having come this far, you have learned enough to create a basic C extension library for Lua. In particular, you've learned the following:

❑   The distinction between embedding Lua and extending it

❑   To use the virtual stack to exchange values between Lua and C

❑   To write and register C functions that can be called from Lua

❑   To call Lua functions from C

❑   Where you can store persistent values in C

❑   To program userdata to create versatile Lua handles that, behind the scenes, can manage C resources

❑   Different ways to layer your extensions to get the most out of C and the most out of Lua

Take some time to test what you've learned by tackling the following exercises. From there, the next chapters will lead you through the use of Lua for database, web, and network access.

Exercises

1. In the `ud_example` Try It Out, you created and used an example handle as follows:

```
local Hnd = ud_example.open(1)
Hnd:set(2)
Hnd:close()
```

What changes would you need to make to the C library so that it would additionally support the following usage?

```
local Hnd = ud_example.open(1)
ud_example.set(Hnd, 2)
ud_example.close(Hnd)
```

2. Add stack diagrams in the form of single line comments to the following C fragment:

```
lua_newtable(L);
lua_newtable(L);
lua_pushstring(L, "Rip Van Winkle");
lua_setfield(L, -2, "Name");
lua_pushvalue(L, -1);
lua_pushcclosure(L, FncA, 1);
lua_setfield(L, -3, "a");
lua_pushcclosure(L, FncB, 1);
lua_setfield(L, -2, "b");
lua_pushvalue(L, -1);
lua_setglobal(L, "test");
```

Now explain what this code accomplishes:

3. Write an extension library for bit operations. The `bit._and` function should return each argument (which must be an integer) linked with and. Similarly, the `bit._or` function should return each argument (which must be an integer) linked with or.

and *and* or *are reserved keywords and cannot be used as names. Nevertheless, you can use them as table keys for your functions, but then you need to invoke your functions as* bit['and'] *and* bit['or'].

For example, the following script:

```
package.path = ""
package.cpath = "./?.so;./?.dll"
require "bit"

print(bit._and(301, 251, 491))
print(bit['and'](301, 251, 491))
print(bit._or(32, 8, 1))
print(bit['or'](32, 8, 1))
```

should print these lines:

```
41
41
41
41
```

Managing Information
with Databases

As a programmer, you'll sooner or later need to store information in between invocations of a program. You can store this information in a text file and decode it with patterns, or you can store it in a Lua file and reloade it with `loadfile`. But sometimes these methods aren't sufficiently fast, powerful, flexible, or scalable, in which case, you should store the information in a database. This chapter is a very brief introduction to databases and database systems. It will cover the following:

- ❏ How data is organized in and retrieved from a database
- ❏ SQL, the special-purpose language used to interact with databases
- ❏ LuaSQL, a set of Lua bindings for a number of popular database systems

Some Basic Relational Database Concepts

This section demonstrates some basic database concepts by having you implement a simple database and a system for retrieving data from it entirely in Lua.

Almost all databases in use today are what are known as *relational databases* because they are designed to work with relationships between things (the previous generation of databases was not good at this). In the following example, the things in question are customers, products, and orders of an imaginary business. The relational aspect is the fact that the orders are defined in terms of the products ordered and the customers who ordered them.

Try It Out   **Creating a Simple Database Entirely in Lua**

1.   Save the following as `join.lua`:

```lua
-- A demonstration of a simple relational database with join
-- functionality entirely in Lua.

-- Example database tables:
Cust = {
  {Id = "C001", NameLast = "Bumppo", NameFirst = "Natty"},
  {Id = "C002", NameLast = "Finn", NameFirst = "Huckleberry"},
  {Id = "C003", NameLast = "Darcy", NameFirst = "Fitzwilliam"},
  {Id = "C004", NameLast = "Bennet", NameFirst = "Elizabeth"},
  {Id = "C005", NameLast = "Marner", NameFirst = "Silas"},
}
Product = {
  {Id = "P001", DescStr = "whatchamacallit"},
  {Id = "P002", DescStr = "gizmo"},
  {Id = "P003", DescStr = "gewgaw"},
  {Id = "P004", DescStr = "thingamajig"},
  {Id = "P005", DescStr = "widget"},
  {Id = "P006", DescStr = "doodad"},
  {Id = "P007", DescStr = "whatsit"},
}
Order = {
  {Id = "O001", CustId = "C003", ProductId = "P002", Count = 52},
  {Id = "O002", CustId = "C003", ProductId = "P004", Count = 87},
  {Id = "O003", CustId = "C004", ProductId = "P001", Count = 12},
  {Id = "O004", CustId = "C004", ProductId = "P003", Count = 8},
  {Id = "O005", CustId = "C004", ProductId = "P005", Count = 20},
  {Id = "O006", CustId = "C002", ProductId = "P004", Count = 2},
}

-- Returns a new database table composed of the selected columns of
-- Tbl1 and Tbl2 where WhereFnc is true:
function Join(Tbl1, Tbl1Select, Tbl2, Tbl2Select, WhereFnc)
  local Ret = {}
  -- For each pairing of rows:
  for _, Tbl1Row in ipairs(Tbl1) do
    for _, Tbl2Row in ipairs(Tbl2) do
      if WhereFnc(Tbl1Row, Tbl2Row) then
        -- WhereFnc is true, so include the selected fields of this
        -- pairing in the result:
        local RetRow = {}
        for _, Tbl1Col in ipairs(Tbl1Select) do
          RetRow[Tbl1Col] = Tbl1Row[Tbl1Col]
        end
        for _, Tbl2Col in ipairs(Tbl2Select) do
          RetRow[Tbl2Col] = Tbl2Row[Tbl2Col]
        end
        Ret[#Ret + 1] = RetRow
      end
    end
  end
end
```

```
    return Ret
end

-- Space-padding helper function for ShowDbTbl:
local function ShowField(Str, Width, Numeric)
  local Pad = string.rep(" ", Width - string.len(Str))
  if Numeric then
    io.write(Pad, Str, "  ")
  else
    io.write(Str, Pad, "  ")
  end
end

-- Displays a database table (an array of associative rows):
function ShowDbTbl(Tbl)
  local ColList = {}
  -- Get the width of each column name and type of each column:
  for ColStr, Val in pairs(Tbl[1]) do
    ColList[#ColList + 1] = {Name = ColStr,
      Width = string.len(ColStr), Numeric = type(Val) == "number"}
  end
  -- Get the maximum width of each column:
  for _, Row in ipairs(Tbl) do
    for _, Col in ipairs(ColList) do
      Col.Width = math.max(string.len(Row[Col.Name]), Col.Width)
    end
  end
  -- Display a column header:
  for _, Col in ipairs(ColList) do
    ShowField(Col.Name, Col.Width, Col.Numeric)
  end
  io.write("\n")
  for _, Col in ipairs(ColList) do
    ShowField(string.rep("-", Col.Width), Col.Width, false)
  end
  io.write("\n")
  -- Display the rows:
  for _, Row in ipairs(Tbl) do
    for _, Col in ipairs(ColList) do
      ShowField(Row[Col.Name], Col.Width, Col.Numeric)
    end
    io.write("\n")
  end
end

-- Demonstration:
CustOrder = Join(Cust, {"NameLast"},
  Order, {"ProductId", "Count"},
  function(Cust, Order) return Cust.Id == Order.CustId end)
print("*** Cust joined to Order ***")
ShowDbTbl(CustOrder)
print()
CustOrderProduct = Join(CustOrder, {"NameLast", "Count"},
  Product, {"DescStr"},
```

```
        function(CustOrder, Product)
          return CustOrder.ProductId == Product.Id
        end)
  print("*** Cust joined to Order joined to Product ***")
  ShowDbTbl(CustOrderProduct)
  print()
  Bennet = Join(CustOrder, {"Count"},
    Product, {"DescStr"},
      function(CustOrder, Product)
        return CustOrder.ProductId == Product.Id
          and CustOrder.NameLast == "Bennet"
      end)
  print("*** All orders by customer 'Bennet' ***")
  ShowDbTbl(Bennet)
```

2. Run it with this:

```
lua join.lua
```

The output will be:

```
*** Cust joined to Order ***
Count   NameLast   ProductId
-----   --------   ---------
    2   Finn       P004
   52   Darcy      P002
   87   Darcy      P004
   12   Bennet     P001
    8   Bennet     P003
   20   Bennet     P005

*** Cust joined to Order joined to Product ***
DescStr           Count   NameLast
---------------   -----   --------
thingamajig           2   Finn
gizmo                52   Darcy
thingamajig          87   Darcy
whatchamacallit      12   Bennet
gewgaw                8   Bennet
widget               20   Bennet

*** All orders by customer 'Bennet' ***
Count   DescStr
-----   ---------------
   12   whatchamacallit
    8   gewgaw
   20   widget
```

How It Works

The word "table" has two meanings in this chapter. The Lua Cust, Product, and Order tables are also *tables* in a database-specific sense. They are called tables because they can be visualized as arrangements of *rows* and *columns*. The columns have names, but the rows don't. For instance, take a look at this table of customers:

```
Cust = {
    {Id = "C001", NameLast = "Bumppo", NameFirst = "Natty"},
    {Id = "C002", NameLast = "Finn", NameFirst = "Huckleberry"},
    {Id = "C003", NameLast = "Darcy", NameFirst = "Fitzwilliam"},
    {Id = "C004", NameLast = "Bennet", NameFirst = "Elizabeth"},
    {Id = "C005", NameLast = "Marner", NameFirst = "Silas"},
}
```

The following table shows how you can visualize this.

Id	NameLast	NameFirst
C001	Bumppo	Natty
C002	Finn	Huckleberry
C003	Darcy	Fitzwilliam
C004	Bennet	Elizabeth
C005	Marner	Silas

An array of associative tables is just one of several ways to conveniently represent a database table as a Lua table.

In another intersection with Lua terminology, database column names (such as NameLast) can also be called *field names*, and particular columns in particular rows can be called *fields*. For example, the NameLast field of the second row in the previous table is "Finn."

The following call does what is known as a *join* between the Cust table and the Order table:

```
CustOrder = Join(Cust, {"NameLast"},
    Order, {"ProductId", "Count"},
    function(Cust, Order) return Cust.Id == Order.CustId end)
```

The Join function takes a database table (a table in the previously described row/column format), a (not necessarily exhaustive) list of field names from that table, another table, a list of field names from *that* table, and a two-argument function. Using nested for loops, it goes through every possible pairing of one row from the first table and one from the second (in this case, five times six = thirty pairings) as follows:

```
function Join(Tbl1, Tbl1Select, Tbl2, Tbl2Select, WhereFnc)
    local Ret = {}
    for _, Tbl1Row in ipairs(Tbl1) do
        for _, Tbl2Row in ipairs(Tbl2) do
            if WhereFnc(Tbl1Row, Tbl2Row) then
```

If a pairing makes WhereFnc return true, then the selected fields of that pairing are added to the table to be returned (which itself is a row/column-formatted database table) like this:

```
            if WhereFnc(Tbl1Row, Tbl2Row) then
                local RetRow = {}
                for _, Tbl1Col in ipairs(Tbl1Select) do
                    RetRow[Tbl1Col] = Tbl1Row[Tbl1Col]
```

453

```
        end
        for _, Tbl2Col in ipairs(Tbl2Select) do
          RetRow[Tbl2Col] = Tbl2Row[Tbl2Col]
        end
        Ret[#Ret + 1] = RetRow
    end
```

So *joining* two tables means getting the selected fields for all pairings of rows where WhereFnc is true (which is why it's called WhereFnc). In the join between Cust and Order, the WhereFnc returns true only if Cust's Id is equal to Order's CustId. Because each row of Order has a unique Id, and each of Order's CustId fields has a corresponding Id field in Cust, this join returns one row for every row in Order. Specifically it returns the following for every order:

❑   The last name of the customer who made the order

❑   The product ID

❑   The quantity of the product ordered

For example, this shows that Huckleberry Finn ordered two of product P004:

```
*** Cust joined to Order ***
Count  NameLast  ProductId
-----  --------  ---------
    2  Finn      P004
   52  Darcy     P002
   87  Darcy     P004
   12  Bennet    P001
    8  Bennet    P003
   20  Bennet    P005
```

This Join function operates on only two database tables at a time, but because the result is itself a database table, it can be joined with yet another table. That's how the product descriptions for each order are retrieved — the join between CustOrder and Product gets every order's customer name, count, and product description as follows:

```
CustOrderProduct = Join(CustOrder, {"NameLast", "Count"},
  Product, {"DescStr"},
  function(CustOrder, Product)
    return CustOrder.ProductId == Product.Id
  end)
```

The result shows that the product (P004) that Huckleberry Finn ordered two of is a thingamajig:

```
*** Cust joined to Order joined to Product ***
DescStr           Count  NameLast
---------------   -----  --------
thingamajig           2  Finn
gizmo                52  Darcy
thingamajig          87  Darcy
whatchamacallit      12  Bennet
gewgaw                8  Bennet
widget               20  Bennet
```

The two joins used their `WhereFnc`s to determine which rows of one table go with which rows of the other. The third join's `WhereFnc` does this, but then it disqualifies some of those rows for not having the right `NameLast` field, as follows:

```
Bennet = Join(CustOrder, {"Count"},
  Product, {"DescStr"},
    function(CustOrder, Product)
      return CustOrder.ProductId == Product.Id
        and CustOrder.NameLast == "Bennet"
  end)
```

The result shows only Elizabeth Bennet's three orders and none of the other customers' orders:

```
*** All orders by customer 'Bennet' ***
Count  DescStr
-----  ---------------
   12  whatchamacallit
    8  gewgaw
   20  widget
```

If a `WhereFnc` always returns `true`, it pairs every row of the first table with every row of the second table, even if those rows have nothing to do with each other. To demonstrate this, run the Lua interpreter (in the same directory as `join.lua`) and type:

```
> dofile("join.lua")
```

The `join.lua` functions and database tables are global, so after it's done printing, you can do the following:

```
> ShowDbTbl(Join(Cust, {"NameLast"},
>>   Order, {"ProductId", "Count"},
>>     function() return true end))
```

This will print out 30 rows. Here are the first 10:

```
Count  NameLast  ProductId
-----  --------  ---------
   52  Bumppo    P002
   87  Bumppo    P004
   12  Bumppo    P001
    8  Bumppo    P003
   20  Bumppo    P005
    2  Bumppo    P004
   52  Finn      P002
   87  Finn      P004
   12  Finn      P001
    8  Finn      P003
```

This (joining every row of one table with every row of the other) is called a *cross join* or *Cartesian product*. It is important for two reasons:

❏ It is the theoretical basis for all other joins. (A cross join will have as many rows as the `Join` function's nested loops have iterations.)

❏ You may sometimes do it by mistake.

An example of doing it by mistake would be leaving out the `CustOrder.ProductId·==·Product.Id` condition in the `WhereFnc` to get all of Elizabeth Bennet's orders:

```
Bennet = Join(CustOrder, {"Count"},
   Product, {"DescStr"},
   function(CustOrder, Product)
     return CustOrder.NameLast == "Bennet" -- UH-OH, CROSS JOIN!
   end)
ShowDbTbl(Bennet)
```

This will print Elizabeth's three orders, mixed in with 18 orders that don't even exist (they're junk generated by the cross join). Another way of putting that is that it prints each of Elizabeth's three orders seven times, with only one of the seven having the right `DescStr`, as shown here:

```
Count  DescStr
-----  ---------------
   12  whatchamacallit
   12  gizmo
   12  gewgaw
   12  thingamajig
   12  widget
   12  doodad
   12  whatsit
    8  whatchamacallit
    8  gizmo
    8  gewgaw
    8  thingamajig
    8  widget
    8  doodad
    8  whatsit
   20  whatchamacallit
   20  gizmo
   20  gewgaw
   20  thingamajig
   20  widget
   20  doodad
   20  whatsit
```

In addition to showing what tables, rows, columns, and joins are, `join.lua` demonstrates a few other things.

One is a principle of database design: don't duplicate information. The `Order` table could have looked like this:

```
Order = {
   {Id = "0001", NameLast = "Darcy", NameFirst = "Fitzwilliam",
     DescStr = "gizmo", Count = 52},
   {Id = "0002", NameLast = "Darcy", NameFirst = "Fitzwilliam",
     DescStr = "thingamajig", Count = 87},
```

```
      {Id = "0003", NameLast = "Bennet", NameFirst = "Elizabeth",
        DescStr = "whatchamacallit", Count = 12},
      {Id = "0004", NameLast = "Bennet", NameFirst = "Elizabeth",
        DescStr = "gewgaw", Count = 8},
      {Id = "0005", NameLast = "Bennet", NameFirst = "Elizabeth",
        DescStr = "widget", Count = 20},
      {Id = "0006", NameLast = "Finn", NameFirst = "Huckleberry",
        DescStr = "thingamajig", Count = 2},
  }
```

This would have made `Cust` and `Product` unnecessary, but if Elizabeth Bennet got married to Fitzwilliam Darcy and needed to change her last name, it would need to be changed in three places rather than one, which is a hassle and an opportunity for error. Also, real-world database systems generally don't do the string interning discussed in Chapter 10, which means that three occurrences of `"Bennet"` take up three times as much space as one.

If you read up on databases, you'll find out about "normal forms," which for the most part are applications of the "don't duplicate information" principle. The principle is sometimes disobeyed for reasons of efficiency and simplicity.

Another lesson of `join.lua` is that a real database system needs to be more optimized. Imagine if there were a thousand customers and one hundred thousand orders. Finding all orders with the last name "Bennet" would make the nested loop in `Join` do *one hundred million* iterations.

This is solved in real database systems by using *indexes*. This is yet another meaning for a word already well-laden with meanings. In this case, you should think of an index in the back of a book, which lets you go right to the page or pages where a topic is mentioned. An index for `Cust`'s `NameLast` field might look like this:

```
  {Bumppo = {1}, Finn = {2}, Darcy = {3}, Bennet = {4},
    Marner = {5}}
```

If `Join` were able to look inside the `WhereFnc` and see that the last name "Bennet" was being sought, the table would tell it that the fourth element of `Cust` had that last name. (The reason the numbers are wrapped in arrays is in case multiple customers share a last name.)

The previous table wouldn't speed up a search for "all customers whose last names start with B," but an index that would speed it up might look like this:

```
  {{NameLast = "Bennet", 4},
    {NameLast = "Bumppo", 1},
    {NameLast = "Darcy", 3},
    {NameLast = "Finn", 2},
    {NameLast = "Marner", 5}}
```

This array is sorted by last name, so a technique called *binary search* can be used to do the following:

1. Jump into the middle of the array.

2. If the array element in the middle's `NameLast` starts with `"B"`, then the B's have been found.

3. If not, repeat these steps with the first half or the second half of the array, depending on whether the just-tested element's `NameLast` starts with a letter after or before `"B"`.

If there are a lot of customers, this method is much faster than searching through every single customer, because with every iteration, the distance to the thing being searched for is halved or more than halved.

Use of database indexes is outside the scope of this chapter, but all serious database systems offer some way to control what indexes are created.

SQL, LuaSQL, and MySQL

Most database systems use a language called SQL to express interaction with a database. (It's pronounced "ESS-CUE-ELL," or sometimes even "SEE-kwuhll," and it stands for Structured Query Language, but nobody actually uses the full name.) SQL was designed specifically for this purpose, and is not really usable as a general-purpose language, so it is generally combined with a language (like Lua) that *is* good for general-purpose programming. A program that needs to interact with a database is written in the general-purpose language, except for those parts of program that deal with the database, which are written in SQL.

There are many database systems, all with their own pluses and minuses (and all with their own slightly different dialects of SQL). One is SQLite, which you met in Chapter 12. Another popular one is MySQL (pronounced "MY-ESS-CUE-ELL").

LuaSQL is a collection of Lua bindings to these and other database systems (PostgreSQL, ODBC, JDBC, Oracle, and ADO). In the remainder of this chapter, you'll be using the LuaSQL binding to MySQL.

> **LuaSQL currently only exists for Lua 5.0. (That's why the examples here use**
> `string.len` **instead of #.)**

MySQL and LuaSQL are available respectively on `dev.mysql.com` and `www.keplerproject.org/luasql/`. You will need to download and install both (according to the instructions on their websites) for the following example to work.

LuaSQL is part of the Kepler project (`www.keplerproject.org`), so if you have Kepler installed, then you already have LuaSQL. The following example assumes that a Lua 5.0 interpreter called `lua50` is in your search path. If this is not the case, give the full path to the interpreter, changing the following line:

```
lua50 mysql.lua Create
```

to this (for example):

```
"C:\Program Files\Kepler\lua50" mysql.lua Create
```

The script `init.lua` in the Kepler directory makes sure that `require` knows where to look for the LuaSQL module. The Kepler installer sets your shell's LUA_INIT environment variable to `@C:\Program Files\Kepler\init.lua` (or something similar, depending on where Kepler is installed). This value for LUA_INIT causes Lua to run `init.lua` before running `mysql.lua`. (`init.lua` has no effect on Lua 5.1.)

Try It Out   Creating a Customers, Products, and Orders Table in MySQL

In this exercise, you programmatically interact with the MySQL database server by means of a Lua script.

1. At your shell, use the following `mysqladmin` function to create a new MySQL database called Lua":

```
mysqladmin -u root -p create Lua
```

You'll be prompted for a password. If you set up a password for the `root` (administrator) account when you installed MySQL, type that one. If no password has been set, press Enter.

2. Invoke the MySQL client application as follows:

```
mysql -u root -p
```

After submitting the MySQL root password, you'll see a `mysql>` prompt.

3. At the `mysql>` prompt, create a new MySQL user account with the username `Lua` by typing the following:

> `'SmPlPaSs'` *is the new account's password in this example.*

```
GRANT ALL PRIVILEGES ON Lua.* TO 'Lua'@'localhost'
  IDENTIFIED BY 'SmPlPaSs';
```

4. Type **exit**, **quit**, or **\q** to leave the MySQL client.

5. With your text editor, create a file with the following contents and save it as `mysql.lua`:

```lua
require("luasql.mysql")

-- Executes all of the the SQL statements in List (stopping if one
-- fails):
function ExecSqlList(Conn, List)
  local Succ, ErrStr
  for _, SqlStr in ipairs(List) do
    Succ, ErrStr = Conn:execute(SqlStr)
    if not Succ then break end -- BREAK ON ERROR.
  end
  return Succ, ErrStr
end

-- Space-padding helper function for ShowCursor:
local function ShowField(Str, Width, Numeric)
  local Pad = string.rep(" ", Width - string.len(Str))
  if Numeric then
    io.write(Pad, Str, "  ")
  else
    io.write(Str, Pad, "  ")
  end
end

-- Displays all the rows in a database cursor, then closes the
-- cursor:
function ShowCursor(Cursor)
```

```
  ---- Get the name of each column and that name's width:
  local ColNames = Cursor:getcolnames()
  local ColWidths = {}
  for I, Name in ipairs(ColNames) do
    ColWidths[I] = string.len(Name)
  end
  -- Find out which columns hold numbers:
  local ColTypes = Cursor:getcoltypes()
  local ColIsNums = {}
  for I, Type in ipairs(ColTypes) do
    if string.sub(Type, 1, 6) == "number" then
      ColIsNums[I] = true
    else
      ColIsNums[I] = false
    end
  end

  -- A wrapper for Cursor:fetch that lets it return a table without
  -- being given one:
  local function RowsIter()
    local Row = {}
    return Cursor:fetch(Row)
  end

  -- Store all rows and the maximum widths of all columns:
  local Rows = {}
  for Row in RowsIter do
    table.insert(Rows, Row)
    for I, Field in ipairs(Row) do
      ColWidths[I] = math.max(ColWidths[I], string.len(Field))
    end
  end
  -- Display a column header:
  for I, ColName in ipairs(ColNames) do
    ShowField(ColName, ColWidths[I], ColIsNums[I])
  end
  io.write("\n")
  for I, ColWidth in ipairs(ColWidths) do
    ShowField(string.rep("-", ColWidth), ColWidth, false)
  end
  io.write("\n")
  -- Display the rows:
  for _, Row in ipairs(Rows) do
    for I, Field in ipairs(Row) do
      ShowField(Field, ColWidths[I], ColIsNums[I])
    end
    io.write("\n")
  end
  Cursor:close()
end

-- Creates the Cust, Product, and Ord tables:
function Create(Conn)
  return ExecSqlList(Conn, {[[
    CREATE TABLE Cust (
```

460

```
        Id INT UNSIGNED NOT NULL AUTO_INCREMENT PRIMARY KEY,
        NameLast CHAR(50),
        NameFirst CHAR(50))]], [[
    CREATE TABLE Product (
        Id INT UNSIGNED NOT NULL AUTO_INCREMENT PRIMARY KEY,
        DescStr CHAR(50))]], [[
    CREATE TABLE Ord (
        Id INT UNSIGNED NOT NULL AUTO_INCREMENT PRIMARY KEY,
        CustId INT UNSIGNED,
        ProductId INT UNSIGNED,
        Count INT UNSIGNED)]]})
end

-- Puts rows into Cust, Product, and Ord:
function Populate(Conn)
  return ExecSqlList(Conn, {[[
    TRUNCATE TABLE Cust]], [[
    INSERT INTO Cust (NameLast, NameFirst) VALUES
        ('Bumppo', 'Natty'),
        ('Finn', 'Huckleberry'),
        ('Darcy', 'Fitzwilliam'),
        ('Bennet', 'Elizabeth'),
        ('Marner', 'Silas')]], [[
    TRUNCATE TABLE Product]], [[
    INSERT INTO Product (DescStr) VALUES
        ('whatchamacallit'), ('gizmo'), ('gewgaw'), ('thingamajig'),
        ('widget'), ('doodad'), ('whatsit')]], [[
    TRUNCATE TABLE Ord]], [[
    -- These CustIds and ProductIds are hardcoded, which means this
    -- INSERT would break if the previous INSERTs' auto-increment IDs
    -- didn't start at 1, but the TRUNCATEs make sure they do:
    INSERT INTO Ord (CustId, ProductId, Count) VALUES
        (3, 2, 52),
        (3, 4, 87),
        (4, 1, 12),
        (4, 3, 8),
        (4, 5, 20),
        (2, 4, 2)]]})
end

-- Does some sample SELECTs (joins) and displays the results:
function Test(Conn)
  local Cursor, ErrStr
  Cursor, ErrStr = Conn:execute([[
    SELECT NameLast, ProductId, Count
    FROM Cust, Ord
    WHERE Cust.Id = Ord.CustId]])
  if Cursor then
    print("*** Cust joined to Order ***")
    ShowCursor(Cursor)
    print()
    Cursor, ErrStr = Conn:execute([[
      SELECT NameLast, Count, DescStr
      FROM Cust, Ord, Product
      WHERE Cust.Id = Ord.CustId
```

```
              AND Ord.ProductId = Product.Id]])
      if Cursor then
        print("*** Cust joined to Order joined to Product ***")
        ShowCursor(Cursor)
        print()
        Cursor, ErrStr = Conn:execute([[
          SELECT Count, DescStr
          FROM Cust, Ord, Product
          WHERE Cust.Id = Ord.CustId
            AND Ord.ProductId = Product.Id
            AND Cust.NameLast = 'Bennet']])
        if Cursor then
          print("*** All orders by customer 'Bennet' ***")
          ShowCursor(Cursor)
        end
      end
    end
  return not ErrStr, ErrStr
end

-- Drops the Cust, Product, and Ord tables:
function Drop(Conn)
  return Conn:execute("DROP TABLE IF EXISTS Cust, Product, Ord")
end

-- Get what the LuaSQL documentation calls an "environment":
local MysqlEnv, ErrStr = luasql.mysql()
if MysqlEnv then
  -- Get a connection to the "Lua" database as the user "Lua":
  local Conn
  Conn, ErrStr = MysqlEnv:connect("Lua", "Lua", "SmPlPaSs")
  if Conn then
    -- Obey the command given as a command-line argument:
    local Cmd = arg[1]
    local Succ
    if Cmd == "Create" then
      Succ, ErrStr = Create(Conn)
      if Succ then
        print("Successfully created Cust, Product, and Ord tables")
      end
    elseif Cmd == "Populate" then
      Succ, ErrStr = Populate(Conn)
      if Succ then
        print("Successfully populated Cust, Product, and Ord tables")
      end
    elseif Cmd == "Test" then
      Succ, ErrStr = Test(Conn)
    elseif Cmd == "Drop" then
      Succ, ErrStr = Drop(Conn)
      if Succ then
        print("Successfully dropped Cust, Product, and Ord tables")
      end
    else
      ErrStr = "A command-line argument of 'Create', 'Populate',"
        .. " 'Test', or 'Drop' is required"
```

```
      end
      Conn:close()
    end
    MysqlEnv:close()
  end
  if ErrStr then
    io.stderr:write(ErrStr, "\n")
  end
```

6.   At the shell, run it with the `Create` command-line argument as follows:

```
lua50 mysql.lua Create
```

It will print this:

```
Successfully created Cust, Product, and Ord tables
```

7.   Run it again with the `Populate` command-line argument as follows:

```
lua50 mysql.lua Populate
```

It will print this:

```
Successfully populated Cust, Product, and Ord tables
```

8.   Run it one more time with the `Test` command-line argument as follows:

```
lua50 mysql.lua Test
```

It will print this:

```
*** Cust joined to Order ***
NameLast  ProductId  Count
--------  ---------  -----
Finn             4      2
Darcy            2     52
Darcy            4     87
Bennet           1     12
Bennet           3      8
Bennet           5     20

*** Cust joined to Order joined to Product ***
NameLast  Count  DescStr
--------  -----  --------------
Finn         2   thingamajig
Darcy       52   gizmo
Darcy       87   thingamajig
Bennet      12   whatchamacallit
Bennet       8   gewgaw
Bennet      20   widget

*** All orders by customer 'Bennet' ***
Count  DescStr
-----  --------------
   12  whatchamacallit
    8  gewgaw
   20  widget
```

How It Works

`require("luasql.mysql")` creates the `luasql` namespace table and puts a function in it called `mysql`. With this function, an object (called an environment in the LuaSQL documentation) is created. This object has a `connect` method, with which a connection is opened to the database Lua as the user Lua with the password SmPlPaSs:

```
Conn, ErrStr = MysqlEnv:connect("Lua", "Lua", "SmPlPaSs")
```

After this connection object is obtained, the command-line argument decides which function to run. The first one run is `Create`, which calls the function `ExecSqlList` with the connection object and a three-element array as arguments. The array's first element is this string:

```
CREATE TABLE Cust (
    Id INT UNSIGNED NOT NULL AUTO_INCREMENT PRIMARY KEY,
    NameLast CHAR(50),
    NameFirst CHAR(50))
```

This is what SQL looks like. SQL keywords, function names, and so on are case-insensitive, but they are often typed in all-uppercase as shown. This is partly to make SQL's rather baroque syntax a bit easier to process visually, and partly just out of tradition. In MySQL, column names are case-sensitive, but database names and table names are only case-sensitive if the filesystem where the database is stored is case-sensitive.

The preceding CREATE-TABLE statement creates a table called Cust with columns Id, NameLast, and NameFirst. In MySQL, as in most database systems (SQLite being a notable exception), a given column can hold only one datatype. The CHAR(50) after NameLast and NameFirst means that those columns can each hold a string of up to 50 characters. The INT-UNSIGNED-NOT-NULL after Id means that Id can hold an unsigned integer, but cannot hold the special value NULL. PRIMARY-KEY has to do with the indexing described at the end of the previous section. (AUTO_INCREMENT will be explained later.)

This and the two other CREATE-TABLE statements are passed to ExecSqlList, which uses the connection object's `execute` method to execute them, creating three tables.

> The Order table from the example earlier in this chapter was renamed Ord here because Order is a reserved word in MySQL.

Next, the Populate function is called, which fills the three tables with data. The TRUNCATE statements clean out anything that's already in the tables (so that things will still work if you run Populate twice), and the INSERT-INTO statements do the actual insertion of data.

Notice that values are inserted into all the columns except for the Id columns. This is because the Id columns of all three tables are *auto-increment* columns, which means that the first row inserted into a given table will get an Id of 1, the next will get an Id of 2, and so on. In this example, where all the data is being loaded at once, it would be just as easy to hard-code the Id fields, but the auto-increment functionality shows its usefulness in more realistic programs, where non-hardcoded rows are added one at a time.

Finally, Test is called. It executes three SELECT statements and uses ShowCursor to display the results. Each of these SELECTs consists of three parts:

❏ A SELECT clause, which names the columns that will be in the result. This is equivalent to the second and fourth arguments of the Join function from earlier in the chapter.

❑ A FROM clause, which names the tables that the previously selected columns are in. This is equivalent to the first and third arguments of Join.

❑ A WHERE clause, which constrains which rows will be in the result. This is equivalent to Join's fifth (WhereFnc) argument. If no WHERE clause is given, but multiple tables are given in the FROM clause, then a cross join is done.

In both the SELECT clause and the WHERE clause, a column can be specified with or without its table name: TblName.ColName or ColName. The first form is mandatory if the same column name is used in two tables named in the FROM clause. This WHERE clause:

```
SELECT NameLast, ProductId, Count
FROM Cust, Ord
WHERE Cust.Id = Ord.CustId
```

could have been written WHERE Cust.Id-=-CustId, because Cust doesn't have a CustId column, but not WHERE-Id-=-CustId, because Ord does have an Id column. (The = in SQL means the same thing as == in Lua.)

More than two tables can be joined by one SELECT statement, by including them all in the FROM clause and the appropriate join conditions in the WHERE clause. If the FROM clause only names one table, then just rows from that table are selected, and no join is done.

These SELECTs are executed by the connection object's execute method:

```
local Cursor, ErrStr
Cursor, ErrStr = Conn:execute([[
   SELECT NameLast, ProductId, Count
```

When execute is given a statement that doesn't return any data, like CREATE or INSERT, it returns a success Boolean. When it is given a SELECT, it returns a *cursor* object that is used to read the SELECT's results. The cursor has the following methods:

❑ getcolnames: Returns an array of the result's column names.

❑ getcoltypes: Returns an array of the datatypes of the result's columns.

❑ fetch: Returns the first row the first time it's called, the second row the second time it's called, and so on. It returns nil when there are no more rows.

❑ close: Closes the cursor.

The fetch method takes two optional arguments. If given no arguments, it returns as many values as there are columns. If given a Lua table as a first argument, it puts the columns of the row being returned into that table and returns it. If the second argument is not given or if it is "n" (for "numeric"), then the returned Lua table is an array indexed by column number such as the following:

```
{"Finn", "4", "2"}
```

If the second argument is "a" (alphanumeric), then the returned table is associative by column name, like this:

```
{NameLast = "Finn", ProductId = "4", Count = "2"}
```

Notice also that LuaSQL's MySQL driver (as of this writing) returns even numeric values as strings.

The ShowCursor function uses these methods to display all the rows in the cursor given to it. Most of the work it does is formatting: getting the maximum width of each column and making sure that strings are left-justified and numbers are right-justified.

If you want to delete the Cust, Product, and Ord tables and start over, use Drop as a command-line argument to mysql.lua.

Summary

This has been a very brief introduction to databases. You haven't even learned about UPDATE and DELETE, the SQL statements that change and remove rows, nor have you learned about the nonintuitive behavior of the SQL value NULL. That information is available in the many books and websites about SQL.

Here are the highlights of what this chapter did cover:

❑   Relational databases store data in tables, which are organized in rows and columns.

❑   Combining the data from multiple tables is called joining those tables.

❑   Combining every single row of one table with every single row of another table is called a cross join.

❑   Duplication of data in a database should be avoided when possible.

❑   Database systems use indexes for faster searching.

❑   SQL is a special-purpose language for interacting with databases.

❑   The SQL CREATE statement creates a table. The INSERT-INTO statement puts rows into a table. The SELECT statement reads rows from a table.

❑   LuaSQL is a set of Lua bindings for a number of popular database systems, including MySQL.

❑   LuaSQL returns the results of a SELECT as a cursor object with getcolnames, getcoltypes, fetch, and close methods.

Before you go on to the next chapter, which is about web programming, check out these exercises. (Answers are in the appendix.)

Exercises

1.   Write a function that takes a LuaSQL cursor and returns a table in the format used by Join (an array of associative tables).

2.   The following SELECT doesn't work — it returns an error message. Why?

```
SELECT Id, CustId, NameLast, ProductId, DescStr, Count
FROM Cust, Ord, Product
WHERE Cust.Id = Ord.CustId
  AND Ord.ProductId = Product.Id
```

Programming for the Web

Although the Internet is the infrastructure for a myriad of protocols, e-mail and the Web are the two services most people associate with it. In this chapter, you'll learn how nicely Lua fits into the Web part of the equation. In this chapter, you learn about the following:

❏　The basic operation of web servers

❏　Generating web content dynamically with Lua

❏　Issues with serving dynamic content

❏　Handling input from users by means of forms

❏　The basics of the Lua-based Kepler web server environment

Along the way, you'll see how Lua can make use of community libraries to dynamically generate attractive, informative web pages.

A Web Server Primer

To generate web pages using Lua, you should have a comfortable grasp on how web servers operate. This understanding will let you develop Lua programs that focus on the Web's strengths and deal with the Web's limitations in as graceful a manner as possible. As you'll see in this chapter, a successful web application draws on many different tools, with the web server itself playing the central role.

Conceptually, a web server is pretty simple. It's an application that runs on a host and listens for inbound connections. It has access to resources, generally web pages, that are handed out in response to requests made by other applications, usually web browsers. These requests and responses conform to a standard known as hypertext transfer protocol, or HTTP. Unlike many other protocols that define how two applications can have an ongoing conversation, HTTP defines a self-contained transaction. It describes how one application, the client, can properly initiate a request and how another application, the server, can properly respond to that request. The lack of dialog is the reason HTTP is often referred to as a connectionless protocol.

The notion of the World Wide Web derives from the presence of many web servers and many web browsers throughout the Internet. The one-shot nature of HTTP transactions simplifies the construction of web servers and allows them to scale efficiently to support frequent requests from many clients. The original intent of the Web as a collection of static, browsable, hyperlinked documents was served quite well by this simple model. The web pages themselves are usually prepared in HTML (HyperText Markup Language), a standard that defines how tags are used to define a page's structure, appearance, and links to other pages.

The request/response model has simplicity going for it, but it's got two drawbacks: poor performance and poor memory. Performance suffers when a client needs to connect repeatedly to the same server to retrieve related resources such as the images, scripts, and style sheets associated with a given page. Version 1.1 of the HTTP standard addresses this by specifying that connections be kept alive by default. The second drawback deals with the server's inability to retain the context of a series of transactions. Each transaction, even one that occurs over a keepalive connection, appears to the server as a brand new request from an unknown client. This is not a problem for static documents, but it becomes an issue for dynamically generated content in which a server response depends on the transactions that precede it. One solution to this deficiency is for the server to embed a limited amount of contextual information in the hyperlinks or HTML forms that are part of a dynamically created page. Requests that are based on these links or forms return this information to the server where it can be used to reconstruct the context of the transaction. Another method is for the server to use a cookie, which is a small packet of information that is optionally stored by a web browser at the request of a server and is returned by the browser when making a request of that server. Often, the information passed between the client and web server is simply a small identifier that indexes more information stored on the server.

Dynamic Web Content

Much of what you see in your web browser is generated on the server after you submit an HTTP request. This is where Lua fits into the picture, because it will be called on to generate web pages dynamically. There are two basic server configurations that are responsible: the embedded web server and the extended web server.

Embedded Web Server

A limited web server is simple enough to embed into even small applications. A growing number of devices, such as network routers, are implemented this way. One advantage of this approach is that managing the user interface can be made trivially easy. Another advantage is that resources such as file handles or database connections can be kept open for the duration of the application. For the purposes of most applications, an embedded web server needs only a small number of features that a mainstream web server would require. Even a file system is not required.

Embedding a web server is suitable for applications of all types, not just hardware devices. For example, using the LuaSocket library, you can write a short Lua script that opens a database connection and begins accepting connections on some specific port. Interaction between the user and the database can occur without the overhead of reestablishing the database connection for each transaction.

Extended Web Server

A general-purpose web server can be extended to run an application that it knows nothing about, as long as it and the application both agree on how to communicate. Mainstream web servers all implement a standard named the Common Gateway Interface (CGI). In this model, when a client requests a resource that specifies a program, the server invokes that program, passing it information about the client, server, and the request itself. The output of the program is then returned to the client. CGI is often associated with HTML forms and user interaction, but at its root, it simply specifies how a web server interfaces with external programs. Much of the dynamically created content on the web is generated this way.

FastCGI is an optimized variation of CGI in which the application and its resources remain active between HTTP transactions.

Creating Content at Run Time with Lua

For many applications, Lua is the ideal language with which to write CGI programs. One complaint that is leveled against CGI is that each request for dynamic content requires an external program to be executed. Large or otherwise slow programs can degrade performance noticeably. Lua, however, is known for its small footprint and its fast loading and execution of scripts, so it fits in nicely with the CGI model. Lua's flexible text handling and ability to connect with low-level libraries are features that definitely enhance the creation of web applications.

Executing CGI Scripts

A key to configuring CGI is to make sure the web server can distinguish programs from static deliverable resources. When a web server identifies a CGI program, it hands the task of actually executing it to the operating system. In order to function properly, the CGI program generally requires some information about the request, network connection, client, and server.

When you tell a web client to request a resource from a server, whether by clicking a hyperlink or using a browser address bar, you are submitting a uniform resource locator (URL, which is pronounced you-are-ell) to the client. Here is an example of a URL:

```
http://localhost/cgi-bin/date.lua?num=3
```

In this example, `http://` is the scheme, `localhost` is the server, `/cgi-bin/date.lua` is the path, and `num=3` is the query. In a hyperlink, the scheme and server are often left out, in which case, the browser uses the values that apply to the page that contains the link. The question mark and query apply only when a dynamic resource is requested and even then only sometimes.

When a web client like a browser contacts a web server, it submits a packet of information that starts with a command that looks like this:

```
POST /cgi-bin/postform.lua HTTP/1.1
```

or this:

```
GET /cgi-bin/submit.lua?name=Natty&number=11 HTTP/1.1
```

Other types of web clients, such as `curl`, can request that the web server accept a file for upload using a command like this:

```
PUT /address.html HTTP/1.1
```

In all cases, the command line is followed by headers that provide more details about the transaction. The web server conveys the command and headers to the CGI program by means of the shell environment, a per-process collection of key/value pairs.

You can recognize the portion of text immediately following the command as the URL with the scheme and server removed. In particular, notice in the GET example that the query is intact. This is one way of transferring user-provided information to the web server.

The other way of conveying information to the server is to include it in the information packet. This is how content is uploaded with the POST and PUT commands. As you can see from the examples of those commands, the information doesn't appear in the HTTP command. In this case, the headers are followed by the submitted data with one blank line in between. This submitted data will be delivered to the CGI program through a standard pipeline. This conduit connects the standard output of the web server to the standard input of the CGI program, permitting a large amount of data to be streamed efficiently.

All of the content that the CGI program generates, regardless of the initial command, is returned to the web server through a similar pipeline in the reverse direction. This model simplifies the creation of CGI programs because it keeps network communication issues with the web server and application details with the external program.

CGI Scripts on Unix-Type Systems

On Unix-type systems, scripts may begin with a line (known as a *shebang*) that specifies the path of the interpreter that is to process the program. For example, if a Lua script is marked as executable and begins with the following line, the system will invoke `/usr/local/bin/lua` with the name of the script as an argument:

```
#!/usr/local/bin/lua
```

The Lua interpreter will skip the first line of a script if it begins with the # character. This can be a convenience for general scripting because it allows you to launch a Lua script directly from a shell prompt without explicitly invoking `lua` itself. With CGI, however, it is imperative, because without the special first line, the system wouldn't know what to do with the script. If you installed Lua in another directory, make the appropriate change.

CGI Scripts on Windows

In general, Windows examines the extension of a script to determine how to launch it. You need to add some entries into the registry to tell Windows how to properly invoke Lua scripts. The following registry script will set things up for you. Make the appropriate changes if you installed Lua in a different location from the one shown here. Create a new file called `lua.reg` and put the following lines into it:

```
REGEDIT4

[HKEY_LOCAL_MACHINE\SOFTWARE\Classes\.lua]
```

```
@="luafile"
"Content Type"="application/lua"

[HKEY_LOCAL_MACHINE\SOFTWARE\Classes\.luac]
@="luafile"
"Content Type"="application/lua"

[HKEY_LOCAL_MACHINE\SOFTWARE\Classes\luafile]
@="Lua script"

[HKEY_LOCAL_MACHINE\SOFTWARE\Classes\luafile\DefaultIcon]
@="C:\\Program Files\\utility\\lua.ico,0"

[HKEY_LOCAL_MACHINE\SOFTWARE\Classes\luafile\Shell]

[HKEY_LOCAL_MACHINE\SOFTWARE\Classes\luafile\Shell\open]

[HKEY_LOCAL_MACHINE\SOFTWARE\Classes\luafile\Shell\open\command]
@="\"c:\\program files\\utility\\lua.exe\" \"%1\""
```

To add the entries to the registry from the Windows Explorer, double-click the file. Alternatively, from the command shell, you can issue this command:

```
start lua.reg
```

In either case, choose Yes when you are asked if you want to add the entries.

Additionally, for recent versions of Windows, an environment variable named PATHEXT can be augmented with the .lua extension so that the system recognizes Lua scripts as executable. The value of this variable is a semicolon-delimited series of extensions including the period. To edit it, go to the environment variables dialog box in the control panel systems applet. After this is done, you can type the name of a script directly without specifying its extension.

Installing a Web Server

You'll need access to a working web server with CGI capability to proceed with the exercises in this chapter. Even if your Internet service provider has given you everything you need to create and run CGI scripts, you'll likely find it beneficial to develop and test your Lua CGI scripts with a local web server. Doing so will obviate the need to frequently upload scripts or edit them remotely.

The following sections focus on Apache and a small Win32 server named TinyWeb. Another excellent multi-platform web server is Abyss from Aprelium Technologies. Abyss is highly configurable using a web browser. Kepler is a Lua-based web server environment that will be covered briefly in a later section.

Apache

Apache is an excellent, free choice for your local web server. It operates smoothly and dependably on a wide variety of platforms. Although it is highly configurable, its default settings should need little or no adjustment after you install it. Should you decide to learn its advanced features, your knowledge can be applied to Apache installations on any platform. Source and precompiled binary distributions are available from `httpd.apache.org`. If you are a Windows user, you'll find the Apache setup program to be a straightforward way of installing this web server on your system.

On Windows, Apache will install an entry in the programs menu. When started, this server will place an icon in the task bar tray. You can right-click this tray icon to restart or stop the server. Apache on Unix-type systems will typically have a script in the `/etc/rc.d` directory to manage starting, restarting, and stopping the server.

After installing Apache, you'll need to make an adjustment to its configuration file, `httpd.conf`, to make it work with Lua.

For security reasons, Apache will not make its own environment fully available to the CGI programs it launches. This means that the usual LUA_PATH and LUA_CPATH environment variables will not be available to CGI scripts by default. One way or another, you'll need to let Lua scripts know where to look for the modules they need. One way would be to explicitly assign values to the `package.path` and `package.cpath` variables at the beginning of scripts that require modules. Alternatively, Apache lets you set environment variables for all or parts of its web directory tree. Here you will make the LUA_PATH and LUA_CPATH variables known throughout the entire tree. First, retrieve the current values of the variables. From a command shell, execute the following to scroll through the environment listing:

```
set | more
```

If your system has `grep`, you can use it as follows to focus the output:

```
set | grep LUA
```

Back up Apache's configuration file, `httpd.conf`, and then open it for editing. You'll find this file in the `conf` subdirectory of Apache's installation directory. Locate the following line:

```
<Directory />
```

Beneath it, add two lines such as the following, making the appropriate substitutions for your system's particular values and platform:

```
SetEnv LUA_CPATH "/usr/local/lib/lua/5.1/?.so"
SetEnv LUA_PATH "?.lua;/usr/local/lib/lua/5.1/?.lua"
```

Restart Apache to make the changes take effect.

TinyWeb

For Windows users looking for a very lightweight web server with CGI capabilities, TinyWeb from Ritlabs may be a suitable choice. It is free, easy to install, and consumes few resources. Obtain the `tinyweb.zip` package from `www.ritlabs.com/en/products/tinyweb`.

In a command shell, set up your server environment as follows:

The instructions shown here assume this will be beneath `c:\program files`.

```
c:
cd "\program files"
md tinyweb
cd tinyweb
md package
md htdocs
md log
cd htdocs
echo Hello from TinyWeb > index.html
md cgi-bin
md images
md scripts
md css
```

To start up properly, TinyWeb needs to find an index file. The one created here is not valid HTML, but it will satisfy the startup requirement.

Unzip the `tinyweb` package in the package subdirectory as follows:

The 7-zip utility is used here, but any unzipping utility should work.

```
cd ..\package
7z x tinyweb.zip
```

Start TinyWeb in its log directory as follows:

```
c:
cd "\program files\tinyweb\log"
start ..\package\tiny "c:\program files\tinyweb\htdocs"
```

The argument to `tiny` specifies the document root. It must be fully specified. You can create a batch file with these lines to facilitate starting the web server.

TinyWeb buffers its log files, so in general, you won't be able to read log entries right after submitting a request to the server or encountering a problem. If you need to do this, obtain `sync`, which is a free command-line program from `www.sysinternals.com`. Place `sync` in a directory that is in the Windows search path, for example the utility directory recommended in Chapter 1. Invoking the following command commits all pending file buffers on the C drive:

```
sync c
```

To stop TinyWeb, terminate it with the task manager.

Every file in TinyWeb's `cgi-bin` directory (and in every subdirectory you may make beneath it) needs to be a program that can be run from the command shell. As long as Lua has been registered properly (as described in the "CGI Scripts on Windows" section earlier in this chapter), you should have no problems running the Lua scripts you place in this directory. TinyWeb does not filter its own environment when executing a CGI program, so it will pass the LUA_PATH and LUA_CPATH variables intact to the Lua scripts it runs. Consequently, nothing special needs to be done to make sure that your Lua CGI scripts will be able to successfully load the modules they need.

Testing Your Web Server with Static Content

In the following sections, you will be accessing your web server by means of a web browser. Make sure your web server has been started before proceeding. The following examples assume you have installed the web server on your own machine. By default, a web server will listen on all network interfaces of the machine on which it is running. For example, if the machine you start the web server on is part of a network and is reachable with the name schubert, then the web server can be reached from a browser with both this:

```
http://localhost/
```

and this:

```
http://schubert/
```

The localhost address works only on the same machine as the web server. The following examples assume this to be the case. Make the appropriate changes if your setup is different.

Make sure that your web server is functioning properly by asking it for a static page. Point your browser to the following URL to verify that it is serving static pages correctly:

```
http://localhost/
```

In the case shown here, the trailing slash following the server name means that you are asking for the default page in the web server's *document root*, a directory that the web server is configured to treat as the topmost folder. Usually this refers to a page named index.html, although this can typically be configured to something else. If your browser reports that it cannot establish a connection with localhost, your web server has not been started or is somehow not listening on the right interface or port. If it reports a permissions problem, then the server doesn't have authority to read the page. In most cases, the error log of the web server will contain more details about the problem than will be reported to the client. Other problems here will almost certainly involve a visit to the web server's documentation.

Serving Dynamic Web Content

When your server is delivering static pages properly, test it to see how it does with CGI scripts. This is where you'll start using Lua in a web server environment.

Try It Out   Creating a Simple Time Server

In this Try It Out, you arrange to have your web server call Lua to fulfill a dynamic resource request. Lua will generate a plain-text page with the appropriate header and a line containing the server time.

1. In your web server's cgi-bin directory, make a file called date.lua with the following line:

```
io.write('Content-Type: text/plain\n\n', os.date(), '\n')
```

2. On Unix-type systems that require scripts to have an interpreter path, insert the following line at the top:

If `lua` *is installed somewhere else on your system, modify this line accordingly.*

```
#!/usr/local/bin/lua
```

3. On Unix-type systems, mark the script as readable and executable by the web server, as follows:

```
chmod a+rx date.lua
```

4. Request the following resource with your web browser:

```
http://localhost/cgi-bin/date.lua
```

The response should be a simple, unformatted display of the system date.

How It Works

If you receive the system date in an unadorned web page, the web server correctly identified `date.lua` as a script, executed it with Lua, and returned the content that the script generated. In this case, the groundwork is in place to develop more advanced CGI programs in Lua. You may want to examine your web server's log to see how it records a successful CGI transaction.

If you don't receive the expected page, note the response that you get instead. Your browser will typically report a status code, but you should consult your web server's error log for more details. The following section covers the problems you are most likely to encounter.

Problems with CGI Scripts

A response from a web server is always accompanied by a three-digit response code. Values in the 200s indicate success; values in the 400s and 500s indicate problems.

When a CGI request goes bad, the error that is reported is generally one of these:

```
400 Bad Request
401 Unauthorized
403 Forbidden
404 Not Found
500 Internal Server Error
```

Problems with CGI scripts usually involve one of the following usual suspects:

❑ The server mistakes the script for a static page. In this case, the server happily returns the file to your browser, which in turn may display the source code or ask you where you want to save it. This is a web server configuration issue. Remedy this by taking the steps needed to convince your web server that it's dealing with a CGI program, which generally entails placing the script in the designated `cgi-bin` directory or configuring the server to allow CGI execution in the script's directory.

❑ The server doesn't have authority to run the script. This stems from a permissions problem with the operating system and results in a `403 Forbidden` response. When it comes to CGI programs, getting permissions right is an important task. You should run the web server as a user with very limited authority, because CGI scripts can be a source of security breaches. On Unix-type systems, this user (often `nobody`) should *never* be a member of groups that would widen its authority. However, this can make it tricky for a CGI developer to assign correct privileges to a

475

script. A reasonable policy is to require all CGI scripts to be cleared by an administrator who has the necessary privileges to place the script in the `cgi-bin` directory and to change the script's permissions to make it executable by the web server.

❏ The script itself has an error. Lua's error message may be reported as a web page, or you may get a rather vague message like `Premature end of script headers`. In the latter case, the web server's error log should contain the full error message. Running a CGI script from the command shell can be a good way to make sure it doesn't contain errors. In general, it's easier to diagnose problems this way than in a web server environment. With a little effort, more sophisticated CGI scripts that depend on environment variables and possibly standard input can be made to work as well. If you are simply interested in catching syntax errors, you can use `luac` to compile it.

❏ Your CGI script may have executed properly, but it sent back content that your browser doesn't know how to render. For example, content of type `text/plain` cannot be displayed by older versions of Internet Explorer.

❏ On Unix-like systems, or on Windows when you have configured Apache to emulate Unix-type behavior, your Lua script may lack or have an improperly specified shebang. This is the first line of the script that looks like `#!/usr/local/bin/lua`.

Asynchronous Calls to the Server

The previous example uses a standard synchronous call to the web server to request the output of the `date.lua` CGI script. Each time you refresh the page, the contents of the page (which is not a whole lot in this example) are entirely replaced. Modern browsers support an asynchronous method of calling the server as well. In this case, your browser issues a standard request of the server, but rather than waiting for the server's response, it returns control immediately. Then, when the server does respond, a handler is called that can programmatically deal with the returned content, often by making localized changes to the displayed page.

In the following examples, a JavaScript page named `AjaxRequest.js` will be used to simplify the process of making asynchronous calls. It can be obtained freely from here:

```
http://www.ajaxtoolbox.com/request/full/AjaxRequest.js
```

If it doesn't already exist, create a directory named `scripts` beneath the document root of your web server. Place `AjaxRequest.js` in this directory. You can test whether it is properly accessible by requesting it explicitly. Point your browser to the following URL and verify that the script is returned:

```
http://localhost/scripts/AjaxRequest.js
```

Try It Out   Implementing the Time Server using AJAX

Enhance the previous server time example with an asynchronous call to the server. To do this, you'll use HTML which links in the AJAX toolkit script.

1. With your text editor, create a new file and copy the following lines to it:

```
<!DOCTYPE html PUBLIC "-//W3C//DTD XHTML 1.0 Strict//EN"
    "http://www.w3.org/TR/xhtml1/DTD/xhtml1-strict.dtd">

<html>
```

```
<head>

  <title>Server time</title>

  <script type="text/javascript" src="/scripts/AjaxRequest.js"></script>

  <script type="text/javascript">

    function NodeReplace(NodeStr, ValStr) {
      var El = document.getElementById(NodeStr);
      var TxtNode = document.createTextNode(ValStr);
      El.replaceChild(TxtNode, El.firstChild);
    } // NodeReplace

    function Get(UrlStr, NodeStr) {
      function LclPrint(Req) {
        NodeReplace(NodeStr, Req.responseText);
      } // LclPrint
      var Req = { 'url':UrlStr, 'onSuccess':LclPrint }
      AjaxRequest.get(Req);
      return false;
    } // Get

  </script>

</head>

<body>

<p><a href="#" onclick="return Get('/cgi-bin/date.lua', 'time');">Server
time</a> <i><span id="time"> </span></i></p>

</body>

</html>
```

2. Save this file as `date.html` in your web server's document root directory. Request the following page with your browser:

```
http://localhost/date.html
```

3. Click the Server Time hyperlink at intervals to update the time display.

How It Works

Clicking the hyperlink initiates a request for the output of the `date.lua` script. Rather than waiting for this call to return, the JavaScript call to the server returns immediately. When the updated system time does arrive, only its designated area (specifically, the span block with the `id` value `"time"`) on the page is updated. Each time you click the server time link, another call is made, and when the response is received, the contents of the time compartment are updated. The browser page history is not modified, which means that clicking your browser's back button will not take you back to a page with the previous time.

AJAX is strictly a client-side mechanism. From the web server's point of view, the synchronous and asynchronous calls to `date.lua` are indistinguishable.

If, as you study this example, you begin to imagine a browser that supports a <script type="text/lua"> script tag and the use of Lua coroutines as an elegant replacement for event handlers, you are not alone. But for now, the province of browser scripting belongs to JavaScript.

For security reasons, an asynchronous call cannot be made to a web server other than the one that served the current page. If it's crucial for you to contact multiple servers from your application, you may need to add a level of indirection by sending all of your asynchronous requests to only one server. This server can then make calls to other web servers and return the content to the original requester.

Producing a Calendar Dynamically

A CGI script is essentially a noninteractive program and can call any library function that applies in that context. The following example demonstrates this by presenting a script that, except for producing HTML rather than plain text, functions just as well in a command shell as a web server environment.

Try It Out   **Displaying a Calendar of the Current Month**

Prepare a script that displays the current month with the current day highlighted. The script will make use of the os.date function to determine attributes of the current month, such as the day of week that the first day of the month falls on.

1.   Save the following file as calendar.lua to your web server's cgi-bin directory:

```
#!/usr/local/bin/lua

local Cn = {}

Cn.HdrStr = [[Content-Type: text/html

<!DOCTYPE html PUBLIC "-//W3C//DTD XHTML 1.0 Strict//EN"
   "http://www.w3.org/TR/xhtml1/DTD/xhtml1-strict.dtd">

<html>

<head>

  <title>Calendar</title>

  <meta http-equiv="Content-Type" content="text/html; charset=utf-8" />

  <link rel="stylesheet" href="/css/general.css" type="text/css" />

  <style type="text/css">

  table.data td {border-right : 1px solid; border-bottom : 1px solid;
  border-color:inherit; color:#404040; background-color:#FFFFFF;
  vertical-align:top; width:14%;}

  table.data td.today {background-color:#f0f0ff;}

  table.data td.name {font-weight:bold; text-align:center; color:#505060;
```

```
    background-color:#f0f0ff;}

    table.data td.edge {width:15%;}

    </style>

</head>

<body>

]]

Cn.FtrStr = "</body>\n\n</html>"

local DaysInMonth = { 31, 0, 31, 30, 31, 30, 31, 31, 30, 31, 30, 31 }

-- For the specified month and year, this function returns the day of week of
-- the first day in the month, and the number of days in the month.

local function Calendar(Year, Month)
  assert(Year > 1900 and Year < 2100, "Year out of range")
  assert(Month >= 1 and Month <= 12, "Month out of range")
  local Rec = os.date("*t", os.time{year = Year, month = Month, day = 1})
  local DayMax = DaysInMonth[Rec.month]
  if DayMax == 0 then
    DayMax = math.mod(Rec.year, 4) == 0 and 29 or 28
  end
  return Rec.wday, DayMax
end

local Today = os.date("*t")
local Dow, DayMax = Calendar(Today.year, Today.month)

io.write(Cn.HdrStr)

io.write('<table class="data shade" border="0" cellspacing="0" ',
  'cellpadding="5" summary="" width="100%">\n',
  '<tbody>\n',
  '<tr><th colspan="7">', os.date('%B'), '</th></tr>\n',
  '<tr>\n')
local Base = 8 - Dow -- Map day to column
for Col = 1, 7 do
  local Wd = (Col == 1 or Col == 7) and ' edge' or ''
  io.write('<td class="name', Wd, '">', os.date("%a",
    os.time{year = Today.year, month = Today.month, day = Base + Col}),
    '</td>\n')
end
io.write('</tr>\n')
local Day = 2 - Dow -- Map day to column
while Day <= DayMax do
  io.write('<tr>')
  for Col = 1, 7 do
    io.write(Today.day == Day and '<td class="today">' or '<td>',
      (Day >= 1 and Day <= DayMax) and Day or ' ', '</td>\n')
```

```
      Day = Day + 1
    end
    io.write("</tr>\n")
  end
io.write('</tbody></table>\n')
io.write(Cn.FtrStr)
```

2. This script and others in this chapter generate web pages that refer to the following style sheet. Create a subdirectory named `css` in your web server's document. Save the following contents to a file named `general.css` in the `css` directory:

```css
body {background-color : #FFFFFF; color : #404040; font: 9pt/13pt arial;
margin-left:4em; margin-top:2em; margin-bottom:1em; margin-right:4em;}

.hdr {padding:3pt; padding-left:1em; font-weight:bold; border-style: solid;
border-width:1px;}

.shade {color:#505060; background-color:#D0D0F0; border-color:#B0B0D0;}

.white {background-color:#FFFFFF;}

.top {vertical-align:top;}

.note {font: 8pt/12pt arial; color: #606060; margin-top: 0px;}

h1 {font: 11pt/15pt arial; color: #606060; font-weight:bold;}

.right {text-align: right;}

span.super {vertical-align: super; font-size: smaller;}

table.data {border-style:solid; border-top-width:1px; border-left-width:1px;
border-right-width:0px; border-bottom-width:0px;}

table.data tbody {border-color:inherit; font: 9pt/13pt arial;}

table.data tr {padding-top:0px; padding-bottom:0px; border-color:inherit;}

table.data th {border-right : 1px solid; border-bottom : 1px solid;
border-color:inherit;}

table.data td {border-right : 1px solid; border-bottom : 1px solid;
border-color:inherit; color:#404040; background-color:#f6f6ff;}

table.data td.in {padding-left:16px;}

form table {border: 1px solid; padding: 6px;}

form table td {border-right: 0px; border-bottom: 0px;}

form table td.label {text-align: right; font-weight:bold;}

form table td.input {text-align: left;}
```

3. Verify that your web server can read this page by requesting the following page:

```
http://localhost/css/general.css
```

Figure 15-1 shows the kind of page you should see when you request the following URL with your browser:

```
http://localhost/cgi-bin/calendar.lua
```

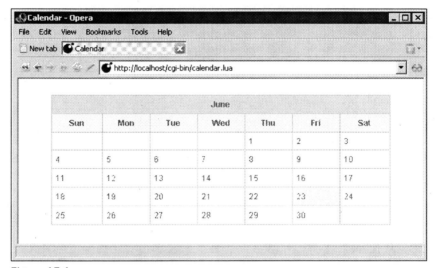

Figure 15-1

How It Works

The calendar script is invoked by the web server as a CGI program. It uses date arithmetics to construct the calendar's attributes, and writes out this calendar using a styled table. Notice that the function `Calendar` is independent of the script's web context. This makes it a prime candidate for inclusion in a general date module.

Producing Charts Dynamically

Charts and other graphs in your web pages are a great way to present at-a-glance data aggregation and to offer insights into informational patterns. The `gd` graphics library that you became familiar with in Chapter 12 is ideally suited for this because with it you can create images programmatically. In this section, you'll learn how to use the `gd` library to generate a bar chart that can be presented in a dynamically built web page.

Usually when you place a graph based on some live data in a web page, you want supporting textual details to accompany it. For example, in a business environment, you may want to produce a web page that details recent customer or vendor transactions. In this page, you may want to place a bar chart that summarizes this activity. Embedding the image right into the dynamically created page would be nice, but this isn't the way HTML works. An image in a web page must be referenced as a separate resource

481

using the `src` attribute with the `<img>` tag. This presents a problem, because you've got two dynamically generated resources — the web page and the chart — that must somehow remain synchronized.

The solution presented here works as follows. When a request is made for a dynamic page, the appropriate CGI script is called. It produces a web page with the appropriate details, usually gleaned from a database. In this page, there is a reference to the image. The `src` attribute of the `<img>` tag identifies a CGI script that will actually produce the graph. The details of what the graph should look like are submitted as part of the query. This way, the web page details and the query that specifies the appearance of the graph are bound together and any synchronization issues are avoided.

In the `cgi-bin` directory of your web server, create a file with the following contents and name it `bar.lua`, marking the file as executable and readable by the web server where necessary:

```lua
#!/usr/local/bin/lua

require "gd"
require "iomode"

io.modeset(io.stdin, "binary")
io.modeset(io.stdout, "binary")

local function LclPng(Str)

   local ValMax = 1 -- Prevent subsequent division by zero
   local ValList = {}
   local ValCount = 0
   local ClrList = {}
   local Factor, Ht, Wd, BarWd, Gap, Hnd, PngStr, ErrStr

   Str = "_" .. string.gsub(string.lower(Str), "_", "__") .. "_"

   local function LclPrm(Prefix, Default)
      local PatStr = "_" .. Prefix .. "(%d+)_"
      local Pos, Pos, NumStr = string.find(Str, PatStr)
      return Pos and tonumber(NumStr) or Default
   end

   Ht = LclPrm("h", 200)
   BarWd = LclPrm("b", 12)
   Gap = LclPrm("g", 4)
   for ValStr in string.gmatch(Str, "_([%.%d%:]+)_") do
      local Pos, NumStr, ClrStr, Val
      Pos, Pos, NumStr, ClrStr = string.find(ValStr, "([%d%.]+)%:(%d+)")
      Val = tonumber(Pos and NumStr or ValStr)
      if Val > ValMax then
         ValMax = Val
      end
      table.insert(ValList, { Val, tonumber(ClrStr) })
      ValCount = ValCount + 1
   end
   if ValCount > 0 then
      Wd = ValCount * (Gap + BarWd) + Gap + 1
```

```
Factor = (Ht - Gap) / ValMax
Hnd = gd.createPalette(Wd, Ht)
if Hnd then
  -- Background is first color allocated
  ClrList.White = Hnd:colorAllocate(255, 255, 255)
  ClrList.Gray = Hnd:colorAllocate(150, 150, 150)
  ClrList.Black = Hnd:colorAllocate(0, 0, 0)
  -- Allocate colors specified in query string
  for Mode, RdStr, GrStr, BlStr in string.gmatch(Str,
    "_([cfl])(%x%x)(%x%x)(%x%x)_") do
    local Clr = Hnd:colorAllocate(tonumber(RdStr, 16),
      tonumber(GrStr, 16), tonumber(BlStr, 16))
    if Mode == 'c' then
      table.insert(ClrList, Clr)
    elseif Mode == 'l' then
      ClrList.Line = Clr
    else
      ClrList.Fill = Clr
    end
  end
  local ClrDef = ClrList[1] or ClrList.Gray
  ClrList.Line = ClrList.Line or ClrList.Gray
  -- By default, background color is the first color allocated. If a fill
  -- color was specified, fill in the image now.
  if ClrList.Fill then
    Hnd:filledRectangle(1, 1, Wd, Ht, ClrList.Fill)
  end
  local X = Gap
  for J = 1, ValCount do
    local Y = Factor * ValList[J][1]
    local ClrPos = ValList[J][2] or 0
    local Clr = ClrList[ClrPos] or ClrDef
    Hnd:filledRectangle(X, Ht - Y, X + BarWd,
      Ht, ClrList.Line)
    Hnd:filledRectangle(X + 1, Ht + 1 - Y, X + BarWd - 1,
      Ht, Clr)
    X = X + Gap + BarWd
  end
  -- Create border around image
  Hnd:line(0, 0, 0, Ht, ClrList.Line)
  Hnd:line(0, 0, Wd, 0, ClrList.Line)
  Hnd:line(Wd - 1, 0, Wd - 1, Ht - 1, ClrList.Line)
  Hnd:line(0, Ht - 1, Wd - 1, Ht - 1, ClrList.Line)
  -- Load image into Lua string
  PngStr = gd.pngStr(Hnd)
  if not PngStr then
    ErrStr = "Error generating PNG image."
  end
  Hnd = nil
else
  ErrStr = "Error creating palette-based PNG image."
end
```

```
      else
        ErrStr = "No values retrieved from query string."
      end
      return PngStr, ErrStr
    end

    local Http, PngStr, ErrStr, QueryStr

    Http = os.getenv("SERVER_SOFTWARE")
    QueryStr = arg[1] or os.getenv("QUERY_STRING")
    if QueryStr then
      PngStr, ErrStr = LclPng(QueryStr)
    else
      ErrStr = "Error retrieving query string."
    end
    if PngStr then
      if Http then
        io.write('Date: ', os.date(), '\r\n')
        io.write('X-Scripting-Engine: ', _VERSION, '\r\n')
        io.write('X-Graphics-Library: ', gd.VERSION, '\r\n')
        io.write("Content-Transfer-Encoding: binary\r\n")
        io.write('Content-Length: ', string.len(PngStr), '\r\n')
        io.write("Content-Type: image/png\r\n\r\n");
      end
      io.write(PngStr)
    else
      io.write(Http and 'Content-Type: text/plain\r\n\r\n' or '', ErrStr, "\r\n")
    end
```

This script uses the gd library to create a simple bar chart in PNG format based only on the arguments that are passed to it. This makes it easy for other dynamic scripts to include charts since no images need to be cached on the server.

Notice the following lines in bar.lua:

```
Http = os.getenv("SERVER_SOFTWARE")
QueryStr = arg[1] or os.getenv("QUERY_STRING")
```

These lines let the script know with a moderate degree of certainty whether it is being run in a web server environment or in a command shell. If Http is not nil, an HTTP header will be written before the PNG file contents. This is the response a web browser expects from its request. This technique is useful when developing a CGI script. It is generally easier to develop a script while working in a command shell than while working with a web server, and this practice permits the script to be run in either environment without modification.

To test bar.lua from a command shell, invoke it as in the following example:

```
lua bar.lua 12_23_34 > test.png
```

The string of numbers delimited with underscores is used by bar.lua to construct a simple bar chart. You can view the resulting test image with a web browser by opening it as a file.

To generate the same chart in a web server environment, request the following:

```
http://localhost/cgi-bin/bar.lua?12_23_34
```

The question mark after bar.lua in this reference separates the resource name from the arguments to be submitted by the web server to the CGI script.

To include a chart in a web page, reference it as follows:

```
<img src="/cgi-bin/bar.lua?12_23_34" alt="Chart" />
```

The arguments to a CGI script are conventionally divided into key/value pairs. For example:

```
height=200&width=500
```

To save some space in the URL, the bar chart script deviates from this practice and uses its own format. The argument string comprises a series of tokens that are separated from one another with an underscore character. Basically, you specify the height of each vertical bar in order. The following sequence creates a chart with bars of height 12, 23, and 34, scaled so that the tallest bar just fits into the height of the chart:

```
12_23_34
```

To specify the same chart with a non-default height, use a sequence like this:

```
H150_12_23_34
```

The token H150 indicates a chart height of 150 pixels.

The following table shows all of the supported tokens. Prefixes and hexadecimal numbers can be specified in either uppercase or lowercase.

Prefix	Numeric Type	Description	Default
H	Integer	Chart height in pixels	200
B	Integer	Bar width in pixels	12
G	Integer	Gap between bars in pixels	4
C	Hexadecimal	Bar color	969696
F	Hexadecimal	Chart background fill color	FFFFFF
L	Hexadecimal	Chart line color	969696
	Float or Integer	Height of bar	

The color prefixes (C, F, and L) are followed by a six-digit hexadecimal number in which the first pair of digits is red, the middle pair is green, and the last pair is blue. For example, the following specifies bright red for the bar color:

```
CFF0000
```

The first bar color value that you specify is used for each of the bars, unless the bar height token is followed by a colon and a bar color position. For example, this sequence results in a chart with three bars, with the first and last bars in red and the middle bar in blue:

```
CFF0000_C0000FF_12_23:2_34
```

Try It Out   Creating a Simulated Report with Bar Chart

1.   Using the bar chart script, generate a live report. Create a new file and copy in these lines:

```lua
#!/usr/local/bin/lua

local Cn = {}

Cn.HdrStr = [[Content-Type: text/html

<!DOCTYPE html PUBLIC "-//W3C//DTD XHTML 1.0 Strict//EN"
   "http://www.w3.org/TR/xhtml1/DTD/xhtml1-strict.dtd">

<html>

<head>

  <title>Bogosity Index</title>

  <link rel="stylesheet" href="/css/general.css" type="text/css" />

</head>

<body>

]]

Cn.FtrStr = "</body>\n\n</html>"

-- This function returns an indexed table and bar chart specifier. The table
-- contains DayCount (default 31) simulated data records. Each record is an
-- indexed table of the form {date, value}. The chart specifier is a string
-- with each value separated by an underscore.

local function LclDataRetrieve(DayCount)
   DayCount = DayCount or 31
   local Lo, Hi, SecPerDay = -0.3, 2.3, 60 * 60 * 24
   local Tm = os.time() - DayCount * SecPerDay
   local ValList, RecList = {}, {}
```

```
    for J = Lo, Hi, (Hi - Lo) / DayCount do
      local DtStr = string.gsub(os.date("%A %d %B", Tm), " 0", " ")
      Tm = Tm + SecPerDay
      local Val = 100 + math.floor(300 * math.sin(J) + math.random(0, 60))
      table.insert(RecList, {DtStr, Val})
      table.insert(ValList, Val)
    end
    return RecList, table.concat(ValList, "_")
end


local Out = io.write
local CnColCount = 3
local List, UrlStr = LclDataRetrieve()
local RowCount = #List
local Split = math.ceil(RowCount / CnColCount)

Out(Cn.HdrStr, '<h1>Recent Bogon Flux Averages</h1>\n',
    '<div><img src="/cgi-bin/bar.lua?h50_cD0D0F0_19090B0_ff6f6ff_', UrlStr,
    '" alt="Bogosity chart" /></div>\n',
    '<p class="note">Average bogon flux values (10<span class="super">9</span> ',
    'bogons / m<span class="super">2</span>) from ', List[1][1],
    ' to ', List[RowCount][1], '</p>\n',
    '<table summary=""><tbody><tr>\n')
local Row = 1
for Col = 1, CnColCount do
  Out('<td><table class="data shade" border="0" cellspacing="0" ',
    'cellpadding="5" summary="">\n',
    '<tbody>\n',
    '<tr><th>Date</th><th>Bogon Flux</th></tr>\n')
  for J = 1, Split do
    local Dt, Val
    local Rec = List[Row]
    if Rec then
      Dt, Val = Rec[1], Rec[2]
      Row = Row + 1
    else
      Dt, Val = " ", " "
    end
    Out('<tr><td>', Dt, '</td><td class="right">', Val, '</td></tr>\n')
  end
  Out('</tbody>\n</table></td>\n')
end
Out('</tr></tbody></table>\n', Cn.FtrStr)
```

2. Save this file as bogosity.lua in your web server's cgi-bin directory. As always, make sure the permissions are set so that the web server can read and execute the script.

3. Request http://localhost/cgi-bin/bogosity.lua in your web browser. Figure 15-2 shows the kind of page you can expect.

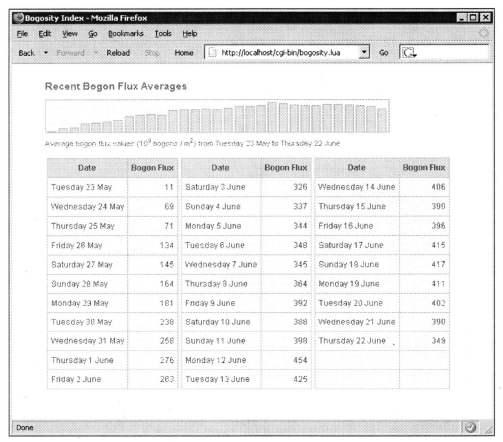

Figure 15-2

How It Works

When you request the bogosity.lua resource, your web server recognizes it as a CGI script. During execution, it obtains a table of information to display. In this case, the data is generated internally, but it would be typical for this information to come from a database, system logs, or some other external source. It then writes out the text of what will become a valid HTML page. Note that the bar chart graphic is not created in this step; it is only specified in the <img> tag. When the browser displays the page, it makes another call to the server to obtain the chart. All of the information needed to produce the graph is passed along with the URL.

Even though the contents of this page are nonsensical, the script provides a good platform on which to base dynamic, informative pages.

A graph generated this way is limited by the amount of descriptive information you can convey to the script that creates it. Browsers and servers may each impose limits on the number of characters that can be transferred as part of URL. If you must submit more information than can fit within several hundred characters, you may need to devise an alternate method of describing the graph. For example, you could encode the bar heights in base 64 (a common method of expressing binary data using a set of 64 characters). Each bar could then be specified with two such characters (allowing a range from 0 to 4095), making the bar height delimiters unnecessary. Additionally, you could predefine a color table in bar.lua and specify colors by table offset rather than 24-bit values.

Interactive CGI Applications

The dynamic pages you've generated so far have not been interactive. You'll now learn about HTML forms that allow you to write scripts that process information provided by the user. HTML forms are rather primitive when compared with most desktop applications, and the simple HTTP request/response model that works so well with static content is decidedly clumsy with interactive content. However, even with its limitations, the interactive web is an integral part of the Internet experience.

CGI Helper Routines

The following file, cgi.lua, includes several routines that simplify writing CGI scripts in Lua. Place it in your server's module directory (as discussed in Chapter 7).

```
local Cgi = {}

-- Return a urlencoded copy of Str. For example,
--    "Here & there + 97% of other places"
-- is encoded as
--    "Here%20%26%20there%20%2B%2097%25%20of%20other%20places"

function Cgi.Encode(Str)
  return string.gsub(Str, '%W', function(Str)
    return string.format('%%%02X', string.byte(Str)) end )
end

-- Returns a urldecoded copy of Str. This function reverses the effects of
-- Cgi.Encode.

function Cgi.Decode(Str)
  Str = string.gsub(Str, '%+', ' ')
  Str = string.gsub(Str, '%%(%x%x)', function(Str)
    return string.char(tonumber(Str, 16)) end )
  return Str
end

-- Returns an escaped copy of Str in which the characters &<>" are escaped for
-- display in HTML documents.

function Cgi.Escape(Str)
  Str = string.gsub(Str or "", "%&", "&amp;")
  Str = string.gsub(Str, '%"', "&quot;")
  Str = string.gsub(Str, "%<", "&lt;")
  return string.gsub(Str, "%>", "&gt;")
end
```

```
-- This function returns an associative array with the parsed contents of the
-- urlencoded string Str. Multiple values with the same name are placed into an
-- indexed table with the name.

local function LclParse(Str)
  local Decode, Tbl = Cgi.Decode, {}
  for KeyStr, ValStr in string.gmatch(Str .. '&', '(.-)%=(.-)%&') do
    local Key = Decode(KeyStr)
    local Val = Decode(ValStr)
    local Sub = Tbl[Key]
    local SubCat = type(Sub)
    -- If there are multiple values with the same name, place them in an
    -- indexed table.
    if SubCat == "string" then -- replace string with table
      Tbl[Key] = { Sub, Val }
    elseif SubCat == "table" then -- insert into existing table
      table.insert(Sub, Val)
    else -- add as string field
      Tbl[Key] = Val
    end
  end
  return Tbl
end

-- Returns an associative array with both the GET and POST contents which
-- accompany an HTTP request. Multi-part form data, usually used with uploaded
-- files, is not currently supported.

function Cgi.Params()
  local PostLen, GetStr, PostStr, KeyList, Obj
  KeyList = {
    'PATH_INFO',
    'PATH_TRANSLATED',
    'REMOTE_HOST',
    'REMOTE_ADDR',
    'GATEWAY_INTERFACE',
    'SCRIPT_NAME',
    'REQUEST_METHOD',
    'HTTP_ACCEPT',
    'HTTP_ACCEPT_CHARSET',
    'HTTP_ACCEPT_ENCODING',
    'HTTP_ACCEPT_LANGUAGE',
    'HTTP_FROM',
    'HTTP_HOST',
    'HTTP_REFERER',
    'HTTP_USER_AGENT',
    'QUERY_STRING',
    'SERVER_SOFTWARE',
    'SERVER_NAME',
    'SERVER_PROTOCOL',
    'SERVER_PORT',
    'CONTENT_TYPE',
    'CONTENT_LENGTH',
    'AUTH_TYPE' }
```

```
    Obj = {}
    for J, KeyStr in ipairs(KeyList) do
      Obj[KeyStr] = os.getenv(KeyStr)
    end
    if not Obj.SERVER_SOFTWARE then -- Command line invocation
      Obj.QUERY_STRING = arg[1]
      PostStr = arg[2]
    elseif "application/x-www-form-urlencoded" == Obj.CONTENT_TYPE then
      -- Web server invocation with posted urlencoded content
      PostLen = tonumber(Obj.CONTENT_LENGTH)
      if PostLen and PostLen > 0 then
        PostStr = io.read(PostLen)
      end
    end
    PostStr = PostStr or ""
    Obj.Post = LclParse(PostStr)
    Obj.POST_STRING = PostStr
    GetStr = Obj.QUERY_STRING or ""
    Obj.Get = LclParse(GetStr)
    return Obj
  end

  return Cgi
```

Your CGI scripts can then make use of this module as follows:

```
local Cgi = require("cgi")
```

The module provides some routines that facilitate the transfer of information between the script and the web server. In particular, the `Cgi.Params` function makes it easy to collect information that a user has submitted in a form. `Cgi.Escape` prepares text for display in an HTML document by replacing the ampersand, less than, greater than and double quote characters with symbolic replacements. Similarly, `Cgi.Encode` makes character substitutions to prepare text for inclusion in a URL. This process is known as urlencoding. `Cgi.Decode` reverses this process to extract information.

The following Try It Out demonstrates how user input is processed by a CGI script.

Try It Out   Specifying a Simple Form

The advantages of inspecting Lua values apply as much to web applications as to other kinds of programs. Here, you will specify a form in a static web page. When you submit the form, a request for the `cgishow.lua` resource is made. This is a CGI program that simply displays the values that are part of this request.

1.   Place the following `form.html` file in the document root of your web server, and then make sure it is readable by the web server:

```
<!DOCTYPE html PUBLIC "-//W3C//DTD XHTML 1.0 Strict//EN"
  "http://www.w3.org/TR/xhtml1/DTD/xhtml1-strict.dtd">

<html>
```

```
<head>

  <title>Simple HTML Form</title>

  <meta http-equiv="Content-Type" content="text/html; charset=utf-8" />

  <link rel="stylesheet" href="/css/general.css" type="text/css" />

</head>

<body>

  <h1>Simple form demonstration</h1>

  <form action="/cgi-bin/cgishow.lua?Number=42" method="get">

  <div><input type="hidden" name="Number" value="42" /></div>

  <table class="shade" summary=""><tbody>

  <tr>

    <td class="label">User</td>

    <td><input type="text" size="20" name="User" /></td>

    <td class="label">Password</td>

    <td><input type="password" size="20" name="Pass" /></td>

  </tr>

  <tr>

    <td class="label top">Site(s)</td><td>

    <select name="Site" size="4" multiple="multiple">
      <option value="1">Abbey of Pomposa, near Ferrara</option>
      <option value="2">Castle del Monte, Apulia</option>
      <option value="3">Cathedral of Pisa, Pisa</option>
      <option value="4">Chancellery Palace, Rome</option>
      <option value="5">Church of San Spirito, Florence</option>
      <option value="6">Doge's Palace, Venice</option>
      <option value="7">Ducal Palace, Urbino</option>
      <option value="8">Florence Cathedral, Florence</option>
      <option value="9">Leaning Tower, Pisa</option>
      <option value="10">Orvieto Cathedral, Orvieto</option>
      <option value="11">Ospedale Degli Innocenti, Florence</option>
      <option value="12">Palazzo Strozzi, Florence</option>
      <option value="13">Pazzi Chapel, Florence</option>
      <option value="14">Piazza del Campo, Siena</option>
      <option value="15">Ponte Vecchio, Florence</option>
```

```
        <option value="16">S. Andrea, Mantua</option>
        <option value="17">S. Maria Della Pace, Rome</option>
        <option value="18">S. Maria Novella, Florence</option>
        <option value="19">S. Maria degli Angeli, Florence</option>
        <option value="20">San Lorenzo, Florence, Florence</option>
        <option value="21">San Sebastiano, at Mantua</option>
        <option value="22">San Zeno Maggiore, Verona</option>
        <option value="23">St. Mark's, Venice</option>
    </select>

    </td>

    <td class="label top">Remarks</td>

    <td><textarea name="Text" rows="3" cols="32"></textarea></td>

</tr>

<tr>

    <td class="label">Artist</td>

    <td colspan="3">

    <input type="radio" name="Artist" value="1" checked="checked" />
      Filippo Brunelleschi
    <input type="radio" name="Artist" value="2" />Leon Battista Alberti
    <input type="radio" name="Artist" value="3" />Donato Bramante

    </td>

</tr>

<tr>

    <td class="label">Art</td>

    <td colspan="3">

    <input type="checkbox" name="Art" value="Arch" checked="checked" />Architecture
    <input type="checkbox" name="Art" value="Paint" />Painting
    <input type="checkbox" name="Art" value="Sculpt" />Sculpture

    </td>

</tr>

<tr>

    <td class="right" colspan="4"><input type="submit" value="Submit" /></td>

</tr>
```

```
  </tbody></table>

  </form>

</body>

</html>
```

2. Place the following `cgishow.lua` file in the web server's `cgi-bin` directory, and then make sure it is readable and executable by the web server:

```lua
#!/usr/local/bin/lua

local Cgi = require("cgi")
require("show")

local Cn = {}

Cn.HdrStr = [[Content-Type: text/html

<!DOCTYPE html PUBLIC "-//W3C//DTD XHTML 1.0 Strict//EN"
  "http://www.w3.org/TR/xhtml1/DTD/xhtml1-strict.dtd">

<html>

<head>

  <title>CGI Environment</title>

  <meta http-equiv="Content-Type" content="text/html; charset=utf-8" />

  <link rel="stylesheet" href="/css/general.css" type="text/css" />

</head>

<body>

]]

Cn.FtrStr = "</body>\n\n</html>"

local Prm = Cgi.Params()
local List = {}
ObjectDescribe(List, Prm, "CGI parameters")
io.write(Cn.HdrStr, '<p class="hdr shade">CGI Environment</p>\n')
for J, Rec in ipairs(List) do
  local Key, Val = string.match(Rec[2], '^%[%"?(.-)%"?%]%s+(.+)$')
  if Key then
    io.write('<div style="margin-left:', Rec[1] * 0.5, 'cm;">',
      '<b>', Cgi.Escape(Key), '</b> ', Cgi.Escape(Val), '</div>\n')
  else
```

```
        io.write(Rec[2], '<br />\n')
   end
end
io.write(Cn.FtrStr)
```

Two files, `show.lua` (introduced in Chapter 7) and `cgi.lua`, need to be located in Lua's module directory.

The `general.css` style sheet (which was used in a previous example) is used by both `form.html` and `cgishow.lua`. It must be located in `css` subdirectory beneath the document root.

3. With your web browser, request the following resource:

```
http://localhost/form.html
```

The resulting page should look like the one shown in Figure 15-3.

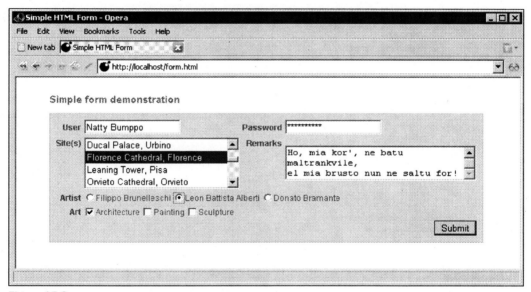

Figure 15-3

4. Fill in the various fields and click the Submit button. Figure 15-4 shows the kind of page you will get.

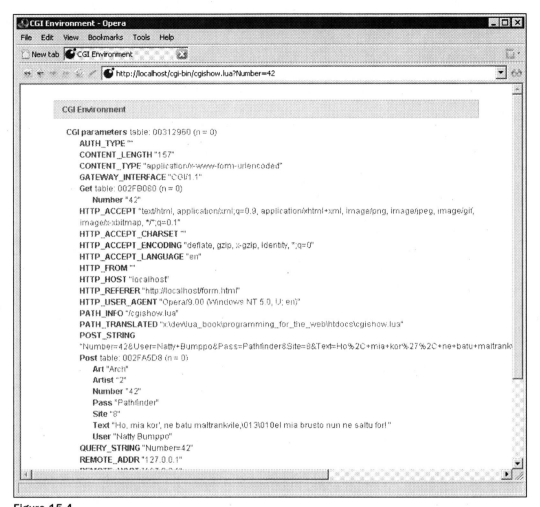

Figure 15-4

How It Works

In `form.html`, the following line specifies where the form contents should be sent (in this case, `/cgi-bin/cgishow.lua`) and in what manner (using the GET command in this example):

```
<form action="/cgi-bin/cgishow.lua" method="get">
```

Because the scheme and server segments are missing from the action URL, the values of the current page (`http://localhost`) are used.

The GET command instructs the browser to append a question mark, followed by the name/value fields from the form, to the end of the URL. The principal advantage of this method is that the full URL can be saved and later used to request the resulting page without needing to revisit the initial form page. This is valuable in the case of a search engine. From another perspective, however, the GET method can be undesirable because it places the form's name/value pairs out in the open where they can show up in server logs and bookmarks. Examine the URL of the cgishow.lua page, and you'll see the unmasked password value. Also, nothing prevents you from pasting a very large amount of text into a form's text field, but limitations with the web browser and web server may prevent your CGI script from actually receiving the complete text.

The POST method places the form's name/value pairs after the HTTP headers, away from the URL. Try changing the form method in form.html from get to post and examine the differences in the CGI parameters table as shown in the resulting page.

A remark should be made regarding the way multiline text appears in the cgishow.lua page. If you type the following into a <textarea> control:

```
Line 1
Line 2
Line 3
```

it will appear as this in the display page:

```
Line 1\013\010Line 2\013\010Line 3
```

The actual data contains carriage returns (\013) and newlines (\010); the backslash notation is used by the show module to present control characters and conforms with Lua's method of embedding binary data in a string.

When you develop a CGI program in Lua, it's helpful to have a glimpse into the data that is transferred to your script. You can temporarily set the action attribute of a form to cgishow.lua in order to examine what your CGI script can expect.

The CGI module presented here supports only urlencoded data uploads. This method is always used with a GET command and is used by default with a POST command. Control characters such a carriage returns are always coded into a printable form in this type of encoding.

If you want to extend the module to accept uploaded files, you'll need to write a routine to handle data that has been encoded with the multipart/form-data method. This type of encoding uses a special form of delimiter that separates the various uploaded field values. These values can contain binary data and, on the Windows platform, special attention must be paid to avoid problems while reading from the standard input stream. Your script, or the revised CGI script, will need to call the following after requiring the iomode module:

```
io.modeset(io.stdin, "binary")
```

Without this, the content read from the standard input stream will have had carriage returns removed. In addition to corrupting binary uploads, this will cause the content to be smaller than the CONTENT_LENGTH value indicates. This discrepancy will cause io.read to block indefinitely as it attempts to read data that isn't there.

Developing CGI Scripts

As helpful as `cgishow.lua` is in developing CGI applications, the cycle of editing a Lua script and then testing it with a web browser can be tedious. Here are some hints to expedite the development process:

❑ Modularize your application by factoring out parts that don't involve the user interface. Place these in modules if appropriate.

❑ Test scripts in a command shell. Any error messages will be displayed in the same console window from which you launch the script, making it unnecessary to examine web server logs.

❑ Make a development replacement for `Cgi.Params` that fills the fields you require with test data.

❑ Make sure your script generates standard HTML. The Html Validator extension for Firefox is a convenient and valuable tool in this regard.

❑ Consider writing a Lua script that automates the testing of your dynamic web pages. Tools such as `wget` or `curl` can be used from the command shell to submit HTTP requests. Both allow you to specify posted content.

Security Issues

The CGI mechanism allows web users to run designated scripts from your web server. Your primary concern when developing CGI scripts is the validity of submitted form data. Put simply, expect the worst. HTML forms support enumerated selections and JavaScript can validate data at the browser, but don't for a moment think that these features do anything except make it easier for a well-intentioned user to enter data.

Lua's `tonumber` function can be used to validate numeric input. Regular expressions, covered in Chapter 5, are very useful in validating and cleaning data in your CGI script. Apply these techniques prior to including any user-provided data into a command to be executed by Lua, a database server, or some other interpreter. For example, if you expect numeric data from a particular field, use a command like this:

```
local Quantity = tonumber(Prm.Post.Quantity)
if Quantity and Quantity >= Cn.QuantityLow and
  Quantity <= Cn.QuantityHigh then
  -- database code goes here
end
```

A very common practice is to construct a database or system command dynamically. When you do this, be especially wary of any quotes that are submitted in form data. Devious quoting can allow a malicious user to alter the intent of your command.

The Kepler Project

Kepler is a versatile Lua-based web server environment that supports a number of extensions that facilitate web applications. It is named after the German astronomer Johannes Kepler (1571–1630), who mathematically described the motion of orbiting bodies. Follow the link to the Kepler project on LuaForge (`luaforge.net/`) to read about Kepler and download the package. A mailing list for Kepler is hosted by LuaForge at `lists.luaforge.net/pipermail/kepler-project`.

Kepler's objective is to provide an integrated web development environment that functions with all mainstream web servers as well as Xavante, its own web server. The project comprises many interrelated components. One of them, CGILua, manages user interface issues, while the others provide support for services such as database connectivity, session management, FastCGI on Apache and platform-independent filesystem access. Kepler is compatible with the LuaBinaries distribution, and a Windows installer for it is available. Lua enthusiasts are encouraged to explore its many features.

CGI the Kepler Way

The following examples assume that you have Kepler installed and are using the Xavante web server with its default configuration. Examine the Lua configuration files for cgilua and xavante to see more details about how Kepler is set up.

CGILua is the layer between the web server and your CGI scripts. With it, you can register handlers to process scripts based on their extension.

As a first step in using Kepler, this Try It Out re-implements the time server covered earlier in this chapter.

Try It Out   **Creating a Time Server with Kepler**

This Try It Out generates a simple page with the current server time. It demonstrates how headers and ordinary content are output in the Kepler web environment.

1. In the Kepler installation directory, locate the subdirectory named web. In this directory, create two new subdirectories named cgi-bin and scripts, as follows:

```
cd web
mkdir cgi-bin
mkdir scripts
```

2. Using your text editor, prepare a CGI script that shows the system date. Save the following file as date.lua in the cgi-bin directory created in the previous step:

```
cgilua.contentheader("text", "plain")
cgilua.put(os.date())
```

3. Copy AjaxRequest.js to the scripts directory created in step 1.

4. With your web browser, request the following:

```
http://localhost/cgi-bin/date.lua
```

You should see the system date displayed in plain text.

5. Copy date.html from the AJAX-based server date example to the web directory and verify that it works as expected with the new date.lua.

How It Works

With Kepler, writing to standard output does not work as it does with the CGI scripts you've seen so far. Instead, Lua scripts use functions in the cgilua namespace. There are many functions and variables in this namespace that help with tasks such as encoding issues and error handling. This module is included automatically with Kepler CGI scripts.

Lua Pages

A Lua page is a hybrid between a static HTML page and a Lua script. In the examples you've worked with so far, you generated HTML output completely within Lua CGI scripts. With Lua pages, that approach is turned around so that you embed Lua code into an HTML page. The Lua page handler in CGILua processes the embedded Lua and replaces each Lua snippet with the content it generates.

Try It Out   Displaying the Server Time Using a Lua Page

1.   Generate an HTML page with the system time using a Lua page. Save the following file as `date.lp` in Xavante's web directory:

```
<!DOCTYPE html PUBLIC "-//W3C//DTD XHTML 1.0 Strict//EN"
    "http://www.w3.org/TR/xhtml1/DTD/xhtml1-strict.dtd">
<html>
<head>
  <title>Server time</title>
</head>
<body>
<p>The system time is <i><% cgilua.put(os.date()) %></i>.</p>
</body>
</html>
```

2.   With your web browser, request this:

```
http://localhost/date.lp
```

The system date is displayed in an HTML page.

How It Works

The Lua page handler in CGILua copies the content of an `.lp` file verbatim, except for the text beginning with `<%` and ending with `%>`. It considers the text between these markers to be Lua code. It executes this code and replaces the entire sequence with whatever content is generated. The Lua code doesn't actually have to generate any content; it can contain variables, even local variables, that are referenced in Lua code elsewhere in the Lua page. For example, near the top of `date.lp` you could have this line:

```
<% local function TimePut() cgilua.put(os.date()) end %>
```

And, in the body of the page, you could have this line:

```
<p>The system time is <i><% TimePut() %></i>.</p>
```

The function declaration doesn't generate any content, so the sequence is replaced with nothing.

CGILua will detect the `<%` and `%>` markers even within Lua strings. If you want to display them in HTML or a Lua string, represent them as `&lt;%` and `%&gt;` respectively.

Summary

In this chapter, you had a chance to use Lua to dynamically generate web content. In particular, you learned the following:

❑   Some details about how the Common Gateway Interface (CGI) works

❑   How to implement CGI scripts in Lua

❑   A method for presenting dynamically generated graphics in your web pages

❑   How to retrieve and examine user-provided data from HTML forms

❑   The rudiments of using Lua pages with Kepler

Before you head to the next chapter, where you'll learn how to use Lua in a wider variety of network applications, try out your new skills with the following exercises.

Exercises

1.   Write a CGI script that displays a message like "Good Afternoon" based on the system time. Follow this with the value of the Name parameter on the URL. For example:

```
http://localhost/cgi-bin/ex1.lua?Name=Kit
```

should result in a message like this:

```
Good afternoon, Kit!
```

2.   Write an HTML form that accepts a name from the user. When the form is submitted, call the CGI script from the previous exercise appropriately.

3.   Modify the calendar script to accept a month and year as follows:

```
http://localhost/cgi-bin/calendar.lua?Month=3&Year=2007
```

If you're feeling ambitious, obtain these values from an HTML form. And if you really want to go the extra mile, set the default values in this form to the current month and year.

Connecting to a Larger World

In the previous chapter, you used Lua in conjunction with web servers and web browsers — applications that take care of networking details and let you focus on dynamic content and presentation. In this chapter, you'll burrow in a little deeper and learn how to manage those communication details using Lua. The principal tool you'll use in doing this is the LuaSocket library. This package lets you connect your Lua scripts to other programs, whether those programs are running on your own machine, on another machine in your home or office network, or on an Internet server located on the other side of the globe. The facets of this library and networking in general that you'll learn about are as follows:

- ❑   Building and installing LuaSocket
- ❑   The rudiments of the Berkeley sockets interface
- ❑   The basics of programming for the Internet
- ❑   Implementing simple client and server scripts
- ❑   Retaining a server-side state with coroutines
- ❑   Sending and receiving e-mail
- ❑   Serving and retrieving web pages
- ❑   Processing content with filters
- ❑   Using standard streams in a networked environment

You'll find the LuaSocket library to be a natural extension of the language that adds an entirely new dimension to your applications. At its simplest, it makes communicating with another program as easy as reading from and writing to a file.

Installing LuaSocket

LuaSocket is the work of Diego Nehab, an active member of the Lua community, and is made available with the same terms as Lua itself. It is widely used on the Linux, Mac OS X, and Windows platforms, and should work fine on all Unix-like systems. In addition to the source package, a package with precompiled dynamic link libraries is available for Windows. Obtain LuaSocket from luaforge.net. The instructions that follow assume version 2.0.1, but you'll want to download a later version if one is available. In the event that a more recent version is available, the instructions regarding the compatibility module may no longer apply.

Compiling LuaSocket

Compiling the LuaSocket library is straightforward. The installable product comprises two core dynamically linked libraries and a number of Lua scripts.

Compiling on Linux and Other Unix-Like Systems

To compile the LuaSocket library on Linux and other Unix-like systems, follow these steps:

1. Extract the downloaded package.

2. Replace /path/to in the following command with the location of the source package:

```
tar xzvf /path/to/luasocket-2.0.1.tar.gz
```

3. Drop into the source package's directory:

```
cd luasocket-2.0.1
```

4. Using your text editor, open the file named config and make the following changes, using values that pertain to your particular system:

```
LUAINC=-I/usr/local/include
INSTALL_TOP_SHARE=/usr/local/lib/lua/5.1
INSTALL_TOP_LIB=/usr/local/lib/lua/5.1
```

5. After saving these changes, open the file named makefile and remove all lines that refer to compat, such as this:

```
$(COMPAT)/compat-5.1.o
```

6. Save your changes and do the same with the src/makefile.

7. Build and install the library:

```
make
make install
```

Compiling on Windows

You can run the following instructions from a Windows command shell. The makefiles that come with LuaSocket are Unix-oriented, so you won't use them here. These instructions assume that you've got your development environment set up as shown in Chapter 1.

Follow these steps:

1. Extract the contents of the luasocket-2.0.1.tar.gz package to the directory in which you will compile the library. To do this with 7-zip, use the following commands, replacing \path\to with the location of the downloaded package:

```
7z x \path\to\luasocket-2.0.1.tar.gz
7z x luasocket-2.0.1.tar
del luasocket-2.0.1.tar
```

2. Drop into the `src` subdirectory of the newly created tree, like this:

```
cd luasocket-2.0.1\src
```

3. The `unix.c` and `usocket.c` files are not used in the Windows version. Effectively remove them from the set by renaming their extension as follows:

```
ren unix.c unix.c00
ren usocket.c usocket.c00
```

4. Compile the C files as follows:

```
cl /c /nologo /Zl /Zd /Yd /MD /W3 /DWIN32 /DWIN32_LEAN_AND_MEAN *.c
```

5. Separate the MIME library module from the others like this:

```
ren mime.obj mime.o
```

6. Link the socket library as follows:

```
link /DLL /out:socket.dll /base:0x67800000 /export:luaopen_socket_core ⤶
    *.obj msvcrt.lib lua5.1.lib wsock32.lib
```

7. Link the MIME library as follows:

```
link /DLL /out:mime.dll /base:0x67700000 /export:luaopen_mime_core ⤶
    mime.o msvcrt.lib lua5.1.lib
```

8. Copy the dynamic link libraries and support scripts to the installation directory as follows:

```
xcopy socket.dll "%LUA_DIR%\socket\core.*"
xcopy mime.dll "%LUA_DIR%\mime\core.*"
xcopy socket.lua "%LUA_DIR%\*.*"
xcopy mime.lua "%LUA_DIR%\*.*"
xcopy ltn12.lua "%LUA_DIR%\*.*"
xcopy ftp.lua "%LUA_DIR%\socket\*.*"
xcopy http.lua "%LUA_DIR%\socket\*.*"
xcopy smtp.lua "%LUA_DIR%\socket\*.*"
xcopy tp.lua "%LUA_DIR%\socket\*.*"
xcopy url.lua "%LUA_DIR%\socket\*.*"
```

Installing Windows Binaries

A binary package of LuaSocket that is compatible with the Window binary package of Lua is available on `luaforge.net`. Download `luasocket-2.0.1-lua5.1-win32.zip` or a higher version if one is available. The zip file's contents are as follows, with directory names shown in italic:

```
lib
  mime
    core.dll
  socket
```

```
      core.dll
lua
  socket.lua
  mime.lua
  ltn12.lua
  socket
    url.lua
    tp.lua
    smtp.lua
    http.lua
    ftp.lua
```

You can use an interactive tool like WinZip to extract the files, or you can use the Windows command shell as follows:

1.   Replace \path\to with the location of the downloaded zip file:

```
7z x \path\to\luasocket-2.0.1-lua5.1-win32.zip
xcopy lua\*.lua "%LUA_DIR%\*.*"
xcopy lua\socket\*.lua "%LUA_DIR%\socket\*.*"
xcopy lib\mime\*.dll "%LUA_DIR%\mime\*.*"
xcopy lib\socket\*.dll "%LUA_DIR%\socket\*.*"
```

2.   Remove the lua and lib directories by executing the following:

```
del /s /q lib lua
```

The del command on older versions of Windows doesn't support these switches. In this case, try the following command instead:

```
deltree lib lua
```

Network Overview

To effectively use the LuaSocket library, you need at least a rudimentary understanding of networks, such as how computers on a network identify one another and how they exchange information.

Virtually all mainstream networks nowadays support the Internet Protocol (IP) as a means of routing data packets from one network device to another. The wide acceptance of this open standard ushered in the Internet boom. IP is just one of the well-engineered layers that allow remote computers to communicate with each other. Beneath it are layers involving standards for low-level protocols — such as communication by means of Ethernet and wireless devices — and above it are layers that coordinate packets and present them in a format suitable for applications like email programs and web browsers. Each of these layers encapsulates its tasks and presents a well-defined interface to adjacent layers, allowing for varied implementations that work well and reliably together. The LuaSocket library doesn't give you access to the lower layers of this model but, as you'll see in the sections that follow, it gives you a lot of control over the upper layers.

Routed Packets

From its inception, the Internet was designed to be fault tolerant. As long as a path exists between two computers on the Internet, they should be able to communicate even if shorter and more direct paths are inaccessible due to equipment failure. The Internet supports this objective by breaking all data transfer into individual packets that make the journey from the originating machine to the destination machine independently. At each step along the way, routers guide a packet closer to its destination based on routing tables and current performance metrics.

Addresses

Each machine with direct access to the Internet is identified with a unique address, either a 32-bit value (the format specified in version 4 of the IP protocol, or IPv4) or a 128-bit value (the format specified by the backwards compatible version 6 of the IP protocol, or IPv6). IPv4 addresses are conventionally expressed in *dotted-decimal* or *dotted-quad* notation in which the individual byte values, or *octets*, are delimited with a dot, for example 192.168.0.1. The most significant portion of the address identifies the network in which a machine resides and the least significant portion identifies the device within the network.

Domain Names

An important level of indirection allows you to use symbolic names like www.lua.org rather than IP addresses. If you were to move the Lua website to another network, its nameserver record would be updated to point to the new address relieving users throughout the world from the need to modify their records. The mechanism that supports this mapping is hierarchical and distributed and is known as *DNS* (Domain Name System). The hierarchy is apparent in the ordering of the dot-delimited names; for example, www is just one of possibly many hosts or subdomains at the Lua site, and lua is just one of many second level domains in the org top level domain. The mappings between host name and IP address are managed by name servers distributed throughout the Internet, each having authority for its own particular domain.

LuaSocket gives you access to DNS, allowing you to obtain host information either by IP address or by host name. There are three functions in the dns namespace (which in turn belongs to the socket namespace):

- ❑ socket.dns.gethostname(): Returns the host name of the machine on which the function is called.

- ❑ socket.dns.tohostname(IP address or host name): Returns, on success, the canonical name corresponding to the specified address followed by a table containing summary information including alias host names. On error, it returns nil followed by an error message. The canonical name is the principal host name registered with an IP address; aliases are alternative host names that resolve to this same IP address.

- ❑ socket.dns.toip(host name or IP address): Returns, on success, the IP address corresponding to the specified address followed by a table containing summary information including alias host names. On error, it returns nil followed by an error message.

The last two functions accept either an IP address or a host name. This is a convenient feature shared by most functions in the LuaSocket library. You should note that the convenience of using host names comes at a cost; a potentially long DNS lookup will need to be made to resolve the name to an IP address. However, subsequent lookups for a given name are usually fast because the name and address association will be cached locally.

Try It Out   **Name and Number, Please**

Usually when you access the principal Lua website, you specify `www.lua.org` and let your browser handle the details of obtaining the site's IP address. Here, you dig a little beneath the surface and use DNS to find out more about this site.

1. With your text editor, create a new Lua file with the following contents:

```
local socket = require("socket")
require("show")

local Ip = {socket.dns.toip("www.lua.org")}

ObjectShow(Ip, "toip")
```

The `ObjectShow` function comes from the `show` module introduced in Chapter 7.

2. Save this file as `dns_test.lua`.

3. While connected to the Internet, run this script from a command shell:

```
lua dns_test.lua
["toip"] table: 00414F28 (n = 2)
   [1] "62.197.40.9"
   [2] table: 00414FD8 (n = 0)
      ["alias"] table: 00410C68 (n = 2)
         [1] "www.lua.org"
         [2] "zeus.pepperfish.net"
      ["ip"] table: 00410C00 (n = 1)
         [1] "62.197.40.9"
      ["name"] "babel.pepperfish.net"
```

How It Works

The `socket.dns.toip` function calls on the services of a *resolver library* to obtain information about the specified host. The first value that is returned is the current IP address of `www.lua.org`; this is followed by a table containing summary information including alias host names, canonical host name and IP address. In this case, you can see that `www.lua.org` is an alias for `babel.pepperfish.net`. Note that this behind-the-scenes information is subject to change; when you run this script, the site hosting `www.lua.org` may have changed.

Identifying Internet Resources

Most resources on the Internet can be named with a URL, which is a standard way of identifying web pages, images, and other resources and the means by which you access them. URLs are described in more detail in Chapter 15. LuaSocket provides support for, according to Diego, "anything you could possibly want to do with" a URL.

If you write an application that works with Internet resources, you can use `url.parse` to get the details you need to connect with a remote server and make a request. This function receives a URL string and breaks it into its constituent parts.

`url.parse(URL string, optional result table)` returns a table with the specified URL's string components keyed with the names url, scheme, authority, path, params, query, fragment, userinfo, host, port, user, and password. If the result table is provided, the components are placed into it rather than a new table. Fields in this table that are not overwritten are left alone.

Try It Out   **Unfurling a URL**

As one example pertaining to the `socket.url` module, use `url.parse` to break a rather contrived URL into its component parts.

1.   Create a Lua file with the following contents:

```
local url = require("socket.url")
require("show")

local UrlStr = "http://natty:pathfinder@www.example.net:8888" ..
  "/susquehanna;loc?date=1793#title"
ObjectShow(url.parse(UrlStr), "URL")
```

2.   Save this script as `url_01.lua`.

3.   Run the script as follows:

```
lua url_01.lua
["URL"] table: 00413760 (n = 0)
  ["authority"] "natty:pathfinder@www.example.net:8888"
  ["fragment"] "title"
  ["host"] "www.example.net"
  ["params"] "loc"
  ["password"] "pathfinder"
  ["path"] "/susquehanna"
  ["port"] "8888"
  ["query"] "date=1793"
  ["scheme"] "http"
  ["user"] "natty"
  ["userinfo"] "natty:pathfinder"
```

How It Works

The `url.parse` function extracts components within the specified URL as substrings. For example, notice that the value of port is saved as a string rather than a number. Also, note that certain intermediate components are stored in the result table as well. For example, in this case the authority field includes the intermediate userinfo field which in turn includes the user and password fields.

Transport Protocols

On top of IP are two protocols to which LuaSocket gives you access: UDP (User Datagram Protocol) and TCP (Transmission Control Protocol). These are so-called *transport* protocols, which means that they're in charge of getting information from one application to another. In a characteristic layered approach, they use IP to handle packet routing details, and IP in turn uses the underlying hardware to handle the physical signal transmission details needed to transfer information.

Here are more detailed descriptions of UDP and TCP:

❑ **UDP:** A short step away from IP is UDP, a protocol that specifies how *datagrams* are exchanged between applications. This protocol has low overhead and is consequently very fast. However, UDP doesn't attempt to straighten out problems with datagrams that are lost in transit, arrive at their destination out-of-sequence, or contain errors introduced in transmission. The high reliability of modern networks has made problems like this less likely to occur than in earlier years. The LuaSocket documentation includes an example client script that uses UDP to connect with a remote daytime server.

❑ **TCP:** The predominant transport protocol of the Internet is TCP. A veritable roster of application protocols with initialized names depend on it: the web (HTTP and HTTPS), mail (SMTP, IMAP, POP), file transfer (FTP), and secure shell (SSH) among many others. This protocol allows applications to send and receive a stream of data without worrying about the problems that may beset the data in transit. When data is transmitted, TCP splits it into packets suitable for conveyance by IP. On the receiving end, TCP requests that missing or corrupted packets be resent, puts arriving packets in their original order, and recombines the packets into a stream of bytes.

Sockets: Streams and Datagrams

A library of routines and data structures that provide applications with abstracted access to the UDP and TCP protocols was developed at Berkeley in the early 80s. The model this library implements is known as the *Berkeley sockets interface* and has become the standard way for applications to communicate with one another on the Internet. In the Berkeley model, a socket represents one end of a connection. It has associated with it an IP address and a port and must be of type TCP or UDP. The IP address must be associated with one of the machine's interfaces; these can be physical such as Ethernet interfaces, or virtual such as the loopback interfaces or virtual private network interfaces. The port number is a two-byte value that identifies a particular service accessible on an interface.

❑ **UDP:** This is sometimes referred to as a *datagram* socket. You generally want to read the entire datagram when receiving data with this type of socket; anything not read is discarded.

❑ **TCP:** This is often referred to as a *stream* or *connection-oriented* socket because, when you connect it to a peer, you can use it for a two way dialog in which streams of bytes are exchanged. Reading data from a remotely connected socket is done with a client socket's `receive` method. On success, `ClientHnd:receive(read pattern, optional prefix)` returns a Lua string containing the received data matching the specified pattern. If the method fails, `nil` is returned followed by an error message and the partial contents of the received data. The first argument to this method indicates how much data is to be read: the next line (the default), the next fixed block of bytes, or everything that is sent by the remote socket until the connection is closed. All patterns have comparable performance, so select the one that is easiest to work with for your particular application. The following table provides a summary of the LuaSocket `receive` patterns.

Pattern	Explanation
*a	Before closing a socket, an application can indicate by means of the `shutdown` method that it is finished sending data. The receiver can detect this condition, or a closed sending socket, and use it to deliver the entire amount of data transmitted.

Pattern	Explanation
*l	LuaSocket reads data up to the next end-of-line marker. This can be a CR (carriage return) LF (linefeed) pair, or a standalone LF. These markers are not returned. Many application protocols are line-oriented. This pattern is used if the pattern argument is missing.
Number	The next available number of bytes is read. In this case, LuaSocket does not translate or interpret end-of-line markers. Blocks of specified length may be useful when reading a header that contains information about the amount of data to follow.

If a prefix is specified, it will be prepended to the returned data string.

Client TCP sockets send data to one another by means of the send method. On success, ClientHnd:send (data string, optional start, optional end) returns the position of the last byte sent. On error, the method returns nil followed by an error message and the position of the last byte successfully sent. You can use the *start* and *end* arguments to send a substring rather than the entire string.

By default, the functions used to send and receive data will block; that is, they will retain control until the operation has completed. A blocking function simplifies programming somewhat, but it can be a trapdoor for the unwary because it can deprive your program of control needed for other connections. The Berkeley sockets interface provides an effective way to deal with this by including a select function that lets you know which sockets in a pool are ready for reading and which are ready for writing. Additionally, LuaSocket lets you set timeout values to bail out of a function if it doesn't respond in the specified time. As you'll see, a combination of these two features makes it possible to write responsive application servers in Lua.

TCP Socket Sociology

A TCP socket is created by calling socket.tcp. If this function succeeds, a new socket handle is returned, otherwise nil followed by an error message is returned. The returned socket is referred to in the LuaSocket documentation as a *master object*, but in some respects it isn't yet even an apprentice; it has a limited skill set and is unable to communicate with peers. There are two career paths open to such a socket: through calls to bind and listen it can become a *server object*, or through a call to connect it can become a *client object*. One thing it cannot do in this phase is transfer information with another socket.

When a TCP socket graduates to client or server status, its associated methods change. LuaSocket lets you know if you attempt to call a method on a socket that isn't of the right type. For example, calling accept on a master socket will result in an error with the following message:

```
calling 'accept' on bad self (tcp{server} expected, got userdata)
```

The tcp{server} notation is how LuaSocket renders a server socket with tostring. In general, a server socket's job is to listen on a well-known port, which is a port that is associated with the service that the application renders. For example, a web server listens on port 80 and an FTP server listens on port 21. When the accept method of a server socket detects an inbound connection request, it creates and returns a new socket that is connected with the remote socket. The returned value is a client socket. The nomenclature can be a little misleading because such a socket is part of a server application, but it's arguably appropriate, because the socket has the same capabilities as a client socket returned from a call to connect.

A client socket created by `accept` and a client socket created by `connect` are *peers*. Their job is to transfer information with each other, and the principal means used to do this are the `send` and `receive` methods. When peers are connected, there is an IP address and a port at each end. The address and port of the server are usually well-known, for example port 80 at www.example.com, but in general the address and port of the connecting client are decided by the sockets library rather than the application itself. The port that the library selects for you is called *ephemeral* because it is recycled after the connection is closed. When using the `socket.connect` shortcut to create a client socket, you can optionally specify an address and port. You might want to do this if you have more than one interface that could be used to connect with the remote server and have some reason to favor one. If you want to specify an address but don't care about the port, you can use 0 as the port value.

Using LuaSocket for Network Communication

The following Try It Outs demonstrate sockets in action. Keep in mind that these examples use LuaSocket at a rather low level; many applications using the package never deal directly with sockets. The first exercise will use Lua scripts for both ends — the server and the client — of a communication link. In the second exercise, you'll implement a very simplistic web server with a Lua script. In this case, you'll use a web browser for the client side of the connection.

Try It Out   Using Two Servers and a Client

LuaSocket gives your Lua scripts access to Berkeley sockets. Here, you'll open up three command shells and explore the basic practice of listening and connecting sockets.

1. With your text editor, create a new Lua file with the following contents:

```
local socket = require("socket")

local Addr = arg[1] or "127.0.0.1"
local Port = tonumber(arg[2] or 11250)
local Str, Len, SckHnd, ClientHnd, ErrStr, BindAddr, BindPort, ClAddr, ClPort
SckHnd, ErrStr = socket.bind(Addr, Port)
if SckHnd then
  BindAddr, BindPort = SckHnd:getsockname()
  io.write("Listening on ", BindAddr, ", port ", BindPort, "\n")
  ClientHnd, ErrStr = SckHnd:accept()
  if ClientHnd then
    ClAddr, ClPort = ClientHnd:getpeername()
    io.write("Connection from ", ClAddr, ", port ", ClPort, "\n")
    Str = string.format("Greetings from %s:%d to %s:%d\r\n",
      BindAddr, BindPort, ClAddr, ClPort)
    Len, ErrStr = ClientHnd:send(Str)
    if Len then
      Str, ErrStr = ClientHnd:receive()
      if Str then
        io.write("Received from client: [", Str, "]\n")
      else
        io.write("Receive error: ", ErrStr, "\r\n")
```

```
        end
        ClientHnd:shutdown("both")
      else
        io.write("Send error: ", ErrStr, "\n")
      end
      ClientHnd:close()
    else
      io.write("Client connection. ", ErrStr, "\n")
    end
    SckHnd:close()
  else
    io.write("Listening socket. ", ErrStr, "\n")
  end
```

2. Save this file as `server_01.lua`.

3. With your text editor, create another new Lua file with the following contents:

```
local socket = require("socket")

local Addr = arg[1] or "127.0.0.1"
local Port = tonumber(arg[2] or 11250)
local SckHnd, ErrStr, Str, ClAddr, ClPort, SrvAddr, SrvPort
SckHnd, ErrStr = socket.connect(Addr, Port, "127.0.0.1", 0)
if SckHnd then
  ClAddr, ClPort = SckHnd:getsockname()
  SrvAddr, SrvPort = SckHnd:getpeername()
  io.write("Connected with ", SrvAddr, " on port ", SrvPort, "\n")
  Str, ErrStr = SckHnd:receive()
  if Str then
    SckHnd:send(string.format("Greetings from %s:%d to %s:%d\r\n",
      ClAddr, ClPort, SrvAddr, SrvPort))
    io.write("Got [", Str, "] from server\n")
  else
    io.error("Error. ", ErrStr, "\n")
  end
  SckHnd:close()
else
  io.write("Connecting socket. ", ErrStr, "\n")
end
```

4. Save this file as `client_01.lua`.

5. Open three command shells and, in each, use `cd` to change to the directory in which the two scripts are saved. If possible, size and arrange each shell display so they are all visible on the screen.

6. In one command shell, invoke the server as follows:

```
lua server_01.lua 127.1.2.3
Listening on 127.1.2.3, port 11250
```

7. In another command shell, invoke another server as follows:

```
lua server_01.lua 127.101.102.103
Listening on 127.101.102.103, port 11250
```

8. In the third command shell, invoke the client script as follows:

```
lua client_01.lua 127.1.2.3
Connected with 127.1.2.3 on port 11250
Got [Greetings from 127.1.2.3:11250 to 127.0.0.1:32822] from server
```

The script in the first shell will terminate after displaying the following line:

```
Connection from 127.0.0.1, port 32822
Received from client: [Greetings from 127.0.0.1:32822 to 127.1.2.3:11250]
```

In general, you'll see an ephemeral port value different than 32822 in the server's response.

9. In the third command shell, reinvoke the client script as follows:

```
lua client_01.lua 127.101.102.103
Connected with 127.101.102.103 on port 11250
Got [Greetings from 127.101.102.103:11250 to 127.0.0.1:32821] from server
```

The script in the second shell will terminate after displaying the following line:

```
Connection from 127.0.0.1, port 32821
Received from client: [Greetings from 127.0.0.1:32821 to 127.101.102.103:11250]
```

As before, you'll likely see a value different than 32821 when you run the script.

How It Works

This example illustrates network connections that take place over your machine's virtual loopback device, effectively connecting your machine to itself. A number of observations can be made from the output of these scripts:

❏ Your machine can listen for incoming connections on the same port as long as the listening sockets are bound to different interfaces. Virtual web servers are set up this way.

❏ A socket-based network connection involves client sockets at each end. The server application creates a client socket when `accept` responds to a connection request, and the client application creates a client socket by calling `connect`.

❏ IP address and port information about the remote socket is available through the `getpeername` method, but this information is not required to conduct a dialog.

A design objective of the World Wide Web was to keep web servers simple. While today's mainstream servers are a good deal more complex than their early predecessors, they are still considerably simpler than web browsers because they don't have to deal with content rendering and the user interface.

Try It Out   Creating a Simple Web Server

LuaSocket has everything you need to script a functional web server. The server you'll build here is light-duty by any definition, but it provides you with a basic framework on which you can add features, including the generation of dynamic content.

1. Create a new Lua file with your text editor and add the following contents:

```lua
local socket = require("socket")
require "show"

local Cn = {}

Cn.Host = "localhost"

Cn.Port = 80

Cn.MimeList = {
  css = "text/css",
  gif = "image/gif",
  htm = "text/html",
  html = "text/html",
  png = "image/png",
  txt = "text/plain" }

local function LclHdrRead(ClSck)
  local Hdr = {}
  local LineStr, ErrStr
  LineStr, ErrStr = ClSck:receive()
  if LineStr then
    -- "GET /page.html HTTP/1.1" -> "GET", "page.html"
    Hdr.Cmd, Hdr.Path = string.match(LineStr, "^(%S+)%s+%/(%S*)")
    while LineStr do
      LineStr, ErrStr = ClSck:receive()
      if LineStr then
        if LineStr ~= "" then
          local Key, Val = string.match(LineStr, "^(.-)%:%s*(.*)$")
          Hdr[string.lower(Key)] = Val
        else
          LineStr = nil -- End loop at first blank line
        end
      end
    end
  end
  if (not Hdr.Path) or (Hdr.Path == "") then
    Hdr.Path = "index.html"
  end
  return Hdr
end

local function LclSend(Client, BodyStr, MimeStr, CodeStr)
  local SendStr =
    'HTTP/1.1 ' .. (CodeStr or '200 OK') .. '\r\n' ..
    'Date: ' .. os.date() .. '\r\n' ..
    'Server: webserver.lua/0.1\r\n' ..
    'Content-Length: ' .. string.len(BodyStr) .. '\r\n' ..
    'Content-Type: ' .. (MimeStr or 'text/html') .. '\r\n\r\n' .. BodyStr
  Client:send(SendStr)
  Client:shutdown() -- We're finished with this transaction
end
```

```
  local function LclSendFile(Client, FileStr)
    local Hnd = io.open(FileStr, "rb")
    if Hnd then
      local Str = Hnd:read("*all")
      if Str then
        local ExtStr = string.lower(string.match(FileStr, "%P+$"))
        local MimeStr = Cn.MimeList[ExtStr] or "application/octet-stream"
        LclSend(Client, Str, MimeStr)
      else
        LclSend(Client, 'Error reading file.', 'text/plain',
          '500 Internal Server Error')
      end
      Hnd:close()
    else
      LclSend(Client, 'Error opening file.', 'text/plain', '404 Not Found')
    end
  end

  local Addr, Port, Server, Client, Hdr, Loop

  Server = socket.bind(Cn.Host, Cn.Port)
  if Server then
    Addr, Port = Server:getsockname()
    if Addr and Port then
      io.write("Waiting for connection from client on ", Addr, ":", Port, "\n")
      local PortStr = Port == 80 and "" or (":" .. Port)
      io.write('To end server, request "http://', Cn.Host, PortStr,
        '/quit" from browser\n')
      Loop = true
      while Loop do
        Client = Server:accept()
        if Client then
          io.write("Got client request\n")
          Addr, Port = Client:getpeername()
          if Addr and Port then
            io.write("Connected to ", Addr, ":", Port, "\n")
            Hdr = LclHdrRead(Client)
            ObjectShow(Hdr, "Hdr")
            if not string.find(Hdr.Path, "..", 1, true) then
              if Hdr.Path == "quit" then
                LclSend(Client, "Shutdown", "text/plain")
                Loop = false
              else
                LclSendFile(Client, Hdr.Path)
              end
            else
              LclSend(Client, 'Unauthorized', 'text/plain', '401 Unauthorized')
            end
          else
            io.write("Could not retrieve client address\n")
          end
          Client:close()
        else
          io.write("Error connecting to client\n")
        end
      end
```

```
      io.write("Ending server loop\n")
    else
      io.write("Could not retrieve server address\n")
    end
    Server:close()
  else
    io.write("Error creating server socket\n")
  end
```

2. Save the file as `webserver.lua`.

3. Before starting the server, create a web page and name it `index.html`. If you want to generate a sample page with a Lua script, you can use the following:

```
local function FncList(Tbl, Name)
  local List = {}
  for Key, Val in pairs(Tbl) do
    if type(Val) == "function" then
      List[#List + 1] = Key
    end
  end
  table.sort(List)
  io.write('<h1>', Name, ' library</h1>\n\n<p>')
  for J, Str in ipairs(List) do
    io.write(Str, " ")
  end
  io.write("</p>\n\n")
end

io.write('<!DOCTYPE html PUBLIC "-//W3C//DTD XHTML 1.0 Strict//EN"\n',
  '"http://www.w3.org/TR/xhtml1/DTD/xhtml1-strict.dtd">\n\n',
  '<html>\n\n<head>\n\n<title>Lua Environment</title>',
  '\n\n</head>\n\n<body>\n\n')

local Namespace = {"coroutine", "debug", "io", "math", "os", "package",
  "string", "table"}

FncList(_G, "base")
for J, Tbl in ipairs(Namespace) do
  FncList(_G[Tbl], Tbl)
end
io.write('</body>\n\n</html>\n')
```

4. Save this file as `env_page.lua` and use it to create an index page as follows:

```
lua env_page.lua > index.html
```

5. Running this script requires that you don't currently have a TCP service listening on port 80 of your machine. If you do, change the value of `Cn.Port` at the top of the script to an unused port number. Fire up the web server as follows:

```
lua webserver.lua
```

6. With your web browser, access `http://localhost/` to test the server. You can add links and references to images and style sheets in your index page to verify that the server returns everything as it should.

How It Works

This script has a very simple structure. First it creates a socket and binds it to the local machine (localhost is associated with the loopback address 127.0.0.1), as follows:

```
Server = socket.bind(Cn.Host, Cn.Port)
```

It then enters a loop in which it blocks on the following line, waiting for a connection request:

```
Client = Server:accept()
```

Because the socket is bound to the loopback device, you can only access the server from the local machine, but if your machine is part of a network, you can modify the value of Cn.Host and access the script from a different machine.

One limitation of this server is that only one request is handled at a time. A fair amount of work is required to address this deficiency in a robust and efficient way. An elegant way to approach this problem with Lua is to use coroutines, but even with these it can be a trick to get a central event dispatcher to conform to the Berkeley sockets model. Another limitation is that it expects each inbound header to occupy only one line. Finally, this implementation does not handle nested directories in the document root robustly.

Handling Multiple Persistent Connections

This section examines an effective way for a server to maintain ongoing connections with clients. When you interact with an FTP or telnet server, your connection is persistent: the server maintains the context of the interaction between transactions until you log off. The emerging SSE (Server-Sent Events) standard will carry this behavior over to web browsers as well.

Using Lua Coroutines with the select Function

Lua coroutines and the LuaSocket select function make it easy for a server application to handle simultaneous connections from multiple clients. In this example, a coroutine is dedicated to each client connection. Each coroutine is uncluttered with connection details or even an awareness of other concurrent connections, allowing it to focus on the ongoing dialog with a particular client.

Follow these steps:

1. Create a new file with your text editor and copy in the following Lua script:

```
local socket = require("socket")

local Cn = {SrvPort = 3072, SrvAddr = "localhost"}

local SckHnd = socket.connect(Cn.SrvAddr, Cn.SrvPort)
if SckHnd then
  local Loop = true
  local CnnSrvStr, CnnSrvPort = SckHnd:getpeername()
  local CnnNameStr = socket.dns.tohostname(CnnSrvStr)
  io.write(string.format("Connected to %s (%s) on port %d.\n",
    CnnSrvStr, CnnNameStr, CnnSrvPort))
```

```
      io.write('Issue .quit to end connection, .shutdown to terminate server.\n')
   while Loop do
     local Str, ErrStr
     io.write("Send: ")
     Str = io.read() or ".quit"
     SckHnd:send(Str .. "\r\n")
     Str, ErrStr = SckHnd:receive()
     if Str then
        io.write("Received: ", Str, "\n")
     else
        Loop = false
        if ErrStr == "closed" then
          io.write("Closing connection to server\n")
        else
          io.write("Error: ", ErrStr, "\n")
        end
     end
   end
   SckHnd:close()
else
   io.write("Error creating client socket\n")
end
```

2. Save this file as `client_02.lua`.

3. Create another new file with your editor and copy in the following Lua script:

```
local socket = require("socket")

local Cn = {HostPort = 3072, HostAddr = "*"}

local function ClientSession(SckHnd)
   local Loop, Str, ErrStr = true
   local Rcv = {}
   while Loop do
     coroutine.yield(Str)
     Str, ErrStr = SckHnd:receive()
     if Str then
        Loop = Str ~= ".quit" and Str ~= ".shutdown"
        if Loop then
          for J = 1, #Str do
            Rcv[string.byte(Str, J, J)] = true
          end
          local SendStr = ""
          for J = 33, 255 do
            if Rcv[J] then
               SendStr = SendStr .. string.char(J)
            end
          end
          SckHnd:send(SendStr .. "\r\n")
        end
     else
        io.write("Error: ", ErrStr, "\n")
     end
   end
end
```

```
      return Str
end


local SckHnd = socket.bind(Cn.HostAddr, Cn.HostPort)
if SckHnd then
  local SckList = {} -- Array of sockets, beginning with accepting socket
  local CoList = {}  -- Table of coroutines keyed by socket
  local Loop = true
  -- Prevent this socket from blocking for too long in call to accept
  SckHnd:settimeout(250)
  SckList[1] = SckHnd
  while Loop do
    io.write('Waiting for connection or data from\n')
    for J, Hnd in ipairs(SckList) do
      io.write('  ', J, ': ', tostring(Hnd), ', ', tostring(CoList[Hnd]), '\n')
    end
    local ReadTbl, WriteTbl, ErrStr = socket.select(SckList)
    for K, SckHnd in ipairs(ReadTbl) do
      if SckHnd == SckList[1] then -- Server socket
        local ClientHnd, ErrStr = SckHnd:accept()
        if ClientHnd then
          local NewPos = #SckList + 1
          SckList[NewPos] = ClientHnd
          CoList[ClientHnd] = coroutine.wrap(ClientSession)
          CoList[ClientHnd](ClientHnd)
        elseif ErrStr ~= "timeout" then
          io.write(ErrStr, "\n")
          Loop = false
        end
      else -- Client connection
        local Cmd = CoList[SckHnd]()
        if ".quit" == Cmd then
          CoList[SckHnd] = nil
          SckHnd:close()
          local L, Pos = #SckList
          while L > 1 do
            if SckHnd == SckList[L] then
              table.remove(SckList, L)
              L = 1 -- Terminate search
            else
              L = L - 1
            end
          end
        elseif ".shutdown" == Cmd then
          io.write("Shutting down server\n")
          Loop = false
        end
      end
    end
  end
  for J, SckHnd in ipairs(SckList) do
    SckHnd:close()
  end
```

```
else
  io.write("Error creating server socket\n")
end
```

4. Save this file as `server_02.lua`.

5. Open a command shell, use `cd` to change to the directory where you saved the scripts, and execute the following server script:

The hexadecimal socket identifier will almost certainly be different in your case.

```
lua server_02.lua
Waiting for connection or data from
  1: tcp{server}: 00658CA0, nil
```

6. Open another command shell, use `cd` to change to the directory where you saved the scripts, and execute the following client script:

```
lua client_02.lua
Connected to 127.0.0.1 (localhost) on port 3072.
Issue .quit to end connection, .shutdown to terminate server.
Send:
```

At this point, the server script prints new information indicating that the client has connected with it:

```
Waiting for connection or data from
  1: tcp{server}: 00658CA0, nil
  2: tcp{client}: 0065BD18, function: 007684A0
```

7. In response to the `Send` prompt, transmit some character sequences to the server, such as the following:

```
Send: ajx
Received: ajx
Send: bky
Received: abjkxy
Send: clz
Received: abcjklxyz
Send:
```

8. Open another command shell, use `cd` to change to the directory where you saved the scripts, and execute the following instance of the client script:

```
lua client_02.lua
Connected to 127.0.0.1 (localhost) on port 3072.
Issue .quit to end connection, .shutdown to terminate server.
Send:
```

The server script will now indicate multiple connected clients:

```
Waiting for connection or data from
  1: tcp{server}: 00658CA0, nil
  2: tcp{client}: 0065BD18, function: 007684A0
  3: tcp{client}: 0065DD8C, function: 0076A1D0
```

9. Alternate between the two client scripts, inputting characters and verifying that the server is returning the set of accumulated characters for the particular connection.

10. End a client session as follows:

```
Send: .quit
Closing connection to server
```

Note that the server prints a summary with one fewer client connection.

11. Terminate the server from the remaining active client as follows:

```
Send: .shutdown
Closing connection to server
```

The server script ends after printing the following:

```
Shutting down server
```

The client script creates a TCP socket and connects it to a server with a well-known port (here, an arbitrarily selected value). This is done in one command:

```
local SckHnd = socket.connect(Cn.SrvAddr, Cn.SrvPort)
```

As presented, the server and clients all run on the same machine, but with the appropriate adjustment to Cn.SrvAddr, you can run the client script on a remotely connected machine. The following lines obtain information about the server for display purposes:

```
local CnnSrvStr, CnnSrvPort = SckHnd:getpeername()
local CnnNameStr = socket.dns.tohostname(CnnSrvStr)
```

A loop is entered in which the following things are done repeatedly:

1. Text is obtained from the user (io.read).

2. The acquired text is sent to the server (SckHnd:send).

3. The server's response is obtained (SckHnd:receive).

4. The response is displayed to the user (io.write).

This loop continues until one of the following occurs:

❑ The user issues the .quit command to end the session.

❑ The user issues the .shutdown command to terminate the server.

❑ Another client issues the .shutdown command. In this case, the client loop won't end until it attempts to send some data to the now defunct server.

Multiple Connections on the Server Side

Things are a little more involved on the server side, but the actual business logic (the code that actually interacts with the client) is refreshingly simple due to coroutines. The actual connection logic is something that you can write once and tuck away in a module.

amazon.com

SDsq5DN7jR

Your order of April 23, 2011 (Order ID:002—4889041—6893815)

Returns Are Easy!
Visit http://www.amazon.com/returns to return any item -including gifts- in unopened or original
condition within 30 days for a full refund (other restrictions apply)

Qty	Item		Item Price	Total
	IN THIS SHIPMENT			
1	**Beginning Lua Programming (Programmer to Programmer)** (** P-3-B55D381 **) 0470069171 : 0470069171 0470069171 **Paperback**		$26.12	$26.12

Subtotal	$26.12
Shipping & Handling	$3.99
Tax Collected	$2.86
Order Total	$32.97
Paid via credit/debit	$32.97
Balance Due	$0.00

This shipment completes your order.

Have feedback on how we packaged your order? Tell us at www.amazon.com/packaging

(1 of 1)

SDsq5DN7jR

784/DSq5DN7jR/-1 of 1-//1M/std-n-us/6477310/0425-15:00/0425-08:24 1A3

amazon.com
and you're done.

The key to handling concurrent client connections is the `socket.select` function. As you saw in Chapter 9, a properly implemented dispatcher forms the basis for properly managing asynchronous events, which are events that originate outside of the application. The feature that you want is the ability to call a function that blocks until an event occurs. In this case, the event can be a connection request by a new client or the arrival of information from an already connected client. The `socket.select` fills this role by blocking until one or more of the sockets you indicate are ready for reading or writing. `socket.select(receive array, send array, optional timeout in seconds)` returns three values: a table of sockets from the receive array that have data waiting, a table of sockets from the send array that are ready to be written to, and an error message. On success the error message is `nil`.

Follow these steps to use `socket.select`:

1. Place the client and server sockets you expect input from into an array (a table indexed with contiguous integers beginning with 1), and pass this table as the first argument.

2. Place all the sockets that you are waiting to write to into another array. If either of these tables is empty, you can use `nil` instead. If you need the function to return after some designated number of seconds in the event that none of the specified sockets become ready for reading or writing, indicate a timeout value as the third argument.

   The returned tables are structured as follows:

```
{
  [1] = tcp{client}: 0065E214,
  [2] = tcp{client}: 0065E394,
  [tcp{client}: 0065E214] = 1,
  [tcp{client}: 0065E394] = 2
}
```

   You can see that each socket is represented two ways in the table: once as an array element and once as an associative key. The script presented here uses an `ipairs` loop to handle only the arrayed sockets.

All incoming connection requests are handled by the server socket. Recall that a server socket calls `accept` to establish a connection and create a new client socket, but does not exchange data with the remote socket. The server socket is kept in the first position of an array that holds all active sockets. Subsequent positions hold client sockets. This array is in the form required by `socket.select` so it is passed as the function's first argument (the receive array) to wait until inbound data or a connection request arrives.

This example is line oriented: the server expects to receive a single line from the client and in return sends back a line. Because of this, there are no special writing considerations and the second argument to `socket.select` (the send array) is passed as `nil`.

Setting Timeout Values for the Server Socket

One quirk in the Windows implementation of sockets is worked around in the multiple-connection example. Generally, a server socket can be included along with client sockets in the receive array, and an inbound connection request for the server socket is treated like inbound data for a client socket. However, Windows is known to occasionally report that a server socket is ready to accept a new connection when in fact it is not. To deal with this, you can do the following:

1. Set a timeout value for the server socket:

```
SckHnd:settimeout(250)
```

This forces a call to `accept` to return in a quarter second if in fact no connection requests are pending.

2. Check the return values of this function to determine whether a viable connection was made. In this example, a timeout condition terminates the main loop. In a real application, you would ignore it.

3. For each new client connection, create a coroutine and associate it with the client socket. When a client connection is terminated, this coroutine is set to `nil` and the client socket is removed from the read array.

The actual dialog between client and server is quite simple. Essentially it is a loop that begins with a yield. This transfers control back to the main script loop where it spends most of its time blocking in a call to `socket.select`. When this mechanism indicates that data has arrived from a client, the associated coroutine is resumed. The client data is read and examined. If it constitutes a termination request (either to end the connection or shut down the server) the dialog loop is terminated and the coroutine returns rather than yields. Otherwise, it processes the data and responds with its own data. In this example, the data returned is simply a string comprising the unique characters received from the client so far. This illustrates the ease with which the dialog state can be retained between transmissions.

The Application Protocols

LuaSocket's C layer interfaces with platform-specific sockets libraries to handle networking details at the TCP and UDP level. LuaSocket also provides a rich interface to the Internet's application protocols such as SMTP, FTP, HTTP and a number of modules to support them.

The application protocols in wide use throughout the Internet are presented in *RFC* (Request for Comments) documents that are informative and generally easy to read. If you need Lua to interact with an Internet server, such as a server that uses NNTP (Network News Transfer Protocol), the relevant RFCs will help you implement a working client. Visit `www.rfc-editor.org` for indexes to all RFCs.

Many application protocols involve transforming data prior to sending it or after receiving it. The following section describes an elegant solution that the LuaSocket libraries bring to this task.

Filtering the Flow of Data

As data is moved from one point to another, it often has to be manipulated to do the following:

❑ Conform with protocol constraints

❑ Enhance transmission efficiency

❑ Accommodate application formats and platform-dependent issues such as end-of-line conventions

LuaSocket includes a framework for flexibly massaging inbound and outbound data. It treats data as a fluid that is pumped from a *source* through a series of *filters* to a *sink*. While Diego Nehab created this framework in conjunction with the development of LuaSocket version 2, it is quite general and has been made into a standalone module named ltn12. An article Diego wrote detailing the principles of this framework (available on the Lua wiki at http://lua-users.org/wiki/FiltersSourcesAndSinks) was evidently slated to become the 12th in a series of *Lua technical notes*. The first eleven of these articles are maintained on the main Lua website; newer contributions by members of the Lua community are placed on the lua-users wiki.

The sources, filters and sinks framework implemented in ltn12 is based on the modification of data chunks rather than transacted data as a whole. This reduces the memory requirements of applications, especially server applications that handle concurrent connections involving large transactions. The basic parts of an ltn12 circuit are shown in the following table.

Component	Explanation
Source	Where data chunks originate. You can supply your own function to do this, or use one of the sources included in the ltn12 module. Of these, ltn12.source.file is convenient if your data is stored in a file or originates from the standard input stream.
Filter	At its simplest, a filter receives a string of bytes and returns a transformed string of bytes. You can use the ltn12.filter.chain function to sequentially combine multiple filters into a single chain. Filters may need to retain some context from chunk to chunk, in which case, a factory is generally used to create a filter as a closure.
Sink	The destination of all data chunks passing through the circuit. As with the source, you can associate a file, (including the standard output stream) with this component.
Pump	A pump function pushes data from a source to a sink. Two pumps are included in the module: ltn12.pump.all blocks until all data has been pumped through the system, and ltn12.pump.step blocks until one chunk has been pumped.

Many of the application protocols in use today were created when only ASCII text was being moved around on networks. To support the transmission of text that includes characters outside of the ASCII range as well as binary data such as images and compressed data, various encoding techniques have evolved to work within the original protocol limitations. MIME (Multipurpose Internet Mail Extensions) standardizes the ways non-ASCII data can be exchanged. Two common encoding methods are Quoted-Printable and Base64, which do the following:

❏ The Quoted-Printable encoding expands non-ASCII characters to a three-character sequence: an equal sign followed by a two-character hexadecimal representation of the out-of-range character. The equal sign itself is given the same treatment, as are tabs and spaces at the end of a line. For text messages that include occasional non-ASCII characters, this method of encoding has the advantage of being readable and compact.

❏ Base64 encoding is suited for transmitted data that includes many non-ASCII characters. In this method of encoding, all data is expanded so that each sequence of three bytes becomes four ASCII characters. In a sense, data is transformed from a 256 character alphabet to a 64 character alphabet.

The `mime` module included in LuaSocket implements encodings from the MIME standard. It requires the `ltn12` module but is independent of the socket routines.

Try It Out   **Text Hydraulics**

The `ltn12` module gives you everything you need to construct a source-to-sink data transformation routine. The `mime` module provides filters for encodings, text wrapping and end-of-line manipulation. Here you'll use both modules to demonstrate the ways to combine a source, filters, sink, and pump to encode and decode a string.

1. Create a Lua file with the following contents:

```lua
local mime = require("mime")
local ltn12 = require("ltn12")

-- This function receives one string and one or more high level filters. On
-- success it returns the filtered string, otherwise nil followed by an error
-- message.

local function Transform(Str, ...)
  -- Source is specified string
  local Src = ltn12.source.string(Str)
  -- Chain all specified filters into one
  local Filter = ltn12.filter.chain(...)
  -- Send all data chunks to table
  local Snk, Tbl = ltn12.sink.table()
  -- Filter chunks before delivering to sink
  Snk = ltn12.sink.chain(Filter, Snk)
  -- Open the valve
  local Code, ErrStr = ltn12.pump.all(Src, Snk)
  return Code and table.concat(Tbl) or nil, ErrStr
end

local function Test(Str, EncodingStr)
  local CodeStr, StatStr
  CodeStr = Transform(Str, mime.encode(EncodingStr)) or ""
  StatStr = Str == Transform(CodeStr, mime.decode(EncodingStr)) and
    "OK" or "Not OK"
  io.write(string.format("%-18s [%s] %s\n", EncodingStr, CodeStr, StatStr))
end

local Str = "Gabriel Garc\237a M\225rquez"
io.write(Str, "\n")
Test(Str, "base64")
Test(Str, "quoted-printable")
```

2. Run the script as follows:

```
lua mime_01.lua
Gabriel García Márquez
base64             [R2FicmllbCBHYXJj7WEgTeFycXVleg==] OK
quoted-printable   [Gabriel Garc=EDa M=E1rquez] OK
```

How It Works

The `Transform` function is a general-purpose routine for applying one or more filters to a string. Receiving and returning whole strings in some respects defeats the purpose of a filtered circuit, but even if the input and output strings are enormous, the actual filtering operations take place on smaller portions of data. The routine illustrates how you can place filters between a source and a sink. In this case, the amalgamated filter is chained to the sink (in `ltn12.sink.chain`), but you could just as easily have chained to the source instead (by using `ltn12.source.chain`).

The `Test` function receives a string to transform and a MIME encoding identifier (either `base64` or `quoted-printable`). It uses this identifier to obtain an encoding filter with which it calls `Transform` to generate an encoded string. To test this, it compares the original string with a decoded version to make sure the process is functioning properly.

Examine the encoded versions of the text. For this example, the Quoted-Printable encoding makes the most sense, as most of the data is already in ASCII characters. The two equal signs at the end of the Base64-encoded string are padding added to make the length of the encoded string a multiple of four.

Accessing Web Pages

The `http` module of LuaSocket lets you retrieve a web resource with one function call. `http.request (URL string, optional post body)` requests a resource from a web server. If there is no second argument, the request is made using the `GET` method; otherwise the second argument is sent to the server as post data and the `POST` method is used. On success, the function returns four response values from the server. In order, these are the web resource body, the status code, the headers and the status line. On error, the function returns `nil` followed by an error message. If the function succeeds, remember to also check the status code.

> When data is posted to the server, it is assumed to be urlencoded. See the section on CGI programming in Chapter 15 for more details.

The following global variables are consulted by `http.request` and can be used to modify its behavior:

- ❑   `PORT` specifies the port used to contact the web server if a value isn't included in the URL.
- ❑   `PROXY` is used as a proxy server. If it is used, it should be in the form `http://proxy.example.com:8080`.
- ❑   `TIMEOUT` specifies the timeout value in seconds of the request.
- ❑   `USERAGENT` specifies the `user-agent` header that will be sent to the server.

An alternate version of the same function gives you finer-grained control over the HTTP request. Instead of submitting a URL to the function, you pass an associative table instead. `http.request(request attribute table)` requests a resource from a web server. Its return values are like the URL string version of this function, except that on success, the first value returned is 1 rather than the resource body.

The request attribute table can have values for the following keys (only the `url` field is mandatory):

- ❑   `url` specifies the URL of the requested resource.

❑   sink indicates where you want the retrieved resource to be stored. Common values are `ltn12.sink.file` to save the resource as a file, and `ltn12.sink.table` to store the retrieved chunks in a table where they can be easily converted to a string using `table.concat`.

❑   method should be `"GET"`, `"HEAD"`, or `"POST"`.

❑   headers is an associative table that includes headers that will be sent to the server in addition to the standard headers. For example:

```
headers = {["content-length"] = 1094}
```

❑   You use source if you are posting data to the server. When using this, you should specify `content-length` in the headers table. For example:

```
source = ltn12.source.string(PostStr)
headers = {["content-length"] = string.len(PostStr)}
```

❑   step enables you to specify a step pump other than the default `ltn12.pump.step`.

❑   proxy allows you to request a resource through a proxy server. You use this like the PROXY global variable.

❑   You can set redirect to false to prevent server redirection.

❑   create specifies an alternate function to create the client socket.

Additionally, you can include any or all of the keys user, password, host, port, and path in the table with appropriate values to override the fields embedded in url.

When `http.request` is called with a table, it saves the retrieved resource to the specified sink rather than returning it.

Try It Out   Grabbing a File

You can conveniently retrieve binary files with `http.request`. Here the table form of the function is used with a file sink.

1.   With your text editor, create a new Lua file with the following contents:

```
local http = require("socket.http")
require("show")

local ResFileStr = "lascii85.tar.gz"
local PathStr = "http://www.tecgraf.puc-rio.br/~lhf/ftp/lua/5.0/"
local ResHnd, ErrStr = io.open(ResFileStr, "wb")
if ResHnd then
  local Req = {
    url = PathStr .. ResFileStr,
    sink = ltn12.sink.file(ResHnd),
    -- proxy = "http://proxy.example.com:8888"
  }
  local Response = {http.request(Req)}
  ObjectShow(Response, "Response")
else
  io.write("Error opening ", ResFileStr, " for writing\n")
end
```

2. Save this file as `http_01.lua`.

3. Run the script as follows:

```
lua http_01.lua
["Response"] table: 0041C6B0 (n = 4)
  [1] 1
  [2] 200
  [3] table: 00429F28 (n = 0)
    ["accept-ranges"] "bytes"
    ["content-encoding"] "x-gzip"
    ["content-length"] "2641"
    ["content-type"] "application/x-gzip"
    ["date"] "Thu, 07 Sep 19:49:29 GMT"
    ["etag"] ""3f60e-a51-3fbb6735""
    ["last-modified"] "Wed, 19 Nov 2003 12:51:01 GMT"
    ["server"] "Apache"
    ["via"] "1.1 tinyproxy (tinyproxy/1.7.0)"
  [4] "HTTP/1.1 200 OK"
```

Some headers may be different when you run the script. When the request completes, the `lascii85.tar.gz` file is saved in the current directory.

How It Works

The table form of `http.request` is used here for extra control over the file retrieval request. To save the downloaded file directly to disk, the `ltn12.sink.file` factory is called with the handle to a file opened for writing. The function this factory returns is called for each chunk of data received. When there is no more data to process, it closes the file handle.

If there are no special request attributes, you can retrieve the file directly into a string with the following call:

```
UrlStr = "http://www.tecgraf.puc-rio.br/~lhf/ftp/lua/5.0/lascii85.tar.gz"
BodyStr, Code, Hdr, StatStr = http.request(UrlStr)
```

Sending and Receiving E-mail Messages

LuaSocket provides high-level support for sending messages with SMTP (Simple Mail Transfer Protocol), which is the standard means of sending Internet e-mail. LuaSocket currently doesn't support email retrieval directly, but its lower-level TCP socket routines let you do this if you follow the protocol — usually POP (Post Office Protocol) or IMAP (Internet Message Access Protocol) — that your mail server uses.

Try It Out   **Sending E-mail**

The `smtp` module comprises two functions: `smtp.message` and `smtp.send`. The first function prepares a message for sending by the second function. Both are used in the following example. This exercise works only with SMTP servers that accept plain-text password authentication.

1. Create a new file with the following Lua script:

```lua
local smtp = require("socket.smtp")

local Recipient = {"<recipient_1@example.net>", "<recipient_2@example.net>"}

-- Run the specified configuration file in an empty environment. On success,
-- returns a table that contains all global variables that are assigned in
-- configuration file, otherwise (nil, error string).

local function Configure(CfgFileStr)
  local Gl, Cfg = getfenv(0), {}
  setfenv(0, Cfg)
  local Code, ErrStr = pcall(dofile, CfgFileStr)
  setfenv(0, Gl)
  return Code and Cfg or nil, ErrStr
end

local BodyStr = [[
Now the hungry lion roars,
  And the wolf behowls the moon;
Whilst the heavy ploughman snores,
  All with weary task foredone.
]]

local Msg = {
  headers = {
    to = "Oberon <oberon@example.com> Titania <titania@example.com>",
    cc = "William Shakespeare <bard@globe.example.org>",
    subject = "Moonlight",
    from = "Puck <puck@example.com>",
  },
  body = BodyStr
}

local Packet = {}
local Code
local CfgFileStr = "smtp.cfg"
local Cfg, ErrStr = Configure(CfgFileStr)
if Cfg then
  if type(Cfg.ServerStr) == "string" and type(Cfg.ServerPort) == "number" and
     type(Cfg.UserStr) == "string" and type(Cfg.PassStr) == "string" then
    io.write("Connecting to ", Cfg.ServerStr, "\n")
    Packet.from = "<puck@example.com>"
    Packet.rcpt = Recipient
    Packet.source = smtp.message(Msg)
    Packet.server = Cfg.ServerStr
    Packet.port = Cfg.ServerPort
    Packet.password = Cfg.PassStr
    Packet.user = Cfg.UserStr
    Code, ErrStr = smtp.send(Packet)
    if Code then
      io.write("Successfully sent messages")
    end
```

```
        else
          ErrStr = "Improper configuration: " .. CfgFileStr
        end
    end
end
if ErrStr then
    io.write(ErrStr, "\n")
end
```

2. Modify the contents of the `Recipient` table to include one or more of your e-mail addresses.

3. Save this file as `smtp_01.lua`.

4. Create a configuration file with your editor and add the following fields, using appropriate values for your SMTP account:

```
ServerStr = "mail.example.com"
ServerPort = 25
UserStr = "user"
PassStr = "password"
```

5. Save this file as `smtp.cfg`

6. Send the message as follows:

```
lua smtp_01.lua
Connecting to mail.example.com
Successfully sent messages
```

7. Use your regular e-mail retrieval software to verify that the message was sent or, if you have POP access to your e-mail account, you can retrieve it programmatically in the next exercise.

How It Works

The e-mail sending process begins by obtaining account particulars (such as the server name, user name, and password) as follows:

```
Cfg, ErrStr = Configure(CfgFileStr)
```

It's a good policy to keep this information out of general-purpose scripts. The technique used in the `Configure` function is to execute the configuration file as a Lua script that does not have access to library functions. Environment manipulation places the global variables it creates into a table that is returned by `Configure`.

After the presence of the fields expected in the configuration table have been verified, a table is prepared that will be used by `smtp.send`. This includes fields such as `from`, `rcpt`, `source`, `server`, `port`, `password`, and `user`.

The `rcpt` table specifies the only addresses to which the message is sent. As shown in this example, the `to` and `cc` fields of the message `headers` table are completely incidental to this process and are included for the purpose of display by the email client. Don't make the mistake of including a `bcc` field. To send a blind copy, simply include the recipient in the `rcpt` table and do not include it in either the `to` or `cc` header fields. This is done in the example.

The `source` field is a simple `ltn12` source. Here, the `smtp.message` factory is used to condition the specified message and generate a suitable source.

Now that you've sent a message, you can retrieve it programmatically if you have POP access to your e-mail account.

Try It Out   Getting E-mail

The POP specification lets you list, retrieve, and delete e-mail that has arrived at your mail server. To do this with LuaSocket, you create a client socket and connect it with a POP server on which you have an account. The following example assumes that your POP server does not require an SSL (Secure Sockets Layer) or the APOP (Authenticated Post Office Protocol) command.

1. Create a new Lua file with the following contents:

```lua
local socket = require("socket")

-- Run the specified configuration file in an empty environment. On success,
-- returns a table that contains all global variables that are assigned in
-- configuration file, otherwise (nil, error string).

local function Configure(CfgFileStr)
  local Gl, Cfg = getfenv(0), {}
  setfenv(0, Cfg)
  local Code, ErrStr = pcall(dofile, CfgFileStr)
  setfenv(0, Gl)
  return Code and Cfg or nil, ErrStr
end

-- Obtain POP server response. On success, return (string), otherwise (nil,
-- error string).

local function LclGet(PopHnd)
  local Str, ErrStr = PopHnd:receive()
  if Str then
    -- All POP responses begin with "+OK " or "-ERR "
    if string.sub(Str, 1, 1) == "+" then
      Str = string.sub(Str, 5)
    else
      ErrStr = string.sub(Str, 6)
      Str = nil
    end
  end
  -- return Ok, string.sub(Str, Ok and 5 or 6)
  return Str, ErrStr
end

-- Send a command to the POP server and obtain its response. Returns (string)
-- on success and (nil, error string) otherwise. The Multi argument is true if
-- the caller expects a multiline response from the POP server. If Multi is
-- true and command succeeds, returns (string, table) where table contains
-- returned data lines, otherwise (nil, error string).
```

```
local function LclTransact(PopHnd, SendStr, Multi)
  local Ok, Str, ErrStr, Tbl
  Ok, ErrStr = PopHnd:send(SendStr .. "\r\n")
  if Ok then
    Str, ErrStr = LclGet(PopHnd)
    if Str and Multi then
      Tbl = {}
      local DataStr
      while Multi and not ErrStr do
        DataStr, ErrStr = PopHnd:receive()
        if DataStr then
          if string.sub(DataStr, 1, 1) == "." then
            DataStr = string.sub(DataStr, 2)
            if DataStr == "" then
              Multi = false
            end
          end
          if Multi then
            Tbl[#Tbl + 1] = DataStr
          end
        end
      end
      if ErrStr then
        Str = nil
      else
        ErrStr = Tbl -- 2nd return value for Multi
      end
    end
  end
  return Str, ErrStr
end

-- Close the connection to the POP server. It is assumed that the server is in
-- a state to receive the "quit" command.

local function LclClose(PopHnd)
  LclTransact(PopHnd, "quit")
  PopHnd:close()
end

-- Connect to the POP server and authenticate user. If this function succeeds,
-- (client socket) is returned, otherwise (nil, error string) is returned.

local function LclOpen(Cfg)
  local Ok, Str, RetHnd, PopHnd, ErrStr
  PopHnd, ErrStr = socket.connect(Cfg.ServerStr, Cfg.ServerPort)
  if PopHnd then
    Str, ErrStr = LclGet(PopHnd)
    if Str then
      if LclTransact(PopHnd, "user " .. Cfg.UserStr) then
        if LclTransact(PopHnd, "pass " .. Cfg.PassStr) then
          RetHnd = PopHnd
        end
      end
```

```
            if not RetHnd then
                ErrStr = "Invalid username or password submitted"
            end
        end
        if not RetHnd then
            LclClose(PopHnd)
        end
    end
    return RetHnd, ErrStr
end

-- This function requests header information for each stored email message. On
-- success, it returns (header table), otherwise it returns (nil, error
-- string). Only the first line of each multiline value is saved.

local function LclHeaders(PopHnd)
    local Ok, Str, ErrStr, RetTbl, ListTbl

    Str, ListTbl = LclTransact(PopHnd, "list", true)
    if Str then
        RetTbl = {}
        for J, Str in ipairs(ListTbl) do
            local HdrTbl, MsgTbl = {}
            HdrTbl.size = tonumber(string.match(Str, "(%d+)$") or 0)
            Str, MsgTbl = LclTransact(PopHnd, "top " .. J .. " 1", true)
            if Str then
                for J, Str in ipairs(MsgTbl) do
                    local KeyStr, ValStr = string.match(Str, "^([%a%-]+)%:%s*(.*)")
                    if KeyStr then
                        HdrTbl[string.lower(KeyStr)] = ValStr
                    end
                end
                RetTbl[#RetTbl + 1] = HdrTbl
            else
                ErrStr = ErrStr and (ErrStr .. ", " .. MsgTbl) or MsgTbl
            end
        end
        if ErrStr then
            RetTbl = nil
        end
    else
        ErrStr = ListTbl
    end
    return RetTbl, ErrStr
end

local Cfg, PopHnd, ErrStr, Ok, HdrTbl, CfgFileStr

CfgFileStr = "cfg"
Cfg, ErrStr = Configure(CfgFileStr)
if Cfg then
    if type(Cfg.ServerStr) == "string" and type(Cfg.ServerPort) == "number" and
        type(Cfg.UserStr) == "string" and type(Cfg.PassStr) == "string" then
```

```lua
      io.write("Connecting to ", Cfg.ServerStr, "\n")
      PopHnd, ErrStr = LclOpen(Cfg)
      if PopHnd then
        io.write("Retrieving headers\n")
        HdrTbl, ErrStr = LclHeaders(PopHnd)
        if HdrTbl then
          for J, Rec in ipairs(HdrTbl) do
            io.write("--- Msg ", J, " ---\n",
                " Subject: ", Rec.subject or "---", "\n",
                " From:    ", Rec.from or "---", "\n",
                " Date:    ", Rec.date or "---", "\n",
                " Size:    ", Rec.size or "---", "\n")
          end
        end
        io.write("Disconnecting from ", Cfg.ServerStr, "\n")
        LclClose(PopHnd)
      end
    else
      io.write("Improper configuration: ", CfgFileStr, "\n")
    end
  end
end
if ErrStr then
  io.write(ErrStr, "\n")
end
```

2. Save this file as `pop_01.lua`.

3. Using your editor, create a new configuration file following this template:

```lua
PassStr = "pass"
ServerPort = 110
ServerStr = "mail.example.com"
UserStr = "user"
```

4. Save this file as `cfg`.

5. Substitute values that apply to your POP account.

6. Run the script as follows:

The particular headers that are displayed may vary according to your POP server.

```
lua pop_01.lua
Connecting to localhost
Retrieving headers
--- Msg 1 ---
  Subject: Moonlight
  To:      Oberon <oberon@example.com> Titania <titania@example.com>
  Cc:      William Shakespeare <bard@globe.example.org>
  From:    Puck <puck@example.com>
  Date:    Thu, 07 Sep 19:52:19 GMT
  Size:    970
Disconnecting from localhost
```

How It Works

Like the previous example, the e-mail header retrieval process begins by obtaining account particulars (such as server name, user name, and password) as follows:

```
Cfg, ErrStr = Configure(CfgFileStr)
```

After the presence of the fields expected in the configuration table has been verified, a connection with the POP server is established. The authentication process shown here involves sending the following lines (where `username` and `secret` are replaced with values from the configuration file):

```
user username
pass secret
```

If the POP server is okay with each of these, a list of the waiting e-mail sizes is requested by sending the `list` command. If this command succeeds, the response will contain multiple lines. In this case, lines are read from the server until a line made up of only a single period is encountered. To address the possibility of such a line being transmitted in an email message, servers conventionally prepend a period to every line beginning with a period. Clients, including the one shown here, remove these initial periods. Based on the retrieved message list, the headers of each waiting message are requested using the `top` command. This is done so that a list of the message details can be presented to the user prior to downloading message bodies. Use the `RETR` command to retrieve the full body of the message. You can delete a message with the `DELE` command. Both of these commands are followed by a space and the one-based position of the message.

For more information about retrieving message bodies and dealing with possible encoding issues, refer to documentation concerning MIME techniques.

Networking with Lua and Streams

In this chapter, you've surveyed some (but by no means all) of the uses of the LuaSocket library. Other viable means of communicating over the Internet exist in the form of programs like `inetd` and `ssh` that handle the networking details for you.

On the Server Side: inetd and Friends

Unix-type systems and the Cygwin system for Windows come with a *super-server* application named `inetd`, `xinetd` or `launchd` that you can configure to listen on various ports. When a connection request arrives on one of these ports, it executes the program associated with the port, mapping the program's standard input, output and error streams to the new socket connection. In this way, your program can receive data from a remote client simply by reading its standard input stream, and send data back to the client by writing to its standard output stream. Many of the issues that arise when writing a full-fledged server application are taken care of by the super-server. These include managing execution privileges and restricting connections by address and frequency. Any program that can read from and write to its standard streams can be registered with a super-server, so what makes Lua special in this regard? In a nutshell, speed. Unlike a dedicated application server that runs continuously as a process, a server application registered with a super-server is executed whenever a new connection for it is made. Lua's small size and rapid loading make it a perfect choice for use in this arrangement.

Try It Out   Creating a Stream-Based Server

If you work on a Unix-type platform, including Cygwin for Windows, you can arrange to have a Lua program act as a network server by registering it with your system's super-server. The example shown here assumes you have xinetd available.

If you use a system with inetd, consult its man page for configuration details. In particular, you need to add an entry in /etc/services to give the listening port a service name. It is this service name rather than the port number itself that is put in the inetd.conf file.

The super-server usually runs as root and executes server programs with minimal permissions to reduce the possibility of a security breach. In the following example, the user nobody (often associated with web servers) is used in this capacity. You may want or need to replace references to nobody in the following files with another suitable low-authority user. In general, you should restrict the writers of server scripts as much as practical. In this example, only root can write to the script.

1. With your text editor, create a new Lua script with the following contents:

```
-- Sample echo server for testing with inetd and cousin xinetd

local Str = "Lua echo server opening / " .. os.date("%T")
while Str and Str ~= "" and Str ~= "\r" do
  io.write(Str, "\r\n")
  io.flush()
  Str = io.read()
end
io.write("Lua echo server closing / ", os.date("%T"), "\r\n")
```

2. Save this file as echo.lua in a suitable directory. (/var/local/lua is used here, but the choice is yours.)

3. As root, modify the permissions of echo.lua so that it is readable by nobody and writeable only by suitable users, like this:

```
chown root:nobody echo.lua
chmod u=rw,g=r,o= echo.lua
```

4. In the /etc/xinetd.d directory, create a new file named lua-echo with the following contents, changing the directory and user if necessary:

```
# description: A sample Lua server

service lua-echo
{
    socket_type    = stream
    type           = UNLISTED
    protocol       = tcp
    user           = nobody
    wait           = no
    server         = /usr/local/bin/lua
    server_args    = /var/local/lua/echo.lua
    disable        = no
    port           = 23032
```

```
    log_type       = FILE /var/local/lua/log
    log_on_success = PID HOST DURATION
    log_on_failure = HOST
}
```

5. Restart the super-server. On some systems this is done with a command like this:

```
service xinetd restart
```

or this:

```
/etc/rc.d/rc.inetd restart
```

Consult the documentation for your particular super-server and platform.

6. Use `telnet` to connect with the server (`localhost` if you are accessing the echo server from the machine on which it will run or the name of the host if you are accessing the script remotely), and submit a blank line when you are ready to terminate the session, as follows:

You can also invoke concurrent connections.

```
telnet localhost 23032
Trying 127.0.0.1...
Connected to localhost.
Escape character is '^]'.
Lua echo server opening / 09:40:56
abc
abc
xyz
xyz

Lua echo server closing / 09:41:08
Connection closed by foreign host.
```

How It Works

When the super-server receives a TCP connection request on port 23032, it makes sure that the remote client is eligible to be connected. If so, it executes the following, with the `stdin`, `stdout`, and `stderr` channels hooked to the socket connection:

```
/usr/local/bin/lua /var/local/lua/echo.lua
```

The echo script begins by writing a welcome message with the time. It then waits for input from the client and, when it receives a non-empty line, writes it back. The loop is broken when an empty line arrives from the client. The script then writes a closing line with the time and terminates. This causes the Lua interpreter to terminate as well, a condition that prompts the super-server to close the network connection.

On the Client Side: ssh and Friends

You can use the Lua `io.popen` function in conjunction with programs like `ssh` and `nc` (sometimes named `netcat`) to do for clients one-half of what super-servers provide for servers. Why one-half? Unfortunately, you can only open the stock `popen` in the C runtime library, on which Lua's `io.popen` is based, in either read mode or write mode but not both together. Here's the way it works: io.popen accepts the name of a program and program arguments as its first argument, and either "w" (or "wb") for writing or "r" (or "rb") for reading as its second argument. The "b" qualifiers indicate binary mode, an important consideration on the Windows platform. Here's an example use of io.popen:

```
Hnd, ErrStr = io.popen("nc server.example.net 4583", "r")
```

In this example, the netcat program (nc) will be invoked with the name of a server followed by the port on which the server is listening. Whatever this program writes to its standard output will be readable from the handle that io.popen returns. In this case, because the pipe is read-only, the launched program has to run without input.

The io.popen function isn't supported on all platforms, including older versions of Windows.

A versatile program named plink can be used with io.popen on Windows and Unix-type systems. This stream-based program is part of Simon Tatham's outstanding PuTTY suite of secure shell client applications. With it, you can connect to a server using the SSH or telnet protocol or use it to transfer data in "raw" mode. The SSH option makes it an excellent tool for accessing servers protected behind a firewall.

Try It Out — Using a Stream-Based Client

In this example, you programmatically connect to the server from the previous example. You need to have either netcat (www.vulnwatch.org/netcat) or plink (www.chiark.greenend.org.uk/~sgtatham/putty) to run the client script.

Because of the one-way nature of io.popen, the stdin channel of netcat or plink will be taken from a file. The stdout channel is attached to the handle returned from io.popen.

1. Create a new Lua script with the following contents. If you run the client script from a machine other than the one the echo server is running on, change the value of ServerStr accordingly. Also, there are two variations of CmdStr — comment or delete the one that doesn't apply depending on which network tool you will use.

```lua
local ServerStr = "localhost"
local Port = 23032
local CmdStr = "nc " .. ServerStr .. " " .. Port
-- local CmdStr = "plink -raw -P " .. Port .. " " .. ServerStr
local SendFileStr = "send.txt"

local Hnd = io.open(SendFileStr, "w")
if Hnd then
  Hnd:write("One\nTwo\nThree\n\n")
  Hnd:close()
  Hnd = io.popen(CmdStr .. " < " .. SendFileStr)
  if Hnd then
    for Str in Hnd:lines() do
      io.write(Str, "\n")
    end
    Hnd:close()
  else
```

```
        io.write("Error executing '", CmdStr, "'\n")
      end
   else
      io.write("Error opening ", SendFileStr, " for writing\n")
   end
```

2. Save this file as `client_03.lua`.

3. Run the script as follows:

```
lua client_03.lua
Lua echo server opening / 10:39:31
One
Two
Three
Lua echo server closing / 10:39:31
```

How It Works

The first order of business for the client script is to prepare some lines to transmit to the echo server. It writes these lines to a file, taking care to include a blank line at the end to signal to the echo server a request to end the session. Putting these lines in a file is necessary because after io.popen is called the script will have no way to send data to the echo server. The network utility, either netcat or plink, is invoked with a call to io.popen. The command uses the < redirector to attach the utility's standard input stream to the file just prepared. After making a network connection with the server, the lines are sent by the utility to the server. Server output is obtained by the client through the io.popen handle. The following line is used to loop through the lines from the server until the session has been ended:

```
for Str in Hnd:lines() do
```

Note that the Lua scripts on both the client and the server have external requirements for network connectivity, but don't require any Lua modules.

The technique of using external tools for network communication can facilitate many tasks. For example, if you administer a number of network hosts, you can write short scripts that collect and print critical information about each script's host. You can register each script with the super-server on its host or, more securely, invoke it through SSH. You can then run a client script to collect this information with one invocation. You can use the plink tool whether you access the scripts in raw mode or through SSH.

When implementing client and server scripts for network operations, moving basic data back and forth in the form of text lines often suffices. This can be limiting, however, for exchanging richly structured data. Currently, the prevailing standard is to exchange data in XML format, and libraries for Lua are available on luaforge.net to read and write in this format. If the scripts exchanging data are both written in Lua, however, another solution may be the easiest. As a data description language, Lua has a very clean and compact notation. Translating the Booleans, numbers, and strings of nested tables to Lua code is a straightforward variation of the ObjectDescribe you worked with in Chapter 7. In addition to being easy to write, data that is received in this format couldn't be easier to read — you let Lua do it for you with the loadstring function. For example, suppose you have a Lua data structure that would be created with the following code:

```
Classes = {
  Laura = {"BIO 102", "SPA 221", "MTH 150", "CHM 100", Id = 120},
  Jasmine = {"ENG 154", "LIT 204", "HUM 120", "PHY 100", Id = 390}
}
```

You can use a routine with the following characteristics to convert this structure back to Lua code:

❑ Special characters like quotes and newlines in strings are properly escaped.

❑ Boolean values are converted to "true" and "false."

❑ Tables are handled by calling the routine recursively, with attention paid to already-defined tables to avoid unbound recursion.

The string that is returned by such a routine might look something like this:

```
['Classes']={Laura={[1]="BIO 102",[2]="SPA 221",[3]="MTH 150",⤶
  [4]="CHM 100",['Id']=120},Jasmine={[1]="ENG 154",[2]="LIT 204",⤶
  [3]="HUM 120",[4]="PHY 100",['Id']=390}}
```

With a little finesse, you could generate a rendition that is more readable. This readability doesn't matter to the receiving machine, but it might be desirable if some type of monitoring by people is required. When the receiving script receives the string, it can reconstruct the data structure as follows:

```
Fnc = loadstring("return {" .. Str .. "}")
if Fnc then
  Tbl = Fnc()
end
```

To avoid the concatenation on the receiving side, wrap the string with return { and } on the sending side instead.

Summary

Network communication with Lua is well-supported by the excellent LuaSocket library and other tools such as the plink utility. In this chapter, you learned about the following:

❑ Berkeley sockets and their use in Internet communication

❑ LuaSocket's support for domain name queries, URL parsing, and socket communication

❑ Sending e-mail with SMTP and receiving it with POP

❑ Requesting web pages and other Internet resources via the Web

❑ The system of filters, sources, sinks, and pumps that can condition data in transit

❑ Using external tools for networking with standard streams

In the next chapter, you'll explore how Lua is used in computer games. But before you leave this chapter, try the following exercises to enhance your Lua networking skills.

Exercises

1. A simple cipher known as *rot13* is often used to casually obscure text. This method is often used in newsgroup postings to veil potentially offensive jokes or the answers to riddles. This forces the reader to intentionally apply the cipher to make the text understandable. Each ASCII character in the text is effectively rotated 13 positions, so that characters in the range from A through M are shifted up to N through Z, and characters in the range N through Z are shifted down to A through M. A similar rotation takes place with lowercase letters. All characters outside of these ranges remain unaffected. The cipher rotates from the midpoint of each character range (that is A-Z and a-z), so it is its own inverse in the sense that applying it to converted text restores the original text.

    Write a simple filter (a function that accepts a string and returns a converted string) that implements rot13. Use the `Transform` function from the Text Hydraulics example to check your filter. The decimal values of the characters A and a are 65 and 97, respectively.

    Tbbq yhpx!

2. Extend the e-mail retrieval example to include the message body when displaying the headers if the size of the message is less than or equal to 4096 bytes. Do this by writing a function named `LclBodyPrint` that is called in the existing header loop as follows:

```
for J, Rec in ipairs(HdrTbl) do
  io.write("--- Msg ", J, " ---\n",
     "  Subject: ", Rec.subject or "---", "\n",
     "  To:      ", Rec.to or "---", "\n",
     "  Cc:      ", Rec.cc or "---", "\n",
     "  From:    ", Rec.from or "---", "\n",
     "  Date:    ", Rec.date or "---", "\n",
     "  Size:    ", Rec.size or "---", "\n")
  if Rec.size <= 4096 then
    LclBodyPrint(PopHnd, J)
  end
end
```

    The POP command to retrieve a message body is RETR position, where position is the value J in the header loop shown above. If the RETR command is successful, it returns the entire message including headers in multiple lines. Use the blank line between the headers and the message body to print only the body.

3. In the Stream-Based Client exercise, you used netcat or plink to pass three lines to an echo server. Do the same using the LuaSocket package rather than an external tool.

Programming Games with Lua

Although Lua was not designed for video game programming in particular, it is quite popular with game programmers — in fact, they were the first programming subculture in which Lua became a household word.

This chapter is only a short introduction to a large topic. It talks about why and when you would want to use Lua in a game, but most of it is occupied with an example: a simple 2-D action game. In this chapter you learn how to do the following:

❑   Program with the SDL library

❑   Define sprites

❑   Make the sprites move, either automatically or in response to user input

❑   Detect collisions between sprites

Understanding Why and When to Use Lua

It is possible to write games entirely in Lua, but generally there's a division of labor between Lua and at least one other language. This is for two reasons:

❑   There are some things (graphics, sound, and interaction with non-character-oriented hardware) that Lua simply cannot do on its own.

❑   As languages of its type go, Lua is very fast, but some games, because of their real-time nature, have speed demands that can only be satisfied by less flexible languages like C and C++.

In parts of a game (or any program, really) where either of those reasons apply, you should use another language. In parts where they don't apply, you can use Lua and benefit from its strong points (that generally aren't shared by languages that beat it in the preceding two departments). The benefits of Lua include the following:

❑ **Lightweight compilation**: In Lua, there's a very short distance between changing a program and seeing the effects of the change. (By loading Lua code at run time, you can even make changes without restarting the program.)

❑ **High-level nature**: Lua includes as basic features things like tables, closures, and coroutines. These allow programs to be written at a higher level of abstraction.

❑ **Ease of learning**: Lua has a simple syntax and type system. It doesn't have a lot of rules that are there just to make things easier for the computer.

This division of labor means that things like graphics are generally written in some lower-level language, and things like game logic, AI for computer-controlled characters, level definitions, and saved-game files can be written in Lua, possibly by different team members than those working in the other language.

You can also use Lua for prototyping. Write as much of the game as possible in Lua, and then translate anything that's too slow (and can't be sufficiently optimized within Lua) to a lower-level language.

The rest of this chapter demonstrates a simple graphical game. So simple, in fact, that it barely deserves to be called a game (there is no scoring or way to win, and the gameplay gets old fast), but this simplicity is intentional — it allows you to examine some basic concepts in more detail than would be possible with a more amusing game.

Simple 2-D Action Game Using SDL

The example game will be entirely in Lua, except for the low-level graphics, which will use the Simple DirectMedia Layer (SDL) library. SDL is a cross-platform library that lets you do graphics, audio, joystick access, and other things that are useful in games. It is licensed under the GNU Lesser General Public License. More information, including documentation, is available at `www.libsdl.org`.

SDL is written in C, but you will be using a Lua binding to it in this chapter. Specifically, you'll be using the binding that comes with LuaCheia. LuaCheia (Portuguese for full moon) is a distribution of Lua that includes a bunch of add-on libraries, including SDL. (LuaCheia's SDL binding was done by Asko Kauppi, and an updated version is included in his Lua distribution LuaX, available at `luaforge.net`.)

> LuaCheia uses Lua 5.0 rather than Lua 5.1, which is why `math.mod` is used instead of the % operator in the following examples.

Installing SDL and LuaCheia

For the SDL examples to work, you need to install LuaCheia. If you are using Windows, then your job is easy, because there's a Windows installer that installs everything you need.

On either platform, first follow these steps:

1. Go to LuaCheia's SourceForge.net page (`sourceforge.net/projects/luacheia/`). Click the Download LuaCheia link, select the file `luacheia5-win32-5.0.1a5.exe` (you may need to scroll down to see it), select a mirror site near you, save the file, and run it. This will install LuaCheia in the directory `C:\Program Files\luacheia` (or somewhere else if your Program Files directory is somewhere else).

2. In the following examples, you access LuaCheia typing **luacheia5** at the shell. For this to work, add `C:\Program Files\luacheia` to your search path (as described in Chapter 1). Alternatively, you can run LuaCheia by typing the following:

```
"C:\Program Files\luacheia\luacheia5"
```

Notice that you use quotes instead of just `luacheia5`.

If you are using a Windows system, you're done. If however, you're using a Unix-like operating system, then you have a bit more work ahead of you. Before installing anything, make sure that you have the following:

❏ gcc or another C compiler

❏ C++ compiler, such as g++ or c++ (because the LuaCheia SDL binding is actually done in C++)

This compiler may be gcc *too, but* gcc *can be installed in a way that doesn't include its C++ components.*

❏ The X Window System, including its header files (usually located at `/usr/include/X11/`)

You may be able to get the following examples to work without the X Window System, using the frame-buffer on Linux or native graphics on Mac OS X, but that's not covered here.

Follow these steps to install SDL:

1. Go to the SDL 1.2 section of `www.libsdl.org` (listed under the Download header) and download the file `SDL-1.2.11.tar.gz` to `/usr/local/src/` or somewhere in your home directory. (If a more recent version is available, it will probably work too.)

2. Unpack the file and use `cd` to change to the directory that unpacking the file creates, as follows:

```
tar xzvf SDL-1.2.11.tar.gz
cd SDL-1.2.11
```

You can remove the `.tar.gz` file after it's unpacked.

3. Build the SDL makefiles as follows:

```
./configure
```

This will print a lot of data. Somewhere in the middle, you should see something like `checking for X... libraries /usr/X11R6/lib, headers`. If you instead see `checking for X... no`, then the X Window System (or its header files) could not be found.

4. Compile SDL as follows:

```
make
```

5. As root, install SDL like this:

```
make install
```

Now follow these steps to compile and install LuaCheia:

1. Go to LuaCheia's SourceForge.net page (`sourceforge.net/projects/luacheia/`). Click the Download LuaCheia link, select the file `luacheia5-5.0.1a5.tar.gz`, select a mirror site near you, and save the file to `/usr/local/src/` or somewhere in your home directory.

2. Unpack the file and use `cd` to change to the directory that unpacking the file creates, as follows:

```
tar xzvf luacheia5-5.0.1a5.tar.gz
cd luacheia5-5.0.1a5
```

You can remove the `.tar.gz` file after it's unpacked.

3. Build LuaCheia's makefiles as follows:

```
./configure
```

This will print a lot of data, including something like this in the middle:

```
checking for sdl-config... /usr/local/bin/sdl-config
checking for SDL - version >= 1.2.5... yes
```

4. Compile LuaCheia as follows:

```
make
```

5. As root, install LuaCheia like this:

```
make install
```

Using SDL

Now that you have LuaCheia installed, it's time to use its binding to SDL in an example program. To make things a little more digestible, two versions of the example program will be given.

Try It Out   **Writing Your First SDL Program**

1. Save the following as `movearound.lua`:

```
-- Simple SDL graphics demo.  Usage: luacheia5 test.lua

assert(cheia.load("SDL"))
assert(cheia.load("bit"))

-- Returns a "screen" (a canvas within a window upon which the
-- sprites will be drawn):
local function MakeScreen()
  local ErrStr
  local Screen = SDL.SDL_SetVideoMode(640, 480, 8,
    bit.bor(SDL.SDL_SWSURFACE, SDL.SDL_ANYFORMAT))
  if not Screen then
    ErrStr = debug.traceback(SDL.SDL_GetError())
  end
  return Screen, ErrStr
end

-- Returns a sprite object; ImgName is the filename of a .bmp file:
```

```lua
local function MakeSprite(Screen, ImgName)
  local Sprite, ErrStr
  local Img = SDL.SDL_LoadBMP(ImgName)
  if Img then
    local Background = SDL.SDL_MapRGB(Screen.format, 0, 0, 0)
    -- Current X and Y positions:
    local CurX, CurY = 0, 0
    -- Tables to be (re)used as rectangle arguments to
    -- SDL_FillRect and SDL_BlitSurface:
    local FillRect = {x = 0, y = 0, w = Img.w, h = Img.h}
    local BlitRect = {x = 0, y = 0, w = Img.w, h = Img.h}
    -- The sprite object:
    Sprite = {}

    -- Moves the sprite; X and Y default to the current position if
    -- they are nil:
    function Sprite:Move(X, Y)
      local Succ, ErrStr
      X, Y = math.floor(X or CurX), math.floor(Y or CurY)
      -- Erase the sprite at its current position:
      FillRect.x, FillRect.y = CurX, CurY
      if SDL.SDL_FillRect(Screen, FillRect, Background) == 0 then
        -- Write it to its new position:
        BlitRect.x, BlitRect.y = X, Y
        if SDL.SDL_BlitSurface(Img, nil, Screen, BlitRect) == 0 then
          CurX, CurY = X, Y
          Succ = true
        else
          Succ, ErrStr = false, debug.traceback(SDL.SDL_GetError())
        end
      else
        Succ, ErrStr = false, debug.traceback(SDL.SDL_GetError())
      end
      return Succ, ErrStr
    end

    -- Give the sprite its initial position:
    local Succ
    Succ, ErrStr = Sprite:Move()
    if not Succ then
      Sprite = nil
    end
  else
    ErrStr = debug.traceback(SDL.SDL_GetError())
  end
  return Sprite, ErrStr
end

-- Returns a function that gets pending events (all it returns in
-- this version is whether to quit):
local function MakeGetEvents()
  -- An SDL_Event structure -- this is how SDL.SDL_PollEvent returns
  -- any event it finds in the event queue:
  local Event = SDL.SDL_Event_new()

  -- Returns whether to quit:
  return function()
```

```lua
      local Quit = false
      -- Consume pending events:
      while not Quit and SDL.SDL_PollEvent(Event) == 1 do
        -- Was the window closed?
        if Event.type == SDL.SDL_QUIT then
          Quit = true -- Break the loop.
        -- Was "q" pressed?
        elseif Event.type == SDL.SDL_KEYDOWN
          and Event.key.keysym.sym == SDL.SDLK_q
        then
          Quit = true -- Break the loop.
        end
      end
      return Quit
    end
end

local function MainLoop(Screen, UserSprite)
  local Succ, ErrStr = true
  -- Put the sprite 32 pixels from the left side, and 0 pixels
  -- from the top, of the screen (window):
  Succ, ErrStr = UserSprite:Move(32, 0)
  if Succ then
    -- Update the entire screen:
    SDL.SDL_UpdateRect(Screen, 0, 0, 0, 0)
    local GetEvents = MakeGetEvents()
    -- GetEvents returns true if the user quits; loop until that
    -- happens:
    while not GetEvents() do end
  end
  return Succ, ErrStr
end

local function Main()
  local ErrStr
  local InitRes = SDL.SDL_Init(SDL.SDL_INIT_VIDEO)
  if InitRes == 0 then
    local Screen
    Screen, ErrStr = MakeScreen()
    if Screen then
      -- The window title is somewhat misleading in this initial
      -- version:
      SDL.SDL_WM_SetCaption("Move Around", "Move Around");
      SDL.SDL_EnableKeyRepeat(SDL.SDL_DEFAULT_REPEAT_DELAY,
        SDL.SDL_DEFAULT_REPEAT_INTERVAL)
      -- Create a sprite (eventually to be controlled by the user):
      local UserSprite
      UserSprite, ErrStr = MakeSprite(Screen, "goodie.bmp")
      if UserSprite then
        io.write("In the new window, press 'q' (or close the",
          " window) to quit.\n")
        io.flush()
        local _
        _, ErrStr = MainLoop(Screen, UserSprite)
      end
    end
    SDL.SDL_Quit()
```

```
      else
        ErrStr = debug.traceback(SDL.SDL_GetError())
      end
      return not ErrStr, ErrStr
   end

   local Succ, ErrStr = Main()
   if not Succ then
     io.stderr:write(ErrStr, "\n")
   end
```

2. Use a drawing program (such as Microsoft Paint or The Gimp) to draw a picture roughly 32 pixels wide by 32 pixels tall, and save it in Windows bitmap format as `goodie.bmp`.

3. On Unix-like systems, start the X Window System if it's not already running.

4. Run `movearound.lua` as follows:

```
luacheia5 movearound.lua
```

As mentioned previously, if you're on Windows and you didn't add the LuaCheia directory to your search path, you'll need to type something like this instead:

```
"C:\Program Files\luacheia\luacheia5" movearound.lua
```

A new window will appear that looks like Figure 17-1. (For this example, the Lua logo was used to create `goodie.bmp`.)

5. Close the window with the mouse or by pressing q.

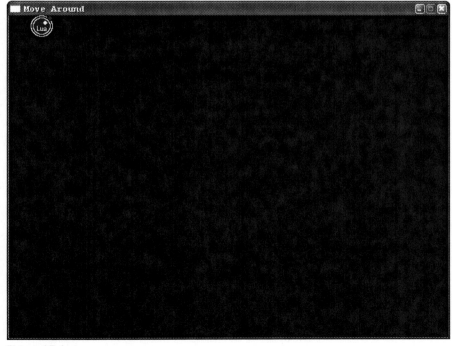

Figure 17-1

How It Works

This is a preliminary version of this example. Despite the name, nothing actually moves around yet.

`assert(cheia.load("SDL"))` loads the SDL library, creating a global table called `SDL`. This table contains the SDL library's functions and constants. `SDL.SDL_Init` is the Lua version of the C function `SDL_Init`, `SDL.SDL_INIT_VIDEO` is the Lua version of the C constant `SDL_INIT_VIDEO`, and so on. Before any of SDL's other functions can be used, `SDL.SDL_Init` is called as follows:

```
local function Main()
  local ErrStr
  local InitRes = SDL.SDL_Init(SDL.SDL_INIT_VIDEO)
```

The `SDL.SDL_INIT_VIDEO` argument tells SDL that you want to initialize the video (graphics) subsystem. (SDL also can do things with sound, joysticks, CD-ROMs, and more.) As documented on the SDL website, the `SDL_Init` C function returns 0 if it succeeds and –1 if it fails. From a Lua standpoint, it would be more idiomatic to return `true` on success and `false` on failure, but this binding is a relatively thin one that doesn't hide SDL's C-ish nature, so the check for success looks like this:

```
if InitRes == 0 then
```

The thinness of the binding also explains why the names are so verbose. The second SDL *in* `SDL.SDL_Init` *is only there because all of the C functions (and constants) start with* SDL_.

After SDL is initialized, the next step is to make a *screen* — a surface that you can draw on, which appears in its own window. This is accomplished with the following:

```
local function MakeScreen()
  local ErrStr
  local Screen = SDL.SDL_SetVideoMode(640, 480, 8,
    bit.bor(SDL.SDL_SWSURFACE, SDL.SDL_ANYFORMAT))
```

For details about the `SDL.SDL_SetVideoMode` *arguments, see the SDL website. For now, just note that this and some other functions take on-off switches (flags) for various behaviors, and that when multiple flags need to be given, they're combined with a bitwise* or. *A bitwise* or *means that two (or more) numbers are treated as binary and a logical* or *is performed on the ones columns, the twos columns, the fours columns, and so on, with 1 used for* true *and 0 for* false. *The bitwise* or *here (*`bit.bor`*) is supplied by the LuaCheia library loaded earlier in the file with* `cheia.load("bit")`. *(This particular set of flags,* `SDL.SDL_SWSURFACE` *and* `SDL.SDL_ANYFORMAT`, *actually could have been handled without a bitwise operation, but other sets of flags you may use cannot.)*

A title is then given to the window, and key repeat is enabled (so that holding down a key is like rapidly tapping it over and over).

Next, a *sprite* is created. A sprite is basically a picture that can be moved around the screen as a unit. SDL has no built-in support for sprites, so they need to be implemented in terms of more basic operations. Specifically, `MakeSprite` returns a table with a `Move` method. When this method is called, the sprite's image (`goodie.bmp`) is erased from its current location on the screen and redrawn so that its upper-left corner is at the given coordinates.

The first coordinate, X, gives the horizontal component of the position, with 0 being the leftmost column of pixels on the screen. The second coordinate, Y, gives the vertical component of the position, with 0 being the topmost row of pixels.

The erasing is done with SDL.SDL_FillRect, whose second argument shows the position and size of the rectangle to be painted with the background color. This second argument is a *rectangle*, which in SDL means a table with x, y, w (width), and h (height) fields.

The redrawing is done with SDL.SDL_BlitSurface. (*Blitting* means copying pixels from one area of memory to another.) SDL.SDL_BlitSurface takes the following four arguments:

❑   The first argument is the source surface which in this example is the surface generated by reading goodie.bmp. (A *surface* is just a chunk of memory viewed as a rectangle of pixels.)

❑   The second argument is a rectangle showing what part of the source surface to copy. If this is nil, the whole source surface is copied.

❑   The third argument is the destination surface, which in this example is the screen.

❑   The fourth arument is a rectangle showing where in the destination surface to copy the source surface to (the w and h fields are ignored).

After the sprite is created, it's given to MainLoop, which moves it to 32, 0 (an arbitrary location chosen for demonstration purposes) and then makes sure that the sprite is visible by calling SDL.SDL_UpdateRect. Until SDL.SDL_UpdateRect is called, there's no guarantee that anything done by SDL.SDL_BlitSurface will be visible — it may be or it may not be. SDL.SDL_UpdateRect is your way of saying that you're done slinging bits around the screen and are ready for what you've done to become visible.

Apart from the surface to be updated, SDL.SDL_UpdateRect takes four arguments: the X position, Y position, width, and height of the rectangular section of the surface that is to be updated. As a special case, if it sees that all four of these arguments are 0, it updates the whole surface (the screen in this case).

The GetEvents function uses SDL.SDL_PollEvent to check for new events. The only events it cares about are the window being closed and the Q key being pressed — if either of these happens, it returns true. If some other event or events occur, or if no events have occurred since the last time SDL.SDL_PollEvent was called, GetEvents returns false. Waiting for the user to quit is the job of the main loop of the program (which MainLoop is named after). This empty-bodied loop just calls GetEvents over and over until it returns true:

```
while not GetEvents() do end
```

Finally, SDL.SDL_Quit is called to shut down SDL, and if an error occurred anywhere along the way, its error message is printed.

———————————

The next version of movearound.lua will still have very low entertainment value as a game, but it will at least live up to its name — you'll be able to control the movement of a sprite. Meanwhile another sprite will be moving on its own.

Putting Sprites in Motion

1.   Make the following changes to `movearound.lua`:

```
-- Simple SDL graphics demo.  Usage: luacheia5 test.lua

assert(cheia.load("SDL"))
assert(cheia.load("bit"))

-- Returns a "screen" (a canvas within a window upon which the
-- sprites will be drawn):
local function MakeScreen()
  local ErrStr
  local Screen = SDL.SDL_SetVideoMode(640, 480, 8,
    bit.bor(SDL.SDL_SWSURFACE, SDL.SDL_ANYFORMAT))
  if not Screen then
    ErrStr = debug.traceback(SDL.SDL_GetError())
  end
  return Screen, ErrStr
end

-- Returns N, or (if N is lower than Min), a number as much above Min
-- as N is below it, or (if N is higher than Max), a number as much
-- below Max as N is above it; also returns a second value telling
-- whether had to return a number other than N:
local function ComputeBounce(N, Min, Max)
  local Fix = false
  if N > Max then
    N = Max - (N - Max)
    Fix = true
  elseif N < Min then
    N = Min + (Min - N)
    Fix = true
  end
  return N, Fix
end

-- Returns N, or Min if N is lower than Min, or Max, if N is higher
-- than Max:
local function Between(N, Min, Max)
  return N > Max and Max or N < Min and Min or N
end

-- Returns 1, 0, or -1 depending on whether N is positive, zero, or
-- negative:
local function Sign(N)
  if N > 0 then
    N = 1
  elseif N < 0 then
    N = -1
  end
  return N
end
```

```
-- Returns a sprite object; ImgName is the filename of a .bmp file:
```

```lua
local function MakeSprite(Screen, ImgName)
  local Sprite, ErrStr
  local Img = SDL.SDL_LoadBMP(ImgName)
  if Img then
    local Background = SDL.SDL_MapRGB(Screen.format, 0, 0, 0)
    -- Current X and Y positions:
    local CurX, CurY = 0, 0
    -- Current velocities along the X and Y axes, in pixels per tick
    -- (minimum -1, maximum 1):
    local VelX, VelY = 0, 0
    -- Velocity increment (the smallest unit by which velocity along
    -- a given axis changes):
    local VelInc = 1 / 32
    -- Tables to be (re)used as rectangle arguments to
    -- SDL_FillRect and SDL_BlitSurface:
    local FillRect = {x = 0, y = 0, w = Img.w, h = Img.h}
    local BlitRect = {x = 0, y = 0, w = Img.w, h = Img.h}
    -- The sprite object:
    Sprite = {}

    -- Moves the sprite; X and Y default to the current position if
    -- they are nil:
    function Sprite:Move(X, Y)
      local Succ, ErrStr
      X, Y = math.floor(X or CurX), math.floor(Y or CurY)
      -- Erase the sprite at its current position:
      FillRect.x, FillRect.y = CurX, CurY
      if SDL.SDL_FillRect(Screen, FillRect, Background) == 0 then
        -- Write it to its new position:
        BlitRect.x, BlitRect.y = X, Y
        if SDL.SDL_BlitSurface(Img, nil, Screen, BlitRect) == 0 then
          CurX, CurY = X, Y
          Succ = true
        else
          Succ, ErrStr = false, debug.traceback(SDL.SDL_GetError())
        end
      else
        Succ, ErrStr = false, debug.traceback(SDL.SDL_GetError())
      end
      return Succ, ErrStr
    end

    -- Call this once for every tick:
    function Sprite:Tick(Ticks)
      local Succ, ErrStr = true
      local NewX
      if VelX ~= 0 and math.mod(Ticks, 1 / VelX) < 1 then
        NewX = CurX + Sign(VelX)
        -- Make sure it doesn't go off the edges:
        local Fix
        NewX, Fix = ComputeBounce(NewX, 0,
          self:ScreenWidth() - self:Width())
        if Fix then VelX = -VelX end
      end
      local NewY
```

```
         if VelY ~= 0 and math.mod(Ticks, 1 / VelY) < 1 then
            NewY = CurY + Sign(VelY)
            -- Make sure it doesn't go off the edges:
            local Fix
            NewY, Fix = ComputeBounce(NewY, 0,
               self:ScreenHeight() - self:Height())
            if Fix then VelY = -VelY end
         end
         if NewX or NewY then
            Succ, ErrStr = self:Move(NewX, NewY)
         end
         return Succ, ErrStr
      end

      -- Accelerates the sprite along the X axis (negative values of
      -- Accel accelerate to the left):
      function Sprite:AccelX(Accel)
         if Accel ~= 0 then
            VelX = Between(VelX + Accel * VelInc, -1, 1)
         end
      end

      -- Accelerates the sprite along the Y axis (negative values of
      -- Accel accelerate upward):
      function Sprite:AccelY(Accel)
         if Accel ~= 0 then
            VelY = Between(VelY + Accel * VelInc, -1, 1)
         end
      end

      -- Stops the sprite cold:
      function Sprite:Stop()
         VelX, VelY = 0, 0
      end

      -- More methods:
      function Sprite:X() return CurX end
      function Sprite:Y() return CurY end
      function Sprite:Width() return Img.w end
      function Sprite:Height() return Img.h end
      function Sprite:ScreenWidth() return Screen.w end
      function Sprite:ScreenHeight() return Screen.h end

      -- Give the sprite its initial position:
      local Succ
      Succ, ErrStr = Sprite:Move()
      if not Succ then
         Sprite = nil
      end
   else
      ErrStr = debug.traceback(SDL.SDL_GetError())
   end
   return Sprite, ErrStr
end

-- Returns a function that gets pending events:
```

```lua
local function MakeGetEvents()
   -- An SDL_Event structure -- this is how SDL.SDL_PollEvent returns
   -- any event it finds in the event queue:
   local Event = SDL.SDL_Event_new()

   -- Returns how much to accelerate to the right, how much to
   -- accelerate downward, and whether to stop or quit:
   return function()
      local AccelX, AccelY, OtherEvent = 0, 0
      -- Consume pending events:
      while not OtherEvent and SDL.SDL_PollEvent(Event) == 1 do
         -- Was the window closed?
         if Event.type == SDL.SDL_QUIT then
            OtherEvent = "Quit" -- Break the loop.
         elseif Event.type == SDL.SDL_KEYDOWN then
            local Key = Event.key.keysym.sym
            -- Was "q" pressed?
            if Key == SDL.SDLK_q then
               OtherEvent = "Quit" -- Break the loop.
            -- If an arrow key was pressed, accelerate the sprite in that
            -- direction:
            elseif Key == SDL.SDLK_LEFT then
               AccelX = AccelX - 1
            elseif Key == SDL.SDLK_RIGHT then
               AccelX = AccelX + 1
            elseif Key == SDL.SDLK_UP then
               AccelY = AccelY - 1
            elseif Key == SDL.SDLK_DOWN then
               AccelY = AccelY + 1
            elseif Key == SDL.SDLK_SPACE then
               OtherEvent = "Stop" -- Break the loop.
            else
               -- Some other key; ignore it.
            end
         end
      end
      return AccelX, AccelY, OtherEvent
   end
end

-- Moves the user sprite and automatic sprite the appropriate
-- distance for the given amount of ticks:
local function Step(UserSprite, AutoSprite, Ticks)
   local Succ, ErrStr = true
   -- Move the sprites:
   Succ, ErrStr = UserSprite:Tick(Ticks)
   if Succ then
      Succ, ErrStr = AutoSprite:Tick(Ticks)
   end
   return Succ, ErrStr
end

-- Are Sprite1 and Sprite2 overlapping?
local function Overlap(Sprite1, Sprite2)
   local Ret = false
   -- This views the two sprites as rectangle-shaped, even if they
```

```lua
    -- look like other shapes.
    local DiffX = math.abs(Sprite1:X() - Sprite2:X())
    local Width = (Sprite1:Width() + Sprite2:Width()) / 2
    if DiffX < Width then
      local DiffY = math.abs(Sprite1:Y() - Sprite2:Y())
      local Height = (Sprite1:Height() + Sprite2:Height()) / 2
      if DiffY < Height then
        Ret = true
      end
    end
    return Ret
end

local function MainLoop(Screen, UserSprite, AutoSprite)
    local Succ, ErrStr = true
    local GetEvents = MakeGetEvents()
    -- Loop until the user quits (or an error occurs):
    local PrevTicks = SDL.SDL_GetTicks();
    local OtherEvent
    while Succ and OtherEvent ~= "Quit" do
      -- Get any and all pending events:
      local AccelX, AccelY
      AccelX, AccelY, OtherEvent = GetEvents()
      -- Update the sprite's velocity:
      UserSprite:AccelX(AccelX)
      UserSprite:AccelY(AccelY)
      -- Get the current number of elapsed ticks -- if it's the same as
      -- the previous number, keep checking until it's different:
      local Ticks = SDL.SDL_GetTicks();
      while Ticks == PrevTicks do
        Ticks = SDL.SDL_GetTicks();
      end
      -- Call Step once for each tick that has happened since
      -- PrevTicks:
      for I = PrevTicks + 1, Ticks do
        Succ, ErrStr = Step(UserSprite, AutoSprite, I)
        if not Succ then break end -- BREAK ON ERROR.
      end
      PrevTicks = Ticks
      if OtherEvent == "Stop" then
        -- Screeching halt:
        UserSprite:Stop()
      end
      -- Are the two sprites overlapping?
      if Overlap(UserSprite, AutoSprite) then
        io.write("GAME OVER (collision)\n")
        break -- EXIT THE MAIN LOOP.
      end
      -- Update the entire screen:
      SDL.SDL_UpdateRect(Screen, 0, 0, 0, 0)
    end
    return Succ, ErrStr
```

```lua
end

local function Main()
  local ErrStr
  local InitRes = SDL.SDL_Init(SDL.SDL_INIT_VIDEO)
  if InitRes == 0 then
    local Screen
    Screen, ErrStr = MakeScreen()
    if Screen then
      -- Set the window title; enable key repeat:
      SDL.SDL_WM_SetCaption("Move Around", "Move Around");
      SDL.SDL_EnableKeyRepeat(SDL.SDL_DEFAULT_REPEAT_DELAY,
        SDL.SDL_DEFAULT_REPEAT_INTERVAL)
      -- Create a sprite to be controlled by the user and another to
      -- be controlled by the program:
      local UserSprite
      UserSprite, ErrStr = MakeSprite(Screen, "goodie.bmp")
      if UserSprite then
        local AutoSprite
        AutoSprite, ErrStr = MakeSprite(Screen, "baddie.bmp")
        if AutoSprite then
          -- Give them their initial positions and velocities:
          local Succ
          local ScreenWidth, ScreenHeight = Screen.w, Screen.h
          Succ, ErrStr = UserSprite:Move(
            ScreenWidth / 3 - UserSprite:Width() / 2,
            ScreenHeight / 2 - UserSprite:Height() / 2)
          if Succ then
            Succ, ErrStr = AutoSprite:Move(
              ScreenWidth * (2 / 3) - AutoSprite:Width() / 2,
              ScreenHeight / 2 - AutoSprite:Height() / 2)
            if Succ then
              -- Go in one of the four diagonal directions depending
              -- on what time it is:
              local Time = math.mod(os.time(), 4) + 1
              local A = 5 -- AutoSprite initial acceleration.
              local AccelX = ({A, A, -A, -A})[Time]
              local AccelY = ({A, -A, -A, A})[Time]
              AutoSprite:AccelX(AccelX)
              AutoSprite:AccelY(AccelY)
              io.write([[
In the new window:
- press the arrow keys to change speed
- press space to stop moving
- press 'q' (or close the window) to quit.
]])
              io.flush()
              Succ, ErrStr = MainLoop(Screen, UserSprite, AutoSprite)
            end
          end
        end
      end
    end
  end
```

```
      SDL.SDL_Quit()
   else
      ErrStr = debug.traceback(SDL.SDL_GetError())
   end
   return not ErrStr, ErrStr
end

local Succ, ErrStr = Main()
if not Succ then
   io.stderr:write(ErrStr, "\n")
end
```

2. Draw another picture roughly 32 pixels wide by 32 pixels tall, and save it in Windows bitmap format as `baddie.bmp`.

3. Run `movearound.lua` as follows:

```
luacheia5 movearound.lua
```

You'll see something like Figure 17-2. The `baddie.bmp` sprite is moving. The `goodie.bmp` sprite is standing still, and pressing an arrow key makes it move in the arrow key's direction. Pressing the key repeatedly makes it go faster and faster in that direction. Pressing the space bar makes it come to a complete stop. Both sprites bounce when they hit the edges of the screen. The program ends when `baddie.bmp` touches `goodie.bmp`.

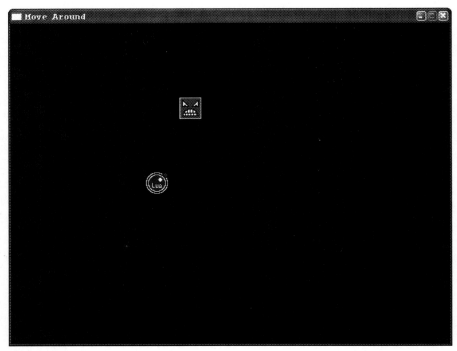

Figure 17-2

How It Works

This version creates two sprites: UserSprite (controlled by the user) and AutoSprite (controlled by the program). They are initially placed respectively to the left and to the right of the screen's center. Then AutoSprite is accelerated (given a push) in a randomly chosen diagonal direction. (The direction is chosen based on what time it is — on Unix-like systems and Windows, os.time returns a number of seconds from a particular date in the past.) This acceleration is done with AutoSprite's AccelX and AccelY methods as follows:

```
-- Go in one of the four diagonal directions depending
-- on what time it is:
local Time = math.mod(os.time(), 4) + 1
local A = 5 -- AutoSprite initial acceleration.
local AccelX = ({A, A, -A, -A})[Time]
local AccelY = ({A, -A, -A, A})[Time]
AutoSprite:AccelX(AccelX)
AutoSprite:AccelY(AccelY)
```

The AccelX method adds the product of its argument and VelInc (1/32) to the sprite's X *velocity* (VelX). Velocity is speed and direction. X velocity is speed along the X axis, but it's negative if the direction is to the left. So, if AccelX is called with an argument of 1, then f 1/32 is added to the sprite's X velocity (which is initialized to 0). AccelX makes sure, though, that the sprite's X velocity never gets lower than –1 or higher than 1, like this:

```
-- Accelerates the sprite along the X axis (negative values of
-- Accel accelerate to the left):
function Sprite:AccelX(Accel)
  if Accel ~= 0 then
    VelX = Between(VelX + Accel * VelInc, -1, 1)
  end
end
```

AccelY does the same thing for the sprite's Y velocity.

MainLoop and the main loop it contains are now more complex. Again, the loop (still a while loop) is based on repeatedly calling GetEvents, but the new GetEvents returns three values. The first two are based on how many times the arrow keys were pressed since the last call to GetEvents. They tell how much UserSprite needs to be accelerated along (respectively) the X and Y axes. The third return value tells whether an event other than an arrow keypress occurred. This third value can be nil, or "Quit" (if the user pressed q or closed the window), or "Stop" (if the user pressed the space bar).

The main loop keeps track of how many *ticks* (milliseconds in SDL) have taken place since its previous iteration. After accelerating UserSprite appropriately, it calls Step once for each elapsed tick:

```
-- Call Step once for each tick that has happened since
-- PrevTicks:
for I = PrevTicks + 1, Ticks do
  Succ, ErrStr = Step(UserSprite, AutoSprite, I)
  if not Succ then break end -- BREAK ON ERROR.
end
PrevTicks = Ticks
```

Step calls each sprite's Tick method with the current tick as an argument.

Actually, it may not be the current tick, but the for I loop lets the Tick method think that it's being called every time a tick occurs, even when several ticks go by in between iterations of the main loop.

In this program, velocity is expressed as the number of pixels to move per tick. Both the X and Y components of velocity have a minimum of –1 (one pixel per tick to the left or upwards) and a maximum of 1 (one pixel per tick to the right or downwards). These values are often fractional, so the Tick method needs to decide on every tick whether or not to move its sprite one pixel. For example, if VelX is 0.25, then Tick needs to move the sprite one pixel to the right on *every fourth tick*. It does this with modulo arithmetic (using the Lua 5.0 function math.mod) as follows:

```
-- Call this once for every tick:
function Sprite:Tick(Ticks)
  local Succ, ErrStr = true
  local NewX
  if VelX ~= 0 and math.mod(Ticks, 1 / VelX) < 1 then
```

"< 1" is used instead of "== 0" to account for the fact that 1 / VelX may not be an integer.

After a new X (always one more or one less than the current X) has been computed, the walls(the edges of the screen) need to be accounted for. If the new X puts part of the sprite offscreen, then it (the new X) is recomputed so that the sprite is fully onscreen, as though it had bounced off the screen's edge, and the sprite's X direction is reversed:

```
NewX = CurX + Sign(VelX)
-- Make sure it doesn't go off the edges:
local Fix
NewX, Fix = ComputeBounce(NewX, 0,
  self:ScreenWidth() - self:Width())
if Fix then VelX = -VelX end
```

Notice that the sprite's width has to be taken into account, because the sprite's X position is actually the position of its left edge.

After doing the same thing for the Y velocity and position, the sprite is moved if necessary:

```
if NewX or NewY then
  Succ, ErrStr = self:Move(NewX, NewY)
end
```

After Step has called each sprite's Tick method, it returns control to MainLoop, which checks whether a "Stop" event has occurred, and responds appropriately:

```
if OtherEvent == "Stop" then
  -- Screeching halt:
  UserSprite:Stop()
end
```

Then the main loop (and after that, the whole program) is exited if `AutoSprite` and `UserSprite` have collided:

```
-- Are the two sprites overlapping?
if Overlap(UserSprite, AutoSprite) then
  io.write("GAME OVER (collision)\n")
  break -- EXIT THE MAIN LOOP.
end
```

If the loop hasn't been exited, then the screen is updated with `SDL.SDL_UpdateRect` and control goes back to the top of the loop. (The loop's `while` expression is responsible for ending things if a `"Quit"` event occurs.)

There are a number of ways you could make this game more interesting. Among other things, you could add the following:

❑   Some sort of goal. This could be as simple as a literal goal — an area of the screen that must be reached, possibly by navigating around fixed obstacles, to win the game. Scoring could be based on how quickly the goal is reached.

❑   More computer-controlled sprites, perhaps with more complex movement patterns. These could all be kept in a table, rather than each having its own variable (as `AutoSprite` does now).

❑   Animation (such as making `AutoSprite`'s eyes blink).

❑   Better collision detection so that sprites are not always considered to be shaped like rectangles.

❑   That old video game standby, shooting things.

You could also improve the interface by making it mouse- or joystick-based, putting it entirely in one window (instead of using `io.write` for messages), and allowing the game to be restarted from the same window.

If any of these changes slowed the game down too much, you could perform optimizations right in Lua, such as minimizing function calls and runtime table creation, and updating only the parts of the screen that need to be updated. If such optimizations weren't enough, you would need to rewrite parts of the game in a lower-level language.

One of the sample programs included with LuaCheia is Meteor Shower by Thatcher Ulrich. This game bears a family resemblance to the arcade classic Asteroids — it demonstrates mouse control, creation of sprites during gameplay, and gravitational physics. On Unix-like systems, you can run it like this:

```
cd /usr/local/src/luacheia5-5.0.1a5/examples/meteor_shower
luacheia5 meteor_shower.lua
```

On Windows, it is one of the choices in the `luacheia` submenu created in the Start menu by the installer.

Summary

In this chapter, you dipped your toes into the deep water of Lua game programming, and learned about the following:

❑ Lua's strong suit in game programming, which is writing the more abstract and less speed-intensive portions of a program

❑ The SDL library

❑ Game programming concepts such as sprites, events, and ticks

❑ The basics of implementing physics concepts like velocity and collisions

As a self-directed exercise, you can make the improvements to movearound.lua suggested in the last section at any time. But for now, here's one exercise to tackle before you move on to the next chapter (about Lua on handheld devices), here's one exercise to tackle. The answer is in the appendix.

Exercise

Here's an SDL program that's not very well commented. Without running it, figure out what it does.

```lua
assert(cheia.load("SDL"))

local function GetImgs()
  local Goodie, Baddie, ErrStr
  Goodie = SDL.SDL_LoadBMP("goodie.bmp")
  if Goodie then
    Baddie = SDL.SDL_LoadBMP("baddie.bmp")
    if Baddie then
      if Goodie.w ~= Baddie.w or Goodie.h ~= Baddie.h then
        Goodie = nil
        ErrStr = debug.traceback(
          "goodie.bmp and baddie.bmp must have the same shape")
      end
    end
  else
    ErrStr = debug.traceback(SDL.SDL_GetError())
  end
  return Goodie, Baddie, ErrStr
end

local function Tile(Goodie, Baddie, Screen)
  math.randomseed(os.time())
  local ErrStr
  for X = 0, 3 do
    for Y = 0, 3 do
      local Img = math.random(1, 2) == 1 and Goodie or Baddie
      if SDL.SDL_BlitSurface(Img, nil, Screen,
```

```
                 {x = X * Goodie.w, y = Y * Goodie.h}) ~= 0
        then
          ErrStr = debug.traceback(SDL.SDL_GetError())
          break -- BREAK ON ERROR.
        end
      end
    end
    return not ErrStr, ErrStr
end

local function WaitForQuit()
  local Event = SDL.SDL_Event_new()
  while Event do
    local Pending = SDL.SDL_PollEvent(Event) == 1
    if Pending
      and (Event.type == SDL.SDL_QUIT
        or Event.type == SDL.SDL_KEYDOWN
        and Event.key.keysym.sym == SDL.SDLK_q)
    then
      Event = false
    end
  end
end

local ErrStr
if SDL.SDL_Init(SDL.SDL_INIT_VIDEO) == 0 then
  local Goodie, Baddie
  Goodie, Baddie, ErrStr = GetImgs()
  if Goodie then
    local Screen = SDL.SDL_SetVideoMode(Goodie.w * 4, Goodie.w * 4, 8,
      SDL.SDL_SWSURFACE)
    if Screen then
      local TileSucc
      TileSucc, ErrStr = Tile(Goodie, Baddie, Screen)
      if TileSucc then
        SDL.SDL_UpdateRect(Screen, 0, 0, 0, 0)
        WaitForQuit()
      end
    else
      ErrStr = debug.traceback(SDL.SDL_GetError())
    end
  else
    ErrStr = debug.traceback(SDL.SDL_GetError())
  end
else
  ErrStr = debug.traceback(SDL.SDL_GetError())
end
if ErrStr then
  io.stderr:write(ErrStr, "\n")
end
```

Carrying Lua with You

Lua's efficiency and small size make it highly suitable for use with the scaled-down resources of a handheld device. This chapter introduces the use of Lua in devices that function with Palm OS, such as PDAs (personal digital assistants) and mobile telephones. The focus will be on Plua, a port of Lua with a very nicely engineered binding to the Palm OS application programming interface. In this chapter, you learn how to do the following:

❑   Obtain and set up Plua on your Palm OS device

❑   Obtain and set up tools to develop Plua applications from your desktop

❑   Save your source code in various formats

❑   Develop Lua modules

❑   Generate artwork programmatically using turtle graphics

❑   Create programs with forms

The flexibility of the Plua package enables you to develop Lua applications right on your Palm device. Alternatively, with the freely available Palm OS Emulator or Simulator, you can build and test your Lua application from your desktop.

Getting Started with Plua

Plua was created by Márcio Migueletto de Andrade and is maintained and copyrighted by him. Currently, version 1.1 and the most recent beta release of version 2.0 are available. The earlier version was a port of Lua version 4.0, and the later version is a port of Lua 5.0. It is the later version, often referred to as Plua2, that's covered here. It is referred to as Plua in this chapter, unless it needs to be distinguished from its predecessor. Because you've been using Lua 5.1 in this book, review the differences between this and Lua 5.0 before developing your own applications with Plua. A summary of these changes can be found near the end of the Lua reference manual. In particular, be aware that in version 5.0 of Lua, there is no # operator and the vararg mechanism uses a table named `arg`.

Obtaining Plua

To obtain an official release of Plua2, you need to be a registered member of the Plua discussion group hosted at `http://groups.yahoo.com/group/plua`. Plua's author is active in this forum and maintains a directory named Plua in the Files section where official releases can be found. Additionally, the Plua community has placed many other contributions such as applications, tutorials, and libraries in other directories of this forum.

From the Plua directory in the Files section of the Yahoo Plua group site, locate and download the most recent plua zip file and examples zip file. Additionally, if a pluac zip file is available for your desktop operating system, you may want to download it as well. This package will allow you to build Plua applications that contain bitmaps and other resources.

Like many other applications, Plua uses MathLib for double-precision math functions. If you don't already have this library, visit `www.radiks.net/~rhuebner/mathlib.html` to download `MathLib.zip`.

Examining the Distribution Contents

Unzip the files you downloaded into a convenient location. For example, assuming you have downloaded `plua-2.0b6.zip` and are using the shell in Windows, the following commands work. Make the appropriate adjustments if the files you have downloaded are of a more recent version or you are on a different platform Replace `/path/to` with the location of the downloaded files.

```
c:
md plua2
cd plua2
7z x /path/to/plua-2.0b6.zip
7z x /path/to/pluac-2.0b6.windows.zip
7z x /path/to/plua-examples.zip
7z x /path/to/MathLib.zip
```

The zip files may be deleted at this point. The extraction process creates a number of subdirectories such as doc, examples, libkit, and prc. The prc subdirectory contains the following three files:

❑ The `program plua2.prc` file includes the Lua compiler, interpreter, library, and editor. If you develop applications directly on your Palm device, you will need to install this file.

❑ The `plua2help.prc` file provides online help for the library functions. This file is highly recommended if you develop program directly on your Palm device.

❑ The `plua2rt.prc` file includes the library and Lua interpreter and is the only file to be distributed with your application.

The `doc` subdirectory contains a file named `pluadoc.htm` that documents various aspects of Plua's use and libraries. Also included here is the Plua2 change log.

The examples subdirectory contains the following subdirectories:

❑ **Aquario**: This example demonstrates the use of animated graphics known as sprites. If you want to include graphics in your application, this is a good example to study.

❑ **LuaCalc**: This example implements a reverse polish notation (RPN) calculator.

❑ **Demo**: This contains the following three example programs:

❏ **Demo1**: This program bundles the various controls that are available in the Plua library. These include check box, selector, button, label, slider, popup, list, and field controls. Make a point of running this program and referring to Demo1.lua to see how controls are programmed and how an event loop is used within a program.

❏ **Demo2**: This demonstrates how various other standard Palm OS windows are invoked. These include the alert, confirmation, text input, color selection, date selection, and time selection windows.

❏ **Life**: This program implements a Palm version of the classic cellular automaton invention of John Conway. This is an adaptation of the script found in the Lua distribution.

The libkit subdirectory includes examples of extending Plua with libraries written in C. You'll need the Palm OS software development kit and a compiler capable of creating Palm executables to build these libraries. You'll want to be familiar with developing Plua applications before venturing into this domain.

Exploring Plua's Features

Using the Palm HotSync Manager, install plua2.prc and plua2help.prc from the prc subdirectory of the Plua2 distribution onto your Palm device. Also, if it isn't already on your device, install mathlib.prc. If you don't have a Palm device or would rather use your desktop or notebook computer to develop Plua applications, see "The Palm OS Emulator" later in this chapter. The instructions in this chapter still apply, except you'll be working with a computer mouse and keyboard rather than with a handheld device.

Running the Plua Application

You should place the Plua application into its own category if you have one available. Select Edit Categories from the main screen's upper right selector. Click the New button, type **Lua** in the text category name field, and tap the OK button. From the main screen menu, select Category and, using the category selector to the right of Plua2, choose the new category. Tap the Done button to approve the action. The online help library is not directly launchable, so it will not show up in this list. Figure 18-1 shows the Lua category screen.

Figure 18-1

In this Try It Out, you tip your hat to Brian Kernighan and Dennis Ritchie, who first published a "Hello, world" program in the 1970s as a means to test the development environment.

1.   Tap the Plua2 icon. You're presented with the screen shown in Figure 18-2.

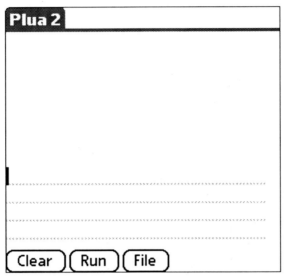

Figure 18-2

2.   On the first dotted line, type the following:

```
print "Hello world"
```

3.   Tap the Run button. The greeting appears in the area above the input section as shown in Figure 18-3. You can repeat the output by tapping the Run button more than once.

4.   Tap the Clear button. The Lua code will be cleared from the input section.

5.   Text in the output section does not automatically scroll when it becomes full, so it is convenient to have this area erased when you clear the input section. To enable this behavior, tap the Palm OS Menu icon (or, alternatively, tap the caption bar) and choose Preferences from the Options menu. Enable the Clear output check box and tap the Done button. Now when you tap the Clear button, both the program and its output are cleared.

How It Works

In this mode, you use Plua much like you do the interactive mode of the Lua interpreter when using a command shell on Windows or a Unix-type system. Unlike the standard Lua interpreter, however, nothing is submitted to the Plua interpreter until you tap the Run button. If you attempt to run an incomplete Lua program, you get an error message.

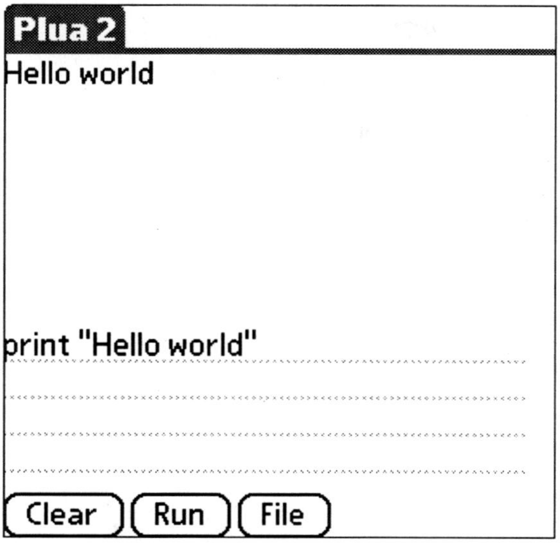

Figure 18-3

Saving Plua Programs

Tapping the File button in the Plua2 program presents a screen where you can create, edit, and run persistent Lua programs. Plua will process a source file in any of the standard ways that text can be saved on a Palm device: as a memo record, a doc file, a stream file, or a file on an expansion card. The particular format is selected from the pop-up menu in the upper-right part of the file screen. Each format has some advantages and disadvantages, as described here:

❏ All memo records on a Palm device belong to a single database. Each record has a fairly modest size restriction of between 4KB to 32KB of text depending on the version of the Palm operating system. A memo record is identified by its first line. Plua will consider as a source file a memo whose first line begins with two dashes, a space, a program name (which may include whitespace), and the extension `.lua.`, like this one:

```
-- Example.lua
```

The advantage of creating a Plua program as a memo record is that it can be edited within the Plua application. Additionally, while you're editing in Plua, an online help system is available that provides documentation for all supported functions and global variables.

❏ Doc files (not to be confused with word processed files with the `.doc` extension) are intended for larger quantities of text than a memo record can have. In fact, many books are available in this standard format. A number of editors, free and commercial, are available for handheld and desktop editing of doc files. The freely available SrcEdit editor is popular for handheld programming because it has amenities for developers such as brace and quote completion. If this program is present on your Palm device, Plua will launch it if you select a doc file and tap the Edit button. However, to return to the file screen, you will need to relaunch Plua.

❑ Stream programs use the File Stream library, a relatively recent addition to the Palm API. This may be a suitable format if you generate Plua source files programmatically.

❑ Storing source files in the virtual file system (VFS) of an expansion card may facilitate the transfer of programs from one device or platform to another. You'll see shortly that this source file format enables you to develop Plua programs from your desktop machine very easily.

Reading the Online Documentation

Plua comes with an online help system that covers the Lua core functions and global variables as well as functions provided by Plua. In the following Try It Out, you explore this handy interactive resource.

Try It Out   Calling for Help

1. In the Files screen of Plua, select Memo from the pop-up menu in the upper-right corner.

2. Tap the New button to create a new Plua program in the memo record format.

3. Type Example.lua in the New File Name field, and then tap the OK button.

4. From the program list, select Example.lua and tap the Edit button. Plua prepares the first line of the program for you. You can change the name, but don't introduce any spaces before the two dashes or add anything after the .lua extension.

5. Tap a line or two below the title line and enter the following:

```
print("Hello from Plua")
```

6. Tap and drag your stylus to select the text print.

7. Tap the Palm OS Find icon. A help screen appears with documentation for the print function, as shown in Figure 18-4.

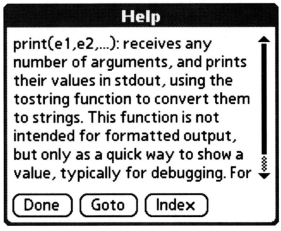

Figure 18-4

How It Works

Plua's online help system is available from the main screen as well. If you tap the Palm OS Find icon when no text is selected, you are presented with a scrolling list of all help topics. To jump to a topic from this list, select the full name of the topic as if this text was in an editor, then tap Goto. If the text you select is not found in the help system, nothing happens when you click the Find icon.

Using Palm OS Streams

The Palm operating system stores data in record-based flat databases. The file stream API is a layer on top of this that removes many of the difficulties of working with databases. As mentioned earlier, Plua can process source code stored as a stream. It also supports the usual reading and writing operations on streams.

In the following Try It Out, you will write a program in stream format. A stream editor on a Palm device is a specialized application that you might not have, so in this example you will use Plua itself to create the program.

Try It Out   Writing a Program with a Program

Write a simple Plua program that generates, in stream format, another simple Plua program.

1. Go to the File section of the Plua application.

2. Select Memo format from the pop-up menu in the upper right corner.

3. Tap the New button and type StreamGen.lua as the new filename. Tap OK.

4. Enter the following program:

    Some of the longer lines will wrap within the editor.

```
local ProgStr = [[
screen.clear()
print("Hello from a stream program!")
gui.event()
]]

local FileStr = "ExampleStream.lua"
local Hnd = io.open(FileStr, "w")
if Hnd then
  Hnd:write(ProgStr)
  Hnd:close()
  gui.alert(FileStr .. " successfully created")
else
  gui.alert("Error creating " .. FileStr)
end
```

5. Tap the Done button when you are finished entering the source code. This should return you to the list of memo programs with StreamGen.lua highlighted.

6.   Tap the Run button. An information box with the text `ExampleStream.lua successfully created` appears. Tap OK to dismiss it.

7.   Select Stream from the pop-up menu in the upper-right corner.

8.   In the resulting list, highlight ExampleStream.lua. Tap Run.

9.   A blank screen with the text `Hello from a stream program!` appears. Tap the screen to exit the program.

How It Works

In this exercise, you created a memo source file directly and a stream source file programmatically. When `StreamGen.lua`, in memo format, was run by Plua, it wrote the text of another short program as a stream file named `ExampleStream.lua`. In a subsequent step, Plua ran `ExampleStream.lua`.

Compiling Applications

So far, you have run your programs from within the Plua development application. Plua lets you compile your programs so that they can be invoked directly from a Palm OS application screen. A program you build this way isn't entirely standalone, however. Either the Plua development application or the Plua runtime library needs to be present on the Palm device for your program to execute. The license for Plua2 clearly states that you are free to distribute the runtime library with your application, but not the development application or its online help library.

In the following Try It Out, you prepare a program that runs outside of the Plua development environment.

Try It Out   Leaving the Nest

1.   From Plua's File screen, select Memo from the pop-up menu in the upper right corner.

2.   Tap the New button and type **standalone.lua** in the New file name input field. Tap the OK button.

3.   Tap the Edit button and, beneath the automatically generated top line, enter the following short program:

```
gui.alert("Look, Ma, no development environment!")
```

4.   Tap the Done button. Test your program by tapping the Run button. Dismiss the message box by tapping the OK button.

5.   Tap the Compile button to open the New PRC Information dialog box (shown in Figure 18-5). (PRC refers to a Palm resource such as an application or library.) Select the App button, and type **LkMa** for the creator ID, **Look Ma** for the name, and **1.0** for the version. Then check the No Title box and tap the OK button.

6.   Tap the Palm OS Home icon.

7.   Optionally, place the Look Ma application into the Lua category. To do this, tap the Palm OS Menu icon or, alternatively, tap the caption bar. Select the Category option, and then locate Look Ma and select Lua for its category.

8.   Locate the Look Ma application and tap its icon. This invokes your application, independent of the development environment.

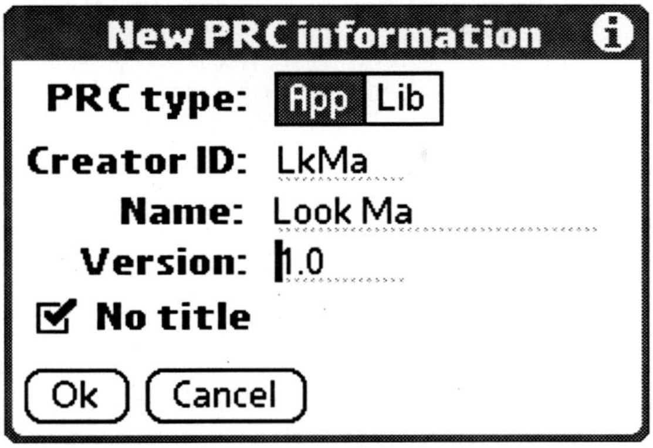

Figure 18-5

How It Works

When Plua builds an application, it compiles your source code and attaches the generated bytecode to a Palm OS application that, at runtime, links with either the Plua development application or the Plua runtime library. No harm is done if both are present. The application that is created is a bona fide Palm OS program that can be distributed like any other. Note, however, that any device that your program is installed on needs to have the Plua2 runtime library onboard. Note also that there is no way to modify the icon that is associated with your standalone application.

Palm OS links an application to its databases with a unique four-character creator ID. Every Palm OS program requires such an ID. Unless you are going to distribute your application, you are reasonably safe just coming up with what looks like a unique value that has at least one upper case character. If your application will be installed on other people's devices, however, you'll want to register your application at the Palm developer's site. Visit palmos.com and follow the links to the developer's pages.

Compiling Libraries

When you built a standalone application, you selected the App option in the compiler dialog box. You can also build Plua libraries that are used much like modules.

Try It Out   Examining Lua Objects with a Library

Here you'll implement a scaled-down version of the show module as a Plua library. This exercise and the ones that follow contain a lot of text. You may prefer to acquire the script from the book's website at wrox.com and transfer it from your desktop system to your Palm device. The next section in this chapter, "Plua on the Mothership," has instructions that tell you how to do that.

1. Create a new file in your preferred format. Copy in the following contents:

```
local function LclVisit(Tbl, Val, Key, Lvl, Seen)
   Seen = Seen or {}
   Lvl = Lvl or 0
   local VtpStr = type(Val)
```

```lua
    local Vqt = VtpStr == "string" and '"' or ''
    local Kqt = type(Key) == "string" and '"' or ''
    local ValStr = tostring(Val)
    ValStr = string.gsub(ValStr, "table:%s*.*$", "(tbl)")
    ValStr = string.gsub(ValStr, "function:%s*.*$", "(fnc)")
    table.insert(Tbl, string.rep('   ', Lvl) ..
      tostring(Key) .. " " .. Vqt .. ValStr .. Vqt)
    if VtpStr == "table" then
      if not Seen[Val] then
        Seen[Val] = true
        local SrtTbl = {}
        for K, V in Val do
          table.insert(SrtTbl, K)
        end
        table.sort(SrtTbl)
        for J, K in ipairs(SrtTbl) do
          LclVisit(Tbl, Val[K], K, Lvl + 1, Seen)
        end
      end
    end
  end
end

function ObjectRender(Val, Key)
  local Tbl = {}
  LclVisit(Tbl, Val, Key, 0)
  return Tbl
end

local function Metrics()
  local Scr = {}
  Scr.Wd, Scr.Ht, Scr.Depth, Scr.Color = screen.mode()
  local Base = Scr.Wd / 160
  Scr.DlgBrd = Base * 2 -- Border
  Scr.ScrollWd = Base * 7
  Scr.ChWd, Scr.ChHt = screen.textsize("X") -- Character size
  Scr.Top = math.floor(Scr.ChHt * 3 / 2)
  return Scr
end

function ObjectShow(Obj, TitleStr)
  local Tbl = ObjectRender(Obj, TitleStr)
  local Scr = Metrics()
  local Wd, Ht = Scr.Wd - 2 * Scr.DlgBrd,
    Scr.Ht - 2 * Scr.DlgBrd
  gui.dialog(0, 0, Wd, Ht, TitleStr)
  local ChWd, ChHt = screen.font(0)
  local Cols = math.floor((Wd - Scr.ScrollWd) / ChWd) - 1
  local Rows = math.floor((Ht - 4 * ChHt) / ChHt)
  gui.control{type = "field", lines = Rows,
    columns = Cols, limit = 30000, editable = false,
    underlined = false, text = table.concat(Tbl, "\n")}
  gui.nl()
  gui.tab()
  local IdOk = gui.control{type = "button", text = "OK"}
```

```
      local Loop = true
      while Loop do
        local Evt, Id = gui.event()
        if Evt == ctlSelect then
            if Id == IdOk then
              Loop = false
            end
          elseif Evt == appStop then
            Loop = false
          end
      end
    gui.destroy()
  end
```

2. Save this file as show.lua.

3. Tap the Compile button to open the New PRC Information dialog box. Select the Lib button, and type **SH11** for the creator ID, **show** for the name, and **1.0** for the version. Then check the No Title box and tap the OK button.

4. Enter the following script into a new file:

```
dofile("show")

screen.clear()
ObjectShow({gui = gui, screen = screen, bin = bin,
  bit = bit, buffer = buffer}, "Plua")
```

5. Save this file as showtest.lua.

6. Tap the Run button. A dialog box appears with a scrolling list of some of the Plua namespace tables, as shown in Figure 18-6.

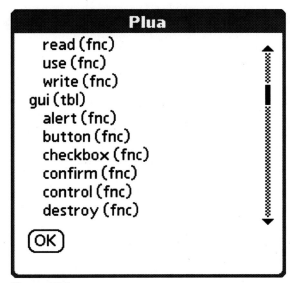

Figure 18-6

How It Works

The Palm version of `ObjectShow` is not as detailed as the full version you first saw in Chapter 7, but it still provides a valuable glimpse into Lua data structures. One of the first function calls made is to `Metrics` to determine certain GUI metrics such as the width of a dialog border. These are needed to size the dialog correctly so that it appears the same on a 160 × 160 pixel device as it does on a 320 × 320 pixel device.

The scrolling list is actually a text input field with the dotted lines and editability disabled. This is done by creating the field with the `screen.control` function. This function receives a table as its only argument. Various key/value pairs in this table are used to pass in information. In this example, the fields `editable` and `underlined` are both set to `false`. Variables such as `ctlSelect` and `appStop` identify events and are available to all Plua programs. (See the Plua documentation for `gui.event` to see a complete list.)

The `ObjectShow` routine implements its own event loop so it will be called as a blocking function. This loop is terminated when the user taps either the OK button or a Palm OS icon to exit the program.

Plua on the Mothership

The ability to program directly on your handheld device opens up many opportunities. It's a simple matter to use Plua to write a quick program to solve a particular task, and you can develop software in situations where even a notebook computer would be cumbersome. However, even with a good handheld editor such as SrcEdit and with well-chosen shortcuts for Graffiti (the Palm method of handwriting), you may yearn for a more familiar development platform. There are three approaches that let you work from your main computer: the `pluac` command-line compiler, the Palm OS Emulator, and the Palm OS Simulator. Each has a particular niche.

The Command-Line Compiler

A Plua2 command-line compiler can be downloaded as a zip file (`pluac-2.0b6.windows.zip` as of this writing) from the same place you obtained the main Plua2 zip file: `groups.yahoo.com/group/plua`. This application runs from a shell window on the Windows platform. (Versions for both Linux and Windows are available for the first version of Plua.)

The Plua command-line compiler is much like the standalone Lua compiler — it is not an interactive or visual tool. It builds an installable Palm OS application that may include additional resources such as bitmaps. It accepts the same command line arguments as the Lua compiler plus a few of its own, as shown in the following table.

Option	Action
-l	Displays the generated bytecode.
-o name	Specifies the name of the generated application or library (the default is `PluaApp.prc`).
-p	Parses the source but don't produce an application or library.
-s	Strips debug information from the generated bytecode.

Option	Action
-v	Displays version information for both Lua and the Plua compiler.
-lib	Generates a Plua2 library instead of an application.
-nt	Specifies that the application not have a title.
-name name	Specifies the name of the application or library as used by Palm OS.
-cid ID	Specifies the unique application or library creator ID. This is coded as a four-character string.
-ver version	Specifies the application or library version, for example 0.6.
--	Stops handling options.

The command-line compiler allows you to bind bitmap resources to your application, something that isn't supported in the handheld version. To do this, you'll need a resource compiler that bundles the images into a Palm OS resource. The freely available PilRC resource compiler, which you can find at pilrc.sourceforge.net, is a good choice. Study the Aquario example that comes with Plua2 to see how images and sprites are programmed. Note that large bitmaps may exceed a resource size limit imposed by Palm OS. In this case, they can be divided into smaller sections that are handled individually.

When you have generated an application with the command-line compiler, you can HotSync it to your Palm device the way you would any other Palm application.

The Palm OS Emulator

An indispensable tool for developing and testing applications on the Palm OS platform is the Palm OS Emulator (POSE). This open-source graphical program runs on Windows and Unix-like systems. As its name implies, it contains software that emulates the hardware of a Palm OS device. The current generation of Palm OS devices uses a processor that is not emulated by POSE, but these devices support programs for the older processors. Plua generates code for older processors, so it and the programs you create with it can run on both the newer and the older Palm OS devices.

Obtaining the Emulator

Visit palmos.com/dev/tools/core.html and download a copy of POSE for your platform. To do this, you'll need to be a registered member of the ACCESS Developer Network. While you are at the Palm OS developer's site, you should download these packages:

❑ Emulator

❑ Emulator HostFS

❑ ROM image for Palm OS version 4 or higher

Ready-to-install binary packages for Windows and Mac OS are available. For other platforms, you'll need to download the source distribution and build POSE from that. The HostFS application enables you to use a directory on your computer as if it is the virtual file system of an expansion card. The ROM image file corresponds to a system that is embedded in an actual device.

Installing on Windows

Create a directory for POSE and extract the contents of the emulator zip file into it. Additionally, in this directory create the following four subdirectories:

- ❏ `autoload`
- ❏ `Card1`
- ❏ `ROM`
- ❏ `skins`

Any Palm OS programs located in the `autoload` subdirectory will be loaded automatically when you start the emulator. Extract the contents of the `HostFS` zip file into the `autoload` subdirectory. Extract the contents of the `ROM` zip file into the `ROM` subdirectory. Then copy `plua2.prc`, `plua2help.prc`, and `mathlib.prc` from your Plua directory to the `autoload` subdirectory.

Configuring POSE

To start POSE, you can use the Run window from the Windows Start button or you can create a shortcut. Either way, you will be executing `Emulator.exe` in the directory you created for POSE.

Figure 18-7 shows what the POSE generic skin looks like. You can download and select graphics that depict other devices.

To configure POSE, follow these steps:

1. Right-click anywhere on the window.
2. From the pop-up menu, select New to invoke the New Session dialog box.
3. Click the ROM File button, and then click the Other option.
4. In the file browser window, locate the ROM file that you downloaded (such as `PalmOS412_FullRel_EZ_enUS.rom`), and then click the Open button.
5. Click the Device button and choose Palm Vx from the menu.
6. Click the RAM Size button and choose 16,384K from the menu.
7. Click OK to approve the session window.

To mount the host-based expansion card, you'll need to active the POSE host file system. Right-click on the POSE window, select Settings, select HostFS, and select Slot 1. Click the Browse button and select the Card1 directory, click the Mounted check box, and then click the OK button. Perform a soft reset of the emulator. To do this, right-click anywhere on the emulator window, select Reset from the pop-up menu, choose Soft reset, and click the Reset button.

Running Plua in the Emulator

The appearance and operation of Plua in the emulator are the same as on a handheld device, although you may notice that the response times may be different between the two. Also, POSE emulates devices with a 160 × 160-pixel screen area, so if you have a device with a higher screen resolution, the Plua application may appear differently on your handheld. The programs you develop with Plua will work fine with devices having any screen resolution as long as you take into account the screen size when you're sizing and positioning elements.

Figure 18-7

<hr>

Try It Out   **Programming Plua with the Emulator**

The emulator host file system makes it easy to develop applications with Plua using your text editor. In the following steps, you create and run a Plua program from your main computer.

1.   In the emulator, tap the Plua2 icon.

2.   Tap the File button.

3.   Select Card from the pop-up menu in the upper-right corner of the screen.

4.   The Card1 subdirectory that you created in the POSE directory will have had some new subdirectories added in it. The directory tree now looks like this:

```
Card1
   PALM
      Launcher
      Programs
         Plua
            src
```

5.   Using your text editor, create a new file with the following contents:

```
screen.clear()
print("Hello from HostFS")
gui.event()
```

6.   Save this file as `hostfs.lua` in the `Card1\PALM\Programs\Plua\src` directory.

7.   In the Plua application, refresh the card list by choosing Memo and then choosing Card from the pop-up menu in the upper-right corner.

8.   Select `hostfs.lua` from the file list and tap Run. The program is executed as if it had been stored in the emulated device's main memory.

How It Works

The following two features are combined to make it very easy to develop applications with Plua running in POSE:

❑   Plua's capability to access Lua files on an expansion card

❑   POSE's emulation of an expansion card file system in the Card1 subdirectory beneath the point where it is installed

Although you needed to refresh the card list in Plua when you created a new file, simply modifying a Lua file that is already present doesn't require this. You can simply tap Run after making a change using your desktop editor, and Plua will load the updated file.

Compiling a Program in the Emulator

You can compile applications and libraries using the emulator just as you can on a handheld device. When you do this, the compiled resource is placed in the main memory rather than the expansion card. How do you get this resource to your hard drive as a .prc file? There are two ways:

❑   You can right-click anywhere on the emulator window to open the main application menu. Then select Export Database and your application or library from the menu. Save the file using the Save As dialog box.

❑   You can tap the Palm OS Applications icon and then the Menu icon, select Copy from the menu, select POSESlot1 in the Copy To menu and Handheld in the From menu, choose your compiled resource from the list, and then tap on the Copy button. The emulator will place the `.prc` file in the `Card1\PALM\Launcher` subdirectory beneath its own installation directory.

Exiting the Emulator

To exit POSE, right-click anywhere on its window and choose Exit from the resulting menu. You are given the opportunity to save the session. Doing so will allow POSE to retain its current state, emulating what a handheld device would do if you turned it off with the power button. However, because you placed your essential files in the POSE autoload subdirectory and set up the host file system, saving the session isn't critical. If you opt not to save your session when exiting, you should store the applications and libraries you write in the autoload subdirectory to assure that they are available when you restart POSE.

The Palm OS Simulator

Like POSE, the Palm OS Simulator is a desktop application that lets you run Palm OS applications. From a user's point of view, its differences are as follows:

❏   It supports Palm OS version 5.0 and higher. (Like the newer generation of Palm OS handhelds, it supports applications and libraries written for older versions.)

❏   It supports 320 × 480 screen resolution and up to 65,536 colors.

❏   It is available only for the Windows platform.

In other respects, it functions virtually the same as POSE. It supports the autoload subdirectory, the host file system mechanism (including the need to issue a soft reset to engage it), and the right-click action to raise the main menu.

Obtaining the Simulator

From `palmos.com/dev/tools/core.html`, download `PalmOS_Garnet_54_simulator.zip` and its associated host file system application, `HostFS_Simulator.zip`. Registration is required. When you extract the simulator zip file on your hard drive, it will create a number of directories, including one named `release`. Create the following two directories in the `release` directory:

❏   `autoload`

❏   `Card1`

Unlike the setup for the Palm OS Emulator, you don't create the `skins` and `ROM` directories.

Using the Simulator

Except for configuration, the instructions for POSE apply to the simulator as well. With the simulator, you don't choose a device to emulate, but you can specify parameters such as memory size, screen resolution, and color depth. Access these by right-clicking anywhere on the simulator window and choosing Settings from the resulting pop-up menu. To terminate the program, select Exit from the main menu.

Programming with Plua

Plua greatly facilitates the programming of many aspects of the Palm OS API, including the handling of data records, expansion card files and directories, image resources and sprites, line and area graphics, and user interface controls and sound. Programming even the simplest Palm application in a low-level language like C can be a daunting task. The Plua programming interface does far more than merely map the Palm OS API to Lua — it encapsulates many details such as memory management and record locking.

In the following sections, you'll have a chance to briefly explore some of Plua's capabilities. Be sure to examine the examples and documentation that come with Plua to find out how much more extensive its scope is than what is covered here.

Generating Graphics

Plua has three functions — `screen.heading`, `screen.turn` and `screen.walk` — that you can use to draw surprisingly intricate graphics with very little code. These are the so-called "turtle" functions that are associated with the Logo programming language.

In this exercise, you'll explore the use of these functions in a loop to draw a repeating pattern.

Try It Out   Turn, Turn, Turn

1. Create a new file (a memo record, a doc file, or a card file — it's your choice) with the following contents:

```
-- graph.lua

local Wd, Ht = screen.mode()
local Turn = 1
local Reduce = 0.98
local WalkLen = Wd
local Color = 0
local ColorInc = 1
local Min = 5

screen.clear()
screen.heading(90)
screen.moveto(0, 0)
repeat
  screen.color(screen.rgb(Color, Color, Color))
  Color = Color + ColorInc
  WalkLen = Reduce * WalkLen
  screen.turn(-(90 + Turn))
  screen.walk(WalkLen)
until WalkLen < Min
gui.event()
```

2. Save the file as `graph.lua`. If you created a memo record, the first line needs to remain intact.

3. From Plua's File screen, select the type of file you created from the pop-up menu in the upper-right corner.

4. Select `graph.lua` from the file list and tap the Run button. The screen shown in Figure 18-8 is displayed.

5. Tap the screen to dismiss the graphic and return to the file selection screen.

How It Works

The program source code begins with the following:

```
-- graph.lua
```

This is a line that the Lua interpreter treats as a comment, but it allows Plua to recognize the file as a Lua program if it is saved as a memo record. Following this, there are several tweakable parameters. Placing these above the main code makes it easier to adjust the program's operation.

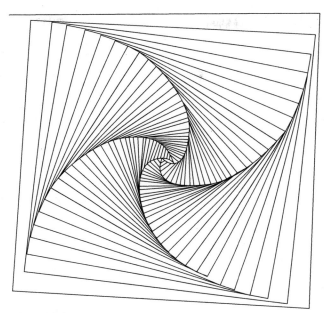

Figure 18-8

The actual turtle instructions follow the parameters. The screen is cleared, the turtle is pointed to the top of the screen with the `screen.heading(90)` call, and the turtle position is set to the upper-left corner of the screen.

A loop is entered in which the turtle is turned clockwise a little more than 90 degrees and then walks, drawing a line as it does so that is a little shorter and lighter than it was in the previous iteration. This continues until the distance walked becomes smaller than some limiting value. After the loop terminates, a call to `gui.event` is made to put the screen on hold until you tap on it or cause some other Palm OS event to occur.

Programming the User Interface

The Palm OS user interface was designed from the start to support brief, punctuated interactions. This allows users to quickly perform a task (such as schedule an appointment or consult the address list) without navigating through complicated program windows. The GUI controls that Plua provides all support this objective. As you'll see shortly, including these controls in your programs is straightforward as well. For example, initializing a list control and keeping it updated is as simple as providing it with a Lua table of strings.

It is often desirable to view detail information as you scroll through a list of names or other key information. In the following exercise, you'll program an application that allows you to add, edit, and delete simple records. The main screen will provide a window for viewing the note attached to the currently selected key.

Creating a Note Viewer

1.   Create a new doc file or expansion card file (a memo record may work, but on older devices the program will exceed its size limit) and include the following contents:

```lua
-- Returns a table in which keys are names and values are associated notes.

local function ListInitialize()
  -- Simulate reading data from a database. This can be replaced with actual
  -- Palm OS database access.
  return {
    Dante = "1265-1321",
    Petrarch = "1304-1374",
    Leonardo = "1452-1519",
    Copernicus = "1473-1543",
    Michelangelo = "1475-1564",
    Cervantes = "1547-1616",
    Galileo = "1564-1642",
    Shakespeare = "1564-1616",
    Donne = "1572-1631",
    Milton = "1608-1674"}
end

-- Stores data from associative data table

local function ListFinalize(List)
  -- Store modified data here.
end

-- Place a button at position X, return button ID

local function LclButton(X, Str)
  local Id
  screen.moveto(X)
  Id = gui.control{type = "button", text = Str}
  gui.nl()
  return Id
end

-- Initialize main form

local function LclForm(Lcl)
  local X, Y
  Lcl.ScrWd, Lcl.ScrHt = screen.mode()
  Lcl.ScrUnit = Lcl.ScrWd / 160
  Lcl.DlgBrd = Lcl.ScrUnit * 2
  screen.clear()
  gui.title(Lcl.TitleStr)
  screen.moveto(1)
  Lcl.ListRowCount = 8
  Lcl.CtlList = gui.control{type = "list", lines = Lcl.ListRowCount,
    columns = 21, selected = 4, list = Lcl.ShowList}
  X, Y = screen.pos()
  gui.nl()
```

```lua
    screen.moveto(1)
  Lcl.CtlNote = gui.control{type = "field", lines = 4, columns = 28,
    limit = 30000, editable = false, underlined = false}
  X = X - Lcl.ScrUnit
  screen.moveto(X, Y)
  Lcl.CtlNew = LclButton(X, "New")
  Lcl.CtlEdit = LclButton(X, "Edit")
  Lcl.CtlDel = LclButton(X, "Delete")
  gui.setfocus(Lcl.CtlList)
end


-- Raises record editor dialog. If NameStr is nil, it will
-- be editable, otherwise noneditable

local function RecDlg(Lcl, NameStr, NoteStr)
  local CtlName, CtlNote, CtlOk, CtlCancel,
    Name, Note
  local New = NameStr == nil
  local Border = 2 * Lcl.DlgBrd
  gui.dialog(0, 0, Lcl.ScrWd - Border, Lcl.ScrHt - Border,
    New and "New record" or "Edit record")
  gui.control{type = "label", text = "Name"}
  gui.nl()
  CtlName = gui.control{type = "field", lines = 1,
    columns = 27, limit = 27, text = NameStr or "",
    editable = New},
  gui.nl()
  gui.control{type = "label", text = "Note"}
  gui.nl()
  CtlNote = gui.control{type = "field", lines = 6,
    columns = 27, limit = 1024, text = NoteStr or ""},
  gui.nl()
  CtlOk = gui.control{type = "button", text = "OK"}
  CtlCancel = gui.control{type = "button", text = "Cancel"}
  gui.setfocus(New and CtlName or CtlNote)
  local Loop = true
  while Loop do
    local Evt, Id = gui.event()
    if Evt == appStop then
      Loop = false
    elseif Evt == ctlSelect then
      Loop = false
      if Id == CtlOk then
        Name = gui.gettext(CtlName)
        if string.len(Name) > 0 then
          Note = gui.gettext(CtlNote)
        else
          Name = nil
        end
      end
    end
  end
  gui.destroy()
  return Name, Note -- May be nil
```

```
  end

-- Returns currently selected name

local function RecName(Lcl)
  local Name, Pos
  Pos = gui.getstate(Lcl.CtlList)
  if Pos then
    Name = Lcl.ShowList[Pos]
  end
  return Name
end

-- Updates note field in main form based on currently selected record

local function NoteRefresh(Lcl)
  local Note, Name
  Name = RecName(Lcl)
  if Name then
    Note = Lcl.DataList[Name]
  end
  gui.settext(Lcl.CtlNote, Note or "")
end

-- Refreshes selection list on main form. Pos specifies new selection. Nil: no
-- change; number: new selection by position; string: new position by name.

local function ListRefresh(Lcl, Pos)
  local J = 1
  for Key in pairs(Lcl.DataList) do
    Lcl.ShowList[J] = Key
    J = J + 1
  end
  Lcl.ShowList[J] = nil
  table.sort(Lcl.ShowList)
  gui.settext(Lcl.CtlList, Lcl.ShowList)
  local PosCat = type(Pos)
  if PosCat == "number" then
    gui.setstate(Lcl.CtlList, Pos)
  elseif PosCat == "string" then
    local J, Count, NewPos = 1, table.getn(Lcl.ShowList)
    while J <= Count and not NewPos do
      if Lcl.ShowList[J] == Pos then
        NewPos = J
      else
        J = J + 1
      end
    end
    if NewPos then
      gui.setstate(Lcl.CtlList, NewPos)
    end
  end
  NoteRefresh(Lcl)
```

```lua
  end

-- Handles addition of new record

local function RecNew(Lcl)
  local Name, Note = RecDlg(Lcl)
  if Name then
    if Lcl.DataList[Name] then
      gui.alert("Duplicate name: " .. Name)
    else
      Lcl.DataList[Name] = Note
      ListRefresh(Lcl, Name)
      Lcl.Modified = true
    end
  end
end

-- Handles modification of existing record

local function RecEdit(Lcl)
  local Name, Note
  Name = RecName(Lcl)
  if Name then
    Name, Note = RecDlg(Lcl, Name, Lcl.DataList[Name])
    if Name then
      Lcl.DataList[Name] = Note
      ListRefresh(Lcl)
      Lcl.Modified = true
    end
  end
end

-- Shift the currently selected record with hardware button

local function RecScroll(Lcl, Key)
  local Pos = gui.getstate(Lcl.CtlList)
  local NewPos
  local Count = table.getn(Lcl.ShowList) -- Lua 5.0
  if Key == hardKeyDown then -- Down
    NewPos = Pos + 1
  elseif Key == hardKeyUp then -- Up
    NewPos = Pos - 1
  elseif Key == hardKey1 then -- Top
    NewPos = 1
  elseif Key == hardKey2 then -- Page up
    NewPos = Pos - Lcl.ListRowCount
  elseif Key == hardKey3 then -- Page down
    NewPos = Pos + Lcl.ListRowCount
  elseif Key == hardKey4 then -- Bottom
    NewPos = Count
  end
  if NewPos then
    if NewPos < 1 then
```

```
        NewPos = 1
      elseif NewPos > Count then
        NewPos = Count
      end
      if NewPos ~= Pos then
        gui.setstate(Lcl.CtlList, NewPos)
        NoteRefresh(Lcl)
      end
    end
  end
end

-- Handles deletion of currently selected record

local function RecDel(Lcl)
  local Name = RecName(Lcl)
  if Name then
    Lcl.DataList[Name] = nil
    ListRefresh(Lcl)
    Lcl.Modified = true
  end
end

-- Main initialization and event loop

local Lcl = {TitleStr = "Notes"}
screen.clear()
Lcl.DataList = ListInitialize()
Lcl.ShowList = {}
LclForm(Lcl)
ListRefresh(Lcl, 1)
local Loop = true
while Loop do
  local Evt, Id = gui.event()
  if Evt == appStop then
    Loop = false
  elseif Evt == ctlSelect then
    if Id == Lcl.CtlNew then
      RecNew(Lcl)
    elseif Id == Lcl.CtlEdit then
      RecEdit(Lcl)
    elseif Id == Lcl.CtlDel then
      RecDel(Lcl)
    end
  elseif Evt == lstSelect then
    NoteRefresh(Lcl)
  elseif Evt == keyDown then
    RecScroll(Lcl, Id)
  end
end
if Lcl.Modified then
  ListFinalize(Lcl.DataList)
end
```

2. Save this file as notes.lua. If you have managed to create this program in a memo record, be sure to include -- notes.lua as the first line.

3. From Plua's File screen, tap the file category from the pop-up menu in upper-right corner. Select notes.lua from the file list.

4. Tap the Run button. Figure 18-9 shows what the main form looks like.

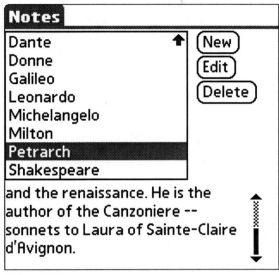

Figure 18-9

5. Experiment with the application: add, edit and delete some records, and use the hardware buttons to scroll through the list.

6. When you are finished with the application, tap the Palm OS Home icon.

How It Works

This example follows a standard application format. It begins with a number of helper functions (including ones that arrange the user interface), followed by an event loop. Here are some key points to note:

❑ Most Plua functions in the gui namespace return immediately. (The exceptions are those like gui.alert and gui.selectdate that put up their own dialog box and implement their own event loop.)

❑ You can call the screen.pos and screen.moveto functions to position the various controls when you're building a form.

❑ You can use the gui.gettext and gui.settext functions with different types of controls to get and set content. In this example, gui.settext is used to assign a table to the list control and to assign text to the note field. Likewise, gui.getstate and gui.setstate work with different types of controls.

❑ The record dialog box for creating a new record or modifying an existing one uses the gui.dialog function. After this function is called, the dialog box is populated with form controls and an event loop is entered. When a terminating event occurs, a call to gui.destroy is made to destroy the dialog box.

In an actual application, information will be stored in a Palm OS database. The program presented here has functions for retrieving and saving the data (`ListInitialize` and `ListFinalize`, respectively) with the assumption that all of the application database records will be loaded into a Lua table when the program begins and saved, if modifications have been made, when the program ends.

At the cost of some program complexity, another approach would be to load only the keys of the database records into a Lua table, and the record IDs into another table. Record insertions, modifications, and deletions would then take place directly in the database.

Accessing Databases

Plua provides a unified approach to input and output with the `io.open` function. With it, you can access standard Palm OS databases, stream files, doc files, memo records, serial port devices, expansion card files, and network devices. Consult the Unified I/O chart in the Plua documentation to see how to format the name of the resource or device when opening it.

In the following exercise, you'll write a script that will access the standard address book database. This demonstrates how you can use the `io` library with Palm OS databases.

Try It Out   **Displaying the Address Book**

Programmatically open the address book on your Palm OS device and, using the list control, display the name and first phone number for each record. Before starting this exercise, make sure you've got at least a couple records in the address book. The Address or Contacts application is used to manage this database interactively.

1.   Open a new file on your handheld and add in the following script:

```
-- address.lua

screen.clear()
local DbStr = "db:/AddressDB"
local ErrStr
local Hnd, Count = io.open(DbStr, "rb")
local List = {}
if Hnd then
  if Count > 0 then
    for J = 0, Count - 1 do
      local RecSize = Hnd:openrec(J)
      if RecSize then
        if RecSize > 0 then
          local RecStr = Hnd:read("*a")
          if RecStr then
            local Rec = bin.unpack("BBBBBBBBBBSSS", RecStr)
            table.insert(List, (Rec[11] or "") .. " " .. (Rec[10] or "") ..
              " " .. (Rec[12] or ""))
          end
        end
        Hnd:closerec()
      end
    end
  end
end
```

```
      else
        ErrStr = "The address book contains no records"
      end
      Hnd:close()
  else
    ErrStr = "Error opening the address book"
  end
  if not ErrStr then
    if next(List) then -- At least one item?
      gui.title("Address")
      gui.list(10, 30, List)
      gui.nl()
      local CtlOk = gui.button("OK")
      local Evt, Id
      repeat
        Evt, Id = gui.event()
      until Evt == appStop or (Evt == ctlSelect and Id == CtlOk)
    end
  else
    print(ErrStr)
    repeat until gui.event() == penDown
  end
```

2.   Save the file as `address.lua`.

3.   Tap the Run button. The resulting screen displays the partial contents of your address book as shown in Figure 18-10.

4.   Tap the Palm OS Home key to exit.

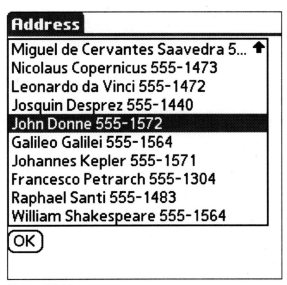

Figure 18-10

How It Works

This example opens the address database on your Palm OS device. The db:/ prefix to the resource name indicates that this is a regular database. The call to io.open returns the handle and record count of the database if it succeeds, or nil otherwise.

The address book record format includes nine bytes of binary information followed by a number of null-terminated strings. (This information can be gleaned from various web resources.) No attempt to read the binary information is made here. In the main record reading loop, a record is opened by position with a call to the openrec method before it can be accessed. After a record has been opened, it is read using the io.read function with the same arguments as if the record itself was a file.

Like most databases on a Palm OS device, the address database has records that are binary and packed — not all fields are text strings, and those that are are contain no trailing unused characters. The bin.unpack function is called with a format string to extract the packed fields into a new record table. Here, the format string contains one B for each binary byte, and one S for each null terminated string. The code in this exercise does not handle missing fields robustly.

Summary

In this chapter, you had a chance to become familiar with Plua, which is a port of Lua to the Palm OS platform. In particular, you've learned to do the following:

- ❏ Use Plua in interactive mode to run quick program snippets
- ❏ Prepare Lua scripts in various source code formats (memo, doc, stream, and expansion card) that Plua can process
- ❏ Access online help while working in the Plua development application
- ❏ Create and write to a Palm OS stream file
- ❏ Compile applications and libraries into Palm OS resources that can be distributed to others
- ❏ Use compiled libraries as modules in your Plua programs
- ❏ Use the Plua command-line compiler
- ❏ Run Plua from your desktop computer using the Palm OS Emulator and Simulator
- ❏ Develop Palm OS programs using turtle graphics, GUI features, and databases

There's a lot more to programming in Plua. The documentation and examples that come with Plua contain information to get you going with network communication, resource graphics, sound, and more.

In the next chapter, you'll take a look at the vibrant community that has arisen around Lua and how you can be a part of it. Before proceeding with that, review the skills you have picked up in this chapter by trying the following exercises.

Exercises

1.   Use turtle graphics to write a Plua script that generates a five-pointed star like the one shown in Figure 18-11.

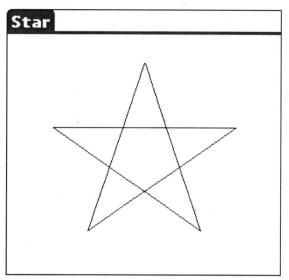

Figure 18-11

2.   Write a simple Lua expression interpreter that accepts a single line of input and displays what Lua returns when that string is submitted to `tostring`. In addition to the Plua GUI functions, plan on using the Lua `loadstring` and `pcall` functions. The screen can look something like the one shown in Figure 18-12.

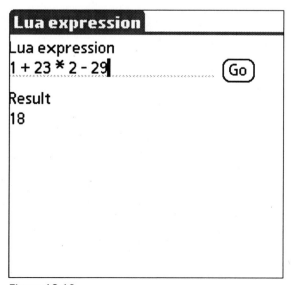

Figure 18-12

3. Write a function named `Barchart` that accepts as arguments a title string and an indexed table containing numbers. The values in the table are to be displayed as bars in a chart. For example, the following call should result in a display that looks like Figure 18-13:

```
Barchart("Example", {12, 34, 23, 25, 67, 45, 23, 7, 5, 54, 48, 50})
```

Use the Plua `screen.box` function to draw the bars, but avoid using `gui.dialog`, because it does not support drawing.

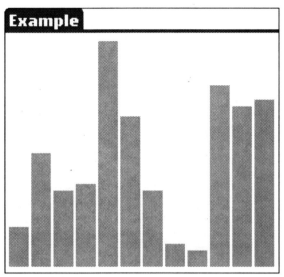

Figure 18-13

Fitting into the Lua Community

You're now familiar with the basics of the Lua language, its core libraries, and a sample of the libraries and applications that developers around the world have made for Lua. The last topic you'll explore in this book involves the vibrant community that has developed around Lua and the resources that can help you with your software development. You'll learn about the following:

❑   The Lua web site

❑   The Lua reference manual

❑   The Lua mailing list

❑   LuaForge, the principal repository for Lua-based projects

❑   The Lua wiki

❑   The Lua chat room

There is a lot of Lua expertise in the community and insight into the way Lua works. Help is available to you in the form of printed and online documents, and discussions on the mailing lists, forums, and chat rooms. The niches these resources fill overlap, sometimes broadly, and you'll find a combination of them is sometimes needed to understand an issue thoroughly. Nevertheless, you can expedite the process of getting over hurdles by selecting the right resources to draw on.

Whether you've got a particular question regarding Lua, you're interested in seeing what people are doing with the language, or you want to contribute in some way to Lua's ongoing success, you'll find a suitable venue among these resources.

The Lua Web Site

The Lua team — Roberto Ierusalimschy, Luiz Henrique de Figueiredo, and Waldemar Celes — maintains a well-organized website at `lua.org` that serves as the official home of Lua. It's where you should go to do any or all of the following:

- ❏ Obtain the most recent source code for Lua
- ❏ Read the *FAQ* (Frequently Asked Questions with answers)
- ❏ View various documents such as articles and memorabilia about Lua
- ❏ Read about recent milestones such as conferences and publications
- ❏ Find links to other websites and resources pertaining to Lua

The Lua website is kept up-to-date, so it's a good place to visit regularly. The community page on the Lua website provides a great launch pad to the sites and resources summarized in this chapter.

The Lua Reference Manual

The terseness and sharp focus of the reference manual are its greatest strengths, but these characteristics can make it a difficult document to read casually. Nevertheless, take the time to read it. Even if you don't absorb all of its details and subtleties the first time through, you'll know where to turn in it later when you want to delve deeper into some topic. If you ever raise a question in one of the dynamic community resources like the chat room or mailing list, it will be assumed that you've studied the manual first.

Although every important facet of Lua and its libraries are covered in the reference manual, sometimes there will be omissions in the corner cases. For example, the documentation for `string.sub` doesn't state what the return value will be for out-of-bound indexes, a condition that might arise in a loop. Don't sweat things like this. First, you can use the Lua interpreter to find out very quickly what this function does, like this:

```
a = string.sub("abc", 0, 0) print(a, type(a))
```

Second, the function's behavior in the current version is almost certainly what it will be in later versions.

The reference manual is not an afterthought. It is an integral part of Lua, and official releases of Lua are not made without an up-to-date manual. Its economy matches that of the language implementation itself, and the Lua authors are to be commended for granting the manual such high significance in the project.

Roberto Ierusalimschy's excellent book *Programming in Lua* (ISBN 8590379825, published by `Lua.org`) is filled with practical applications and insights into the concepts presented in the manual.

An online version of the manual in HTML format is included in the source distribution of Lua. You're encouraged to purchase a bound copy as well. It's often more convenient to have a printed book, and the proceeds help the Lua project. Follow the links on the Lua website or LuaForge to order a copy.

Framing Questions

A big part of working through software development problems is knowing not only where to ask but how to ask. Some articles on the web address this head on. For one of these, follow the link on Lua's mailing list page to an article named, "How To Ask Questions The Smart Way," by Eric Steven Raymond and Rick Moen. Before reporting issues with software, you should read the excellent online article named, "How to Report Bugs Effectively." written by Simon Tatham (`www.chiark.greenend.org.uk/~sgtatham/bugs.html`).

A common theme with these articles is to narrow the scope of the problem. Take the time to strip away all extraneous content in order to present the smallest possible program that demonstrates the issue. *You* may be intimately familiar with every part of your large program, but don't brazenly expect someone else to ferret out a particular problem you are having with it. More often than not, the process of distilling a problem to its bare essentials will allow you to present your question more intelligently if not solve it completely.

The Lua Mailing List

A central and active part of the Lua community is the mailing list. Messages sent to the mailing list are in turn sent to all subscribers electing to receive them. Although the mailing list has steadily grown since Roberto posted the first message in 1997, it is still of a manageable size, handling usually fewer than a few dozen messages per day. The messages themselves are generally focused and friendly, with subjects ranging from beginning to advanced.

Here are a number of ways to read the messages that are sent to the mailing list:

- ❑ Receive e-mails from the list server
- ❑ Access a web interface site with your web browser
- ❑ Access a net news interface site with your newsreader
- ❑ Download daily, recent, and full archives of messages for reading offline

Viewing and Searching the Archives

Before subscribing to the Lua mailing list, take a look at the archives to get a feel for the topics that are discussed.

Try It Out   Visiting the Message Museum

Over the years, a huge amount of ground has been covered in the Lua mailing list. You can search through the accumulated messages to see if a particular question you've got has been discussed. Here's how:

1. With your web browser, access `www.lua.org`.

2. Click the community link, the mailing list link, and finally the search archive link.

3.　In the Search field, type the following:

The and *is implied so it doesn't have to be specified, but the terms do need to be separated from the parentheses by at least one space.*

```
( ipairs or pairs ) and next
```

4.　Select the Score option as the sorting method. This will place the messages with the greatest algorithmically-determined relevance at the beginning.

5.　Click the Go button. The results page highlights the search terms, hyperlinks the subject lines of the retrieved messages, and displays the author, date of post, and the first couple lines of the message contents.

6.　Click one of the subject hyperlinks to view the complete message. A diagram showing the context of the post is displayed beneath the message body. It shows, with hyperlinks, the follow-up messages and references to the message as well as index links.

7.　Click the Date Index link. This displays a flat list of all messages that were posted in the same month as the message you were reading sorted by date.

8.　Click your browser's back button and then click the Thread Index link. The messages that were posted in the same month as the selected message are hierarchically arranged by subject. This view gives you a great way to follow the *thread* of a discussion and shows you the context of a particular message.

9.　Click the back button of your browser a few times to return to the search page. Retry your query with different terms and sorting options.

10.　The matrix beneath the search box is a hyperlinked summary showing the number of messages archived by month and year. Click a particular value to bring up a sequential list of hyperlinked message headers for that month.

How It Works

Lua's mailing list server acts not only as a message dispatcher, but also as an archiver. Searching the archives can be done with plain-text terms and Boolean operators, and with wildcards (as in `luaP_*`) and regular expressions. If you want to restrict your search to particular authors or subject line terms, use `+from:` and `+subject:` notation. For example, the following finds messages written by one of the mailing list's top gurus containing the term `coroutine`:

```
+from:lake coroutine
```

Downloading the Archives

The Lua website has a download area from which you can obtain source packages (including older versions) and mailing list archives. The download area is duplicated (or *mirrored*) regularly by a number of sites around the world to distribute server load. A link to a page listing these mirror sites is available on the mailing list page of Lua's website.

The archives are provided in standard mbox text format so you can view them in an editor and most e-mail programs and can easily process them with Lua itself. A complete archive is available as well as one containing messages from the last month or two and one containing messages from the most recent complete day.

Using a Web Browser to Access the List

The mailing list page on the Lua web site maintains links to sites that host a web interface to the mailing list. The Gmane (the G is silent) site displays posts in threaded form. You can submit messages with this interface, but you have to be a Lua mailing list subscriber for them to be accepted.

Using a Newsreader to Access the List

A huge number of Internet *newsgroups* are supported by the Usenet system, some of which have been active since the early 1980s. Unlike a mailing list that distributes e-mail, you access newsgroups anonymously with a newsreader, which is a component of many modern e-mail clients. Generally, the newsreader will show you only unread messages and present them in threaded format. A message is posted directly to a news server from which it propagates to other news servers.

Gmane (the same project that provides a web interface to the Lua mailing list) lets you access a large number of mailing lists, including the Lua list, as if they were newsgroups. You might consider this approach if you would rather pull mailing list messages at your convenience than have them pushed at you right after they are posted. Posting to the mailing list through Gmane is easy, but just as with the web interface, you will need to be a list subscriber for your messages to be accepted.

Subscribing to the List Server

If you want to contribute to the mailing list, you'll need to subscribe to it. This assures a certain level of accountability so that any abuse of the system can be tracked and dealt with. Even as a subscriber, you can elect not to receive e-mails if you prefer to access the list by some other means.

To subscribe to the Lua mailing list, visit the community page at the Lua website, and click the Mailing List link and then the Subscribe link. At the mailing list subscription page, you need to provide a valid e-mail address and a password. You will receive a confirmation notice at this address that you'll need to respond to in order to subscribe. By following the link in this confirmation message, you'll be able to configure a number of options such as whether you to receive posts that you submit to the list and whether to receive acknowledgment when you post. Here are two of the more important options:

❏   Whether you want to receive e-mails: If you'll be unable to collect e-mail for a length of time and don't want your mailbox to fill up, or you intend to read messages by some other means, you should disable e-mail delivery. If you are temporarily disabling message delivery, you can always catch up on messages with one of the other methods of reading posts.

❏   Whether you want to receive messages bundled into digests: This option lets you reduce the possible disruption of having individual messages trickle in as they are posted. The server can be told to accumulate messages, usually about a day's worth, and send them to you as a single digest.

Posting Messages

When you send a message to the Lua mailing list, it will be promptly dispatched to over a thousand subscribers around the world and will be accessible in searchable archives for the foreseeable future. Before pressing that Send button, make sure you've followed the guidelines as presented on the mailing list page of the Lua website and the web pages it references. These are summarized here:

❏   If you are submitting a new post rather than a follow-up, make sure that you aren't bringing up something that's covered in the documentation or has been discussed and resolved before. Take the time to search the archives. If the question or subject isn't covered elsewhere, expend the effort to present the smallest possible example that illustrates it.

❏   Send your message in plain-text format. Formatting in HTML and including multipart MIME attachments adds extraneous baggage to your post. This can be annoying to readers, many of whom use e-mail clients that display markup tags and MIME content verbatim. It can degrade the accuracy of searches on list archives. Your e-mail software may be converting the messages you send to HTML automatically, in which case, it is unlikely that you'll notice that they've been marked up when you read your post. Configure your e-mail software to use plain text when sending messages to the list server.

❏   Practice *netiquette*, the art of keeping Internet interactions polite. The Lua mailing list is quite free of damaging flame wars or even extended sidetracks. To do your part in keeping it this way, be sure to "remember the human" when posting.

❏   Take the extra time to quote material from previous posts properly. Your message will receive more attention if you include only the previous material that directly pertains to your response. If needed for clarity, break up the quoted text into sections with your responses directly beneath. You can configure many e-mail programs to indent and prepend angle brackets to quoted material to make it easier to frame your response.

❏   Don't depend on mail readers to automatically wrap long lines. Some web interfaces treat messages as preformatted content, requiring the reader to scroll horizontally to read paragraphs. Wrap the text of your message so that lines don't exceed 60 or 70 characters.

❏   Post your message in the right context. You've seen the hierarchical arrangement of messages in the threaded index view of the list archive and possibly in your e-mail software. This tree format is very helpful for showing where a message fits in a discussion thread. Although it may appear that these threads are based on subject lines and timestamps, they are in fact based on internal message headers named `Message-ID`, `References` and, less often, `In-Reply-To`. There are two rules to follow here. First, when you are starting a new topic, don't reply to an existing message and change the subject thinking that this will begin a new thread. Instead, send a new message to the list server. Second, when posting a response, don't send a new message with a copied-in subject line. Instead, use the reply feature of your e-mail software and let it handle the internal headers.

Joining the Lua mailing list is a great way to participate in the Lua worldwide community. The Lua authors are frequent contributors as are a number of undisputed gurus and other elders of the tribe.

The Lua Chat Room

Lua programmers can get together on Lua's Internet Relay Chat (IRC) channel. The kind of interaction that occurs here is more spontaneous than that on the mailing list. To participate, you'll need an IRC client such as the one integrated into Opera or the Chatzilla extension for Firefox. Follow the `irc` link from the Lua website's community page for connection details.

Like participation in the mailing list, certain rules apply to the chat room. These include the following:

❑ If you're asking a question, trim it down to the smallest possible size first. If you need to display source code, you should cut-and-paste it to the designated pasting site. This site will keep your snippet for a limited length of time and give you a temporary URL that you can in turn copy-and-paste to your chat submission. Other participants can then access the URL to examine your code.

❑ Avoid requesting communication with a participant one-on-one. Private messaging is intrusive.

Long lulls can occur on the Lua IRC channel, but people always seem to be present to step in when an interesting topic comes up.

Forums

A topic that surfaces with some regularity on the Lua mailing list is whether to abandon the mailing list in favor of a *forum*, which is a website that hosts ongoing discussions in various topics. Ultimately, it's the community itself that decides these things, and the continued activity on the mailing list is a strong indication that the list is the favored means of community interaction.

Nothing prevents a site from hosting a Lua forum, however, and one such site, `www.icynorth.com/forums/index.php?c=8`, has its share of participants.

The Lua Wiki

The `lua-users.org` site is maintained by users of Lua and serves as an unofficial repository for all things Lua. In addition to maintaining the mailing list archives, it provides, in the form of a wiki, an extensive collection of web pages devoted to tutorials, code, links, and patches. You can visit these pages at `http://lua-users.org/wiki`. The wiki pages are contributed and maintained by members of the community, making it a collaborative endeavor.

Navigating the wiki is a matter of clicking the hyperlinks interspersed throughout the content. From the home page, you can explore many pages, including a tutorial on programming in Lua, an unofficial FAQ page, many links for Lua-related projects and libraries, and much more.

You can add and modify wiki pages by clicking the Edit link at the lower-left corner of each page. Rather than editing directly in HTML, your contributions are made in simplified format. The wiki engine behind the scenes takes care of converting it to HTML for use by browsers. To learn how to style your pages, check out the formatting examples page. Click the WikiHelp link on the wiki home page, and then click the WikiFormattingExamples link. The basic rules are as follows:

❑   Make a large header by surrounding text with three equal signs. For example:

    === Large Header ===

    Or, make a smaller header by using two equal signs instead.

❑   Place a blank line between paragraphs.

❑   Italicize text by surrounding it with two consecutive single quotes.

❑   Make text bold by surrounding it with three consecutive single quotes.

❑   Make text monospace by surrounding it with {{ and }}.

❑   Add a horizontal rule by putting ---- on a line of its own.

❑   Create a link to an internal page by referring to its name. Each wiki page has a name that is the concatenation of two or more terms where each term begins with one uppercase letter and is followed by one or more lowercase letters, as in MyPage. This is sometimes referred to as *camelback* format.

❑   Create a new page by using a camelback name that doesn't refer to an already existing page. When you view a page that contains an unresolved page reference, it will be shown with a question mark link. Click this link to edit the new page.

❑   Refer to an external link by using square brackets as in this example:

    [http://www.lua.org/ Lua]

❑   Make a bulleted list by preceding items with an asterisk. Make a sublist by indenting the asterisk with a tab or eight spaces.

❑   Surround source code with {{{ and }}}, each on their own line. This disables wiki markup handling. For example, identifiers in camelback form will be presented verbatim rather than being treated as internal links. Indent the opening braces to indent the entire code block.

Before you modify a page on the wiki, spend some time getting used to the format and procedure by visiting the sandbox. From the WikiHelp page, click the SandBox link. The sandbox page exists solely for practice of this kind.

LuaForge

Several references to the LuaForge site at luaforge.net have been made throughout this book. This site is managed by André Carregal and has been of indispensable value to the Lua community by providing a single repository of many Lua-related projects.

LuaForge's home page shows recent news, lists the most active current projects, and contains links to various pages such as the project catalog tree. Reading the news lets you know of new products and releases, and scanning the activity lists lets you keep a pulse on what people are using Lua for.

Access a project detail page by drilling into the Project Tree page, clicking one of the news or activity links, or using the keyword search field at the top of the home page. This will bring you to the summary page for the project, with information about the project developers, latest file releases, news, source code management, and access to areas associated with the project such as forums and mailing lists. If the project has a home page, there will be a link to it from the summary page.

Some projects such as Kepler maintain one or more mailing lists. Such lists are more appropriate than the general Lua mailing list for discussions related to the project. The participants of these mailing lists are generally quite aware of the project's details and the message topics are focused. When visiting a project summary page, look for a Lists tab or, alternatively, a Mailing Lists link in the Public Areas section. In the page referenced by these links, you can read archived messages and register to participate in the list. Subscribers receive new posts and are able to post their own messages to the list.

If you've got a project that uses Lua, you can host it with LuaForge. You'll be provided with everything you need to give your project a good home on the Internet with great exposure, including web space and the opportunity to host forums, mailing lists, and a source code repository. You'll need to set up an account before registering your project. Even if you choose to host your project on another site, you can still register it with LuaForge for the exposure it can provide.

Annual Workshops

In recent years, Lua enthusiasts have had the chance to get together and actually meet the people behind the names on the mailing list and wiki. By all accounts, these Lua workshops are informative, fun, and worthwhile. Participation is free, but attendees need to register because of seat restrictions.

The stated goals of the Lua workshops are to provide a forum for discussing all aspects of Lua and to increase professional and academic awareness of Lua. Like the mailing list and wiki, participants hail from all parts of the globe. The workshops have so far been two-day events with structured programs comprising presentations by participants, with enough free time to become acquainted with one another and engage in unformatted discussion. Most presentations are 30 minutes and cover a spectrum of topics. Past presentations have included talks by Lua team members, library authors, and other technology professionals.

Summary

This chapter gave you an overview of Lua's community resources. Lua has a rich global support system made possible by enthusiasts who share their time and expertise in a variety of ways, including the following:

- ❑ Wiki articles

- ❑ Mailing list, forum, and chat room discussions

- ❑ Lua-related software projects

- ❑ Workshop presentations and participation

In this book, you've gotten to know about Lua itself and the power it can provide to your software projects. Its small size, high speed, and ease of integration make it eminently suitable for an extensive array of applications including, hopefully, yours.

Answers

Chapter 2

Exercise 1 Solution

Because the "p" in print needs to be lowercase.

Exercise 2 Solution

```
"ABC123"
```

Exercise 3 Solution

Because it reduces to the following, and the attempt to concatenate a Boolean value will trigger an error:

```
false .. 123
```

Exercise 4 Solution

One (the first one). More than one branch of an if is never executed. The first branch when a true test expression is executed, and after that, the if is exited.

Exercise 5 Solution

```
for N = 10, 2, -2 do
  print(N)
end
```

Chapter 3

Exercise 1 Solution

```
function TypedToString(Val)
  return type(Val) .. ": " .. tostring(Val)
end
```

Exercise 2 Solution

```
function SumProd(A, B)
  return A + B, A * B
end
```

Exercise 3 Solution

It will print the following:

```
6        10        25
```

(SumProd(3, 3) returns 6, 9, which is adjusted to one value. SumProd(5, 5) returns 10, 25, and both values are used.

Exercise 4 Solution

It prints North America. (The Continent inside F is local — assigning to it has no effect on the global Continent.)

Exercise 5 Solution

For the functions returned to be closures (and thus have private state), Dots needs to be local. Because it's global, all the functions returned share the same state, so they all do the same thing. The fix is simply this:

```
function MakeDotter(N)
  local Dots = ""
  for I = 1, N do
    Dots = Dots .. "."
  end
  return function(Str)
    return Str .. Dots
  end
end
```

As mentioned earlier, forgetting to make a variable local is a common source of bugs.

Chapter 4

Exercise 1 Solution

```
C
```

To figure this sort of thing out, work from left to right: figure out what D is, then what D.C is, and then what D.C["B"] is.

Exercise 2 Solution

The main trick to this is to compare things other than numbers and strings by their tostring value, as follows:

```
CompAll = function(A, B)
  if type(A) ~= type(B) then
    -- If they're of different types, sort them by type:
```

```
      A, B = type(A), type(B)
    elseif type(A) ~= "number" and type(A) ~= "string" then
      -- If they're something other than numbers or strings,
      -- sort them by their tostring representation:
      A, B = tostring(A), tostring(B)
    end
    return A < B
  end
```

Exercise 3 Solution

`table.concat` does most of the hard work:

```
-- "String print" -- returns a string of the form output by
-- print:
function Sprint(...)
  local Args = {...}
  -- Using select and a numeric for makes sure that no nils
  -- are missed:
  local ArgCount = select("#", ...)
  for I = 1, ArgCount do
    Args[I] = tostring(Args[I])
  end
  return table.concat(Args, "\t") .. "\n"
end
```

Exercise 4 Solution

```
-- Rotates self N elements to the left:
function Methods:RotateL(N)
  N = N or 1
  if #self > 0 then
    self.Pos = OneMod(self.Pos + N, #self)
  end
end
```

Exercise 5 Solution

Here's one way to do it:

```
function SortedPairs(Tbl)
  local Sorted = {} -- A (soon to be) sorted array of Tbl's keys.
  for Key in pairs(Tbl) do
    Sorted[#Sorted + 1] = Key -- Same as table.insert.
  end
  table.sort(Sorted, CompAll)
  local I = 0

  -- The iterator itself:
  return function()
    I = I + 1
    local Key = Sorted[I]
    return Key, Tbl[Key]
  end
end
```

Chapter 5

Exercise 1 Solution

```
-- Returns an array of Str's characters:
function StrToArr(Str)
  local Ret = {}
  for I = 1, #Str do
    Ret[I] = string.sub(Str, I, I)
  end
  return Ret
end
```

Exercise 2 Solution

```
Frmt = "%6s\n"
```

Exercise 3 Solution

```
-- Does a "dictionary order" less-than comparison:
function DictCmp(A, B)
  -- "Fold" each argument by deleting all non-alphanumeric
  -- characters then lowercasing it:
  local FoldedA = string.lower(string.gsub(A, "%W+", ""))
  local FoldedB = string.lower(string.gsub(B, "%W+", ""))
  -- Only compare the folded versions if they're unequal:
  if FoldedA ~= FoldedB then
    return FoldedA < FoldedB
  else
    return A < B
  end
end
```

Exercise 4 Solution

```
-- Reads lines, evaluates them as expressions, prints the
-- results:
function ExprInterp()
  io.write("expression> ")
  local Line = io.read()
  while Line and Line ~= "quit" do
    -- Convert the expression to a statement, convert the
    -- statement to a function, call the function, and print
    -- its results:
    Line = "return " .. Line
    local Fnc = loadstring(Line) -- Missing error check.
    print(Fnc()) -- Missing error check.
    io.write("expression> ")
    Line = io.read()
  end
end
```

It could also be written with `io.lines`, like this:

```
function ExprInterp()
   io.write("expression> ")
   for Line in io.lines() do
     if Line == "quit" then
       break -- QUIT.
     end
     -- Convert the expression to a statement, convert the
     -- statement to a function, call the function, and print
     -- its results:
     Line = "return " .. Line
     local Fnc = loadstring(Line) -- Missing error check.
     print(Fnc()) -- Missing error check.
     io.write("expression> ")
   end
end
```

Exercise 5 Solution

Here's one way to do it:

```
-- Trims leading whitespace:
function TrimLeft(Str)
   return (string.gsub(Str, "^%s+", ""))
end
```

Exercise 6 Solution

No. If there's whitespace starting at the subject's first character, it deletes it all and searches no more. If there's no whitespace there, it does nothing and searches no more.

Exercise 7 Solution

```
-- Turns $XYZ into the value of the global variable XYZ (XYZ
-- is any identifier):
function Interpolate(Str)
   return (string.gsub(Str, "%$([%a_][%w_]*)",
     function(Ident)
       return tostring(getfenv()[Ident])
     end))
end
```

Chapter 6

Exercise 1 Solution

The `debug.traceback` function is called (by Lua) while setting up the arguments to `print`, which is before the `print` function is actually called.

Exercise 2 Solution

Here is one way:

```
debug._traceback = debug.traceback

debug.traceback = function(Str)
   return debug._traceback('Programmer error: ' .. Str)
end
```

Exercise 3 Solution

```
local function zpcall(Fnc, Err, ...)
   local Args = {...}
   local function Relay()
      return Fnc(unpack(Args))
   end
   return xpcall(Relay, Err)
end

-- Test

local function Fnc(A, B, C)
   print("Here in Fnc.", A, B, C)
   print(A + B + C)
end

print(zpcall(Fnc, debug.traceback, 1, nil, 3))
```

Chapter 7

Exercise 1 Solution

Here's one solution. Add the following line near the top of show.lua:

```
local Object = Object or {}
```

This assigns the local variable Object to a global value of that name if it exists; otherwise this assigns the variable to a newly created empty table.

Find this function header:

```
function ObjectDescribe(Tbl, Val, Key, TruncLen)
```

and change it to this:

```
function Object.Describe(Tbl, Val, Key, TruncLen)
```

Correspondingly, change ObjectShow to Object.Show, and ObjectDescribe to Object.Describe.

Finally, add the following to the bottom of the module:

```
return Object
```

This new version of show.lua can be used as follows:

```
local Obj = require("show")

Obj.Show(_G, "_G")
```

Exercise 2 Solution

The following error message is displayed:

```
lua: nomod.lua:1: cannot find module xyz
```

Lua first examines "?.lua", replacing "?" with "xyz". It doesn't find xyz.lua, so it then examines "nomod.lua", replacing all occurrences of "?" with "xyz". This results in "nomod.lua" (there are no "?" characters to replace), so it looks for nomod.lua, finds it, loads it, and runs it, resulting in the error message.

Note that Lua already has a superior mechanism to report an unfound module. The message it generates lists all of the filenames it attempted to locate before failing.

Chapter 8

Exercise 1 Solution

```
Meta = {
  -- Returns a reverse-order copy of an array:
  __unm = function(Arr)
    local Ret = {}
    for I = #Arr, 1, -1 do
      Ret[#Ret + 1] = Arr[I]
    end
    return Ret
  end}
```

Exercise 2 Solution

```
-- Makes Tbl read-only (and returns it):
function Protect(Tbl)
  -- Tbl will be used as a proxy table; transfer all its
  -- pairs to OrigTbl:
  local OrigTbl = {}
  for Key, Val in pairs(Tbl) do
    OrigTbl[Key] = Val
    Tbl[Key] = nil -- Clear the soon-to-be proxy.
  end
  -- __newindex prevents writes to the table; __index allows
  -- reads from the (original) table; __metatable prevents
  -- metatable trickery:
  local ProtectMeta = {
    __newindex = function()
      error("attempt to assign to a protected table")
    end,
```

```
        __index = OrigTbl,
        __metatable = true}
    -- As well as setting Tbl's metatable, return it (for
    -- convenience):
    return setmetatable(Tbl, ProtectMeta)
  end
```

These techniques can be used to rewrite ring.lua (from Chapter 4) to protect the object returned by MakeRing from tampering.

Chapter 9

Exercise 1 Solution

The script prints this:

```
0
1
1
2
3
5
8
13
```

These are the first eight numbers in the number series named after Leonardo Fibonacci, the medieval Italian mathematician. Beginning with 0, 1, each value is the sum of the two before it.

Exercise 2 Solution

This is one solution:

```
function JoinPairs(AList, BList)
  local function Iter()
    local Pos = 1
    local A, B = AList[Pos], BList[Pos]
    while A ~= nil and B ~= nil do
      coroutine.yield(A, B)
      Pos = Pos + 1
      A, B = AList[Pos], BList[Pos]
    end
  end
  return coroutine.wrap(Iter)
end
```

Notice that the iterator is generic in the sense that it doesn't care what value or type each array element is.

Exercise 3 Solution

Here is one solution:

```lua
    local function LclConsumer(Evt)
      print("Consumer: initialize")
      while Evt ~= "end" do
        print("Consumer: " .. Evt)
        Evt = coroutine.yield()
      end
      print("Consumer: finalize")
    end

    local function LclProducer()
      print("Producer: initialize")
      local PutEvent = coroutine.wrap(LclConsumer)
      -- Simulate event generation
      local List = {"mouse", "keyboard", "keyboard", "mouse"}
      for J, Val in ipairs(List) do
        local Evt = string.format("Event %d (%s)", J, Val)
        print("Producer: " .. Evt)
        PutEvent(Evt)
      end
      PutEvent("end")
      print("Producer: finalize")
    end

    LclProducer()
```

Notice how little the overall structure of the program is changed from the original.

Chapter 10

Exercise 1 Solution

Somehow, the character "\27" (an ASCII escape character) has been left at the beginning of the file, causing Lua to try (and fail) to treat it as bytecode.

Exercise 2 Solution

This function boils down to: See if it's a local; if not, then see if it's an upvalue; if not, then see if it's a global. It's getting all the details right that's hard. Here they are:

```lua
    -- Gets the value of the named variable from its calling
    -- scope:
    function GetVar(Name)
      local CallerInfo = debug.getinfo(2, "uf")
      local Caller, Nups = CallerInfo.func, CallerInfo.nups
      local Found, FoundVal
      -- Look at the variables local to the caller; the last hit
      -- (if any) will be the desired one:
      local LclIndex = 1
      local Loop = true
      while Loop do
        local MaybeName, MaybeVal = debug.getlocal(2, LclIndex)
```

```
    if MaybeName then
      if MaybeName == Name then
        -- Found one hit (of possibly several):
        Found, FoundVal = true, MaybeVal
      end
      LclIndex = LclIndex + 1
    else
      -- No more locals; break the loop:
      Loop = false
    end
  end
  -- If it wasn't found as a local, search the caller's
  -- upvalues:
  if not Found then
    for UpIndex = 1, Nups do
      local MaybeName, MaybeVal = debug.getupvalue(Caller,
        UpIndex)
      if MaybeName == Name then
        -- FOUND IT! -- RECORD THE VALUE AND BREAK THE LOOP:
        Found, FoundVal = true, MaybeVal
        break
      end
    end
  end
  -- If it wasn't found as either a local or an upvalue, get
  -- it as a global (from the caller's environment):
  if not Found then
    FoundVal = getfenv(2)[Name]
  end
  return FoundVal
end
```

Chapter 12

Exercise 1 Solution

The following script is one solution.

```
require "sqlite3"

local Cn = {}
Cn.DbStr = "test.db"
Cn.InitStr = [[
  BEGIN TRANSACTION;
  DROP TABLE IF EXISTS T1;
  CREATE TABLE T1(A, B, C);
  INSERT INTO T1 VALUES (12, 91, 40);
  INSERT INTO T1 VALUES (27, 79,  5);
  INSERT INTO T1 VALUES (32, 66, 53);
  END TRANSACTION;
]]

local DbHnd, ErrStr = sqlite3.open(Cn.DbStr)
```

```
    if DbHnd then
      if DbHnd:exec(Cn.InitStr) then
        DbHnd:set_function("format", -1, string.format)
        print(DbHnd:first_cols("SELECT FORMAT('%05d %05d', 12, 34)"))
        for Row in DbHnd:rows("SELECT FORMAT('A %05d, B %05d, C %05d', A, B, C) " ..
          "AS Rec FROM T1") do
          print(Row.Rec)
        end
      else
        io.write("Error initializing ", Cn.DbStr, "\n")
      end
      DbHnd:close()
    else
      io.write("Error opening ", Cn.DbStr, ": ", tostring(ErrStr), "\n")
    end
```

This simply registers `string.format` as a SQLite multivalue query function. The -1 value indicates a variable number of arguments. The `string.format` function meets the criteria for a `lua-sqlite3` user function, so it didn't need to be wrapped in a user-written function.

Exercise 2 Solution

Copy the following script to a file named `pngchunk.lua`:

```
require "pack"

local PngFileStr = arg[1] or "logo.png"

local function LclFileGet(FileStr)
  local Str
  local Hnd, ErrStr = io.open(FileStr, "rb")
  if Hnd then
    Str = Hnd:read("*all")
    Hnd:close()
  end
  return Str, ErrStr
end

local function printf(FrmtStr, ...)
  io.write(string.format(FrmtStr, ...))
end

local PngStr, ErrStr = LclFileGet(PngFileStr)
if PngStr then
  local PngSize = string.len(PngStr)
  local DataLen, DataStr, HdrStr, Crc
  -- Documented PNG signature
  local SignatureStr = string.char(137, 80, 78, 71, 13, 10, 26, 10)
  local Pos = string.len(SignatureStr)
  if SignatureStr == string.sub(PngStr, 1, Pos) then
    Pos = Pos + 1
    printf("Header Length  CRC\n")
    printf("------ ------  ----------\n")
```

```
        while Pos and Pos < PngSize do
          Pos, DataLen, HdrStr = string.unpack(PngStr, ">LA4", Pos)
          if Pos then
            -- print("unpack_1", Pos, DataLen, HdrStr)
            if DataLen > 0 then
              Pos, DataStr, Crc = string.unpack(PngStr, ">A" .. DataLen .. "L", Pos)
            else
              Pos, Crc = string.unpack(PngStr, ">L", Pos)
              DataStr = ""
            end
            -- print("unpack_2", Frmt, Pos, string.len(DataStr), Crc)
            if Pos then
              printf("%s %8u  0x%08X\n", HdrStr, DataLen, Crc)
              if HdrStr == "IEND" then
                Pos = nil -- End of loop
              end
            end
          end
        end
      else
        io.write("Error: ", PngFileStr, " does not have expected signature\n")
      end
    else
      io.write("Error: ", ErrStr, "\n")
    end
```

Pass the name of the PNG file as an argument to the script. For example, if the PNG file you want to summarize is named chart.png, run the script as follows:

```
lua pngchunk.lua chart.png
```

Note that this script actually reads each chunk's data field. To do this, it uses the A specifier concatenated with the data length. It implements a special case for zero-length data fields. An alternative method is to read the data length and chunk header fields in the first call to string.unpack, adjust the starting position value based on the data length, and call string.unpack again to retrieve the CRC field.

Chapter 13

Exercise 1 Solution

In the luaopen_ud_example function in ud_example.c, copy the following lines from the MetaMap array and place them unmodified into the Map array:

```
{"close", LclExampleClose},
{"get", LclExampleGet},
{"set", LclExampleSet},
```

Exercise 2 Solution

Here is the code with possible comments:

```
// Stk: ...
lua_newtable(L);
// Stk: ... Namespace
lua_newtable(L);
// Stk: ... Namespace Upvalue
lua_pushstring(L, "Rip Van Winkle");
// Stk: ... Namespace Upvalue NameStr
lua_setfield(L, -2, "Name");
// Stk: ... Namespace Upvalue
lua_pushvalue(L, -1);
// Stk: ... Namespace Upvalue Upvalue
lua_pushcclosure(L, FncA, 1);
// Stk: ... Namespace Upvalue FncA
lua_setfield(L, -3, "a");
// Stk: ... Namespace Upvalue
lua_pushcclosure(L, FncB, 1);
// Stk: ... Namespace FncB
lua_setfield(L, -2, "b");
// Stk: ... Namespace
lua_pushvalue(L, -1);
// Stk: ... Namespace Namespace
lua_setglobal(L, "test");
// Stk: ... Namespace
```

The code creates a global namespace table called `test` that includes two functions: `"a"` and `"b"`. Each of these functions has one upvalue: a table that is accessible only to the two functions. Inside this table is the string `"Rip Van Winkle"` keyed by the string `"Name"`. The namespace table is left on the stack as a possible return value.

Exercise 3 Solution

Here is one possible solution:

```
#include "lua.h"
#include "lualib.h"
#include "lauxlib.h"

/* * */

static int BitOr(
  lua_State *L)

{ // BitOr
  int Val, J, Top;

  Top = lua_gettop(L);
  Val = 0;
  for (J = 1; J <= Top; J++) Val |= luaL_checkinteger(L, J);
  lua_pushinteger(L, Val);
  return 1;
} // BitOr

/* * */

static int BitAnd(
```

```
    lua_State *L)

{ // BitAnd
  int Val, J, Top;

  Top = lua_gettop(L);
  Val = Top > 0 ? -1 : 0;
  for (J = 1; J <= Top; J++) Val &= luaL_checkinteger(L, J);
  lua_pushinteger(L, Val);
  return 1;
} // BitAnd

/* * */

int luaopen_bit(
  lua_State *L)

{ // luaopen_bit
  static const luaL_reg Map[] = {
    {"_and",  BitAnd},
    {"and",   BitAnd},
    {"_or",   BitOr},
    {"or",    BitOr},
    {NULL, NULL}
  };

  luaL_register(L, "bit", Map);
  return 1;
} // luaopen_bit
```

Chapter 14

Exercise 1 Solution

```
-- Converts a cursor to an array of associative tables:
function CursorToTbl(Cursor)
  local Ret = {}

  -- A wrapper for Cursor:fetch that lets it return a table
  -- without being given one:
  local function RowsIter()
    local Row = {}
    return Cursor:fetch(Row, "a") -- alphanumeric/associative
  end

  -- Get each row:
  for Row in RowsIter do
    table.insert(Ret, Row)
  end
  Cursor:close()
  return Ret
end
```

Exercise 2 Solution

All three tables have an Id column. The database system doesn't know which one you want, so it returns the error message Column 'Id'-in-field list-is-ambiguous. You can fix this by specifying the following table:

```
SELECT Ord.Id, CustId, NameLast, ProductId, DescStr, Count
FROM Cust, Ord, Product
WHERE Cust.Id = Ord.CustId
  AND Ord.ProductId = Product.Id
```

The column will still be called "Id" (not "Ord.Id") in the result. SQL offers a way to make it appear under another name — the AS keyword:

```
SELECT Ord.Id AS OrdId, CustId, NameLast, ProductId, DescStr, Count
FROM Cust, Ord, Product
WHERE Cust.Id = Ord.CustId
  AND Ord.ProductId = Product.Id
```

That gives the following result:

```
OrdId   CustId  NameLast  ProductId  DescStr           Count
-----   ------  --------  ---------  ----------------  -----
    6        2  Finn              4  thingamajig           2
    1        3  Darcy             2  gizmo                52
    2        3  Darcy             4  thingamajig          87
    3        4  Bennet            1  whatchamacallit      12
    4        4  Bennet            3  gewgaw                8
    5        4  Bennet            5  widget               20
```

Chapter 15

Exercise 1 Solution

Save the following file as ex1.lua in your web server's cgi-bin directory:

```
#!/usr/local/bin/lua

local Cgi = require("cgi")

local Cn = {}

Cn.HdrStr = [[Content-Type: text/html

<!DOCTYPE html PUBLIC "-//W3C//DTD XHTML 1.0 Strict//EN"
   "http://www.w3.org/TR/xhtml1/DTD/xhtml1-strict.dtd">

<html>
<head>
  <title>Greeting</title>
  <link rel="stylesheet" href="/css/general.css" type="text/css" />
</head>
```

```
<body>

]]

Cn.FtrStr = "</body>\n\n</html>"

local Rec = os.date("*t")
local Hr = Rec.hour
local Str
if Hr >= 3 then
  if Hr >= 12 then
    if Hr >= 18 then
      Str = "Good evening"
    else
      Str = "Good afternoon"
    end
  else
    Str = "Good morning"
  end
else
  Str = "Good night"
end
local Prm = Cgi.Params()
Str = Str .. ", " .. (Prm.Get.Name or "Unknown user") .. "!"
io.write(Cn.HdrStr, '<p class="hdr shade">', Cgi.Escape(Str), '</p>', Cn.FtrStr)
```

Exercise 2 Solution

This solution calls the CGI script from the previous exercise using the GET method. Save the following file as ex2.html in your web server's document root directory:

```
<!DOCTYPE html PUBLIC "-//W3C//DTD XHTML 1.0 Strict//EN"
   "http://www.w3.org/TR/xhtml1/DTD/xhtml1-strict.dtd">

<html>

<head>
  <title>Greeting Form</title>
  <meta http-equiv="Content-Type" content="text/html; charset=utf-8" />
  <link rel="stylesheet" href="/css/general.css" type="text/css" />
</head>

<body>
  <h1>Greeting Form</h1>
  <form action="/cgi-bin/ex1.lua" method="get">
  <table class="shade" summary=""><tbody>
  <tr>
  <td class="label">Name</td>
  <td><input type="text" size="20" name="Name" /></td>
  <td><input type="submit" value="Submit" /></td>
  </tr>
  </tbody>
  </table>
  </form>
</body>

</html>
```

Exercise 3 Solution

Here is one solution. It uses one CGI script handle both the request form and the calendar presentation. Save the following file as ex3.lua in your web server's cgi-bin directory:

```
#!/usr/local/bin/lua

local Cgi = require("cgi")

local Cn = {}

Cn.HdrStr = [[Content-Type: text/html

<!DOCTYPE html PUBLIC "-//W3C//DTD XHTML 1.0 Strict//EN"
  "http://www.w3.org/TR/xhtml1/DTD/xhtml1-strict.dtd">

<html>

<head>

  <title>Calendar</title>

  <meta http-equiv="Content-Type" content="text/html; charset=utf-8" />

  <link rel="stylesheet" href="/css/general.css" type="text/css" />

  <style type="text/css">

  table.data td {border-right : 1px solid; border-bottom : 1px solid;
  border-color:inherit; color:#404040; background-color:#FFFFFF;
  vertical-align:top; width:14%;}

  table.data td.today {background-color:#f0f0ff;}

  table.data td.name {font-weight:bold; text-align:center; color:#505060;
  background-color:#f0f0ff;}

  table.data td.edge {width:15%;}

  </style>

</head>

<body>

]]

Cn.FtrStr = "</body>\n\n</html>"

local function CalendarShow(Year, Month)

  local DaysInMonth = { 31, 0, 31, 30, 31, 30, 31, 31, 30, 31, 30, 31 }

  -- For the specified month and year, this function returns the day of week of
  -- the first day in the month, and the number of days in the month.

  local function Calendar(Year, Month)
```

621

```lua
      assert(Year > 1900 and Year < 2100, "Year out of range")
      assert(Month >= 1 and Month <= 12, "Month out of range")
    local Rec = os.date("*t", os.time{year = Year, month = Month, day = 1})
    local DayMax = DaysInMonth[Rec.month]
    if DayMax == 0 then
      DayMax = math.mod(Rec.year, 4) == 0 and 29 or 28
    end
    return Rec.wday, DayMax
  end

  local Dow, DayMax = Calendar(Year, Month)

  io.write(Cn.HdrStr)

  io.write('<table class="data shade" border="0" cellspacing="0" ',
    'cellpadding="5" summary="" width="100%">\n',
    '<tbody>\n',
    '<tr><th colspan="7">', os.date('%B %Y', os.time{year = Year,
      month = Month, day = 1}), '</th></tr>\n',
    '<tr>\n')
  local Base = 8 - Dow
  for Col = 1, 7 do
    local Wd = (Col == 1 or Col == 7) and ' edge' or ''
    io.write('<td class="name', Wd, '">', os.date("%a",
      os.time{year = Year, month = Month, day = Base + Col}),
      '</td>\n')
  end
  io.write('</tr>\n')
  local Day = 2 - Dow
  while Day <= DayMax do
    io.write('<tr>')
    for Col = 1, 7 do
      io.write('<td>', (Day >= 1 and Day <= DayMax) and Day or ' ',
        '</td>\n')
      Day = Day + 1
    end
    io.write("</tr>\n")
  end
  io.write('</tbody></table>\n')
  io.write(Cn.FtrStr)

end

local function CalendarRequest(ScriptStr)
  io.write(Cn.HdrStr, '<h1>Calendar Request</h1>\n',
    '<form action="', ScriptStr, '" method="get">\n',
    '<table class="shade" summary=""><tbody>\n',
    '<tr>\n',
    '<td class="label">Month</td>\n',
    '<td>\n',
```

```
          '<select name="Month" size="1">\n')
      local Today = os.date("*t")
      for J = 1, 12 do
        local AttrStr = Today.month == J and ' selected="selected"' or ""
        local MonthStr = os.date("%B", os.time{year=2000, month=J, day = 1})
        io.write('<option', AttrStr, ' value="', J, '">', MonthStr, '</option>\n')
      end
      io.write('</select>\n',
        '</td>\n',
        '<td class="label">Year</td>\n',
        '<td>\n',
        '<select name="Year" size="1">\n')
      for J = Today.year - 12, Today.year + 12 do
        local AttrStr = Today.year == J and ' selected="selected"' or ""
        io.write('<option', AttrStr, ' value="', J, '">', J, '</option>\n')
      end
      io.write('</select>\n',
        '</td>\n',
        '<td><input type="submit" value="Submit" /></td>\n',
        '</tr>\n',
        '</tbody></table>\n',
        '</form>\n',
      Cn.FtrStr)
  end

  -- If UserMonth and UserYear were passed in and are valid, present the
  -- requested calendar, otherwise present a request form.

  local Prm = Cgi.Params()
  local UserMonth, UserYear
  local ShowForm = true
  UserMonth = tonumber(Prm.Get.Month)
  if UserMonth and UserMonth >= 1 and UserMonth <= 12 then
    UserYear = tonumber(Prm.Get.Year)
    if UserYear and UserYear >= 1970 and UserYear < 2038 then
      ShowForm = false
    end
  end

  if ShowForm then
    if Prm.SCRIPT_NAME then
      CalendarRequest(Prm.SCRIPT_NAME)
    else
      io.write(Cn.HdrStr, "<p>Error: could not determine name of script.</p>\n",
        Cn.FtrStr)
    end
  else
    CalendarShow(UserYear, UserMonth)
  end
```

Chapter 16

Exercise 1 Solution

The following is one of many possible solutions:

```
local ltn12 = require("ltn12")

local function Transform(Str, ...)
  -- Source is specified string
  local Src = ltn12.source.string(Str)
  -- Chain all specified filters into one
  local Filter = ltn12.filter.chain(...)
  -- Send all data chunks to table
  local Snk, Tbl = ltn12.sink.table()
  -- Filter chunks before delivering to sink
  Snk = ltn12.sink.chain(Filter, Snk)
  -- Open the valve
  local Code, ErrStr = ltn12.pump.all(Src, Snk)
  return Code and table.concat(Tbl) or nil, ErrStr
end

-- Return the rot13 cipher of the character Ch

local function Rot13Char(Ch)
  local Val = string.byte(Ch)
  return string.char(Val < 65 and Val or
    Val < 78 and Val + 13 or
    Val < 91 and Val - 13 or
    Val < 97 and Val or
    Val < 110 and Val + 13 or
    Val < 123 and Val - 13 or Val)
end

-- Filter that returns a rot13 cipher of the string Str

local function Rot13(Str)
  return Str and string.gsub(Str, "(%a)", Rot13Char)
end

local Str = "The quick brown fox jumps over the lazy dog"
local CnvStr = Transform(Str, Rot13)
io.write(Str, "\n", CnvStr, "\n",
  Str == Transform(CnvStr, Rot13) and "OK" or "Not OK", "\n",
  Str == Transform(Str, Rot13, Rot13) and "OK" or "Not OK", "\n")
```

Exercise 2 Solution

The following is a possible solution:

```
local function LclBodyPrint(PopHnd, Pos)
  local Str, Tbl
  Str, Tbl = LclTransact(PopHnd, "retr " .. Pos, true)
```

```
   if Str then
     io.write(Str, "\n")
     local Show
     for K, Str in ipairs(Tbl) do
       if Show then
          io.write(Str, "\n")
       elseif Str == "" then
          Show = true
       end
     end
   else
     io.write('Error: ', Tbl, "\n") -- Tbl is error message
   end
end
```

Exercise 3 Solution

The following script sends three lines, displays the echoed response, and sends an empty string to terminate the session:

```
local socket = require("socket")

local Cn = {SrvPort = 23032, SrvAddr = "localhost"}

local SckHnd = socket.connect(Cn.SrvAddr, Cn.SrvPort)
if SckHnd then
  local RcvStr, ErrStr = SckHnd:receive()
  if RcvStr then
    io.write(RcvStr, "\n")
    local SendList = {"One", "Two", "Three", ""}
    for J, Str in ipairs(SendList) do
      SckHnd:send(Str .. "\r\n")
      local RcvStr, ErrStr = SckHnd:receive()
      if RcvStr then
         io.write(RcvStr, "\n")
      elseif ErrStr ~= "closed" then
         io.write("Error: ", ErrStr, "\n")
      end
    end
  else
    io.write("Error: ", ErrStr, "\n")
  end
  SckHnd:close()
else
  io.write("Error creating client socket\n")
end
```

Chapter 17

Exercise Solution

It displays a 4×4 grid of goodies and baddies in random order.

625

Chapter 18

Exercise 1 Solution

Here is one solution:

```
-- star.lua

screen.clear()
local Wd, Ht = screen.mode()
gui.title("Star")
local X, Y = screen.pos()
screen.moveto(Wd / 2, Y + Ht / 10)
screen.heading(252)
for J = 1, 5 do
  screen.walk(2 * Wd / 3)
  screen.turn(144)
end
gui.event()
```

Exercise 2 Solution

A possible solution is as follows:

```
-- lua_expr.lua

screen.clear()
gui.title("Lua expression")
local X, Y
local Wd, Ht = screen.mode()
gui.label("Lua expression")
gui.nl()
local CtlExpr = gui.control{type = "field", lines = 1, columns = 24,
  limit = 256, editable = true, underlined = true}
local CtlGo = gui.control{type = "button", text = "Go"}
gui.nl()
gui.label("Result")
gui.nl()
local CtlResult = gui.control{type = "field", lines = 1, columns = 28,
  limit = 256, editable = false, underlined = false}
gui.setfocus(CtlExpr)
local Loop = true
while Loop do
  local Evt, Id = gui.event()
  if Evt == appStop then
    Loop = false
  elseif Evt == ctlSelect then
    if Id == CtlGo then
      local Fnc
      local Str = gui.gettext(CtlExpr)
      if string.len(Str) > 0 then
        Fnc, Str = loadstring("return tostring(" .. Str .. ")")
        if Fnc then
          local Status
```

```
            Status, Str = pcall(Fnc)
          end
          gui.settext(CtlResult, tostring(Str))
        end
      end
    end
end
```

Exercise 3 Solution

Here is a solution:

```lua
-- barchart.lua

function Barchart(TitleStr, Tbl)
  local Count = table.getn(Tbl) -- Lua 5.0
  if Count > 0 then
    local ScrWd, ScrHt, ScrDepth = screen.mode()
    local ScrBase = ScrWd / 160
    screen.clear()
    gui.title(TitleStr)
    local X, Top = screen.pos()
    local BarWd, GapHrz, GapVrt = 3, 3, 4 * ScrBase
    if Count * (BarWd + GapHrz) - GapHrz <= ScrWd then
      BarWd = math.floor((ScrWd + GapHrz - (Count * GapHrz)) / Count)
      local Lf = math.floor((ScrWd + GapHrz - Count * (BarWd + GapHrz)) / 2)
      local Max = Tbl[1]
      for J, Val in ipairs(Tbl) do
        if Val > Max then
          Max = Val
        end
      end
      if Max > 0 then
        local Mlt = (ScrHt - Top - GapVrt - GapVrt) / Max
        local Clr = screen.rgb(128, 128, 128)
        X = Lf
        for J, Val in ipairs(Tbl) do
          local Ht = math.floor(Val * Mlt)
          screen.box(X, ScrHt - GapVrt - Ht, BarWd, Ht, Clr)
          X = X + BarWd + GapHrz
        end
        gui.event()
      else
        gui.alert("Values must be positive")
      end
    else
      gui.alert("Too many elements")
    end
  else
    gui.alert("Table is empty")
  end
end

Barchart("Example", {12, 34, 23, 25, 67, 45, 23, 7, 5, 54, 48, 50})
```

627

Nice extensions to this routine would include the following:

❏ Bar colors

❏ Interactive use, in which tapping a bar would result in detail information for the corresponding value

❏ A scale

Index

Symbols and Numerics

... (ellipsis). *See* `vararg`
. (dot) character class, **193, 209**
' (apostrophe character, single quote), **33**
_ (underscore), **30**
* (asterisk) character, **195–198, 200, 209**
^ (carat) character
  for anchoring patterns, 188, 203
  description of, 209
$ (dollar sign) character, **209**
- (hyphen) character
  in bracket classes, 190
  description of, 209
  in pattern matching, 197, 198, 200
(length operator) character, **46, 123**
(number) character, **139, 470**
+ (plus) character, **194, 198, 200, 209**
? (question mark) character, **198, 200, 209**
% (percent) character classes
  in bracket classes, 192
  descriptions of, 209
  as formatting placeholder, 175–178
  in patterns, 187, 192
= (equal) sign, **29, 34**
*1 pattern, **511**
`1stThing` identifier, **30**
`1tn12` module, **525**
2-D action game, **544**
8-bit clean, **383**

A

*a pattern, **510**
absolute value, function for, **266, 358**
abstraction
  benefits of, 70
  defined, 69
  discussed, 69–70
  functions and, 70
  statements and, 70
`accept` method, **511, 512**
accumulator, **101**
`activelines` field, **312**
actual argument, **84**
addition, **24**
address, **507**
adjusted value, **40**
adjustment function, **358–360**
aggregate function, **409**
AJAX
  time server implementation with, 476–478
  toolkit, 476–478
algebraic equal sign, **29**
`ambiguous syntax` error, **215**
anchor, **188**
and operator
  discussed, 42–43
  `nil` value from, 43
  side effects and, 93
de Andrade, Marcio Migueletto, **565**
angle conversion function, **361**
anonymous function, **104**
ANSI C, **281, 338**
Apache, **471–472**
  defined, 1
  on Windows system, 472
API (application program interface), **1, 379**
APOP (Authenticated Post Office Protocol), **532**
apostrophe character (single quote), **33**
application program interface (API), **1, 379**
application protocol, **524–536**
Aquario, **566, 577**
archive (mailing list)
  downloading, 598–599
  viewing and searching, 597–598
argument. *See also* Actual argument
  actual, 84
  formal, 84
  keyword, 143–144
  variable scope of, 84

arithmetical operation
- addition, 24
- discussed, 23
- division, 24
- exponentiation, 24
- interpreter interaction for, 24–25
- multiplication, 24
- nonintuitive actions of, 27–28
- notations for, 25–26
- rounding, 28
- subtraction, 24
- in tables, 249–257

array(s)
- with gaps, 123
- length of, 123–124
- receive, 523
- send, 523
- splicing, with concatenation operator, 250–253
- tables and, 121–124

ASCII characters, 174, 192

assert function
- described, 333–334
- for errors, 220

assertion failed message, 220

assignment(s)
- defined, 29
- discussed, 29–30
- functions as, 103–105
- of global variables, 244–245
- multiple, 31
- variables on right side of, 31

associative table, 121

associativity, 49–51

assumption of errors, 219–221

asynchronous call, 476–478

Authenticated Post Office Protocol (APOP), 532

autoexec.bat, 5, 6

average function
- discussed, 74, 137
- returning values from, 73–74

B

backslash escaping
- for pattern matching, 189
- with quoted strings, 35–37

backtracking, 197

balanced delimiter, 202

base case, 97

Base64 encoding, 525

base-two number system, 44

bash shell, 4

basic output, of core library, 333

Berkeley sockets interface, 510

binary mode, 182

binary packages, prebuilt
- discussed, 18
- installing, on Unix-type systems, 19–20
- installing, on Windows systems, 20–21
- selection of, 18–19

binding, 375, 407

blitting, 551

block
- as chunk, 89
- defined, 86

blocking function, 288

Boole, George, 37

Boolean operator
- discussed, 41
- not unary operator (unary minus), 44–45
- and operator, 42–43
- or operator, 43–44

Boolean value
- comparing numbers with, 37–38
- comparing strings with, 38–40
- defined, 37
- discussed, 37

Boutell, Thomas, 395

bracket classes, 187, 190–191
- hyphen character in, 190
- percent character in, 192

break statement
- discussed, 63–65, 75
- return statement vs., 75

building
- discussed, 2–3
- gd graphics library, 395–397
- libcurl, 389–392
- luacurl, 392–393
- lua-gd, 397–399
- lua-sqlite3, 407–409
- with Microsoft Visual C++, 12–14
- with MinGW package, 16–18
- pack library, 383–384
- SQLite 3, 405–407
- with Tiny C Compiler (TCC), 14–16
- in Windows, 12–18

built-in function(s)
- discussed, 102–103
- replacing, 102–103

byte, 37, 46–47

byte order, 303

bytecode(s)
- chunks and, 81
- discussed, 299
- with luac, 299–303
- modules and, 241–242
- source codes and, 81, 302
- for troubleshooting, 302

bytecode interpreter, 81

C

C++. See Microsoft Visual C++

C compiler, 1, 2

C programming language
- calling Lua from, 421–423
- communicating between Lua and, 415–421
- defined, 1
- embedding Lua in, 414–415
- extension library of, 441–447
- format placeholders in, 179
- function environments in, 439
- indexing values in, 436–438
- libraries written in, 234
- modules with, 247
- obtaining functions in, 421
- retaining values in, 438–441
- stack of, 415
- upvalues in, 439–440
- userdata basic type in, 423–436
- using Lua in, 413–414

C runtime library, 375
C stack, 96
calendars, dynamic, 478–481
call stack. *See* stack
callback, 130, 394
calls and calling
    of anonymous functions, 104
    asynchronous, 476–478
    functions, 108
    of functions, in C, 421–423
    for Lua, from C, 421–423
    to web server, 476–478
captures, 198–201
Carregal, Andre, 602
case-insensitive tables, 259–261
case-sensitivity
    in filenaming, 241
    of identifiers, 30
cc command, 8
C/C++ compilers, 12
Celes, Waldemar, 596
CGI application, interactive
    discussed, 489
    for forms, 497
    helper routines, 489–498
    Kepler for, 499
    security issues of, 498
CGI scripting
    developing, 498
    executing, 469–470
    for images, 482–484
    privileges in, 475–476
    problems with, 475–476
    on Unix-type systems, 470
    on Windows systems, 470–471
character(s)
    absence of, 39
    conversion of, to character codes, 173–174
    defined, 32
    discussed, 173–174
    magic, 209
    for pattern-matching, 209
character class, 189, 197–198
character code, 173–174
chart(s)
    dynamic, on Web, 481–489
    gd graphics library for, 481
    in web pages, 485
chat room, for Lua, 601
chunk(s)
    as block, 86
    compiling and, 81
    defined, 75, 89
    discussed, 81–82
    as functions, 81–83
    in lua.exe, 82–83
    mechanics of, 82–83
    strings executed as, 83
chunk-loading function, 328–330
ChunkSpy, 301, 302
churn, memory pool, 305
client connections, 523
Client for URLs. *See* cURL file transfer library
client object, 511
client side networking, 538–541
client socket, 512
close (filehandle), 366

closure
    defined, 109
    discussed, 108–109
    storage in, 109
    for upvalues, 440
cmd shell, 27
Coco (patchset), 280
code error, 220
"collect" action, 332
collectgarbage function, 304–305
colon syntax, 136
color, 401, 486
columnar data, 174–179
columns
    data in, 174–179
    packaging, 441–442
command-line argument, 141–142
command-line compiler, 576–577
command-line interface (shell)
    defined, 3
    discussed, 3
    environment (variables) of, 4–6
    features of, 4
    on Unix and Unix-like systems, 3
    on Windows systems, 3
command-line interpreter, 81
comma-separated value (CSV) format, 441–447
comments, 52–53
Common Gateway Interface. *See under* CGI
communication
    discussed, 503
    with LuaSocket, 503–518
    network, 512–518
    by networking, 536–541
community resources
    chat room, 601
    discussion group, 566
    forums, 601
    LuaForge, 602–603
    for LuaSocket, 508–509
    mailing lists, 597–600
    mirror sites for, 598
    question and answer, 597
    reference manual, 596
    web site, 596
    wiki pages, 601–602
    workshops, 603
compile-time error, 215
compiling
    applications, in Plua application, 572–573
    chunks and, 81
    defined, 7
    discussed, 2–3, 7–18
    libraries, in Plua application, 573–576
    on Linux and Unix-like systems, 8–12
    Lua tarball and, 7–8
    LuaSocket, 503–505
    in Palm OS emulator, 580
    on Windows systems, 12–18
compound statement
    break statement, 63–65
    discussed, 54–65
    do statement, 63–65
    if statement, 54–58
    for loop, 60–62
    repeat loop, 62–63
    while loop, 58–59

concatenation. *See string concatenation operator*
concatenation operator, 250–253
concurrent tasks
  client connections, 523
  management of, with coroutines, 281–282
`Configure` function, 531
connection handling (LuaSocket), 518–524
connection-oriented (stream) socket, 510
constants, 363–364
control
  altering, with return values, 74–76
  coroutines for, 271–272
  flow of, 74–76
  transferring, with coroutines, 273
control character, 32
control sharing, coroutines for, 273–275
control structure, 54
control variable, 159
conversion
  automatic, 48–49
  of characters to character codes, 173–174
  functions for, 171–173
  of operands, 48–49
  of strings, 171–173, 173–174
cooperation, of coroutines, 273–278
copying tables, 148–152
core library
  basic output of, 333
  chunk-loading functions in, 328–330
  discussed, 325–335
  environment functions in, 326
  error-condition functions in, 333–334
  error-containment functions in, 330–331
  garbage-collections functions in, 332
  metatable functions in, 326–328
  module functions in, 331
  table traversal functions in, 334–335
  type and conversion functions in, 333
  `vararg`-related functions in, 335–336
coroutine(s)
  call stack of, 272
  for concurrent tasks management, 281–282
  for control sharing, 273–275, 277–278
  control transference by, 273
  cooperation of, 273–278
  defined, 271, 272
  discussed, 271
  dispatching, 280
  for event handling, 287–297
  event loop, 288–295
  functions vs., 272
  instantiated, 272
  iterating, 286–287
  for multitasking, 273–278
  for program control, 271–272
  programs vs., 272–273
  recursion and, 281
  requirements for, 279–281
  restrictions on, 280
  for retaining state, 282–287
  with `select` function, 518–522
  status of, 278–279
  thread of, 272–273
  tokenizing, 282–286
  variable scope in, 280
  wrapping of, 273
  yielding of, 279–280, 296–297

coroutine library, 336–337
`coroutine.create` function, 272, 273, 278, 336
`coroutine.resume` function, 272, 273, 336
`coroutine.running` function, 273, 336
`coroutine.status` function, 336
`coroutine.wrap` function, 272, 279, 336
`coroutine.yield` function, 272, 273, 275
cosine functions, 346, 352
"count" action, 332
CPU timing, 368
`create` key, 528
credit card numbers
  formatting type for, 186
  validating, 187–193
CSV (comma-separated value) format, 441–447
`csv.parse` function, 447
cURL (Client for URLs) file transfer library
  discussed, 389
  `libcurl`, 389–392
  `luacurl`, 392–395
`curl.new`, 395
curly braces, 202
`currentline` field, 312
Cygwin system, 2

D

data error, 220
data structure, 117
database
  access to, with Plua application, 590–592
  discussed, 449
  LuaSql, 458
  MySQL, 458–465
  relational, 449–458
  SQL, 458, 464–468
datagram socket, 510
datatype, 40
date functions, 368–369
"dead" status, 278
debug library
  for call stack, 216
  discussed, 308–321, 370–373
  functions in, 321, 371–372
  hooks in, 315–321
  running code in, 308–315
`debug.debug` function, 309, 371
`debug.getfenv` function, 371
`debug.gethook` function, 321, 371
`debug.getinfo` function, 311, 314, 371
`debug.getlocal` function, 309, 310, 371
`debug.getmetatable` function, 371
`debug.getregistry` function, 371
`debug.getupvalue` function, 314, 371
`debug.setfenv` function, 371
`debug.sethook` function, 319, 371
`debug.setlocal` function, 310, 372
`debug.setmetatable` function, 265–266, 372
`debug.setupvalue` function, 314, 372
`debug.traceback` function, 167, 217, 229, 310, 372
decimal-point notation, 28
degrees in radians, function for, 361
delimiters, 202
Demo subdirectory, 399, 566
Demo1 subdirectory, 567
Demo2 subdirectory, 567

Denom field, 255
digest newsgroup, 599
Dijkstra, Edsger, 76
discussion group, 566
dispatching, 280
division
    discussed, 24
    by zero, 27–28, 48
DLL (dynamic-linked library)
    configuration options for, 376–377
    discussed, 376–377
DLL (dynamic-linked library)
    external references of, 376
    in TCC, 16
DNS (Domain Name System), 507
dns namespace, 507
do block, 86
do statement, 63–65
doc files, 569
doc subdirectory, 8
document root, 474
documentation, for Plua application, 570–571
dofile function, 328, 330
Domain Name System (DNS), 507
domain names, 507–508
doskey utility, 27
dotted-decimal notation, 507
dotted-quad notation, 507
double quotes, 32–33
duplicate lines, 183–185
dynamic linked library. See DLL
dynamic Web calendar, 478–481
dynamic Web chart, 481–489
dynamic Web content
    for asynchronous calls to server, 476–478
    calendars, 478–481
    CGI scripts, problems with, 475–476
    charts, 481–489
    discussed, 468
    on embedded web server, 468
    on extended web server, 469
    run time, 469
    serving, 474–475

E

e-mail, LuaSocket for, 529–536
embedded web server, 468
embedding Lua, 414–415
empty string, 33
encoding, 525
end arguments, 511
end-of-file (EOF), 26
end-of-line character, 35
environment (variables)
    of command-line interface, 4–6
    discussed, 4
    on Unix-like systems, 4–5
    on Windows systems, 5–6
environment functions, 326
EOF (end-of-file), 26
ephemeral, 512
equality, of tables, 144–145
error(s)
    ambiguous syntax error, 215
    anticipating conditions for, 222

assert function for, 220
    assumptions of, 219–221
    in Boolean values, 38
    in call stack, 216–217
    code, 220
    compile-time error, 215
    containment of, functions for, 227–230
    data, 220
    default behavior of, 218–219
    defining conditions for, 221–222
    discussed, 213
    functions for, 220–221
    with global variables, 111
    handling, 218
    kinds of, 213–218
    locating, 230
    program termination and, 220
    return values and, 222–224
    runtime, 217–218
    stack overflow, 98–99
    stack tracebacks, 220
    structuring code and, 224–227
    syntax, 213–216
    unexpected symbol, 215
    unfinished string, 215
    in user-written scripts, 230
    with vararg, 215
error file, standard, 182
error function, 220–221, 334
error handler, 422
error-condition function, 333–334
error-containment function, 330–331
escape sequence, 36
etc subdirectory, 8
evaluated expression, 56
event handling, 287–297
event loop, 288–295
explicit nil value, 90
exponent function, 354–355
exponentiation, 24, 49
expression, 53–54
extended web server, 469
extending Lua, 414–415
extension function, 415
extension library
    of C programming language, 441–447
    layering, 441–447
external local variable. See upvalue
extracting tarballs, 6–7

F

Fact, 98–99, 102
factorial, 59
false, 43, 266
de Figueiredo, Luiz Henrique, 596
file handles, 366–367
File Stream library, 570
file transfer protocol (FTP), 510
filenaming, 241
files
    input/output for, 181–184
    mode setting for, 430–436
    naming of, 241
    writing and reading from, 181–184
filesystem function, 369

filter, 524–525
filtering, of data flow, 524–527
floating point representation, 360
floating-point rounding, 28
flow of control, 74–76
`flush` **(filehandle), 366**
`for` **loop**
  as block, 86
  discussed, 60–62
  local variables in, 85–86
  loop variable of, 111
  variable scope of, 84
formal argument
  discussed, 84
  function definitions with, 103
format code, 386
format placeholders, 175–179
formatting
  for credit card numbers, 186
  numbers, 174–179
  pattern matching for, 186–187
  strings, 174–179
formatting placeholder, 175–178
forms
  CGI for, 497
  JavaScript in, 498
  validation of, 498
forums, for Lua, 601
fractional integers, function for, 362
FTP (file transfer protocol), 510
"full" mode, 367
`func` **field, 312**
function(s)
  as assignments, 103–105
  built-in, 102–103
  in call stack, 96
  call stack for, 95–97
  calling, in C, 380–383, 421–423
  for calling functions, 95–102
  chunks as, 81–83
  closures, 108
  code inside, 71
  comparing, 103
  coroutines vs., 272
  for creating functions, 108–109
  in debug library, 371–372
  defining, 108–111
  discussed, 69–72
  for functions, 95–102, 108–109
  limits on, 105
  local, 105–106
  local variables in, 85–86
  for modules, 245–247
  multiple, 104
  obtaining, in C, 421
  printing, 103
  with private state, 110–111
  recursive, 97–98
  replacing, 102–103
  replacing, of built-in, 102–103
  for return values, 73–74
  for returning values, 72–80
  semicolons in, 107–108
  with side effects, 91–93
  side effects of, 91–95
  stack frame of, 109

  stack overflow and, 98–99
  tables and, 128–136, 147–148
  tail calls, 99–102
  upvalues, 108
  as values, 102–106
  variable scope and, 84–91, 111–113
  whitespace and, 106–107
`function argument error`**, 215**
function call, 108
function expression, 103–104
`function` **identifier, 30**
function plot, 402–405
function type, 421

G

game programming, with SDL
  for 2-D action game, 544
  discussed, 543
  installing programs for, 544–546
  LuaCheia for, 544–546
  reasons for, 543–544
  sprites in, 551–561
  writing programs for, 546–551
gaps, arrays with, 123
garbage collection
  discussed, 303
  mechanics of, 304–307
  metamethods for, 267
  usage of, 304
garbage-collection function, 332
`GarbageTest`**, 304, 307**
`gd` **graphics library**
  building, 395
  building, on Unix-like systems, 396
  for charts, 481
  defined, 395
  discussed, 395–405
  installing, on Windows systems, 396–397
  `lua-gd`, 397–405
`Get`**, 136**
GET command (forms), 496–497, 527
`GetEvents` **function, 551**
`getfenv` **function, 326**
`getmetatable` **function, 326**
global environment, 167
global variable(s)
  assignments of, 244–245
  avoiding, in namespaces, 244–245
  defined, 89
  errors with, 111
  local variable definition and, 111
  metatables for, 246–247
  in namespaces, 244–245
  shadowing, 89–90
  in tables, 163–168
  variable scope of, 91
Gmane, 599
GNU Readline History libraries, 27
Goldberg, David, 28
graphic generation, 582–583
graphical user interface (GUI)
  modal programs vs., 287
  shell access with, 3
graphics library. *See* `gd` **graphics library**

greedy characters, 197–198
gsub, 186. *See also* `string.gsub`
GUI (graphical user interface)
  modal programs vs., 287
  shell access with, 3
`gui` namespace, 589
`gui.destroy`, 589
`gui.dialog`, 589
`gui.getstate`, 589
`gui.gettext`, 589
`gui.setstate`, 589
`gui.settext`, 589
`.gz` extension, 6–7

H

handheld device, Lua on, 565
handle, 180
hash part, 307
hashing, 307
`headers` key, 528
helper routines (CGI), 489–498
hexadecimal color codes, 486
hexadecimal number, 49
highlighting (text editor), 21
history feature, 27
`HISTORY` file (tarball), 7
hook, 315–321
hook count, 320
HostFS, 577
HTML, 174, 176, 204, 467–468
HTML forms, 489, 491–497
`http.request` function, 527–529
hyperbolic angle, functions for, 351–353
hyperbolic functions, 351–353

I

identifier, 29–30
Ierusalimschy, Roberto, 596
`if` statement
  as `block`, 86
  discussed, 54–58
image tag (HTML), 481–482, 488
IMAP (Internet Message Access Protocol), 529
implementation, 233–234
implicit `nil` value, 90
`Inc`, 136
`include` directory, 14
indexed values
  in C programming language, 436–438
  retrieving, in C, 436–437
  setting, in C, 437–438
indexing metamethod, 258–265
`inetd` (`sinetd`, `launchd`), 536
inheritance, 264–265
initializing variables, 40
inner scope, variables from, 87–88
input file, standard, 182
input/output (I/O)
  discussed, 180
  functions for, 364–367
  mechanics of, 184–185
  for writing and reading from files, 181–184
input/output (I/O) library, 364–367

`INSTALL` file (tarball), 7
installation
  location of, 12
  of Lua, 1–3
  of LuaCheia, 544–546
  of LuaSocket, 503–506
  of `pack` library, 385
  of Palm OS emulator (POSE), 578
  of SDL, 544–546
instance (universe), 379
instantiated coroutine, 272
instantiated object, 134
integer (whole number), 26
integer exponent, function for, 360
integers, functions for, 358–359
interactive CGI application. *See* CGI application, interactive
interface
  discussed, 233–234
  preservation of, 236–240
interfacing Lua, 413
interned string, 307
Internet Message Access Protocol (IMAP), 529
Internet Protocol (IP), 506
Internet Relay Chat (IRC), 601
interpreter
  defined, 1, 81
  interaction for arithmetical operations, 24–25
  quitting, 26
  shortcuts for, 26–27
interrupt signal, 26
intializing loops, 59
inverse cosine function, 349
inverse sine function, 348
inverse tangent function, 350
inverse trigonometric function, 348–350
I/O. *See* input/output
`io.close` function, 364
`io.flush` function, 364
`io.input` function, 364
`io.lines` function, 364
`io.open` function, 223, 226, 364
`io.output` function, 365
`io.popen` function, 366, 539, 540
`io.read` function, 365
`io.stderro`, 182
`io.stdin`, 182
`io.stdout`, 182
`io.tmpfile` function, 365
`io.type` function, 365
`io.write` function, 365
IP (Internet Protocol), 506
`ipairs` function, 161, 260, 334
IRC (Internet Relay Chat), 601
`Iter` function, 158
iterating
  of coroutines, 286–287
  of pattern-matching, 204–207
iterator, 158–159
iterator factory, 158–159
Ittner, Alexandre Erwin, 397

J

JavaScript, for form validation, 498
junk value, 30

K

Kepler, James, 498–499
Kepler project
  for CGI, 499
  defined, 1
  discussed, 498–499
  for Lua pages, 500
  mailing lists for, 603
keys, for tables, 119–120
KeyToNums, 264
key-value pair, 118
keyword argument, 143–144
keywords (reserved words), 29
Klein bottle, 275

L

lastlinedefined field, 312
launchd (inetd, inetd), 536
layering, of extension library, 441–447
left-associative operator, 49
length operator, 46–47
less command, 7
less filter (Linux), 239
lib directory, 14
libcurl
  building, 389–390
  building, on Unix-like systems, 390
  building, on Windows systems, 391–392
  discussed, 389
libkit subdirectory, 567
libraries
  building, from source code, 377–379
  core library, 325–335
  coroutine library, 336–337
  cURL file transfer library, 389–395
libraries
  debug library, 308–321
  debugging library, 370–373
  defined, 375
  discussed, 325, 375–376
  DLL (dynamic-linked libraries), 376–377
  gd graphics library, 395–405
  input/output (I/O), 364–367
  input/output (I/O) library, 364–367
  interaction of Lua with, 379–383
  math library, 345–364
  operating system library, 368–370
  pack library, 383–389
  package library, 338–340
  shared, 376
  from source code, 377–379
  SQLite database library, 405–411
  string library, 340–343
  table library, 344
Life subdirectory, 567
"line" mode, 367
linedefined field, 313
lines (filehandle), 366
linker, 7
lint-type program checker, 303

Linux systems
  compiling Lua on, 8–12
  compiling LuaSocket on, 503
  less filter in, 239
list(s). See array(s)
literal strings, 266
literal value, 54
load function, 328
loader function, 415
loadfile function, 328
loadlib function, 338
loadstring function
  description, 328
  function return by, 168
  for multiple return values, 83
  use of, 83
local function
  discussed, 105–106
  variable scope of, 89
local variable(s)
  discussed, 85–90
  in functions, 85–86
  global variable and, 111
  for global variable shadowing, 89–90
  initializing multiple, 90
  in for loop, 85–86
  numbering of, 310
  in stack, 109
  storage of, 109
  variable scope of, 85–90
locale, 39
logarithm function, 356–357
Logo programming language, 582
long string, 34–35
loop variable, 111
loop(s) and looping
  with custom-made loops, 158–163
  defined, 58
  intializing, 59
  for loop, 60–62
  repeat loop, 62–63
  through tables, 124–128, 158–163
  while loop, 58–59
low watermark, 288
Lua
  building, 2–3
  communicating between C and, 415–421
  compiling, 2–3, 7–18
  installation of, 1–3
  interfacing, with other languages, 413
  prebuilt, 3
  using, 543–545
  versions of, 2
  web site for, 596
Lua API stack, 96
Lua C interface, 1, 379
lua interpreter (lua.exe), 2, 24
  chunks in, 82–83
  defined, 81
  make command affecting, 9
  testing, 10
Lua mailing list
  accessing, with newsreaders, 599
  accessing, with web browsers, 599
  discussed, 597
  downloading archives of, 598–599
  newsreaders for accessing, 599
  posting messages to, 600

subscribing to, 599
viewing and searching archives of, 597–598
web browsers for accessing, 599
Lua pages, Kepler for, 500
Lua tarball, 7–8
Lua technical notes, 525
luac
  bytecode with, 299–303
  `make` command affecting, 9
  mechanics of, 300–303
LuaCalc, 566
LuaCheia, 544–546
lua_close, 414
luac.out, 302
luacurl
  building, on Unix-like systems, 392
  building, on Windows systems, 393
  discussed, 392
  mechanics of, 394–395
  using, 393–394
lua.exe. See lua interpreter; lua interpreter
LuaForge, 602–603
lua-gd
  building, on Unix-like systems, 397–398
  building, on Windows systems, 398–399
  discussed, 397–405
  mechanics of, 401–402, 404–405
  using, 399–404
LuaSocket
  addresses in, 507
  application protocols for, 524–536
  compiling, 503–505
  for connection handling, 518–524
  domain names in, 507–508
  for e-mail, 529–536
  for filtering flow of data, 524–527
  installing, 503–506
  Internet resources for, 508–509
  for network communication, 512–518
  networks and, 506
  routed packets in, 506–507
  `select` function in, 518–522
  sockets in, 510–512
  transport protocols, 508–509
  for web page access, 527–529
  Windows binary package for, 505–506
LuaSql, 458
lua-sqlite3
  building, 407
  building, on Unix-like systems, 407–408
  building, on Windows systems, 408–409
  discussed, 407–411
  using, 409–411
lynx character-mode web browser, 7–8

M

mad.rad function, 361
magic character
  for pattern matching, 198
  for pattern-matching, 188–189, 209
  punctuation characters, 189
  punctuation characters as, 189
mailing list
  for Kepler project, 603
  for Lua. See Lua mailing list

main thread, of coroutine, 272
make utility, 9–10
makefile utility, 9
Man, Kein-Hong, 301
mantissa, function for, 360
manual, reference, 596
master object, 511
matching. See pattern matching
math library
  adjustment functions in, 358–360
  angle conversion functions in, 361
  constants in, 363–364
  discussed, 345
  exponent functions in, 354–355
  floating point representation in, 360
  hyperbolic functions in, 351–353
  inverse trigonometric functions in, 348–350
  logarithm functions in, 356–357
  maximum functions in, 363
  minimum functions in, 363
  modulus functions in, 362–363
  pseudo-random number functions in, 362
  trigonometric functions in, 345–347
math.abs function, 358
math.acos function, 349
math.asin function, 348
math.atan function, 350
math.atan2 function, 350
math.ceil function, 359
math.cos function, 346
math.cosh function, 352
math.deg function, 361
math.exp function, 354
math.floor function, 360
math.fmod function, 362
math.frexp function, 360
math.huge function, 363–364
math.ldexp function, 360
MathLib, 566
mathlib.prc, 567
math.log function, 356
math.log10 function, 357
math.max function, 363
math.min function, 363
math.modf function, 362
math.pi function, 364
math.pow function, 355
math.random function, 362
math.randomseed function, 362
math.sin function, 345
math.sinh function, 351
math.sqrt function, 355
math.tan function, 347
math.tanh function, 353
maximum function, 363
memo record, 569
metamethod
  applicability of, 268
  concatenation and, 249–258
  defined, 251
  discussed, 249
  for garbage collection, 267
  indexing, 258–265
  non-syntactical, 267
  nontables with, 265–267
  relational, 257–258
  syntactical, 265

metatable(s)
  defined, 251
  for global variables, 246–247
  mechanics of, 251–253
  for userdata, 423
metatable function, 326–328
method key, 528
Microsoft Visual C++. *See also* **C programming language**
  building Lua with, 12–14
  modules of, 247
Microsoft Visual C++ 6.0 SDK, 12
mime module, 526
MIME notation, 600
MinGW package
  building Lua with, 16–18
  for Windows-Unix compatibility, 2
minimum function, 363
mirror sites, for resources, 598
modal programs, 287
modal windows, 288
modularization technique, 244
module(s)
  bookkeeping for, 240–241
  bytecodes and, 241–242
  with C programming, 247
  defined, 233
  directory for, 235–236
  discussed, 233
  function for, 245–247
  implementations, 233–234
  interface preservation, 236–240
  interfaces, 233–234
  namespaces and, 242–245
  placement of, 235–236
  require function and, 234–235
  using, 234–235
module directory, 235–236
module function
  in core library, 331
  discussed, 245, 331
  in math library, 362–363
  mechanics of, 245–247
modulo operator, 47–48
Moen, Rick, 597
Monotone (revision control system), 22
MSVCRT.DLL, 12
MSYS, 16
multiple assignments, 31
multiple connections (LuaSocket)
  on sever side, 522–523
  timeout values for, 523–524
multiple-character string, 39
multiple-valued function, 78–79
multiplication, 24
multitasking
  with coroutines, 273
  coroutines for, 273–278
  preemptive, 276
mutable tables, 144, 305
mutating, 144
MySQL, 458–465

N

Nakonechnyj, Alexandre, 399
name field, 313

namespace
  creating, 242–243
  discussed, 242–245
  global variables in, 244–245
  modules and, 242–245
  reusing, 242–243
namewhat field, 313
natural exponent, function for, 354
nc (netcat) program, 539
Nehab, Diego, 503, 524–525
netcat (nc) program, 539
netiquette, 600
network communication (LuaSocket), 506, 512–518
Network News Transfer Protocol (NNTP), 524
networking
  on client side, 538–541
  on server side, 536–538
newsgroup, 599
newsreader, 599
next function, 334
nil value(s)
  addition of, 97
  discussed, 40–41
  implicit/explicit, 90
  from I/O function, 185
  from and operator, 43
  replacement function returning, 204
NNTP (Network News Transfer Protocol), 524
"no" mode, 367
nonalphanumeric character, 189
nongreedy character, 197–198
nonpunctuation character, 189
non-syntactical metamethod, 267
nontable, with metamethods, 265–267
"normal" status, 278
not unary operator (unary minus), 44–45
notation
  for arithmetical operations, 25–26
  RPN, 566
  scientific, 25
notation, decimal-point, 28
null byte, 37
Number pattern, 511
numbers
  comparing, with Boolean values, 37–38
  comparing, with relational operators, 37–38
  formatting, 174–179
  rational, 255–256
Numer field, 255
NumToKeys, 264
nups field, 313

O

object-oriented programming, 133–136
octets, 507
OneMod function, 157
one-operand (unary) operator, 44
online documentation, 570–571
opaque handle, 282
operands
  automatic conversion of, 48–49
  defined, 42
operating system library
  CPU timing in, 368
  discussed, 368

filesystem functions in, 369
other functions in, 370
time and date functions in, 368–369
optimizing rings, 156–157
or operator
discussed, 43–44
side effects and, 93
ordered table, 261–265
os.date function, 368
os.difftime function, 368
os.execute function, 370
os.exit function, 26, 370
os.getenv function, 370
os.remove function, 369
os.rename function, 369
os.setlocale function, 370
os.time function, 368–369
os.tmpname function, 369
outer scope, 87–88
output file, standard, 182
overflow, 27–28. See also stack overflow
overlapping, of pattern matching, 194

P

pack library
building, in Unix-type systems, 383–384
building, in Windows systems, 384
discussed, 383–389
installing, 385
mechanics of, 389
testing, 384–385
using, 385–389
package library functions, 331
package.cpath function, 339
package.loaded function, 339–340
package.loadlib function, 338
package.path function, 338–340
package.preload function, 338–340
package.seall function, 338
packaging, in columns, 441–442
pairs function, 260, 334
Pall, Mike, 280
Palm API, 570
Palm HotSync Manager, 567
Palm OS emulator (POSE)
compiling programs in, 580
configuring, 578
discussed, 577
exiting, 580
installing, 578
obtaining, 577
for Plua application, 577–580
programming Plua in, 579–580
running Plua in, 578–579
Palm OS simulator
discussed, 581
obtaining, 581
for Plua application, 581
using, 581
Palm OS stream, 571–572
parameter (term), 84. See also Formal argument
parentheses
as delimiter, 202
for literal strings, 266

within pattern, 199
use of, 80
parser, 286
pattern(s)
anchor of, 188
receive, 510–511
pattern (substring), 185
pattern item, 189
pattern matching
for any of several characters, 186–193
of balanced delimiters, 202
captures and, 198–201
discussed, 185
for formatting, 186–187
iterating, 204–207
magic characters for, 188–189, 198, 209
overlapping of, 194
searching and, 186
for specific strings, 186
with string.find, 203
with string.gsub, 203–204
with string.match, 203
tricks for, 207–208
for varying lengths, 193–198
pattern-based string function, 340–342
pcall function, 227–229, 330, 422
PDF (portable document format), 383
peers, 512
percent-escaped character, 189
pi, function for calculating, 364
plink, 539
Plot function, 405
Plua application
command-line compiler for, 576–577
compiling applications in, 572–573
compiling libraries in, 573–576
contents of, 566–567
database access with, 590–592
discussed, 565
features of, 567
graphic generation in, 582–583
on main computer, 576
obtaining, 566
online documentation for, 570–571
Palm OS emulator for, 577–580
Palm OS simulator for, 581
in Palm OS streams, 571–572
programming with, 581–592
running, 567–568
saving, 569–570
user interface programming with, 583–590
Plua2, 565, 566
plua2help.prc, 566, 567
plua2.prc, 567
plua2rt.prc, 566
Pluto (persistence library), 149
PNG format, 484
pop, 382
POP (Post Office Protocol), 529, 532–536
PORT variable, 527
portable document format (PDF), 383
POSE. See Palm OS emulator
position capture, 200
POST method (forms), 497, 527
Post Office Protocol (POP), 529
posting messages
to Lua mailing list, 600

prebuilt binary packages. *See* binary packages, prebuilt
prebuilt Lua, 3
precedence, 49–51
preemptive multitasking, 276
`print` function
    discussed, 103
    for input/output, 180
    quoting and, 32
private state, functions with, 110–111
privileges
    in CGI scripts, 475–476
    root, 11
program control, coroutines for, 271–272
program termination error, 220
program writing, 571–572
`Programmer` error, 220
programming, 581–592
Programming in Lua (Ierusalimschy), 596
`programplua2.prc`, 566
programs, coroutines vs., 272–273
protected calls (C), 422–423
`proxy` key, 528
proxy table, 261
`PROXY` variable, 527
pseudo-index, 438
pseudo-random number function, 362
punctuation characters, 189
push, 382

Q

questions, phrasing, 597
Quoted-Printable encoding, 525
quoting strings
    backlash escaping with, 35–37
    discussed, 32
    with double quotes, 32–33
    with single quotes, 33
    with square brackets, 33–35

R

radians, functions for calculating, 361
random numbers, function for, 362
rational numbers
    defined, 255
    defining, 253–255
    mechanics of, 255–256
`rawequal` function, 326
`rawget` function, 326
`rawset` function, 326, 328
Raymond, Eric Steven, 597
read (filehandle), 366
read mode, 182
`README` file (tarball), 7
`RealTbls`, 264
`receive` array, 523
`receive` patterns, 510–511
`recurse.lua`, 215–216
recursion
    coroutines and, 281
    discussed, 97–98
recursive calls, 99
recursive descent, 286
recursive function, 97–98

redirect key, 528
redirection operators, 185
reference manual (Lua), 596
referencing value (C), 440–441
register (temporary storage), 301
registering variables, 379–380
registry, retaining values with (C), 438
regular assignment, 91
relational database, 449–458
relational metamethod, 257–258
relational operator
    comparing numbers with, 37–38
    comparing strings with, 38–40
    discussed, 37
`release` directory, 581
`repeat` loop
    as block, 86
    discussed, 62–63
replaying, of captures, 201
Request for Comments (RFC), 524
`require` function
    defined, 331
    `loadlib` function vs., 338
    modules and, 234–235, 241, 247
reserved words (keywords), 29
resolver library, 508
resources. *See* community resources
"restart" action, 332
retaining values, in C, 438–441
`return` statement
    to alter control flow, 74–76
    defining functions for, 73–74
    errors and, 222–224
    for flow of control, 74–76
    functions for, 72–74
    for multiple values, 77
    with no value, 76–77
    tail call as, 101
    using functions for, 72–73
    value lists for, 78–80
`ReturnArgs` function, 78–79
`reverse` argument, 144
reverse polish notation (RPN), 566
`ReverseIpairs`, 159
revision control system, 22
RFC (Request for Comments), 524
right-associative operator, 49
ring (data structure), 153–157
root privileges, 11
Roth, Michael, 407
rounding, 28
routed packet, 506–507
rows, 441–447
RPN (reverse polish notation), 566
run time, 469
"running" status, 278
runtime, 217–218
runtime error, 217–218

S

`SampleWindow` function, 296
sandboxing, 165
saving, 569–570
scientific notation, 25
scope, variable. *See* variable scope

`screen.heading`, 582
`screen.moveto`, 589
`screen.pos`, 589
`screen.turn`, 582
`screen.walk`, 582
scripts
    CGI. *See* CGI scripting
    for form validation, 498
    JavaScript, 498
    user-written, 230
    as `vararg` functions, 140–143
SDK. *See* software development kit
SDL. *See* Simple DirectMedia Layer library
search path (Windows), 5–6, 11
searching
    pattern-matching and, 186
    strings, 185–186
    substrings, 185
secure shell handling (SSH), 510
secure sockets layer (SSL), 390
security issues
    in Apache, 472
    with asynchronous calls, 478
    of CGI applications, 498
seek (filehandle), 366
`select` function
    described, 335
    in LuaSocket, 518–522
Selene Unicode Library, 192
semicolons, in functions, 107–108
send array, 523
server object, 511
server side
    multiple connections on, 522–523
    networking on, 536–538
Server Sockets Layer (SSL), 532
`set` command, 4
`setfenv` function, 164–167, 326
`SETGLOBAL` instruction, 244–245
`setmetatable` function, 326
"setpause" action, 332
"setstepmul" action, 332
`setvbuf` (filehandle), 366
shadowing, of global variables, 89–90
shallow copy, 148–149
shared library, 376
shebang (Unix), 470
shell. *See* command-line interface
short-circuit evaluation, 93–95
`short_src` field, 313
show module, 237–240
side effects
    discussed, 91–95
    of functions, 91–95
    functions with, 91–93
    ordering of, 91–93
    short-circuit evaluation and, 93–95
`sieve.lua`, 281
Simple DirectMedia Layer (SDL) library
    defined, 544
    for game programming. *See* game programming, with SDL
    installing, 544–546
Simple Mail Transfer Protocol (SMTP), 529
sine functions, 345, 351
`sinetd` (`inetd`, `launchd`), 536
single quote (apostrophe character), 33
single-character string, 39

sink, 524–525
sink key, 528
SMTP (Simple Mail Transfer Protocol), 529
smtp module, 529
`smtp.message` function, 529
`smtp.send` function, 529
socket namespace, 507
`socket.dns.gethostname` function, 507
`socket.dns.tohostname` function, 507
`socket.dns.toip` function, 507, 508
sockets
    Berkeley sockets interface, 510
    in LuaSocket, 510
    TCP sockets, 511–512
    types of, 510–511
    in Windows system, 523
`socket.select`, 524
`socket.tcp`, 511
software development kit (SDK)
    Microsoft Visual C++ 6.0 SDK, 12
    need for, 1
    for Windows, 12
source, 524–525
source code
    building libraries from, 377–379
    bytecodes and, 81, 302
source field, 313
Spolsky, Joel, 192
sprite
    defined, 550
    in game programming with SDL, 551–561
SQL (structured query language), 458, 464–468
SQLite 3. *See* SQLite database library
SQLite database library (SQLite 3)
    building, 405
    building, on Unix-like systems, 405–406
    building, on Windows systems, 406–407
    discussed, 405–411
    `lua-sqlite3`, 407–411
square brackets
    as delimiter, 202
    quoting strings with, 33–35
    use of, 209
square root, function for calculating, 355
`squeeze` function, 193–198
`src` subdirectory, 8, 9
SSH (secure shell handling), 510
SSL (Server Sockets Layer), 532
SSL (secure sockets layer), 390
stack (call stack)
    for C function calls, 96
    debug library for, 216
    defined, 95
    errors in, 216–217
    for functions, 95–97
    functions in, 96
stack diagrams, 416
stack frame, 109
stack overflow, 98–99
stack overflow error, 98–99
stack traceback
    defined, 97
    discussed, 220
`stack traceback` function, 218
`stack.look` function, 420
standard error file, 182
standard input file, 182

standard output file, 182
start arguments, 511
state, 282–287
stateful iterator, 159
stateless iterator, 159
statement(s)
  abstractions and, 70
  compound, 54–65
  defined, 70
  discussed, 53–54
"step" action, 332
step key, 528
"stop" action, 332
storage
  in closures, 109
  temporary, 31
stream programs, 570
stream (connection-oriented) socket, 510
stream-based server, 537–538
strict.lua module, 244
string(s)
  of character codes, 173–174
  of characters, 173–174
  comparing, with Boolean values, 38–40
  comparing, with relational operators, 38–40
  conversion functions for, 171–173
  conversion of, 173–174
  defined, 32
  discussed, 32, 171, 307
  executed as chunk, 83
  formatting, 174–179
  implementation of, 307
  interned, 307
  length of, 173
  multiple-character, 39
  pattern-matching for, 185–209, 186
  quoting, 32–35
  searching, 185–186
string concatenation operator
  discussed, 45–46, 49
  metamethods and, 249–258
  on tables, 249–257
string library
  discussed, 340
  pattern-based string functions in, 340–342
  string-conversion functions in, 342–343
string.byte function, 173–174, 342
string.char function, 174, 342
string-conversion functions, 342–343
string.dump function, 185, 302, 342
string.find function
  captures return from, 200
  described, 340–341
  pattern matching with, 196, 203
  string.match function vs., 200
  for zero-length match, 196
string.format, 174–179, 342–343
string.gmatch function, 204–206, 341
string.gsub function
  bytecode and, 305
  captures within, 201
  defined, 186
  described, 341
  pattern matching with, 196–197, 203–204
  of squeeze, 194
string.len function, 173, 343
string.lower function, 171–172, 343

string.match function
  described, 341
  features of, 199, 203
  string.find vs., 200
string.pack function, 385, 386
string.rep function, 172, 343
string.reverse function, 172, 343
string.sub function, 172–173, 343
string.unpack function, 386
string.upper function, 172, 191, 343
structured query language. See SQL
structuring code, 224–227
subject (string), 185
substring, 185
subtraction, 24
sudo command, 10
super-server application, 536
surface, 551
"suspended" status, 278
SWIG, 416
syntactic sugar, 134
syntactical metamethods, 265
syntax, 134–135, 214, 303
syntax error, 213–216
system thread, 276

T

table(s)
  altering contents of, 120–121
  arithmetical operations in, 249–257
  arrays and, 121–124
  associative, 121
  building data structures in, 152–158
  case-insensitive, 259–261
  changing content of, 144
  content, changing, 144
  contents of, altering, 120–121
  copying, 148–152
  defined, 117, 118
  discussed, 117–119, 307
  equality of, 144–145
  functions and, 128–136, 147–148
  global variables in, 163–168
  implementation of, 307
  keys for, 119–120
  keyword arguments in, 143–144
  looping through, 124–128, 158–163
  mutable, 144, 305
  object-oriented programming with, 133–136
  ordered, 261–265
  vararg functions in, 136–143
  variables in, 145–147
table constructor, 122
table fields, 121
table library
  discussed, 128
  table.concat function, 131
  table.maxn function, 132–133
  table.remove function, 132
  table.sort function, 128–131
table traversal functions, 334–335
table.concat function, 131, 344
table.insert function, 130, 132, 156, 344
table.maxn function, 132–133, 344
table.remove function, 132, 156, 344

`table.sort` function, 128–131, 224, 344
tail call
  defined, 100
  discussed, 99–102
  stack frame of, 109
tail calls, 99
tail recursive, 101
tail return, 320
tangent functions, 347, 353
`.tar` extension, 6–7
tar utility, 8
tarball
  contents of, 7
  discussed, 6
  extracting, 6–7
Tatham, Simon, 597
TCC. *See* Tiny C Compiler
TCP (Transmission Control Protocol), 509–510
TCP sockets, 511–512
technical notes, 525
termination, program, 220
`Test` function, 527
text editor, 21
`.tgz` extension, 6–7
`this-var` identifier, 30
thread, of coroutines, 272–273
time function, 368–369
time server
  creating, 474–475
  implementing, with AJAX, 476–478
timeout value, 523–524
`TIMEOUT` variable, 527
timing, 368
Tiny C Compiler (TCC)
  building Lua with, 14–16
  discussed, 3
  web site for, 14
TinyWeb, 472–473
token
  coroutine, 282–286
  defined, 204
  discussed, 204
  `string.gmatch` as, 204
  supported, 485
`tonumber` function, 333
tools
  revision control system, 22
  text editor, 21
`ToString`, 157
`tostring`, 174
`tostring` function, 333
total order, 258
`Transform` function, 527
Transmission Control Protocol (TCP), 509–510
transport protocol, 508–509
trigonometric function, 345–347
troubleshooting, bytecodes for, 302
"turtle" functions, 582
type and conversion function, 333
`type` function
  described, 333
  returning values from, 72–73

U

UDP (User Datagram Protocol), 509–510
unary minus (`not unary`) operator, 44–45
unary (one-operand) operator, 44
`unexpected symbol` error, 215
`unfinished string` error, 215
Unicode, 192
Unicode (UTF-8 format), 192
uninitializing variables, 40
universe (instance), 379
Unix/Unix-like system
  CGI scripts on, 470
  command-line interface on, 3
  compiling Lua on, 8–12
  compiling LuaSocket on, 503
  environment of, 4–5
  `gd` graphics library on, 396
  `libcurl` on, 390
  libraries on, building, 378
  `luacurl` on, 392
  `lua-gd` on, 397–398
  `lua-sqlite3` on, 407–408
  `pack` library in, 383–384
  prebuilt binary packages on, 19–20
  SQLite 3 on, 405–406
  Windows system and, 2
`unpack` function, 139, 335–336
`until` expression, 86
upvalue (external local variable)
  in C programming language, 439–440
  closures for, 440
  in functions, 108, 109
`url` key, 527
`url.parse` function, 508–509
User Datagram Protocol (UDP), 509–510
user interface programming, 583–590
`USERAGENT` variable, 527
userdata
  in C programming language, 423–436
  metatables for, 423
user-written script, errors in, 230
`usr` subdirectory, 14
UTF-8 format (Unicode), 192

V

validation, of credit card numbers, 187–193
value(s)
  in C, 436–438, 438–441
  defined, 118
  discussed, 51–52
  functions as, 102–106
  indexing, 436–438
  multiple, 77
  none, 76–77
  retaining, 438–441
value list
  adjusting, 78–80
  defined, 78
  discussed, 78
  multiple-valued functions in, 78–79
  for return values, 78–80
value-less function, 79, 80

vararg (...)
  defining, 136–140
  discussed, 136
  errors with, 215
  for `loadstring`, 83
  as placeholder, 240
  scripts as, 140–143
  in tables, 136–143
vararg-related function, 335–336
variable(s)
  defined, 28
  discussed, 28, 51–52
  global, 91, 163–168, 244–245
  initializing, 40
  from inner scopes, 87–88
  local, 85–90
  in namespaces, 244–245
  from outer scopes, 87–88
  registering, 379–380
  on right side of assignments, 31
  in tables, 145–147
  uninitializing, 40
  variable scope, 85–91
variable scope
  arguments, 84
  in coroutines, 280
  determining, 111
  discussed, 84
  functions and, 84–91, 111–113
  global variables, 91
  of `local` function, 89
  local variables, 85–90
  of `for` loop, 84
  tricky situations involving, 111–113
velocity (Velx), 559
VFS (virtual file system), 570
virtual file system (VFS), 570
virtual machine, 299
virtual stack, 415
Visual C. See C programming language
Visual C++. See Microsoft Visual C++
Visual C++ 6.0 SDK, 12

W

watermark, low, 288
WaveForm function, 405
weak key, 305
weak value, 306
Web applications
  CGI applications, interactive, 489–498
  CGI scripts, execution of, 469–471
  discussed, 467
  dynamic content for, 468–469, 474–489
  Kepler project, 498–500
  run time, 469
web browser
  for Lua mailing list access, 599
  `lynx` character-mode, 7–8
Web content, dynamic. See dynamic Web content
web page
  access to, with LuaSocket, 527–529
  charts in, 485
web server
  Apache, 471–472
  creating, 514–518

  discussed, 467–468
  embedded, 468
  extended, 469
  installing, 471–473
  testing, with static content, 474
  TinyWeb, 472–473
wget program, 8
what field, 313
while loop
  as block, 86
  discussed, 58–59
whitespace
  functions and, 106–107
  squeezing, 193–198
whole number (integer), 26
wiki pages, for Lua, 601–602
Win32 subdirectory, 20
Window.Close, 296
Windows binary package, 505–506
Windows system
  Apache on, 472
  CGI scripts on, 470–471
  character processing in, 430
  command-line interface on, 3
  compiling Lua on, 12–18
  compiling LuaSocket on, 503–504
  control code processing in, 365
  environment of, 5–6
  filenaming in, 241
  `gd` graphics library on, 396–397
  `libcurl` on, 391–392
  libraries on, building, 378–379
  `luacurl` on, 393
  `lua-gd` on, 398–399
  `lua-sqlite3` on, 408–409
  `pack` library in, 384
  prebuilt binary packages on, 20–21
  SDK for, 12
  search path mechanism of, 5–6
  settings recommended for, 6
  sockets in, 523
  SQLite 3 on, 406–407
  Unix-type systems and, 2
Window.Show, 296
Wirth, Niklaus, 214–215
workshops, for Lua, 603
World Wide Web, 468
wrapping
  of coroutines, 273
  of messages, 600
write (filehandle), 367
write mode, 182

X

X Window System, 288
XNextEvent function, 288
xpcall function, 229, 330

Z

zero, division by, 27–28, 48
zero-length match, 196
Zeus programmer's editor, 415